THIRD EDITION

ADOLESCENCE
Continuity, Change, and Diversity

Nancy J. Cobb
California State University, Los Angeles

MAYFIELD PUBLISHING COMPANY
Mountain View, California
London • Toronto

Copyright © 1998 by Mayfield Publishing Company

LIBRARY OF CONGRESS CATALOGING-IN-PUBLICATION DATA

Cobb, Nancy J.
    Adolescence : continuity, change, and diversity / Nancy J. Cobb—3rd ed.
        p.   cm.
    Includes bibliographical references and index.
    ISBN 1-55934-946-8
    1. Adolescence.   2. Adolescent psychology.   3. Teenagers—United
States.   I. Title
HQ796.C596   1997
305.235—dc21   97-31566
                                                                         CIP

Manufactured in the United States of America
10   9   8   7   6   5   4   3   2   1

Sponsoring editor, Franklin C. Graham; developmental editor, Barbara Armentrout; production editor, Melissa Kreischer; manuscript editor, Jennifer Gordon; text and cover designer, Claire Seng-Niemoeller; design manager, Susan Breitbard; art manager, Robin Mouat; photo researcher, Brian Pecko; illustrators, Judy & John Waller; manufacturing manager, Randy Hurst. Cover photo, © Adam Peiperl. The text was set in 10.5/12 Legacy Serif Book by GTS Graphics, Inc. and printed on acid-free 45# Quebecor Matte by Quebecor Printing Book Group.

Brief Contents

CONTENTS

CHAPTER 2   Theoretical Foundations of Adolescent Development   41

CHAPTER 6   Adolescents and Their Friends   247

CHAPTER 11   Facing the Future: Values in Transition   471

CHAPTER 12   The Problems of Youth   507

RESEARCH FOCUS BOXES

To the Instructor

First things first! The most important question about this edition is, What's new? Four major changes stand out. First, this edition features a new chapter, "Protective Factors in Adolescence." By focusing on sources of support and guidance within the family, the community, and society at large, Chapter 13 concludes the study of adolescent development on a positive note rather than a problem-oriented one. The second major focus of the revision is the greater prominence of the constructive approach to adolescent development. This perspective is evident throughout the book, from the very first page of Chapter 1, which illustrates how cultural context informs the adolescent search for identity with an example of a Chinese American girl's dreams of being a woman warrior. Chapters include new discussions of how adolescents construct, or give shape to, the events they experience. Adolescent development is the result not only of what the individual has experienced but of how he or she has interpreted the experience. With the contextual approach comes the appreciation that development involves a fragile balance that brings not only new strengths and a new way of understanding but also new vulnerabilities. The third big change is that over half the research focus boxes are new to this edition. Although we have retained the format and focus of this well-received element of the text, we know that no matter how good an example is, it can become dated. For a complete listing of the research methods and specific studies profiled in these boxes, turn to the last page of the table of contents. Finally, as is fitting for this course, we have designed the book with an entirely new look and richly illustrated it throughout with four-color photographs. This change does not affect the cost to the student, but it will add to the appeal of the text and help students relate what they read to their own memories of what it was like to be an adolescent.

The purpose of *Adolescence: Continuity, Change, and Diversity* is twofold: It provides a comprehensive, up-to-date survey of the research findings and theories of adolescent development, and it shows how this information can be applied to help adolescents meet the challenges they face as they grow into adulthood. The book is distinctive in four important ways: First, it treats early and late adolescence as two distinct periods of development. Second, it relates each aspect of adolescent development to the unifying theme of identity formation, highlighting important gender differences when these exist. Third, it integrates discussion of cultural differences throughout rather than relegating such coverage to special focus boxes or an isolated chapter. Fourth, it views adolescence within a lifespan developmental perspective.

Early and Late Adolescent Development   The primary developmental issues and experiences of early adolescents differ markedly from those of late adolescents. Early adolescents are just one step beyond the comfortable routine of grade school; high school students are one step away from the responsibilities of adult life. Early adolescence is identified with the onset of puberty and the changes that transform the body into that of a mature adult. Maturation of the reproductive system and a growth spurt put the adolescent eye to eye and nose to nose with his or her parents. Early adolescents must integrate these changes into a new sense of themselves. By late adolescence, puberty is no longer the dominant theme; instead, late adolescents must deal with changes in their relationships and take steps toward the commitments that will define their adult social roles. For early adolescents, a major issue is achieving autonomy; for late adolescents, the issue becomes one of consolidating the changes that accompany autonomy into a mature personality structure. The social world of friends changes as well, from circles of same-sex friends to couples seeking to establish a more mature, intimate sexual identity. In the intellectual realm, early adolescents develop the ability to think abstractly; late adolescents use this ability to formulate a set of values and an ethical system to guide their behavior. By virtue of its organization, this textbook aims to make these and other important distinctions between early and late adolescence clearer than any other textbook currently available.

Identity Formation and Gender   A second key feature of this textbook is the theme of adolescence as a search for a stable personal identity, a search often affected by differences in the ways adolescent females and males define themselves. All adolescents face the task of achieving a sense of themselves, but the contexts in which this process takes place, as well as cultural definitions of maturity, may differ significantly for males and females. Many developmental theories assume the experiences of males to be normative for both sexes, even though current research increasingly shows this assumption to be in need of revision.

It is also important to examine gender similarities. Scholars have long accepted that self-definition for males characteristically involves increasing autonomy and separation from others, along with strong occupational and ideological commitments. Few books, however, give much attention to females' need for increasing autonomy, especially in their work roles and their sexuality. Conversely, the close interpersonal relationships and the sense of connectedness with others that are commonly viewed as hallmarks of female maturity are increasingly being recognized as aspects of male maturity as well. The interplay in this book between established developmental theory and recent challenges to it should spark the reader's interest and convey the dynamic nature of this field of inquiry.

Cultural Diversity   A third feature of this book is its emphasis on the ways that ethnic and cultural backgrounds affect adolescents' development. Although the cultural and ethnic composition of the United States is rapidly changing, most developmental theories fail to reflect or address such change. Erik Erikson, perhaps better than any other current theorist, captures the dialectical interplay between a changing self and an evolving society, and yet he speaks of identity largely in terms of a White male society even though he has examined the impact of social conditions on a number of ethnic groups.

The developmental challenges faced by minorities and females are remarkably similar. Frantz Fanon speaks of the "colonization of the unconscious" in describing the incorporation of dominant White values by members of the Black minority. Ethnic minorities and adolescent females face a similar problem: how to forge a sense of self in the context of social norms that reflect White-male-defined characteristics, which often differ significantly from their own. The field still lacks a systematic examination of prevailing cultural images and their impact on minority and female adolescents. To the extent possible, this textbook considers developmental theory in the light of what is in known about class, ethnic, racial, and sex differences.

The Lifespan Perspective Our understanding of the psychological, biological, social, and historical forces that shape individual development throughout life has grown immensely during the 1980s and 1990s. Yet few textbooks seek to integrate these multidisciplinary findings into a cohesive portrait of adolescence within the lifespan. This book views adolescence as a period of both the consolidation (continuity) of developmental tasks and the establishment of new foundations (change) for the future of the maturing adult.

Organization Part One provides the foundation for the study of adolescence. Chapter 1 introduces the basic definitions and then places adolescence in historical context. Adolescence has not always existed as it does today in technological societies; even in today's world, there are cultures in which only two stages of life are recognized: childhood and adulthood. Chapter 2 introduces theories and models of adolescence and relates these to the broad developmental issues discussed throughout the book.

Rather than introducing the topic of research methods at the very beginning, when students are least interested, this book treats them one by one in "Research Focus" boxes in every chapter, as the methods become pertinent to specific problems, and then more comprehensively in a final chapter. Each Research Focus box starts with a practical problem and illustrates how researchers used a particular approach to solve it. Taken together, the boxes present the full range of topics important for an understanding of the methodologies employed by developmental researchers.

Parts Two and Three are the core of the textbook. Part Two opens with puberty (Chapter 3) and traces the changes adolescents undergo intellectually (Chapter 4), within their families (Chapter 5), with peers (Chapter 6), and at school (Chapter 7). These chapters provide a foundation for understanding adolescents in the various contexts of their lives. Part Three opens with a chapter on identity and intimate relationships (Chapter 8), in which the changes covered in Part Two are examined in light of the central task of adolescence, that of identity formation. The next three chapters examine the various aspects of identity separately: gender roles and sexuality (Chapter 9), vocational choices or preparation for these through college (Chapter 10), and the development of values and beliefs (Chapter 11). Part Three closes with chapters on the problems of youth (Chapter 12), on factors that promote healthy development (Chapter 13), and research methods and issues (Chapter 14).

Learning Aids

Each chapter begins with a personal vignette that provides insight into how adolescents perceive their world or deal with its challenges. These vignettes are intended to engage the reader and focus attention on themes within the chapter.

In addition, each chapter ends with a summary and a list of key terms. Key terms appear in bold type in the chapter and are defined in the glossary at the end of the book. To clarify and reinforce essential points, the text is also illustrated extensively with charts, tables, drawings, and photographs.

Supplemental Teaching Aids

A Resource Book for Adolescent Development provides suggestions for teaching about gender and ethnic diversity, additional readings for each chapter, lists of audiovisual and online resources, and exercises that can be used in group or individual projects. Also included are handouts about how to read a journal article on adolescence and how to write a paper on adolescent research, as well as review charts of the core theories and models of development. The resource book also contains transparency masters to supplement class lectures.

An extensive test bank, by Dr. Andrea Weyerman of Augusta State University, is available in printed form and on computer disk in the Chariot testing system for IBM compatibles and Macintosh. For each chapter, there are multiple-choice items, true/false questions, fill-in or short-answer questions, and essay questions. Page references are provided for each question.

Acknowledgments

So many people have contributed to the writing of this book. I am especially grateful to sponsoring editor Frank Graham for expecting the best and having little patience with anything less. His confidence in the project made it possible to write about the field of adolescence in new ways, and many of his ideas appear throughout the manuscript. To developmental editor Barbara Armentrout, special thanks for the creative energy and time she put into this book. Special thanks, too, are due to production editor Melissa Kreischer for the care and competence with which she saw this book through production. Thanks also go to Susan Breitbard, design manager; Robin Mouat, art manager; Brian Pecko, photo researcher; and to the manuscript editor, Jennifer Gordon, for all their work.

The reviewers who contributed countless helpful comments and suggestions at varying stages in the writing of this book also deserve a note of thanks. Those who helped in reviewing the manuscript include: Radhi H. Al-Mabuk, University of Northern Iowa; Belinda Blevins-Knabe, University of Arkansas at Little Rock; Terry Bontrager, Rhode Island College; Stephanie Clancy Dollinger, Southern Illinois University at Carbondale; Mary Ann Drake, Mercer University; Daniel Fasko, Morehead State University; G. Alfred Forsyth, Millersville University; Peggy Forsyth, Millersville University; Gregory T. Fouts, University of Calgary; Larry Jensen, Brigham Young University; Nancy Kalish, California State University, Sacramento; Lynn F. Katz, University of Pittsburgh; Alan Krasnoff, University of Missouri at St. Louis; Judith Rae Kreutzer, Fairmont State College; Lissa Mathews, Arizona State University; Elizabeth Mazur, Eastern Kentucky University; Merle McElroy, Southeastern Oklahoma State University; David S. Moshman, University of Nebraska at Lincoln; Christine (Coco) Readdick, Florida State University; Lee B. Ross, Frostburg State College; Toni Santmire, University of Nebraska at Lincoln; Lawrence G. Shelton, University of Vermont; Lisa Smulyan, Swarthmore College; Debra Steckler, Mary Washington College; Sheila J. Vaughn, University of California, Irvine; and Frank Vitro, Texas Women's University.

Revising a text is in some ways as demanding as first writing it. To all my friends at First Pres in Burbank, thank you for your prayers, and to Abba, Father God, thank you for the gracious ways You answered them. To Bill, for e-mail and nostalgia; to Michael—wise and witty beyond words—for always being there and for simply being who you are; and to Joshua and Jenny, who remain as amazing to me in adulthood as you did in adolescence—I celebrate your creativity and courage.

TO THE STUDENT

Think about adolescents you know. Or try to remember yourself as an adolescent. Whether thinking about those you know or your own adolescence, one thing is certain: you cannot recapture the excitement, the anguish, or those many "firsts" you experienced then. As adults, our perspective is different, balanced by having "firsts" followed by seconds and thirds. Because we recognize that our adult perspective is so different, we have a new appreciation for the special contexts of adolescent development. Today, we have a better appreciation for the context of adolescence, a context simultaneously shaped by the forces of continuity, change, and diversity.

This perspective allows us to see that, despite the many similarities between adolescents and adults, striking differences often separate our understanding of the world from theirs. The differences can be dramatic:

> A 14-year-old, when asked by her mother why she's been acting so dreamy lately, replies, "You wouldn't understand, Mom, you've *never* been in love!"

> A frightened 16-year-old tells his mother that because he hadn't had sex "enough times" with his girl, that he didn't think she could get pregnant. "Girls just don't get pregnant that way, not by having sex just once, just that one time!"

> A gifted 17-year-old who can think circles around most adults still feels like a child inside and becomes anxious at the thought of leaving home for college.

Thoughts and feelings like these point to the very deep differences in the ways adolescents and adults perceive and relate to their worlds. This textbook examines the many contexts of adolescent experience and development: the physical changes brought on by puberty, the growth of intellect and logic, relations with family and friends, sexuality, and the larger worlds of school and work. The goal is to present information in a way that helps the reader appreciate the complexity of adolescent interactions with adults and others. Only through understanding what is meaningful in adolescent development can we become positive influences in the lives of today's adolescents and tomorrow's adults.

A Focus on Meaningful Differences   Just as we distinguish phases of childhood and adulthood, such as toddlers from school-age children, or young adults from middle-aged adults, we also can distinguish early adolescents from late adolescents. Early adolescents' first steps take them out of childhood. Late adolescents stand at the threshold of adulthood. Early adolescents struggle with puberty, a new awareness of their sexuality, and with changing relationships with parents. Late adolescents grapple with identity issues, stepping into adult roles by getting a job or going to college, and integrating sexuality into their relationships.

Increasing your understanding of the many aspects of adolescent behavior is the objective of this textbook. Yet many questions will remain unanswered. The study of adolescent development is a young field and has not been investigated as extensively as other developmental periods, such as infancy or early childhood. Many interesting questions have not even been asked, let alone answered.

Some of your questions will remain unanswered for another reason. To obtain answers one would have to study adolescents in ways that are simply not possible. Many factors interact to make adolescents the individuals they are. Some factors are undoubtedly inborn; others are shaped by the contexts of their lives—by families, friends, schools, and communities. Many of the research methods that contribute to our understanding of adolescence isolate a behavior for closer study and then extrapolate from the findings to other developmental contexts. Although isolating behavior in order to study it increases our knowledge, it can also lead to distortions, because a person's behavior always assumes a somewhat different form in each different context. Compensating for such distortions is at best an inexact science. In the chapters that follow, you will find information that increases your understanding of adolescence, but you are cautioned that such knowledge is subject to future revision as more research is conducted and applied.

Other questions cannot be answered because of ethical limitations. For instance, does assignment to a lower academic track lead to poorer learning and increased risk of dropping out of school? To answer such a question, we would have to assign adolescents at random to either a lower or higher track, and compare their academic performance. Investigators who believe that assignment to a lower academic track might adversely affect learning could not ethically conduct such a study. Researchers have therefore chosen to study naturally occurring groups instead. But they face still other problems when they do. For example, some unknown factor could be the cause of the differences between groups. Consequently, there are many questions for which we do not have—and are unlikely to get—definitive answers.

Extending Knowledge to Practical Outcomes   Many of you will become teachers, nurses, social workers, or counselors. Most of you will establish families of your own, if you have not done so already, and will face the immensely important challenge of raising adolescents. One way or another, you will come into contact with adolescents who will affect your lives. This textbook will help you make connections between learned concepts and everyday situations. Throughout each chapter, development is discussed within the context of practical applications. The examples used to establish these connections illustrate in concrete ways the situations faced by adolescents of different ages, sexes, and cultural backgrounds.

Finally, I want to stress that research often has meaningful applications to adolescents' lives. The Research Focus boxes in each chapter isolate recent studies that warrant special attention. These boxes will help you to distinguish various kinds of research and to become familiar with issues researchers face. In addition, they present the practical applications of research that can make a difference in the lives of adolescents.

The Place of Values Developmentalists attempt to study adolescents in a value-free context in order to objectively observe and record what they see. Yet values affect their observations if only through their choice of what they consider important enough to observe. Observations that confirm our expectations are usually not subjected to the same critical tests, or followed up with further observations, as are those that are unexpected. Such expected observations often reflect gender and ethnic stereotypes, however unintentionally. Thus, when research finds that males use rules more effectively than females to regulate and prolong their play, few questions are asked. Similarly, studies finding that minority adolescents are more likely to be in noncollege than college tracks in high school are not questioned. Each finding reflects an expected outcome.

But when we look beneath the surface of studies such as these, we often find that other conclusions are equally supportable. Take the case of the use of rules. Is it simply a matter of males being "better" at using rules than females? Hardly. But it takes a different perspective to look for other answers. When one does, one finds that females interpret the need to settle their differences through rules as a sign that the friendship is in jeopardy, and they end the game to protect their relationship. Similarly, a closer look at the larger numbers of minority students in noncollege tracks supports alternative conclusions. Research controlling for background variables, such as minority status and intelligence, finds that students assigned to noncollege tracks still do more poorly than those in the college tracks. Assignment to the track itself, rather than ability or minority status, is a key factor in determining a student's investment in learning.

It is only fair to point out that this textbook is not free of values. It makes a deliberate effort to take a second look, to determine whether expectations concerning gender and ethnicity contribute to the conclusions researchers make. Many psychological theories have been formulated on the basis of data collected only from males. Others implicitly assume a male perspective. And nearly all theories assume the perspective of the dominant culture. This book explicitly points out these shortcomings when they occur and organizes the coverage of topics within chapters to include issues of gender and ethnicity.

Even so, an additional set of values will color what you are reading. These are your own values. They operate in much the same way as those of the developmentalists who collected the initial observations. As a student, you need to be a discerning reader. Think about how you are reacting to what is stated. You may be surprised to find that many of your assumptions about adolescents run counter to what you are reading.

Your understanding of adolescence will have increased immensely by the time you finish the final chapter of this textbook. For those of you planning to work or share some part of your lives with adolescents, the knowledge you gain will be both meaningful and practical. Above all, you will have gained a sense of the immense richness of diversity in the human experience.

For
Willa Cobb

PART ONE

Foundations of Adolescent Development

Metamorphosis, change, transition. Adolescents experience all of this. In just a few years, nearly everything changes, from the way they think to how they look and feel. At times, it may seem as if sorcery is involved. Or perhaps it is a mystery of nature. For like caterpillars, adolescents shake out their wings and fly when the time arrives.

Even with the many changes adolescents experience, there is also continuity to their lives, both in their physical growth and in the general patterns to their development. Adolescents remain the same individuals, in fundamental ways, that they were when children and will be when adults. Whether it's coping with stress, solving a problem, daydreaming, or planning, the approach they adopt and the outlook they take bears a characteristic stamp that identifies each as an individual, whether at 6, 16, or 63. The adaptive mechanisms that individuals acquire in childhood are generally the ones through which they cope as adolescents and adults.

As a group, adolescents live with more diversity than did their parents or grandparents. The number of ethnic and racial minorities in the United

States has been increasing steadily over the past several generations. Two generations ago, minorities made up approximately 10% of the population. Before this generation of adolescents reaches its twenties, that figure will be just under 17%. All adolescents are affected by increasing cultural diversity: The experiences of majority as well as minority adolescents will be colored by the diversity that marks our culture.

Change, continuity, diversity. Each of these characterizes the lives of adolescents today. The major themes of the text are introduced in Chapter 1. The first of these—achieving a sense of oneself—threads its way through each of the chapters, highlighting significant gender differences and taking a constructivist-contextualist perspective. A second theme of the text spotlights the increasing cultural diversity that characterizes our society. A third theme organizing the text, a lifespan developmental perspective, places the age-specific changes of adolescence within the context of developments throughout the life cycle. A fourth and final theme distinguishes early and late adolescence as two dis-

tinct periods of development. Parts Two and Three examine the major developments within each of these stages.

Chapter 2 introduces the developmental theories that guide research in adolescence. Many theories have focused on males, assuming their experiences are normative for both sexes. Current research increasingly shows this assumption needs revision. Chapter 2 presents alternatives to prevailing developmental theories, as well as established developmental thought.

The first of many Research Focuses appear in these opening chapters. These boxes highlight procedures that developmentalists use when conducting research on adolescence. Each Research Focus opens with a practical problem, then examines the particular approach taken by those who studied this problem. Together, they cover the full range of topics one would expect to find in an in-depth treatment of developmental methodology. Separate Research Focuses cover the many types of research, discuss issues unique to developmental research, and present issues common to all research.

CHAPTER 1

Perspectives on Adolescence

Each culture has its stories. They offer a way of understanding ourselves and our lives. Most of us accept the stories our culture tells us—stories we've heard since childhood. It is daring to live lives that are too different from these stories. But in adolescence, one may dream the daring. Listen to the story told by a Chinese American girl who dares to dream for herself the exploits reserved for boys—initiation into the rites of a warrior:

> After I returned from my survival test, the two old people trained me in dragon ways. . . . Tigers are easy to find, but I needed adult wisdom to know dragons. "You have to infer the whole dragon from the parts you can see and touch," the old people would say. Unlike tigers, dragons are so immense, I would never see one in its entirety. (Kingston, 1977, p. 34)

So Maxine Hong Kingston describes the fantasies of a Chinese American girl who dreamed of avenging her people as a fierce and beloved warrior.

Adolescents still dream of dragons. Fantastic? Of course. But in another sense, dragons are made of common stuff. They are what looms large when one feels small. So, too, with dreams. This girl's dreams were not that different from those of other adolescents. Dreams and dragons alike are personal. The dragon was spun from remarks surrounding her youth: "Better to raise geese than girls." "When you raise girls, you're raising children for strangers." The dream, of course, was to slay the dragon—and prove them wrong.

Each culture offers up its dragons. The Chinese are no different in this respect. The trick is to recognize a dragon when one finds it. As Maxine Hong Kingston tells us, they are too large ever to be seen. In studying the youth who pursue them, though, we will have occasion to examine some of

3

their parts. These are rarely the same from one culture to the next, or even within the same culture when it is as diverse as ours.

All cultures have one part of the dragon in common. They hold up one set of stories for females and another for males, offering a different set of experiences to their youth depending on their sex. Adolescents of either sex, as a result, are likely to follow different developmental paths to maturity. Tracing the impact of these gendered paths on adolescent development is a theme of this text.

Similarly, adolescents' lives reflect, in intimate ways, their cultural backgrounds. These cultures affect everything from which foods taste good to which language they use when talking to their grandmothers. Cultures, like dragons, are too big to be seen by those who live within them, even though the very rituals, beliefs, and rhythms of one's culture provide the perspective from which one views the world. Members of a culture, because they share its tastes, its rhythms, and its stories, share expectancies that give shape to the events they experience. Experience, you see, rather than being taken in raw, is interpreted, and culture, like a pair of eyeglasses, provides the interpretive lenses through which one looks. Just as with glasses, one sees *through* the lenses, missing the culture that makes that view of reality possible. The influence of ethnicity and culture on adolescents' development is a second theme of this text, illustrating a **contextual perspective** on development.

Perceiving the world—whether it's listening to someone talk or making sense of what we are seeing—is an active process. Reality does not come at us packaged for passive absorption. In order to experience a coherent, meaningful world, a person must construct or assemble it from the moment, from less coherent raw material. I remember, for instance, frequently having difficulty understanding my mother-in-law, who spoke English with a heavy Yiddish accent. It's not that I couldn't ever understand her, but I had to know which language to "listen" in. If it were Yiddish, there was simply no hope of understanding, because I didn't know the language. But even with English, if I *thought* it was Yiddish, I also didn't understand. Only when she was speaking English, and I expected to hear English, could I make out what she had said—knowing which sounds to listen for, knowing that "vehdink" could be heard as "wedding," that "voo-manh" could be "woman." This view of perception as an active, constructive process—referred to as a **constructive perspective**—will inform the pages of this text.

A lifespan developmental perspective organizes our study of adolescence. The lifespan reveals continuity as well as change with the years. Traditionally, developmentalists have not allowed themselves this broad a view of their field. Until fairly recently, we have lifted a particular span of years out of the life cycle for closer observation. But in doing so, we often missed the similarities these adolescent years held with other ages. The **lifespan perspective** is multidisciplinary, providing several perspectives from which to view adolescence. Psychology, sociology, education, history, and anthropology all bring insights to this field of study.

The text also distinguishes two distinct periods in adolescence. Early adolescents must contend with puberty, changing gender roles, developing more autonomous relationships with parents, and more mature relation-

Adolescence spans the years from 11 to 19, a time of dramatic physical, emotional, and intellectual changes. Some of the cast members in this school play still look like children, and others seem nearly adult.

ships with peers. Late adolescents face the need to integrate their sexuality into their relationships, prepare for adult work roles, arrive at a set of values to guide their behavior and, through each of these, achieve a sense of their own identity.

The chapters themselves are organized around these distinct periods of **early adolescence** and **late adolescence.** The first half of the book focuses on development in early adolescence, from approximately age 11 to 15, considering first the physical changes of puberty (Chapter 3), the intellectual changes (Chapter 4), the changing relationships within the family (Chapter 5), the world of peers (Chapter 6), and school (Chapter 7). The second half of the book examines development in late adolescence, from approximately age 16 to 19, which is organized around the central task of achieving an identity (Chapter 8). The next four chapters examine various aspects of identity: defining gender roles and intimate relationships (Chapter 9), preparing for work (Chapter 10), and developing a set of values by which to live (Chapter 11). Chapter 12 examines some of the problems of youth, and Chapter 13 addresses the supports adolescents need to grow into adulthood. Finally, Chapter 14 summarizes the research issues discussed in the various Research Focuses throughout the text.

Chapter 1 begins our study by examining the many faces of adolescents. We look first at differences between the sexes and then turn to cultural and ethnic differences. Sex differences become more pronounced in adolescence than they were in childhood; however, the differences among adolescents of the same sex remain larger than those between the sexes. The same is true for ethnicity. Just as with gender, differences among adolescents within any ethnic group are greater than those that exist among the groups themselves. Perhaps as a consequence, the basis for distinguishing among ethnic groups is difficult to maintain at other than a superficial level, and definitions of ethnicity and race are still evolving (Phinney, 1996).

Adolescence itself is not easy to define. Think for a moment of a 17-year-old boy who has just graduated from high school. He's as tall as his dad and can beat him in arm wrestling. He has a driver's license but isn't allowed to drink alcoholic beverages in his state. He's old enough to enlist in the army, but can't vote for another year. It's clear that he is no longer a child, but is it just as clear that he is an adult? Even though he can drive a car and carry a gun, he is not old enough to vote or drink. Adolescence abounds with paradoxes such as these. We will look at biological, psychological, and sociological definitions of adolescence.

The chapter moves to a consideration of the various perspectives—constructive, contextual, and lifespan—from which adolescence can be viewed. Each brings an advantage to the study of adolescence. A glance at history informs us that adolescence has not always existed as we know it today; nor, for that matter, has childhood or adulthood.

Despite the tremendous diversity of experience among adolescents today, all face the task of gaining a sense of themselves. Adolescence is frequently discussed as a transitional stage. The lifespan perspective suggests that adulthood is equally transitional, as are other developmental periods. We look to adolescents and parents, and their parents, for similarities and differences in developmental issues. Perhaps we can think of adolescence—like every other age—as a developmental lens that focuses the past onto the future.

ADOLESCENTS IN A CHANGING POPULATION

There are almost 19 million 10- to 14-year-olds and another 18 million 15- to 19-year-olds in the United States (U.S. Bureau of the Census, 1996a). Adolescents make up approximately 14% of the population. Many of these adolescents are the children of the baby boomers who were born in the years following World War II, from 1946 to 1964. As their parents' generation has been squeezing its way through the population, the population has been ever so slightly aging with it. The median age for the population in 1982 was 30.6. By 1990 it had risen to 32.9; by the year 2000, this figure should be 36.3, and by 2030 it will reach 40.8 and continue to climb (U.S. Bureau of the Census, 1992a). We can see these trends in the population pyramids shown in Figure 1.1. The pyramid for 1982 was still a bit bottom heavy, that is, relatively youthful. By 2000 the baby boomers will all be over 35, and the nation's median age will lift appreciably.

Presently, a second trend is under way, with more children and preadolescents attending elementary and secondary schools than ever before (Youth Indicators, 1996). Such population changes can affect adolescents more immediately than one might think. With increasing numbers of stu-

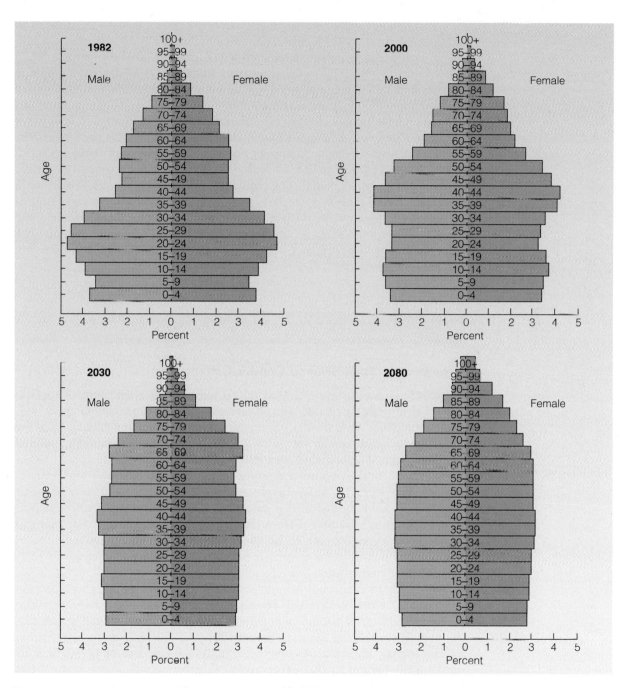

FIGURE 1.1   Population Pyramids for the Years 1982, 2000, 2030, and 2080. *Source:* U.S. Bureau of the Census. (1984). *Current population reports, Series P-25, No. 952, Projections of the population of the United States by age, sex, and race: 1983–2080.* Washington, DC: U.S. Government Printing Office.

dents in school, there is a growing demand for teachers and social services, thereby increasing potential jobs. The downside to these trends is that competition for such jobs will increase among those reaching the age to fill them.

Family characteristics are also changing. More families are headed by single parents. In 1993, more than twice as many children under 18 (25%) lived with a single parent than a generation ago (Youth Indicators, 1996). This figure is even higher for minority children and adolescents. Approximately 29% of Hispanic and 60% of African American children lived with a single parent (Youth Indicators, 1996). By far, most single parents are women. These figures contain a hidden dimension for many adolescents—poverty. Over half of the families with children under 18 that are maintained by single women qualify as poor (Youth Indicators, 1996). Slightly over 20% of children under 18 years live below the poverty level (U.S. Bureau of the Census, 1996a). The difficulty of making it on one's own while maintaining a family has, in part, accounted for other changes in families. Many single parents live with a relative, usually one or both of their parents, to make ends meet. As we turn the corner to the twenty-first century, it may be with a grandparent at the wheel and mom and the kids in the backseat.

THE MANY FACES OF ADOLESCENTS

One Face or Two? Sex and Gender Differences

Few differences are more important to adolescents than those associated with being male or female. Yet few are as likely to be misunderstood. Misunderstandings arise from a basic confusion—that of sex with gender. Sex refers to whether one is biologically female or male and is determined at the moment of conception. **Sex differences** are biologically based. Examples include differences in the reproductive systems of males and females, or differences in the average height and body proportions of each sex. Gender refers to the distinctions a culture makes in what it considers masculine or feminine. **Gender differences** are socially determined. For example, our culture expects males to be strong and rational and females to be intuitive and helpful. One is *born* female or male, but one is *socialized* to be feminine or masculine.

A quick tour through a high school reveals many differences between students of either sex. It also reveals the difficulty we face in interpreting these differences. Walk into a math class, such as trigonometry or calculus, and you'll see more males than females. Why? Is the male brain better suited to math than the female brain, or are males expected to be better in math and simply live up to that expectation? In other words, is this a sex difference or a gender difference? Continuing the tour, we'd probably find more females than males in a home economics class. You might ask, "Is it in one's genes to be domestic?" (a sex difference). Or "Are females encouraged to be domestic in ways that males are not?" (a gender difference).

Gender stereotypes are the beliefs most people hold concerning what is a typical male or female. These stereotypes encompass traits, roles, and occupations. For the most part, characteristics perceived as typically masculine are the opposites of those seen as feminine (Constantinople, 1973).

Why are so few girls in
advanced science and
math classes? Are boys
naturally better at
these subjects, or are
they simply behaving
according to gender
stereotypes?

Males, for example, are thought to be independent, active, and rational. Females, on the other hand, are perceived as dependent, passive, and emotional. As a result of this either/or approach, gender stereotypes can be problematic for adolescents, when their being different from the stereotype of their own sex brings them closer to the stereotype for the other sex. Consider a boy who approaches situations intuitively rather than rationally. Not only is he seen as less masculine than boys who adopt rational approaches, he is also seen as more feminine (Lips, 1997).

On a more positive note, gender roles are more flexible today than in the past, allowing adolescents to express both feminine and masculine qualities. Adolescents of either sex can be sensitive and assertive, gentle and self-reliant. These adolescents are called **androgynous** ("andro" for male and "gyno" for female). However, fashioning one's own gender role in this way usually occurs in late adolescence because it requires a degree of self-knowledge and confidence beyond the reach of most early adolescents.

Whether based on sex, race, or even age, stereotypes usually reflect differences due to status as well. In our society, males frequently have positions of higher status than females. Behaviors of females and males that are attributed to their gender can often be explained by differences in their status. The masculine stereotype, for instance, includes qualities such as independence, decision-making skill, and risk taking. The confusion of status differences and gender differences becomes clear when we think of reversing the roles typically held by females and males. When status roles are reversed, as in the case of a male secretary and a female boss, the differences attributed to their gender often disappear. Who is more likely to make decisions, and who to be helpful? Or who will likely take risks, and who will be more dependent? Differences between the sexes exist in a social context, and this context will affect our interpretation of them (Lips, 1997).

Before leaving this discussion of gender differences, one final point is important. Gender differences are much smaller than individual differences. That is, the differences that exist *between* adolescents of either sex are much smaller than those that exist *among* adolescents of the same sex (Lips, 1997).

Social context gives rise to another difference facing adolescents: their cultural backgrounds. Increasing numbers of adolescents in the United States belong to ethnic minorities. All adolescents—those within the majority as well as those in minorities—are affected by increasing cultural diversity.

The Colors of Change: Ethnic Diversity

Adolescents of both sexes are coming of age in a culture that is ethnically diverse. The proportion of adolescents belonging to ethnic groups of color—including African Americans, Asian and Pacific Islander Americans, Hispanics, and Native Americans—has been steadily increasing. In 1950, ethnic minorities made up 10.7% of the population. By 1970, this figure increased to 12.4%, and by the turn of the century it should be just under 17%. By the year 2020, 40% of youth in the United States will be members of an ethnic minority group, with Hispanics making up nearly 20% of the population under age 18, African Americans approximately 15%, and Asian and Pacific Islander Americans approximately 4% of the population under age 18 (U.S. Bureau of the Census, 1996b; Youth Indicators, 1996).

The term *ethnicity* has been used to include adolescents who differ racially as well as culturally, for several reasons. Both genetic and behavioral

On school days, dual-culture adolescents blend in with the mainstream teenage culture of their friends, but with their family they partake of traditional customs and may even speak a different language.

variation among individuals of European, African, and Asian descent are greater *within* any racial classification than *between* classifications (Lewontin, 1982; Rowe, Vazsonyi, & Flannery, 1994; Zuckerman, 1990). The *significance* of race can best be understood from a contextual perspective. The community and cultural contexts in which people live and the responses of others to racial features such as skin pigmentation and facial characteristics are what contribute to one's sense of identity (Phinney, 1996).

Ethnicity can affect adolescents in many ways. Adolescents who belong to a minority are more aware of the racial or ethnic differences that distinguish them than are those who belong to the majority. Majority adolescents may even be unaware that they are also members of a racial group. Thomas Kochman (1987) found that Whites distinguished each other in terms of ethnicity, but not race. They would, for example, refer to themselves as Irish or Polish, never as "White." The terms *minority* and *majority* are relative, of course. Whites are actually in the minority throughout the world, though in the majority in the United States. Similarly, within this country, White adolescents can experience minority status if they live in a community or attend a school in which some other ethnic or racial group predominates (Phinney, 1996).

But what does it mean to belong to an ethnic group? Jean Phinney (1996), a psychologist at California State University, Los Angeles, points out that ethnicity cannot be thought of simply in terms of labels for groups of people who are neatly distinguished from one another. People using the same label often differ widely from one another, including the ways in which they interpret and use the very terms by which they identify themselves. Rather than sorting people into categories, it is necessary to examine ethnicity with respect to at least three *dimensions* along which individuals vary: their cultural values and attitudes, their sense of belonging to the group, and their experience of being a member of a minority.

Although culture, the first dimension of ethnicity, is central to the identity of an ethnic group, there are such large differences in lifestyles and traditions within any group that culture alone is not enough to distinguish members of one group from those of another. The term *Hispanic*, for instance, includes not only Mexican Americans but also people from more than a dozen South American countries, each with its own distinctive culture. Hispanic carries a different meaning for each of those cultures. What is important is that individuals belonging to the group are seen by others, and by themselves, as a separate group within society for whom their common heritage continues to be a significant part of their lives. Thus ethnicity is more than ancestry; it almost always involves culture, or the socially shared values, beliefs, and norms that determine one's way of life and that are passed on from one generation to the next (Betancourt & Lopez, 1993).

Individuals within an ethnic group differ as well in the degree to which they identify with their group, or in their **ethnic identity,** the second dimension of ethnicity. Ethnic identity itself is multifaceted, including how one labels or identifies oneself, as well as one's sense of belonging to a group and the degree to which one values and participates in one's group. Furthermore, one's ethnic identity can be seen to change developmentally, from

Research Focus

Archival Research: Racial Socialization—Survival Tactics in a White Society?

With Michael Wapner

Parents reflect the values of their society, and in doing so, pass them on to their children. Psychologists refer to parents as socialization agents. As "agents" of society, they also communicate the statuses and roles that make up the social order, and prepare their children to participate accordingly as adults. So far so good.

So what's the bad part? Minority parents face a special problem when they encounter societal values that can diminish the self-esteem of their children and, if internalized, could prevent them from realizing their potential. How do minority parents prepare their children for entrance into a society that frequently views their group negatively?

In a sense, they become "double agents." In addition to socializing their children into the values of the broader society, minority parents interpret that society's values in ways that shield their children from harm. By explicitly speaking against negative stereotypes, by serving as models themselves, and by exposing their children to cultural experiences that reflect the strengths of their own background, they inculcate feelings of worth and group pride. In Black society, this process is termed *racial socialization*.

The way Black parents perceive society, and communicate those perceptions to their children, should reflect their own position in it. Yet we know little about the influence of demographic variables on racial socialization. Frequently a single study lacks the scope to address such issues. Tapping into existing databases, often collected from national samples, offers a useful alternative. *Archival research* does just that: It uses existing information to obtain answers to research questions.

Archives exist in many forms: Vast databases collected from national samples, written records such as books or newspapers, and publicly maintained records are examples. The databases maintained by the U.S. Census Bureau are an obvious source of archival information, illustrating the first of these forms. How might one use books or newspapers to answer research questions? Consider, for example, the question of whether school materials reinforce traditional sex-role stereotypes. To answer, one might sample textbooks and analyze their content for the frequency of female and male characters, their activities, and the settings in which they appear (such as home or work). Is living together prior to marriage more common today than a generation ago? One can look at marriage license applications for common addresses, to determine an answer.

An obvious advantage to archival research is *accessibility*: The data have already been collected. Another advantage is that many archives, such as

an initial stage in which ethnicity is simply taken for granted, through a period of exploration into the significance of belonging to a group, to a secure sense of oneself as a member of that group (Phinney, 1989, 1993).

Being a member of an ethnic group typically brings with it the experience of minority status, the third dimension of ethnicity, although not always. For instance, in Canada, English-speaking and French-speaking people are both members of dominant groups, yet each is a different ethnic group (Phinney & Rotheram, 1987). At this point, the term *minority* deserves closer attention. It might seem, for example, that members of the majority would always outnumber those of a minority. Yet such is not always the case. In certain areas of the United States, people of one race outnumber those of another yet are not considered part of the majority. In some counties of Mississippi, the ratio of Blacks to Whites is three to one, yet the lat-

Research Focus *(continued)*

the U.S. Census data, are more complete than any data that could be collected in a single research study. A further advantage is that the measures are *unobtrusive.* Subjects do not know they are being studied and therefore do not change their behavior or their answers to questions (as they might, for instance, if asked whether they are living together). Unobtrusive measures are *nonreactive:* They do not change the behavior they are measuring.

Disadvantages to using archival data also exist. Information may be lost over time. The quality of record keeping can change with time, causing unsuspecting researchers to infer that changes have occurred when in actuality none have. Computers, for example, allow better record keeping by police. As a result, crime may appear to have increased, whereas in actuality it is only being recorded more precisely.

What does archival research tell us about racial socialization? Do most Black parents act as double agents to shield their children from harm by the larger society? Michael Thornton, Linda Chatters, Robert Taylor, and Walter Allen (1990), analyzing data from a national survey of African Americans, found that they do. Nearly two-thirds of all Black parents engage in some racial socialization. What demographic variables predict racial socialization? These investigators found that sex, age, marital status, and region of the country all predict the likelihood of racial socialization. Mothers are more likely than fathers to prepare their children for the realities of minority

status. So, too, are older parents, those who are married (versus never married), and those who are more educated. Regional differences also predict socialization approaches. Black parents living in the Northeast, more so than those in the South, engage in racial socialization.

For most Black parents, race is a salient issue in the socialization process. Most feel the need to prepare their children for the minority experience of living in our society. Yet just like jewelers refining a precious metal, they may find that gold appears beneath the surface dross. The dross? Children learn of racially based restrictions, such as job and housing discrimination. And the gold? They learn that they must work hard, get a good education, and, above all, be proud of who they are.

What other groups can you name in which children and adolescents need *corrective socialization?* Can you think of any groups where it is needed but not generally available? Who teaches gay male and lesbian adolescents how to deal with negative stereotypes? Their heterosexual parents? What can mentally handicapped or intellectually gifted adolescents learn from their parents of average intelligence? Who socializes adolescents in more androgynous sex roles? Traditional parents?

Source: M. C. Thornton, L. M. Chatters, R. J. Taylor, & W. R. Allen. (1990). Sociodemographic and environmental correlates of racial socialization by black parents. *Child Development, 61,* 401–409.

ter are considered the majority. It could be argued that the majority status of the Whites is determined not by local ratios, but by those for the country as a whole. Yet a look at other countries suggests that qualifiers other than sheer numbers are involved in determining majority status. The British, for example, although vastly outnumbered in India, retained their majority status, as did Whites in South Africa (Simpson & Yinger, 1985).

The Research Focus, "Archival Research: Racial Socialization," explores some of the ways that minority parents prepare their children for life in the broader society. Minority status has less to do with numbers per se than it does with the distribution of power within a society, being associated, at least for those of color, with lower status and less power, whether in positions of leadership or, even when education is equated, in annual income (Dovidio & Gaertner, 1986; Huston, McLoyd, & Garcia Coll, 1994). Stanley

Sue (1991) argues that the very term *minority* connotes the unequal relationships that exist among various groups within a society, and that to fully understand the minority experience, one must understand the ways in which these relationships define patterns of exploitation.

Minority status also signifies, for one reason or another, a failure to be fully assimilated into the dominant culture. Louis Wirth (1945) defines a **minority** as

> a group of people who, because of their physical or cultural characteristics, are singled out from the others in the society in which they live for differential and unequal treatment, and who therefore regard themselves as objects of collective discrimination. The existence of a minority in a society implies the existence of a corresponding dominant group with higher social status and greater privileges. Minority status carries with it the exclusion from full participation in the life of the society. (p. 347)

Minorities can be set apart by race, religion, nationality, or other defining features. (Box 1.1 gives a personal account of minority socialization.) In fact, Wirth's definition of a minority could also include women, the elderly, the disabled, or adolescents themselves.

Perhaps nothing captures the vagaries of ethnicity and race better than the experiences of biracial adolescents whose lives embrace two different cultures. In *Life on the Color Line,* Gregory Williams (1995), presently dean of a law school, has written of growing up White in a segregated town in the 1950s, before discovering that his dark-skinned father was actually Black and not of Italian descent, as he and his brother had been led to believe:

> As the bus bumped into gear, I felt a tinge of doubt. He leaned closer and spoke very softly. "There's something else I want to tell you."
>
> "What?" I groaned.
>
> "Remember Miss Sallie who used to work for us in the tavern?"
>
> Dad's lower lip quivered. He looked ill. Had he always looked this unhealthy, I wondered, or was it something that happened on the trip? I felt my face—skin like putty, lips chapped and cracked. Had I changed, too?
>
> "It's hard to tell you boys this." He paused, then slowly added, "But she's really my momma. That means she's your grandmother."
>
> "But that can't be, Dad! She's colored!" I whispered, lest I be overheard by the other white passengers on the bus.
>
> "That's right, Billy," he continued. "She's colored. That makes you part colored, too, and in Muncie you're gonna live with my Aunt Bes. . . ."
>
> I didn't understand Dad. I knew I wasn't colored, and neither was he. My skin was white. All of us are white, I said to myself. But for the first time, I had to admit Dad didn't exactly look white. His deeply tanned skin puzzled me as I sat there trying to classify my own father. Goose bumps covered my arms as I realized that whatever he was, I was. I took a deep breath. I couldn't make any mistakes. I looked closer. His heavy lips and dark brown eyes didn't make him colored, I concluded. His black, wavy hair was different from Negroes' hair, but it was different from most white folks' hair, too. He was darker than most whites, but Mom said he was Italian. That was why my baby brother had such dark skin and curly hair. Mom told us to be proud of our Italian heritage! That's it, I decided. He was Italian. I leaned back against the seat, satisfied. Yet the unsettling image of Miss Sallie flashed before me like a neon sign. (pp. 32–33)

Box 1.1   Socializing African American Children

When strangers stop me on the street or at airports, often it is to comment on the essays I write about my family. Those about life in our old home in Brooklyn provide the most response. "It is obvious," a nun in a brown habit said one day, "that yours was a house of joy." I loved the phrase, but it troubled me.

It was not, I started to say to her, always so joyful. In fact, there were times that were painful, as there might be in any family. Some of our dinner-table discussions touched sensitive subjects. For example, our parents often struggled to help us understand and battle racial rejection. It was not always easy for them, proud immigrants in a new land.

One of the heroes of our family in the late 1940s was Dr. Ralph J. Bunche. He was then this nation's highest-ranking black diplomat. He was also a leading academic. His field at Harvard had been international organization, a subject of special interest to our family. It was at the time of the formation of the United Nations. There must have been a dozen pictures of Dr. Bunche around our home. We owned at least one copy of everything published under his name.

The difficult time came the night of Dr. Bunche's public humiliation. He was denied entry to the Forest Hills Tennis Club, then the scene of the most prestigious matches in the world of tennis. Dr. Bunche's rejection became our own. . . .

The idea that it would reject the hero of our family meant it had rejected each of us. . . .

As one of my three sisters, a tennis player, began to put her troubled thoughts into words, tears welled up in her eyes, and she stopped talking. My mother's eyes met my father's. I could tell they had been discussing this between themselves.

"I want you children to understand what you are seeing here." He pointed across to a side table where the *New York Daily News* lay. The story of Dr. Bunche's rejection was prominently displayed. "I know you feel sorry about Dr. Bunche, but I tell you my prayers tonight are for those men who have humiliated them. . . .

"People who create special rules of exclusiveness think they are showing the rest of us what great status they have achieved. In fact they are telling us the very opposite. . . ."

"The very opposite." My mother repeated my father's last phrase for special emphasis. They often reinforced each other's points by repeating a few of the exact words.

"In fact," my father continued, "when people need racial exclusiveness in their social lives, it is usually to prove to others they have 'arrived.' But that's not how I read such men. I read them as socially insecure. Have you ever noticed that truly confident people walk and work among all with ease? The strong do not need that sort of status; the wealthy but weak do."

"Dr. Bunche," my mother said with a wry smile, "is fortunate he will not have to associate with such people." At last we laughed.

Source: Adapted from R. C. Maynard. (1990, August 5). An example of how Afro-American parents socialize children. *The Oakland Tribune.*

THE CONSTRUCTIVE PERSPECTIVE

The constructive perspective assumes that we actively construct what we know of the world, interpreting our experiences, composing or making sense of the events to which we react. One person's reality is not necessarily shared by others. Reality is not a given. In a very real sense, we make it up. Despite what his father said or how he looked, despite the image of Miss Sallie or knowing that she was his father's mother, Gregory Williams still thought his father must be Italian. Yet the reality of Miss Sallie could not be denied, nor the reality of his father's words. Those were facts. It's just that these facts didn't fit his world.

Foundations of
Adolescent
Development

We interpret the be-
havior of others based
on our own contex-
tual perceptions.
Some may perceive
this teen as upset
while others may think
he's concentrating.

Gregory Williams had grown up in a segregated world, living in a White neighborhood and going to White schools. His reality reflected a logic of its own, one that was internally consistent and through which he made sense of his life. The simple fact of a Black grandmother wilted in the face of this. He would need new experiences—a new neighborhood, new schools, an expanded family—before this fact could become real, before he could see his father's tanned skin and black, wavy hair as other than Italian.

How do we go about constructing the events to which we respond? How are we to understand such a constructive process? We can begin an explanation by examining the activity you are engaging in now—reading. The constructive approach assumes that perception is an active process. To perceive the letters that make up a sentence, we must do something other than simply keep our eyes open and on the page. The nature of this perceptual activity takes the form of scanning the lines that form the letters to determine which features are present. Features are characteristics of letters, such as whether lines are straight or curved, open or closed, or angular. Perceptual scanning is directed by expectancies as to what a letter *might* be, based on what has preceded it. (Given that there are 26 letters in the alphabet, each of which is defined by a combination of features, there are simply too many features to scan for otherwise.)

Look at Figure 1.2. Are there right angles? Could that letter be a *B*? An *E*? An *E* has the same number of right angles as a *B*, but lacks curvilinear lines. Are there curvilinear lines? Research on letter recognition lends substantial support to this type of analysis. Confusion errors in tasks calling for individuals to quickly identify letters flashed on a screen confirm that the more features two letters have in common, the more likely they are to be confused with each other (Neisser, 1967).

If you are still not convinced that we actively "construct" the events to which we respond, take a moment to look at Figure 1.3. Notice that the very same lines that form the letter *B* in the top row also form the number

FIGURE 1.2   Letter Recognition

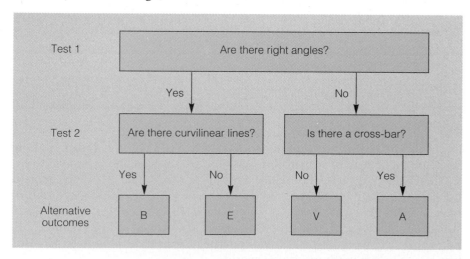

FIGURE 1.3
The same physical
arrangement of
lines that forms
the letter B also
forms the number
13.

13 in the bottom row. What determines whether you will see these lines as a letter or as a number? The answer, obviously, is not in the physical arrangement of the lines themselves, because this arrangement is the same in either case. Rather, it is your, the reader's, expectancy to see one or the other figure that determines how the arrangement of lines will be read. This expectancy, in turn, is derived from the context in which the lines appear—that context being either a row of letters or a row of numbers.

This same active, constructive process occurs at each of many levels of human functioning, from the relatively micro level of perceptual processing that has just been examined to the macro level of social interactions. An experiment by John Condry and David Ross (1985) illustrates that the same constructive process occurs in the perception of social behavior. These investigators showed college students a videotape of two children engaged in rough and tumble activity in the snow. The actual sex of the children couldn't be determined because of their bulky snowsuits; some viewers were told the children were boys and others that they were girls. Viewers who believed the children to be boys perceived the children's behavior to be playful. However, those who thought they were looking at girls saw the identical behavior (remember, they all viewed the same videotape) as aggressive. Boys' play, you see, is expected to be rough, and actions such as wrestling or pummeling each other with snowballs fit the viewers' expectations of how boys play. In other words, it was easy for them to "read" such actions as playful. Conversely, girls' play is expected to be quiet. Given that expectancy, wrestling and pummeling could only be perceived as aggressive.

What determined what each viewer saw? Just as in the previous example, the answer is not to be found in the videotape of the two children. The same videotape was seen by all subjects. Rather, it is to be found in the expectancies of the viewers. What they saw is what they constructed, guided by their expectancies, as these gave meaning to the activity they were viewing. The Research Focus, "An Experiment," provides a further example of research into the ways that people give meaning to the behavior of others.

Research Focus

An Experiment: "Who You Pushin', Buddy!" Perceptions of Aggressiveness

By Michael Wapner

People interpret experience by literally constructing or piecing together the events to which they respond. One of the most important manifestations of this interpretive construction occurs in determining the intentions of others. Even when an action is so obvious that it leaves little to interpretation, the motives behind the action still need to be understood, and this usually requires a good deal of cognitive construction. Observers may all agree that George bumped into Ira. But what the observers feel and do about it depends more on why they think George did it than the mere fact that he did. If George stumbled and could not keep from bumping Ira, that's one thing. But if George bumped Ira to get ahead of him in line, that's entirely different.

What is it that determines how observers interpret the intentions behind an act? Mary Lynne Courtney and Robert Cohen (1996) designed an experiment to investigate this question. In particular, they looked at the contribution of two variables to the interpretation of intention: (1) prior information and (2) the personality of the observer. These two variables, in addition to influencing an observer's interpretation of the intentions behind an action, illustrate, by their difference, something fundamental about the design of experiments in general.

Briefly, boys between 8 and 12 were shown a videotape of two boys playing tag on a playground. At a critical point in the middle of the tape, the boy being chased falls down after being tagged by the other boy. The fallen boy slowly gets up and resumes the game. The variables were introduced as follows:

(1) PRIOR INFORMATION: AN INDEPENDENT VARIABLE

Previous research, and common sense, would suggest that observers' interpretation of the intention behind an act should depend on what else they know about the actors. Thus, one would guess that the subjects would more likely attribute hostile intent to the tag that caused the fall if they were told beforehand that the two boys were enemies and had just recently been fighting. Conversely, the likelihood of seeing the tag as accidental should increase if the observers believed the boys to be good friends. But what if the observers knew nothing about the boys? These three conditions—let us call them benign, hostile, and ambiguous—constitute the independent variable in the experiment.

In an *experiment,* each group of subjects is treated differently than the others. In all other respects the groups are equivalent. If the groups differ afterward, we can assume the difference is due to the way they were treated. In order to be confident about this assumption, however, we must be sure that the groups are the same at the outset. The simplest way to ensure this would be to start with identical groups. But because no two individuals are ever the same in all respects, such a tactic is impossible. An equally good approach is to make sure the groups don't differ in any *systematic* way. We can accomplish this by assigning individuals at random to each condition. If each person has the same chance of being assigned to each group, and if we assign enough people to each, the differences among the people would balance out among the groups. *Random assignment* will distribute any initial differences more or less evenly among the groups. Contrast

Research Focus (*continued*)

this type of independent variable with a second variable these investigators studied.

(2) AGGRESSIVENESS OF THE OBSERVER: A CLASSIFICATION VARIABLE

Aggressive boys have been found to attribute hostile intentions to the actions of others more frequently than less aggressive boys. Courtney and Cohen incorporated the variable of aggressiveness by having classmates rate each boy for aggressiveness. Notice that unlike assignment to the prior knowledge variable, aggressiveness scores could not be assigned randomly. Rather, subjects were *classified* based on judgments of a preexisting characteristic—that is, aggressiveness. Thus, if we find a difference between aggressive and unaggressive boys, we cannot be sure that the difference is due to something else that might be correlated with aggressiveness.

Now let's look at the results of the study. The subjects (randomly assigned and classified as described above) were shown the videotape and asked to "segment" the action by pressing a button whenever one action stopped and another began. These points of segmentation are labeled "breakpoints." Of course, most natural behavior does not have discrete breakpoints. Rather, one activity flows into another. Thus, segmenting the flow of action is not simply marking what already objectively exists; rather, it is an act of cognitive construction and will vary from observer to observer.

A dramatic example of segmentation as a cognitive construction lies in the fact that we hear our native language spoken in discrete, word segments although the sound issuing from the speaker's mouth is continuous, as can be demonstrated by visualizing normal speech on the screen of an oscilloscope. It is our knowledge of the rhythms and sounds of our native language, as well as familiarity with the vocabulary and current context, that allows us to segment accurately. You can test this proposition. Rent a film in an unfamiliar foreign language. Then gather a few friends who are equally ignorant of the language and all try to count the number of words spoken in two minutes of dialogue. You will be surprised at the wildly different counts.

Segmenting the action in Courtney and Cohen's videotape is roughly the same kind of cognitive task. But unlike speech, there is no cultural consensus as to where the breakpoints belong. Because the number of breakpoints should increase when an individual is seeking more information, it was expected that identifying breakpoints would be a function of how much information the boys had about the action. Recall, each boy got information from two sources: (1) from what he was told about the boys' friendship (the condition of prior information to which he had been assigned) and (2) from what he assumed (based on his level of aggressiveness). When subjects were given information that the boys were enemies, aggressiveness did not predict the amount of segmentation. Everyone "knew," in other words, what was going on and didn't have to look for it. When subjects were told the boys were friends, or were told nothing at all, subjects who were more aggressive identified more breakpoints than less aggressive ones, suggesting that their perception of ongoing behavior differed from that of less aggressive boys. Aggressiveness relates not only to the motives one attributes to others, but also to the ways in which one organizes one's perception of ongoing events.

Source: M. I. Courtney & R. Cohen. (1996). Behavior segmentation by boys as a function of aggressiveness and prior information. *Child Development, 67,* 1034–1047.

THE CONTEXTUAL PERSPECTIVE

Just as adolescents put together, or make sense of, the separate events making up experience, they also construct, or give meaning to, the larger contexts in which these events take shape—virtually guaranteeing that one person's world will never completely be shared by others. Adolescents growing up in the same family, going to the same schools, living in the same community can experience quite different contexts. It is not so much the actual, objective context—whether family, school, or community—that affects development as it is how that context is *perceived* by the individual (Bronfenbrenner, 1979, 1994).

What aspects of our environment are we likely to perceive and incorporate into our reality? Urie Bronfenbrenner, a psychologist at Cornell University, identifies three features of one's environment, each of which, rather than being a static aspect of the physical setting, involves the person in a dynamic exchange with it. First, Bronfenbrenner points out that individuals are most likely to attend to and notice what they are doing, the ongoing *activity* they are engaged in at the time. Much of this activity involves us with others, in *interpersonal relations* that take the form of what we say and do when we are with other people. And last, being with others invariably implicates us in a *role,* with expectations for certain behaviors depending on the setting or the relationship.

At this point, it is important to highlight the interpersonal and very intimate nature of one's environment. The environment is not to be found in rooms, or streets, or stores. Nor is it in books or clothes, or the presence or absence of one resource or another. It is all of these, but also something more. The environment, in fact, is not that which is outside the person or separate from the person. Rather than being something outside the self, the environment always *includes* the self, in the form of how we experience ourself in relation to something else, usually another person. Bronfenbrenner emphasizes this point when he stresses the importance of a young person developing a meaningful relationship with an adult who finds that young person "somehow special, especially wonderful, and especially precious" (Bronfenbrenner, 1990, p. 31). Such a relationship becomes a springboard from which adolescents can step into other contexts, determining how they will be perceived.

Bronfenbrenner adds that the environment does not exist as a simple, unified context, but takes the form of overlapping spheres of influence, much like a set of nested Russian dolls (Figure 1.4). At the innermost and most immediate level of environmental influence, that of the **microsystem,** are the various settings in which the adolescent moves throughout the day: at home, at school, with friends, at work. A characteristic of the microsystem is that the activities, interpersonal relations, and roles involve the adolescent in face-to-face interactions with others. It's relatively easy to imagine how such interactions might affect an adolescent, whether they take the form of supportive eye contact from a friend or a verbal exchange with a parent.

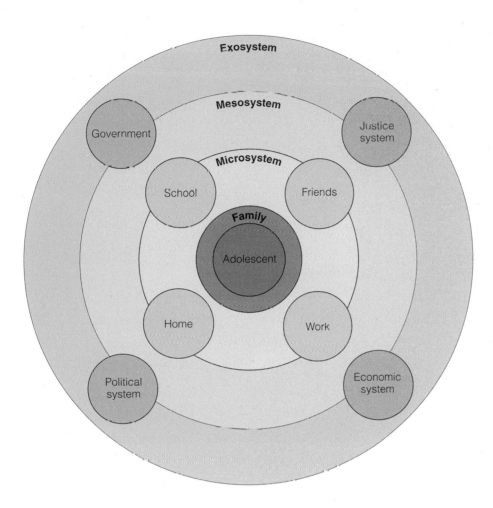

FIGURE 1.4
Bronfenbrenner's
Environmental Model

Bronfenbrenner maintains that adolescents are affected not only by immediate influences such as these, but also by various relations among the microsystems of daily life, influences at the level of the **mesosystem.** For example, a parent's involvement with school can significantly improve the adolescent's academic performance (Comer, Haynes, Joyner, & Ben-Avie, 1996).

In addition to the microsystem and mesosystem, adolescents can be affected by environments in which they are not present but that affect their immediate surroundings. Bronfenbrenner refers to such influences as the **exosystem.** Conditions in a parent's workplace, for instance, can affect the amount of time the parent has to spend with the family or the amount of stress introduced into family life, thereby affecting the adolescent.

The **macrosystem,** which consists of the underlying social and political climate, is even further removed from adolescents' daily experiences, yet it impinges on their lives in very real ways. Laws concerning compulsory education, the mainstreaming of students with special needs, and the separation of grades into elementary, junior high, and high schools all illustrate the direct ways the macrosystem can affect the lives of adolescents.

Although these middle-school students may all be the same age, they're not necessarily all adolescents yet. The start of adolescence is signaled by puberty rather than by a particular chronological age.

THE LIFESPAN PERSPECTIVE

The lifespan offers a unique perspective from which to view adolescence. Issues that arise in adolescence can be traced back to childhood and followed into adulthood. Issues of autonomy and competence, for example, are immensely important to adolescents. Both are also significant issues facing two other age groups: the elderly and toddlers. We can see continuities such as these, and also note the more obvious changes that occur within the age category itself.

The lives of a teenager and a grandparent appear, and are, very different, yet beneath the surface each person may be coping with similar issues. The teenager, for example, may be trying to get the keys to the family car, whereas the grandparent may be facing the need to surrender them after a lifetime of use. The issue for both is the same: independence. If we were to study either of these ages apart from the other, we would miss the important developmental threads that weave their way through the fabric of life.

Similarly, adolescents and middle-aged parents must cope with changing body images. An adolescent boy and his father will both experience changes in physical development. The adolescent is experiencing rapid muscular development, noticing a new "buffed" look, and pulsing with vitality. His father may be noticing signs of aging: a slight paunch around the middle and the tendency to become winded faster than he remembers. Despite the differences in their ages and in the particular changes they encounter, there are similarities in their experiences as well. Subtle changes in strength and energy level create a new awareness of their bodies and themselves and a need to integrate these changes into the self that each has always known.

The lifespan approach defines development from a number of perspectives. Four of these are especially helpful for understanding adolescence: the biological, psychological, sociological, and historical.

A Biological Definition of Adolescence

The *biological* and physical changes of **puberty** quite literally transform children into sexually and physically mature adults (Hyde, 1990). These changes occur in all adolescents no matter what their culture and are, in fact, the only universal changes of adolescence. They are caused by a heady hormonal cocktail served up by Mother Nature herself. Sometimes increasing by as much as twentyfold with the onset of puberty, hormones account for puberty's dramatic events.

Beginning in early adolescence, puberty takes anywhere from two to four years to complete. Several growth processes are involved, each one regulated by different hormones and frequently occurring at different rates, resulting in **sexual dimorphism,** a term for the physical differences between males and females. These include differences in height, weight, and body proportions, as well as differences in the reproductive system itself (Strong & DeVault, 1997).

Some changes, such as growth of the ovaries or uterus, go unnoticed. Other changes, such as the appearance of facial hair or breasts, though of less reproductive significance, are more dramatic. By age 10 or 11, nearly all preteens begin to look for signs of change in themselves. The events most closely associated with puberty—menstruation in girls and ejaculation in boys—actually occur fairly late in the process. Which changes will occur first and just when they will happen is hard to say for any one person. Wide variations exist in the timing and sequence of development from one individual to the next. Also, development is not necessarily even; some functions mature at a faster rate than others. However, some general statements can be made about the most likely course of events.

The physical growth spurt, one of the first noticeable changes for girls, is a period of accelerated growth beginning just after age 10 and peaking at about age 12. Boys begin to grow approximately two years later, peaking at about age 14. During this period girls grow approximately 3½ inches a year and boys slightly more. Growth in height is accompanied by a corresponding gain in weight and an increase in the rate of muscular development. Body proportions also begin to change, as girls' hips widen and boys' shoulders become broader.

Changes in the reproductive system and the appearance of secondary sex characteristics can also be charted. For boys, changes in the testes and scrotum and the appearance of pubic hair are among the first noticeable changes. For girls, the growth of breast buds and pubic hair typically coincide with growth of the uterus and vagina. Development of the external genitalia also typically occurs in the first year of puberty. Midway through puberty most girls begin to menstruate, usually coinciding with a peak in the growth spurt. Also midway through puberty boys will first experience ejaculation, which may or may not be accompanied by orgasm. Most adult males usually experience orgasm at the same time as ejaculation; however, these are independent processes and may occur separately. Boys, in fact, typically experience erections and sometimes orgasm well before the time they first ejaculate (Hyde, 1990).

Toward the end of puberty, secondary sex characteristics find full expression. Some are long awaited, such as breasts in girls and facial hair in boys; others less so, such as the development of sweat glands and oil glands in the skin, which can be responsible for embarrassing odors and acne. Related to the production of the hormone androgen, these latter events affect boys and girls alike, although boys suffer more than girls because of the higher levels of androgen in their systems.

Even though puberty serves as a convenient, if somewhat imprecise, marker for the onset of adolescence, the changes we have described are completed well before adolescence ends. The task of specifying an end to adolescence is more difficult, and we must turn to psychological and sociological definitions.

A Psychological Definition of Adolescence

Imagine, for the moment, the world of a 15-year-old boy. Video games, comics, and friends fill after-school hours. Old toys and a skateboard are scattered about his room; two pet rats sleep in a cage on the bureau. A notice about a summer program in math for the college-bound is pinned to a bulletin board. He hates math, doesn't know if he wants to go to college, and can't imagine working. His childhood seems to be slipping away, and adulthood remains impossibly distant.

How do adolescents maintain a sense of themselves when faced with changes such as these? The answer gives us a *psychological* perspective on adolescence. Each adolescent reaches a point when it is not possible to continue living out the same life patterns he or she did as a child. The task facing adolescents is to forge a stable identity, to achieve a sense of themselves that transcends the many changes in their experiences and roles. Only then will they be able to bridge the childhood they must leave and the adulthood they have yet to enter.

The task arises naturally from forces present in adolescence: puberty, cognitive growth, and social expectations. The first force to make itself felt is usually puberty. In addition to visible changes in height, weight, and body proportions, puberty brings an inner world of sexual stirrings. These bodily changes are accompanied by adolescents' new awareness of themselves and others' reactions to them; the period is marked by rapid cognitive as well as physical growth. Social expectations subtly change as well. Parents and others expect a new maturity from adolescents. They expect adolescents to begin planning for their lives and thinking for themselves. In short, they expect them to be more responsible—to be more adult.

The convergence of physical maturation with changing personal and social expectations confronts adolescents with new **developmental tasks.** These tasks represent our culture's definition of normal development at different points in life (see Table 1.1 on page 36). Because our sense of ourselves comes in part from our awareness of how others see us, cultural norms give shape to personal standards. Biological maturation contributes more heavily to some tasks, such as adjusting to an adult body, whereas cultural norms contribute more to others, such as developing social skills.

Adolescents face eight developmental tasks. The first four are primarily the concern of early adolescence, the latter four of late adolescence. Each, however, can be thought of as a facet of one central task: achieving a continuing and stable sense of self (Havighurst, 1972).

1. *Achieving new and more mature relations with age-mates of both sexes.* Physical maturation plays an important part in this developmental task. Whether adolescents keep pace with age-mates in physical development or fall behind can affect their friendships and influence membership in social groups. Those who mature much slower, or faster, will be dropped from the group. The groups themselves function as a sort of social laboratory in which adolescents try out and learn new ways of being with others, ways that are more adult. Approval by the others in the group and by age-mates in general becomes especially important as adolescents experiment with new forms of behavior.

Adolescents develop a stable identity by trying out new roles and relationships, such as taking part in a neighborhood cleanup project.

2. *Achieving a masculine or feminine social role.* Although puberty provides the biological basis for this task, cultural expectations are equally important in determining behaviors regarded as masculine or feminine. Well-defined gender roles await adolescents, reflecting our culture's view of characteristic male and female behavior. Most adolescents will conform in large measure to these expectations. Most, too, will tailor their gender roles, taking a tuck here or there, to achieve the best fit. Our culture expects males to be strong, active, assertive, and independent, and females to be the weaker, passive, and dependent sex. Every Tarzan, in other words, needs a Jane. Fortunately for both Tarzan and Jane, as well as the rest of us, these roles have become more relaxed over the past several decades.

Patterns of work, marriage, and child care are changing rapidly for women. We can see corresponding changes in their gender roles as they move out of the home and into the workforce, combining careers with more traditional roles. The socially defined role for men has changed less rapidly, although they, too, face adjustments if only because the roles for women are changing, and the roles of each sex are defined in relation to the other.

3. *Accepting one's physique and using the body effectively.* Puberty again provides the biological basis for this task, as it transforms the bodies of adolescents into those of adults. Girls are slightly ahead of boys in this respect, maturing about a year or two earlier. Tremendous variations characterize physical maturation, both within and between individuals. This variability gives puberty a special mystery for the adolescent, who is "the fascinated, charmed, or horrified spectator that watches the developments, or lack of developments, of adolescence" (Tanner, 1972, p. 1).

The cultural basis for this task is given by well-defined stereotypes of the perfect body for females and males. The ease with which adolescents come to terms with their bodies will in part reflect the degree to which they match these images.

4. *Achieving emotional independence from parents and other adults.* Puberty plays a less well-defined role in this task, although increases in physical size and strength are undoubtedly important. Children derive much of their strength by internalizing, or taking on, their parents' attitudes and values. The strength provided by having their parents within them enables them to step out into the world. An implication of the process, however, is that at some point each of us must redefine our sources of personal strength. Adolescence is the time when most of us do.

As adolescents become responsible for more areas of their lives, they experience new personal strengths. Redefining responsibility, however, redefines their relationships with parents. Both parties are likely to greet these changes with mixed feelings. In return for self-reliance, adolescents must trade in a comfortable dependence. Parents must in turn trade a final say in things for trust in adolescents' judgment. The process is painful for both; it is difficult to shed familiar roles when new roles are not well defined or fully understood.

5. *Preparing for marriage and family life.* Although most adolescents will eventually marry and have children of their own, marriage today is more of

Adolescents typically are torn between the desire for emotional and financial independence from their parents and the reluctance to give up the comforts of dependence.

an option than it has been in the past. At present, there are more single adults in the United States than ever before (U.S. Bureau of the Census, 1992a).

Sexual maturation provides the biological basis for this developmental task. Although sexual maturation usually takes place in early adolescence, most individuals do not achieve a fusing of genuine intimacy with sexual feelings until late adolescence or early adulthood.

6. *Preparing for an economic career.* Perhaps nothing better signifies adult status than being able to support oneself. This developmental task has become increasingly problematic for adolescents today because of the many years of education required prior to assuming many kinds of jobs. The President's Science Advisory Committee has commented, "As the labor of children has become unnecessary to society, school has been extended for them. With every decade, the length of schooling has increased, until a thoughtful person must ask whether society can conceive of no other way for youth to come into adulthood" (Coleman, 1974, p. vii).

7. *Acquiring a set of values and an ethical system as a guide to behavior—developing an ideology.* Thought undergoes profound changes in adolescence. Adolescents can consider abstract principles and hypothetical situations that are beyond the grasp of children. These changes make it possible for adolescents to think of their beliefs and values as part of a larger system that they can evaluate in terms of new principles. Some psychologists believe that the development of conscience and moral thought parallels intellectual development. Others point to important sex differences in moral thought.

8. *Desiring and achieving socially responsible behavior.* Adolescence is a stepping-off point. Children view the world from the window of the family; adolescents and young adults, from their places of work and new social roles. So, too, children know themselves primarily through their relationships within the family; adults, through their status within the community. Once adolescents achieve emotional independence from parents and become economically independent, whether through occupation or marriage, they become members of a larger community.

Each of these eight developmental tasks confronts adolescents with the larger task of achieving a sense of themselves. A new independence from parents, preparation for adult roles of work and family, and formation of a set of values by which they can relate to their communities are necessary steps into adulthood. Even teenagers who master these steps, however, find the gateway to adulthood locked and must wait for someone to come along with the key. The lock is sprung not by biological or even psychological maturity. The final tumbler is keyed to a sociological definition of adolescence.

A Sociological Definition of Adolescence

Sociologists define individuals in terms of their status within society, reflected in large measure by their self-sufficiency. From a *sociological* perspective, adolescents emerge as individuals who are neither self-sufficient, and hence not adult, nor completely dependent, and thus not children. Adolescence becomes a transitional period whose end is marked by legislation specifying age limits for the legal protection of those not yet adult. David Bakan (1971) suggests that complex social conditions require the prolongation of childhood or, rather, the delay of entrance into adulthood. These conditions can be traced to the way this nation produced its goods.

The United States remained an agrarian and rural society well into the first half of the nineteenth century. With industrialization, both of these conditions changed. Mills and factories drew people like magnets to growing urban centers. Many were new immigrants drawn to the country by a recent labor shortage. Rising numbers of immigrants and unrest in new urban centers focused attention on the need for government to oversee the education and socialization of individuals into a new way of life. Three social movements surrounding industrialization contributed to the emergence of adolescence as a distinct new age group.

Compulsory education laws were introduced for children between ages 6 and 18 on a widespread basis in the United States in the late nineteenth century. Previously, children attended school, or did not, as their parents saw fit. Just as children had worked alongside their parents on farms and in fields when additional hands were needed, they now accompanied them to the factories. Their presence in the factories created certain problems. The hours were long and jobs were increasingly scarce, as the nation found that machines could indeed do the work of ten people. The cheap labor of children became an economic liability to the adults in the labor force. Compulsory education laws ensured basic skills among future workers—and also protected the jobs of adults in the work force.

Similarly, **child labor laws** specifying minimum ages for different types of work restricted the numbers of children who could hold full-time jobs. In 1832, 40% of the factory workers in New England were children. These young factory workers became a liability to the nation rather than an asset, as industrialization solved the labor-shortage problem. Child labor laws ensured humane working conditions for children, but at the same time they protected the jobs of adults in the workforce (Bakan, 1971).

Finally, laws instituting separate legal proceedings for juveniles, giving us a separate system of **juvenile justice,** were introduced at about this time. These laws were intended to free the courts from punishing children as adults, and to allow them to offer corrective measures instead. Bakan points out, however, that these laws also suspended important legal rights guaranteed to adults, such as due process and the presumption of innocence. This legislation, just as that governing child labor and education, specified an age group. Each social movement targeted the population to which it applied in terms of age. Adolescence emerged as a period in life bounded at one end by puberty and at the other by legal age requirements.

Each of the three definitions of adolescence that we have considered is incomplete by itself, but together they give us a fairly good sense of adolescence in total. Adolescence is a period in life that begins with biological maturation, during which individuals must accomplish certain developmental tasks, and that ends when they achieve a self-sufficient state of adulthood as defined by society. With this definition in hand, let us now turn our attention to the ways in which adolescence and other periods in the life cycle have been viewed at different points throughout history.

LIFE STAGES THROUGHOUT HISTORY

How many different ages are there in life? That was the riddle of the Sphinx: "What walks on four legs in the morning, on two at noon, and on three in the evening?" We all do, according to Homer. However, as with many questions, the answer one gets depends on who one asks. Homer divided the lifespan into three ages: infancy, youth, and old age. Shakespeare gave us six: "the infant mewling and puking . . . the whining schoolboy . . . the lover, sighing like a furnace . . . a soldier, full of strange oaths . . . the justice, in fair round belly . . . the sixth age shifts . . . with spectacles on nose . . . turning again toward . . . second childishness." Infancy, childhood, adolescence, young adulthood, middle age, and old age. Our conception of aging has expanded distinctly over the centuries.

Even though the pattern of growth is the same for each generation, people age in different ways depending on when they are born. Their year of birth defines their **cohort** group. Members of a cohort group undergo similar experiences in the course of their development, experiences they share and that frequently set them apart from other cohorts. One group may experience war, another economic depression, and another prosperity. Such

Although historians are not all in agreement, life stages seem to have been defined in different ways in different periods. As the clothing of the children in this seventeenth-century Dutch family indicates, childhood has not always been a clearly different stage of life.

societal changes in turn affect the availability of jobs or scholarships, the number of potential mates, the quality of schools and housing, and innumerable other life circumstances.

Societies, like individuals, change with time. Our society has changed in significant ways even within our lifetime. These changes affect us at every stage of the lifespan. Adolescence, or, for that matter, any life stage, is as much a product of our society as video games or personal computers. For one thing, adolescents today are growing up in an aging society. Couples are having fewer children and adults are living longer than ever before. The percentage of the population 65 and older has more than doubled in the last 80 years. If these trends continue, half the population will be middle-aged or older by the year 2100 (U.S. Bureau of the Census, 1992a).

A Time Before Childhood?

Philippe Aries, a French historian, traces changes in attitudes toward various age groups by noting the words by which a group has, or has not, been identified. He notes that at certain points in history there were no words to refer to childhood. In the Middle Ages, a single word served for infancy, toddlerhood, childhood, and adolescence. Aries maintains that the absence of specific words for different ages implies that people did not feel it necessary to distinguish between them (Aries, 1962).

Barbara Hanawalt (1986) argues that Aries's view of children stepping immediately into adulthood is too starkly drawn. According to Hanawalt's analysis of the Middle Ages, "The patterns of work and play, the rather late age of majority and premarital sexual flirtation all point to teenage years not unlike our own" (p. 188).

Even though a period separating childhood and adulthood may have been recognized, the ages of life nonetheless were defined quite differently. For instance, English laws in the sixteenth century defined "young people" as single people below the age of 30. Similarly, in colonial America, although youth was distinguished from childhood and adulthood, this period could last well into one's twenties or even thirties, ending only when one married. Even then, one might not be considered fully adult until the death of one's own parents. Until then even married children were only marginally independent (Moran, 1992).

Neil Postman (1982) argues that childhood became a recognizably distinct stage in life only when conditions prompted a redefinition of adulthood. Postman argues that childhood was born in the mid-1400s, to strange parents: a goldsmith named Gutenberg and a converted winepress. If the invention of the printing press created childhood, it did so by default. What it really created, maintains Postman, was adulthood. Adults came to be defined as those who could read the new documents, maps, charts, manuals, and books that were quickly becoming available. The concept of adulthood was based on reading competence, and childhood on reading *incompetence*. Before this time, adulthood directly followed infancy, which was considered to end at about age 7, when children mastered spoken language. Postman adds:

> In a literate world to be an adult implies having access to cultural secrets codified in unnatural symbols. In a literate world children must *become* adults. But in a nonliterate world there is no need to distinguish sharply between the child and the adult, for there are few secrets, and the culture does not need to provide training in how to understand itself. (p. 13)

Printing brought about the concept of authorship, and with it, a new awareness of individuality. Postman believes this heightened sense of individual importance was critical in the development of childhood. "For as the idea of personal identity developed, it followed inexorably that it would be applied to the young as well" (Postman, 1982, p. 28). Prior to this point there was a striking lack of individuality, compellingly illustrated by the frequent practice of calling children within a family by the same name. Four sons might all be named John and distinguished only by order of birth.

The "knowledge gap" that developed with printing—something like 8 million books were printed in the first 50 years—created the need for schooling. Improving economic conditions made it possible for more families to send their children to school, and a new age group emerged in societies throughout Europe (Postman, 1982).

The Creation of Adolescence

In a similar way, adolescence emerged from childhood in the middle of the nineteenth century. This time industrialization gave birth to the new age group. As we read earlier in the chapter, David Bakan (1971) suggests that adolescence emerged as a response to social conditions that required the prolongation of childhood. The machines of an industrialized society demanded skills as well as physical strength, and the entrance of young workers into the workforce was delayed until they had acquired those skills (Kett, 1977).

Other conditions sped the arrival of adolescence. Industrialization created a shift in the rural and urban population distribution. Large numbers of youths of the same age became concentrated in one place, a phenomenon unheard of in the days of the one-room schoolhouse. It became possible to have separate classes for youths of different ages. Finally, much as with the arrival of childhood, a growing middle class made it possible for parents to send their children to school in order to secure for them the better jobs that were becoming available. The first high schools were formed in these urban centers in the early 1900s, and the youths who attended them became a noticeable new age group.

A New Age: Youth

Kenneth Keniston (1970) points out that more recently another age group has emerged for much the same reason. This group spans the years between adolescence and adulthood. Postindustrial technology has increased the demand for education, and prosperity has enabled parents to support their children longer. Consequently, the entrance of many young people into the workforce has been further delayed. These young people are no longer adolescents but not yet adults. They are no longer struggling with the problems of achieving a personal identity, yet they have not yet assumed the commitments of marriage, parenting, and a career. Keniston uses the term **youth** to refer to this group.

Adulthood in Change

Views of adulthood are also changing. Until fairly recently, adulthood was regarded as a continuous stretch of time lasting from the end of adolescence through old age. We now distinguish three phases of adulthood—early, middle, and late—with different experiences common to each. Young adults establish intimate relationships, usually—though not always—by marrying and having children. For men, and for many women as well, the twenties and thirties are devoted to career advancement. In the midlife years—the late thirties, forties, and early fifties—adults experience nearly as much change as they experienced in adolescence. Such phrases as "midlife crisis" and "male menopause" reflect the transitional nature of this period. Higher levels of health and widespread prosperity have prolonged the period of middle adulthood and have delayed the onset of old age. Adults in the middle years begin to look back and question how well they are prepared to face the future.

Attitudes toward old age have changed as well. Until relatively recently in history, most people did not live beyond their fifties; the age of 40 was considered old. Today, reaching 40 merely signals the passing of youth. Prior to the 1800s, only 2% of the U.S. population reached the age of 65. Not until the 1900s did substantial numbers of people live into their sixties. Now many people live healthy lives well into their seventies and eighties (Aries, 1962).

Increased numbers of pension plans have led to earlier retirement for millions of workers in the United States. In 1900, two out of three men who were 65 or older were still working. By 1960, only one out of three worked, and in 1980, one out of five. With increased longevity, individuals will spend approximately one-quarter of their adult lives in retirement (Riley, 1986). As fewer older adults stay in the work force, new norms of work and leisure are established, contracts are changed, and expectations for achievement are reshaped.

An Era of Unisex and Uni-Age

Some of the voices that chronicled the arrival of childhood and adolescence predict that these ages may soon disappear. We will always have 4- and 15-year-olds, to be sure, but we may lose the developmental markers by which they are distinguished.

Childhood exists when there are separate domains for adults and children. The business of children, in other words, is to prepare themselves for adulthood. Postman (1982) suggests that just as the printing press created separate domains, a more recent invention has begun to merge them. The Gutenberg of our times is Samuel Morse, inventor of the telegraph (Postman, 1982).

The telegraph ushered in the age of electronic communication and, with this, a parallel revolution from print to images. Images, unlike books, are readily available to those of any age. They require no interpretation and no years of preparation for their mastery. The "knowledge monopoly" that previously separated children and adults was broken. Postman writes:

> The essential point is that TV presents information in a form that is undifferentiated in its accessibility, and this means that television does not need to make distinctions between categories of "child" and "adult." . . . This happens not only because the symbolic form of television poses no cognitive mysteries but also because a television set cannot be hidden in a drawer or placed on a high shelf, out of the reach of children; its physical form, no less than its symbolic form, does not lend itself to exclusivity. (1982, pp. 79, 80)

Television, movies, and home videos disclose secrets that were previously the domain of adults. For that matter, printed books did much the same thing 500 years ago when they broke the monopoly of the privileged few who could read and write. The difference is that literacy also established an obstacle that could only be overcome by years of preparation, as children learned to read and understand ever more complex forms of written expression. Television, however, tells all to anyone who may be watching; its images are self-explanatory. This point becomes important if one believes that groups are defined in significant ways by the exclusivity of the information available to their members. Lawyers are distinguished from doctors, students from teachers, or, in this case, children from adults by what they know. If the authority of adults derives, in part, from their ability to initiate children into their secrets, adult authority is diminished to the extent that there are no secrets (Postman, 1982).

David Elkind (1984) also notes that many of the visible markers that distinguish age groups are fading. A generation ago, children, adolescents, and adults dressed in characteristically different ways. Jeans and sneakers marked the appearance of adolescence just as suits or high heels marked adulthood. Today, designer jeans and name-brand gym shoes are worn by people of all ages. Even infants wear designer labels and babies can outgrow their first Reeboks before ever taking a step. Transition markers, such as short to long pants for boys or knee-highs to stockings for girls, are gone.

Preteens enjoy the same types of music and entertainment as adolescents. Similarly, team sports that were once the domain of adolescents, signifying their movement into adulthood, are organized for children. In the past, children would practice in back lots to "make the team" in high school. Now they have their own teams, complete with umpires and uniforms. Beauty pageants for toddlers and martial arts for elementary schoolers similarly blur age distinctions (Elkind, 1984).

Another marker of maturity that is quickly disappearing is access to sexual information. Although information about sex is more available than ever before, its availability to children as well may lessen its significance for adolescents. So, too, with violence, once reserved for the mature (Elkind, 1984).

To the extent that adolescence and childhood are becoming less distinct as life stages, loss of markers for adulthood may follow. Ages are given definition in relation to one another. Current media images of parents are noticeably different from those of a generation ago, as in the "child-adult," a carefree, irrepressible parent to a competent and responsible child or adolescent. This adult need only be compared with TV images of adults in the 1950s, such as in *Leave It to Beaver* (Elkind, 1984).

A look at cultures other than our own assures us that wide differences can exist in the organization of the life course; life stages are socially constructed. Whether age has become more or less important in regulating the transitions between stages, however, is still in debate. Some assert that life stages are more clearly demarked and passages are more tightly organized by age than ever before. Others argue that age is less relevant to life experiences now than in the past. Increases in technology and gains in the sophistication of information require periodic retraining. Career paths structured by age do not hold up to rapid technological change. The information explosion, when coupled with increasing longevity, can lead to changes in our existing pattern of education, work, and retirement. It can also lead to reversals in age-grading as the young get ahead of older workers, especially in information technologies such as the computer and entertainment industries (Held, 1986).

Family roles also structure the life course, but recent trends suggest that these roles are less closely related to chronological age than before. There is

Although adolescents have the longest list of developmental tasks, people at every age—childhood, middle age, old age—must adapt to developmental changes

greater variation in age when marrying, remarrying, and having children in a first or second marriage. Age-grading may remain relatively tight in public roles, whereas in private family roles it is becoming looser. This asynchrony poses interesting questions. One can only wonder how each of these sectors, public and private, will contribute to individuals' senses of themselves. We may be approaching a time when the private sector of marriage and children defines one not so much through social roles with a semipublic identity as through a set of experiences that allow one to explore the self (Held, 1986).

Although the age categories we presently identify within the lifespan are tied to changing social and historical conditions, development throughout the lifespan reveals consistencies as well. In the section that follows we will look for continuities in the experiences of adolescents and their parents and grandparents.

TABLE 1.1   Developmental Tasks

INFANCY AND EARLY CHILDHOOD	Learning to walk
	Learning to take solid foods
	Learning to talk
	Learning to control the elimination of body wastes
	Learning sex differences and sexual modesty
	Forming concepts and learning language to describe social and physical reality
	Getting ready to read
MIDDLE CHILDHOOD	Learning physical skills necessary for ordinary games
	Building wholesome attitudes toward oneself
	Learning to get along with age-mates
	Learning appropriate masculine or feminine social roles
	Learning fundamental skills in reading, writing, and calculating
	Developing concepts necessary for everyday living
	Developing conscience, morality, and a scale of values
	Achieving personal independence
	Developing attitudes toward social groups and institutions
ADOLESCENCE	Achieving new and more mature relations with age-mates of both sexes
	Achieving a masculine or feminine social role
	Accepting one's physique and using the body effectively
	Achieving emotional independence from parents and other adults
	Preparing for marriage and family life
	Preparing for an economic career
	Acquiring a set of values and an ethical system as a guide to behavior—developing an ideology
	Desiring and achieving socially responsible behavior

EARLY ADULTHOOD	Selecting a mate	Managing a home
	Learning to live with a marriage partner	Getting started in an occupation
	Starting a family	Taking on civic responsibility
	Rearing children	Finding a congenial social group

MIDDLE AGE	Assisting teenaged children to become responsible and happy adults
	Achieving adult social and civic responsibility
	Reaching and maintaining satisfactory performance in one's occupational career
	Developing adult leisure-time activities
	Relating to one's spouse as a person
	Accepting and adjusting to the physiological changes of middle age
	Adjusting to aging parents
LATER MATURITY	Adjusting to decreasing physical strength and health
	Adjusting to retirement and reduced income
	Adjusting to the death of a spouse
	Establishing an explicit affiliation with one's age group
	Adopting and adapting social roles in a flexible way
	Establishing satisfactory physical living arrangements

Source: R. J. Havinghurst. (1972). *Developmental tasks and education.* New York: David McKay.

ADOLESCENCE: A UNIQUE AGE?

Table 1.1 lists Robert Havighurst's (1972) developmental tasks for different ages in life. The sheer length of the columns for adolescence and middle childhood show these stages to be active times of change. A second look, however, shows middle age to be nearly as active, just one task short of adolescence. Parents may believe stress stalks in the form of adolescence, but it is just as likely to assume the form of middle age.

Interesting parallels exist between the tasks of both adolescents and their parents. Adolescents must accept their physical types (or physiques, to use Havighurst's term), whereas their parents must come to accept and adjust to the physiological changes of middle age. Adolescents face the tasks of achieving emotional independence from parents and other adults; a parallel task for parents is assisting their teenage children to become responsible and happy adults, while simultaneously adjusting to the needs of their own aging parents. A task of adolescence is to prepare for marriage and family life; that of middle age is to relate to one's spouse as a person. Just as adolescents face the task of preparing for an economic career, their parents face the task of reaching and maintaining satisfactory performance in their occupations. Adolescents must achieve socially responsible behavior, whereas their parents face the need to achieve civic responsibility.

No cause for surprise, then, that relationships between adolescents and parents are occasionally tense. But despite sources of potential tension, most adolescents report surprising levels of satisfaction with their parents. Most agree with the way they have been parented and report that they hold many of the same values as their parents (Youth Indicators, 1993).

Parallels exist for adolescents and grandparents as well. Both groups must come to terms with rapidly changing bodies and the resulting changes to their sense of themselves. Both, too, face the need to redefine the self in terms of an occupation. For adolescents this task assumes the form of commitment to a career, and for grandparents, adjustment to retirement, often from a job that has been an important source of self-definition. Similarly, the issue of economic independence faces both groups. Adolescents may have to postpone work while they continue education; recently retired grandparents often face radically reduced incomes. Most adolescents are looking forward to marriage at a time when grandparents begin to worry about losing a spouse. Both face the task of adapting social roles to changing life circumstances. Finally, both face the need to establish satisfactory living arrangements, a problem for many adolescents who continue to live at home while they pursue their education, as well as for grandparents who may not be able to maintain a separate residence of their own and face moving in with their children.

The many developmental tasks of adolescence confirm it to be a transitional period. However, to see adolescence just, or even primarily, as a transition is to miss the point: Transition characterizes every age. It is, in fact, what allows us to distinguish each age from the preceding one. Middle age is no less a transition, nor is later maturity. To view adolescence as a transition is to fail to see adolescents themselves. Adolescents are not just in the process of becoming someone else. They are individuals in their own right.

SUMMARY

Adolescents in a Changing Population

Adolescents make up approximately 14% of the nation's population. The median age of the population itself has been increasing, a change that has far-reaching effects on adolescents. Adolescents today constitute a relatively smaller percentage of the population than they did a generation ago.

Family characteristics are also changing. With increasing numbers of divorces, more families are headed by single parents. Adolescents in single-parent families are more likely to experience economic hardships than those in dual-parent homes.

The Many Faces of Adolescents

Sex and gender differences, though vitally important to adolescents, are frequently confused. Sex differences are the physiological differences associated with being female or male. Gender differences are the cultural expectations that surround each sex. Gender stereotypes are important components of gender; these are shared beliefs that some qualities characterize one sex and others characterize the opposite sex.

Today's adolescents are also growing up in an ethnically diverse society. The strength of their identification as a member of a particular ethnic group depends on the extent to which they share the cultural values and attitudes of the group, feel they belong to the group, and experience being a member of a minority.

The Constructive Perspective

Adolescents are diverse not only because of ethnicity and gender, however. Diversity is also a result of individual differences in the way they each make sense of and respond to their experiences and environment. According to the constructive perspective, we each construct our own reality, actively interpreting experiences and reacting to them on the basis of our interpretation.

The Contextual Perspective

According to the contextual perspective, we each interact in a different way with the various levels of our environment, from the microsystem to the macrosystem, and those interactions in turn influence who we are.

Defining Adolescence

Three sets of definitions together are needed to give a comprehensive view of adolescence. A biological definition emphasizes the events of puberty that transform the bodies of children into those of sexually and physically mature adults. A psychological definition distinguishes adolescence in terms of the developmental tasks to be accomplished. Each of the tasks adolescents face relates to the central task of achieving a stable personal identity. A sociological definition defines adolescents in terms of their status within society. Specifically, this approach views adolescence as a transitional period between childhood and adulthood.

The Lifespan Perspective

The lifespan gives us a unique perspective on adolescence. One can see that many of the issues arising in adolescence are common to other ages as well. Continuities in developmental experience, as well as the more obvious differences, emerge.

The lifespan approach looks at development from four perspectives: biological, psychological, sociological, and historical.

Life Stages Throughout History

Our conception of age has changed distinctly over the centuries. During the Middle Ages, people may not have distinguished childhood from adulthood. Childhood as a distinct age may have emerged with widespread literacy and the need for schooling. Adolescence occurred with the industrial revolution in response to social conditions that required the prolongation of childhood. A new age of youth has recently emerged with the prolongation of education and the postponement of the commitments of adulthood. Adulthood also has recently undergone change. We can distinguish three distinct phases: early, middle, and late.

Many of the developmental markers distinguishing different ages in the lifespan are disappearing. As age distinctions blur, adolescents face a more difficult task in establishing markers signifying their more mature status.

Adolescence: A Unique Age?

Parallels exist between the developmental tasks of adolescents and their middle-aged parents. Both must come to terms with changing bodies. As adolescents face the task of unraveling their emotional dependence on their parents, their parents must adjust to the changing needs of their own aging parents. Similar parallels exist for adolescents and their grandparents.

KEY TERMS

contextual perspective	androgynous	puberty
constructive perspective	culture	sexual dimorphism
lifespan perspective	ethnic identity	developmental tasks
early adolescence	minority	compulsory education laws
late adolescence	microsystem	child labor laws
sex differences	mesosystem	juvenile justice
gender differences	exosystem	cohort
gender stereotypes	macrosystem	youth

CHAPTER 2

Theoretical Foundations of Adolescent Development

A theory is like a bridge that connects an island of understanding to the mainland of life. In this case, the island is adolescence and the mainland is the whole of human life. Imagine the limitations in going to and coming from such an island if there were but one theory to connect adolescence to the rest of development. But there are many theories, and each theoretical bridge approaches adolescence from a particular direction. Depending on which theory you take, different landforms appear. Some theories reach deep within the personality, others drop you off at the shores of behavior. Still others feed into the traffic of thought and intellect. Taking just one approach would give a limited view of adolescence. Together, they provide access to a panorama of thoughts, feelings, and behaviors. This chapter is like a number of short trips into adolescence, each one crossing a different bridge. Crossing all of the theoretical bridges will give us as complete a picture of adolescence as is possible at the present time.

Like bridges, theories are functional. The first section of the chapter looks at the functions theories serve and at the models that generate them. Beneath the surface of every scientific theory are the beliefs we hold about the world we live in. We believe, for instance, that males and females *are* different. Many of us believe that there *has to be* a difference. Many of us believe that without differences the human species would be less viable than it is. Although we hold many beliefs, only a few belief systems have produced developmental theories. When a belief system does produce a complete model of behavior, it is given a name. Thus, we have in adolescent development the environmental and organismic models. From these it is possible to view the whole outline of what we know about adolescence.

Once the developmental models are discussed, the theories that guide our view of adolescent development are treated in some detail. It is important to keep in mind that not every theory focuses on the same aspects of development. Each theory has its own view of what influences are most important and least important to our behavior. For instance, some theories stress the importance of feelings and personality development, whereas others emphasize thought and judgment. Also, a single theory may fail to cover all the things one might want to understand about adolescents. Almost no theory, for example, allows us to chart the development of females as well as males. And although many theories acknowledge the influence of culture on personality development, few have explored its implications for particular ethnic or racial minorities.

MODELS AND THEORIES

A Model Defined

Models are the bedrock on which theories rest. Scientists build their theories around basic assumptions, or models, about the nature of human functioning. These assumptions can be so fundamental that they go unnoticed, yet they exert powerful influences on the theories they generate. For one thing, assumptions determine which questions appear reasonable and which seem foolish. If a scientist assumes that human behaviors are primarily reactions to events in the environment, then it makes sense to inquire how the events differ that immediately precede different behaviors. If another scientist assumes that behavior reflects goal-directed decisions, then it is reasonable to ask people about their goals and how they make their decisions. Notice that the first scientist—we can use the label "behaviorist"—is likely to observe *what* people do and what's going on around them when they do it. The second—a cognitive psychologist—is likely to ask people *why* they do what they do. In each case, the beliefs that direct scientific investigation are collectively called a **model.** It is important to know just what a model is and how it serves our understanding of adolescence.

You might think that only scientists have models of human behavior. Actually, we all do. Do you think behavior is rational and goal-directed, or does it simply reflect past reinforcements? What motivates us? A succession of rewards and punishments? Inner goals? How much are we influenced by our biology? Do hormones and genes shape our interests and drives? Or do our interests and drives reflect acquired tastes and passions?

Not all of us share the same model. Models are easiest to see when the differences between them are extreme. Consider a teenage babysitter putting a young child to bed. The child lost a tooth that day and insists on placing it under his pillow. The child's belief system (model) includes tooth fairies. The babysitter's does not. What would the babysitter think if the child were to run up to her later with money in his hand and explain that he found it under the pillow? The teenager would question her sanity before admit-ring to anything like the tooth fairy—and with good reason. Scientists and teenagers alike base their theories on assumptions about what is real and what is not, and most adolescents assume that fairies are not real (Kuhn, 1962; Reese & Overton, 1970).

Models are useful because they generate theories. But models themselves are too general and often too vague to test. Theories, on the other hand, are specific explanations of particular phenomena that can be confirmed or disconfirmed. The babysitter dismisses the child's explanation because she assumes that a person, not a fairy, must have put the money under the pillow. We can even imagine her reviewing each alternative: "The money was there all along . . . I put it there and forgot . . . His mom or dad put it under the pillow before leaving . . . He took the money from his piggy bank just to put one over on me!" Each possibility reflects a model in which *people* put money under pillows, a model that bestows reality on some events—whether they be people, quarks, or electromagnetic fields—and nonreality on others.

A Theory Defined

Mention the word *theory* and many people mentally close up shop and take a walk. The word sounds too abstract to suggest any help with day-to-day problems. Images of bespectacled academics come to mind. Yet each of us comes up with any number of "minitheories" every day. In its simplest form, a theory offers an explanation by relating something that we don't understand to something else that we do.

Theories reflect the models from which they derive. A look at our example shows us why. A **theory** consists of statements arranged from the very general to the very specific. The most general statements derive directly from the model and are called **axioms;** they are the assumptions one never thinks to question. An axiom that might be derived from the teenager's belief system would be that only things occupying space and existing in time are real. This axiom would exclude all but the most substantial of fairies. A **law** is at the next level. Derived from axioms, laws state relationships that are either true or false. Careful observations inform us of the validity of laws. A law from the above example might be that inanimate objects (such as teeth) remain stationary unless moved by some external force. Laws make it possible to predict specific events. We might predict that a tooth placed under a pillow would be there the next morning unless someone moved it.

All developmental theories have one thing in common: Each is an attempt to explain the constancies and changes in functioning that occur throughout the life course. Rather than embrace all aspects of functioning, developmental theories have limited themselves to particular aspects. Some, for instance, are concerned with personality development, others with social or intellectual development, still others with moral and ethical development. Whatever their focus, each theory looks at the similarities and differences that occur with age and attempts to explain them in terms of their sources or causes (Lerner, 1986).

Questions concerning the source of development have traditionally divided theorists into two camps. The division reflects their position on the

Foundations
of Adolescent
Development

How much are our
interests and abilities
due to inherited traits,
and how much are
they due to our envi-
ronment? Compar-
isons of the life course
of twins have provided
important informa-
tion but no definitive
answers about the rel-
ative influences of na-
ture and nurture.

nature–nurture controversy: Is nature—that is, heredity—primarily responsible for development, or is nurture—that is, the environment—
responsible? Those who view nature as organizing developmental variables
emphasize the importance of factors such as genetic inheritance and maturation. Developmentalists who look to nurture for explanations emphasize
conditions such as the home environment and learning.

A second issue, following from the first, also distinguishes developmental theories. This issue concerns the nature of the developmental laws
that relate behavior to either source: the **continuity–discontinuity issue.**
Can one explain behavior at any, and every, point in the life cycle without
formulating new sets of laws? Do the same laws apply to other species as
well (continuity)? Or do lawful relationships change with age and across
species (discontinuity)? Developmentalists who stress the importance of genetic inheritance and maturation typically assume that different sets of laws
are needed for species with different genetic endowments, and within a
species, at different points in development due to maturation. These theorists see development as occurring in discrete stages. Conversely, those who
trace development to environmental sources are more likely to see these
forces as exerting the same influence independent of age or species (Lerner,
1986).

Finally, developmentalists differ in the assumptions they make when explaining the occurrence of new behavior. Those who assume that the same
set of laws are sufficient to describe behavior at all points in the life cycle
believe in **reductionism,** which is an attempt to explain complex behavior
by reducing it to its simpler components. Developmentalists who assume
that new laws are needed at different ages argue from the standpoint of **epigenesis,** holding that new complexities in development emerge that cannot
be predicted from earlier forms (Lerner, 1986).

Differences in these sets of assumptions characterize two models of behavior: the environmental and the organismic. The first considers the environment to be the primary source of behavior, assumes continuity to developmental laws, and is reductionist in nature. The second looks to genetic or maturational forces—that is, nature—to explain development, assumes a noncontinuity position, and views development as epigenetic. All the theories deriving from a model bear a strong "family resemblance." Even so, you will find in reading through this chapter that the degree to which they reflect the assumptions characterizing the model will vary. Some theories reflect each of the model's assumptions perfectly; others are only a good approximation.

The Environmental Model

The environmental model focuses on environmental forces in explaining development. These forces affect behavior in lawful ways; the laws are assumed to apply at all levels of development. The assumption of continuity to behavioral laws underlies a strong reductionist approach in environmental theories. Because everything from silicon chips to bones and brain tissue is made of atoms and molecules, the laws that describe their actions should describe the functioning of humans as well as the workings of a computer. To explain vision, an environmentalist would speak of the amount of light necessary to stimulate receptors in the retina, or of the exchange of sodium and potassium ions across the membrane of a neuron as the impulse is propagated along the neural fiber. Everything from a toddler taking first steps to the virtuosity of a concert cellist playing a Bach fugue is understood as a sequence of simpler reactions, each prompted by the completion of the last, and all traceable to an external force. In other words, "there is nothing special about the complex pattern of events we call psychological functioning. In the final analysis these events involve the functioning of the very same atoms and molecules that are involved in the workings of a liver, a kidney, or a shooting star" (Lerner, 1986, p. 45).

Reductionism reduces psychological phenomena to simpler components that operate, in principle, no differently than those in a machine. The metaphor of a machine, such as a computer, is helpful in understanding the environmental model, because it translates otherwise abstract assumptions into an everyday example. Based on what we know about the example, we can predict certain outcomes and events that otherwise might remain unclear.

In order to get a computer to work, you have to start it; a computer does not start on its own. You have to plug it in, push a button, or whatever. This sets off a chained sequence of events that takes the same form each time it unfolds. As long as the parts bear the same relationship to one another, tripping one will set the next in motion. A computer does only what it was programmed to do. But if you know what software you have, and just what point in the sequence is unfolding, you should be able to predict what it will do next.

Is human behavior as predictable? The environmental model assumes it is—ideally. In actuality, it is difficult, if not impossible, to specify the myriad parts that make up the human machine. Even if one could, must our actions be prompted by events external to ourselves, or is behavior self-initiated? The environmental and organismic models give us different answers (Reese & Overton, 1970).

If the model of the machine is correct, actions are primarily *re*actions to forces external to us. The environment becomes a primary source of our behavior. We, like computers, remain quiescent until stimulated to act. The burden for explaining and changing behavior remains with the environment. Is an adolescent disruptive in class? Look for the events in the classroom that cause this behavior. Is a teenager anxious in new situations? Have that person list situations from the most to the least anxiety-producing, then tackle the easiest. Success will make the next one more approachable. Although it is often difficult to trace behaviors to the events that occasion them, it is infinitely easier than it would be if organisms could, at any moment, choose to alter what they were doing just because they felt like it. Human behavior is, at least in the abstract, predictable for those who hold to this model.

Before leaving this model, we will look at how it explains the way we perceive our world. The environmental model holds that knowledge is a direct copy of reality. Copy theory maintains that, rather than interpreting our sensations or in other ways trying to make sense of experience, our sensory systems do this for us. You recognize the letters in this sentence through receptors in the retina that fire in a pattern corresponding to the physical configuration of the letters. In a sense, the retina can be thought of as a film that retains the patterns of light to which it was exposed. Receptors carry the physical pattern of the letters through neural pathways to appropriate centers in the brain. All you need to do is simply keep your eyes open and make sure there's enough light to "expose the film."

For those of you who think you take a more active role in defining your world, read on. The organismic model differs sharply from the environmentalist position.

The Organismic Model: The Constructive Perspective

The organismic model provides the framework for the constructive perspective adopted in this text. This model takes the living, biological system as its metaphor for human behavior. This model explains human development in terms of variables closely tied to the nature of the organism and governing its growth. Organismic theorists differ sharply from environmentalists, practically point by point, in their views of human nature. (Table 2.1 shows these contrasts.)

Three points summarize these differences. Organismic theorists view the human organism as active rather than passive. They believe this activity to be internally organized, rather than a reaction to external events. Finally, they understand behavior as the unfolding of genetically programmed processes, which produce discontinuous development, marked by qualitatively different stages. Environmentalists, on the other hand, view developmental change as continuous, with ever more complex behaviors being constructed from the same simple building blocks (Lerner, 1986; Reese & Overton, 1970.)

TABLE 2.1   Comparison of Developmental Models

	Environmental Model	Organismic Model
ORGANISM IS	Reactive	Active
BEHAVIOR IS	Structured by environment	Internally organized
DEVELOPMENT IS DUE TO	Behavioral conditioning	Environmental-genetic interactions
FOCUS IS ON	Behavior	Cognition, perception, motivation
DEVELOPMENTAL STAGES?	No	Yes

The Active Organism   Organismic theorists point out that environmental events become clear only when we respond to them. It takes an action from us to define the conditions that will then be perceived as events. Noam Chomsky (1957), a psycholinguist at MIT, has pressed this argument effectively (John Dewey made the same argument in 1896). Chomsky argued that many sentences appearing to have a single meaning actually have many. They appear clear because we have *already* assumed a context in which they are unambiguous. Consider the sentence, "They are eating apples." Seems clear enough. What are they doing? They are eating apples. Yet if the sentence is a response to the question "What kind of apples are those?" its meaning changes. There are different kinds of apples. Some are for cooking and others for eating. And what are those? They are eating apples.

Organized Activity   Perhaps the description of a simple experiment will illustrate the point best. Individuals heard a click every 20 seconds for several minutes. With the first click, heart rate, brain-wave activity, sensory receptivity, and electrical conductance of the skin changed. These changes make up the orienting response, a general reaction to novel events. With each recurrence of the click, the orienting response decreased until it barely occurred at all (Sokolov, 1963). When **habituation,** or decreased response, had been pretty well established, the click was stopped, and everyone reacted with a full-scale orienting response. What was the stimulus for their reaction? Could it have been the *absence* of sound? The same silence, however, did not produce a reaction before the procedure began.

   The phenomenon of habituation tells us that organisms detect regularities in their surroundings and anticipate them. Events that match, or confirm, their anticipations provoke no further reaction. Those that do not conform prompt a reaction. Notice that our definition of a stimulus has changed. The stimulus is no longer an external event. Nor is it simply an internal event. It is a product of both. The stimulus is the match, or mismatch, of input with what is anticipated. As such, the original meaning of stimulus, as a goad or prod to action, is lost (Miller, Galanter, & Pribram, 1960).

Developmental Stages   Organismic theorists argue that as we age, we organize experience in different ways than we did during the preceding period of development. Each period is a separate **stage** with its own characteristics. For example, Jean Piaget, a Swiss developmentalist, described several stages in the development of thought, the last of which begins in adolescence. In the first stage, infants do not have symbols through which they can represent their experiences, and thought in the absence of symbols is very different from the symbolic thought of adults, or even of slightly older children. When language first develops, young children organize their experience in very personal ways, not according to the linguistic categories used by older children or adults (Piaget, 1952b, 1954).

You can see this difference for yourself with a simple procedure. Just ask a preschooler and an adolescent to say the first word that comes to mind after hearing each of two words. To "fork" the preschooler is likely to say "eat"; the adolescent will most likely say "spoon." To "chair" the preschooler will likely respond "sit"; the adolescent, "table." Preschoolers organize experience in terms of what they do with things. They answer with functional categories: One eats with a fork and sits on a chair. Adolescents organize experience in terms of linguistic categories: "Fork" and "spoon" are both utensils and "chair" and "table" are furniture.

Similarly, psychoanalytic theories, such as that of Freud, hold that development is organized around stages that take form as maturation enables the organism to interact with its surroundings in new ways. Freud, for example, assumed that young boys experience horror when they first see a little girl naked, believing that she has been castrated. Their reaction to this experience both reflects and redirects inner psychic forces. Freud (1925b) would argue that maturation has brought them to a stage in which sexual tensions receive genital focus and also involve them in a dangerous rivalry with their fathers. To protect themselves from a fate similar to the girl's, boys must repress their sexual fantasies, thus resolving the Oedipal complex and moving them into the next stage of development. (The Oedipal complex is further discussed later in this chapter.)

For psychoanalytic theorists, life is a battle, and we are all on the front lines. Two opposing forces, one within us and the other outside, fight for control. Because each is an integral aspect of our personalities, the victory of either one means a sure defeat to the individual. Instead, we must achieve a balance between internal biological instincts and external social constraints. We achieve this balance only with time and at some personal cost. As in any war, there are casualties. True spontaneity may be the first to go. The second loss takes the form of compromise: We learn to make do with lesser delights to avoid the anxiety provoked by indulging our first instincts. There are victories as well. We gain control over instinctual urges that otherwise, these theorists say, could destroy us and our civilization (Hall, 1954).

A final point before leaving this model concerns the way we know our world. Recall that the environmental model views perception as a copy of reality. The organismic model maintains, predictably enough, just the opposite—that perception is an active, constructive process. In order to perceive the letters that make up this sentence, we scan them to see whether certain features are present. We look for angles or curves, vertical or horizontal lines. Detecting certain of these leads us to "see" one letter or another. Recall the example given in Chapter 1, in which the very same

physical configuration of lines can be read either as a *B* or a *13* in one context or another, depending on what the reader expects.

Is perception simply the stimulation of sensory receptors, as copy theory asserts? If so, you should not be able to see the very same lines as either a *B* or a *13*. Organismic theorists argue that context—whether a succession of clicks or a series of numbers—establishes an expectancy that directs the extraction of information. Put a slightly different way, they are saying that we actively "construct" the events to which we respond (Neisser, 1967, 1976).

Is the organismic model better because it offers sophisticated approaches to cognition and perception? Or perhaps the environmental model is more "scientific," because it focuses on behaviors that can be observed and precisely manipulated? Comparisons all too frequently lead to evaluations, and someone usually ends up holding the short end of the theoretical stick. Comparisons can also be misleading. Each model addresses different aspects of human functioning. We need both to begin unraveling the knotty problems of adolescence. The organismic model helps us understand motives and feelings that otherwise would never see the light of day. The environmental model gives us objective and readily testable theories of behavior. Unless we are willing to settle for theories about adolescents who act but don't think and feel, or teenagers who think and feel but can't act, we need the insights each model offers.

According to the organismic model, physiological and cognitive readiness is the key. The environmental model also acknowledges the importance of developmental readiness, but this model stresses behavioral conditioning.

But what about the developmental theories spawned by these models? Remember, a single model can parent many theories. We will look at several theories for each. Examining more than one theory should help distinguish the assumptions of the model from the particular form they take in a theory. We will consider environmental theories first, then turn to organismic, or constructive, ones. Among the latter, we will first look at theories focusing on intellectual development, then those addressing emotional and motivational aspects of development, and finally those focusing on the social or interpersonal aspects of development.

ENVIRONMENTAL THEORIES

Focus on the Intellectual: Havighurst

Robert Havighurst, an educator from the University of Chicago, stressed the importance of learning in giving shape to development. "One learns to walk, talk, and throw a ball; to hold down a job, to raise children; to retire gracefully. . . . These are all learning tasks. To understand human development, one must understand learning" (Havighurst, 1952, p. 1).

Havighurst maintained that each of us masters a succession of tasks throughout our lives. These tasks reflect social expectations for more mature behaviors as we age. Physical maturation frequently sets the pace for what is expected of us. For example, we expect children to be toilet trained once they develop control over the sphincter, the muscle used in elimination. We don't expect infants to stay dry through the night, or to let us know when they will soil a diaper. Similarly, we don't expect adolescents to hold down full-time jobs and be self-supporting. Yet we do expect them to develop more mature relations with age-mates once puberty confers mature bodies and interests (Havighurst, 1952).

Havighurst called these learning experiences **developmental tasks.** (These tasks are listed in Table 1.1 on page 36.) He defined a developmental task as "a task which arises at or about a certain period in the life of the individual, successful achievement of which leads to . . . happiness and to success with later tasks, while failure leads to unhappiness in the individual, disapproval by the society, and difficulty with later tasks" (Havighurst, 1952, p. 2). Thus the successful mastery of each task lays the foundation for the next.

Despite the importance he gave to learning, Havighurst recognized that we can only master a new skill when we are physically ready to perform it. He spoke of "the teachable moment." Biological maturation prepares us for certain experiences that will have an optimal impact only if they occur when we are ripe to receive them. The very same experiences will have practically no effect at all if they come too early or if the moment is lost by their coming too late.

A second environmental theorist, B. F. Skinner, considered every moment to be teachable.

Radical behaviorist B. F. Skinner (1904–1990) contended that behavior is determined by external forces and can be explained only in terms of what can be actually observed. The subconscious urges described by Sigmund Freud have no place in Skinner's theories.

Explaining the Motivational: Skinner

B. F. Skinner, an American psychologist, referred to actions as **operants,** pointing out that actions can be thought of as ways of operating on one's environment. Examples of operants might be reading a book, eating a meal, or choosing to wear a purple shirt. You might say that one is prompted to read a book by seeing it. Yet there are also numerous times when one notices a book and does not read it, or when one will look for a book that one has not seen. Operants can be brought under the control of environmental events. Skinner studied this simple form of learning—**operant conditioning**—extensively (Skinner, 1938, 1953, 1961).

Skinner's ideas have influenced countless psychologists and educators and infuriated others, for the same reason: Skinner reduced the nuances and complexities of human behavior to the events that follow it rather than to what might have preceded it. His approach is a radical departure from the way most people understand their behavior. Most of us think that what we do is a response to inner states, to our feelings and thoughts. Skinner told us our behavior is under the control of external events. He called his approach radical behaviorism.

Skinner said it is senseless to talk about inner states such as motives and intentions. We can't measure or observe them. He believed we can understand behavior only by describing the conditions under which it occurs. When antecedent conditions cannot be identified, he suggested looking at what follows the behavior. When we do, lawful relationships emerge.

Skinner's first subjects were rats. He constructed a small box with a metal lever protruding from one wall, and selected a simple behavior— pressing the lever—for study. Because there was little for an animal to do in such a small space, its explorations soon brought it near the lever. Skinner waited until the animal touched the lever, then dropped a food pellet into a chute that ended in a dish beneath the lever. Each time the rat pressed the lever, a pellet of food dropped into the dish. In no time the rat began to steadily press the lever. Skinner had brought a voluntary behavior—putting a paw on a metal lever and depressing it—under the control of its consequences. By making food contingent on lever pressing, he controlled the frequency with which the rat pressed the lever (Skinner, 1938).

Critics reacted by saying that humans are different from animals, or at the very least different from rats. Our behavior reflects motives and intentions, not contingencies. Skinner's reply to these objections was that our intentions reflect our reinforcement histories. Consider a teenager who has a favorite color—purple, for instance—and buys many of her clothes in that color. Skinner would explain this preference for purple in terms of past reinforcements when wearing purple. She may have worn a purple skirt one day and received several compliments. When next shopping for clothes, she tried on several items that were purple, finally buying one. She spent a few extra minutes with her appearance the day she wore her new clothes and once again received several compliments. Skinner would suggest that this history of reinforcements shaped her preference for purple.

We can analyze many social interactions in terms of positive and negative reinforcement. Sometimes such an analysis seems especially appropriate with adolescents and parents. Let's look at an exchange between an adolescent and his mother. She has just told him to pick his clothes up from the living room floor. He responds "Sure, Mom," with a slightly sarcastic edge to his voice. She reacts quickly and sharply, with more animation than he has seen all day. He picks up his clothes and carries them off to his room.

Now take a closer look at what has just taken place. The mother reinforced her son when she allowed herself to become engaged by his sarcasm. She paid more attention to him than she had all day. Attention is a powerful reinforcer. Even though this may not be the kind of attention the teenager, or anyone, seeks, if it is more than he usually gets, and if he is frequently sarcastic when his mother scolds, she is very likely reinforcing a behavior that in fact annoys her.

Also notice that *he* reinforced *her* scolding. By picking his clothes up when she scolded (removing something that displeased her), he negatively reinforced her scolding—the very behavior that maintains his sarcasm. We can analyze many parent–adolescent interactions in terms of the reciprocal effects of positive and negative reinforcement. Adolescents frequently develop the very behaviors their parents find most objectionable. According to behaviorists such as Skinner, this is no accident. Those are the very behaviors parents are most likely to notice.

Reinforcement is a powerful force in shaping and maintaining behavior. But must we actually do something or receive reinforcement in order to learn? Critics of radical behaviorism point out that we can know *what* to do before we ever do it. Many actions are novel, yet they unfold in smooth, successful sequences, not in the on-again, off-again manner one would expect if trial and error governed their performance. Language itself is perhaps the most intricate of all human activity, and the most difficult for Skinner to explain. We produce endless numbers of novel sentences each day. Has each been shaped through reinforcement? How is radical behaviorism to account for each of these?

Albert Bandura, a psychologist at Stanford University, stresses the social nature of learning; his approach is called social-cognitive theory.

Focus on the Social-Interpersonal: Bandura

Bandura believes that most human learning is **observational learning,** not conditioning, and occurs by *observing* what others do and *imitating* what one sees. One need not actually perform the behavior oneself. Inner processes such as attention and memory focus behavior. This theory departs from strict environmentalist assumptions by emphasizing inner, cognitive processes by which individuals interpret their experiences. Bandura supported his position in a dramatic study of aggression in children.

Children at play watched a model punch and kick a large inflated doll in very unusual ways (Bandura, Ross, & Ross, 1963). The model sat on it, shouted "Sock him in the nose" and punched the doll, then hit it with a hammer and yelled "Pow!" Later, when the children were left alone with the doll and other toys, they imitated the same unusual sequences, often copying exactly what they had seen. Other children who had watched a model play with Tinkertoys showed none of the same aggressive behaviors. Numerous studies support the importance of observation and imitation in human learning (Bandura, 1977, 1980).

Social-cognitive theorists are willing to talk about many of the same processes as organismic theorists, processes such as thoughts and motives.

Young adolescents learn new behaviors by closely watching how other people behave and trying out those new behaviors themselves, either in actuality or in their imagination. For social-cognitive theorists the most important element of learning is observation; for behaviorists, it is performing the behavior.

Many of these processes suggest that the learner actively processes information, instead of being a passive receiver of input. Yet social-cognitive theorists, just as other environmentalists, assume that developmental changes are continuous. They do not, like organismic theorists, explain change as a succession of stages distinguished by qualitatively different features. Organismic theorists give us a very different view of things.

ORGANISMIC THEORIES: ADOLESCENTS CONSTRUCTING THEIR WORLDS

Focus on the Intellectual: Piaget and Kegan

Jean Piaget   Perhaps because Piaget was first interested in biology, he approached human intelligence with questions a biologist might ask if discovering a new organism. How does a creature adapt to its surroundings? What does it do that allows it to survive? How is it changed by the processes that maintain it? For Piaget, intelligence was a means of adapting to one's environment, and only those forms of thought that promoted adaptation survived with increasing age.

By the time Piaget completed his doctorate, he had published extensively on mollusks (acquiring an international reputation in this field while still a teenager). After getting his degree in biology, he turned his interest to psychology, but instead of poking for life along the edges of waters, Piaget went to Paris to work with Alfred Binet, standardizing questions for Binet's scales of intelligence. His inquisitive mind guaranteed that he would still poke around for interesting new life forms, but in Paris these took the shape of children's ideas about their world.

Piaget's theory of intelligence illustrates the central assumptions of the organismic model, and the constructive perspective, perhaps better than any other. He viewed the individual as active, not passive. He saw developmental change as successive *re*organizations of experience, each of which could be viewed as a stage that differed qualitatively from the one that preceded it.

Not surprisingly, Piaget viewed intelligence as biologically based. He assumed that the sequential nature of intellectual stages reflects an underlying maturation of the nervous system (Piaget, 1971). This emphasis did not prevent him from giving equal importance to environmental contributions. In fact, a singularly distinctive feature of his theory is the manner in which it accounts for intellectual development through the interaction of environmental and biological forces. Rather than viewing maturation as providing "ready-made knowledge" or "preformed structures," Piaget viewed it as "open[ing] up new possibilities . . . which still have to be actualized by collaboration with the environment" (Piaget, 1971, p. 21).

Piaget believed knowledge to be more than a copy of reality, as it might be if all it reflected were a faithful detecting and recording by an ever more mature nervous system. On the contrary, Piaget assumed that we actively construct what we know of the world; that is, that we are active, not passive,

Jean Piaget (1896–1980) developed his theory that we actively construct what we know of the world based on four stages of cognitive development.

organisms. He also assumed that we organize our experiences in qualitatively different ways with age, leading to distinct stages in the development of thought.

The Active Organism   Piaget assumed that all knowledge is based initially on actions. Actions are transformed into thought through a process of **reflective abstraction,** in which features of the actions become abstracted so that they can be applied in other contexts (Piaget, 1954). The way we interact with our environment changes with age, and as a result, our experience also changes. Initially, infants have no way of holding experience in mind, and their awareness is limited to immediate sensations. Through repeatedly interacting with things around them, infants develop ways of representing these experiences, though at first the objects they recall are not distinguished from the activities leading to their discovery. For example, an infant who delights in a game of finding a toy hidden under a pillow may again look under the pillow even though she has just watched the parent hide the toy in a new place. Why? Because seeing the toy is part of the same experience as pulling away the pillow. With time, children separate the way they have come to represent their world from the way they act on it. As adolescents, once they can free their ideas from objects, they can relate these ideas to other ideas, and thought becomes abstract. Each form of knowledge evolves from the preceding one. In all, Piaget argued that we progress through four stages. These are discussed on the following page.

Organized Activity   Piaget regarded intelligence as an adaptive process through which we maintain an equilibrium with our environment. Adaptation takes place through two related processes, assimilation and accommodation. **Assimilation** is the process by which individuals fit new information into their present ways of understanding, as when they act on a new object in a way that is similar to previous actions on other objects. Quite often—but not always—we can understand new experiences in terms of what we already know. And sometimes the actions by which we attempt to gain understanding are modified by the process of gaining it. **Accommodation** is the process by which cognitive structures are altered to fit new experiences.

The processes of assimilation and accommodation must be complementary for us to remain in equilibrium with the environment. If assimilation predominates, the organism imposes its own order on the environment, and if accommodation predominates, the converse occurs. Neither one by itself represents the homeostatic state of balance between organism and environment that characterizes adaptation. Thus with each assimilation, accommodation must occur. Piaget referred to the balance thus achieved as **equilibration:** the process responsible for the growth of thought.

Stages of Cognitive Development   Table 2.2 presents the major characteristics of each of Piaget's four stages: **sensorimotor thought, preoperational thought, concrete operational thought,** and **formal operational thought.** These stages illustrate characteristics common to all stage theories:

1. *Emergent properties.* New structures or functions appear that were not previously present.

2. *Qualitative difference.* Each stage of thought is qualitatively different from the preceding one. Differences do not reflect the gradual accumulation of experience, but result from a transformation of experience through the reorganization of underlying structures. According to Jerome Kagan (1971), a Harvard psychologist, each stage has "its own unique attributes, catalyzed into manifest form by a delicate marriage of biological maturation and experience" (p. 997).

3. *Invariant sequencing.* Stages of development occur in the same order for all individuals. Each stage evolves from the preceding one and builds on its achievements.

4. *Universality.* Biological maturation is assumed to play a part in movement to the next stage. Because all members of a species share the same biology, stages should occur universally among all members.

Critics of Piaget question the usefulness of his stages for explaining changes in thought with age. They do not take issue with the characteristics that Piaget describes for each stage, only with his ability to tie these to presumed differences in an underlying competence that forms the basis for each stage. They question, that is, whether he has adequately tied performance to its theoretical moorings. Many of Piaget's measures of formal thought can be solved without the logic he assumed to underlie it. For example, just because adolescents can come up with all the logical possibilities for any situation (a characteristic of formal thought) does not mean they arrive at these through the logical combinations Piaget had in mind. Despite objections to his concept of intellectual stages, however, Piaget has given us a sophisticated way of understanding how individuals make sense of their surroundings (Lourenco & Machado, 1996).

TABLE 2.2   Piaget's Four Stages of Cognitive Development

Stage	Description
Sensorimotor (birth–2 years)	Infants' awareness of their world is limited to their senses, and their reactions to general action patterns, e.g., sucking, grasping, through which they incorporate their experiences.
Preoperational (2–7 years)	Children can use symbols such as words and images to think about things, but confuse the way things appear with the way they must be.
Concrete operational (7–11 years)	Thinking becomes more flexible, allowing children to consider several dimensions to things simultaneously, realizing that though an object may look different, it has not necessarily changed (conservation).
Formal operational (11 years–adulthood)	Thinking becomes abstract, embracing thought itself; adolescents can consider things that are only possible, as well as those that are real.

Piaget studied many aspects of cognitive development, from understanding time and space to the use of rules in children's games. He regarded the latter as important because he believed they provided the foundation for later social and moral development. His approach was always the same, whether studying children's concept of number or of social justice: He watched children and asked them questions about what they were doing. In the matter of moral development, Piaget watched children play marbles, a game common at the time. When he questioned them about the rules of the game, he began to construct a view of the stages of cognitive and moral thinking.

Younger and older children answered his questions in different ways. The youngest boys (the players were rarely girls) regarded the rules as absolute and didn't think they could be changed. When asked where the rules came from, they assumed they had always existed in their present form. They didn't realize that rules are important only for the purpose they serve, making it possible to continue with the game when disagreements arise. Older boys knew that rules are a matter of convenience and are worked out by the players. They also knew rules can be changed if all agree (Piaget, 1965).

Piaget found that girls and boys approached rules differently. Girls were more lax, more practical, and willing to break the rules as the need arose. Piaget believed the girls' approach was not as well developed as that of the boys, who had a better sense of the legal function of rules. Because Piaget believed this sense to be critical for moral development, this difference has important implications for our view of the sexes, especially when held by one of the single most influential theorists in child development (Piaget, 1965).

Piaget is not the only theorist to measure females against a yardstick developed with males (marbles is a boys' game) and find them lacking. Two other giants of personality theory, Freud and Erikson, have done the same. Carol Gilligan (1982), commenting on psychological theorists in general, writes:

> Implicitly adopting the male life as the norm, they have tried to fashion women out of a masculine cloth. It all goes back, of course, to Adam and Eve—a story which shows, among other things, that if you make a woman out of a man, you are bound to get into trouble. In the life cycle, as in the Garden of Eden, the woman has been the deviant. (p. 6)

Robert Kegan Building on the constructive process elaborated by Piaget, Robert Kegan (1982, 1994), a psychologist at Harvard University, argues that the most central human activity is that of "meaning making," of constructing from the moment a reality that makes sense given the balance one has already struck with the world. Such a balance, as represented in Piaget's stages, is the qualitatively different reality the individual achieves at different ages. This reality is shaped by mental structures that give form not only to our ways of thinking, as Piaget discovered, but to our ways of feeling, our ways of relating to others, and our ways of relating to ourselves. These four dimensions, the cognitive, the affective, the interpersonal, and the intrapersonal, constitute the meaning-making arenas of the "self" (Kegan, personal communication).

Kegan suggests that, at all ages, individuals continuously "parse" experience into that which is "me" and that which is "not me," into "subject" and "object." Development occurs when aspects of the "me" become *differentiated* from the "not me," enabling us to perceive and relate to things that we had failed to see because they had been too much a part of us. Thus growth or development is a process by which those aspects of meaning making that we *cannot* see gradually move to a place where we *can* see them, and be in charge of them. The aspects move from "having us" to our "having them," from "subject" to "object." For example, young children in Piaget's stage of pre-operational thought may think that a can of soda poured into a tall thin glass is actually more than when poured into a short wide glass because it reaches a higher level in the first glass. These children are "subject to," or embedded in, their *perceptions* of the physical world. When they evolve a more complex mental structure that enables what Piaget calls concrete operations, they "have" perceptions, and their view of reality is no longer determined by how things appear. They can realize that the soda only *looks as if* it is more. In the same way, these young children are emotionally more impulsive, have a hard time waiting their turn or delaying any desire once it appears in their minds. They are "subject to," or embedded in, their *impulses,* and when they gradually evolve the same deeper mental structure which allows them to differentiate from their *perceptions,* what we call "concrete operations," they will also be able to differentiate from their *impulses,* what we call "impulse control" (Kegan, personal communication).

Kegan argues that this broader structure, which usually develops in the elementary school years, allows children to think concretely, control their impulses, and recognize that others have a point of view distinct from their own. All in all, it permits a more durable sense of self in which the child's desires are organized as ongoing dispositions or preferences rather than moment-to-moment, highly changeable affairs (Kegan, 1982). But typical 10-year-olds are also embedded in the concrete (they cannot think abstractly) and embedded in their own needs and point of view (they cannot subordinate their own needs to the needs of a relationship). These are the changes of mind we expect in adolescence, and they require yet another transformation in our meaning-organizing principle (Kegan, 1994). According to Kegan, adolescents gradually are able to think more abstractly when the concrete way of knowing moves from "subject" to "object," when it becomes a way of knowing they "have" rather than a way of knowing they "are." And similarly, they are gradually able to relate more mutually, and less instrumentally, when their own needs and point of view become ways of knowing they "have" rather than ways of knowing they "are" (Kegan, personal communication). Consider a 12-year-old boy who has difficulty separating his growing need for independence from his perception of his father, whom he sees as domineering and controlling. Because of his inability to see his own struggle with issues of dependence, he sees his father as continually trying to micromanage his life. As a consequence, he finds it difficult to comply with any requests his father may make. As this boy becomes more confident in himself, and sees that he is able to make decisions and function independently, his perception of his father will most likely change as well. For him to relate to his father in a different way, however, he must first be able to see himself differently to develop an ongoing sense of himself in which he can see his needs for what they are, rather than see himself and his father *through* his needs.

Focus on the Motivational: Freud and Horney

Sigmund Freud   As a young physician with a private practice in neurology, Sigmund Freud might have been more surprised than anyone at the direction his career would take. Were it not for some of his patients who complained of mysterious ailments, he might have remained an obscure but successful Viennese doctor.

The mysterious symptoms were no different from those he saw daily, such as numbness and paralysis from damaged nerves. But the nerves in these patients were unaffected; he found only healthy neural tissue when he examined them. How could patients suffer neurological symptoms with no physical damage? Fortunately, a Frenchman named Jean Charcot had just concluded a series of studies in which healthy people were told under hypnosis that they would awake with physical symptoms (among those suggested were numbness and paralysis). When they awoke, they had no memory of the suggestion, yet they exhibited the symptoms, just as Freud's patients did (Thomas, 1979).

Sigmund Freud (1856–1939), the founder of psycho-analysis, defined five stages of psychosexual development. These particular stages have been subject to much debate, but many theorists have built on his general concept of developmental stages.

The Unconscious   Freud eventually solved the mystery, but only by tossing aside current notions about the mind. He asserted that we have an active mental life of which we remain completely unaware, an unconscious that affects our actions in very direct ways. Thoughts, feelings, or problems that are too disturbing to face or that cannot be solved immediately are pushed out of the conscious mind, repressed to the unconscious realm of thought. Although **repression** momentarily reduces the distress, it does not get rid of the problem. The thoughts and feelings continue to exist and continue to push for expression, like a teapot that has been brought to a boil: If you cover the spout, the pressure within continues to build until the steam is released through some other opening, perhaps by blowing off the lid. The repressed ideas and feelings escape in many ways—in dreams, actions, or even physical symptoms, as with Freud's patients. The only requirement limiting their expression is that the person remain unaware of their true meaning, thereby protected from the distress they occasion. The treatment that Freud eventually devised involved discovering the unconscious source of the patient's distress and bringing it to light in the safe atmosphere of therapy (Freud, 1954).

Freud formulated his theory of personality development while treating these unusual symptoms. He believed that they resulted from an inner war between conflicting aspects of the personality. Although Freud first noticed these aspects of the personality in his patients, he believed them to be present in all of us.

Stages of Psychosexual Development   Like other organismic theorists, such as Piaget and Kegan, Freud believed that development occurs over distinct stages. These were thought to unfold in different zones of the body, focusing the expression of a psychic energy. This energy, which Freud termed **libido,** takes different forms depending on the body zone through which it is channeled. Expression of the libido moves from the region of the mouth in infancy (*oral stage*), to the sphincters in toddlerhood (*anal stage*), to the genital region in early childhood (*phallic stage*). Because genital expression of the libido in early childhood is associated with tremendous anxiety, it goes underground (*latency stage*), so to speak, and does not arise again until it emerges full-force with puberty (*genital stage*), once again pressing for genital expression (Freud, 1954). Different aspects of the personality express or inhibit these libidinal impulses. The **id** demands immediate gratification of the biological impulses that it houses. It operates according to the pleasure principle. The expression of libido is highly pleasurable (assuming a sexual nature even in infancy), and the pressure resulting from its blockage is painful. The id, however, has limited means of gratifying libidinal impulses. The infant can only cry its displeasure or fantasize about the food and comforts it desires.

The **ego** soon emerges as a means of realistically satisfying these instinctual impulses. The ego can distinguish the id's fantasies from actual goals, and can negotiate the realities of the environment. It also realizes that although some forms of expression will be tolerated, others will bring more pain than they're worth. The ego seeks to gratify as many of the id's demands as possible without bringing on the wrath of parents, peers, and society. It operates according to the reality principle, both facilitating and blocking the expression of the libido. The functions of the ego—such as evaluating, comparing, and planning—emphasize the active role we take in structuring our experiences.

A final aspect of the personality, emerging from the ego when the child is about 4 or 5, contains the moral values acquired from our culture and dictates what we should and should not do. Freud called this the **superego.** It has two aspects, the conscience and the ego-ideal. The conscience embodies the "should-nots," those thoughts and actions for which we have been punished in the past; the ego-ideal represents the "shoulds," the positive values we have learned as children. These two aspects of the superego gradually assume the controls that once had to be exercised by parents and others, so that with the ego, behavior becomes self-regulated. The superego also introduces us to the human drama that Freud believed laid the foundation for adult sexuality, and to his view of the differences between men and women (Hall, 1954).

Formulation of Gender Differences   Freud called this drama the **Oedipal complex** after the Greek myth of a young man who murdered his father and married his mother. Freud believed that every boy falls in love with his mother, and every girl with her father. The resolution to this love triangle lays the foundation, according to Freud, for fundamental differences between the sexes. We shall look at the Oedipal complex in boys first, because Freud framed his theory around the male experience.

During the phallic stage, the third of Freud's stages of personality development, the libido seeks expression through the genitals. The young boy derives sexual pleasure from masturbating. This activity imbues his penis with such significance that when he first notices a girl without one, he is horrified and assumes she has been mutilated. He also thinks that the same could happen to him if he is not careful. Before you think he is overreacting, consider the reason for his fears. His feelings for his mother transform his father into a rival. Castration would be a fitting punishment for his sexual longing for his mother. Freud believed the boy's fear (termed castration anxiety) to be so great that he represses his sexual desire for his mother. In yielding to his father, he identifies with him, and in the process, takes on his values. Thus the boy's fear of castration motivates him to move beyond his incestuous desires, repressing these and identifying with the father. The superego that emerges from this process is strong, because it reflects the power that the boy sees in his father.

The girl falls in love with her father and views her mother as a sexual rival. For her the Oedipal, or Electra, complex revolves around a different set of motives. Instead of anxiety, she experiences longing and inferiority. She sees that she has "come off badly" in comparison with boys and feels inferior because she does not have a penis. She wants her father to give her one, too. Of course, these longings (which Freud calls penis envy) cannot be satisfied, and are finally replaced by a compensatory wish: that her father give her a baby. Freud writes, "Her Oedipus complex culminates in a desire, which is long retained, to receive a baby from her father as a gift—to bear him a child" (Freud, 1925, p. 124). Freud believed that the girl's longings for a penis and a child intermingle in the unconscious and prepare her for her future roles of wife and mother.

Notice that the girl never cleanly resolves the Oedipal complex; she retains a lingering longing in the unconscious that imbues her personality with its essential feminine features, one of which is a feeling of inferiority. Freud believed that the woman moves from feelings of personal inferiority to contempt for all women. Once she realizes that her lack of a penis is not a personal form of punishment for something she has done, but is shared by all women, "she begins to share the contempt felt by men for a sex which is the lesser in so important a respect" (Freud, 1925, p. 253).

Freud was ahead of his time in many ways in his acceptance of women. He freely admitted women into his analytic circle and frequently referred patients to women analysts (Tavris & Wade, 1984). However, his theory of the feminine personality is uniquely uncomplimentary. Freud believed females to be masochistic, vain, and jealous. The masochism (deriving pleasure from pain) stems from their frustrated longing for their fathers. The vanity and jealousy he attributed to penis envy. "If she cannot have a penis, she will turn her whole body into an erotic substitute; her feminine identity comes to depend on being sexy, attractive, and adored. Female jealousy is a displaced version of penis envy" (Tavris & Wade, 1984, p. 182).

Finally, Freud believed that the female superego is not as strong as that of males; the implication is that females are less moral. Two things account for their weaker superegos. Females are never as highly motivated as males to resolve Oedipal issues, because they literally do not have as much to lose, and they identify with a weaker figure than do males: The mother is more nurturant, and less threatening and powerful, than the father.

Anna Freud, his daughter, extended Freud's theory by focusing on the unique demands that adolescence places on the ego. She contended that the adult sexual drives that emerge with puberty strain the child's organization of the personality and require new and stronger defenses against the incestuous threats that these drives reintroduce. She noted that intellectual developments in adolescence make such defenses possible, namely in the form of *intellectualization,* or the ability to justify one's behavior in highly abstract terms. Even with new defenses, however, adolescents must create additional distance between themselves and their parents. In doing so, they establish social relations with age-mates, with whom expression of the genital drive becomes appropriate (Freud, 1969).

Karen Horney   Karen Horney, a contemporary of Sigmund Freud and his daughter Anna, objected to Freud's interpretation of the feminine personality. She countered that he had not properly taken into consideration the male-dominated society in which his patients lived. Although women might want the power and privileges that men have, this is a very different matter from Freud's penis envy. Further, women's economic dependence on men creates a psychological dependence and a need to have men validate their self-worth (Horney, 1967).

Although Karen Horney initially accepted Freud's ideas, she eventually came to question many of them. Most importantly, she asserted that our personalities take shape through adapting to life situations, not through dealing with primitive instincts. She also viewed the personality as a whole, rather than as compartmentalized into id, ego, and superego. She stressed the creative potential present in all of us, and at least the possibility for living lives that are in harmony with our surroundings, whereas Freud maintained that conflict between instinctual forces and societal inhibitions is inevitable (Munroe, 1955).

Horney also viewed the early influence of the family differently than Freud. She traced healthy personality development, which she viewed in terms of the ability to value oneself and to see that one is valued by others, to the child's first experiences of warmth and affection from parents. Conversely, she traced neurosis to the absence of true warmth and affection from parents. Though she considered early experiences to be important, she did not see them as having the determining effect on later personality that Freud did. Thus Horney placed less stress on biological instincts than Freud, giving more emphasis to the impact of culture. Nonetheless, she retained a firm belief that development reflects inner sources of growth (Horney, 1937).

Horney (1967) took issue with Freud's interpretation of the Oedipal drama. She contended that it is impossible to test Freud's concept of penis envy as long as women do not have the same status in society as men. Though from wealthy families, Freud's female patients lived in a male-dominated society. They were economically dependent first on their fathers and later on their husbands, enjoying few outlets for creativity or productivity. Did they envy a man for his penis? Or did they envy him for his privileged position in society?

Horney also questioned Freud's assertion that masochism is a central feature of the female personality. Freud maintained that because the Oedipal complex was never fully resolved in the girl, she retains a frustrated desire for her father, which becomes associated with later sexual pleasure.

Karen Horney (1885–1952) was a psychoanalyst who took issue with Freud's views on personality development in women. She believed that culture, as much as biological instincts, was responsible for many of the characteristics of the female personality.

Horney pointed out that not all women obtain pleasure by sacrificing themselves to the needs of others, whereas some men do (Tavris & Wade, 1984).

Horney further objected that Freud's analysis of the female personality
not only ties their social condition to their biology, thereby making it un-
alterable, but it also suggests that they secretly desire to be in this state. She
then reversed Freud's analysis of penis envy and asked why men would fear
and envy women. She pointed out that the very social conditions that suggest women's inferiority can also be seen as an active attempt by men to
keep women in a one-down position (Tavris & Wade, 1984).

Horney mentioned that numbers of her male patients expressed envy
and fear concerning pregnancy and childbirth. She suggested that men cope
with these feelings by reacting with compensatory emotions. Rather than
feeling inferior because they are not able to become pregnant, they feel contempt for women for not having a penis. Rather than fearing women's
power to give birth, they feel contempt for their weakness.

Despite the force of Horney's arguments, hers remains a minority opinion. Although other female analysts made similar objections (Miller, 1973,
1976), the baton Freud carried was passed to a successor who also viewed
development as unfolding in a single, universal sequence for females and
males alike—a sequence that again takes a male perspective.

Focus on the Social: Erikson, Chodorow, and Gilligan

Erik Erikson   Theories often reflect the personalities of their originators.
Havighurst, who was an educator, saw development as a series of tasks to
be learned. Piaget, who was intellectually precocious himself, developed a
theory of intelligence. Horney stressed cultural contributions to development, as she reacted to the male bias in her society. Erikson as well developed a theory that reflected a personal issue. In his case the issue was a
search for personal identity.

Erik Erikson's parents separated before he was born. Rather than take
the name of his biological father or his stepfather, Erikson named himself
after his given name (Erik-son). As a young man, he traveled about Europe,
earning a living as an artist, and eventually teaching art in a school for
young children. The position at the school proved to be a turning point in
his life, for the school was established by the Freuds for the children of patients. Erikson studied with Freud's daughter Anna, who was herself a talented analyst. His theory takes off where Freud's ends, at adolescence with
a search for oneself. It reflects his own awareness of the need to develop an
inner sense of self.

Erikson built on Freud's analysis of the personality into id, ego, and
superego and on his stages of psychosexual development. Yet he differed
from Freud in several important respects. Perhaps the most significant is
Erikson's emphasis on the healthy personality. Erikson stressed the social
functions of the ego that allow individuals to cope successfully. These functions assume central importance in adolescence, as adolescents question
who they are and where they are going.

Identity is a central aspect of the healthy personality, reflecting both an
inner sense of continuity and sameness over time and an ability to identify
with others and share in common goals, to participate in one's culture.

Erik Erikson (1902–
1994) built on Freud's
theory of psychosexual
development and
formulated a psycho-
social theory of devel-
opment. According to
his theory, people
move from one stage
to the next in response
to social demands.

Research Focus

Erikson's Psychohistorical Approach: A Clinician's Notebook from the Dakota Prairies

With Michael Wapner

When we neared the simple, clean homestead, the little sons were playing the small Indian boy's favorite game, roping a tree stump, while a little girl was lazily sitting on her father's knees, playing with his patient hands. Jim's wife was working in the house. We had brought some additional supplies, knowing that with Indians nothing can be settled in a few hours; our conversation would have to proceed in the slow, thoughtful, shy manner of the hosts. Jim's wife had asked some women relatives to attend our session. From time to time she went to the door to look out over the prairie which rolled away on every side, merging in the distance with the white processions of slow-moving clouds. As we sat and said little, I had time to consider what Jim's place among the living generations of his people might be. (Erikson, 1963, pp. 120–121)

So begins Erikson's description of the conversations that contributed to his understanding of the Sioux's early childhood experiences and their difficulty as adults in finding meaning to life. More generally, these observations led to his understanding of the ways in which one's society influences the course of each person's development.

Erik Erikson developed a unique style of research that combined the tools of clinical analysis with those of fieldwork. His insights into human development reflected the same psychoanalytic training that Freud and others practiced in urban European offices. Erikson took these skills to the rolling plains of the Dakotas, and later to the forested dwellings of the Yurok in the Northwest, and in doing so, opened new vistas in our understanding of human development.

His observations made him keenly aware that human development takes place within a social community. Each community raises its children to participate in the world as adults—but there are as many worlds as there are communities. Children are indulged or controlled, taught to give away or to hoard, and so on, depending on the wisdom of their group—a wisdom that reflects the peace their group has made with the realities of geography and the historical moment. The area in which one lives determines the form life takes, whether in the specifics of what one eats or wears or in abstractions such as notions of goodness and propriety (Coles, 1970).

The Sioux, for instance, value generosity and regard the accumulation of wealth as tantamount to evil. Erikson traces these attitudes to a nomadic life in which they followed the buffalo across the plains. The buffalo existed in great numbers and the Sioux rarely experienced need. As nomads, the Sioux learned to live lightly, without the encumbrances of possessions.

Erikson (1963) believed that identity develops as adolescents assume commitments to future occupations, adult sex roles, and personal belief systems. It is no accident that identity assumes importance as individuals step from childhood into adulthood and, with this, into their culture. It is also no accident that identity emerged as a central concern to a young artist in search of himself. The Research Focus, " Erikson's Psychohistorical Approach," offers a vivid look at group identity development.

Psychosocial Stages of Development   Erikson (1963) believed that new aspects of the person emerge through inner growth, making new types of social encounters possible. As with other stage theorists, he assumed that development occurs in the same set sequence for all, reflecting an internal ground plan in which each stage has its own period of ascendence, a time in which the individual is especially vulnerable to certain influences and in-

Research Focus (*continued*)

Generosity, because it reflected a more basic harmony with their surroundings, was a virtue. Conversely, the Yurok value thrift and a meticulous management of resources. They live in settlements along the Klamath River. Once a year, when the salmon return to breed, they experience the abundance that the Sioux lived with in every season. For the rest of the year, they must cautiously manage that brief harvest to avoid hunger and need.

These particular differences are less important than the common function served by the communal practices of either group. Ritual ways of living provided each with a group identity. It is from this group identity that members of the community derived a sense of their own identity. Erikson arrived at this observation after noting what he referred to as a "cultural pathology" among the present-day Sioux Indians. He traced this problem to their inability to find "fitting images to connect the past with the future" (Erikson, 1963, p. 117). The Sioux's lifestyle had been tied to the buffalo, the provider of meat for food; pelts for clothing and shelter; bones for needles, ornaments, and toys; and even dried droppings for fuel. The destruction of the buffalo herds by White settlers resulted in the destruction of the Sioux's way of life—and of the group identity from which new generations could derive a sense of themselves. Speaking of the present generation of Sioux, Erikson noted that

the majority of them have as little concept of the future as they are beginning to have of the past. This youngest generation, then, finds itself between the impressive dignity of its grandparents, who honestly refuse to believe that the white man is here to stay, and the white man himself, who feels that the Indian persists in being a rather impractical relic of a dead past. (1963, p. 121)

If Erikson's theory is correct, that without "fitting images to connect the past with the future" young people are lost, what are the images that performed this function for you? Is there any single or even small set of recurrent experiences that anchor you in your community and physical environment the way the buffalo anchored the Sioux? Is it possible that society in the U.S. at the end of the twentieth century has no such single image? Perhaps these images belong to subgroups rather than the culture as a whole. For instance, is the gang for the East Los Angeles gang member in any way analogous to the buffalo for the Sioux? What functions would the gang have to fulfill for its members to qualify as an image? If it is an image in the Eriksonian sense, then what will it take to discourage gang membership in East Los Angeles and similar urban communities?

Sources: R. Coles. (1970). *Erik Erikson: The growth of his work.* Boston: Little, Brown. E. Erikson. (1963). *Childhood and society.* New York: Norton.

sensitive to others. (This assumption is known as Erikson's **epigenetic principle.**) Society challenges us with new demands as we age. We experience these as crises. Each takes a slightly different form and gives each age its unique characteristics. Table 2.3 presents and describes each of Erikson's life stages.

Each of the first four crises equip adolescents to meet the central challenge of achieving an ego identity. Trust establishes the confidence in themselves and in others that is needed to begin the task. Autonomy gives self-direction and purpose, the ability to follow goals that one sets for oneself rather than those set by others. Initiative allows adolescents to explore the options that open up with adolescence, and industry allows them to realistically evaluate these options and select the ones they will commit themselves to (Erikson, 1963, 1968).

The establishment of identity involves the individual in a succession of

TABLE 2.3   Erikson's Developmental Stages

Stage	Psychosocial Crisis
BIRTH TO ADOLESCENCE	
Infancy	Trust versus mistrust. Realization that needs will be met leads to trust in others and self.
Toddlerhood	Autonomy versus shame and doubt. Physical maturation gives sense of being able to do things for self.
Early childhood	Initiative versus guilt. Increasing abilities promote exploration and expand experience.
Middle childhood	Industry versus inferiority. Accomplishments and skills provide basis for self-esteem.
ADOLESCENCE TO OLD AGE	
Adolescence	Identity versus identity diffusion. Biological and social changes of adolescence occasion a search for continuity of self.
Early adulthood	Intimacy versus isolation. Sense of self provides the basis for sexual and emotional intimacy with another adult.
Middle adulthood	Generativity versus stagnation. Concern for children and future generations reflects need to leave something of oneself.
Late adulthood	Integrity versus despair. Acceptance of one's life as having meaning gives one a sense of dignity.

Source: E. Erikson. (1963). *Childhood and society*. New York: Norton.

commitments to life goals that serve to define the self. The young adult faces the crisis of sharing that self with another—of intimacy, first with a mate and then, for most, with children. Middle adulthood extends the adult's concerns beyond this intimate group to others in the community. Older adults face a final crisis of reviewing their lives and accepting the decisions they have made. Erikson calls this last crisis one of personal integrity.

Like Freud's, Erikson's theory reflects a male bias. Erikson considers the achievement of identity to be the central crisis of adolescence, even though he asserts that a different sequence exists for females. Most females resolve the crisis of intimacy, which Erikson places in early adulthood, *before* they complete identity issues. Their sense of themselves derives more from their relationships than from commitments to work and ideology. Although Erikson notes these differences, he does not change his sequence of life stages; that is, he equates the male experience with development in general (Bardwick & Douvan, 1971; Gilligan, 1982).

Nancy Chodorow   Another theorist, also influenced by Freud, gives us a very different view of development. Nancy Chodorow offers an alternative to the universal developmental sequence charted by Erikson. Chodorow (1978) attributes psychological differences in the makeup of women and men to the social fact that for most children the first intimate relationship is with a woman—their mother. This initial relationship has very different consequences for girls than it does for boys.

Chodorow asserts that infants experience themselves as continuous with the mother. They live within the boundless security of her presence, little caring which smile is theirs or whose hand reaches out to the other, all of it part of the same encircling awareness. Mothers, too, empathically relate to their infants and experience a continuity with them.

> In a society where mothers provide nearly exclusive care and certainly the most meaningful relationship to the infant, the infant develops its sense of self mainly in relation to her. Insofar as the relationship with its mother has continuity, the infant comes to define aspects of its self . . . in relation to internalized representations of aspects of its mother. (Chodorow, 1978, p. 78)

Important to Chodorow are the necessary differences in the way children of either sex develop beyond this point. Girls can continue to define themselves within the context of this first relationship. Mothers, as well, can see their daughters as extensions of themselves. Girls can experience a continuing attachment to the mother while still defining themselves as females. None of this is possible for boys. They must separate themselves from the mother much earlier than girls in order to develop as males. Mothers, too, experience their sons as separate and different from themselves, unlike their daughters. Thus, boys embark on a developmental path marked not by attachment but by separation and increasing individuation.

Chodorow argues that because the primary caregiver is the same sex for girls, there is less need for the girl to differentiate herself in terms of ego boundaries. Chodorow brings us to a point made earlier by Freud: The

Nancy Chodorow's research challenges Freud's and Erikson's assumptions of a universal development sequence. Because boys must define themselves outside their relationship with their mother but girls define themselves within that relationship, the course of identity development is fundamentally different for the two sexes.

A growing body of research can describe the differences in identity development for these two students due to their gender. Few researchers, however, have explored differences in identity development for various racial or ethnic groups.

personalities of women are frequently less differentiated than those of men, and are more closely tied to their relationships. But she sees this difference as an asset, as a strength rather than a weakness. Girls can experience continuity with others and relate to their feelings. Chodorow points to the heavy costs males pay for their greater individuation. In curtailing their emotional attachment to the mother, they also limit their ability in general to relate empathetically to others. Thus, differences in ego boundaries lay a foundation for a greater capacity for empathy in females. In fact, Chodorow sees the capacity for empathy to be a core part of the feminine personality, giving them a sense of connectedness with others (Chodorow, 1978).

Carol Gilligan   Taking up Chodorow's point, Carol Gilligan, a psychologist at Harvard University, notes striking differences in the ways males and females think of themselves. These differences extend to the ways they resolve issues involving others. Gilligan finds that males tend to see themselves as separate from others; females describe themselves in terms of their relationships with others. These themes of separation and connectedness appear over and again in her research, whether she is studying morality and choice, descriptions of the self, or interpersonal dynamics (Gilligan, 1982).

Notice the way two of Gilligan's subjects, an 11-year-old boy and an 11-year-old girl, describe themselves, as shown in Box 2.1.

Jake describes himself at length. He first identifies himself by his age and name and then his status within his community. We never know what his mother does, but we know that doesn't contribute to his sense of position as does his father's occupation. He then identifies his abilities and interests. He ends with a description of an important physical characteristic. We get the impression of a distinct personality from this description. Gilligan agrees. Jake has described himself in terms of the things that distinguish him from others. His self-description emphasizes his uniqueness and separateness.

Amy's description of herself is brief. We know only that she enjoys school and wants to be a scientist. Otherwise she describes herself in terms of her relationships with others. We know nothing about Amy apart from the qualities she believes will allow her to help others. Short, tall, freckled, funny, well-off, or disadvantaged—things that set her apart from others receive little attention. Gilligan stresses that this sense of responsibility for and connectedness to others frequently appears in girls' and women's descriptions of themselves. It is, she notes, a very real difference between most women and men.

We see this difference clearly when Jake and Amy are asked how one should choose when responsibility to oneself and responsibility to others conflict (Box 2.2). Jake believes we are mostly responsible to ourselves. Being independent means taking care of ourselves and making sure that our actions don't hurt others ("If you want to kill yourself, use a hand grenade instead of an atom bomb so you don't take your neighbors with you!"). Jake starts with the assumption that individuals are separate and proceeds with the need for rules to protect each person's autonomy. Thus for Jake, responsibility is not doing certain things.

Amy's answer is much longer than the one she gave in describing her-

Carol Gilligan, a psychologist at Harvard University, has focused her research on female development and challenged the definition of developmental stages by Kohlberg and other developmentalists whose theories are based primarily on the experiences of male subjects.

Box 2.1   Self-Descriptions of Two Adolescents

How would you describe yourself to yourself?

Jake: Perfect. That's my conceited side. What do you want—any way that I choose to describe myself?

Amy: You mean my character?

What do you think?

Well, I don't know. I'd describe myself as, well, what do you mean?

If you had to describe the person you are in a way that you yourself would know it was you, what would you say?

Jake: I'd start off with eleven years old. Jake [last name]. I'd have to add that I live in [town], because that is a big part of me, and also that my father is a doctor, because I think that does change me a little bit, and that I don't believe in crime, except for when your name is Heinz; that I think school is boring, because I think that kind of changes your character a little bit. I don't sort of know how to describe myself, because I don't know how to read my personality.

Amy: Well, I'd say that I was someone who likes school and studying, and that's what I want to do with my life. I want to be some kind of a scientist or something, and I want to do things, and I want to help people. And I think that's what kind of person I am, or what kind of person I try to be. And that's probably how I'd describe myself. And I want to do something to help other people.

If you had to describe the way you actually would describe yourself, what would you say?

I like corny jokes. I don't really like to get down to work, but I can do all the stuff in school. Every single problem that I have seen in school I have been able to do, except for ones that take knowledge, and after I do the reading, I have been able to do them, but sometimes I don't want to waste my time on easy homework. And also I'm crazy about sports. I think, unlike a lot of people, that the world still has hope. . . . Most people that I know I like, and I have the good life, pretty much as good as any I have seen, and I am tall for my age.

Why is that?

Well, because I think that this world has a lot of problems, and I think that everybody should try to help somebody else in some way, and the way I'm choosing is through science.

Source: C. Gilligan. (1982). *In a different voice* (pp. 35–37). Cambridge, MA: Harvard University Press.

self. She puts her responsibility to others first. Not always, of course; but she differs in an important way from Jake in her view of responsibility. Amy sees responsibility as an action, as a positive response. She assumes a connectedness with others. She talks about people and caring, all on a very personal level, whereas Jake mentions the community and seems to imply a need for rules to regulate the actions of its members.

Amy and Jake have taken different paths through childhood. They are likely to follow different paths into adulthood. Amy experiences herself in

Box 2.2   Choosing Between Responsibility to Self and Responsibility to Others

When responsibility to oneself and responsibility to others conflict, how should one choose?

Jake: You go about one-fourth to the others and three-fourths to yourself.

Amy: Well, it really depends on the situation. If you have a responsibility with somebody else, then you should keep it to a certain extent, but to the extent that it is really going to hurt you or stop you from doing something that you really, really want, then I think maybe you should put yourself first. But if it is your responsibility to somebody really close to you, you've just got to decide in that situation which is more important, yourself or that person, and like I said, it really depends on what kind of person you are and how you feel about the other person or persons involved.

Why?

Jake: Because the most important thing in your decision should be yourself, don't let yourself be guided totally by other people, but you have to take them into consideration. So, if what you want to do is blow yourself up with an atom bomb, you should maybe blow yourself up with a hand grenade because you are thinking about your neighbors who would die also.

Amy: Well, like some people put themselves and things for themselves before they put other people, and some people really care about other people. Like, I don't think your job is as important as somebody that you really love, like your husband or your parents or a very close friend. Somebody that you really care for—or if it's just your responsibility to your job or somebody that you barely know, then maybe you go first—but if it's somebody that you really love and love as much or even more than you love yourself, you've got to decide what you really love more, that person, or that thing, or yourself.

And how do you do that?

Well, you've got to think about it, and you've got to think about both sides, and you've got to think which would be better for everybody or better for yourself, which is more important, and which will make everybody happier. Like if the other people can get somebody else to do it, whatever it is, or don't really need you specifically, maybe it's better to do what you want, because the other people will be just fine with somebody else so they'll still be happy, and then you'll be happy too because you'll do what you want.

Box 2.2   (continued)

What does responsibility mean?

Jake: It means pretty much thinking of others when I do something, and like if I want to throw a rock, not throwing it at a window, because I thought of the people who would have to pay for that window, not doing it just for yourself, because you have to live with other people and live with your community, and if you do something that hurts them all, a lot of people will end up suffering, and that is sort of the wrong thing to do.

Amy: That other people are counting on you to do something, and you can't just decide, "Well, I'd rather do this or that."

Are there other kinds of responsibility?

Well, to yourself. If something looks really fun but you might hurt yourself doing it because you don't really know how to do it and your friends say, "Well come on, you can do it, don't worry," if you're really scared to do it, it's your responsibility to yourself that if you think you might hurt yourself, you shouldn't do it, because you have to take care of yourself.

Source: C. Gilligan. (1982). *In a different voice* (pp. 35–37). Cambridge, MA: Harvard University Press.

terms of her connection with others, Jake through his separateness. Each is also developing different strengths: Amy in interpersonal relations, Jake in functioning autonomously. At this point, the strengths of one are the weaknesses of the other.

Susan Pollack and Gilligan (1982) noticed unusual violence in men's fantasies about seemingly peaceful, intimate scenes. When asked to tell a story about a couple seated on a bench, over one-fifth of the men described some act of violence—murder, rape, kidnapping, or suicide. Very few of the women did. Gilligan reminds us that men, from an early age, define themselves through their separateness and uniqueness. Intimacy and closeness with others pose threats to their sense of themselves, and they may react to this danger with themes of violence.

Women experience themselves through their relationships with others, and experience danger in impersonal settings. Gilligan points out that 20 years earlier Matina Horner (1968) had noted unexpected themes of violence from women who were asked to complete a story about a young medical student, Anne, who finished the term at the top of her class. Women reacted to her success with fear. The tough competition of medical school that ended with Anne's success also signaled failure for others. Would the other students react with anger, ostracizing Anne? Isolation is a dangerous consequence of success, to the extent that it sets women apart from others and can trigger fears of isolation and rejection.

Gilligan suggests that because of the difference between females' and males' capacities for empathy, males should experience more problems with relationships and females with individuation. Because human development is charted, to date, in male terms—that is, in terms of increasing separation and individuation—when women have problems with individuation, these are seen as a sign of developmental immaturity. Men's problems with relationships, however, do not evoke a parallel interpretation. Gilligan pointedly notes that "women's failure to separate then becomes by definition a failure to develop" (Gilligan, 1982).

Gilligan points out that science has not been neutral. Our theories reflect "a consistent observational and evaluative bias." We tend to interpret "different" as either better or worse, because we have a tendency to work with a single scale. Because most scales are also standardized in terms of male development, male behavior is taken as the norm and female behavior as a departure from the norm. This approach is perpetuated by the fact that most research is done by males, with many important studies using only males as subjects (Gilligan, 1982; Yoder & Kahn, 1993).

Gilligan offers us a challenge: Can we see human behavior from other than this single perspective? She dares us to ask not only why women's feelings "get in the way" of their reasoning when thinking about others (a quality she does not regard as a weakness), but also why men's feelings do not.[1] Instead of asking why more women than men have problems with individuation, we need also to ask why more men have problems with intimacy and relationships. Until we begin to ask and find answers to all of these questions, our psychology of human development will remain incomplete.

Gilligan brings a new awareness to the study of personality. She identifies two unique perspectives on human experience, each more dominant in one sex than the other. The first is individualistic, defining the self in terms of its uniqueness and separateness. Relationships with others are governed by a consideration of individual rights, rules, and the application of an impartial justice. Gilligan finds this approach more characteristic of males. The second perspective reflects a sensitivity to and connectedness with others. The self is defined through interpersonal relationships. Rather than rights and rules governing relationships, a sense of responsibility toward others arising out of one's connectedness with them shapes relationships. An ethic of care—rather than abstract justice—dictates personal responsibility in dealings with others. This second approach is more characteristic of females. The Research Focus, "Projective Measures," describes one of Gilligan's studies about the differences in the way men and women perceive social realities.

Gilligan's theory has generated considerable interest and debate. Its strength lies in giving us a more complete picture of the human condition, one that gives equal attention to the experiences that organize a characteristically female perspective. Its weakness, to date, is in the equivocal support it has received from the research it has stimulated (for example, Walker, 1984, 1986; but see Baumrind, 1986).

Before leaving Gilligan's approach, let's go back to a point raised earlier when discussing Piaget: the differences he observed between girls' and

---

[1]Freud's (1925) observation that females have a lesser sense of justice than males and are more influenced by their feelings received later support by Kohlberg and others in that females' moral judgments were more likely to reflect interpersonal concerns and males' to reflect abstract principles (Kohlberg & Kramer, 1969).

boys' use of rules. Gilligan cites research by Janet Lever (1976, 1978), which found that boys' games occur in larger groups, are more competitive, and last considerably longer than girls' games. Of special interest is the fact that although boys quarreled throughout the games, they never let the quarreling disrupt their play. They were always able to settle their disputes through the rules of the game. Girls play in smaller, more intimate groups, usually with a best friend. When disagreements occur among girls, they tend to stop the play.

On the face of it, these findings seem to support Piaget's contention that boys' moral (and social) development outpaces girls'. Gilligan interprets the data differently. She points to different priorities in the play of either sex. The game has first priority for boys, and rules enable them to continue it. With girls, the relationship comes first, and the need for rules to negotiate play signals danger. Girls will end the game in order to preserve the relationship. Is this a less-developed sense of morality? Surely not. But it *is* a very different dynamic, one that has been addressed by only a handful of developmental theorists to date.

THE WORLDS OF ADOLESCENTS: A CONTEXTUAL PERSPECTIVE

In Chapter 1, we discussed the various overlapping contexts in which development takes place, from the moment-by-moment, face-to-face interactions that make up the "real stuff" of life, to the unseen, yet palpably present social and political climate, experienced in such things as the availability of jobs, whether lawns in one's neighborhood are mown or go to seed, the condition of parks and libraries, and the number of computers at school. As Urie Bronfenbrenner has pointed out, each of these contexts affects us in numerous ways. For them to do so, however, they must be responded to and made sense of. In other words, the events to which adolescents respond do not have meaning until they are interpreted.

Internalizing the Context: Vygotsky and Rogoff

Lev Vygotsky   Lev Vygotsky, a Russian psychologist living in the early part of this century, stressed the ways in which individuals internalize aspects of their surroundings. Vygotsky, like Piaget, believed that individuals acquire knowledge of their world simply in the course of doing whatever they happen to be doing, without having to be formally instructed. But Vygotsky differed from Piaget in an important respect. For Vygotsky (1978), this process is fundamentally social in nature, taking place under the tutelage of another, simply as a natural consequence of working alongside someone who has already discovered a better way of doing things. Vygotsky pointed out that for much of the time, as children and adolescents play or engage in their tasks, they frequently do so in the presence of someone who is older— and more skilled in the activity in which they are engaged. The discoveries of others, what Vygotsky refers to as cultural tools, get passed on

Research Focus

Projective Measures: If Shakespeare Had Been a Woman, Romeo and Juliet Might Have Survived Romance

With Michael Wapner

Picture a couple sitting quietly beside a river. The spires of a town rise in the distance. What thoughts run through their minds in this peaceful setting? Homicide? Betrayal? Death? Stabbing? Rape?

Impossible?

Yet when late adolescent males were asked to tell a story about a scene such as the one above, over one-fifth spoke of violent acts such as these; very few females did. What are we to make of this violent imagery—or its absence?

Explanations of gender differences in aggression have typically assumed that females repress "normal" levels of aggression, that is, the levels seen in males. Susan Pollack and Carol Gilligan (1982) suggest another explanation for this gender difference. They suggest that differences in aggression reflect the way individuals of either sex perceive social realities. Males and females alike will respond with violence when they perceive

danger, but each perceives danger in different settings.

Males are socialized to be independent and self-sufficient. Settings that limit their independence, by involving them in emotional connections with others, can challenge their sense of self. Will males see danger in situations that involve affiliation? Females are socialized to be interdependent and form connections with others. Will females perceive danger in situations in which they are isolated from others? Would settings of competitive achievement arouse fears of isolation by setting individual females apart from the group?

Deep-seated feelings such as reactions to danger are often difficult to observe and measure. Pollack and Gilligan used a *projective measure*—the Thematic Apperception Test (TAT)—to get at these feelings. This measure consists of a series of ambiguous pictures; subjects are asked to tell a story about each. It is assumed that they will project themselves into the situation they are describing and actually tell about their own thoughts and feelings.

Projective measures such as the TAT give a rich, complex record of an individual's feelings. Often the individual is unable to verbalize these feelings and may even be unaware of them.

to them in this social context, without breaking the flow of the activity or being labeled "learning." Through this process, individuals internalize the cultural wisdom of their society.

Take, as an example, a weekend project of painting a room. Everyone pitches in, the room finally gets painted, and the furniture is moved back into place. Mom, a veteran of many painted rooms, heads over to the window with a razor blade in her hand, handing one to her son on the way. He watches her slide the blade under the dried paint on the pane, and does the same, until they have cleaned paint off all the panes. The use of a tool—not the razor blade, but the wisdom that it is easier to scrape paint *off* than it is to put masking tape *on*—has been acquired in a social context, without the need for direct instruction.

Both Piaget and Vygotsky analyze, or view, the course of cognitive development in terms of progressive adaptations to one's environment. But they differ in what they take as the proper unit of analysis (Rogoff, 1990). Piaget takes as this unit the solitary individual, gaining a sense of his or her world through inspecting the objects that make it up. By observing what a

Research Focus (*continued*)

Because individuals respond to their interpretations of events rather than to the events themselves, projective measures have an additional advantage in that they let us see these interpretations.

TAT measures have a number of disadvantages as well. Extensive training is required before one can interpret the responses. Reliability and validity for these measures are frequently low; that is, the measure does not necessarily give the same "reading" each time it is used, and may not always tap what it was designed to measure. These problems are common with subjective measures such as the TAT, in which there is always a danger that the investigator may be reading his or her own feelings into the subject's answers.

Pollack and Gilligan used two TAT cards that portrayed affiliation and two portraying achievement. Individuals wrote stories to all four cards. When the investigators analyzed the stories, they found that males wrote many more violent stories to the affiliation cards than to the achievement ones—more than three times as many. The opposite pattern emerged for females; nearly three times as many females wrote violent stories to the achievement cards as to the affiliation ones.

These findings support the hypothesis that males and females perceive danger in different settings. More specifically, the very relationships females seek in order to protect themselves from isolation—a setting they regard as dangerous—are the ones that males perceive as dangerous, because they involve connection with others.

William Shakespeare foresaw only doom and death in the adolescent love affair between Romeo and Juliet. Had Juliet taken the pen from his hand, we might have had a happier ending.

Are adolescents still writing scripts that reflect these gender-specific fears? Or have changing sex roles spelled the end to this particular gender difference? Do the purveyors of popular culture know how males' fears differ from females'? Do they use them? Movie and television producers may not have read Pollack and Gilligan, but when was the last time you saw a movie where the heroine chose career over love or the hero walked away from worldly success to start a family? If you do recall such a film or TV show, was it a commercial success? Would you pay to see such a movie?

Source: S. Pollack & C. Gilligan. (1982). Images of violence in Thematic Apperception Test stories. *Journal of Personality and Social Psychology, 42,* 159–167.

person does and says, Piaget "enters" the mind of the individual and examines the processes by which that person grasps hold of his or her reality. Thinking, for Piaget, is a mental activity taking place in the mind of a person as that person adapts to his or her environment. As such, thinking is a *property* of the individual (Rogoff, 1990).

Vygotsky takes as his unit of analysis not the solitary individual, but a social person playing or working alongside others, engaging in activities that are characteristic of the group, whether these are learning the best way to remove paint from window panes or how to program the VCR. By observing people as they acquire the skills of those with whom they live—that is, of their culture—Vygotsky identifies thought in terms of the "tools" that enable the members of the culture to "grasp" things more easily. Thinking, for Vygotsky, develops as a person internalizes these tools through interacting with people who already use them. As such, thinking is a *process,* one that is fundamentally social in nature, that occurs as a result of living within a social group. The "mind" that Piaget observed within the individual (that is, the individual's grasp on reality) exists, for Vygotsky, in the society in which that person lives, in the form of the cultural wisdoms that the child internalizes through its interactions with those who are already skilled in their use. Thinking takes the form of the person's internalization of these cultural "tools." It is no accident that Vygotsky (1978) entitled the book in which he set forth this theory "Mind *in* Society" (italics added).

Vygotsky believed that the mind of the apprentice learner grasps these cultural wisdoms, just as the hands would grasp tools. He believed, as did Piaget, that this acquired knowledge changes the way the mind apprehends reality, but unlike Piaget, Vygotsky did not regard cultural tools as being forged anew by the individual, through her or his own interaction with the physical world. Instead, he saw these tools as handed down from those who are more skilled to those who are less skilled in their use.

For something to be passed on in this manner, the person must be close enough to reach out for it. Vygotsky termed this closeness the **zone of proximal development.** This zone is the distance separating the person's current performance from what that optimally might be. *Proximal* means "near" or "close to." Thus, in order for people to profit from working alongside those who are more skilled, their own performance must come close to, or approximate, the behavior of others. The zone represents the range of skills that individuals must possess in order to profit from exposure to those who are more skilled. We see this zone illustrated in the example of removing paint from the windows. This boy was able to internalize the cultural wisdom that it's easier to scrape the paint off than to put something else on only because his own behavior was sufficiently close to the behavior he eventually acquired; that is, he was already skilled in using tools such as the one his mother handed him.

Barbara Rogoff   Regarding the expertise of a culture as tools to be used by its members has implications for the way one thinks of intellectual development. Barbara Rogoff, a psychologist at Stanford, speaks of this development as an "apprenticeship" in thinking.

The term *apprenticeship* suggests that development is fundamentally a social process and that thinking, rather than being a private event occurring within a person's head, is an activity that is shared with others. Thinking, in other words, is not so much a process by which we "produce thoughts" as one that guides "practical action" (Rogoff, 1990). This action can be as playful as it is practical when it involves children and caregivers. Rogoff describes a scene in which 9-month-old twins, who were eating dry Cheerios in their high chairs, were surprised when their mother walked by and popped some of their cereal in her mouth. How silly for mom to be eating their food! Each time the mother snatched some cereal, the twins would laugh. The mother then put a Cheerio in Valerie's, one of the twin's, fingers and, opening her mouth, bent down "close to Valerie. Valerie began putting the Cheerio in her own mouth reflexively but stopped abruptly when her mother opened her mouth. Valerie looked at her mother's open mouth and began laughing hilariously with her hand poised in midair" (Rogoff, 1990, p. 17). This child's thought (I could pop this in *mom's* mouth!) arises out of the shared activity of their game.

For Rogoff, as for Vygotsky, the unit of analysis is the activity in which

These adolescents at basketball camp hope to improve their performance on the basketball court by following the behavior of the professionals.

the individual is engaged. For Vygotsky, however, this activity is initially only a social activity, taking place outside the person, and must be internalized in order to regulate behavior as thought. Rogoff does not make such a distinction. Rogoff's focus on the *shared* activity as the crucible of development avoids the age-old developmental question of what is on the outside and what on the inside of the child. Rogoff does not regard the child, the mother, or the social context (the game) as separable elements, but sees each as a part of the other. Instead of thinking of context as an influence *on* behavior, Rogoff sees behavior as embedded *in* context, taking its particular shape and direction from context. The activity (popping Cheerios into mouths) is the unit of analysis—not the child, not the Cheerio, and not the child *and* the Cheerio. By focusing on the activity, and not the Cheerio (or mom's mouth), for instance, we can predict that once the child knows that the Cheerio can be popped into mom's mouth, the child also knows that she can pop it into her brother's mouth—and she knows that other digestibles (and indigestibles) can be similarly popped.

Rogoff does not need to explain how this knowledge is internalized, that is, to explain how it moves from a social realm outside the individual to a realm of thought that is inside. Such a distinction would suggest a barrier of some kind across which the activity must pass, changing form in the process. Instead, Rogoff sees individuals as appropriating features of an activity in which they are already engaged with another. What they have practiced with the other is not on the outside, nor does it need to be brought inside, or internalized. Says Rogoff, "The 'boundaries' between people who are in communication are already permeated; it is impossible to say . . . 'whose' a collaborative idea is" (1990, p. 195). Valerie was already putting her Cheerios into her own mouth—as was her mother. Popping a Cheerio into her mother's mouth was appropriated from, or fit into, this activity. Both activities, in other words, were on the same side of the "barrier."

Valerie's discovery illustrates Rogoff's concept of **guided participation.** This concept extends Vygotsky's concept of the zone of proximal development. Guided participation captures the notion that the child or adolescent shares with an adult an activity in which both participate to decrease the distance between their respective contributions to the activity. Rogoff focuses more than Vygotsky on the ways in which children and adolescents actively participate in their development. She says, "Children see, structure, and even demand the assistance of those around them in learning how to solve problems of all kinds" (1990, p. 16). She also places greater emphasis than Vygotsky on the importance of tacit or unspoken forms of communication, as in the example of Valerie and the Cheerio.

Rogoff points out that an individual's strategies for learning its culture are the same one would recommend to any visitor to a foreign culture: Stay close to your guide, watch what the guide does, get involved whenever you can, and pay attention to what the guide may tell or show you. The "guide" complements the individual's activity by adjusting the difficulty of the activity to match the person's abilities, modeling the behavior that is sought while the person is watching, and accommodating his or her own behavior to what the person can grasp.

Rogoff views development as multidirectional. Unlike Piaget, for instance, she does not see development as moving toward a single endpoint, toward a universal set of achievements, such as Piaget's formal thought. Instead, the course of development can take any of a number of forms, depending on the types of skills that are valued in one's culture. These skills, whether they be literacy or goat herding, establish the developmental goals that are local to each culture. Thus, Piaget's developmental endpoint of logical, abstract thought reflects our society's value of scientific reasoning. Formal thought, in other words, represents the "local" goals of Western societies.

The Significance of Context: Protective Versus Risk Factors

Richard Lerner (1996), a psychologist at Boston University, points out that development, to be understood, must be studied in the many contexts of daily life, contexts that not only influence individual development, but are themselves changed by that individual's presence. Lerner asserts, in other words, that developmental influences are bidirectional, or reciprocal. Individuals are both influenced by their families, friends, and teachers, and also exert an influence on these very same contexts. Additionally, Lerner, just as Bronfenbrenner, analyzes the many features of one's environment in terms of overlapping spheres of influence, simultaneously operating at the biological and physical, psychological, and sociocultural levels. Lerner suggests that in order to know what research questions to ask, or even to fully understand the implications of our findings, we must study children and adolescents in real life settings, in their families, neighborhoods, and classrooms. This approach, known as **developmental contextualism,** makes it possible to integrate developmental research with policies and programs designed to meet the practical needs of youth and their families.

Lerner raises a warning call to our society, pointing out that increasing numbers of children and adolescents, currently over 20%, are growing up in poverty. Although poverty in itself does not necessarily place adolescents at risk for developmental problems, it is associated with other **risk factors** that do: substandard housing, deteriorating neighborhoods, inadequately funded schools, neighborhood gangs, unemployment, and crime, to mention a few. The list goes on, of course (Emshoff, Avery, Raduka, Anderson, & Calvert, 1996).

Most research on adolescence focuses on risk factors such as these and on the problems that attend them (Blyth & Leffert, 1995; Moore & Glei, 1995; Zeldin & Price, 1995). Relatively little research has studied **protective factors,** the conditions that protect adolescents from potential missteps. These can include factors at the level of the individual, family, and the community (Emshoff et al., 1996).

Emily Werner and her colleagues (1989) conducted a 30-year longitudinal study of all infants born in a single year on the island of Kauai, some 698 infants in all. The majority of these children grew up in stable homes with supportive relationships; 10%, however, were identified as "high risk" children because of the presence of multiple risk factors, such as congenital problems, poverty, uneducated parents, family strife, alcoholism, or mental illness. Despite the many strikes against them, fully a third of these high-risk children grew up to become competent adults who "loved well, worked well and played well."

One of the protective factors consistently noted in the lives of these individuals, illustrating the influence of context at the psychological level, was the establishment of a close emotional bond with at least one other person who took care of them, someone who, in Urie Bronfenbrenner's words, regarded them as "somehow special, especially wonderful, and especially precious" (1990, p. 31).

Resilient individuals also received considerable emotional support from outside their families. This support could come from teachers, classmates, a church group, or might take the form of extracurricular activities such as working on the school newspaper or playing in the school band (Werner, 1989).

Constitutional factors such as temperament, which illustrate the influence of context at the biological level, also serve as protective factors. Individuals who are easygoing, affectionate, active, and even-tempered are likely to prompt positive responses from others. These individuals, in a sense, establish their own supportive contexts, making friends at school and in the neighborhood, frequently making school a home away from home, a retreat from an otherwise chaotic life.

Supportive contexts, whether given or created, give the sense that life is manageable and meaningful. The ability to effectively cope, with the help of one's friends, provides a sense of mastery as well as feelings of hopefulness. As adults, Werner found these resilient individuals' lives to be characterized by determination, competence, a supportive relationship with at least one other person, and a strong religious faith (Werner, 1989).

SUMMARY

Models and Theories

Models are sets of assumptions about the nature of reality. These assumptions are too general to be tested; however, theories, which derive from models, are more specific explanations of phenomena and can be confirmed or disconfirmed. Theories serve four major functions: (1) They serve as a guide to formulating questions; (2) they describe phenomena by allowing isolated facts to be related to a body of knowledge; (3) they make it possible to predict new behavior based on explanations of previous actions; and (4) they suggest ways for changing the behavior they describe by allowing antecedent events to be identified.

Two models of human behavior are the environmental and the organismic models. The environmental model views humans as passive and sees their actions as *re*actions to environmental events. It uses the metaphor of the machine to describe behavior. People are assumed to remain quiescent until something stimulates them to act. Behavior is linked to external events through simple associations; these are formed through respondent and operant conditioning.

The organismic model takes the living, biological system as its metaphor for human behavior. Theories derived from this model assume that variables tied to the nature of the organism structure development. Organismic, or constructivist, theorists assume that the human organism is active and does not passively await stimulation, and that activity is internally organized instead of structured by environmental events. Behavior is seen as an unfolding of developmental stages, each of which is qualitatively different from the last.

Environmental Theories

Robert Havighurst traces development across a succession of developmental tasks that reflect social expectations for more mature behavior with age; physical maturation sets the pace for these expectations.

The theory of B. F. Skinner is a radical departure from the way most people understand their behavior. Skinner assumes that behavior is under the control of the events that follow it instead of reflecting preceding motives or intentions. Skinner refers to these antecedent events as reinforcers.

Albert Bandura also emphasizes the importance of learning in development but believes that most human learning occurs through observing others rather than through direct conditioning. Inner processes such as attention and memory are important in Bandura's social-cognitive theory.

Organismic and Constructivist Theories

Jean Piaget viewed intelligence as a means of adapting to one's environment, with only those forms of thought that promote adaptation surviving over the years. Piaget viewed intelligence as biologically based. He assumed that knowledge, rather than being a simple copy of reality, is an active construction of what we know of the world. He also assumed that our experiences are organized in qualitatively different stages with age.

Robert Kegan has built on the constructive process described by Piaget. Kegan argues that the most central human activity is meaning making, or constructing a reality that corresponds to our sense of self in relation to events and other people. Development, for Kegan, is a cumulative process of differentiating the "me" from the "not me." As our sense of "me" changes, so do our ways of relating to others and responding to events—and those changes lead to further changes in our sense of self.

Freud assumed that all thoughts and actions are motivated by the life force termed the libido. Different aspects of the personality control the expression of the libido. The id, present from birth, has limited means for gratifying libidinal impulses. The ego, next to develop, seeks to gratify as many libidinal impulses as possible within social constraints. The last aspect of the personality to develop, the superego, contains the moral values of one's culture and dictates what one should and should not do.

Karen Horney considered the development of a healthy personality in terms of the ability to value oneself and see that one is valued by others. Horney placed less emphasis than Freud on biological instincts and more stress on the impact of one's culture. Though she, like Freud, considered early experiences important, she did not view them as having the determining effect on later personality that Freud did. In particular, Horney reinterpreted Freud's analysis of the feminine personality as a reflection of living in a male-dominated society and of women's economic dependence on men.

Erik Erikson assumed, as did Freud, that personality develops through a sequence of stages, but he carried these through the lifespan. He assumed that society challenges us with new demands as we age and that we experience these as crises. Each crisis takes a slightly different form and gives each stage its unique characteristics. Achievement of a personal identity is the central crisis of adolescence; this involves adolescents in a set of commitments to life goals that give definition to the self.

Nancy Chodorow builds on a foundation provided by Freud but attributes gender differences to the social fact that for almost all children the first intimate relationship is with a female—the mother. Girls can continue to define themselves within the context of this first relationship, but boys must separate themselves in order to develop as males. As a consequence, girls' development is characterized by attachment, and boys' by separation and individuation.

Carol Gilligan also notes striking gender differences in the ways individuals of either sex define themselves. Males tend to view themselves as separate from others; females typically describe themselves in terms of their relationships with others.

Contextual Theories

Like Piaget, Lev Vygotsky believed that events do not have meaning until people actively interpret and internalize them. He differs from Piaget, however, in his notion that thinking and learning are fundamentally social in nature, rather than the result of individual experience. For Vygotsky, cognitive development is the internalization of the tools of cultural wisdom.

Barbara Rogoff extends Vygotsky's concept of the zone of proximal development with her concept of guided participation; the child doesn't simply copy the adult's behavior but actively participates in the activity. Rogoff, unlike Piaget, sees development as multidirectional, depending on the goals and values of the particular culture.

Richard Lerner adds that developmental influences, involving parents, friends, and teachers, are bidirectional; that is, they not only influence an individual's development but are also changed by that individual's presence. This approach, known as developmental contextualism, has given impetus to research to identify not only risk factors affecting adolescent development but also protective factors.

KEY TERMS

model	operant conditioning	id
theory	observational learning	ego
axiom	reflective abstraction	superego
law	assimilation	Oedipal complex
nature–nurture controversy	accommodation	identity
continuity–discontinuity issue	equilibration	epigenetic principle
reductionism	sensorimotor thought	zone of proximal development
epigenesis	preoperational thought	guided participation
habituation	concrete operational thought	developmental contextualism
stage	formal operational thought	risk factors
developmental task	repression	protective factors
operant	libido	

PART TWO

Continuity and Diversity in Early Adolescent Development

Part Two begins, as does adolescence itself, with puberty. The years of early adolescence from 10 through 14 differ in important ways from those of late adolescence, from 15 through 19. Whether we consider physical and intellectual changes, relationships with family or with friends, or the extended social world of adolescents, clear differences between early and late adolescence emerge.

Early adolescents are adjusting to changing bodies, new intellectual skills, a new school setting, and changing relationships with parents and friends. While they approach greater autonomy in their relationships with parents, they're also moving toward heterosexual relationships with friends. In contrast, by late adolescence, the wrinkles of puberty have ironed themselves out, the need for autonomy has been supplanted by the more pressing need to consolidate a personal identity, and decisions about college and jobs that seemed distant indeed to early adolescents press for resolution. Early adolescents are just stepping out of childhood; late adolescents stand on the threshold of adulthood.

The chapters in Part Two—Chapters 3 through 7—follow an "inside-out" approach in tracing the changes of adolescence. We begin by considering changes within the individual, both biological and intellectual, then discuss the interpersonal worlds of family and friends, and finally focus on the extended interpersonal context of the school.

Pubertal changes clearly set early adolescence apart as a distinct time of life. These changes start a year or two earlier in girls than in boys. These changes transform their bodies into those of adults. Puberty is just the beginning, but one that's hard

for adolescents to miss. Chapter 3 traces the sequence of these physical developments and considers their implications for young adolescents.

The intellectual changes that take place in early adolescence are, in their own way, as dramatic as the biological ones. Early adolescents begin to think in ways that are more like adults than like children just a few years younger. They can imagine the impossible, dream about the future, and entertain all manner of thoughts about the simplest of everyday situations. They are no longer limited to thinking about actual, concrete experiences. Adolescents can think in the abstract and possess a new self-awareness. Their ability to examine their thoughts and to imagine the thoughts of others contributes to this process. Chapter 4 looks at the intellectual changes of adolescence.

Changing relationships with parents also contribute to adolescents' new sense of themselves. An increase in autonomy and a greater role in decision making are common in early adolescence. Chapter 5 looks at the characteristics of families that facilitate the development of autonomy and lay a foundation for the development of identity. Families are changing in our society. Increasing numbers of adolescents experience divorce, single parenting,

and stepparenting, and more live in homes in which both parents are wage earners. This chapter examines the effect of these trends on adolescents.

For adolescents, friendships and school are the primary social settings outside the family. Friends contribute to early adolescents' developing sense of self. Close friends are the emotional supports to whom adolescents turn; in larger numbers, peers are socialization agents, guiding adolescents into more adult roles. Early adolescent friendships differ in distinct ways from those of late adolescence; these differences reflect the tasks adolescents face at each age. Chapter 6 looks at adolescents and their friends.

The everyday world of early adolescents expands at school, as they leave the comfortable familiarity of elementary school and enter a middle school or junior high. They have different teachers throughout the day, and cannot always count on having a close friend in class with them. Having options in the classes they can take emphasizes the larger issues of defining their own goals and arriving at workable plans for their lives. Chapter 7 covers these issues, closing the section on biological, intellectual, and social changes of adolescence.

CHAPTER 3

The Biological Context of Development
Puberty

She checked herself in the mirror again. Maybe she'd wear the new shirt. Or maybe she'd put the bag it came in over her head, and go to school that way. Glasses . . . braces . . . and two more pimples! Wonder what Helen of Troy had looked like at 13? She had probably been cute—and short. This face wouldn't get a rowboat off the beach. And she was taller than everyone in her class—including the teacher. Being different was lonely at times. Sometimes she felt left out altogether.

Feeling left out and being rushed into changes too quickly are common for adolescents. Although both of these things happen to all teenagers, the process of change is faster for some than for others. In the space of a few years, adolescents exchange the bodies of children for those of adults—complete with a full set of emotions and fancy accessories. But none of the equipment is road-tested as yet. And for most adolescents, it seems someone else must have the owner's manual.

This chapter maps the journey into maturity. The first stop takes us deep within the body, to the headquarters of an elaborate communications network, the endocrine system. This network of glands and hormones plays a significant role in regulating the changes of puberty. A finely tuned feedback system triggers the onset of puberty and then shuts it down, much as a thermostat signals a furnace to click on and off once the temperature reaches a preset level. This biological thermostat regulates delicate changes within the body that transform immature sexual organs into those capable of sexual reproduction. The endocrine system is also responsible for everything from a remarkable growth in height to the nose becoming disproportionately large for one's face. (Although it stays this way only briefly, it can leave a lasting dread of what surprises the body might bring next.)

The second stop checks out the remarkable changes that take place in height, weight, and body contours. Puberty involves a surge of growth that brings adolescents eye to eye and nose to nose with their parents. Adolescents add inches in a single year at the peak of their growth. Sex differences become noticeable with changing body proportions and gains in weight; girls add more subcutaneous fat than boys do, and boys add more muscle mass than girls. Not all adolescents grow the same amount, or at the same rate. Nor do they start at the same age; some will begin years ahead of others. And to the confusion of all, different parts of the body mature at different rates. Yet trends exist, and we will review them.

Many factors affect the rate at which growth proceeds. Conditions as diverse as diet, amount of exercise, psychological stress, and even altitude can affect the rate of growth during puberty. And of course one's particular genetic inheritance plays a part as well. The growth spurt ends in sexual dimorphism, the characteristic physical differences between sexually mature females and males. We will explore these differences before moving to a discussion of the secular trend, a trend toward earlier and faster development that has occurred over the past several centuries.

Changes as significant as those of puberty can have far-reaching psychological and social effects, and these effects are discussed in the third part of the chapter. The changes themselves may not be as important as when they take place for a particular individual. Staying the same when all one's friends are changing can be every bit as stressful as going through the changes. The timing of puberty is important, along with its end results. Early and late maturers face different challenges.

Sexual decision making brings adolescents several steps closer to adulthood. These steps can be problematic for a number of reasons. Adolescents must integrate their sexuality into a sense of self. Most receive little guidance in this task, and many lack the information needed to make responsible decisions. Even when they are informed, many adolescents find it difficult to make decisions responsibly due to their own emotional and intellectual immaturity.

Some adolescents will limit their experiences to necking, others will go further. Each decision involves others. We examine adolescents' sexual attitudes about masturbation, petting, oral-genital sex, and sexual intercourse.

Sex means different things to different people. To a lover, it is the stuff of dreams. To a biologist, it is a means of reproduction. Adolescents are better lovers than biologists, and only a few consistently take care not to reproduce. The chapter ends with a consideration of contraception use, and programs aimed at helping adolescents make sexual decisions.

THE ENDOCRINE SYSTEM

The **endocrine system** consists of glands within the body that produce hormones and structures in the central nervous system that regulate their activity. It is part of a larger feedback system that controls the timing of puberty. The production of **hormones,** chemical messengers that travel through the bloodstream, increases during late childhood. A dramatic rise in sex hormones (androgens in males and estrogens in females) and in the hormones that govern their release occurs in early adolescence. The action

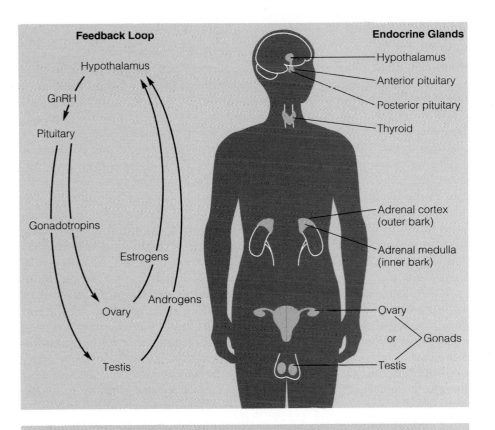

FIGURE 3.1
The Major Endocrine
Glands Involved
in Puberty

TABLE 3.1   Endocrine Glands and Hormones Regulating Pubertal Change

Glands	Hormones	Target or Function
Pituitary	Gonadotrophic hormones: Luteinizing hormone (LH) Follicle-stimulating hormone (FSH)	Stimulates gonads to produce sex hormones; menstrual cycle (females)
	Adrenocorticotrophic hormone (ACTH)	Stimulates adrenals to release androgens
	Growth hormone	Growth
	Thyroid-stimulating hormone (TSH)	Stimulates thyroid to release thyroxine
Adrenals	Androgens	Body hair
Thyroid	Thyroxine	Growth spurt
Gonads:		
Ovaries	Estrogens	Development of reproductive system and secondary sex characteristics
Testes	Androgens	

of these hormones is part of a complex chain of events that triggers the onset of puberty (Kulin, 1991a). Table 3.1 lists the major glands of the endocrine system affecting puberty, and the hormones each one secretes. figure 3.1 shows where the glands are located in the body.

Hormonal Activity

Because of the complexity of the hormones themselves and the changes that accompany their production, hormonal action is difficult to study. As hormone production increases, for instance, the sensitivity of the tissues they stimulate also changes. These changes differ for different types of tissues. Tissues that form the male reproductive organs are most sensitive to **androgens,** the male hormones, and tissues forming female organs are most sensitive to **estrogens,** the female hormones. The chemical composition of the sex hormones, however, is similar, allowing the body to convert one hormone into another as needed. Thus progesterone, which plays an important part in the female menstrual cycle, forms the basis for androgen, which in turn can be converted into estrogen (Daniel, 1983; Higham, 1980). Individual differences from one adolescent to the next also complicate the study of hormonal action. Adding to the complexity, the production of hormones changes with the time of day and day of the month, as well as with stress, diet, weight, altitude, exercise, and medications (Frisch, 1983; Warren, 1983).

The effectiveness of hormones depends on many things. In addition to the sensitivity of different tissues to their action, also important are the levels at which hormones circulate through the blood, and whether they exist in bound or unbound form. Hormones are molecules that act by attaching themselves to receptor sites on target tissues. Bound hormones have other molecules attached to them and are not free to act on their targets. Frequently the presence of one hormone will bind another, inhibiting its action. Some research suggests that the onset of puberty may be related to the emergence of a binding agent at the time of puberty (Horst, Bartesh, & Dirksen-Thedens, 1977; Petersen & Taylor, 1980).

The Timing of Puberty

The timing of puberty is intimately connected to centers within the brain tucked beneath the cortex (the "gray matter"), a few inches behind the bridge of the nose. The most important center in puberty is the hypothalamus. The **hypothalamus** has sometimes been called the body's master clock, because it serves as a control center for biological rhythms, including the ones of puberty. The **pituitary,** an endocrine gland, hangs from the hypothalamus by a slender stalk (the infundibulum). The pituitary has two lobes, or sections. The one closer to the nose is the anterior (front) lobe. The one farther is the posterior (back) lobe.

The hypothalamus is actually very small, just one three-hundredths of the brain's total size. Yet it is involved in many aspects of bodily functioning and plays a central role in regulating the events of puberty. Most of what we know about the hypothalamus comes from experiments with laboratory rats. For example, if the blood supply from the hypothalamus to the pituitary is cut off, a rat's reproductive organs soon begin to wither and the animal becomes sterile (Restak, 1984). But what is this important substance carried in the blood?

Research has shown that the hypothalamus secretes a hormone called gonadotropin-releasing hormone (GnRH), which tells the anterior pituitary to manufacture gonadotrophic hormones, which act directly on the gonads.

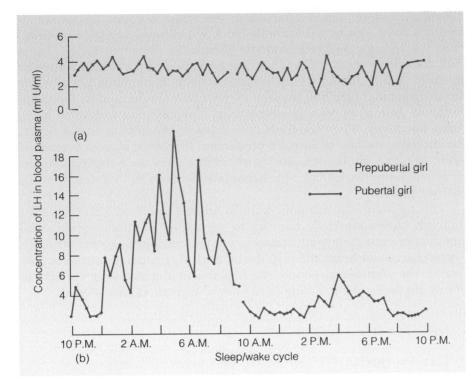

(a)

(b)

Prepubertal girl

Pubertal girl

Concentration of LH in blood plasma (ml U/ml)

Sleep/wake cycle

10 P.M.   2 A.M.   6 A.M.   10 A.M.   2 P.M.   6 P.M.   10 P.M.

FIGURE 3.2
Release of LH During
Waking and Sleep
Cycles in (a) a Pre-
pubertal Girl and
(b) a Pubertal Girl

Source: Adapted from M. P.
Warren. (1983). Physical and
biological aspects of pu-
berty. In J. Brooks-Gunn &
A. C. Petersen (Eds.), *Girls
at puberty: Biological and psychosocial perspectives.* New
York: Plenum Press.

The **gonads** are the sex glands—the ovaries in females and the testes in
males. Two gonadotrophic hormones—luteinizing hormone (LH) and follicle-
stimulating hormone (FSH)—stimulate the gonads to produce their own
sex hormones, estrogens in females and androgens in males. The whole system acts sort of like a row of dominoes. Knocking the first one over trips
the second, which affects the third, and so on. In the laboratory rats, when
the blood supply from the hypothalamus failed to reach the anterior pituitary, the anterior pituitary stopped producing the hormones that stimulate the gonads. When the gonads were no longer stimulated, they shut
down and withered, reverting to an earlier state (Restak, 1984).

The hypothalamus functions like a clock by measuring out its signals
in rhythmic pulses. A single pulse of GnRH normally reaches the anterior
pituitary each hour. The timing of these pulses is critical. If the pulses decrease to one every several hours or even increase, the mechanism breaks
down and the anterior pituitary fails to release its gonadotropins into the
bloodstream; the gonads will not develop (Knobil, 1980; Kulin, 1991a).

Both LH and FSH circulate through the bloodstream in low levels during childhood. Levels of each increase prior to puberty, starting at about
age 8 or 9 in girls. By the beginning of puberty, pulses occur more frequently
during sleeping than waking hours, especially for LH. Figure 3.2 illustrates
the marked difference in prepubertal and pubertal LH release, with the
sleep-associated release occurring only during puberty. By the end of puberty and throughout adulthood, LH is again released evenly over waking
and sleep cycles (Cotman & McGaugh, 1980; Cutler, Comite, Rivier, Vale,
Loriaux, & Crowley, 1983; Knobil, 1980).

A Feedback System   The level at which hormones circulate in the bloodstream is controlled by a delicate feedback system involving the hypothalamus, the anterior pituitary, and the gonads, as shown in Figure 3.1. A feedback system sends information from one point in a sequence back to an earlier point, thereby regulating later activity. A gonadostat, much like the thermostat controlling the heat in your home, is located in the hypothalamus. Instead of sensing temperature, it senses the presence of circulating hormones. When the levels drop too low, the hypothalamus signals the anterior pituitary to increase production of gonadotrophic hormones, which in turn stimulate the gonads to produce more sex hormones. As levels of sex hormones increase, the hypothalamus decreases its signals to the anterior pituitary.

During childhood, the gonadostat is set at a low level. This makes the feedback system especially sensitive to circulating hormones. Even small amounts prompt the hypothalamus to cut back its signals to the pituitary. This low set-point keeps the prepubertal level of circulating hormones low. Late in the prepubertal period, the hypothalamic gonadostat is reset, allowing the levels of circulating hormones to increase (Kulin, 1991a).

THE PHYSICAL CHANGES OF PUBERTY

Puberty brings about the physical differences that distinguish females and males. Differences in the reproductive system itself, such as growth of the ovaries in females and the testes in males, constitute **primary sex characteristics.** Other changes, such as the growth of pubic hair, the development of breasts in females and facial hair in males, represent **secondary sex characteristics.** Not all of these changes occur at once, of course, and not all are viewed as equally important by adolescents. The changes that occasion most fascination, such as menstruation in girls or facial hair in boys, are not usually the first to occur, although the timing of these changes varies considerably (Petersen, Crockett, Richards, & Boxer, 1988).

The sequence of changes varies less than their timing. One adolescent can be almost fully matured before another has begun to develop, yet each will experience the events of puberty in roughly the same order (Tanner, 1974).

The changes of puberty are easiest to follow if we chart them separately for each sex (Figure 3.3). Girls are generally two years ahead of boys. We will start with them first, as nature has done. A fictitious adolescent named Sarah will serve as our model.

Recollections of an Adolescent Girl

Sarah reports that the first change she noticed was in her breasts. She was in the fifth grade at the time, not quite 11 years old. It was such a small change that she almost didn't notice it at first. A slight mound had appeared just below each nipple. Sometime later the skin around the nipple darkened slightly. She couldn't see any difference when she was dressed, but by the

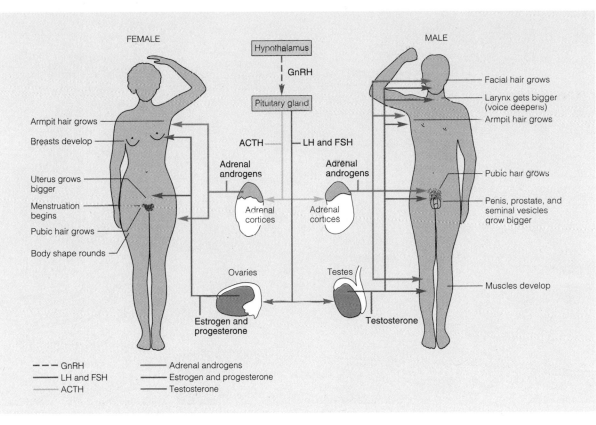

FIGURE 3.3   Effects of Hormones on Physical Development and Sexual Maturation at Puberty. *Source:* P. Insel & W. T. Roth. (1998). *Core concepts in health* (8th ed). Mountain View, CA: Mayfield.

time school let out for the summer, she felt a bit self-conscious in a bathing suit.

Sarah remembers the day she discovered a few wisps of pubic hair. It seemed as if they had appeared overnight. Actually, they had been growing for quite some time, but she hadn't noticed because they were unpigmented and very soft. Other changes were occurring within Sarah that she would never see. Her uterus and ovaries were enlarging and developing as the level of hormones circulating through her bloodstream increased.

She didn't notice anything else until the sixth grade. By then it became obvious how much faster she was growing, compared to before. By winter vacation, most of her fall back-to-school clothes were too short, and she was taller than most of the boys in her class. She spent a lot of time that vacation shopping for clothes. By the end of the sixth grade, she had grown several inches since the previous year.

Just before spring vacation, when she was in the seventh grade and 12 years old, Sarah had her first menstrual period. She had known for a while that it could happen at any time. A number of her classmates had begun menstruating this year, as had one or two the year before. She knew girls in the ninth grade who had not begun to menstruate. Her mother told her that a girl could start as early as 10 or as late as 16.

Although young adolescent boys may be self-conscious about their bodies if the signs of puberty are late in coming, young adolescent girls are more likely to feel self-conscious if they start to mature physically before most of their peers.

She stopped growing as quickly as she had started—a relief, because she'd started to identify with the giants in children's stories. She had also begun using an underarm deodorant and was shaving under her arms. Actually, she remembered thinking she looked pretty mature. Her figure had begun to fill out, and no one asked her age at PG-13 movies.

Recollections of an Adolescent Boy

Alfred will talk about his experiences of puberty. He, too, is a fictitious adolescent and just as typical for boys as Sarah is for girls. Alfred recalls being very impatient for something to happen. With mixed emotions, he first noticed a change in his scrotum. It was slightly larger and a bit darker than it had been. This was in the seventh grade, just after he had turned 12. Very shortly after, wisps of pubic hair appeared at the base of his penis. Despite these early signs of his manhood, his penis remained the same size. He remembers having some problems with acne once he started the seventh grade. Other changes had begun within his body, but Alfred remained unaware of them. His testes were growing and secreting more androgen than before, and his seminal vesicles and prostate were developing. Maturation of the testes would be necessary for the ejaculation of seminal fluid, the wet dreams he had heard so much about.

By the end of the seventh grade, he had started to grow. It had begun slowly at first, but during the eighth grade, he grew 3 inches in a single year.

His parents complained they couldn't keep him in clothes: As soon as they bought new ones, he outgrew them. During the eighth grade he noticed, too, that his penis had started to grow longer. What a relief. He remembers dreading gym class; he couldn't face the showers. A few of the guys in there looked as mature as his father. Of course, others still looked like kids.

Alfred recalls continuing to grow a lot in the ninth grade. By then he was 14 and his voice was starting to change. He experienced his first ejaculation at about this time, too. He had the sexiest dream with it. His pubic hair was now thick and curly, and he had started to get some axillary (underarm) hair. He was still growing but says he started to slow down a bit after the ninth grade. He still didn't have any hair on his face. He was 15 before he noticed a few hairs growing in over his upper lip. His mom called it peach fuzz. He didn't have a real beard until he was 16. By then he also

Hormones contribute to more than the physical changes of puberty. Exuberant, inexperienced, and self-centered thinking, especially in young adolescent boys, can lead to risk-taking behavior. These boys know their behavior is risky, but they do not seem to understand that they could be seriously hurt.

TABLE 3.2 Summary of the Changes of Puberty and Their Sequence

Characteristic	Age of First Appearance (Years)	Major Hormonal Influence
GIRLS		
1. Growth of breasts	8–13	Pituitary growth hormone, estrogen, progesterone, thyroxine
2. Growth of pubic hair	8–14	Adrenal adrogen
3. Body growth	9½–14½	Pituitary growth hormone, adrenal androgen, estrogen
4. Menarche	10–16½	Hypothalamic releasing factors, FSH, LH, estrogen, progesterone
5. Underarm hair	About 2 years after pubic hair	Adrenal androgens
6. Oil- and sweat-producing glands (acne occurs when glands are clogged)	About the same time as underarm hair	Adrenal androgens
BOYS		
1. Growth of testes, scrotal sac	10–13½	Pituitary growth hormone, testosterone
2. Growth of pubic hair	10–15	Testosterone
3. Body growth	10½–16	Pituitary growth hormone, testosterone
4. Growth of penis	11–14½	Testosterone
5. Change in voice (growth of larynx)	About the same time as penis growth	Testosterone
6. Facial and underarm hair	About 2 years after pubic hair appears	Testosterone
7. Oil- and sweat-producing glands, acne	About the same time as underarm hair	Testosterone

Source: B. Goldstein. (1976). *Introduction to human sexuality* (p. 80). Belmont, CA: Star.

had a fair amount of hair on his body. Alfred says he didn't actually stop growing until his early twenties. He also developed more hair on his chest, back, and stomach all through his late teens.

The typical sequence of these events appears in Table 3.2, along with their age ranges. Sarah and Alfred are typical adolescents. However, other adolescents can pass through these changes at different ages, or even in different sequences, and still be just as normal. You can see that for some

In addition to obvious
differences in muscle
mass, males develop
larger hearts and lungs
and higher systolic
blood pressure and
carry more oxygen in
their blood than fe-
males do. These differ-
ences may reflect the
increase in males' ac-
tivity levels and the
decrease in females'
during adolescence.

events, such as menstruation in girls or body growth in boys, some adolescents can be as much as six years ahead of others and each will be within
a range considered normal for development. With differences like these, the
exception is almost the norm.

The Growth Spurt

Females   Growth is regulated by the growth hormone (secreted by the anterior pituitary) and the sex hormones (secreted by the gonads). The growth
hormone affects the timing and amount of growth mostly by serving as a
"gate crasher" for amino acids, the body's building blocks, helping them
cross cell membranes and promoting cell multiplication. This results in a
dramatic spurt of growth. The growth hormone also affects changes in the
bones during puberty. In childhood, bones contain segments of cartilage,
which hardens at puberty (Cech & Martin, 1995). Girls experience a period
of rapid growth in height starting at about age 11. The **growth spurt** usually lasts a little over two and a half years. For some girls it can be as brief
as one and a half years, and for others it can last up to four years. Girls gain
about 8 to 10 inches in height from the start of the growth spurt until they
have finished growing. The most rapid growth occurs before **menarche,** the
beginning of the menstrual cycle (Malina, 1990).

Body proportions begin to change even earlier. About one and a half
years before the growth spurt, girls' legs start to grow faster than their bodies, giving them a long, leggy look. Most of the early gain in height is due
to a lengthening of the legs. The shoulders also widen before the actual
growth spurt. Somewhat later, during puberty itself, the hips widen. These

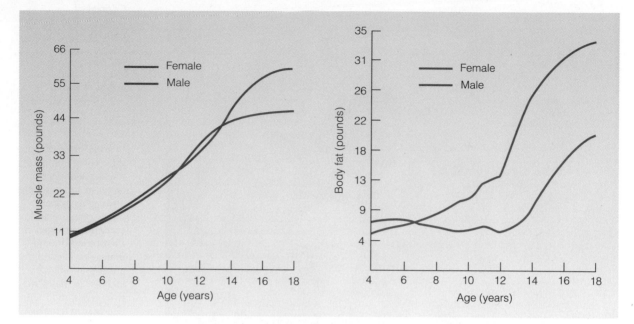

FIGURE 3.4 Development of Muscle Mass and Body Fat for Females and Males

Source: Adapted from D. B. Cheek. (1974). Body composition, hormones, nutrition, and adolescent growth. In M. M. Grumbach, G. D. Grave, & F. E. Mayer (Eds.), *Control of the onset of puberty.* New York: Wiley.

growth patterns give young adolescent girls a characteristic look: relatively long legs, slender bodies, wide shoulders, and narrow hips—our present standard of beauty. Puberty changes all this (Faust, 1983).

Males The growth spurt can begin anywhere from age 10½ to age 16 in boys. Boys grow for a longer time than girls, reaching their peak rate in growth two years later than girls reach theirs. The average height of boys prior to the height spurt is 58 inches. They add another 12 or 13 inches during the growth spurt. Most of this increase is due to a lengthening of the trunk, because the legs began to grow earlier.

Striking sex differences begin to appear in muscle mass and body fat. Figure 3.4 shows the dramatic increase in muscle mass that accompanies the height spurt in males, and the corresponding increase in body fat for females (Petersen, Crockett, Richards, & Boxer, 1988). In addition to obvious differences in muscle mass, males also develop larger hearts and lungs; they have higher systolic blood pressure, can carry more oxygen in their blood, and can dispose of the chemical by-products of exercise more efficiently than females. They also have more red blood cells. These differences, although genuine sex differences, can reflect differences as well in activity levels between females and males that become more pronounced during adolescence. The most obvious change, however, is in the shape of the body itself: In males, the shoulders widen relative to the hips (Petersen & Taylor, 1980).

The Reproductive System

Females   During puberty, the uterus, ovaries, and vagina all increase in size. The **uterus** is a muscular sac shaped like an upside-down pear, enclosed at the neck by the **cervix,** which opens into the vagina. Some girls think the uterus is an empty space within them. Figure 3.5 shows that the walls of the uterus lie against each other; they remain this way unless pushed apart by a fetus. During pregnancy, the uterus holds the fetus. The length of the uterus doubles during puberty, growing to about 3 inches at maturity (McCary & McCary, 1982).

The **ovaries** flank either side of the uterus. Each is about the size of a walnut. They have two major functions. The first is to house the immature eggs, or **ova** (singular **ovum**), which each infant girl stores from the time of birth. The second function is to produce estrogens and progesterone. The ovaries begin to grow at a slightly faster rate at about the age of 8. About a year before any of the visible signs of puberty, gonadotropins from the anterior pituitary stimulate the ovaries to accelerate their production of estrogens. These gonadotropins—FSH and LH—also stimulate the follicles, individual chambers housing each ovum, to develop.

The **fallopian tubes** feed into either side of the uterus from the ovaries. Each tube is approximately 4 inches long, and is lined with tiny hairs called cilia that move in a sweeping motion and set up currents within the fluid in the tubes. These currents catch the mature egg as it is released from the ovary and sweep it into the oviduct, where it is carried to the uterus. If live sperm are present to fertilize the egg, fertilization will take place at the top of the oviduct. If no sperm are present, the egg passes outside the body along with the lining of the uterus, which is prepared monthly for a fertilized egg.

FIGURE 3.5
Female Reproductive System. *Source:* P. M. Insel & W. T. Roth. (1998). *Core concepts in health* (8th ed.). Mountain View, CA: Mayfield.

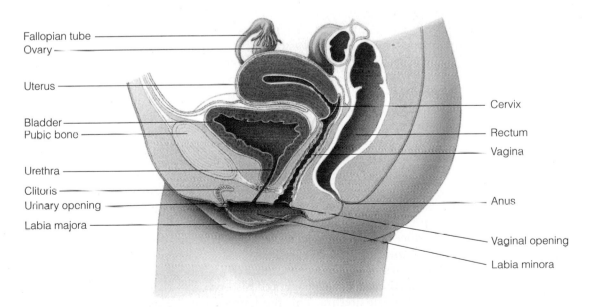

Fallopian tube
Ovary
Uterus
Bladder
Pubic bone
Urethra
Clitoris
Urinary opening
Labia majora

Cervix
Rectum
Vagina
Anus
Vaginal opening
Labia minora

The **vagina** is a muscular tube leading to the uterus. During puberty it lengthens to its adult length of 4 to 6 inches, and becomes more flexible, developing a thick lining. Two glands on either side of the vaginal opening, Bartholin's glands, also develop during puberty. These secrete a lubricant during sexual arousal. The walls of the vagina touch each other (just as do those of the uterus), unless they are separated by something such as a tampon, a penis, or a baby during birth.

Many girls mistakenly think of the vagina as a hollow tube leading to an even larger space inside. This misunderstanding can cause some teenage girls to be fearful of losing tampons in some vast, unknown space within. In actuality, the vagina is closed off at the inner end by a tight, muscular gate, the cervix. Menstrual fluids or semen can pass through, but the cervix must be dilated (opened) for anything larger to pass.

The opening to the vagina is partially covered by a fold of skin called the hymen, sometimes referred to as the "cherry." This delicate membrane is frequently torn or stretched during childhood. Activities ranging from bicycle riding to using tampons can stretch the hymen. Folklore holds that first intercourse ruptures the hymen, causing some bleeding and discomfort, and that an intact hymen is a sign of virginity. Relatively few females today survive their active childhoods with the hymen intact. Even when it remains, stretching the hymen through intercourse rarely produces discomfort.

The **clitoris,** not the vagina, is the primary source of sexual stimulation. The clitoris is similar to the penis; both have a glans, a shaft, and a prepuce. The **glans** is supplied by an extensive network of nerve endings, making it the most sensitive part of the clitoris. Hidden beneath the skin and connected to the glans is the **shaft.** Numerous blood vessels, which develop during puberty, feed into the shaft. During arousal, these become engorged with blood, causing the clitoris to become erect. A thin covering of skin, the **prepuce,** covers the glans.

Males   The epididymis, vas deferens, seminal vesicles, prostate gland, and Cowper's gland form the internal male sex organs (Figure 3.6). The **epididymis** is a long, oval mass sitting near the top of each testis that receives the sperm produced by the testis. The epididymis leads into the **vas deferens,** long, coiled tubes that carry the sperm to the **seminal vesicles** where they are stored. Tiny hairlike cilia line the walls of the epididymis and the vas deferens, just as they do the fallopian tubes in females, and move the immature sperm on their way to the seminal vesicles.

Both the seminal vesicles and the **prostate gland** produce **semen,** a milky white fluid in which the **sperm** are suspended. This fluid is ejaculated during an orgasm. The prostate gland begins to develop at around 11 years of age, at about the time the testes begin to develop. Sperm can be found in the urine of boys by about the age of 14 (Kulin, 1991b). A single ejaculate of approximately 3.5cc contains upward of 200,000,000 sperm. A mature male will produce several hundred million sperm each hour (Gilbert, 1994).

The **Cowper's glands** begin to mature at about the same time as the prostate. These glands secrete a lubricating fluid that facilitates passage of the sperm through the urethra and also protects them from the acidic environment of the urethra. This fluid appears at the opening of the glans of

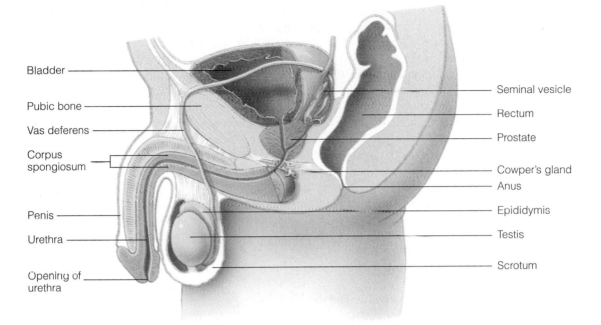

Bladder

Pubic bone

Vas deferens

Corpus
spongiosum

Penis

Urethra

Opening of
urethra

Seminal vesicle

Rectum

Prostate

Cowper's gland

Anus

Epididymis

Testis

Scrotum

FIGURE 3.6
Male Reproductive
System. *Source:* P. M. Insel
& W. T. Roth. (1998).
Core concepts in health (8th
ed.). Mountain View, CA:
Mayfield.

the penis during sexual arousal, and frequently contains some sperm. Intercourse, even with no ejaculation, can result in pregnancy just from the presence of sperm in the lubricating fluid (McCary & McCary, 1982).

At puberty, increases in FSH, LH, and prolactin (the same hormones that stimulate the ovaries to develop and produce estrogen) stimulate the testes to develop and produce testosterone. Levels of circulating testosterone increase twentyfold during puberty. The combination of testosterone and FSH stimulates the testes to produce sperm. Two types of cells line the tubes in which they develop: sperm-producing cells (germinal epithelial cells) and nurse cells (Sertoli cells). Division of the germinal cells produces sperm; one part remains behind for later cell divisions, allowing a male to produce sex cells throughout his life. Sertoli cells function as "nurses" for the immature sperm, which nestle among them to receive nourishment while they develop.

When the developing sperm at last split off from their nurses, they travel with many others through the dark fluid canals of the testes into the epididymis. Sperm may take three weeks to travel the length of the congested epididymis; during this time they continue to mature. The growing throng reaches the vas deferens, the tube leading to the seminal vesicles. Mature sperm are discharged in an ejaculate, or they gradually lose vitality and are reabsorbed by the body.

The **penis,** like the clitoris in females, is the primary source of sexual stimulation. It has three major parts: the glans, the shaft, and the prepuce. The glans, or rounded head of the penis, is the most sensitive, as it is richly supplied with nerve endings. The shaft of the penis is filled with spongy pads of erectile tissue surrounding the **urethra,** the canal for urine and semen. An extensive network of blood vessels feeds into these tissues. During sexual arousal, blood fills cavities within the tissues, causing the penis to become hard and erect. In a nonaroused state, the penis is soft and flaccid. Erections occur throughout infancy and childhood. They can be triggered by many forms of stimulation, such as washing, needing to urinate, tight clothing, or masturbation. The frequency of spontaneous erections without ejaculation increases once the penis starts to grow (Levitt, 1981).

The penis doubles in length and thickness during puberty, growing to about 3 to 4 inches. Adolescent boys frequently express concerns about the size of their penis. These concerns almost surely reflect the considerable variability in size that exists from one boy to the next, and the mistaken belief that the size of the penis is related to masculinity and sexual prowess.

The prepuce, sometimes called the foreskin, is a thin fold of skin that covers the glans of the penis. The prepuce is frequently removed surgically, usually right after birth, in a procedure known as **circumcision.** Circumcision is widely practiced for hygienic purposes as well as for religious reasons. A thick secretion known as **smegma** collects around the glans under the prepuce of males who are not circumcised. Germs breed here and can cause infections, unless the prepuce is pulled back when washing to expose the glans.[1]

The **scrotum** is the sac that hangs just beneath the penis and houses the **testes,** the two glands that produce sperm and testosterone. The testes start to grow at about age 11 and more than double in length during puberty. One of the first changes of puberty for boys is an increase in the size of the scrotum, as the testes within begin to grow. The testes themselves are about the same size, but the left testis frequently appears larger, perhaps because it hangs a bit lower than the right.

The scrotal sac protects the testes from harm. One might argue that they would be even safer if tucked securely inside the body, as indeed they would. However, the temperature within the body is a few degrees too high for the optimal production of sperm. The range of temperatures ideal for the breeding of sperm is relatively narrow. The scrotal sac accommodates to temperature fluctuations by contracting or relaxing, adjusting the distance of the testes from the warmth of the body cavity. Adolescent males may notice that the scrotum contracts in the cold, drawing the testes closer to the body. In hot weather, or after a hot shower, it hangs lower, keeping the testes farther from the body.

Menarche

Menarche is the term for a girl's first menstrual period. The average age for reaching menarche is presently about 12½ in the United States (Brooks-Gunn & Warren, 1985). The menstrual cycle is regulated by the feedback

---

[1]Although **female circumcision** bears the same name, the procedure is in no way comparable. In female circumcision, more accurately referred to as female genital mutilation, the clitoris of the young girl is cut out, usually without benefit of anesthesia or sterile conditions, and frequently the outer labia are sewn together, leaving only a small opening for the passage of urine. The procedure is comparable to cutting off the penis! It robs the female of the source of sexual pleasure and makes even simple acts, such as walking, sitting, or urinating, difficult. This procedure is practiced upon millions of girls in non-Western nations today, and has recently entered the United States with those immigrating from these nations.

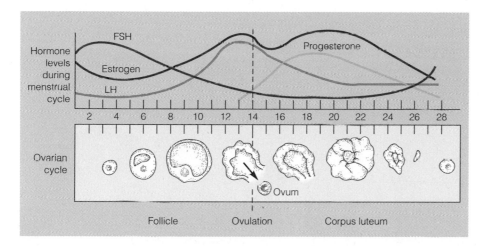

FIGURE 3.7   Hormonal Feedback Loop Controlling the Menstrual Cycle. *Source:* Adapted
from R. A. Levitt. (1981). *Physiological psychology.* New York: Holt, Rinehart & Winston.

loop between the ovaries, the anterior pituitary, and the hypothalamus. At
the beginning of the cycle (counting from the first day of the menstrual period), the level of estrogen circulating in the bloodstream is low; this
prompts the release of FSH by the anterior pituitary. Figure 3.7 shows how
the production of FSH drops off as the follicle is stimulated to produce
more estrogen. A second hormone, LH, is sent out by the anterior pituitary
beginning around the second week of the cycle and works with estrogen to
prepare the follicle to release its egg. Levels of LH and estrogen peak at
about the 14th day of the cycle, causing the follicle to burst and release its
egg (Hood, 1991).

The empty follicle begins to produce progesterone (shown on the bottom of the graph) and continues to produce estrogen. Progesterone inhibits
the release of any more LH. If the ovum is not fertilized in about a week,
the follicle decreases its production of hormones, and the levels of progesterone and estrogen drop. The uterus, sensitive to low levels of these hormones, contracts when the levels bottom out on about day 29. These
contractions shake loose the lining that has formed to receive the egg, if it
were fertilized. The shedding of this lining by the uterus is the menstrual
flow. The hypothalamus also reacts to the low level of estrogen by signaling
the anterior pituitary to send out FSH, thus initiating the next monthly cycle (Hood, 1991).

Menstrual cycles sometimes occur without the release of an egg; such
cycles are called *anovulatory*. They feel no different from those in which an
egg is released, and occur only because the hormonal feedback cycle is not
sufficiently developed to release an egg each time. Up to half of a girl's cycles can be anovulatory for the first several years, but only about one-fifth
are by the end of her teens.

It is impossible to say with any certainty when a girl will ovulate. Ovulation usually occurs 14 days before the next period starts. If a girl's menstrual periods occur regularly every 28 days, she would ovulate on the 14th
day of the cycle. Most adolescents do not have regular cycles, at least at first,
and some evidence even suggests that a girl may occasionally ovulate sev-

Although they may not share their feelings with friends, some girls may feel ambivalent about menarche, whereas others accept it as a natural part of maturing. The difference is due in large part to how parents prepare their daughters for the physical changes of puberty.

eral times during a cycle. Variability in the timing and frequency of ovulation has at least one practical implication: It is not possible for the adolescent to identify a time during her cycle when she *cannot* become pregnant (Apter & Volko, 1977; McCary & McCary, 1982).

Reaching a certain proportion of body fat appears to trigger menarche. The chronological age for menarche varies considerably from one girl to the next, but each achieves about the same percentage of body fat just prior to menarche (Frisch, 1991). Aside from the estrogen produced by the ovaries, estrogen is converted from androgens in fatty tissues (Frisch, 1991). Additional support for the importance of body fat to menarche comes from girls who are athletes or dancers. These girls have proportionately less fat for their total weight—and they also tend to have delayed menarche and irregular periods (Frisch, 1991).

Most girls have mixed feelings about menarche. They look forward to it so they can be like others, but they also report wanting to postpone the "hygienic hassles" it entails (Ruble & Brooks-Gunn, 1982). Girls are reluctant to discuss their menstrual experiences right away. After telling their mothers, most wait several months before talking with friends (Brooks-Gunn & Ruble, 1982).

Mothers are the most frequent source of information. Nearly all girls report receiving some information from their mothers. However, older sisters and friends are also important. Two-thirds of adolescent girls with older sisters get some information from them, and even more say they receive information from friends. Fathers play a small role. Only about 20% of girls receive information from their fathers. It may be that they are less willing to discuss menstruation than their fathers are. More than three-quarters say they would not report their menstrual status to their fathers, whereas a small sample of fathers who were interviewed said they would be comfortable talking with their daughters. It is interesting that girls who tell their fathers, or who know their mothers have told them, report fewer menstrual symptoms such as cramps or other discomfort. This inclusion of the father may reflect a more open, relaxed attitude about menstruation or perhaps a more open attitude at home in general (Brooks-Gunn & Ruble, 1983).

The source of a girl's information is related to her experience of menstruation. Different sources may give different types of information and communicate different attitudes about menstruation. Girls who are informed by their mothers generally have fewer symptoms. Mothers may be more positive, stressing menarche as a sign of growing up, and friends may be more likely to discuss the hassles of menstruation. No matter how well prepared a girl is, however, she is invariably surprised by menarche (Brooks-Gunn & Ruble, 1983). With respect to secondary sexual characteristics such as breast development and the appearance of pubic hair, girls are more likely to react positively—reporting feelings of pride and maturity—than negatively, although they experience some embarrassment at having their father know about such things as menarche or a first bra (Brooks-Gunn, Newman, Holderness, & Warren, 1994).

Spermarche

Spermarche, a boy's first ejaculation of seminal fluid, usually occurs early in his teens, by about 13 (Stein & Reiser, 1994). For some, it will occur spontaneously in a **nocturnal emission** (also known as a wet dream); for others, through masturbation or intercourse. Relatively few boys are likely to have anyone explain all this to them. Peers and books or magazines are the most likely sources of information, boys learning more about menarche than about ejaculation in their health classes. Despite the relative lack of preparation, most boys are not alarmed, although most do admit to being surprised. Generally, reactions are positive, boys reporting feeling excited, grown up, and glad (Gaddis & Brooks-Gunn, 1985; Stein & Reiser, 1994).

Boys are not likely to discuss their experience with friends or with their fathers. This reaction to ejaculation contrasts sharply with that of girls to menarche, most of whom tell their mothers immediately and share their new status with friends several months later (Ruble & Brooks-Gunn, 1982; Stein & Reiser, 1994). The difference may reflect the closer association of first ejaculation with masturbation for boys. Neither boys nor girls seem to discuss masturbation. For girls, the lack of any association of menarche with masturbation may account for their greater willingness to discuss it. Or it may be that they have had discussion modeled for them by their mothers, because most are prepared for menarche, whereas most boys have not been prepared for first ejaculation by their fathers (Gaddis & Brooks-Gunn, 1985).

Most adolescent boys receive considerably less information than girls about the reproductive nature of pubertal changes. Few fathers explain nocturnal emissions to their sons, and neither parent is likely to explain menstruation. A survey of college males found that many had gotten much of their information about menstruation as young adults from female friends,

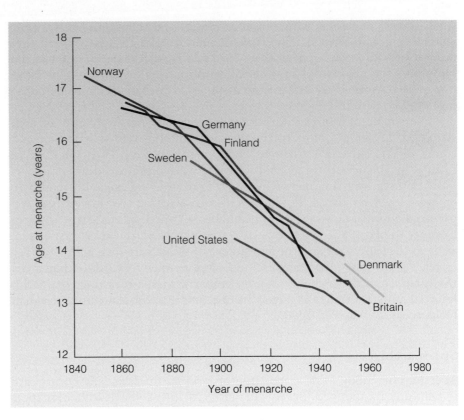

**FIGURE 3.8
Trends in the Age
of Menarche.** *Source:*
Adapted from J. M. Tanner.
(1968). Earlier maturation
in man. *Scientific American,
218*, 26.

once the security of early adulthood permitted such discussions (Brooks-Gunn & Ruble, 1986). Perhaps because of inconsistency in the way males get their information about menstruation, this information more frequently reflects negative cultural beliefs.

The Secular Trend

Quite a bit of evidence indicates that puberty begins earlier today than it did in the past. This downward shift in age is called the **secular trend.** The greatest changes occurred from the mid-1800s to the mid-1900s. The trend appears to have leveled off. The average age for menarche in the United States is about 12½. In Britain during the mid-1800s, menarche occurred between 15½ and 16½ years (Frisch, 1983). Figure 3.8 shows a striking drop in age at menarche over a period of 130 years for a number of countries. Age at menarche has dropped by about three to four months every ten years (Tanner, 1991).

Adolescents not only begin puberty earlier than in previous generations, they also grow faster. We have only scanty records from earlier centuries, but the pieces fit a predictable pattern. In the nineteenth century in Britain, females reached their adult height at about 21. Adolescent girls stop growing today by 16 to 18. British men in the nineteenth century continued growing well into their mid-twenties, reaching their adult height at 23 to 25. Adolescent boys today reach their adult height by 20 to 21 (Frisch, 1983).

Adolescents also grow to be larger than they once did, girls growing half an inch to an inch taller than their mothers and weighing about 2 pounds more. For boys these differences could be even greater. Generational differences are startling when we make comparisons across centuries. American sailors during the War of 1812 were probably just an inch or two over 5 feet tall, because the decks of the USS *Constitution* were only 5'6" high. Similar evidence from medieval armor, old clothing, and antique furniture all point to a dramatic increase in stature over the centuries. The seats of La Scala opera house in Milan, for example, built in 1776, were 18 inches wide. Most seats today are 24 inches wide (Muuss, 1975; Tanner, 1991).

A number of conditions probably contribute to the secular trend. Improved nutrition is almost surely an important cause of the accelerated growth patterns. Despite the prevalence of fast foods and junk foods, diet today is immeasurably better than in the past. Rose Frisch (1983, 1991) suggests that the earlier age for menarche today is due to the faster rate at which children grow; they simply get bigger sooner today. She argues that menarche occurs when girls reach a critical weight, and they reach this weight sooner today than in centuries past. She adds that the secular trend should level off as nutrition and child care reach optimal levels. This may be happening now (Wyshak & Frisch, 1982).

THE PSYCHOLOGICAL AND SOCIAL IMPLICATIONS OF PUBERTY

Even experiences as close to a biological ground zero as those of puberty do not necessarily have the same significance from one adolescent to the next. Adolescents continually interpret the biological frontiers they are crossing, reading the reactions of friends and family for the meaning of the changes they are going through. Nor are they alone in doing so. Their parents, siblings, friends, and teachers also read significance into the biological script unfolding before them. Not surprisingly, puberty affects adolescents' closest relationships in intimate ways.

Reed Larson and Maryse Richards (1994) were able to document the details of adolescents' lives by having them wear beepers and paging them at random intervals throughout the day and evening, when they would report on their activities and feelings. These investigators remind us of what we too easily forget about our own lives—that even the simplest activities that make up a day, things such as having breakfast or hassling over kitchen responsibilities, are often suffused with emotion. They also remind us that such activities, when they involve more than one member of the family, are rarely experienced in the same way by each of them, that there are as many realities to be experienced as individuals to experience them. This reminder should strike a familiar note at this point, illustrating one of the central assumptions of the constructive approach taken in this text. Namely, that we continually interpret our experiences, putting events together in ways that make sense to us, constructing the reality to which we eventually respond.

Heightened Emotionality

Larson and Richards point out that tensions are greatest in early adolescence, when puberty tips the psychosocial balance established throughout childhood. As adolescents' bodies assume more adult proportions, those around them, particularly parents and teachers, expect them to behave in more adult ways as well. Crowding in on the heels of puberty are additional stressors such as starting junior high, navigating problematic relationships with peers, redefining relationships with parents and, for many, facing increasing pressures to experiment with sex and drugs. Because of the secular trend, adolescents as young as 10 or 11 begin to face these pressures of puberty, often before either they or their parents are ready for them (Larson & Richards, 1994).

How do adolescents react to these changes? A common stereotype is that, with puberty, adolescents become moody, their emotions swinging from one extreme to another with little predictability. Larson and Richards indeed found some support for heightened emotionality in adolescence. Figure 3.9 shows that adolescents more frequently report experiencing extreme states than do their parents. They also report a wider range of emotions. In addition to simply feeling happy, for instance, adolescents report feeling great, free, cheerful, proud, accepted, in love, friendly, and kindly. They also report a wider gamut of negative feelings, describing themselves as unsure, lonely, awkward, ignored, and nervous, or as Larson and Richards put it, "a whole array of painful feelings that remind us adults why we never want to be adolescents again" (1994, p. 83). Even though they feel self-conscious and embarrassed two to three times as often as their parents, they are also bored more, perhaps because they feel less in control and less invested in the moment, often saying they would rather be doing something else. Furthermore, despite the advantage of youth, adolescents are more likely to say they feel tired, weak, and have little energy. These differing inner realities, as well as the more visible differences of their exterior lives, virtually ensure that misunderstandings with parents will arise.

Relationships With Parents

Good relationships with parents can provide a powerful buffer against the stresses of life. Adolescents who see their parents as warm and loving, for instance, experience fewer emotional or behavioral problems (Wagner, Cohen, & Brook, 1996). For most adolescents, however, closeness with parents temporarily decreases and conflict increases with the onset of puberty. Adolescents begin to demand a greater role in family decision making and more freedom in areas that their parents still believe require parental oversight, such as the adolescents' well-being (see Chapter 5). For their part, parents may see that the ways they have always parented are no longer appropriate, yet they have no ready substitutes for outmoded forms of discipline and guidance. The resulting scuffles, though often uncomfortable, lay the groundwork for renegotiated relationships. With few exceptions, however, studies of these changes have all involved White middle-class families.

Brooke Molina and Laurie Chassin (1996) compared parent–adolescent relationships in Hispanic and non-Hispanic families. These investigators

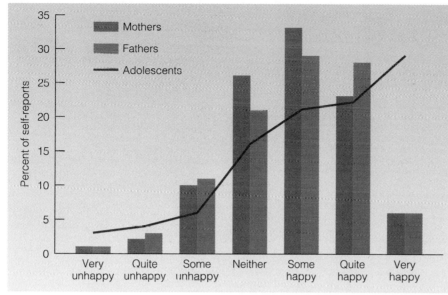

FIGURE 3.9
**Frequency With Which
Family Members Feel
Gradations of Happiness and Unhappiness.**
Source: Adapted from
R. Larson & M. Richards.
(1994).

found increased conflict and decreased closeness with pubertal onset only in White adolescent boys. For Hispanic boys, just the opposite occurred, with puberty actually bringing parents and sons closer together. Hispanic boys reported less conflict and greater emotional support from their parents once they began puberty. This increased closeness may reflect the value Hispanic families place on the traditional male role. Supporting this interpretation, Hispanic girls did not experience a comparable improvement in their relationships with parents.

The Timing of Change: Early and Late Maturers

Differences in the timing of pubertal change from one adolescent to the next, or within any adolescent, are collectively known as **asynchrony.** Asynchrony simply means that all changes do not occur at the same time. For adolescents who believe changes should occur together, the fact that they haven't, or that they occurred together but at the wrong time, can have enormous implications. Many changes receive cultural as well as personal interpretation. These interpretations affect the way adolescents feel and think about themselves. Change can be difficult enough when all goes according to schedule, but when adolescents develop faster or slower than their friends and classmates, or at obviously uneven rates within their own lives, differences can be hard to ignore.

It is common for adolescents to experience asynchrony today. In fact, our society seems to foster adolescent asynchrony. Most adolescents are biologically and intellectually mature by their mid- to late teens, yet many remain emotionally and socially dependent on parents while they obtain the education they need to succeed in an increasingly technological society. Little information exists on the possible effects of these asynchronies on personality

Continuity and
Diversity in
Early Adolescent
Development

Early maturing boys
often show off their
strength at the ex-
pense of smaller, later
maturing boys. Will
their different rates
of maturation affect
the development of
self-image in these
two boys?

development. Certainly, we need more research on this important topic, because it affects the lives of millions of adolescents and their parents.

We know most about the effects of asynchrony as it concerns differences in the rate of maturation among adolescents. Even here, the findings
are not easy to interpret. Probably the most influential set of studies comes
out of research conducted at the University of California, Berkeley, in the
1950s and 1960s by Mary Cover Jones, Nancy Bayley, and Paul Mussen.
Looking at the relationships between the timing of maturation and personality measures, they observed some important differences (Jones, 1957,
1958, 1965; Jones & Bayley, 1950; Jones & Mussen, 1958; Mussen & Jones,
1957).

Early and Late Maturing Boys   The Berkeley research found that boys who
matured early appeared more adult and more attractive to their peers and
to adults than boys who matured later. Early maturing boys were also more
popular and achieved more recognition in activities ranging from captain
of the football team to class president. Personality measures showed further
differences between early and late maturing boys. Early maturers were more
self-confident and less dependent. The late maturers often appeared more
rebellious and more concerned with rejection. Some differences persisted
into adulthood. These, too, favored the early maturers, who by then were
men in their thirties.

Other investigators report similar findings, suggesting that early maturation offers distinct advantages, and that late maturation may even handicap boys in relatively permanent ways. These beliefs have received little

challenge, despite the fact that in some studies only a few of the comparisons between early and late maturers are statistically significant, and even these do not support the notion of a handicap.

Research by Harvey Peskin (1967, 1973) challenges these pictures of early and late maturing boys. His data give us an alternative perspective on the effects of timing. Peskin is one of the first to suggest that early maturation may have its own disadvantages. Recall that adults and peers react to early maturing boys as adults much sooner than they do to late maturers. Early maturing boys may feel pressured into prematurely committing themselves to goals and life choices in order to live up to the expectations of others, whereas their late maturing cohorts have more opportunity to explore personal alternatives. Perhaps late maturers can better reflect on their feelings, both positive and negative, maybe leading to greater insight as well as a heightened awareness of negative feelings—for example, the rejection and rebellion frequently found in later maturers in earlier studies.

The work of John Clausen (1975) gives us yet another way to interpret differences between early and late maturing males. Clausen suggests that the importance of early maturation may be greater among working-class boys, but that more general differences in body type, height, and intelligence better predict personality differences than timing per se. He suggests, for instance, that adults as well as peers tend to look to boys with muscular bodies (mesomorphs) as leaders, and are more likely to perceive boys who are especially thin (ectomorphs) as timid and less assured.

Just how important is rate of maturation or body type to personality development? Efforts to disentangle the effects of such factors are complicated by the fact that the significance of physical characteristics can change even within a culture from one ethnic group to another or from one generation to another. An attribute such as body type may not be equally valued by all segments of society. The stereotype of the computer hacker may be as popular to one group as that of the varsity linebacker is to another.

Early and Late Maturing Girls   Clear gender differences exist in the effects of timing. Early maturing girls do not share the advantages of early maturing boys (Brooks-Gunn, 1991). Many are self-conscious about their adult bodies and lack the poise of late maturing girls. Their height, menarcheal status, and developing breasts can be sources of embarrassment among classmates who have the bodies of children. The picture brightens with junior high. Early maturing girls are no longer set apart by their adult bodies. They enjoy a new prestige and, with this, frequent popularity. Socioeconomic status appears to be important in mediating the effects of timing for girls as well. Early maturation is a more positive experience for middle-class girls than for working-class girls (Clausen, 1975).

Several factors contribute to the difficulties generally experienced by early maturing girls. For one thing, early maturing girls are less likely to be prepared for pubertal changes than late maturers because most will begin to menstruate before they learn of menstruation either from their mothers or in a health class. They are also less likely to have close friends with whom they feel comfortable discussing the changes they are experiencing. In general, early maturers have more negative attitudes concerning menstruation, poorer body image, and more eating problems. The latter may be due to being somewhat heavier in a culture that values thinness (Brooks-Gunn, 1991; Tschann, Adler, Irwin, & Millstein, 1994).

Some effects persist into adulthood for females, just as they do for males. Researchers have found that early maturing girls are more introverted and experience more emotional conflict as young adults. Early maturing females appear to come into their own in middle adulthood, when they surpass late maturers on many measures of mental health (Peskin, 1973; Petersen & Taylor, 1980).

Explaining the Differences Several hypotheses explain the psychological effects of timing. The *deviance hypothesis* suggests that timing has a psychological impact by changing adolescents' status relative to their peers. Adolescents who mature either way ahead of or way behind their peers become deviants. According to this position, early maturing girls are the most deviant and experience more disadvantages. Girls generally mature several years ahead of boys. Thus, girls who mature the earliest are the most anomalous group among their age-mates. Late maturing boys are the second most deviant group, because they are at the other end of the developmental parade. Early maturing girls and late maturing boys do in fact have the hardest times (Petersen & Crockett, 1985).

A second explanation suggests that early maturers do not have as much time as other adolescents to complete the developmental tasks of middle childhood. The *stage termination hypothesis* predicts more difficulty for those facing the demands of adolescence first, that is, early maturing girls. A positive note for these adolescents is that they have more time to complete the tasks of adolescence. The early years of adolescence, however, can be expected to be rough, as early maturers cope with new experiences, expectations, and feelings when they have not yet completely resolved the problems of middle childhood (Peskin & Livson, 1972).

A third explanation, the *adult status hypothesis,* suggests that the advantages or disadvantages of early and late maturation depend on the status that awaits adolescents when they become adults (Block, 1978). Adult males generally enjoy a higher status in society than females. They are frequently the decision makers within the family and have positions of greater power and influence in society. Early maturing boys enjoy the higher status afforded males when they attain the adult bodies of males. Movement toward adulthood for girls does not carry the clear advantages it does for boys. At best, the advantages are mixed. Girls can anticipate the greater independence enjoyed by adults, but female adult models are frequently financially and emotionally dependent on males. Physical maturation has more of a sexual meaning for girls than boys, perhaps because adult women traditionally have been defined through their roles as wife and mother. Maturity does not move them into positions of leadership, financial independence, and physical prowess.

Is this what life is all about? Perhaps not, but such are the values of society. Consequently, the adult status hypothesis can explain why early maturation is more advantageous for middle-class than working-class girls. More of the former can expect to achieve positions of independence and prestige as adults.

Between the ages of
10 and 14, girls are
usually taller than
boys of the same age.
Because girls reach
physical maturity ear-
lier than boys, social
interactions between
them can be awkward
at times.

Body Image

Among boys, early maturers have more positive body images. Just the opposite is true among girls: Late maturers feel more positive about their bodies and more attractive than early maturers do. As we have seen, how
satisfied adolescents are with their bodies depends a lot on how others react to them. Adolescents' self-images reflect the attitudes of others, or their
perceptions of these attitudes, as well as their own evaluations of how attractive a particular trait may be. Body images are reflected by social mirrors and always capture comparisons with others.

These images can get pretty distorted at times, especially in adolescence,
when bodies change in so many ways. In early adolescence, physical changes
contribute heavily to adolescents' senses of themselves. Adolescents' self-
images are strongly tied to their body images; this is true for both sexes.
Furthermore, just how satisfied adolescents are with their bodies roughly
predicts their levels of self-esteem, especially for girls. Superficial or not, this
relationship reflects something of a social reality, because peer acceptance
is related to body type (Stiles, Gibbons, Hardardottir, & Schnellmann, 1987;
Tobin-Richards, Boxer, & Petersen, 1983).

In general, boys have more positive body images than girls (Brooks-
Gunn, 1991; Duke-Duncan, 1991). Girls tend to be critical of the way they
look, believing themselves to be heavier than they are and wanting to be
thinner. Boys, on the other hand, are content with their appearance, wanting, if anything, only to be somewhat more muscular. Girls' tendency to
overestimate their weight declines after mid-adolescence; however, their dissatisfaction with their bodies continues to increase through late adolescence
(Phelps, Johnston, Jimenez, Wilczenski, Andrea, & Healy, 1993).

TABLE 3.3 Body Satisfaction Among African American and European American Adolescent Girls	
African American Girls	European American Girls
70% express satisfaction with their bodies.	90% express dissatisfaction with their bodies.
64% believe it is better to be somewhat overweight than somewhat under-weight.	62% report dieting within the past year.

Source: S. Parker, M. Nichter, M. Nichter, N. Vuckovic, C. Sims, & C. Ritenbaugh. (1995). Body image and weight concern among Afro American and White adolescent females: Differences that make a difference. *Human Organization, 54,* 103–115.

Fitting a new body image into a sense of self is an important developmental task of early adolescence, and more girls experience difficulty than boys. In a longitudinal study of over 600 adolescents, Roberta Simmons and Dale Blyth (1987) found consistent gender differences in body image and self-esteem during early and mid-adolescence. Girls are less satisfied with their weight, their general body type, and consider themselves less attractive than do boys. These differences appear as early as the sixth grade and persist into the tenth. Perhaps not surprisingly, girls have lower self-esteem than boys at each of these grades and are more self-conscious. Girls not only evaluate their looks more negatively than boys, they place more value on personal appearance than do boys (Wood, Becker, & Thompson, 1996).

Important racial differences exist among adolescent girls in terms of body image—African American girls view their bodies quite differently than European American girls do. A team of researchers at the University of Arizona, studying junior high and high school students, found that although nine out of ten European American girls are dissatisfied with their body weight, seven out of ten African American girls are satisfied. Additionally, whereas 62% of European American girls said they had been on a diet within the past year, a comparable percentage of African American girls, many of whom also had dieted, nonetheless believed it to be better to be somewhat overweight than underweight (Parker, Nichter, Nichter, Vuckovic, Sims, & Ritenbaugh, 1995). Table 3.3 summarizes the results of this body satisfaction survey.

Are the pounds adolescents add simply excess fat from the Big Macs, Whoppers, fries, and shakes they consume, or are they the muscle and subcutaneous fat that will transform their bodies into those of adults?

EATING DISORDERS

Some adolescents mistake the natural changes of maturation for unwanted fat, and diet to regain their former shapes. Others, perhaps unsure whether they are ready for adulthood, attempt to delay its appearance by literally starving themselves. Still others turn to food when stressed and become obese.

Dieting

Dieting is not an eating disorder, and most adolescents who lose weight do so in healthy ways, such as by eating fewer snacks, and decreasing their intake of fat (French, Perry, Leon, & Fulkerson, 1995). However, most girls believe they are too fat, even when they are not, and place themselves on diets (Ledoux, Choquet, & Manfredi, 1993; Phelps et al., 1993). One study of ninth-graders found that 25% of the girls were currently on diets, and 75% reported having been on a diet at some prior time. Many skipped breakfast and ate salads as their main meal. All knew which foods were high in calories and stayed away from them. Boys were untroubled about their weight; 80% said they had never tried to lose any weight (Leon, Perry, Mangelsdorf, & Tell, 1989).

Cultural messages on the importance of being thin are clear: To be considered attractive, females need to be thin. For instance, nearly three-quarters of the female characters on television are actually underweight; most of the males, however, are of average weight (Silverstein, Perdue, Peterson, & Kelly, 1986). Those most susceptible to this message, and most likely to experience eating problems, are girls who were early maturers who are less likely to be thin than late maturers (Smolak, Levine, & Gralen, 1993; Swarr & Richards, 1996).

Television is not unique in communicating to females the importance of being thin. Silverstein, Perdue, Peterson, and Kelly (1986) sampled advertisements in popular women's and men's magazines for messages about body shape. Ads for diet products in women's magazines outnumbered those in men's magazines 60 to 1. Despite the clear message to stay thin, women's magazines contained over 1,000 advertisements for food; 10 appeared in all the men's magazines.

Adolescent females today face a standard of beauty that is considerably thinner than in the past. Models of feminine beauty—whether actresses, performers, or individuals advertising products—are thin indeed, compared to their curvaceous counterparts of generations past. The flapper era of the 1920s was the only other time during this century when the popular images of women were as thin as they are at present. Developmentalists note with some alarm that eating disorders became epidemic among young women then, and warn that, with respect to eating disorders, history may be repeating itself.

Bulimia and Anorexia

Both bulimia and anorexia have increased significantly over the past 10 to 15 years, and both are more common among females than males (Tobias, 1988). **Bulimia** is characterized by binge eating: consuming large amounts of food in a short time, usually in less than two hours. Binges are usually accompanied by the fear that one cannot stop oneself and are followed by self-deprecating thoughts. They tend to be done in secret and usually end only because of abdominal pain or falling asleep.

Anorexia is a disorder in which individuals severely limit their intake of food, dieting to the point of actual starvation. Actual starvation has mental and emotional, as well as physical, effects, and anorexics can be apathetic

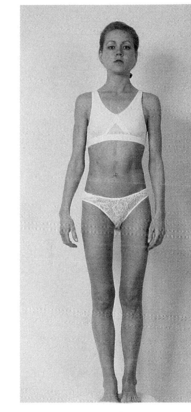

Anorexics severely limit their intake of food; some lose up to 25% of their body weight. However, they usually have a distorted body image; even though they look dangerously emaciated to friends and family, to themselves, they still do not feel thin enough.

and irritable. Due to the loss of body fat, anorexics frequently become amenorrheic, ceasing to have menstrual periods.

Most bulimics are aware that their eating patterns are abnormal, and most make continued attempts to lose weight through highly restrictive diets, self-induced vomiting, and use of laxatives or diuretics. Anorexics deny that they have any problem and reject help (American Psychiatric Association, 1994).

Less than 5% of high school students are thought to be bulimic; the percentage of those who are anorexic is even smaller (French, Perry, Leon, & Fulkerson, 1995). Whereas anorexia is more common in young adolescents, bulimia is more common in older adolescents and young women (Johnson, Steinberg, & Lewis, 1988).

Though bulimics can be of any weight, they are rarely fat (Ledoux, Choquet, & Manfredi, 1993). Usually their weight fluctuates widely, sometimes by as much as 20 to 30 pounds over a period of just several months. Anorexics are excessively thin, frequently losing up to 25% of their body weight.

Anorexia and bulimia are closely related disorders. Both involve an obsession with food and a morbid fear of being fat. Both also share an obsessive need to be thin. Many anorexics engage in binging and purging, and many bulimics start with an initial anorexic phase. Most bulimics usually begin self-induced vomiting approximately a year after they start binging (Fairburn & Cooper, 1982). Due to the large numbers of calories bulimics consume, they can only maintain their weight by alternating binges with highly restrictive diets, or by purging what they have eaten through self-induced vomiting, laxatives, or diuretics.

Bulimics are likely to live with the disorder for a number of years before seeking help. During that time they suffer physical as well as emotional symptoms, such as fatigue, weakness, and constipation. Dental caries and erosion of the enamel of the teeth are also common from frequent contact with stomach acids through self-induced vomiting (Johnson, Steinberg, & Lewis, 1988). Anorexics have a distorted body image and are not likely to seek help even when they become emaciated through self-starvation.

Bulimics often have low self-esteem and a history of depression (Ledoux, Choquet, & Manfredi, 1993). These adolescents are likely to feel self-conscious around others, be sensitive to rejection, have difficulty expressing their feelings directly, and share a number of personality characteristics with individuals who are identity-diffused as described in Chapter 8 (Auslander & Dunham, 1996). Both bulimics and anorexics are likely to have high standards and expectations for themselves and be overly critical when they fail to meet them.

Both disorders are more common among adolescents from European American, middle-class, upwardly mobile homes who are typically good girls seeking approval and love by pleasing others. Both disorders require professional intervention. Each is a serious threat to health and reflects underlying emotional problems that need treatment (Tobias, 1988).

Eating Disorders and Family Conflict Amy Swarr and Maryse Richards (1996) followed a sample of adolescent girls over a two-year period and found that adolescents who enjoyed close positive relationships with their parents had healthier attitudes both toward their weight and toward eating. Eating

Research Focus

Bias and Blind Controls: Eating Disorders

"You always shut yourself off in your room," her mother said, somewhat angrily.

"I just want to be left alone," she pleaded, the hint of a whine in her voice. The teenager was 17, and her dark eyes communicated a sulky resentment.

The research assistant on the other side of the one-way mirror quickly coded the girl's response: "asserting," "appeasing," "separating," and "interdependent."

"Some message!" he thought, as he watched the family in front of him.

The girl was trim, neither overweight nor underweight. He couldn't tell from her appearance which type of disorder she suffered from; he only knew that this project was about adolescents with eating disorders. For all he knew, she could be part of the control group.

Why keep this graduate student in the dark about the families he is observing? Why not assume that the more he knows, the better he'll understand and more accurately record their behavior? Investigators have found from painful experience that their expectations all too often influence what they see—sometimes even causing them to read things into a person's behavior that just aren't there. Their expectancies can *bias*, or systematically alter, the results of the study.

Whenever investigators know the condition of which a subject is part, they can bias the outcome of the research either by unconsciously treating subjects in that condition differently or by interpreting—that is, scoring—their behavior differently. If, for example, this graduate student believed that the parents of girls with a certain type of eating disorder were harsh and demanding, he might read hostility into their remarks even when it wasn't there, or perhaps be less friendly with them when introducing them to the experiment. The latter difference might lead to tensions in family interactions that otherwise would not be present, thus unintentionally confirming initial expectations.

Investigators can eliminate experimenter bias by conducting the experiment "blind." In a *single-blind control* procedure, such as the one above, the investigator is unaware of the condition of which each subject is part; expectations cannot contribute to any of the observed differences. A single-blind control is adequate in many experiments. Some, however, require a *double-blind control,* in which both the subjects as well as the experimenter are ignorant of which condition each subject is in. Double-blind controls are frequently used in drug studies in which it is necessary to control for the patients' as well as the doctor's expectations that they will get better if they take an experimental medication. In double-blind drug studies, *all* subjects are given a pill, but half receive a *placebo*, or sugar pill.

Let's get back to the other side of the one-way mirror. Do families of girls with different eating disorders interact in characteristically different ways? Laura Humphrey (1989) observed 74 adolescent girls with their parents. Sixteen were *anorexic*, 16 were *bulimic*, 18 were both *bulimic and anorexic*, and 24 were normal controls. All of those in the first three categories were patients who had been hospitalized long enough so that one could not distinguish the anorexics by their appearance.

Parents of anorexics were both more nurturing and comforting *and* more ignoring and neglecting than were those of bulimics or controls. The anorexic girls were the most submissive of the group when they were with their parents. Bulimics and their parents were more likely to engage in mutual grumbling and blaming and to exchange disparaging remarks. Interactions of normal controls and their parents were characterized more by helping, protecting, trusting, and simple enjoyment of each other.

These findings underscore the importance of treating the family as a whole, as well as working individually with the adolescent when treating eating disorders. Most eating disorders are associated with a pattern of disturbed family interactions.

Source: L. L. Humphrey. (1989). Observed family interactions among subtypes of eating disorders using structural analysis of social behavior. *Journal of Consulting and Clinical Psychology, 57,* 206–214.

disorders, when they occur, hide deeper, underlying problems in which family experiences play an important role. Four characteristics of families that lead to the expression of psychological problems as physical symptoms frequently characterize the families of anorexics and bulimics (Minuchin, Rosman, & Baker, 1978; Tobias, 1988). *Enmeshment* exists when boundaries between family members are not clear. In enmeshed families, everyone is involved in everyone else's life, making it difficult to be independent or autonomous. *Overprotective* families show an inappropriate concern for the welfare of family members. Families characterized by *rigidity* have a need to maintain the status quo and are unable to face change. These qualities make adolescence, a time of many changes, especially difficult. Finally, families in which there is *inadequate conflict resolution* avoid conflict, with the result that differences are never cleanly resolved and members continue to impinge on each other. An eating disorder may be the only way in which adolescents from such families can gain a sense of maintaining control over their lives (Tobias, 1988). The Research Focus, "Bias and Blind Control," describes another study of the families of girls with eating disorders.

Obesity

Physical appearance is perhaps never more important than during adolescence. Body image contributes significantly to self-image for most adolescents. Those who are obese tend to have less-positive self-images and lower self-esteem than adolescents of average weight. **Obesity** is defined as being 20% above the average weight for one's height. Approximately 15% of all adolescents meet this criterion; this figure makes obesity the most common eating disorder of any age (Grandjean, 1988).

Obesity has multiple causes. The likelihood of a genetic component is strong in that obese children tend to have obese parents. This relationship is difficult to interpret in any simple way, because parents and children share eating habits and lifestyles as well as genes. Also, the eating patterns of obese adolescents differ from those who are of average weight. Obese adolescents are more likely to eat irregularly, missing meals and snacking. These habits make it difficult to maintain a balance between hunger and satiation. Obese adolescents are also more likely to eat rapidly, to eat somewhat larger portions, and to eat food that is denser in calories (Lucas, 1988).

Perhaps the biggest difference between obese adolescents and those of average weight is in how active they are, not how much they eat. Obese adolescents are considerably less active than their peers of average weight. A low level of activity can contribute as much to obesity as excess eating. Once again, separating cause from effect is difficult. Are obese adolescents less active because of their weight; that is, are they less likely than their peers to be chosen for the team or to be good at sports? Or do adolescents who are inactive simply run a greater risk of becoming obese (Lucas, 1988)?

The relationship between obesity and inactivity highlights the importance of exercise in weight reduction programs. Exercise increases the body's metabolism, allowing the body to burn excess calories more rapidly; in moderate amounts, exercise also depresses appetite. Dieting alone can have paradoxical effects, frequently causing a preoccupation with food, which in turn can prompt reactive overeating (Lucas, 1988; Satter, 1988). Ellen Satter (1988) recommends programs that incorporate procedures that foster a reliance on internal cues rather than on external constraints, such as counting calories and diets. The latter force one to continually think about food and ways of avoiding it.

Adolescents attempting to lose weight often have unrealistic expectations. Many view their weight as central to all their problems and expect that once they lose weight, their problems will be solved—they will become popular, make the team, and so forth. When their problems do not roll away with the pounds, adolescents can become frustrated and fall off their diets. The most successful programs are multifaceted. The success of a weight control program for adolescents almost always depends on successfully integrating the family into the treatment program. As with bulimia and anorexia, obesity is often a symptom of underlying conflicts within the family.

MAKING SEXUAL DECISIONS

Puberty brings new sexual feelings and emotions, and the natural need to integrate these into a sense of oneself. Doing so can be difficult, especially because many of these feelings have been labeled in childhood as "forbidden" or "bad." Adolescents cannot simply add new sexual feelings to an old self. They must revise that self so that what they add fits. In other words, adolescents cannot continue to see themselves as children and simply add sexual feelings and behaviors to this self-image. "Sexy children" is a contradiction in terms in most societies—to be sexual is to be adult. To integrate sexuality into their sense of themselves, adolescents must take a big step toward adulthood—and away from childhood. For many, this step is a hard one to take, not so much for what they are stepping into as for what they are leaving behind.

Not surprisingly, adolescents frequently experience conflict when contemplating their own sexuality. Conflict isn't necessarily bad, but it can interfere with responsible sexual decision making, often leading to avoidance and denial. Translated into the terminology of sexual decision making, adolescents who experience conflict may deny that they are assuming a stance that is any different from that which they have always taken. Rather than consciously thinking through the consequences of becoming actively sexual, these adolescents will engage in sex without planning to do so—and without doing so responsibly.

The lack of consistent adult guidance makes the transition to adult forms of sexual behavior even more difficult. The transition itself occurs in several steps, but, unlike the first steps of toddlers, these are not taken with a parent's guidance and support. Adolescents usually cross this terrain guided by someone their own age. They rarely, for instance, cite parents as their principal source of information, being much more likely to mention a sibling (Ansuini, Fiddler-Woite, & Woite, 1996). As a consequence, sexual decision making reflects considerable misinformation.

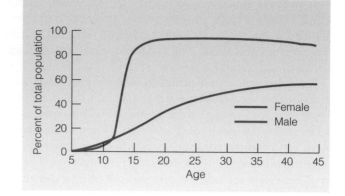

FIGURE 3.10
Frequency of Mastur-bation in Males and Females of Different

Ages. *Source:* Adapted
from J. S. Hyde. (1990).
Understanding human sexual-ity (4th ed.). San Francisco:
McGraw-Hill.

Unlike many attitudes, those surrounding sex are not likely to be openly discussed, especially with parents. In itself, that may not be surprising, but adolescents also find it hard to talk openly about sex with friends, and even with sexual partners. Those who do talk with their parents are not as likely to begin their sexual experiences early, or to engage in high-risk behavior once they have begun (Baumeister, Flores, & Marin, 1995). Similarly those who can talk openly with their sexual partners engage in sex more responsibly (Darling & Hicks, 1982; Leland & Barth, 1993).

Mary Jo Nolin and Karen Kay Petersen (1992) asked mothers, fathers, and adolescents to indicate how much they talked to each other about sexuality. They found that parents talked much more with their daughters than with their sons, and that mothers were more likely than fathers to talk with their children. As a result, sons had less opportunity than daughters to discuss sexual matters with the same-sex parent. When discussions did occur between parents and sons, they were less likely to touch on issues of morality or values than were discussions with daughters. Of course, values can be communicated in many ways, not necessarily through talking. One important way is by teaching adolescents to be responsible for their actions and to have respect for others. Parents also influence their teenagers' sexual practices by maintaining strong bonds with them, thereby lessening their need for peer approval (DiBlasio & Benda, 1992; Miller & Fox, 1987).

Masturbation

The sexual practice that evokes the most concern among adolescents is **masturbation;** most adolescents masturbate, and most regard the practice with mixed feelings. Figure 3.10 shows the increase in this practice with age. Because adolescents initiate all forms of sexual behavior earlier today than in the past, these trends, extrapolated from Kinsey's data, probably should be moved ahead by several years (Hyde, 1990; Kinsey, Pomeroy, & Martin, 1948; Kinsey, Pomeroy, Martin, & Gebhard, 1953).

Even though 80% of boys and almost as many girls say they approve of masturbation, many feel anxious and guilty about masturbating. Novelist Philip Roth (1969) depicts these concerns in a boy:

It was at the end of my freshman year of high school—and freshman year of masturbating—that I discovered on the underside of my penis, just where the shaft met the head, a little discolored dot that has since been diagnosed as a freckle. Cancer. I had given myself cancer. All that pulling and tugging at my own flesh, all that friction, had given me an incurable disease. And not yet fourteen! In bed at night the tears rolled from my eyes. "No!" I sobbed. "I don't want to die. Please—no." But then, because I would shortly be a corpse anyway, I went ahead as usual and jerked off.

Attitudes toward masturbation have changed radically. Past generations were taught that masturbation was morally wrong and were warned that excessive masturbation could result in physical deformities or disease—even insanity (Hall, 1904). Adolescents today learn that masturbation is a normal sexual outlet with no harmful effects and some positive ones. Masturbation can help both females and males learn how their bodies respond sexually. Although most adolescents no longer believe that masturbation is abnormal or dangerous, most still view it with mixed feelings; such feelings may be the only negative effects associated with masturbation.

Stages of Heterosexual Behavior

As individuals move through adolescence, more of them engage in heterosexual activity and do so with greater frequency. Most White adolescents follow a predictable progression that starts with necking, moves to feeling breasts over clothing, feeling breasts directly, touching the female's genitals, touching the male's genitals, to intercourse (Hyde, 1990; Miller, Christopherson, & King, 1993; Smith & Udrey, 1985). For Black adolescents this progression is not necessarily normative; more are likely to engage in intercourse than in directly touching breasts or genitals. Adolescents of both races consider a wider range of behaviors acceptable for couples who are emotionally committed to each other than for those who are casually dating (Thornton et al., 1990).

For most adolescents kissing is their first sexual experience, and an important one. "An adolescent's first erotic kiss often proves to be an unforgettable experience. . . . It is largely through kissing that we learn to be sexually intimate, to be comfortable with physical closeness, and to give and take sexual pleasure" (Strong & DeVault, 1997).

Petting also is an acceptable sexual outlet for most adolescents, though sexual practices lag somewhat behind acceptance. Males are more likely to be the ones to touch their partners than vice versa, perhaps because males experience more permission to be sexually active than females. In fact, a girl needs more commitment in a relationship in order to touch her partner than to allow the boy to touch her. This fact suggests that it is quite difficult for most girls to assume an active role in sexual encounters even when most hold positive attitudes about the behaviors in question.

Attitudes toward oral sex are more positive than they were in previous generations, and this activity has increased in frequency among adolescents (Wilson & Medora, 1990). Adolescents also engage in intercourse at earlier ages today than in the past. A national sample of over 10,000 high school

Starting with a kiss, all adolescents follow a predictable progression of sexual behavior as they grow older, although the progression varies somewhat among ethnic and racial groups.

TABLE 3.4   Percentage of High School Students
Who Have Had Sexual Intercourse

	Ever Had Sexual Intercourse	Have Had Four or More Sex Partners	Currently Sexually Active*
SEX			
Female	52.1	14.4	40.4
Male	54.0	20.9	35.5
GRADE			
9	36.9	12.9	23.6
10	48.0	15.6	33.7
11	58.6	19.0	42.4
12	66.4	22.9	49.7
RACE OR ETHNICITY			
White	48.9	14.2	34.8
Black	73.4	35.6	54.2
Hispanic	57.6	17.6	39.3

*Of those who had ever had sexual intercourse, the percentage who had had intercourse during the 3 months preceding the survey.

Source: Centers for Disease Control. (1996a, September 27). CDC surveillance summaries. *Morbidity and Mortality Weekly Report, 45,* no. SS-4.

students revealed that by the ninth grade almost 40% are sexually experienced and by the twelfth grade nearly 70% are (Table 3.4) (Centers for Disease Control, 1996a). By the age of 19, 70% of girls and 80% of boys have had intercourse (Strong & DeVault, 1997). Surveys such as these necessarily rely on adolescents' self-reports, which, though generally consistent when given by the same adolescents in longitudinal research, may nonetheless be somewhat unreliable when reporting their age at first intercourse (Capaldi, 1996).

Within each ethnic group fewer girls are sexually experienced than boys at each age, although again wide differences exist from one group to another. This difference holds across all groups, with from 40% to 52% of 17-year-old females and 53% to 66% of 17-year-old males being sexually experienced (Benda & DiBlasio, 1994).

Despite the fact that teenagers are more likely to be sexually active today than before, many adolescents engage in intercourse infrequently (Jensen, de Gaston, & Weed, 1994). Some adolescents appear to have had their first sexual experiences for reasons not necessarily sexual but as a rite of passage, an act of rebellion, or to satisfy their curiosity. Once they have proven themselves or discovered what they wanted to know, they abstain until they become involved in a relationship. Adolescents who are romantically involved are most likely to engage in intercourse on a regular basis. Most adolescents practice serial monogamy, limiting their experiences to a single partner at any time.

First intercourse occasions many feelings. In general, these are more uniformly positive for boys than girls. A majority of adolescent boys report feelings of happiness, excitement, satisfaction, and even joy. Adolescent girls are more likely to experience guilt or fear. Many are disappointed. As one 19-year-old girl put it, "Was *that* what we waited so long for?" (Aitken & Chaplin, 1990, p. 24). But not all are disappointed, and one survey found a majority of girls felt excitement and romance (Weis, 1983).

Reactions such as the above emphasize one of the most important differences in the sexual experiences of males and females. Adolescent males find sex itself exciting. For females, romance still seems to be a necessary part of the erotic equation. Females are more likely than males to report being in love with their first sexual partner. However, even this gender difference is changing. Patricia Koch (1988) reports that fewer girls expect to marry their first sexual partner than before, and that boys are more likely than before to be in love. The Research Focus, "Coding Descriptive Responses," explores gender differences in beliefs about sexual desire.

Despite such gender differences, Doreen Rosenthal and Rachel Peart (1996) found that the strategies adolescents use to communicate either their interest in having sex, or in avoiding unwanted sex, differ little for females and males. In either case, the rules for encouraging sex are more clear-cut than those for avoiding sex, and boys as well as girls report difficulty in getting out of unwanted sexual situations. It is interesting that more than half of the boys, in addition to four-fifths of the girls, reported at one time or another wanting to avoid sex. Girls were more likely to use more direct strategies than were boys, over 80% of girls saying that they had been able to clearly tell their partners when they had gone far enough. It is interesting that, despite the use of similar strategies, boys perceive themselves as being less able to say no than girls—28% of boys versus 9.6% of girls saying they definitely or probably could not say no to unwanted sex (Zimmerman, Sprecher, Langer, & Holloway, 1995).

CONTRACEPTION USE

One might think that early sexual activity among adolescents would be accompanied by an equal sophistication concerning contraception, but data suggest this is not the case. More than a million adolescent girls become pregnant every year. Most of them do so unintentionally. Yet adolescents can select from a wide range of birth control measures. The most effective of these all but eliminate the possibility of pregnancy. Why aren't they effective for teenagers? The answer, it seems, is that most sexually active teenagers do not systematically use contraceptives.

Only 27% of sexually active 13- to 18-year-olds say they always use some form of birth control (Benda & DiBlasio, 1994). Sporadic use of birth control, however, is higher. In a national survey of high school students, over 54% of the sexually active respondents reported they or their partner had used a condom during their most recent sexual intercourse, and 17.4% said

Coding Descriptive Responses: Gender Differences in Beliefs About Sexual Desire

What causes sexual desire? Is desire aroused by the characteristics of the person one is with, such as a good body or a dynamic personality? Might it be the situation one finds oneself in, such as being alone with a date in a parked car? Or does it have more to do with oneself, apart from who one is with? Do males and females even attribute desire to the same causes? When it comes to beliefs as to what fans the fires of desire, we are just beginning to get answers to some very basic questions. Social scientists have put most of their energy into defining sexual desire, spending relatively little time exploring people's beliefs about what causes it. Yet beliefs are closely tied to what people do, and knowing their beliefs brings us one step closer to predicting their behavior. So what *do* people think are the causes of sexual desire?

Pamela Regan and Ellen Berscheid (1995) asked college students to describe, in their own words, what causes sexual desire in men and women. This approach involves the use of *free-response data* or *descriptive data*. When researchers begin to investigate an area in which relatively little is known, they will frequently simply observe what people do in natural settings, or, when this is impossible given the sensitive nature of the behavior, they will listen to what people have to tell them. Open-ended questions such as those used by Regan and Berscheid are useful when one wants to know what people are thinking (Cozby, 1997). Another advantage to descriptive responses is that they generate a rich source of data, useful in formulating future research questions. An additional advantage is the increased *external validity* of the research, or the likelihood that the answers one gets are representative of the way people actually think.

There are disadvantages to the use of descriptive free responses as well. Perhaps the most formidable of these is the need to *code,* or classify, the specific answers that people give into broader classes of answers. Instead of attempting to work with everything people say, for instance, one looks at categories of answers. This approach makes it easier to detect relationships. Patterns emerge showing the frequency of different types of answers for different people, such as those given by females versus males. How does one arrive at the codes to be used in analyzing descriptive responses? One might simply decide in advance to look for certain types of answers, given what other investigators have found. One might also look at the actual answers that are given by a sample of the respondents, grouping specific answers into larger categories based on similarities in their meaning. Regan and Berscheid had two independent raters code each of the response protocols; each rater was ignorant of the sex of the respondent whose answers he or she was reading. The use of more than one coder makes it possible to determine the *reliability* with which answers are coded, or the degree to which the two raters working independently of each other agree in their coding.

The use of free-response or descriptive data is a time-intensive procedure. Raters must be trained to identify responses accurately, and this takes time. The actual scoring of the data also takes more time. In a sense, one enters a stream of behavior with a net—ready to catch (code) certain specimens of interest—but there is little way of speeding up the rate at which the behaviors flow by.

Do college students believe the causes of sexual desire differ for males and females? The answer is a clear yes. Sexual desire in males was believed to be caused by erotic factors, such as looking at a woman with a sexy body, more than by romantic ones, whereas desire in females was thought to be caused more by romantic factors, such as love or intimacy. Significant numbers of students also attributed sexual desire in males simply to their being male, or to their maleness. Conversely, none of them considered femaleness to be a cause of sexual desire in women. Interestingly, in matters romantic, as is so often the case, the sexes often get their signals crossed. For instance, males—but not females—believed that power and status made a male sexually desirable. On the other hand, females—but not males—believed that femininity made a female sexually desirable. Adolescents and young adults spend hours cultivating the right image. All too often this image fits their own perception of sexual desire but not that of their partner.

Source: P. C. Regan & E. Berscheid. (1995). Gender differences in beliefs about the causes of male and female sexual desire. *Personal Relationships, 2,* 345–358.

they or their partner had used birth control pills during last sexual intercourse (Centers for Disease Control, 1996a). Those least likely to use a condom are early adolescents and those who do not believe that responsibility for contraception is shared. Males who have a close relationship with their sexual partners are more likely to use a condom. Condom use may be a transitional behavior; couples who are going steady or engaged are twice as likely initially to use a condom as to use a female method, but for their most recent experiences they are twice as likely to use a female method (Sonenstein, Pleck, & Ku, 1989). Even so, condoms remain important as protection from sexually transmitted diseases, even when other forms of contraception are used.

It is important to know why contraceptive use is at best sporadic for most adolescents. A number of possible reasons exist. Three of the more likely are lack of information, inability to accept one's sexuality, and cognitive-emotional immaturity.

Lack of Information

Most adolescents are surprisingly misinformed about their own reproductive capabilities. Some surveys have shown that as many as two-thirds of adolescent girls believe it isn't necessary for them to take any precautions because they are too young to get pregnant, or because they have not had intercourse enough times to become pregnant. An equal number of adolescents appear to be so anxious about their sexual activities that they are not able to deal with the associated issues in any practical way (Strong & DeVault, 1997).

What is the relationship between what adolescents know about reproduction and how likely they are to use some form of contraception? Findings here are inconclusive. Much research suggests that the more adolescents know about the risk of pregnancy, the more likely they are to use a contraceptive (Hayes, 1987). Other findings suggest that knowledge and behavior are unrelated. Pleck, Sonenstein, and Swain (1988), for example, found that 18% of adolescent males with no sex education used a condom—the same percentage as those who *did* have sex education. Perhaps the reason that sex education does not increase condom use is that using a condom correctly requires a certain amount of skill, which if not acquired beforehand, is not likely to be mastered in the heat of the moment. Most sex education programs do not offer students experience in gaining skill in condom use (Barth, Fetro, Leland, & Volkan, 1992).

Most adolescents do not receive any information about reproduction or contraception from their parents. Most are also not likely to disclose their concerns to their parents. How likely adolescents are to talk to their parents depends on the quality of the relationship they have with them (Papini, Farmer, Clark, & Snell, 1988), as well as their levels of self-esteem and individuation (Papini, Snell, Belk, & Clark, 1988). This last point suggests that young adolescents especially will not bring their sexual concerns to their parents because they are still in the early stages of the process of individuation.

One study of communication between adolescents and parents found that adolescents are least likely to talk with parents about sexual concerns once they have decided to become sexually active and most likely to talk to parents only when their attitudes are not well formed (Papini, Farmer, Clark, & Snell, 1988). Adolescents appear to talk to parents as a way of clarifying their own attitudes, but once they have done so, they disclose little to their parents or to their friends. This study suggests that once adolescents become sexually active, they are even less likely to get the information they need from parents. Once sexually active, they are guided only by their peers, who are likely to be blatantly misinformed, and some by a need to deny their own sexuality.

Inability to Accept One's Sexuality

First sexual encounters can occasion considerable conflict in many adolescents, especially in girls. A number of reasons exist for this conflict. Sexual behavior is closely tied to moral issues, which are not likely to be openly examined and discussed. In some homes sexual matters are cloaked with secrecy, and discussions of sexual concerns are infrequent or absent entirely. Many adolescents simply are uncomfortable discussing their sexuality, even those who are sexually active. Adolescent girls who *can* accept and talk about their own sexual behavior are more likely to use contraceptives effectively.

Cause for conflict among many adolescent girls can be found in current stereotypes of femininity and masculinity. Compare these components of the feminine stereotype—yielding, shy, sensitive to the needs of others, childlike, and compassionate—with those of the masculine stereotype—makes decisions easily, is self-reliant, independent, assertive, and willing to take risks. Who is most likely to make decisions, be self-reliant, or assertively insist on the use of a condom? Although most males are not likely to use a condom, many females will fail to use a contraceptive because it simply isn't feminine to plan to have sex or to take precautions against getting pregnant.

Cognitive-Emotional Immaturity

One of the hallmarks of cognitive development is the ability to think about things that have not been experienced. Thought that is limited by experience is limited to what has happened before. Most adolescents are just entering a form of thought in which they can consider events that may only exist as possibilities for them. Most have never been pregnant before either.

Despite the emergence of new mental skills that enable adolescents to imagine things they have never experienced, things that exist only as abstractions or possibilities, these skills appear at different times for different individuals. Some adolescents may be facing sexual decisions while still approaching daily problems in a concrete fashion, their thinking limited to what is immediate and currently apparent (see Chapter 4). Thus a 13-year-old girl flattered by the attentions of an older boy may not have the cognitive maturity, in the pressure of the moment, to consider distant consequences. The concrete problem is, "What will make him like me now?" Pregnancy and disease belong to the world of tomorrow, and tomorrow is but dimly represented in concrete thought.

Even among those adolescents who can think more abstractly, the absence of practical experience and accurate information can make imagined consequences hard to evaluate. Many adolescents are able to conceive of problems intellectually yet feel personally immune to them. To these individuals disease and pregnancy are possible but not real, and it's hard to take dangers seriously if they believe such things only happen to others.

Early adolescents tend to think that other people are as interested in what they are thinking and doing as they are themselves (Elkind, 1967; Lapsley, FitzGerald, Rice, & Jackson, 1989). In doing so they create an imaginary audience. Imagining that others are aware of their feelings or activities can mean that their private fantasies about sex risk becoming public knowledge. The imaginary audience can also give adolescents the feeling that they are special (the personal fable). Why else would everyone be so aware of what they are feeling and doing? Being special carries the implication that what happens to others will not happen to you. Thus many girls believe they will not get pregnant even though their friends do. As one 18-year-old said:

> Like when I'm having sex, I don't really connect it with getting pregnant cause I've never been pregnant, you know, and a lot of my friends have but I just can't picture it happening to me. And like you really don't connect it, you know, until once you've been pregnant. Because when it's never happened you say "Why should it happen?" or, "It's never happened yet," you know. You always look at the other person and say, "It happened to them, but it'll never happen to me." And I . . . I don't really kinda put it together. I don't . . . you just don't worry about it. You don't believe it can happen to you. (Sorenson, 1973, p. 324)

Teenage pregnancies will almost surely continue to be a major problem until courses in sex education integrate facts about the biology of reproduction with approaches that make sense to the adolescents involved. Specifically, they must address the attitudes that adolescents and their parents have about being sexual. We also need to consider sexual decision making in light of what we know about adolescents' ability to understand things that may, at the moment, exist for them only as possibilities.

SEX EDUCATION: WHAT ADOLESCENTS NEED TO KNOW

Where do adolescents get information about sex? Where can they go to find out what feelings are normal, what their own reproductive capabilities are, how sexual expression relates to other feelings, what issues surround sexual intimacy, and the associated hazards? Adolescents who want answers to all of their questions soon find that no single source suffices.

Sources of Information

As we have already discussed, most adolescents do not get their information from their parents because they are generally uncomfortable talking with them about sexual concerns. But if not to parents, whom can they talk to? Most adolescents get their information from friends, many of whom are misinformed themselves (Barth, Fetro, Leland, & Volkan, 1992; deAnda, Becerra, & Fielder, 1988).

Nearly 90% of adults favor sex education in the schools (Harris, 1988), as do most adolescents themselves. Almost 90% of large school districts offer some form of sex education (Kenny, Guardado, & Brown, 1989). The goals of the programs differ. Nearly all provide information designed to prepare adolescents to make informed sexual decisions; most also teach material about the reproductive system as a means of achieving this goal. Few that are offered in junior high cover contraceptive techniques, perhaps assuming that doing so would communicate approval of teenage sexuality. However, this information, not that about reproduction per se, is related to the likelihood that adolescents will use some form of contraception (Scott-Jones & Turner, 1988). Most programs focus on information and provide little opportunity for students to interact with the information in ways that would make it most meaningful to them.

The information covered by many courses may be so technical, textbookish, and abstract that teenagers fail to make the connection between what they are learning and their own bodies—or at the very least what they need to know and do in order to practice effective contraception. One 16-year-old girl recalled, "We had to memorize the parts of the body—the fallopian tubes . . . and how all that is connected. Which was a big help, let me tell you. I didn't know what I needed to know, but that wasn't it" (Aitken & Chaplin, 1990, p. 24).

The Effectiveness of School Programs

More programs are involving parents, with the assumption that doing so will improve communication within the family. Some train students to listen to peers and to help them find information. These programs assume that teenagers are more comfortable discussing sexual matters with each other than with adults. Which approaches work best? Information on the effectiveness of programs is limited, and not always consistent. Involving parents may improve communication between adolescents and their parents, but such an approach appears to be most effective with younger children. Peer counseling programs appear to be effective, but primarily by raising the awareness of adolescent counselors to sexual issues rather than by reaching other students (Hayes, 1987).

Do sex education programs that include information on contraception make it more likely that adolescents in these programs will engage in sexual activity? Evidence suggests they do not, and that teenagers who are already engaging in sex are likely to have intercourse somewhat less often and more likely to use condoms (Barth, Fetro, Leland, & Volkan, 1992). Other studies have found no relationship between contraception use and sex education courses (Kirby, 1984, as cited in Hayes, 1987; Pleck, Sonenstein, & Swain, 1988).

An important factor contributing to the success of a program almost surely is the degree to which it allows adolescents to actually practice the skills they will need either to abstain or to successfully use contraception.

Richard Barth, Joyce Fetro, Nancy Leland, and Kevan Volkan (1992) incorporated homework assignments such as talking with parents or pricing birth control methods, and classroom role playing of sexual encounters in a program covering both abstinence and birth control. Although adolescents completing the program were no less likely to engage in sexual intercourse, they were more likely to use birth control.

A number of programs stressing abstinence have reported some success in changing adolescents' attitudes, with more adolescents, after taking such a program, believing that their sexual urges were controllable and that there were good reasons to wait until marriage before engaging in sex (Eisenman, 1994). The success of sex education programs stressing abstinence, however, is significantly affected by how committed teachers are to the objectives of such programs (de Gaston, Jensen, Weed, & Tanas, 1994).

Programs that teach adolescents assertiveness and decision-making skills offer an attractive supplement to information-based programs. These programs approach sexual decision making by building interpersonal and problem-solving skills. Sex *is* problematic for most adolescents, and it is highly interpersonal. Many adolescents feel pressured into sexual encounters that they would otherwise avoid or postpone if they felt comfortable stating how they felt. These pressures affect adolescents of both sexes. Adolescent males frequently feel pressured into making sexual overtures simply because they assume it's expected of them or that everybody else is having

What should be taught in this sex education class? sexual anatomy? sexual functioning? contraceptive methods? Although most adults—and most adolescents—favor sex education in the schools, the content of such programs is controversial, especially if they are perceived to condone or encourage teenage sexuality.

sex. One of the ways in which sex education programs can be effective is to correct perceptions such as these (Barth, Fetro, Leland, & Volkan, 1992).

The few data we have on assertiveness and decision-making programs suggest that they are effective. Problem-solving and communication skills improve, as does knowledge of reproduction. Data suggest that contraception use also improves among adolescents enrolled in such programs. Only small numbers of adolescents have been involved, and more research is needed (Hayes, 1987).

SUMMARY

The Endocrine System

The endocrine system consists of glands within the body that produce hormones and of structures within the central nervous system that regulate their activity.

Endocrine activity is regulated by a feedback system that controls the timing of puberty. The hypothalamus and the anterior pituitary are the brain centers most closely related to the timing of pubertal events. The hypothalamus secretes a hormone that stimulates the anterior pituitary to produce hormones that act directly on the gonads. These in turn produce the sex hormones—estrogens in females and androgens in males. The hypothalamus is sensitive to levels of circulating hormones and adjusts its signals to the anterior pituitary whenever these get too high or too low.

The Physical Changes of Puberty

Puberty ushers in a growth spurt and maturation of the reproductive system. Primary sex characteristics involve changes in the reproductive system itself; other changes, such as the appearance of pubic hair, represent secondary sex characteristics. Considerable variability exists from one adolescent to the next in the timing and, to a lesser degree, the sequence of these changes.

In girls, the appearance of pubic hair is one of the first visible signs of change. Breasts begin to develop at about the same time. The uterus, vagina, labia, and clitoris all develop simultaneously with the breasts. The ovaries also grow as the ova within mature.

Boys begin puberty an average of two years later than girls. The first sign of change is an enlargement of the scrotum, followed by the appearance of pubic hair. The penis starts to grow a year later. Internal organs—the testes, seminal vesicles,

Cowper's glands, and prostate gland—also mature, and levels of circulating testosterone increase markedly during puberty. The height spurt precedes a change in voice and the appearance of facial and underarm hair.

Girls experience a period of rapid growth and add subcutaneous fat before reaching menarche, the onset of menstrual periods that occurs midway through puberty. Most girls reach menarche in their 12th year. The menstrual cycle is regulated by a feedback loop involving the ovaries, the anterior pituitary, and the hypothalamus. When levels of estrogen reach a peak at midcycle, ovulation occurs. Most adolescent girls have irregular cycles at first, many of which do not involve the release of an ovum.

In boys, the presence of testosterone and other hormones stimulates the testes to produce sperm. Both the seminal vesicles and the prostate gland produce semen, the fluid in which sperm are suspended. Most boys experience spermarche, the first ejaculation of seminal fluid, by mid-adolescence.

Puberty begins earlier today than in past generations. Adolescents also grow faster and grow to be larger than in the past, a trend known as the secular trend. Improved nutrition is a likely cause of the secular trend.

The Psychological and Social Implications of Puberty

The significance of puberty is different for each adolescent, depending on how the adolescent interprets the changes he or she is going through and how friends and relatives react to those changes. Puberty usually comes at about the same time as starting junior high school, coping with changes in relationships with peers and parents, and facing pressures to experiment with sex and drugs. Adolescents react to these changes with a heightened emotionality. Tensions are common between adolescents and parents and lead to renegotiated relationships.

Biological, intellectual, emotional, and social maturation occur at different times during adolescence, and rates of maturation are also different from one adolescent to the next. Both early and late maturation seem to affect how adolescents see themselves and how others see them. In particular, adolescents' self-image is tied to their body image. Females generally have less positive body images than males and experience more eating disorders.

Making Sexual Decisions

Adolescents must revise their self-concepts to include new sexual feelings and behaviors. This process is problematic for those who experience conflict in leaving their childhood behind them. Changing social attitudes and values are reflected in the sexual decisions adolescents make.

Attitudes toward sex are becoming more permissive. Changes in the sexual behavior of females have been primarily responsible for a decrease in the double standard of sexual conduct.

Sexual practices change in predictable ways with age. Most adolescents begin to masturbate in their early teens. Boys begin earlier than girls and masturbate more frequently.

Adolescents move through stages of heterosexual activity as they grow older. Most start with kissing, progress to French kissing and petting, and then engage in intercourse and oral-genital sex. Boys begin their sexual experiences earlier than girls, though adolescents in general are becoming sexually experienced at earlier ages than in the past. Ethnic differences in the timing of sexual experiences can be large.

Contraception Use

Most adolescents do not systematically use contraceptives because they lack adequate information. Many also do not practice responsible sex because they are unable to accept their own sexuality. Many more engage in unprotected sex due to their cognitive and emotional immaturity.

Sex Education

Most adolescents do not talk to their parents about their sexual concerns. Sex education programs in the schools are a common source of information for many adolescents. Although most programs are effective in communicating information, many are not effective in changing behavior.

KEY TERMS

endocrine system
hormones
androgens
estrogens
hypothalamus
pituitary
gonads
primary sex characteristics
secondary sex characteristics
growth spurt
menarche
uterus
cervix
ovaries
ova (ovum)

fallopian tubes
vagina
clitoris
glans
shaft
prepuce
epididymis
vas deferens
seminal vesicles
prostate gland
semen
sperm
Cowper's glands
penis

urethra
circumcision
smegma
scrotum
testes
female circumcision
spermarche
nocturnal emission
secular trend
asynchrony
bulimia
anorexia
obesity
masturbation

CHAPTER 4

Cognitive Development
Processes and Transitions

Yaun-Pin—Pete, to his friends—read alternatives "b" and "c" again. He knew this material. He had distinguished his family with good marks in this very subject before coming to this country. Yet he couldn't understand the question. The two choices seemed the same to him. He could feel the heat rising in his face as the words danced and mocked him. Blindly, he marked "c" and moved on. The bell would ring soon. So much depended on him. He would have to study his English again tonight after he and his father closed the shop. No time for hanging out, for video games or the sit-coms his friends watched each night. No wonder they thought he was a loner. Sometimes he thought he was crazy. How could he explain one world to the other? Or to himself?

Sehti's mind wandered as she stared at the quiz. She was still angry that she hadn't been able to study more last night. She'd had to help her mother with dinner. Why had her uncle and aunt picked that night to visit? And why couldn't her brothers have helped? They didn't have half the homework she had, and they never had to help. Her mother said it was women's work, that she should leave her brothers alone. The bell—oh, no! She quickly marked alternative "b." Why couldn't she concentrate?

Joe looked at the quiz: 15 questions. He knew the answers to all of them—all but number 11. Actually, it was the way the question was worded. He could make an argument for either "b" or "c." Joe loved junior high. Math, social studies, drama, English lit—each left him more excited than the last. By the end of the day, he was filled with ideas, ideas he framed easily in words that he spoke with quiet confidence. The bell! He chose "b" and wondered how successful he'd be in convincing Mr. Allen of his reasoning if his teacher had keyed "c" as correct.

You have just met three students, each competent, each standing on the threshold of a new world of thought and experience. All adolescents embark on the journey these three are beginning. Not all travel the same distance. Yuan-Pin, Sehti, and Joe probably will not either. They aren't likely to get the same grade on this quiz, or to do equally well in junior high. Is this unfair? Differences in their grades will not necessarily reflect their capabilities. Yuan-Pin is still learning English; he doesn't have a chance to show what he knows. Sehti's concentration is scattered by conflicting demands at home and at school. Intellectual performance almost always reflects more than what one knows. Motives, interests, and even expectations held by others can affect performance.

Early adolescents face intellectual changes that are very bit as profound as the biological changes discussed in the last chapter. These changes usher in adult forms of thought, just as the latter usher in adult bodies. Adolescents can plan for the future, imagine the impossible, catch multiple meanings to words and situations, understand nuance, follow a philosophical discussion, and respond to a simple question with an answer that would make the captain of a debating team proud. We will look at the nature of these changes, and at explanations that have been offered for them. We will also consider conditions that affect intellectual performance in adolescents such as Yuan-Pin, Sehti, and Joe.

Piaget offers a constructive developmental analysis of intellectual development. Adolescence marks the last of his four stages. For Piaget, the ability to imagine the possible, rather than thinking only of the actual, is the most important quality of mature thought. With this step, thought becomes abstract. It also becomes logical and systematic. Adolescents can think of problems in terms of the variables that define them, isolating first one and then the other, until they come up with all possible combinations.

Some developmentalists believe that what Piaget identifies as new forms of thought may only reflect continuous growth in abilities already present. Because these abilities are known to increase with age, one could explain Piaget's formal thought in terms of age changes in general intelligence. This approach, known as a psychometric approach, focuses on the abilities that underlie general intelligence and on how these are measured.

We will look at how intelligence tests are constructed, what they measure, and some of the problems they introduce when not interpreted correctly. The greatest strength of intelligence tests is in predicting academic success. This strength is also a weakness. The paradox arises from our inability to distinguish what success reflects: the general abilities presumed to be tapped by the tests, or the degree of familiarity with the culture required to understand the questions? Just as Yuan-Pin experienced difficulty on his math quiz, he would have difficulty with many of the items on the intelligence test.

A final approach to cognitive and intellectual development focuses on age-related changes in the strategies people use to catalogue and process information. Robert Sternberg analyzes intellectual functioning into three components: one that organizes strategies for thinking, another that does the actual work, and a third that gathers new information when needed. Howard Gardner suggests there are seven different forms of intelligence. He

This child and teenager represent two different stages of cognitive development. The child thinks only in concrete terms; she doesn't understand "yesterday" or "tomorrow." The adolescent's thinking is qualitatively different—it has reached the stage that Piaget calls formal thought—and she can mentally manipulate abstractions and imagine events that may never happen.

divides intelligence into areas as diverse as bodily-kinesthetic intelligence and logical-mathematical intelligence.

Throughout the chapter, we will look at the practical side to intellectual development in adolescence: Adolescents can study new things in school, support their ideas with adult arguments, experience new emotions, think about themselves in new ways, plan for their futures, and understand the complexities of social relations in more subtle ways.

HOW ADOLESCENTS THINK

Thought takes interesting turns in early adolescence and carries teenagers places children don't easily go. Adolescents can think about things that don't exist and may never exist. They can think about what is possible as well as what actually is. Thinking becomes highly systematic and logical. This is not to say that adolescents are always logical and that children never are, or that children never consider possibilities as well as realities, or that adolescents always reason in the abstract. It is, rather, that adolescents do so more often, and with greater ease. Each of these characteristics of adolescent thought—thinking abstractly, thinking hypothetically, and thinking logically—is discussed in the sections that follow.

Science Project

Ms. Jones has asked her seventh-grade class to consider the following problem: Imagine that scientists have just discovered a new planet. A research team has been given the task of determining all possible life forms that may exist on this planet. A space probe has returned with data suggesting that life could exist either in bodies of water (aquatic) or on land (terrestrial). The team suspects that life on this planet, as on ours, could either be vertebrate or invertebrate. What are all the possible forms that life might take?

Children think of four types by combining the four separate forms: terrestrial vertebrates, aquatic vertebrates, terrestrial invertebrates, and aquatic invertebrates. Adolescents come up with twelve more possibilities. They think not only to combine the separate forms of life but also to combine the combinations! The original four combinations, plus the separate life forms, give them a total of sixteen possibilities. One of these is the possibility of no life at all.

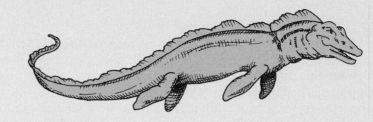

1. Terrestrial vertebrates (TV)
2. Aquatic vertebrates (AV)
3. Terrestrial invertebrates (TI)
4. Aquatic invertebrates (AI)
5. Only vertebrates (TV and AV)
6. Only invertebrates (TI and AI)
7. Only terrestrial animals (TV and TI)
8. Only aquatic animals (AV and AI)
9. TV and AI
10. AV and TI
11. TV, AV, and TI
12. TV, AV, and AI
13. TV, TI, and AI
14. AV, TI, and AI
15. TV, AV, TI, and AI
16. No animals at all

**FIGURE 4.1
Classification of
Thoughts by Adoles-
cents and Children**

Source: Adapted from J. M.
Hunt. (1961). *Intelligence
and experience.* New York:
Ronald Press.

Thinking Abstractly

"How is a horse like a goldfish?" If you ask adolescents this question, they are likely to come up with any number of answers. They might say, "Well, a horse and a fish are both animals," or "Both have to eat to live," or "Both take in oxygen and give off carbon dioxide." Children are more likely to stare you down. You can almost hear them think, "That was a stupid question!" In any event, they are not likely to think of any similarities. Why is their response so different from that of adolescents?

Children tend to think of things in terms of their physical properties. With horses and goldfish, this approach doesn't take them very far. If you had asked how a horse was like a dog, they would have had no problem: Both have four legs. They could tell you how a horse is like a cow: Both are large and eat grass. But as long as their thoughts are bound by the physical characteristics of things, fish remain worlds removed from horses. Adolescents can think of things as members of classes, and can even think of ways to classify those classes (Drumm & Jackson, 1996). An adolescent can say, for example, "Both are animals, and animals can be either aquatic or terrestrial." Figure 4.1 shows an example of the type of science project adolescents can solve because they can think in terms of classes.

Thinking Hypothetically

Thinking abstractly is related to another characteristic of adolescent thought: hypothetical thinking. Adolescents can turn a problem around in their minds and come up with possible variations it might take (Figure 4.2).

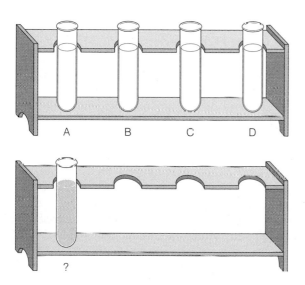

FIGURE 4.2
A Problem Involving Chemical Solutions That Requires Hypothetical Thinking to Solve. *Source:* Adapted from B. Inhelder & J. Piaget. (1958). *The growth of logical thinking from childhood to adolescence.* New York: Basic Books.

In one measure of hypothetical thinking, adolescents see a rack of four test tubes, each containing a clear liquid. A second rack holds a single test tube with a clear yellow liquid. The problem is to find the combination of colorless liquids that produces the yellow color. Adolescents can think of all the possible (i.e., hypothetical) combinations, whereas children simply combine the chemicals.

Models of atomic structures and other abstract concepts are meaningful only to students who have reached a level of cognitive development that enables them to use symbolic representations to evaluate the logical consistency of ideas.

Only then do they start to work, testing each possibility to find the one that applies in that situation. Being able to imagine what is possible, instead of thinking only of what is real, allows adolescents to think hypothetically.

Children, in contrast, focus on the actual, perceptible elements of a situation and rarely speculate about possibilities they cannot generate by actually doing something. They are more likely to jump in and do something with no plan of attack. Even if they succeed in solving the problem, they are not likely to have kept a record of what they did. John Flavell, a psychologist at Stanford University who has written widely on cognitive development, remarks that the school child's "speculations about other possibilities—that is, about other potential, as yet undetected realities— occur only with difficulty and as a last resort. An ivory-tower theorist the elementary school child is not" (Flavell, Miller, & Miller, 1993).

Thinking Logically

As thought becomes abstract, adolescents are able to test different ideas against one another to establish their truth. They become aware of the logical relations that exist among ideas and can use logical consistency to determine whether a statement is true or false. Children check their ideas

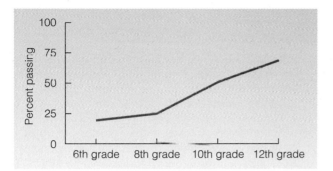

FIGURE 4.3
Adolescents Passing
Piaget's Measures of
Formal Thought

Source: S. C. Martorano.
(1977). A developmental
analysis of performance on
Piaget's formal operations
tasks. *Developmental Psychology, 13,* 666–672.

against hard facts; so do adolescents, but logical consistency is equally compelling for them.

This difference is dramatically illustrated in a simple experiment. Adolescents and children are shown poker chips and asked to judge whether statements about the chips are true or false. Sometimes the chips are hidden in the experimenter's hand; at other times they are clearly visible. The experimenter has just picked up a green chip and holds it in clear view. He says, "The chip in my hand is either green or it's not green." Both the adolescent and the child agree that the statement is true. Next the experimenter holds up a chip that is hidden in his hand and says, "The chip in my hand is either red or it's not red." The adolescent knows the statement must be true and agrees. The child says, "I can't tell," and asks to see the chip! Children evaluate statements such as these by comparing them to what they can see, not realizing that they could still evaluate their truth based on logical properties. Adolescents know that thoughts can be checked against themselves for logical consistency (Osherson & Markman, 1975).

One might assume, at this point, that all adolescents think and solve problems alike. But thinking, like every other aspect of development, is highly individual. Tremendous differences exist among early adolescents in the rate at which they acquire new reasoning abilities, and many adolescents do not reason in these ways even by the end of junior high (Figure 4.3). Instead, thinking improves with age throughout adolescence (Arnett & Taber, 1994). As the Research Focus, "Correlational Research," indicates, the development of thinking—specifically, the ability to interpret the thoughts, feelings, and motives of oneself and others—also shows some gender differences.

Biological Bases to Intellectual Development

It's common knowledge that most 14-year-olds know more, reason faster, and remember better than most 10-year-olds. They can solve harder problems, think through abstract dilemmas, understand complex social situations, and even spell better. What interests developmentalists is not *if* there is a difference between the way adolescents and children think, but what to make of that difference. Is it only that each additional year adds a bit more to what one knows? Or does a more fundamental change occur somewhere between childhood and adolescence to account for this difference?

Research Focus

Correlational Research: How Accurately Do Adolescents Perceive Others and Themselves?

Children think about things they can see and touch. Adolescents classify things and then think about the classes. The classes don't actually exist—except in their minds. Does the ability to think abstractly affect the way adolescents think about other things? about themselves? about others? How might a developmentalist go about answering questions such as these?

One would first need to measure abstract thinking in individuals of different ages, to determine whether thinking does indeed become more abstract with age. Then one could look for changes in the ways adolescents think about themselves and others that relate to these differences. Research that classifies individuals according to characteristics they possess, to determine what relationship these have to other variables, illustrates the *correlational method*. Instead of independent variables, this research works with *classification variables*. Age is a classification vari-

able, as is gender, and ethnicity. A simple rule of thumb allows us to distinguish an independent variable from a classification variable: Can you assign subjects at random to the conditions you are interested in? If so, you have an independent variable. If not, you have a classification variable.

When changes along one variable correspond to changes along another, the variables are said to be *correlated. Correlation coefficients* are statistics that reflect the degree of relationship between variables. *Scatterplots* show this relationship pictorially. In the figure, the scatterplot on the left illustrates no relationship (r = 0); the one on the right shows a strong relationship (r = +1.00). One could have an equally strong relationship but in the opposite direction (r = −1.00); that is, variables can be either *positively* or *negatively* correlated. In the first case, increases along one variable match increases along the other. In the second case, increases along one are accompanied by decreases along the other. Let's look at how one group of investigators used a correlational approach to determine the relationship between abstract thinking and thinking about the self and others.

Robert and Sherry Hatcher, Meryl Berlin, Katherin Okla, and Jill Richards (1990) gave fifth-, eighth-, and twelfth-graders two measures

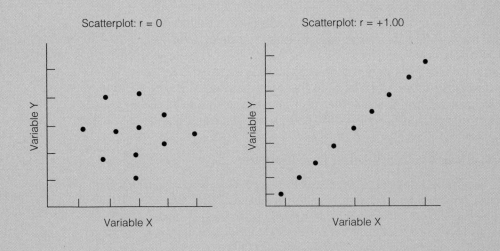

Scatterplot: r = 0

Scatterplot: r = +1.00

Variable Y

Variable X

Variable Y

Variable X

Research Focus (*continued*)

of abstract thinking. They found large increases in abstract reasoning from one grade to the next (that is, grade and abstract thinking are positively and highly correlated), and no relationship between abstract reasoning and gender (gender and abstract reasoning are not correlated). Are there corresponding differences in the ways adolescents think about others? about themselves?

This is where fairy tales enter the picture. Adolescents listened to shortened versions of fairy tales and answered questions about the thoughts, feelings, and motives of the characters. "Why was Cinderella so nice to people who were mean to her?" "Why were the stepsisters so mean to Cinderella?" "Why did the emperor believe that he was wearing a beautiful new outfit?" "The little boy was the one to say that the emperor wasn't wearing any clothes. Why did he say it instead of a grownup?" Their answers were scored for perception of others (PO). They assessed self-observational skills (PS) by showing adolescents ambiguous yet evocative pictures and asking them to write what the characters thought and felt. Psychologists assume that individuals identify with the characters in the pictures and that their stories about the characters reflect their own thoughts and feelings.

Do observational skills increase with age? Data relating PO and PS scores to age show that they do—dramatically (see the figure). They also show that girls are more skilled at interpreting the thoughts, feelings, and motives of themselves *and* others than are boys (see the discussion of Gilligan in Chapter 2). Yet PO and PS do not correlate in any direct or simple way, a fact that suggests these are measures of quite different skills.

What can we say about the gender differences these investigators found in adolescents' observational skills? Although not definitive, these investigators guess that adolescents become skilled in observing others when they become able to think abstractly. In girls, these skills most likely take the form of a general social competence that also includes self-observational skills (see Chapter 6), but in boys they remain linked to general abstract reasoning.

Source: R. Hatcher, S. Hatcher, M. Berlin, K. Okla, & J. Richards. (1990). Psychological mindedness and abstract reasoning in late childhood and adolescence: An exploration using new instruments. *Journal of Youth and Adolescence, 19,* 307–326.

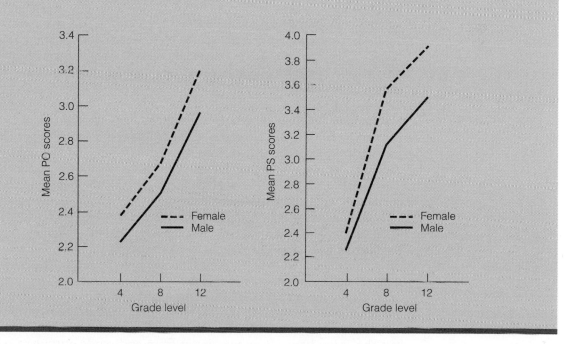

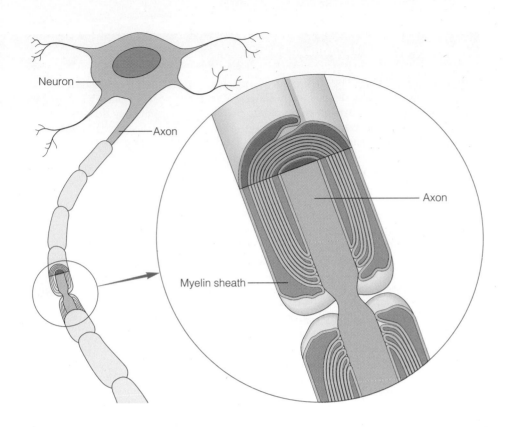

FIGURE 4.4
Myelin Sheath
Coating Axon

Considerable data suggest that biological maturation of neural structures is responsible.

Brain development continues well into adulthood, with different regions developing at different rates at different points in life (Greenough, Black, & Wallace, 1987). This development takes three forms of continued myelination of neural fibers, increases in synaptic connections, and increases in specialization of function.

Myelination Myelin is a fatty substance that coats the axon, the long filament extending out from the cell body, by which the neuron makes contact with other nerve cells (Figure 4.4). Fibers coated with a myelin sheath conduct impulses at higher speeds than those without a myelin covering. The sequence in which fibers in different areas of the brain are myelinated correlates with the timing of anticipated use of the pathways involved. Myelination of most neural fibers is largely completed by about the age of 7, the age, by the way, at which children move into Piaget's stage of concrete operations (see Box 4.1, page 144). However, myelination continues until early adolescence in four additional regions of the brain: the reticular formation, nonspecific thalamic radiations, corpus callosum, and fibers of the cortical association areas. These brain regions all play a role, in one way or another, in abstract thought, integrating neural input from various areas.

The *reticular formation* sits in the core of the brain and ramifies throughout the entire brain. It receives input from and sends output to every portion of the nervous system, performing numerous integrative functions. The *nonspecific thalamic radiations,* an extension in the forebrain of the reticular formation, integrate influences from the reticular formation with specific higher level sensory and motor functions. The *corpus callosum* connects the two hemispheres of the brain, uniting and integrating their functions. The fibers of the cortical association areas do for the integration of local areas what the previous structures do for more distant areas. Common to each of these areas, in which myelination precedes and may play a role in ushering in new ways of thinking, is the integrative role each serves (Reinis & Goldman, 1980).[1]

Synaptic Connections   Synapses, the connections between neurons responsible for the conduction of neural messages, continue to increase in the prefrontal cortex until about the age of 14 (Greenough, Black, & Wallace, 1987). The prefrontal cortex lies at the very front of the brain, right behind the forehead. We know about its functions primarily by seeing what happens when the prefrontal areas are injured. This area of the brain is primarily responsible for abstract thought, enabling us to hold on to information long enough to relate it to something else. For this reason, the prefrontal cortex is involved in planning—either on a short-term basis, such as generating an answer for Piaget's chemical solutions problem (see Figure 4.2), or longer term, such as envisioning the consequences of one's actions, planning for one's future, or, even more generally, worrying.

Increased Specialization of Function   Greenough, Black, and Wallace (1987) suggest that the brain responds to stimulation in two quite different ways, depending on different types of experience. For experiences that are idiosyncratic, differing from one person to the next, *experience-dependent mechanisms* establish new connections between neurons, enabling us to hold on to the new information. For experiences that are common to virtually all humans, however, more neural connections exist initially than are needed, and excess connections are "pruned" through *experience-expectant mechanisms,* those that are not stimulated dying out. This selective pruning continues until mid-adolescence in the frontal areas, a region of the brain that is important for abstract thought (Huttenlocher, 1990). Perhaps the most general index of neural organization, however, is the brain-wave activity known as EEG, as measured by an electroencephalogram, which refers to the periodicity of neural activity in different regions of the brain. The frequency of EEG waves changes from the low-frequency waves characteristic of childhood to the high-frequency waves characteristic of adults, starting from 10 to 13 years of age (Cech & Martin, 1995).

Thus, changes in each of the ways in which the brain continues to grow can be observed at about the age at which adolescents begin to show characteristic changes in thinking, lending strong support to a biological basis for their occurrence.

---

[1] I am indebted to Michael Wapner for his explanation of these regions.

A Constructive Interpretation of Cognitive Development

A number of years ago, there was a particularly scary horror movie, *A Nightmare on Elm Street*, in which the villain, Freddy Krueger, reached his victims through their minds, appearing to them in their dreams. Unlike other dreams, these took on a chilling reality because they didn't end when the person woke up. The villain was able to step into one's waking life, through a door in one's mind, making the villain as close as a heartbeat and only a thought away. Children across the country didn't sleep for nights after watching this movie. Freddy Krueger had a power to terrorize that other villains lacked. Other monsters could be more easily separated from one's self.

The idea that thought gives substance to reality is a powerful one, taking different forms depending on one's age, and even at different times in history. The ancient Hebrew alphabet, for instance, lacked symbols for vowels. These had to be supplied by the reader. Unlike consonants, which are formed as the tongue or teeth stop the flow of air, vowels are unstopped breaths. In Hebrew, the word for breath is the same as the word for spirit, *ruach*. In reading, one had to breathe life into the message, fleshing it out with the thoughts that made one vowel more probable than another. Similarly, ancient texts, even up to medieval times, lacked punctuation, making it necessary for a reader to interpret the text in order to decipher it. Because reading was such an active, even creative, process, a person would often initial a text after reading it.

The constructive perspective that informs this text assumes that individuals must continually interpret, or make sense of, all experience— whether deciphering printed words on a page, recognizing a familiar face, or listening to a conversation. In fact, this perspective argues that events remain ambiguous *until* we respond to them. Only by responding does the meaning of an event become explicit. Noam Chomsky (1957), a psycholinguist at MIT, illustrates this point by asking the meaning of the sentence, "flying planes can be dangerous." Does this mean that it is dangerous to fly a plane? Or that it is dangerous to be around planes that are flying? We rarely notice such ambiguities because we, just as the readers of ancient texts, breathe life into our experiences on a moment-by-moment basis. Pilots will hear Chomsky's sentence one way, and those living near airports will hear it another, the expectancies of each giving shape to their experience. Only when one is new to a task do expectancies fail, making it necessary to assemble understanding piece by piece. As any 5-year-old would tell you, reading is hardly automatic, even today.

Five-year-olds will also tell you that their dreams come in through the window at night, and, if asked whether someone else in the room could also see their dream, they would agree that another could, an admission that bespeaks a fuzzy distinction among thoughts, dreams, and reality (Piaget, 1954). This distinction, however, lies at the very heart of cognitive development.

Piaget and Kegan

Piaget adds a developmental twist to the constructive perspective. Fascinated by differences in the way children and adults understand their world, he assumed not only that we actively construct what we know of the world, but that we organize this understanding in qualitatively different ways with age, each way resulting in a distinctly different stage of thought. (Box 4.1 summarizes Piaget's stage theory of intelligence.) These stages differ in the nature of the equilibrium which we maintain with our environment (Piaget, 1971). This equilibrium, or adaptive balance, is maintained through two complementary processes: assimilation and accommodation. Through assimilation, the individual is able to interpret new experiences in familiar ways, ways that are already a part of the self, fitting the new into what one already knows. Through accommodation, in order to understand something new, one must change the way one views things; one must work at understanding, sounding out the experience as a new reader does with a word, a process that also changes one ever so slightly, making the other familiar only by changing the self.

We have seen that preschool-age children, school-age children, and adolescents think differently about their worlds, but what is the developmental process that accounts for these changes? Building on the constructive process elaborated by Piaget, Robert Kegan (1982, 1994) argues that intellectual growth takes place through a process of **differentiation** of self from other, a process that has the effect of simultaneously defining new aspects of one's surroundings and of one's self. In a manner similar to Isaac Newton's second law of motion, in which every action has an opposite and equal reaction, when one gives meaning to events out there, one's sense of self in relation to these events also changes.

Kegan gives the example of two young boys, 5 and 9 years old, surveying a street scene from the observation deck of a skyscraper. They exclaim their wonderment in different ways. The younger one says, "Look at the people. They're tiny ants." The older one says, "Look at the people. They look like tiny ants." There is a complexity to the older boy's remark that is lacking in the younger boy's. We hear in his remark a comment that has to do as much with *how* he is perceiving as with *what* he has perceived. His awareness of people looking *like* ants, rather than simply being the size of ants, adds a reflective quality in which the percept, or object being perceived, is evaluated. In other words, he is aware both of the percept and of the evaluating self—both of what he is seeing and of himself seeing it.

Kegan speaks of differentiation as a "moving-over" in the subject–object balance that we have struck with the world, a balance that represents our current grasp on reality. In order to envision this process, it might help to think of an actual balance, the old-fashioned kind with two pans positioned on either side of a fulcrum, or balance point. For the scale to balance, whatever is placed in one pan must be countered by an equivalent weight in the other pan (illustrated in Figure 4.5).

Differentiation, just as with weights in a scale, adds something to each "pan" of the subject–object balance. Consider again the example of the two boys looking down at people on the street below. Differentiation has

Box 4.1   Piaget's Stage Theory of Intelligence

Development, for Piaget, is a gradual freeing of thought from experience. Once thought becomes removed from the limitations of immediate experience, one is able to consider possibilities that do not exist and perhaps never will. This quality characterizes adolescent thought, which Piaget believes develops at approximately 11 years of age. Follow along as we trace Piaget's evolution of intelligence.

SENSORIMOTOR THOUGHT (BIRTH TO 2 YEARS)

In infancy, thought is limited to what is experienced through one's sense and actions: It is *sensorimotor.* To know something is to anticipate what will happen when one takes a certain action or to know the characteristics of an object, how it feels, tastes, smells. It is to know, for instance, that something held in one's hand will drop if released or that candy is sweet. Piaget maintains that, at first, infants cannot represent these experiences in their minds. As a consequence, he assumes infants do not realize that objects continue to exist when they no longer see them; that is, they do not have a concept of **object permanence.** Infants expand their world through countless daily experiments, such as dropping, sucking, or banging, which allow them to discover what things do. Piaget calls actions such as these **schemes.** A scheme is a class of actions that infants can apply to any number of objects; the precise form of the action varies slightly from one object to the next. After all, it's not as easy to wrap one's mouth around a rubber ball as it is a rattle or a cookie. But in each case, the baby explores an object by bringing it to the mouth.

PREOPERATIONAL THOUGHT (2 YEARS TO 7 YEARS)

In the preschool years, children develop the capacity to represent their experiences symbolically. Despite this ability, there are characteristic limitations to thought. The first of these is **centration,** the tendency to think of something in a single way, to the exclusion of others. If another way is pointed out, children lose sight of the first. If one of two balls of clay is rolled into a sausage, preschoolers argue that the amount changes, focusing either on the length of the one or the fatness of the other.

There is a "stuck" quality to preoperational thought, an apparent inability to move something around in one's mind and catch it from another angle. As a result, thought is often dominated by how things look. Young children have difficulty moving beyond appearance to how things *might* be. Thus, preschoolers cannot get from the sausage back to the ball; they cannot mentally **reverse,** or undo, the previous action by rolling the sausage into a ball again and envisioning how the two are really the same.

Young children often fail to realize that their view of something may not be shared by others, another quality of preoperational thought called **egocentrism.** They are not aware that what they see is a perspective, assuming the way they see things is the way everyone does.

CONCRETE OPERATIONAL THOUGHT (7 YEARS TO 11 YEARS)

In middle childhood, children become able to imagine actions that can be carried out in their heads and then reversed or undone. These **mental operations** allow children to take a mental step off the spot from which they have viewed a problem and gain a new perspective on it. Being able to relate different aspects of a problem to one another allows them to impose a new order on experience instead of taking it as a given. Thought becomes more integrated and logical.

Operations have a second quality that, like reversibility, makes thought more flexible. Each operation belongs to a set of operations, making it possible to see how one is related to another. Think, for a moment, what it means to understand the concept of "six." One knows, for example, that six pencils, six buttons, and six pennies are alike in that all are "six things." One can imagine moving the pencils, buttons, and pennies into groups of threes, or twos. A mental operation such as this allows one to appreciate relationships between the class of "six things" and other classes, such as classes of "two things" and "three things." One realizes not only that six is larger than three, but also that six is the same as two threes, and so on. The dawning of operations burns through the mists of childhood thought like the morning sun. New skills follow as the day follows night.

Box 4.1   (*continued*)

Mathematical concepts such as multiplication emerge from addition, concepts such as one's home state can be understood as larger than one's hometown and smaller than one's nation, and stamp albums, baseball cards, and doll collections reflect a new ability to mentally order one's world.

Despite the flexibility of the child's thought, it is still limited. Children do not think easily about things they cannot see. Thought is concrete, not abstract. Children can think of things that are absent only through simple extensions of their thoughts about those things that are present. Thought is still prompted by the here and now. Operations may organize experience and at times even extend it, but they do not create for the child, as they do for the adolescent, another world in which "the real becomes a special case of the possible" (Flavell, 1963; see Lourenco & Machado, 1996, for a defense of Piaget's theory).

FORMAL OPERATIONAL THOUGHT (11 YEARS AND OLDER)

Formal operational thought begins at about age 11. In a sense it is simply an extension of the concrete operations children have used all along in sorting and classifying the objects around them. In another sense it is an extension that quite literally opens up new worlds of possibilities for adolescents. The extension is a simple one: Adolescents can extend their earlier operations on classes of *objects* to classes of *classes*. The adolescent mind can include itself in the things it considers. Adolescents can think about their thinking.

Because most junior high school students are in transition from concrete operational thought to formal operational thought, they need a lot of hands-on activities in the classroom.

enabled the older boy to see as an object that which previously had been embedded on the subject side of the balance—that is, something has moved over from the "self" to the "other" pan. He can distinguish his own viewing perspective (they only *look* as small as ants) from the people. This moving-over is balanced by a comparable "weight" that is added to the subject side of the scale. He is aware not only of what he is looking at—the size of the people below—but also of the way he perceives them. This second awareness, of his own perceptual activity—distinct from the people he is perceiving—is the weight that is added to the subject side of the balance.

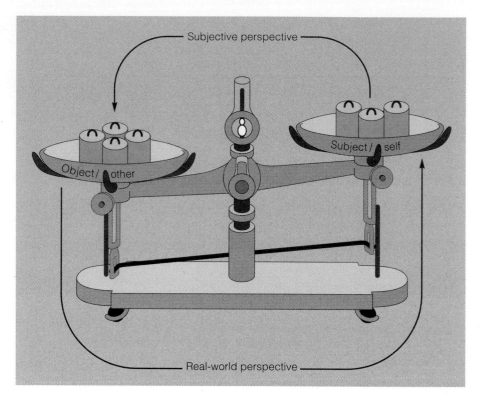

FIGURE 4.5
A Representation
of the Process of
Differentiation

In one of Piaget's most dramatic tests of **conservation,** which he used
to demonstrate whether children knew that things remained unchanged
even when they appeared to be different, he poured liquid from a short,
wide glass into a tall, narrow one, causing the level of the liquid to rise, and
asked if the liquid was still the same. Younger children, such as the younger
boy in our example, are unable to distinguish how the liquid *looks* from how
it *is* and say there is more in the taller glass. Older children, however, agree
that the amount of liquid in either container must be the same. They say
things such as, "I could pour the liquid back and it would look the same,"
a mental operation that Piaget referred to as "negation," or "This glass may
be taller, but it's also narrower, and the one makes up for the other," which
Piaget called "reciprocity." It is this ability to move from one perspective to
another, and back again, using either of these operations, that enables them
to understand that the liquid is unchanged, giving their world stability,
"concreteness."

To understand what takes place in adolescence, let's look at what enabled the older child, in the preceding example, to see that the people on
the street below only *looked* as small as ants. He became aware not only of
what he was seeing, but of how he was seeing it—of his perceptions. The
change allowed the boy to "own" his part in the tiny-ness of the people. In
the metaphor of the balance, he put into the "other" pan the perspective
that he previously did not distinguish from himself, and took back onto his
side the attribute of size that he earlier could not separate from the object

itself. The ability to separate himself from his perceptions enabled him to see them for what they were—as ways of seeing or perspectives. When perspectives emerge for the child's inspection, the child can move from one perspective to another and back again, seeing that the object has not changed even though its appearance may. This understanding gives the child a new grasp on things. Things that previously expanded and shrank when seen from different vantage points, like reflections in a fun house mirror, now hold still and become concrete (Kegan, 1982).

Just as older children become aware of their perspectives, adolescents become aware of how these can be coordinated. They can see that the liquid is the same either because one could always pour it back or because the width of the second glass compensates for its height. They can also see that, not only is the *liquid* similar in the two glasses, but so are the *ways* by which they arrive at this understanding similar—that is, that negation and reciprocity are comparable. Because each of these operations is a way of thinking, adolescents are able to think about thinking.

What "moves over" that enables adolescents to view the world differently than do school children? What must they "own" in order to see the child's concrete world differently? Differentiation occurs when adolescents become aware of their part in creating this stability. When they put into the "other" pan the way different perspectives can be coordinated, the concrete world of stable objects moves over and can be seen for what it is, as one of the many ways they might see their world. Adolescents take back to the "subject" side of the balance the attribute of concrete realness that they previously could not distinguish from their world.

The ability to think about thought allows adolescents to arrive at possibilities they could never reach otherwise. We can see this quality of thought at work in one of Piaget's tasks, a game in which balls are shot onto a gameboard with a spring launcher. The balls differ in size and in the smoothness of their surfaces. Eventually each stops rolling, the larger and rougher ones first. Piaget asks adolescents to explain why they stop. At first adolescents identify wind resistance and friction as important. But they soon realize something else: that the balls would roll forever if neither of these was present. This conclusion can be reached only through thought, because the conditions under which the event would occur are never actually present (flavell, Miller, & Miller, 1993; Ginsburg & Opper, 1988).

How does all of this relate to Freddy Krueger's power to terrorize? For 5-year-olds, who have difficulty separating their perceptions from themselves (whose perceptions are on the "subject" side of the balance), how things appear is how they *are*. People are tiny ants, and Freddy Krueger is in the room with them! When perceptions "move over" and become part of the "object" side of the balance, as they do for school children, these children become aware not only of what they are seeing but of themselves seeing it, of watching a monster in a horror movie. Freddy Krueger is still scary, but at heart school children know they are reacting to a character in a movie. Adolescents' awareness that the villain in the movie is simply one of any number of monsters that could be imagined, that Freddy Krueger is the product of someone's imagination, makes it possible and even fun for them to think of ways to make him scarier.

These adolescents contradict Piaget's assumption that once formal thought emerges, individuals think logically all the time. Even though these young women are certainly aware of the health risks of smoking, their behavior does not reflect their ability to reason logically or to envision the long-term consequences of their actions.

Contextual Effects and Formal Thinking

Does differentiation progress at the same rate and take the same form independent of the larger context in which adolescents find themselves? Quite a lot of evidence suggests that it does not. Perhaps the first place in which to look for contextual influences on cognitive development is school.

Piaget believed that the changes he chronicled were not simply due to learning, but became possible only with the biological maturation of underlying mental structures. Yet Lavee Artman and Sorel Cahan (1993), working with large numbers of fourth-, fifth-, and sixth-graders, found that schooling contributed more to their success on certain Piagetian-type problems than did age.

The assumptions we bring to a problem, irrespective of how it may be presented to us, also affect the type of logic we bring to bear in solving a problem. These assumptions are formed through daily experiences with everyday objects. Consider the problem illustrated in Figure 4.6. People are told to pretend they are postal workers sorting letters. Their job is to determine whether the following rule has been broken: "If a letter is sealed, it has a 32-cent stamp on it" (i.e., If there is a P, then there is a Q). Subjects are told to select just those letters they would have to turn over to determine whether they broke the rule. Even adults have difficulty with problems of this type—with or without formal thought. The most frequent mistake

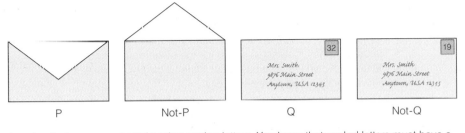

Imagine that you are a postal worker sorting letters. You know that sealed letters must have a
32-cent stamp. Among the letters that appear above, select just those you would need to turn
over to determine whether they break this rule. The answer appears at the end of the chapter.

FIGURE 4.6   Logical Thinking About a Concrete Problem. *Source:* Adapted from
P. C. Wason & P. N. Johnson-Laird. (1972). *Psychology of reasoning: Structure and content.* Cambridge, MA:
Harvard University Press.

is to pick P and Q even though Q gives no information about whether the
rule is broken. One has the tendency to check to see whether, if P is not
present, Q is not either. However, the initial premise says nothing about
what happens when P is *not* present; it only states what should be the case
when it *is* present (Wason & Johnson-Laird, 1972).

Perhaps reasoning is less than optimal in problems such as the above
simply because of their difficulty. Yet when adults are asked simple, even
though misleading, questions designed to test conservation of weight, many
still fail to reason in even a concrete operational way. Gerald Winer and
Chadd McGlone (1993) asked individuals questions such as "When do you
weigh more, when you are standing up or lying down (moving or being still;
running or walking)?" Approximately 70% of those who, moments before,
had correctly answered a more obvious misleading question gave at least one
wrong answer to the weight question, suggesting that their failure could not
be explained simply on the basis of acquiescing to an absurd situation.
Rather, when faced with a situation that is initially confusing, even adults
at times fall back on more intuitive forms of thinking, a tendency that becomes even more likely when considering the weight of their own body versus that of some other object (Winer, Craig, & Weinbaum, 1992).

Adolescents do not always test hypotheses in systematic and reasonable
ways. Depending on the context, logic can break down. Tschirgi (1980) gave
individuals stories to read such as the one in Figure 4.7. For some, the story
had a successful outcome ("The cake turned out great, it was so moist").
For others it did not ("The cake turned out just terrible; it was so runny").
Tschirgi found that, depending on the outcome, individuals evaluated hypotheses for why the cake turned out as it did in different ways.

A logician would tell us that the same strategy applies in either case.
The most logical approach is to attempt to disconfirm the hypothesis being considered by changing the condition presumably responsible for the
outcome, while holding everything else constant. In the example in Figure
4.7, this would mean selecting alternative (a). Adolescents follow this
approach with negative outcomes, for example, when the cake "turned out
terrible." But when the cake is delicious, they abandon the logic of

John decided to bake a cake. But he ran out of some ingredients. So:
- He used margarine instead of butter for the shortening;
- He used honey instead of sugar for the sweetening, and
- He used brown whole-wheat flour instead of regular white flour.

The cake turned out great; it was so moist.

John thought the reason the cake was so great was the honey. He thought that the type of shortening (butter or margarine) or the type of flour really didn't matter.

 = Great Cake

What should he do to prove this point?

(a) He can bake the cake again but use sugar instead of honey, and still use margarine and brown whole-wheat flour.

(b) He can bake the cake again but this time use sugar, butter, and regular flour.

(c) He can bake the cake again still using honey, but this time using butter and regular white flour.

FIGURE 4.7
Different Strategies, Based on Outcome, to Evaluate Hypotheses. *Source:* J. E. Tschirgi. (1980). Sensible reasoning: A hypothesis about hypotheses. *Child Development, 51,* 1–10.

philosophers: The desire to maintain the condition that led to success can override the simplicity of formal logic. Wason and Johnson-Laird (1972) also found that the type of reasoning one uses depends on what one is thinking about. It was easier for individuals to solve the logic problem when the alternatives referred to types of envelopes than when they were logical options simply referred to as P, Not-P, Q, and Not-Q.

Does practicing the
guitar develop intelli-
gence? The answer
depends on whether
intelligence is a single
innate capacity, or
one of several specific
abilities, such as musi-
cality or numerical
ability.

Although research indicates that thinking changes dramatically with
adolescence, it is equally clear that individual differences are large and that
even adolescents who use formal logic do not apply it in all situations. Some
critics of Piaget's constructive developmental approach suggest that measures of formal reasoning actually reflect the more general abilities that contribute to intelligence at all ages (Keating, 1980). This argument brings us
to a second approach to intellectual development, one that comes out of
the intellectual testing movement.

A PSYCHOMETRIC APPROACH TO INTELLIGENCE

Robert Sternberg, a psychologist at Yale University, tells an amusing story
that illustrates some of the difficulties in measuring intelligence using the
psychometric approach. A team of psychologists tested people from a Third
World country with some of the tasks typically included on standard tests
of intelligence. One of the tasks involved sorting pictures. In Western cultures, the most intelligent approach to this task is to sort categorically, to
put a picture of a robin under that of a bird, and so on. Cross-cultural com-

parisons such as this one frequently find that people from Third World nations are not as "intelligent" as those from Western countries.

The people in this study were no exception. Instead of sorting the pictures categorically, they sorted them functionally. For example, they placed the picture of the robin with that of a worm, explaining that robins eat worms. No amount of encouragement or hinting from the research team could get them to sort categorically. finally, in exasperation, one of the psychologists told them to sort the pictures the way someone who *wasn't* intelligent would do it. Each person executed a perfect categorical sort! These people were clearly intelligent enough to sort categorically. They just thought that it wasn't a smart way to sort (Baron & Sternberg, 1987).

Intelligence: What Is It?

Intelligence is a term that most of us use almost daily. Out of sheer familiarity, one might think it would be easy to define. But it is not. In fact, even experts in the field have come up with widely differing views of what it is. Yet most agree that intelligence allows us to profit from our experiences and adapt to our surroundings, and that it frequently involves abstract reasoning.

Differences among the experts as to the nature of intelligence are primarily between the "lumpers" and the "splitters," those who view intelligence as a single, general capacity versus those who view it as numerous specific abilities (Mayr, 1982).

The measures that we have—intelligence tests—are simply collections of questions that reflect the information and abilities of the average person in our society. Depending on which questions are included, people with different experiences will do either better or worse on the tests.

Figure 4.8 shows the percentage of individuals falling in each of seven classifications of intelligence. These percentages reflect the performance of nearly 2,000 people tested during the most recent standardization of the WAIS-R (Wechsler Adult Intelligence Scale-Revised), the most widely used intelligence scale for adults and adolescents 16 years old and older.[2] The **WAIS-R** is constructed so that the intelligence quotient for the average person at any age will be 100. Notice that performance is distributed relatively evenly above and below the average score; scores ranging from 90 to 109 are considered average. The figure shows the percentages of individuals falling at different points from the mean IQ of 100. Approximately two-thirds of all adults score between 85 and 115. Ninety-five percent score between 70 and 130, and over 99% score between 55 and 145 (Wechsler, 1981).

A Closer Look: The WAIS-R

One way of understanding intelligence is to take a look at what is measured by an intelligence test. We will use WAIS-R as our example, because it is ap-

---

[2]Widely-used scales for children and early adolescents are the Wexler Preschool and Primary Scale of Intelliegence-Revised (WPPSI-R), for ages 3–7, the Wexler Intelligence Scale for Children-Third Edition (WISC-III), for ages 6–16, and the Stanford Binet Intelligence Scale: Fourth Edition (SB:FE), which has been standardized for use with children as young as 2 years of age (Cohen, Serdlik & Phillips, 1996).

FIGURE 4.8
Percentage of Individuals and Intelligence Classifications at Different Points From the Mean IQ of 100

Source: D. Wechsler. (1981). *Wechsler Adult Intelligence Scale—Revised.* San Antonio, TX: Psychological Corporation.

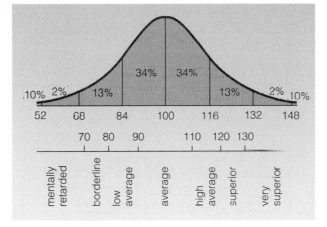

propriate for adolescents as well as adults and is one of the most commonly used measures of intelligence. The WAIS-R includes 11 subtests, grouped into Verbal and Performance Scales (described in Box 4.2). Despite these different scales, David Wechsler was a "lumper." Each scale contributes to an overall IQ score. His inclusion of a performance scale was an attempt to correct the heavy reliance of other measures on verbal items.

Rather than ask questions that reflect academic knowledge, such as "What is the distance between the earth and the sun?" Wechsler asked questions that reflect general information. Questions on the Information subtest, for instance, tap the type of information average people are expected to acquire on their own. Examples of such questions are "What is the distance between London and San Francisco?" and "How tall is the average American man?" (Wechsler, 1981).

Notice that members of some groups are more likely to have the information required to answer these questions than others are. Sehti, one of the adolescents in the introduction to this chapter, might be more familiar with the height of men in another culture than with that of men in the United States, for example. And Yuan-Pin might be able to estimate the distance between Peking and Bombay more accurately than the distance between London and San Francisco. In addition to information that is general knowledge in a culture, one also must be familiar with cultural expressions, and even with a cultural sense of humor. One must know, for example, that "The apple of one's eye" is not the same as "The pear of one's ear," and that our culture pokes fun at men and women in different ways than others. The henpecked husband is humorous in our culture, but not in all.

Questions are arranged in each subtest in order of increasing difficulty. A question is considered to be good if the frequency with which it is correctly answered increases with the intellectual level of those answering it. Not all questions discriminate equally well among all levels of ability. Some, for instance, nicely distinguish at the lower levels ("How many months are there in a year?") but not at higher levels. Other questions distinguish at higher levels ("What is the Koran?") but not at lower levels, being missed by nearly all individuals below a certain level of intelligence. It is interesting that as our culture includes more individuals from different ethnic and

Box 4.2 Subtests on the WAIS-R

VERBAL SCALE

1. **Information**
   Individuals answer questions requiring information that one would gain from living in a culture.
   - "How many weeks are there in a year?"
   - "How many miles is it from New York City to San Francisco?"

2. **Digit Span**
   Individuals hear a random string of digits, which they must repeat back in order. Performance reflects immediate memory.
   - 2—9—5—1—3—8

3. **Vocabulary**
   One must define words related to daily experience. Performance is highly related to academic performance.

4. **Arithmetic**
   One is given 14 arithmetic problems to solve. Quantitative reasoning and knowledge of basic arithmetic are reflected.
   - "If a rocky-road big scoop is 75 cents and you buy three, how much change will you get back from $5.00?"

5. **Comprehension**
   Individuals must answer simple questions designed to tap practical knowledge and judgment.
   - "Why would one boil water at a campsite before drinking it?"

6. **Similarities**
   One must tell how pairs of items are similar. The test reflects abstract thinking.
   - "In what way are a snake and a lizard alike?"

PERFORMANCE SCALE

7. **Picture Completion**
   Individuals look at pictures of common objects; they are to identify an important aspect of each one that is missing. Performance reflects visual alertness and attention to detail.

Box 4.2   (*continued*)

8. **Picture Arrangement**
   Subjects look at a set of cards printed with pictures. They must arrange the pictures so they tell a story. The test reflects understanding relations.

   [Figure 4.10 illustrates this type of task.]

9. **Block Design**
   One duplicates geometric patterns with a set of colored blocks. The test taps general analytic skills and correlates highly with general mental ability.

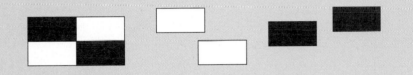

10. **Object Assembly**
    One must assemble picture puzzles of common objects. Visual-motor coordination underlies performance on this subtest.

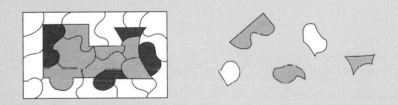

11. **Digital Symbol**
    One sees a row of boxes, each with a symbol that corresponds to a digit in a box beneath. One must fill completely the row of digits to reflect the code above. The test reflects attentiveness and persistence.

☆	→	←	●	$	●	←	☆	$	→
1	2	3	4	5					

Sources: Adapted from L. R. Aiken. (1987). *Assessment of intellectual functioning.* Boston: Allyn & Bacon. D. Wechsler. (1981). *Wechsler Adult Intelligence Scale—Revised.* New York: Psychological Corporation.

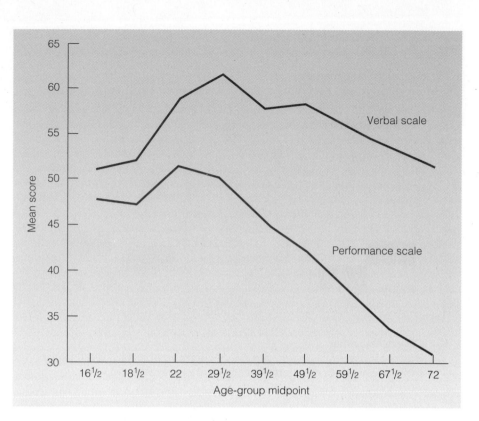

FIGURE 4.9
Changes With Age in
Performance on the
WAIS-R. *Source:* L. R.
Aiken. (1987). *Assessment
of intellectual functioning.*
Boston: Allyn & Bacon.

religious backgrounds, questions such as this last one may lose their discriminating power at the higher level, as they reflect a broader base of knowledge among the population in general.

Does Intelligence Change With Age?

Performance on measures of intelligence varies with age. Figure 4.9 shows these trends. Performance on the WAIS-R increases dramatically in late adolescence through the twenties and early thirties, after which it declines with age. Performance drops sharply on subtests of the Performance scale and considerably less so on subtests of the Verbal scale (Wechsler, 1981).

K. Warner Schaie, a "splitter," identifies six primary abilities that he has traced across the adult years. Some abilities, such as perceptual speed, peak in early adulthood, whereas others, such as numeric ability, peak in middle adulthood. All decline with age, though again at different rates and not all starting at the same time (Schaie & Willis, 1993). Such differences in the developmental courses of abilities have been taken as support for the position that they represent discrete forms of intelligence. The Research Focus, "Cross-Sectional and Sequential Designs," discusses the question of whether intelligence slips with age.

Crystallized and Fluid Intelligence   Two other "splitters," John Horn and Raymond Cattell (1967), distinguish two forms of intelligence, each with a different developmental course. **Crystallized intelligence** reflects the broad

Crystallized intelligence is expressed in knowing the rules, such as how a single element behaves in nature. But to excel in science, these adolescents must also have fluid intelligence, the ability to reason through complex processes and anticipate results.

base of knowledge people gain through living in their culture, including specific skills acquired in school. **Fluid intelligence** taps people's abilities to reason through situations on the spot, to use their heads. Fluid intelligence is thought to be biologically based and declines more markedly with age in adulthood than does crystallized intelligence, which reflects cultural learning (Schaie & Willis, 1993).

We began our discussion of intelligence with a warning that intelligence tests have an arbitrary quality to them. The questions they contain don't only tap the capacities with which one is born; they also tap a general knowledge gained by living in a culture. People from different cultures, though theoretically just as able, will not do quite as well as those from our own. If different questions were included, one that reflected their particular cultural experiences, their performance would improve, whereas that of the average North American would drop slightly. These differences do not reflect ability so much as the nature of the questions themselves. When adolescents from different cultures are tested in their own countries on equivalent tests of primary abilities, their performance is remarkably similar (Li, Sano, & Merwin, 1996). Adolescents' cultural backgrounds, then, can be expected to affect their perspective on and approach to problems.

Research Focus

Cross-Sectional and Sequential Designs: Does Intelligence Slip With Age?

With Michael Wapner

Does intelligence decline with age? When can adolescents expect to peak intellectually? Putting it more bluntly, just how many good years do they have ahead of them? And why can't we give them any straight answers to questions such as these?

Straight, unambiguous answers are possible only with research that allows us to rule out alternatives. In such research, investigators manipulate variables by randomly assigning individuals to the conditions they are observing. Why can't we say for certain whether intelligence increases, decreases, or stays the same with age? Simply put, age cannot be manipulated. Individuals come to the laboratory with a certain age; they cannot be assigned one. People who differ in chronological age—that is, are of different cohort groups—also differ in other ways, namely, in their social and historical backgrounds. These differences don't always have to affect the way they respond to the measures we are taking, but

they might. Cohorts are more likely to have similar cultural experiences than people of different ages. Adolescents today live in relatively plentiful times, and most grow up in urban or suburban settings. Adolescents born in 1930 grew up in the shadow of the Depression and were more likely to live in rural areas. Differences such as these appear in all sorts of attitudes and behaviors and can easily be confused with age changes. They are known as *cohort differences*.

Most of the studies finding that intelligence declines with age are cross-sectional. *Cross-sectional* research tests groups of individuals of different ages all at the same time. An obvious advantage to this approach is that one need not wait around while individuals grow older. A disadvantage is that differences between the groups can reflect either age changes or cohort differences. In contrast to longitudinal research, in which age is confounded with times of measurement, cross-sectional research confounds age with cohort differences.

Is there any way around the difficulties inherent in cross-sectional and longitudinal designs? *Sequential designs* provide a solution. These designs combine cross-sectional and longitudinal approaches. They test several cohort groups at several times of measurement. In a way, the

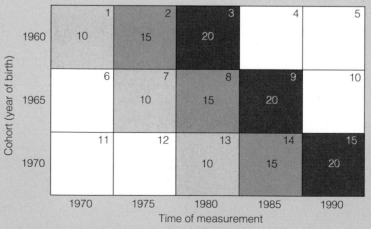

A Sequential Design
The cells are numbered in the upper-right hand corner. The numbers in the centers of the cells are ages.

Research Focus (*continued*)

sequential design can be thought of as a number of longitudinal studies, each starting with a different age group.

You might ask, "Won't *both* cohort and time of measurement effects be present?" Yes. But because they are, we can measure them and estimate their contribution. By subtracting these estimates from our estimates of age differences, we can statistically isolate these confounds from genuine age changes. The resulting design appears in the figure.

By looking at the cells that form the diagonals, we can compare 10-year-olds with 15-year-olds and 20-year-olds. Cells 1, 7, and 13 are groups of 10-year-olds. Cells 2, 8, and 14 are 15-year-olds. And cells 3, 9, and 15 are 20-year-olds. "That's our age effect," you note. Not so fast. Even though the means of the diagonals reflect the performance of different ages, they can also contain cohort effects (e.g., any differences that might exist between 10-year-olds who were born in 1960 versus 1965 versus 1970) as well as differences due to time of measurement (depending on whether they were tested in 1970, 1975, or 1980). If all we had were the diagonals, we couldn't say anything about the relationship of intelligence to age.

But sequential designs give us more. We have vertical and horizontal means as well. The first of these, the column means, allow us to estimate differences due to time of measurement, and the

second, the row means, the effect for cohorts. Comparing performance measured in 1975 (cells 2 and 7), with performance measured in 1980 (cells 3, 8, and 13), with that in 1985 (cells 9 and 14) provides an estimate of the amount of variability in intellectual functioning that is contributed by time of measurement. Differences among row means allow us to estimate the size of a cohort effect. By subtracting each of these estimates from the diagonals, we end up with an estimate of age effects.

Does intelligence slip with age? Sequential designs find that age effects are minimal. Simply put, adolescents can expect to hold on to their smarts as they enter adulthood. But what shall we make of the cross-sectional data indicating (erroneously as it turns out) that intelligence declines in adulthood? Obviously, some measures of intelligence confound the period in which one lives, the historical context, with attributes of the individual. The result of that confusion is to stigmatize older people. Sound familiar? This problem is reminiscent of similar complaints that intelligence tests penalize ethnic and racial minorities because they confound cultural and economic conditions with attributes of the individual.

Source: A. Anastasi. (1988). *Psychological testing* (6th ed.). New York: Macmillan.

Are There Social-Class, Ethnic, and Racial Differences in Intelligence?

Imagine the following scene of a teenager taking the Picture Arrangement subtest of the WAIS-R. She is Japanese American. The examiner places a set of four cartoon drawings on the table in front of her and tells her to arrange them so that they tell a story (Figure 4.10). One drawing shows a man fishing by a river. A second shows a woman pointing at a garden while the man looks on. The third shows the man digging and discovering a worm, and the fourth shows him getting out the gardening tools. The girl tries first one arrangement, then another. None seems right to her. Finally the time runs out. You are puzzled. Why was this difficult for her? You quickly arrange the pictures mentally in this order: the second, the fourth, the third, the first. The story? The man has been told by his wife to garden, gets out the tools, discovers a worm as he works, and, reminded of more pleasant pursuits, goes off fishing. It's easy for most North Americans—unless they

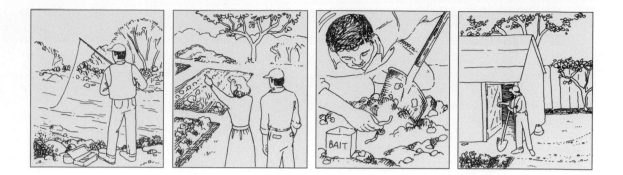

FIGURE 4.10

Example of a Type of Item in the Picture Arrangement Subtest of the WAIS-R

happen to be of Japanese descent. In Japan, wives don't give chores to their husbands. This girl knew that, and the pictures made no sense to her (Wechsler, 1981).

Performance on measures such as the one above reflect not only a person's ability but also the extent to which that person's background is similar to that of the dominant culture. If one belongs to certain minorities, one is not as likely to do as well as someone from the dominant culture. Differences exist even among individuals within the same culture but from different social classes. Adolescents from lower-income homes can score as much as 15 to 20 points below their age-mates from the middle class. Ethnic and racial differences can be equally as large, and the latter have prompted considerable debate.

Arthur Jensen (1969, 1985) argues that up to 80% of one's intelligence is determined by heredity, and that racial differences in intelligence are largely genetic. Most other experts place the contribution of heredity considerably below this figure, estimating its contributions to be about equal to those of environment. These investigators maintain that enriched environments should actually raise a child's IQ and impoverished ones should lower it. Scarr and Weinberg (1983), for instance, report that Black children born to lower-income parents and adopted by White upper-middle-income parents scored an average of 20 points higher than children who remained in lower-income homes. Even if the genetic component of intelligence *were* closer to Jensen's estimate than most experts believe, cultural differences could still account for very large differences in IQ. A fictitious adolescent with an IQ of 100 (up to 80% of which Jensen believes to be inherited) would be expected to have an IQ as high as 120 if reared under the best of conditions, or as low as 80 under the worst—a difference of 40 IQ points due to environment!

Thomas Sowell, a behavioral scientist at Stanford University, points out that the performance of minorities today closely resembles that of other minorities in the early 1900s, whether of European or non-European descent, before they assimilated into the culture (Sowell, 1978). Sowell focuses on African Americans, highlighting three distinct patterns that characterize their performance. He notes first that they do most poorly on the most abstract items on the tests. Investigators have concluded from this pattern that lower performance is genetically based, because abstract items should not

Will standardized performance tests fully reveal this young woman's abilities? Many researchers believe that such tests may be weighted with questions based on experiences of the dominant culture and that the scores from such tests may not accurately represent the capabilities of adolescents from nondominant cultures.

reflect information specific to a culture. Sowell notes that European American ethnic groups experienced a similar difficulty with abstract items when they immigrated to this country. Yet when members of these same ethnic groups were tested several generations later, they performed no differently from the population in general on the same items.

Sowell identifies a second pattern in the test performance of African Americans: a decline in the intelligence of children as they age. Again, this decline occurred among children of European immigrants. finally, Sowell compares the performance of African American women with that of women from European American ethnic groups when they first immigrated. All scored higher than the men in their ethnic groups. This pattern exists even though intelligence does not differ appreciably between men and women for the population in general. Gender differences in intellectual functioning among early immigrants show the same pattern: higher scores for women. Recent comparisons with Mexican Americans and Puerto Ricans also show the same trend.

Sowell suggests that degree of assimilation, not racial or ethnic differences, best predicts a group's level of functioning on measures of intelligence. Those groups that are upwardly mobile—one of our best indices of assimilation—show marked increases in intelligence from one generation to the next. Groups that assimilate more slowly do not show an equivalent increase with time.

One last set of differences deserves our attention before we leave this approach to intelligence. These differences concern the sexes. It is only natural to ask whether males and females differ in their intellectual functioning.

Are There Gender Differences in Intelligence?

Does intelligence differ in females and males? Popular belief holds that it does. We hear, for instance, that males are more logical and females more intuitive, that males are better at numbers and females at language. Some differences have been noted, but they are not large nor are they always the ones stereotypes would lead us to expect (Lips, 1997).

Before we look more closely, keep in mind that there are no gender differences in overall intelligence. In fact, intelligence tests are constructed so that there will not be. Questions that are answered more accurately by females are balanced by other questions that favor males. There is also no evidence linking intellectual functioning to specific biological factors, such as prenatal hormones or the presence of the X or Y chromosome, that would differ for either sex (Lips, 1997).

Several specific gender differences exist. The first of these is verbal ability. Females do somewhat better on measures of verbal reasoning and fluency, comprehending written passages, and understanding logical relations (Li, Sano, & Merwin, 1996). This difference first appears in infancy as children learn to speak. Boys soon catch up, and the difference disappears by about age 3. Performance during the grade-school years shows no differences. By early adolescence, girls again perform better on measures of verbal ability. This difference persists throughout the remainder of adolescence and adulthood. Despite the consistency of the findings from one study to the next, the difference attributable to gender is always quite small, accounting for less than 1% of the variability between scores (Hyde, 1981).

Gender differences in spatial ability also exist. Males do better on tests that require one to mentally manipulate things or remember a visual figure in order to find it in a more complex figure (Schaie & Willis, 1993). Most research has found this difference to be small, accounting for less than 5% of the variability among individuals. A comparison of males' and females' spatial abilities found some measures to account for 15% of the variability among individuals of either sex (Krasnoff, 1989). However, none of the published differences are large enough to explain the preponderance of males in professions that might tap these abilities, such as engineering or architecture (Hyde, 1981).

A third gender difference favors males: math. Differences do not appear until early adolescence; then boys begin to do better than girls on measures of quantitative ability. The overall difference, once again, is small, accounting for 1% to 5% of the variability among adolescents. Despite the slight advantage held by boys, girls may still get better grades in math at school. Some studies have found that among the most able students in mathematics, those with the higher scores are more likely to be boys. Their findings are dramatic, yet they should be interpreted with caution. Comparisons at the very highest levels of ability often involved only small numbers of adolescents (Benbow & Stanley, 1980, 1982, 1983). Carol Dweck (1986) interprets these differences to reflect gender differences in motivational patterns that occur when adolescents encounter new and initially confusing material (see Chapter 7). Schaie and Willis (1993) report differences in adulthood, although only on some measures.

Being good at math is expected more of adolescent males than adolescent females in this culture. Differences in mathematical ability emerge in adolescence, when individuals become aware of cultural sex roles. Also, gender differences disappear when prior mathematical experience is controlled. Of course, it is possible that by limiting comparisons to samples of girls who have had as much mathematical experience as boys, one is drawing samples that are not representative of girls in general. Nonetheless, the overall difference between males and females is so small as to be negligible, and certainly does not allow one to predict success or failure in mathematics courses in school or, later, in a mathematics-related profession on the basis of gender. One authority on gender differences pointedly asks,

> Has it been our intent to divide the population into the pinks and the blues and to develop one set of cognitive skills in the pinks and another set in the blues? If this is not our intent, the educational and social practices that have occurred "naturally" will need reexamination. (Sherman, 1978, p. 66)

The psychometric approach to intelligence has done much to further our understanding of intelligence. A more recent approach, to which we turn next, has contributed considerably to our understanding of the processes that underlie intellectual functioning in all individuals, regardless of sex or culture.

Are males more logical and females more intuitive? Are males better at numbers and females better at language? Does any difference matter between males and females, or between any two individuals regardless of sex, when it comes to mastering the computer?

As adolescents grow older, they can retrieve items from memory more quickly, use memory strategies more effectively, and because of greater content knowledge, assimilate new information more readily.

BEYOND IQ: INFORMATION PROCESSING

Have you ever caught yourself missing what someone just said after hearing your name mentioned in another conversation? Or have you ever asked a person to repeat something, only to find you know what that person said before hearing it again? How many times have you repeated a phone number until you could write it down, or noticed that you know what you *don't* know in addition to what you *do* know?

Robert Siegler (1991), summarizing two fundamental characteristics of cognition, points out that thinking is both limited and flexible. Simply put, we are limited in just how much we can attend to at any point in time, as the examples above illustrate; and we are very good at adapting the way we think to the demands of the task or the moment, also illustrated above. With age, we develop increasingly efficient processes for overcoming these cognitive limitations.

Three memory systems, the *structural characteristics* of the information-processing system, exist at all ages. These are sensory memory, short-term memory, and long-term memory. We see little change in these systems from one type of task to the next or from one person to the next. Other aspects of information processing vary with the task and with the person, reflecting the particular *processes* that may or may not be carried out.

Sensory memory is very brief, lasting for half a second or less. This is the memory that allows you to reconstruct that lost snippet of conversation you asked someone to repeat. **Short-term memory,** though longer, is also brief for memory (lasting under a minute) and limited in how much it can hold. You can manage only about seven items—about the size of a phone number—without losing some. **Long-term memory** lasts from a minute to a lifetime. Because of the vast information it contains, you need to categorize. Scanning the categories allows you to know what you know and what you don't. Research suggests that few important changes occur with age in these three structural aspects of memory, whereas age has a dramatic effect on the processes involved with memory (Siegler, 1991).

Just as computers differ in capacity, speed, and in the types of software they can handle, information-processing theorists think of intellectual functioning as changing with age in comparable ways. Four factors thought to contribute to developmental change are (1) basic processes, such as the speed with which information is processed, (2) the use of strategies, (3) metacognitive skills, such as knowing what one knows or needs to know, and (4) knowledge, or the actual information that is stored (Brown & De-Loache, 1978; Siegler, 1991).

Sensory memory appears to have the same capacity and duration limitations for people of all ages. And because it is so brief, with little time to consciously process information, few developmental changes occur in sensory memory (Siegler, 1991).

Information is held only briefly in short-term memory unless one does something to keep the material alive, such as repeating it over and over to oneself. This procedure is called **rehearsal** and illustrates the use of a memory *strategy*. As one might expect, given the limits of how many items one can repeat without losing track of some of them, short-term memory is only helpful in remembering a few items at a time. Unlike either sensory or long-term memory, we are usually aware of the items in short-term memory.

Strategies are not equally effective at all ages. Young children, for example, are not likely to repeat items in order to remember them. Even older children do not rehearse as effectively as adolescents, but tend to repeat each item to be remembered in isolation from the others. Adolescents repeat each new word with the last few in the list. The latter strategy leads to much better recall (Ornstein, Naus, & Liberty, 1975).

In addition to strategies, changes in *basic capacities,* such as speed of processing, account for differences in cognition. As children get older, they get faster at retrieving items from short-term memory (Hale, Fry, & Jessie, 1993; Kail, 1991). Speed of processing, in turn, influences the effectiveness of strategies such as rehearsal, making it possible for more words to be refreshed before returning again to the first (Kail, 1992).

Information is semantically **encoded,** or stored according to meaning, in long-term memory. To hold onto long-term information, one must relate it to things one already knows. Even though long-term memory has no time or capacity limitations, there is no guarantee that one will always be able to use the information that is encoded in it. Retrieving information is the biggest problem. Imagine misplacing a book in a large city in a public library. How likely are you to recover the book if you can't remember which part of the library you were in when you put it down? The book is likely still there, but you can't retrieve it without using the system by which it was coded.

We also find age differences in long-term memory, a number of which reflect speed of processing—in this case, how quickly one can reach and retrieve information as it is needed. Items stored in long-term memory, because they are encoded according to meaning, are named and stored by category. In one experiment, 11- and 19-year-olds responded to pairs of letters that appeared on a computer screen by indicating whether they were the "same" or "different." The letters could differ either in name or in appearance, that is, whether they were typed in uppercase or lowercase. Subjects who were told to respond according to the physical appearance of the letters had to perceptually scan their features—Are they the same size? Do they both have right angles?—but did not need to locate them in memory by name. Subjects who were told to respond to the letters categorically, according to name regardless of how they were typed, had an additional step that involved retrieving information (the letters' names) from long-term memory. It takes longer to respond on the basis of a name (or category) than on physical appearance. Because this step involves retrieving information from long-term memory, it also shows that older subjects needed less time to retrieve information from long-term memory than younger ones (Hale, Fry, & Jessie, 1993).

Age differences in long-term memory also include knowledge about one's memory. Early adolescents know more than children about their memories, and they use their knowledge to monitor what they do. This knowledge is called **metamemory.** Adolescents know the limits of their memories; for example, just how long a passage can be before they must reread it in order to remember it, or whether they are familiar with a name and hence likely to recall information about it. They know what strategies work best for them, are aware of using them, and realize how much they help. In contrast, younger children must often be told to use a strategy and then be shown how it has helped in order to continue to use it (Siegler, 1991).

In addition to developmental changes in strategies, basic processes, and metacognition, *knowledge* also changes with age. Adolescents simply know more than younger children. This knowledge provides a context for assimilating new information, increasing the likelihood that relevant features will be processed and encoded. Because information can be related more easily to what one already knows, it has more meaning and is more easily remembered.

STERNBERG'S COMPONENTIAL INTELLIGENCE

Compared to younger children, adolescents process information faster and use more intelligent and efficient strategies. They also know more about the limitations of their memories, and adapt their strategies to compensate for anticipated failings. Robert Sternberg, a psychologist at Yale, accounts for these differences, as well as others, by analyzing intellectual functioning in terms of the processes, or components, that operate on information. Sternberg identifies three kinds of components: metacomponents, performance components, and knowledge-acquisition components (Sternberg, 1984).

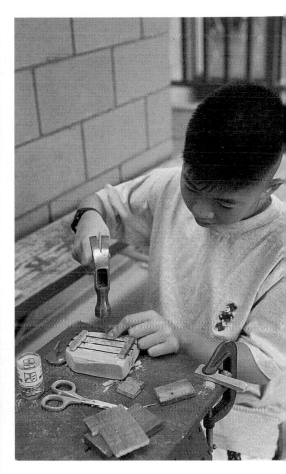

According to the research of Howard
Gardner, these adolescents are demonstrating different types of intelligence.
Gardner has identified seven forms
of intelligence, including not only the
logical-mathematical domain measured by IQ tests but also interpersonal, bodily-kinesthetic, and spatial
intelligence.

Metacomponents decide when more information is needed and whether a particular strategy should be used or another one constructed, and monitor and keep track of one's progress. *Performance components* carry out the actual procedures selected by the metacomponents. If metacomponents are the supervisors, performance components are the actual workers. Performance components might decipher information in sensory memory, encoding this as names of letters. They might compare elements, inferring similarities or differences, or apply a procedure completed in one domain to another aspect of the problem. *Knowledge-acquisition components* acquire new information as it is needed. They sift through information, picking out that which is relevant to the problem and integrating it with what one already knows, giving it new meaning.

We can apply this analysis to the way people solve problems. Sternberg studied analogies because they reveal interesting age differences. An example of an analogy is the following: "Swift is to *Gulliver's Travels* as Pope is to: (a) the *Baedecker,* (b) 'The Rape of the Lock', (c) the Vatican." To construct an analogy, one must choose the term that completes the second pair so that the two terms bear the same relationship to each other as the terms in the first pair.

To begin, one must encode each item: Does "Swift" refer to speed, or is it someone's name? (Encoding is a performance component.) The word *Travels* suggests the first alternative, and you know that the *Baedecker* is a travel guide. But then what is Pope? You may decide at this point that you need more information (a metacomponent) and search your memory for anything related to travel. You remember that *Gulliver's Travels* is the name of a book; then Swift could be the name of its author. Notice that one uses inference (another performance component) to determine the relationship between the first two terms. Encoding Swift as an author's name would mean that Pope is the name of an author. This last step has involved another performance component, mapping, or using the relationship between the first two terms to establish a relationship between the last two. Thus the fourth term must refer to something that Pope wrote. This extension rules out the Vatican, and because the *Baedecker* travel guide bears the name of its author, you are left with "The Rape of the Lock." You justify your selection by noting that the terms are all capitalized, as they would be in a title, and respond with alternative (b).

People of all ages use the same components to construct analogies, but spend different amounts of time on each (Sternberg & Rifkin, 1979). Adolescents and adults spend proportionately more time encoding the items than doing any of the other steps, whereas children spend relatively little time encoding. How does this fact relate to the characteristics of adolescent thought we reviewed earlier? Recall that adolescents tend to think of all the possible forms something might assume before they begin to work with any of them. They generate a world of possibilities, whereas children latch on to the first thing that comes to mind, their time for encoding being relatively brief. Sternberg also finds that with age, people spend much more time planning how to solve a problem than actually carrying out the steps (Sternberg, 1981, 1984). Once again, this difference reflects the tendency of adolescents to generate a strategy, and contrasts with the tendency of children to jump right in and move things about.

Notice, too, that analogies might be difficult for children because they require one to find the appropriate class for each term and then map the relationship between the classes of one set to those of the other. This higher-order, or abstract, form of thought awaits adolescence. Most children have as much success with analogies as they do in relating horses to goldfish (Sternberg, 1984).

Sternberg's componential analysis gives us an expanded view of intelligence. Rather than ranking one person relative to another in terms of a single number, such as IQ, we get a picture of intelligence at work: setting priorities, allocating resources, encoding information, monitoring feedback, and so on. But is it a single intelligence that works for us, or does intelligence take more than one form?

GARDNER'S SEVEN FACETS OF THE MIND

Howard Gardner, a psychologist who has written extensively on the development of intellect and creativity, proposes not one but seven forms of intelligence: musical, bodily-kinesthetic, logical-mathematical, linguistic, spatial, interpersonal, and intrapersonal. Gardner, like others, defines intelligence in terms of one's ability to solve problems as they arise, but the range of problems that he accepts as legitimate for the study of intelligence is much broader than it is for others (Gardner, 1983).

Gardner points out that most measures of intelligence tap a limited range of abilities, which he identifies as logical-mathematical. Because these measures are also good at predicting success at school, they continue to be used. But what about problems that don't call for logical-mathematical analysis, such as finding our way back to a parking lot in a new area of town, or recognizing the composer of a piece of music? Do these tasks call upon intelligence? Do musicians, athletes, or surgeons have more of some talent in common than the rest of us? Gardner would answer yes to both.

Of course, one could list endless problems or talents and claim a separate intelligence for each one. Gardner uses several criteria to isolate legitimate intellectual domains. He points out that a domain must be universal to all humans and should show development with age. Each intelligence should be capable of being expressed in its own symbol system, for example, words for language, equations for mathematics, or notes for music (Walters & Gardner, 1986).

Evidence for separate intellectual domains also comes from child prodigies, idiot savants, and people who have suffered brain damage. In each case we can see an uneven profile of abilities. Prodigies such as Mozart or Yehudi Menuhin showed musical genius at an early age, yet remained quite ordinary in other domains. Cases have been reported of autistic children who could perform rapid mental calculations yet not be able to carry on a conversation or dress themselves. Similarly, people who have suffered brain trauma may have some areas of functioning spared (Gardner, 1983). Table 4.1 shows Gardner's seven forms of intelligence and corresponding potential professions.

TABLE 4.1   Gardner's Seven Forms of Intelligence and Corresponding
Potential Professions

Form of Intelligence	Potential Professions
Musical	Musician
	Music teacher
Bodily-kinesthetic	Dancer
	Athlete
Logical-mathematical	Scientist
	Mathematician
	Teacher
Linguistic	Interpreter
Spatial	Artist
	Architect
	Landscape designer
Interpersonal (understanding others)	Psychologist
	Counselor
Intrapersonal (understanding the self)	Poet
	Writer

Source: H. Gardner. (1983). *Frames of mind.* New York: Basic Books.

Gardner anticipates objections to labeling these domains as intelligence. But he replies that nothing is sacred about the word *intelligence*. His choice of the term over other equally suitable ones, in fact, is deliberate. It emphasizes his point that present measures of intelligence are limited because they place logical-mathematical and linguistic abilities on a pedestal above other abilities, such as musical and interpersonal ones. In doing so, our measures of intelligence reflect our culture's bias in favor of logical and verbal abilities over abilities such as kinesthetic or artistic ones. Gardner argues that to call one type of ability "intelligence" and another "talent" reflects this bias. He challenges us to consider them all talents or to consider them all intelligence (Gardner, 1983).

Practical Intelligence

Gardner is not alone in viewing present measures of intelligence as overly narrow and related more to academic than real life experiences. Some psychologists speak of a *practical intelligence,* which they distinguish from the academic intelligence tapped by intelligence tests. Neisser (1976) defines this type of intelligence as "responding appropriately in terms of one's long-range and short-range goals, given the actual facts of the situation as one discovers them" (p. 137). He points out that the problems one must solve on tests that tap academic intelligence share a number of features: They are designed by someone else, are usually not very interesting, and have nothing to do with daily experience. Also, most test problems are well defined; they have a single answer and only one way of arriving at it (Wagner & Sternberg, 1986). In contrast, practical intelligence applies when one must discover the problem, instead of having it defined by someone else. Another difference is that finding the solution is frequently pleasurable. finally, usually a number of approaches will work, each leading to a slightly different solution.

How much has our view of intelligence been influenced by the tests we use to measure it? Probably too much. Even though these tests can predict academic success, they often have little or no connection to other areas of life. Nothing illustrates this last point better than adolescents themselves, who may reach a pinnacle of intellectual achievement as measured by tests of intelligence, only to be pulled up short by the simplest of life's situations. Despite arriving at the cutting edge of thought, adolescents frequently nick themselves in the process.

THOUGHT AND THE ADOLESCENT

Pseudostupidity

Many of the intellectual advances of early adolescent thought have their down side. The ability to hold a problem in mind and consider it from all possible perspectives occasionally leads teenagers to make things more complicated than they actually are. David Elkind (1978), a psychologist who writes extensively on thinking in childhood and adolescence, suggests that frequently teenagers fail to see the obvious not because the task is too hard for them, but because they have made a simple task more complicated than it actually is. He refers to this tendency as **pseudostupidity.** While a teenager is mentally ticking off all the oddball but nonetheless possible alternatives, someone else usually comes up with the obvious. Teenagers can feel stupid, asking themselves, "Why didn't I think of that?"

Early adolescents also frequently read complex motives into situations where none exist. A simple request such as, "Would you hand me the paper on your way out?" can be viewed with skeptical eyes. The teenager may wonder, "Is this just another attempt to control?" To avoid being controlled, the adolescent may consider refusing, but may also suspect that the need to refuse is merely another response to control. Neither able to comply nor to refuse, the teenager shoots back an angry remark to the effect that the news isn't worth the ink it takes to print it and storms out, leaving the parent to wonder what would have been done with something as loaded as "How was your day?"

An Imaginary Audience

One of the hallmarks of adolescent thought is the ability to think in the abstract, and nothing is more abstract than thought itself. Adolescents can think about thinking, not only their own thoughts but those of others. This ability can bring its own problems. Elkind (1967, 1985) assumes that this

Continuity and
Diversity in
Early Adolescent
Development

Adolescents assume that everyone is as preoccupied with them as they are with themselves. This self-focused perception often leads to extreme self-consciousness and an intense need for privacy as well as a feeling of being unique and special.

ability underlies a new form of egocentrism in adolescence. Early adolescents frequently lose perspective as to what concerns them and what concerns others. Because so many of their concerns focus on themselves, they can have the feeling that others, too, are thinking about them. Elkind refers to this loss of perspective as the **imaginary audience.** Adolescents can have the feeling that every eye is on them and every thought is about them. The imaginary audience may explain adolescents' exaggerated feelings of self-consciousness, as well as their intense need for privacy.

Very few of us command the type of attention that adolescents feel they capture. Those who do are special; they are political figures, athletes, entertainment personalities, or in some other way notable. The imaginary audience gives adolescents this same feeling of specialness. Elkind (1978) calls this feeling the **personal fable.** It is a belief that we are different and special, and that what happens to others won't happen to us. Elkind reminds us that this story we tell ourselves isn't true.

The personal fable can have some very personal consequences for adolescents. One is a confusion over what they have in common with others and what is genuinely unique to themselves. Confusions such as this lead to the belief that no one else can understand their feelings, because they are the only ones to have ever felt this way. It's not unusual, for example, for early adolescents to tell their parents that they couldn't possibly understand how it feels to be in love!

Another consequence is a mistaken assumption that everyone else shares their concerns. Jim may feel that his nose is too big for the rest of his face and not want to go anywhere because he's afraid he'll be kidded about it. In fact, no one else notices his nose or particularly cares what size it is. Convincing him of this, however, may be next to impossible. Adolescents caught in this form of the personal fable are not dissuaded by reasoning. Elkind suggests agreeing with them. If one were to agree with Jim that his nose was too big, he might end up defending himself.

Elkind (1978) suggests that the personal fable explains many of the tragic cases of adolescents who appear to be self-destructive. Their behavior may not be motivated as much by a desire to destroy themselves as by their belief that what they see happening to others won't happen to them; that because they are unique, they are invulnerable to the events that touch others' lives.

The capacity of adolescents to catch glimpses of themselves in the eyes of others may be important to gaining a sense of themselves. Erikson (1968) speaks of identity formation as a process by which adolescents come to see themselves as individuals and at the same time as members of a social group. Even while assessing their individual worth, adolescents use the standards and norms shared by members of their social group. How they see themselves will reflect the way they measure up in the eyes of others. The ability of adolescents to examine their thoughts and to imagine the thoughts of others underlies a new awareness of their own separateness from others and of what they have in common with others through shared values and behaviors.

New Emotions

How one feels depends on the interpretations one gives to experience. "Did that person just brush me off, or simply fail to notice that I was going to say something?" Depending on which interpretation one gives, the encounter can occasion either feelings of irritation or no feelings in particular. Intellectual development in adolescence makes it possible for teenagers to react emotionally in new ways. Children focus on the immediate elements of the situation: To a compliment they react with pleasure; to a present, with happiness. Adolescents do all this and more.

Adolescents can consider what a situation might mean as well as the way it appears. By being able to turn something around in their minds, they can assign more than the obvious meaning to social encounters. Adolescents do not always complicate life in this way, but they do so more than children and also more than most adults. A compliment can be the occasion for anger if seen as an attempt to win a favor. Or a present can cause depression if seen as an emotional bribe. Adolescents also experience emotions that are relatively foreign to children; they get high on themselves, moody, depressed, or elated (Hirsch, Paolitto, & Reimer, 1979). Unlike children, adolescents relate their feelings to their experience of themselves as well as to the events that may prompt the feelings, adding an extra level of magnification to their view of the world.

One evening during a discussion, parents may suddenly realize that their adolescent's arguments are better constructed and more difficult to refute. Her improved ability at argumentation may at times be frustrating, but it is also a sign that she is learning to manage her emotions.

Arguing

The ability of adolescents to consider the possibilities in any situation affects more than their emotions. An immediate consequence is that adolescents can argue better than children can. To carry out an argument, whether in a debating class at school or with a parent in the kitchen, one must come up with ideas for or against something. Adolescents are not limited, as are children, to testing their ideas against facts; they can test them against other ideas. (Remember the experiment with the green and red poker chips?) This new ability makes it possible for adolescents to argue for or against an idea regardless of whether they actually believe in it. The test of the argument is whether it has an inner logic. Children are limited to arguing either for things they believe in or against those they do not. The only test they can apply is to compare what they say with how things really are for them—how they feel, or what they believe.

Because of their literal approach, children cannot consider that a statement could mean something other than it says it does: It's simply taken at face value. A father's complaint, "If we had no dandelions, this would be a fine lawn" will bring a response of "But we have lots of dandelions, Dad," or "I like our lawn." Adolescents can consider statements about things that are contrary to the way they presently are or about things that don't exist. They can imagine a lawn that is free of dandelions, or even a lawn of *nothing but* dandelions. Perhaps this ability to divorce thought from fact, to think in ideals, even when these are counter to fact, provides the basis for the new ability of adolescents to plan and to gain new perspectives on themselves, their families, and their friends.

Doubt and Skepticism

Prior to formal thought, children believe that knowledge comes simply with exposure to the facts, never considering that factual information can be interpreted in more than one way. As a consequence, differences of opinion are treated as one person being wrong and the other one right. With formal thought, adolescents realize that what they have regarded as truth is simply one fix on reality, and that other equally compelling interpretations are possible. The result can be a profound skepticism in which they come to doubt the possibility of ever knowing anything in this "newly created world of wholesale uncertainty" (Boyes & Chandler, 1992).

Understanding Others

Adolescents gradually become better able to understand others as they become able to consider another person's perspective. Robert Selman (1976, 1980) outlines several levels in the development of **social understanding** (Table 4.2), reflecting differences in one's ability to infer the views of another and to coordinate that view with one's own (Small, 1990). At the highest level, level 4, one can infer how another might be thinking *and* anticipate how that person will react to one's reactions to them. An adolescent, for example, might get angry with her friend upon hearing that the friend used cocaine after swearing he'd stay off it, but may keep her anger to herself, guessing that her friend is also afraid and angry with himself and will not confide in her in the future if she loses her temper. Compare that type of understanding with that of a young child at the first of these levels, level 0, who would unthinkingly assume that others feel and think as she does.

TABLE 4.2 Selman's Levels of Social Understanding		
Level	Name	Age
0	Egocentric viewpoint	Early childhood
1	Social-informational	Ages 6 to 8
2	Self-reflective	Ages 8 to 10
3	Mutual	Ages 10 to 12
4	Social and conventional system	Ages 12 to 15 and older

Source: R. L. Selman. (1980). *The growth of interpersonal understanding.* New York: Academic Press.

Considering the perspective of another person reflects more general role-taking abilities. Selman speaks of these as understanding "the self and others as subjects, . . . [reacting] to others as like the self, and . . . to the self's behavior from the other's point of view" (Selman & Byrne, 1974, p. 803). Prior to being able to consider another's perspective, young children do not realize that others' thoughts and feelings are different from their own. Nor do they understand the relationship between a person's actions and that person's feelings. Selman calls the lack of perspective that characterizes early childhood an *egocentric viewpoint* (level 0).

As thought becomes more flexible (from ages 6 to 8, with the beginning of concrete operational thought), older children realize that another person might view a situation differently than they do, but they cannot imagine that the other person could understand how they feel. Children at this level assume that they would have to tell the other person how they feel for the other to know. At this level, they can observe themselves or the other, but are not aware that the other can also observe them. Selman calls this initial awareness the *social-informational* level, or level 1.

At the *self-reflective* level, level 2 (ages 8 to 10), children are able to put themselves in the other's place and understand their feelings, realizing that the other can understand theirs as well. Thus, in addition to observing themselves or the other person, they can observe the other observing them. With this, they can evaluate their own actions from the other's point of view. They still can't coordinate that view with their own and consider a situation from both points of view. They are not able, in other words, to step outside the situation and see the interaction as a third person might.

At the *mutual* level, level 3, of role taking (ages 10 to 12), early adolescents can see things from both their own and the other's perspective, and understand that the other person can do the same. The adolescent "discovers that both self and other can consider each party's point of view simultaneously and mutually . . . [and knows that each] can put himself in the other's place and . . . view himself from that vantage point before 'deciding' how to react" (Selman, 1976, p. 805). This third-person perspective makes it possible for early adolescents to reflect upon the self, to see themselves as they might appear to others.

At level 4 (12 to 15 and older), the third-person perspective becomes generalized and reflects adolescents' understanding of social conventions and laws. Rather than viewing a situation simply from the eyes of another person such as a parent or teacher, adolescents see that interactions are guided by social rules. They realize that because all members of the society understand the rules, individuals can regulate their interactions regardless of the particular points of view or experiences of those involved. Selman calls this last perspective the *social and conventional system*.

Selman finds that individual adolescents progress through these levels at different rates (Selman & Byrne, 1974). As a consequence, some may be able to adopt a third-person perspective in dealings with friends (level 3) while others of the same age may not yet understand that their friends can appreciate their point of view unless they tell them how they feel (level 2). Research suggests that a majority of preadolescents function at level 2 (about 60%), and that level 3 understanding does not characterize the social understanding of most adolescents until mid- to late adolescence (Selman, 1980; Selman & Byrne, 1974).

Selman's levels of social cognition give us another way of understanding the imaginary audience. Elkind assumes that the latter occurs with formal thought. However, the developing ability of adolescents to understand themselves in relation to others may be involved as well. The third-person perspective that develops with level 3 allows adolescents to anticipate others' reactions to them (Lapsley & Murphy, 1985). This understanding means that they can imagine how they must look to a third person when interacting with someone else. This perspective gives them a heightened awareness of the self, especially as they are seen through the eyes of another (Lapsley, FitzGerald, Rice, & Jackson, 1989).

Lapsley and his colleagues (1989) note that research is equivocal in supporting Elkind's contention that formal thought underlies the imaginary audience. A number of studies find that the imaginary audience is more pronounced with concrete operational thought than with formal thought; others find that the imaginary audience actually decreases with the appearance of formal thought, or is unrelated to formal thought (Goossens, 1984; Gray & Hudson, 1984; Lapsley, Milstead, Quintana, Flannery, & Buss, 1986). Lapsley himself views the imaginary audience as a reflection of the difficulties adolescents sometimes experience as they attempt to understand themselves in relation to others (Lapsley, FitzGerald, Rice, & Jackson, 1989). Partial support for Lapsley's position comes from research by Heather Jahnke and Fredda Blanchard-Fields (1993). These investigators assessed egocentrism, formal reasoning, and interpersonal understanding in adolescents and young adults and found that the development of interpersonal understanding, and not formal reasoning, was related to the personal fable.

Despite significant developments in social understanding such as the ones chronicled by Selman, adolescents often fail to consider the impact their remarks can have on others. Joan Newman (1985) describes a family conversation about where the Russian satellite "Cosmos" might fall. Neither parent had any idea where this might be, but the teenage son knew that it had already fallen, landing ENE of the tiniest island southwest of Madagascar. So impressed was he with his superior knowledge that he ridiculed the rest of the family saying, "You don't know anything, do you?" Yet this same teenager couldn't find his math homework or remember where he left his sneakers that morning.

ADOLESCENTS IN THE CLASSROOM

High school courses in mathematics, science, and literature require increasingly abstract and logical thought. Adolescents taking algebra, for instance, must solve problems in which they let x equal 5, or y equal -14. They know better than to assume that x really *is* 5 or y really *is* -14 (Bjorklund, 1989). Literature courses ask them to discuss the nuances of motives and meaning in characters that live only in the pages of their books. In physical science, they must make observations, generate explanations for these, then systematically test each one out, controlling for extraneous conditions as they do.

Inductive Reasoning

These problems are the sort Piaget claimed require formal thinking, where both inductive and deductive reasoning come into play. **Inductive reasoning** takes one from the particular to the general, from specific events to the class to which these belong, that is, to an explanation. For instance, to find that water in a closed container boils at several degrees below the point at which it boils in an uncovered container is a single observation resulting in a single fact; interesting, perhaps, but of limited value to science or the student. The logical thought process that enables a student to extrapolate from this single fact to a general rule (that there is an inverse relationship between the pressure exerted on a liquid and its boiling point) is an example of inductive reasoning.

Similarly, the adolescent who must write an essay analyzing why Hamlet was so slow to avenge his father's murder is also confronted with a task of induction. Shakespeare describes specific events in the life of Hamlet—conversations, thoughts, actions. To explain Hamlet's motives, the student must use induction to arrive at his character, that is, the source (class) of likely actions and the rules of their occurrence. The events Shakespeare actually shows us are analogous to the individual observations of a chemistry experiment such as the one above, and the step from these particulars to a general personality is as much an act of induction as formulating the rule relating pressure on a liquid to its boiling point.

Deductive Reasoning

Deductive reasoning works the other way, going from the general to the particular, that is, checking a hypothesis by seeing what happens when conditions change. Thus, starting with the rule that the boiling point of water drops by a certain amount with every increase of pressure, one can deduce (predict) any particular boiling point for any given pressure. Likewise, given the diagnosis of Hamlet as indecisive but impulsive (the general personality or rule from which spring all his actions), one can predict (deduce) that left to himself Hamlet will have difficulty formulating a plan of action, but once provoked, will act quickly and rashly.

The ability to think logically, abstractly, and hypothetically increases with age throughout adolescence, as does the speed at which adolescents process information (Hale, 1990; Overton, Ward, Noveck, Black, & O'Brien, 1987; Ward & Overton, 1990). Even on simple deductive tasks, we see a definite developmental progression in the use of formal reasoning. Figure 4.11 shows this trend quite clearly. Ward and Overton (1990) gave sixth-, ninth-, and twelfth-graders propositions such as the ones in Box 4.3. Only 16% of the sixth-graders used formal reasoning, whereas 56% of the ninth-

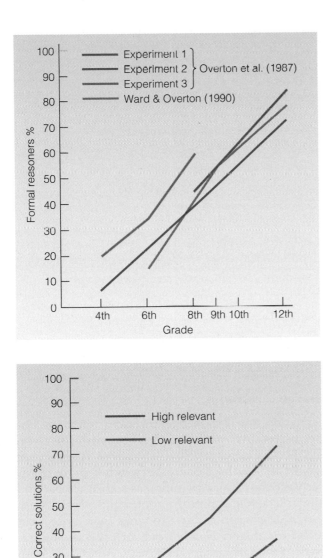

FIGURE 4.11
**Percentages of
Fourth- to Twelfth-
Graders Capable of
Formal Reasoning**

Sources: W. F. Overton, S. L. Ward, I. A. Noveck, J. Black, & D. P. O'Brien. 1987. Form and content in the development of deductive reasoning. *Developmental Psychology, 23,* 22–30. S. L. Ward & W. F. Overton. (1990). Semantic familiarity, relevance, and the development of deductive reasoning. *Developmental Psychology, 26,* 488–493.

FIGURE 4.12
**Deductive Reasoning
for High-Relevant
(Sensible) and Low-
Relevant (Nonsensi-
cal) Propositions**

Source: S. L. Ward & W. F. Overton. (1990). Semantic familiarity, relevance, and the development of deductive reasoning. *Developmental Psychology, 26,* 488–493.

graders did, as did 80% of the twelfth-graders. Propositions that made sense were solved more readily than nonsensical ones (see Figure 4.12). However, until formal reasoning develops, even familiar and sensible content does not help. Figure 4.12 shows that sixth-graders found sensible (high-relevant) propositions to be nearly as difficult as those with little relevance.

Box 4.3   Deductive Reasoning: Sensible and Nonsensical Propositions

Propositions that make sense (in which the first statement is relevant to the second):

> If a person is drinking beer, then the person is 21 years of age.
>
> If a person is driving a motor vehicle, then the person is 16 years of age.
>
> If you are caught running in the halls, then you will be punished.
>
> If a student strikes a teacher, then the student is suspended.

Propositions that make little sense (little relevance of the first statement to the second):

> If a person is drinking beer, then the person goes to church.
>
> If a person is driving a motor vehicle, then the person is a schoolteacher.
>
> If you are caught running in the halls, then you are wearing sneakers.
>
> If a student strikes a teacher, then the alarm goes off.

Source: Adapted from S. L. Ward & W. F. Overton. (1990). Semantic familiarity, relevance, and the development of deductive reasoning. *Developmental Psychology, 26,* 488–493.

Minority Adolescents in the Classroom

Minority adolescents face an additional challenge: to find a way to reconcile the often contradictory perspectives presented at school with their own life experiences. Dick Gregory once remarked that he and his friends used to root for the Indians against the cavalry, because they didn't think it was fair for textbooks to characterize the cavalry's winning as a great victory and the Indians' winning as a massacre. Many minority adolescents would agree. For them, life experiences frequently run counter to what they must learn at school. Will *Tom Sawyer* or *Huckleberry Finn* be read with the same interpretation, or with sensitivity to the same issues, by African American, Asian American, or Native American adolescents as by European American adolescents? Which students' experiences are more likely to be reflected by their teachers?

Similarly, carpetbaggers have traditionally been portrayed as low-life opportunists who turned the chaos following the Civil War to personal advantage. Yet if one believes that members of the White majority at that time, or the present, have opportunistically taken advantage of minorities, this portrayal does not raise meaningful distinctions, or at least does not evoke the same sensitivities as it would for those whose views reflect the dominant culture.

Consider the westward expansion on the North American continent. Numerous treaty violations with Native Americans led to the eventual decimation of these people. The internment of Japanese Americans during World War II violated all their civil rights. How are these events covered in most U.S. history books? Do textbooks, or teachers, simply adopt the dominant cultural perspective, and if they do, can we expect minorities to un-

High school courses demand a greater degree of abstract and logical thinking than do classes in elementary and junior high school. In science classes, for instance, students must make observations, explain them, and test their explanations.

derstand the facts presented in class as easily as students for whom these facts present no cultural conflict?

Textbooks used in courses such as history and literature frequently present a narrative account that evolves from a single frame of reference—a European American perspective. Many teachers uncritically adopt this same perspective. Students who do not share this view of history, as many minorities do not, will fail to experience these courses as "making sense." Yet teachers and textbooks are the authoritative sources, and students who cannot remember the facts as presented will be seen as problems.

Can Adolescents Think Like Scientists?

Early adolescents can marshal facts to support or oppose principles, generate a realm of possible alternatives for any situation, think in abstractions, and test their thoughts against an inner logic. These abilities set them apart from children. They also make new forms of learning possible in the classroom. Adolescents' systematic approach to problems, for one thing, lends itself especially well to science.

Much of the excitement of science involves discovery. Often the first discovery is the nature of the problem itself. Alexander Fleming, for example, documents the discovery of penicillin by telling of a mold that had formed in one of his petri dishes. He noticed that the bacteria surrounding the mold had died. Instead of cleaning out the dish and starting a new culture, fleming was puzzled (that is, he had discovered a problem). Why had only the bacteria around the mold died?

One could identify other, less interesting, problems, such as, "What did I do wrong?" Perhaps Fleming did, too, but he chose to move on to why the bacteria surrounding the mold had died. What Fleming saw illustrates the first step in solving a problem. One must analyze a situation to discover its salient features (what a scientist would call the relevant variables). Only when these have been isolated can a strategy be formulated. Given a strategy, one can begin to test each of the features to see which produce a solution. finally, one must be able to reach conclusions based on these tests (Ginsburg & Opper, 1988).

Notice that the success of the whole endeavor rests on the ability to think the situation through before starting to work on it. Adolescents can do this. They can identify each of the possible variables, then generate combinations. Remember that a characteristic of adolescent thought is to think in terms of possibilities. In doing so, they are also generating a strategy, because each possibility must be tested.

A strategy makes for a systematic approach to problems. Adolescents know, for instance, that they must hold all of the conditions constant except the one they are testing. Only then can they be sure their test reflects the possibility they have in mind instead of some other. They know, too, that frequently an effect can result from more than one combination of conditions. Even though they may discover that the bacteria die under one particular combination of conditions, they will continue with their tests, exhausting all the possibilities.

The above is fine for adolescents who have reached formal thought. But many adolescents have not. Science teachers may need to combine abstract approaches that illustrate isolating variables with concrete examples, to bring their points home to thinkers who do not use formal thought. The example in Box 4.4 of a discussion in a science class illustrates this point. Notice how the discussion revolves around common objects such as a Frisbee, a shoe-box lid, and the cover to a tin can. Even concrete thinkers can wrap their minds around these examples.

Study Skills and Knowing What You Don't Know

One of the factors contributing to better learning is that adolescents, more so than children, are aware of what they don't know and adjust the way they study to accommodate for the gaps in their knowledge. Children, on the other hand, often fail to realize when they have not learned what they have been studying. Campione and Brown (1978) observed fifth-graders through college students as they studied material in a textbook. Younger students focused on the same information each time they reviewed the material, whereas older students, realizing what they had missed, directed their attention to that material on subsequent readings. The development with age of metacognitive skills, and the consequent use of strategies, underlies this improvement.

Students who fail to monitor their performance can be taught to do so. Poor readers who were shown how to assess their reading comprehension by noting what they have missed climbed from the 20th percentile to the 56th percentile (Palinscar & Brown, 1984).

Similarly, Hiller Spires, Joan Gallini, and Jan Riggsbee (1992) found that fourth graders who were taught to attend to cues such as chapter headings and other pedagogical tools or to focus on cues embedded in the passages themselves (such as "in comparison to" or "on the other hand") improved in their comprehension.

Metaphors and Meaning: When Is a Ship a State?

Children interpret remarks literally; adolescents can understand multiple levels of meaning. When asked to interpret an expression such as, "His bark is louder than his bite," for example, children might answer that "You can't hear a dog bite," or that "Some dogs bark loudly." Adolescents can understand the expression to mean that some individuals bluff their way through situations. Their ability to understand figurative uses of language makes many types of literature accessible that previously were not.

Adolescents can also appreciate *metaphor;* a metaphor makes an implicit comparison between ideas or objects to show some hidden similarity. They understand that when politicians refer to a government as a "ship of state," they are communicating that the fate of all citizens is bound together, just like the fate of passengers and crew on a ship at sea. Similarly, the phrase "evening of life" communicates that life is drawing to an end, just like the day at the approach of evening. Early adolescents easily understand expressions such as these; children do not (Geller, 1985).

Early adolescents also begin to understand irony, sarcasm, and satire. Their ability to think in terms of hypothetical situations as distinct from actual ones makes an understanding of these concepts possible. Being able to consider the perspective of another and anticipate the other's intended effects by their remarks almost surely contributes to this new appreciation. Adolescents can appreciate the irony in passages from works such as *Pilgrim at Tinker Creek,* in which Annie Dillard writes the following:

> Somewhere, and I can't find where, I read about an Eskimo hunter who asked the local missionary priest, "If I did not know about God and sin, would I go to hell?" "No," said the priest, "not if you did not know." "Then why," asked the Eskimo earnestly, "did you tell me?" (Dillard, 1974)

The ability of adolescents to appreciate the irony in this story may be especially acute. They, like the Eskimo, face a challenge to change because of what they know. In the chapter that follows, we examine the way changing perceptions of themselves and others affect adolescents' family relationships.

Answer to the problem in Figure 4.6: P and Not-Q.

Box 4.4 Science in the Classroom: Analysis of a Frisbee

The teacher in this science class has told students to bring in something that flies. One student brought in a Frisbee.

Teacher: Okay, let's consider some explanations now. Why is the Frisbee built this way? Look back at our list of structural features on the blackboard and see if you can explain one of them. Why is the Frisbee designed the way it is? I'd like to see almost everyone's hand up with one idea.

Student 1: Well, it's round so you can spin it.

Teacher: Okay. How many other people were thinking something like that? Now let's take this a little bit further. Could you spin it if it weren't round?

Student 1: No. Well, I guess you could. But it wouldn't work very well.

Teacher: How come? What would go wrong?

Student 1: It would flop around; it wouldn't sail smoothly.

Teacher: Can you give another model case of that?

Student 1: Well, I can't think of anything.

Teacher: Can anyone think of an example of something shaped like a Frisbee a little bit, but not round? What has a rim like a Frisbee but isn't round?

Student 2: Maybe the lid of a shoe box. You know, it's shaped like a rectangle but it has sides like a Frisbee.

Teacher: And what would happen if you spun it like a Frisbee?

Student 2: Well, it wouldn't go very far.

Teacher: Why not?

Student 2: I don't know. I guess it's not so heavy. The air slows it down maybe.

Teacher: Good. Anyone else have some ideas about why it slows down?

Student 3: It doesn't spin well because the sides of the box lid hit the air.

Teacher: Good point. When it's not round, the sides hit the air and slow it down. That's a reason for a Frisbee being round. But that leads to another question: Why is spin so important? [No one raises a hand.] Let me ask the question this way, and again I'd like almost everyone to think of an answer. What happens if you throw a Frisbee without spinning it, versus throwing the Frisbee with a spin? [Most hands go up.]

Student 4: It flops if you don't spin it. So I guess the spinning keeps it straight.

Teacher: How many other people had a similar answer? [Several raise their hands.] Anyone have a different answer?

Student 5: It's like a gyroscope that we studied last week.

Teacher: That's very good. How many others noticed that connection? [Two or three hands go up.] Could you explain?

Student 5: Well, we learned that the gyroscope effect keeps something in the same position, so it doesn't tilt or wobble. So the gyroscope effect keeps the Frisbee from toppling over.

Box 4.4   (*continued*)

Teacher: Very good. So a Frisbee is round so it can spin fast without slowing down when its edges hit the air. And it needs to spin to keep it from tumbling. What about some other feature on the structure list? Who has an explanation for something else? . . .

Student 6: It's rounded on top. I mean it isn't perfectly flat. That maybe helps it to fly.

Teacher: A very interesting idea. Anyone else have that one? So a Frisbee is a kind of spinning wing. The spinning keeps it straight and the wing shape helps it to stay up. How much does that shape help it to stay up, though? [No answer.] Can anyone think of other things you can throw somewhat like a Frisbee? Maybe we can see whether they fly just as well.

Student 7: A discus.

Student 8: A tin-can lid. You can throw those by spinning them.

Teacher: Interesting examples. I wonder if we can see whether the rounded shape of a Frisbee really gives it more lift than something that's flat.

Student 9: But a discus is pretty heavy; so are tin-can lids.

Teacher: That's a good point. When you worry about a difference like that, you're worrying about what scientists call control of variables. That means that when you're making a comparison, you want it to be fair. If you're comparing how much the rounded top helps, you don't want the comparison messed up by other differences, like weight. So a discus is a good idea but, thinking about it, we see it's too heavy. Is there any way we could make a fairer comparison? Could we test the Frisbee against itself somehow?

Student 10: How about cutting off the rim?

Teacher: Could be. A good idea. You're thinking up ways to compare it with itself. Let's think if it's a fair comparison.

Student 10: I guess not. Cutting off the rim would make it lighter.

Teacher: Well, that's a point. Can we test it against itself without making it lighter?

Student 11: How about throwing it upside down? If the rounded top really helps it to stay up, it shouldn't fly as well upside down.

Teacher: That's a good idea. Is it a fair comparison?

Student 11: Sure, because it weighs the same right-side up and upside down.

Teacher: Okay, so we have a good idea for controlling the variables. It's a fair test because everything is the same except what we're interested in—the rounded top. We have a Frisbee here, so let's try the experiment.

Source: D. N. Perkins. (1987). Knowledge as design: Teaching thinking through content. In J. B. Baron & R. J. Sternberg (Eds.), *Teaching thinking skills: Theory and practice.* New York: Freeman.

SUMMARY

How Adolescents Think

Three advances characterize adolescent thought. (1) Thought becomes more abstract; adolescents can think of things in terms of class membership and can classify the classes. (2) Thought becomes hypothetical; adolescents can think of things that are only possible but not real. (3) Thought becomes more logical; adolescents can test one thought against another. These changes in the way adolescents think are prompted by the biological maturation of the brain.

A Constructive Interpretation of Cognitive Development

According to the constructive perspective, we continually interpret experience. Piaget applies this constructive perspective to development by suggesting that we organize how we understand the world in qualitatively different ways as we grow older. Sensorimotor thought is limited to what the infant experiences through its senses and actions. Preoperational thought, though symbolic, is dominated by the appearance of things. Concrete operational thought is more flexible and allows children to move beyond how things look to how they must be. Only with formal operational thought can adolescents think of abstract ideas and consider hypothetical situations.

Kegan builds on Piaget's stage theory by suggesting that intellectual growth takes place through a process of differentiation of self from other. Differentiation progresses at different rates in each individual because of different contextual influences and daily experiences. Rogoff suggests a variant of Piaget's stage theory: Cognitive development does not move toward a single endpoint but instead has the potential to take any number of forms depending on the skills that are valued in the child's culture.

A Psychometric Approach to Intelligence

Common measures of intelligence reflect the knowledge and abilities of the average person in our society. Intelligence increases during late adolescence and early adulthood and decreases in later adulthood. Age changes follow different developmental courses for crystallized and fluid intelligence. The former taps cultural knowledge and increases with age; the latter reflects one's ability to think on the spot and decreases with age.

Most intelligence tests reflect one's familiarity with the culture. Racial and ethnic differences in intelligence exist and may reflect different rates of assimilation into the dominant culture. Gender differences in intelligence may also reflect different socialization experiences.

Beyond IQ: Information Processing

Few important changes occur with age in the structural features of memory; individuals of all ages have sensory, short-term, and long-term memories.

Different control features appear at different ages. Adolescents are more likely to use strategies to remember, to use more efficient strategies, and to retrieve information faster than younger children. They also know more about their memories and use their knowledge to monitor what they do.

Sternberg's Componential Intelligence

Sternberg analyzes intellectual functioning in terms of components, or processes that operate on information. He distinguishes among three types of components: (1) metacomponents allocate processing resources, (2) performance components carry out the actual procedures, and (3) knowledge-acquisition components require new information as it is needed.

Gardner's Seven Facets of the Mind

Gardner defines intelligence as one's ability to solve problems as they arise, but includes problems from a much broader domain than most experts in the field. He argues for seven forms of intelligence: musical, bodily-kinesthetic, logical-mathematical, linguistic, spatial, interpersonal, and intrapersonal.

Thought and the Adolescent

Adolescents frequently make problems more complex than they are and feel stupid when someone else comes up with the obvious solution. Elkind refers to this tendency as pseudostupidity. Elkind believes that the ability of adolescents to think about thinking leads them to create an imaginary audience in which they feel themselves to be the center of everyone's attention. More sophisticated forms of thought affect adolescents' emotions and their ability to argue for what they believe in.

Selman traces the development of social understanding through five levels, reflecting differences in one's ability to infer the views of another person and to coordinate that view with one's own. At the egocentric level, one is not able to take another's perspective. At the social-informational level, one realizes that another's view of a situation may differ from one's own. Individuals at the self-reflective level can put themselves in another's place and understand that person's feelings, and at the mutual level they can understand that the other can do the same. At the highest level, the social and conventional system, one can infer how another might be thinking and anticipate how that person will react to one's reactions to them. Changes in considering another person's perspective may explain the concept of the imaginary audience.

Adolescents in the Classroom

Adolescents' ability to think hypothetically makes it possible for them to study science, and their ability to appreciate multiple levels of meaning broadens their understanding of literature. They can understand irony, sarcasm, satire, and metaphor.

KEY TERMS

object permanence

schemes

centration

reverse

egocentrism

mental operations

differentiation

conservation

intelligence

WAIS-R

crystallized intelligence

fluid intelligence

sensory memory

short-term memory

long-term memory

rehearsal

encoding

metamemory

pseudostupidity

imaginary audience

personal fable

social understanding

inductive reasoning

deductive reasoning

CHAPTER 5

Adolescents in the Family

Annie is 15 and standing in the dark on her aunt's doorstep. It's 2:30 in the morning. Only blocks away, Annie's frantic mother has called the police to say that her daughter has run away. That morning Annie's mother, looking for the medical card she had given Annie to use, found two joints in Annie's purse. When she confronted Annie about them, Annie screamed that her mother was spying on her, grabbed the purse and said that she was leaving for good. Annie's mother stood in the doorway and said they had to talk, but Annie pushed past her and nearly knocked her over. Later, when the police, Annie's mother, and Annie all converge in her aunt's living room, Annie tells them she ran away because her mother is cold, selfish, demanding, and doesn't love her. Annie's mother describes Annie as bright and sweet, but immature, irresponsible, and thoughtless. Each has nothing to say that will reach the other.

If asked to describe herself, Annie's mother would never use words such as *cold* or *selfish*, nor would she say that she didn't love her daughter. Nor would Annie describe herself as immature or thoughtless. How can the two of them see things so differently? What has gone wrong? How much of their difficulty is because of Annie? How much is because of her mother? And how much is because Annie is 15?

Eddie, 13, is sitting in his room waiting for his father to open the door. His little sister went running to get him after she saw all the hair in the bathroom and found her mother crying in the kitchen. It hadn't been all that good around the house lately. Things came to a head, literally, when Eddie shaved both sides of his head, leaving a swath down the middle, which he dyed green and spiked with hair gel. His mother said she had never seen anything like that. Who knows what his father will say. Or do. Eddie tells himself he doesn't care. He has never felt so alone in all his life.

How is it possible for Eddie to feel alone with his family all around him? And what possessed him to give himself a green Mohawk?

A CONSTRUCTIVE INTERPRETATION OF RELATIONSHIPS

In the preceding chapter we explained the intellectual changes that take place in adolescence as a consequence of an active constructive process by which the individual gives meaning to experience. Robert Kegan (1982, 1994) argues that, at every age, individuals partition experience into two "rough cuts" of reality—that which is "me" and that which is "not me." Development occurs when aspects of the "me" become differentiated from that which has been regarded as "not me." This differentiation has the effect of simultaneously defining new aspects of our surroundings and of our self. When we give meaning to events out there, our sense of self in relation to these events also changes. For adolescents, this process of differentiation carries the promise of profound changes in their most significant relationships, changes that start within the family.

What prompts this differentiation? Why are relationships with parents renegotiated in adolescence and not, say, in middle childhood or early adulthood? Puberty gives us one answer. The biological changes discussed in Chapter 3 have important implications for the way adolescents and their parents interact. Among European American adolescents in our culture, puberty ushers in increased conflict and decreased closeness with parents. As adolescents develop the bodies and feelings of mature adults, their and their parents' expectations change. Adolescents, for their part, expect to be treated in more adult ways, to be given more autonomy and a greater say in family decision making. Parents, in turn, expect adolescents to be more responsible and to act in more adult ways. Conflict frequently results.

These trends are not universal, and the importance of the way a culture interprets, or constructs, biological events such as puberty cannot be overemphasized. Puberty, for instance, is associated with very different changes among Hispanic adolescents, at least for boys, for whom relationships with parents actually improve, perhaps reflecting the value their families place on the traditional male role (Molina & Chassin, 1996).

A second factor contributing to a renegotiation of relationships in early adolescence is the way adolescents begin to think. The intellectual changes discussed in the preceding chapter give adolescents new perspectives from which to view themselves and their relationships with others. Adolescents can no longer see themselves as they always have. What sense, then, are they to make of themselves?

In giving meaning to their experiences, individuals actively construct the events to which they respond, putting together a reality that makes sense, given the way they perceive their world. One's worldview changes, as we have seen, in adolescence. In the preceding chapter, we examined these changes in terms of adolescents' intellectual grasp on reality. In this chapter, we will consider changes in the meaning adolescents make of themselves. In particular, we will look at how their meaning of self changes in relation to their families.

How does a constructive perspective help us understand adolescents such as Annie and Eddie? Despite other differences between them, both Annie and Eddie have one thing in common. Both have organized their meaning of the self in terms of their relationships with their parents. If asked to talk about herself, Annie would likely say something such as, "The problem's not me so much as it is my mother. She doesn't really care about me and wants to control me." Annie has a hard time separating her feelings from how she sees her mother, her *self* from the *other*. One could say that she simply is not being honest. But the truth is, she is being honest. This is the way things are for her. In order for her to relate differently to her mother, she must be able to see *herself* differently. She must be able to distinguish her needs and feelings of the moment from her larger sense of who she is, from her sense of self. Kegan characterizes this differentiation as, "'I' no longer *am* my needs . . . I *have* them." This distinction brings with it the possibility of not only coordinating her needs but coordinating them with the needs of others, ushering in the potential for mutuality. In recognizing the needs of her mother as well as her own, and the obligations of each toward the other, she will have stepped out of the role of a child with a parent, into a relationship characterized by greater mutuality (Kegan, 1982).

And what about Eddie? How are we to understand his feelings of loneliness? The differentiation that eventually leads to greater mutuality in relationships with parents takes years to achieve. Eddie didn't have years to spend on differentiation that afternoon. He knew he wasn't a child, like his sister, but he was not sure what it was that made him different from children her age or, for that matter, different from adults such as his parents. He didn't want to be seen as a kid anymore, nor did he want to be like his parents. At 13, scissors and paint, cutting and pasting, promised a quick fix to an identity. Why, then, was he feeling so lonely? Eddie had lost something. He had lost the self he had known himself to be, and he had not put together a way of being to step into when he stepped out of the other.

In life, one frequently finds oneself in the middle of something without knowing exactly what it is one is doing, or precisely what one wants to get out of it—not at all a new experience for adolescents as they attempt to understand themselves in new ways. Change at any age doesn't come easily, and the more people who are involved, the more difficult it is, for as adolescents define themselves in new ways, so, too, must those around them, most notably their parents.

Why *is* it so hard to forge a new meaning of the self in adolescence? In part, it is because adolescents must gain hold of a new way of being. But they must do something else as well. They must also let go of, or be willing to lose, the self they have always known. Just how easy or difficult it is for adolescents to gain a new sense of themselves and let go of the old one will depend on the type of support they receive from the environment in which this process takes place—their relationships with their parents. The first section of this chapter examines the way adolescents put together their experiences within the family to give a new sense of self.

CHANGING RELATIONSHIPS WITH PARENTS

Is emotional turmoil necessary for healthy development? Does adolescence so disrupt one's sense of self and one's relationship to the rest of the world that emotional tumult, mood swings, and unpredictable behavior inevitably result? Or can adolescents continue to maintain positive and satisfying relationships with parents while developing as individuals?

Turmoil and Change

Is turmoil inevitable? According to psychoanalytic theorists, it is. They maintain that adolescents must separate from their parents in order to develop as their own persons, and that this separation is inevitably conflictual. Sigmund Freud believed that dramatic increases in hormones during adolescence reactivate earlier incestuous feelings (see Chapter 2). He felt that the only way adolescents can defend against these repressed Oedipal impulses is to distance themselves from their parents. This distancing creates the emotional separation necessary for further psychological growth (Blos, 1967, 1979; S. Freud, 1954). Anna Freud (1969) felt so convinced that emotional turbulence was a natural consequence of adolescence that she considered it *ab*normal for adolescents to maintain their emotional balance.

The psychoanalytic view has received considerable support from clinical psychologists who work with troubled adolescents, and also from those working with adult patients who, during the course of therapy, refer to problems they experienced as adolescents (Blos, 1967, 1979; A. Freud, 1969). Most developmentalists simply assumed that they could generalize clinical data to a normal population—that all adolescents experienced emotional turmoil. Theoretical support for such assumptions was strong, because prevailing theory maintained that adolescence was a time of intense conflict. Why *not* study troubled adolescents for insights into this time of life?

Calm and Continuity

Research with normal adolescents gives us a different picture of adolescents' relationships with their parents. These studies point to continuing, close relationships (Larson, Richards, Moneta, Holmbeck, & Duckett, 1996; Offer, Ostrov, & Howard, 1981). Even though conflicts become more frequent in adolescence, they do not prevent adolescents and parents from remaining close. In fact, the most autonomous adolescents are also most likely to say that their parents remain an important influence in their lives and that they continue to seek their advice (Fuligni & Eccles, 1993).

Daniel Offer and his associates found little evidence of emotional turmoil in the adolescents they studied, or of conflict in their relationships with their parents. Most adolescents described themselves positively, as happy and self-confident. The majority did not feel that there were any major problems between themselves and their parents. They reported feeling close to their parents and believed their parents were proud of them. These investigators point out that adolescents' positive feelings toward their parents appear to be extensions of similarly positive feelings as children. Sum-

marizing their findings concerning adolescents and their parents, they state that their "most impressive findings ... are that eighteen out of nineteen items strongly indicate that the adolescents have positive feelings toward their families" (Offer, Ostrov, & Howard, 1981).

Change and Continuity

Can both of these characterizations of parent–adolescent relationships be true? Are some changes so significant that to deny them is to deny what adolescence is all about, and do most adolescents remain close to their parents while going through these changes? Recent research answers yes. Relationships with parents remain important in adolescence, *and* these relationships are renegotiated (Baumrind, 1991a).

Reed Larson, Maryse Richards, Giovanni Moneta, Grayson Holmbeck, and Elena Duckett (1996) had adolescents wear pagers for a week, asking them to record what they were doing and how they were feeling when beeped at random intervals during the day and evening. Larson and his associates noted both dramatic changes as well as important continuities in the ways adolescents interacted with their families. Perhaps the most striking change was the amount of time adolescents spent with their families. In contrast to fifth-graders, who spent about 35% of their waking hours with their families, twelfth-graders spent only 14%. (However, these investigators caution that the adolescents in this study were all from European

Are disagreements between adolescents and their parents an inevitable part of growing up? Research says they are, but also that most adolescents and parents stay close despite conflict.

Research Focus

Sampling: How Emotional Are Adolescents?

Do words such as *impulsive, moody,* and *intense* capture something special about adolescence as a time of life? Are adolescents more emotional than their parents? Parents and educators have come to expect emotional turmoil with the onset of adolescence, but what evidence is there that the daily emotional states of adolescents are different from those of children or adults?

Reed Larson and Maryse Richards (1994) tackled this difficult question in an unusual way. They asked fifth- to ninth-graders and their parents to wear beepers for one week. Each time they were beeped, they filled out a one-page form indicating their emotional state. You might ask, "How can we be sure these investigators caught all the emotional states adolescents and parents experience? If they beep each person only a few times each day, they will catch only a few emotional states and perhaps reach the wrong conclusions. How do we know the emotions they recorded are representative of all adolescents' and parents' feelings?"

"Beeping" adolescents and their parents is a way of *sampling* emotional states. Larson and Richards could not ask individuals to record each and every feeling every moment of the day. Instead, they sampled from this larger population of emotions. The *population* is the entire group of people or events, or, in this case, emotional states, in which one is interested. The *sample* is a subgroup drawn from this population. If the sample is drawn at random from the population, we can be reasonably certain that it will be *representative* of that population. This is because in random sampling, each person or event has an equal chance of being chosen. How might this procedure apply to emotional states?

Larson and Richards first limited the population to waking states between the hours of 7:30 A.M. and 9:30 P.M. They organized these into four 2-hour blocks of time from 7:30 A.M. to 3:30 P.M. and four 90-minute blocks between 3:30 P.M. and 9:30 P.M. (The more frequent sampling during later afternoon and evening hours provided better sampling of family time together.) They randomly beeped each adolescent once within each of the eight blocks of time. This procedure ensures that each of the 120, or 90, minutes within each block has an equal chance of being sampled. To imagine how this might work, think of a hat containing 120, or 90, slips of paper, one for each minute in the block of time. The time written on the slip you pull would be the time the adolescent is beeped.

What did the samples show? Are adolescents more emotional than their parents? These investigators found that adolescents are in fact more emotional than their parents. When sampled, adolescents reported extremes of highs and lows much more frequently. Adolescents reported feeling "very happy," for instance, five times more often than their parents did. Similarly, they reported more intense lows than their parents, their beepers catching them as "very unhappy" three times more often than their parents. Larson and Richards conclude that the inner life of adolescents differs significantly from that of their parents, adolescents "ascending higher peaks of rapture and tumbling into deeper crevasses of dejection" (p. 83). Differences such as these make it easier to understand how misunderstandings can so easily arise between adolescents and parents. As Larson and Richards put it, "They are on different wavelengths."

Source: Adapted from R. Larson & M. H. Richards. (1994). *Divergent realities.* New York: Basic Books.

American backgrounds, and this trend may not be characteristic of adolescents from other backgrounds.) Adolescents' emotional experiences when they were with their families also changed with age—the positive feelings of fifth- and sixth-graders becoming negative by junior high, especially during conversations, only improving again toward the end of high school. The

Research Focus, "Sampling," describes a similar study by Larsen and Richards that used pagers to sample the emotional state of young adolescents and their parents throughout the day.

Contrary to psychoanalytic theory, withdrawal from family life does not appear to be due to dynamics within the family. Decreases in family time were unrelated to increases in conflict, or to decreases in such things as family cohesion and closeness to parents, or even to the feelings adolescents had when they were with their families. Instead, other factors appeared to be responsible. The need to be alone was important for early adolescents, who spent much of their time alone in their rooms, even though they were not necessarily happier there than with the family. Once in high school, however, outside attractions, such as after-school activities and going out with friends, became more important. Having access to a car, a job, and permission to stay out later all related to decreases in family time.

The continuities? Adolescents and parents actually found ways to make up for the lost time together. Even though older adolescents participated less in family activities involving little or no communication, such as watching television, they spent just as much time as they had before in conversations with family members. In fact, twelfth-graders spent the same amount of time alone with each of their parents as fifth-graders did, suggesting that adolescents and parents actively attempt to maintain closeness. Conversations also became more mutual, older adolescents reporting, for instance, that they gave a direction to the conversation as frequently as one of their parents. Thus, even though the time adolescents spend with the family decreases with age, this time involves more direct, one-on-one interaction, greater mutuality, and, once the negativity of early adolescence is past, is experienced in even more positive ways than previously.

Relationships between younger children and parents, however, are relatively one-sided in their distribution of power and responsibility, even in families where parents involve the children in family decisions. Several conditions cause adolescents to press for change in this family arena.

One condition is adolescents' new awareness of themselves. The ability to think abstractly contributes to this awareness (see Chapter 4). Teenagers can imagine how someone else might see their interactions with others. They can get a feeling for how their actions and intentions are seen not only by the person they are with, but by others in general. This ability sharpens their sense of themselves as separate from others. They begin to appreciate the many ways they are different, even though they do the same things, share the same tastes, and have similar preferences as their friends.

The very same ability that allows teenagers to see themselves through the eyes of others also allows them to see themselves with their parents in a new light (Eisert & Kahle, 1986). They see how their relationships with their parents differ from the ones they have with their friends (Eccles, Buchanan, Midgley, Fuligni, & Flanagan, 1991). The latter are egalitarian and mutual; friends arrive at decisions jointly. James Youniss (1980) suggests that adolescents become conscious that they live in two very different social worlds: one with friends, in which they participate on an equal footing, share in decision making, and negotiate differences; the other with parents, in which they have little power, make few decisions, and conform to parental expectations. Adolescents face the need to achieve a single sense of them-

Box 5.1   Strategies for Better Family Communication

Central to any effective communication is one's acceptance of the other person. Frequently, there isn't any need to offer help or give advice; all that's needed is simply to listen. Parents' comments are usually motivated by good intentions: They only want to help their children learn new skills ("Here's how you should do that") or to prevent them from making unnecessary mistakes ("Watch out for that car in the intersection"). However, such comments communicate nonacceptance, letting the adolescent know that the parent's way is better. Active listening offers an alternative.

LISTENING TO ADOLESCENTS: ACTIVE LISTENING

Active listening is a way of drawing people out and helping them explore their feelings by feeding their message back to them. In the process, you find out if you have understood what they said. Consider the following example:

ALLEN: Do I have to get up? [He has just been told it's nearly time to leave for a baseball game.]

FATHER: You don't feel like playing baseball today?

ALLEN: I'll miss messing around with my friends.

FATHER: You'd rather mess around with your friends than play baseball?

ALLEN: Yes. We have fun together

FATHER: It's not fun to play baseball?

ALLEN: No. Sometimes the other guys razz me when I don't get a hit.

FATHER: You don't like being teased?

ALLEN: It makes me feel like I'm not a very good player.

FATHER: You'd like to be good at baseball?

ALLEN: Yes, I felt terrific that day I got that base hit.

FATHER: Would you like to practice before the game?

ALLEN: Hey, Dad, that'd be great. I'll get dressed.

Notice how Allen is able to discover how he really feels when his father actively listens. Notice, too, that his father does not offer a solution, give advice, or do anything other than feed back what his son is saying.

An essential ingredient to active listening is communicating acceptance to the other person. The paradox in accepting people as they are is that as they feel accepted, they are free to change. Many parents, and adolescents for that matter, communicate nonacceptance, believing that if you want someone to change, you must let the other person know what needs improvement. Telling adolescents, or parents, that they need to improve

selves that holds across *all* the social situations they enter; as a first step, they press for fuller participation in relationships within the family. As adolescents move toward a more equal relationship with their parents, communication becomes increasingly important. Box 5.1 offers suggestions for improving family communications.

Box 5.1   (*continued*)

communicates that they are not all right the way they are. This communication puts the person on the defensive—and closes off the conversation.

Active listening takes time. Each must be willing to let the other feel his or her way through a problem. If you don't have the time, it is important to say so and arrange some other time to talk. Parents must also genuinely want to let the adolescent find a solution to the problem and not use active listening merely as a way to get her or him to do what they think should be done. They must accept the problem as the adolescent presents it and accept the adolescent's feelings about it. Parroting words without reflecting feelings is not active listening. You need to feed back all of the message, and feelings are an important part of it.

TALKING TO ADOLESCENTS: YOU-MESSAGES AND I-MESSAGES

Let's turn the situation around and look at how parents can talk so that adolescents will listen to them. The simplest approach would be to let adolescents know how they feel, but parents rarely do that. Instead, they are likely to tell adolescents what to do ("Pick up your clothes"), warn them what will happen if they don't ("If I have to tell you one more time, you've lost your clothes allowance"), moralize ("You should contribute your share of the work around the house"), or make a suggestion ("Why don't you put your clothes in the hamper when you take them off?"). Each of these approaches is usually met with resistance. After all, who likes being told what to do, warned, or made to feel wrong?

The parental comments in the preceding paragraph are examples of **you-messages.** They communicate that parents do not expect adolescents to be helpful unless they are told to be. And by offering a solution without letting adolescents help in defining the problem, such remarks subtly communicate that parents don't think adolescents can help or are willing to find a solution.

An **I-message** tells adolescents how their actions make others feel. Adolescents can hear such messages as a fact about the parent, not as an evaluation of themselves, and thus they have little need to be defensive. A parent who says "I can't hear what she's saying to me when you interrupt" communicates a different message than one who says "It's rude of you to interrupt." I-messages let adolescents know how their behavior affects others. These messages also communicate to adolescents that parents trust them to find a solution, and put the responsibility for change with the recipient. Because I-messages do not accuse, suggest, or warn, they are easier for adolescents to hear.

Source: Adapted from T. Gordon. (1972). *Parent effectiveness training.* New York: New American Library.

Perhaps at no time are their changing roles more evident than when parents and adolescents discuss their perceptions of family conflicts. Judith Smetana and Rusti Berent (1993), at the University of Rochester, asked seventh-, ninth-, and eleventh-grade adolescents and their mothers to respond to vignettes describing typical conflicts that occur at home, such as those involving household chores, keeping one's room clean, or personal appearance. Each conflict was presented both from the parent's perspective and the adolescent's, by giving justifications each might use in appealing to the other. (Table 5.1 shows the different perspectives.)

Perhaps not surprisingly, given their responsibility for maintaining family ways, mothers considered conventional justifications to be more adequate in resolving conflict than did adolescents. Adolescents, on the other hand, saw this type of reasoning as a source of conflict. This was especially true of mid-adolescent ninth-graders, for whom family conflict is likely to have reached a peak as gains in autonomy are won by questioning parental authority.

Mothers also considered appeals to authority and threats of punishment to be more effective in getting adolescents to comply with their wishes than did adolescents, a difference that increased with the adolescents' age. Adolescents, on the other hand, appealed to practical considerations, perhaps because such arguments are less likely to be challenged by parents. Smetana has found that, although adolescents may believe their position can be justified by appeals to personal jurisdiction ("It's my room and I can keep it as I like"), they will use pragmatic reasons ("It doesn't matter if it's messy; I can find whatever I need") when arguing with a parent. Parents are not as likely as adolescents to view the behaviors in question as rightfully within the adolescents' purview (Smetana, Braeges, & Yau, 1991).

Adolescent appeals to social convention in resolving family conflict are likely to generate more conflict than they settle, usually because the conventions referred to are those of their peers, perhaps already a sore point for many parents.

The complexity derives from the fact that different domains of authority exist within the family. Only in some domains is there a shift in parental authority. In others, parents continue to be perceived as having a legitimate say, both by themselves and by adolescents. Conflict arises over which issues lie within which domains: Adolescents and parents, in other words, don't always see things eye to eye (Smetana & Asquith, 1994).

Judith Smetana and Pamela Asquith (1994) asked sixth- through tenth-graders and their parents to indicate the legitimacy of parental authority concerning various hypothetical issues, shown in Table 5.2. Almost all adolescents and parents agreed that parents have the authority, even the obligation, to set rules concerning *moral issues,* in which a person's actions can affect the well-being of another. Similarly, most adolescents and parents considered *conventional issues* to be the legitimate province of parental decision making, although parents saw themselves as having more authority here than did adolescents. These perceptions, by the way, did not change with age, suggesting that parents are seen as rightfully the ones to establish and maintain the social as well as the moral order and adolescents as the ones seeking greater autonomy within this.

There was similar agreement between adolescents and parents about *personal issues,* both believing that adolescents should have the say concerning these. When disagreements arose, they were most likely to concern *friendship issues, multifaceted issues* (involving both personal and conventional concerns), and *prudential issues,* which involved adolescents' well-being or possible harm.

TABLE 5.1   Differences in the Parent's and the Adolescent's
Attempts to Resolve Conflict

The examples below are responses to a typical conflict:
Mother wants Anne to wear something else, but Anne doesn't want to.

	Type of Justification	Example
PARENT	Conventional	Reference to behavior standards, arbitrarily arrived at by family members, e.g., "I'd be embarrassed if any of my friends saw you looking like that."
	Pragmatic	Consideration of practical needs or consequences, e.g., "You'll catch a cold."
	Authoritarian	Reference to authority and punishment, e.g., "I'm your parent, and I say you can't dress like that."
ADOLESCENT	Conventional	Reference to standards of behavior shared with peers, e.g., "My friends would think I'm weird."
	Pragmatic	Consideration of practical needs or consequences, e.g., "I'm comfortable in these clothes."
	Personal	Portraying the issue as one of maintaining personal jurisdiction in an area, e.g., "The way I dress is an expression of me and my personality."

Source: J. G. Smetana & R. Berent. (1993). Adolescents' and mothers' evaluations of justifications for disputes. *Journal of Adolescent Research, 8,* 252–273.

Adolescents, for instance, believed their friendships to be matters of personal choice, whereas parents considered these to more legitimately fall within their domain, feeling obligated to step in when they disapproved of certain friends. Similarly, even though parents and adolescents agreed that parents had the authority and were even obligated to set down rules concerning prudential issues, disagreements arose over which specific issues fell within this domain, with parents seeing themselves as having more authority to govern adolescents' behavior than adolescents did. The large differences in parents' and adolescents' perceptions of these issues indicate where the struggle for autonomy is fought—not on moral or even conventional grounds, but on what constitutes the personal prerogatives of adolescents.

In general, for both adolescents and parents, the realm of issues considered to be properly the domain of adolescents increased with age, with more items being considered personal as adolescents got older, thus expanding the sphere of adolescent autonomy (Bosma et al., 1996; Smetana & Asquith, 1994). Smetana and Asquith point out, however, that this sphere remains narrower for parents than for adolescents, the former continuing to see themselves as legitimately setting rules governing adolescents' bodies, physical appearance, and choice of friends.

To what extent are adolescents' appeals to personal prerogative in resolving conflicts with their parents specific to our own highly individualistic culture? Can we generalize findings such as these to other cultures, such

TABLE 5.2   Issues Concerning Parental Authority

MORAL ISSUES

Taking money from parents without permission

Hitting brothers and sisters

Lying to parents

Breaking promises to parents

CONVENTIONAL ISSUES

Not doing assigned chores

Calling parents by their first names

Eating with elbows on table

Cursing

MULTIFACETED ISSUES

A boy wearing an earring

A girl wearing heavy makeup

Not cleaning one's room

Not putting clothes away

FRIENDSHIP ISSUES

Going to a movie alone with a boyfriend or girlfriend

Seeing a friend whom parents do not like

Having a party when parents are away

Inviting a boyfriend or girlfriend over when parents are away

PERSONAL ISSUES

Watching cartoons on TV

Choosing own clothes

Spending allowance money on games

Listening to heavy metal music

PRUDENTIAL ISSUES

Smoking cigarettes

Eating junk food

Drinking alcohol

Driving with friends who are new drivers

Source: J. G. Smetana & P. Asquith. (1994). Adolescents' and parents' conceptions of parental authority and personal autonomy. *Child Development, 65,* 1147–1162.

as Chinese or Hispanic cultures, which are more collectivistic and place a greater value on interpersonal obligations and harmonious relationships? Jenny Yau and Judith Smetana (1996) interviewed seventh-, ninth-, and twelfth-graders from Hong Kong, asking them to describe the types of conflicts they experienced with their parents and listening to the reasons they gave as to why they and their parents felt as they did. They found that these Chinese adolescents talked about conflicts with their parents in very much the same way as North American adolescents, supporting their positions with appeals to personal jurisdiction. This finding suggests that bids for autonomy take place in similar ways despite other differences between these cultures. It should be noted, however, that although these adolescents talked about conflicts with their parents in much the same way as did North American adolescents, they reported far less conflict—just under two disagreements per month—as compared with nearly four and a half for North American adolescents. Even so, when conflicts occurred, they involved the ordinary, everyday issues as those between parents and adolescents in North America: what they could do in their free time, chores, homework, friends, and the like.

Samuel Vuchinich, Joseph Angelelli, and Antone Gatherum (1996), at Oregon State University, followed 63 families in a two-year longitudinal study of family problem solving, making their first observations when the children were in the fourth grade. These investigators found that the struggle for autonomy begins in preadolescence, even before the ages observed by Smetana and Asquith. Families were videotaped as they discussed an issue that had been a problem in the family during the past month. As preadolescents got older, from 9½ to 11½ years, problem solving became less effective, with family members finding it more difficult to reach a solution or even take the other's perspective. With age, preadolescents became more negative. Fathers, especially, appear to react negatively to this, mothers being more the "peacemaker." Consistent with the findings of Smetana and Asquith, difficulties in communicating were not so much a matter of *what* was being discussed, mundane issues generating as much difficulty as significant ones, as was the age of the child.

Parents themselves initiate many of the changes that occur in relating to their adolescent children. They expect adolescents to be more assertive and independent than when they were younger. They think teenagers should get around more on their own, whether going to the library or to a part-time job, and have ideas of their own, from what to wear to how to study for a test. Even so, many parents react with ambivalence to adolescents' bids for independence. For some adults, their sense of themselves is strongly tied to their parenting roles, and to include adolescents in more family decisions, they must redefine those roles.

PARENTS AND ADOLESCENTS

People learn to parent not from reading books or taking courses, though both can be helpful, but from the way *they* were parented. As such, we should find the characteristics of parents to be related to those of their children.

Styles of Parenting

Diana Baumrind (1967, 1971, 1991a), at the University of California, Berkeley, has distinguished four *styles of parenting* in terms of differences in parental responsiveness and demandingness (shown in Table 5.3). *Responsiveness* refers to how sensitive, supportive, and involved parents are, and *demandingness* to the degree to which parents hold high expectations for their

TABLE 5.3   Parenting Style and Social Competence

Parenting Style	Characteristics	Adolescent Social Behavior
Authoritative	Demanding, encourages independence; responsive, warm and nurturing; disciplines with explanation; maintains open dialogue	Social competence and responsibility
Authoritarian	Demanding; consistent in enforcing standards; restrictive, controlling	Ineffective social interaction; inactive
Indulgent	Responsive, warm, and nurturing; undemanding; uses punishment inconsistently and infrequently; exercises little control	Social competence, well-adjusted; peer oriented; misconduct
Neglectful	Unresponsive, little warmth or nurturance; undemanding, sets few limits and provides little supervision	Poor orientation to work and school; behavior problems

Source: Adapted from D. Baumrind. (1991). The influence of parenting style on adolescent competence and substance use. *Journal of Early Adolescence, 11,* 56-95.

adolescents' behavior and supervise their activities, monitoring them in terms of where they are going and who they are with.

Authoritative parents are both responsive and demanding. They are warm and nurturant, listen openly to their children's ideas and plans, and yet are willing to assert their own authority and do so by consistently enforcing their standards. These parents stress self-reliance and independence, maintain an open dialogue with their children, and give reasons when they discipline. **Authoritarian parents** are equally demanding but less responsive than authoritative ones. They, too, are consistent in enforcing their standards but, perhaps because they value obedience over self-reliance, are less open and responsive to the other's perspective. Instead, they expect their children to do as they are told and not to question. Rather than backing up their discipline with reasons, they are more likely to use force. **Indulgent parents** are responsive to their children, as are authoritative parents; however, they are not demanding. These parents are warm and nurturant, making few demands for responsible behavior, punishing infrequently and inconsistently, and exercising little control or power over their children's decisions. A fourth group of parents, **neglectful parents,** are neither responsive nor demanding. These parents provide little nurturance or supervision, are cold and uninvolved, and set few limits, letting their children do whatever they choose.

Both authoritarian and authoritative parents provide strong models, but in different ways. Authoritarian parents attempt to control their children, authoritative ones to guide them. In line with this difference, the latter place greater value on autonomy and self-discipline and the former on obedience and respect for authority. Both types of parents define limits and set standards. Authoritative parents, however, are more willing to listen to reasons and arguments, tending to draw the line around issues rather than set absolute standards.

Authoritative parents, in contrast to authoritarian and permissive ones, try to balance tradition with innovation, cooperation with autonomy, and tolerance with firmness. The children of such parents tend to be socially competent and responsible.

Authoritative parenting carries clear advantages, which persist into adolescence. Adolescents raised in authoritative families are more socially competent, more self-reliant, do better academically, and have a better work ethic. They also show fewer signs of psychological distress, such as anxiety or depression, and fewer problem behaviors, such as truancy or the use of drugs (Kurdek & Fine, 1994; Steinburg, Lamborn, Darling, Mounts, & Dornbusch, 1994). Laurence Steinberg, Susie Lamborn, Nancy Darling, Nina Mounts, and Sanford Dornbusch (1994) found these advantages to remain relatively stable during the high school years. Similarly, the profile of adjustment for adolescents reared by authoritarian parents changed little during high school. These adolescents continued to do well in school and had few behavior problems but were less self-reliant and had less positive conceptions of themselves. The Research Focus, "Questionnaires," describes a study of the relation between parenting style and children's involvement in schoolwork.

A different picture emerges over time for adolescents raised by indulgent parents. These adolescents are well adjusted and socially competent

Research Focus

Questionnaires: Parenting Styles and Flow

By Michael Wapner

For too many students, schoolwork is drudgery. Even good students may find some classes and a good deal of homework boring. But there are those great occasions when a student finds a course fascinating—when the topic is so engrossing that an hour's lecture seems to last only 10 minutes and when television can't compete with the assigned reading. This experience of intrinsically rewarding immersion in an ongoing activity is termed *flow,* and you will not be surprised to find that students who frequently have this experience in school tend to learn well and achieve much.

Research suggests that episodes of flow occur when individuals experience a balance between the challenges of a task and their abilities to meet that challenge. That is, the task must be sufficiently demanding to present a challenge, but students must also experience their talents as up to the task. If the task requires less than the available skills, then it will be boring. If skills are not up to the task, then individuals will experience anxiety.

Kevin Rathunde (1996), of the University of Utah, wondered whether there was a connection between students' likelihood of experiencing flow while engaged in schoolwork and their relationship with their parents, in other words, whether a particular family context corresponds to adolescents' experience of flow at school. The question arose from theorizing about the effects of various patterns of parenting. Based on the work of other investigators, Rathunde identified two dimensions of the parent–adolescent relationship and hypothesized that conditions at home had to be favorable on both dimensions to maximize the likelihood of flow experiences at school. On the one hand, parents who are *supportive* and patient give the student the security to risk involvement in new and engaging tasks. On the other hand, parents who are *challenging* and expect the adolescent to assume more mature responsibilities motivate achievement. It is both the confidence to try and the motivation to achieve, Rathunde guessed, that gives rise to the experience of flow in academic contexts.

But how might one go about testing this idea? Rathunde had high school students wear pagers (a technique described in the Research Focus on sampling), allowing him to sample the quality of their experiences as they worked. He also asked students and their parents to fill out a questionnaire assessing dimensions of family interaction. *Questionnaires,* along with interviews, are a type of *survey research.* Surveys obtain information from large numbers of people, through the use of personal reports. Rathunde, for instance, surveyed 165 adolescents *and* their parents—a total of 400 people. The use of personal reports has its strengths and weaknesses. A ma-

and, if anything, even more oriented toward their peers than other adolescents. However, during high school, their interest in school declined, and forms of misconduct, such as truancy, increased. The most serious declines, however, occurred among adolescents reared by neglectful parents. These adolescents showed even poorer orientations over time toward work and school and significantly more problem behaviors, suggesting a downward trajectory of disengagement at school and emerging behavior problems (Steinberg et al., 1994).

Despite the superiority of authoritative parenting, this type of parenting is not simple, nor is it stress-free. In fact, parenting authoritatively seems to be distinguished by the presence of tensions produced by the need to balance opposing forces: tradition with individualistic innovation, cooperation with autonomous behavior, and tolerance with principled firmness.

At times it may seem easiest to simply appeal to authority or threaten

Research Focus (continued)

jor strength of this type of data is the chance it offers to study behavior that otherwise could not easily be observed. Parenting, for instance, is a behavior that extends over time, rather than occurring in a limited, and easy to observe, time frame. Having adolescents and their parents report on parenting by filling out a questionnaire offers a convenient alternative to many hours of observation. Personal report data, as obtained through questionnaires, is also useful for private behaviors, such as sexual activity, or even illegal ones, such as drug use. A related advantage to the use of questionnaires, unlike face-to-face interviews, is the *anonymity* they offer individuals, who at times may be asked to disclose very personal information. Because most questionnaires rely on *closed-ended questions,* ones that supply individuals with alternative answers from which to choose, data are easy to score; in contrast, data obtained from interviews require elaborate preprocessing or coding before being analyzed. Because of the ease of scoring answers, questionnaires can be given to large numbers of people at relatively little expense to the investigator.

There also are disadvantages to the use of questionnaires. They can only be given to people who can read, thus eliminating their use with very young children or others with limited reading skills. Nonnative English speakers may also find them difficult. Individuals also appear to find it less interesting to fill out a questionnaire than to be interviewed, making participation somewhat less likely than with the use of personal interviews. A more serious disadvantage, however, is the investigator's inability to interpret questions for an individual who might not understand or might misinterpret the questions' meaning, as can be done in an interview, thereby ensuring that each participant has answered the questions as they were intended. Another disadvantage to questionnaires is the opportunity for distortion, either by deliberately changing information (as might occur in surveys on drug use among adolescents) or by failing to remember events as they really happened. Our memories are notably better for pleasant events or occasions in which we come off looking good. This type of distortion is known as the *social desirability effect.*

What did Rathunde find about parenting correlates of flow? As he anticipated, students whose parents both supported and challenged them reported more optimal experiences when working at school tasks. Specifically, the dimension of parental support was related to students' reports of feeling open, excited, and involved in what they were doing, or to flow, and the dimension of parental challenge was related to their goal directedness.

Sources: P. C. Cozby. (1997). *Methods in behavioral research* (6th ed.). Mountain View, CA: Mayfield. M. Csikszentmihalyi. (1990). *Flow: The psychology of optimal experience.* New York: Harper & Row. K. Rathunde. (1996). Family context and talented adolescents' optimal experience in school-related activities. *Journal of Research on Adolescence, 6,* 605-628.

punishment, both characteristic of authoritarian parenting. Smetana and Berent (1993) found that, although each of these alternatives has the short-term payoff of being effective in achieving compliance, adolescents and parents alike see them as having the potential for causing conflict, especially with older adolescents. William Cook (1993), at the University of Texas, Austin, characterizes this conflict as a downward spiral in which coercive attempts to get adolescents to behave in desired ways result in greater negativity among adolescents, causing parents to feel even less in control of the situation than before.

As a group, children of authoritative parents are more competent and independent, and are less likely to be rebellious, than those of other parents (Baumrind, 1991b). Their parents have stressed self-reliance and have paved the way for independence by involving their children in decision making from early childhood on. Interestingly, the conditions that lead to rebelliousness in adolescence, or childhood, are not necessarily rigorous demands, but arbitrary ones. Parental strictness per se does not appear to be the issue; rather it is the willingness, or lack thereof, to give adolescents a voice in decision making (Fuligni & Eccles, 1993). Andrew Fuligni and Jacquelynne Eccles, at the University of Michigan, found that early adolescents who perceive their parents as unwilling to relax their control or allow them to participate in decisions often turn to friends for support and advice, even when maintaining such relationships involved some personal cost. Parents encounter rebelliousness, it seems, when they fail to leave room for autonomy, do not give reasons for their actions, or are inconsistent in their punishment. Inconsistency can also take the form of different parenting styles from each parent, as when one parent is authoritative and the other permissive. This type of inconsistency is associated with lower self-esteem and lower school achievement in adolescents (Johnson, Shulman, & Collins, 1991).

Parenting styles vary little with the gender of adolescents, but they do change with their age. In a study of nearly 8,000 high school students, Sanford Dornbusch and his colleagues (1987) found that authoritarian parenting decreases as adolescents get older; similarly, permissiveness increases. Interestingly, authoritative parenting does not vary with adolescent age. The reason, Dornbusch and his associates suggest, is that authoritative parenting reflects an ideological commitment on the part of parents and is not a simple response to what adolescents do. Also, being more democratic than authoritarian parenting, it continues to be appropriate in adolescence.

Styles of Parenting and Ethnicity

Research with European American adolescents clearly links measures of adjustment and school success to parenting styles, with authoritative parenting being the best predictor of adolescent adjustment and authoritarian parenting more frequently being associated with negative outcomes. Many ethnic minority families prove an exception to this general finding. Yet it has been difficult to determine what might be responsible for the differences. To what extent, for instance, are the cultural differences associated with ethnicity responsible? Or are the differences due to the resources of one's community, resources—such as the quality of schools, libraries, and parks—that also frequently differ with ethnicity?

Susie Lamborn, Sanford Dornbusch, and Laurence Steinberg (1996) assessed adjustment in more than 3,500 African American, Asian American, European American, and Hispanic 14- to 16-year-olds over a two-year period. These investigators drew their samples of adolescents from two types of communities: ethnically mixed communities and predominantly White, somewhat more affluent, communities. They found little to support the possible mediating role of community context. Instead, the advantages of authoritative parenting were equally visible for African American adolescents, whether they came from one type of community or the other, and the disadvantages associated with authoritarian parenting were similar for European American adolescents, irrespective of their community. Authori-

Chinese American
parents may appear
to be controlling or
strict, but they differ
from authoritarian
parents in that control
is bidirectional.

tarian parenting was unrelated to adolescent adjustment for either Asian American or Hispanic adolescents, for either type of community.

Ruth Chao (1994), at the University of California, Los Angeles, argues that parenting styles cannot be separated in any simple way from their cultural contexts. She points out that Chinese American parenting, often referred to by developmentalists as "authoritarian," "controlling," or "strict," nonetheless is very different from the authoritarian style of parenting identified by Baumrind. "Strictness" and "control" simply do not exist as ways of interacting for most Asian parents. For instance, control, instead of taking the form of a unidirectional exercise of power by parents over the child, in Asian cultures is bidirectional, carrying with it an obligation to nurture and support the child. Thus, parents are as much governed by the child's needs as the child is under the control of the parents. This manner of parenting, by the way, is associated with high levels of academic achievement among Asian American students.

Chao refers to this harmonious parenting relationship as *chiao shun,* or child "training." In practice, this type of parenting takes the form of providing an exceptionally supportive environment for the child. If anything, it comes closer to authoritative parenting, as this is practiced by European American parents, which is also characterized by high degrees of responsiveness and support and high expectations in terms of the child's behavior. Chao, in fact, found that the immigrant Chinese American mothers she studied did not differ from European American mothers in the degree to which they endorsed statements indicative of authoritative parenting. David Crystal and Harold Stevenson (1995) have found as well that adolescents in China do not differ from European American adolescents in their perceptions of the disruptiveness of conflict in the family, suggesting that Chinese parents may be more open to dialogue with adolescents (also a characteristic of Baumrind's authoritative parents) than previously thought.

Parenting is not an activity limited to mothers and fathers; many ethnic minority, as well as majority, families include a grandparent or other relative living in the home. Adolescents who have contact with grandparents, aunts, and uncles, whether under the same roof or close enough to visit, typically benefit from their support. Ronald Taylor (1996), at Temple University, found that adolescents whose families frequently got together with relatives, and who could count on them for advice and support, were more self-reliant and successful in school and had fewer problem behaviors.

Robin Jarrett (1995), at Loyola University, identifies such supportive adult networks as a key element for low-income families, an element that can make a difference in buffering the adolescent from the risks associated with poverty. The excerpt that follows describes such a relationship between an adolescent girl, Ruth, and her oldest sister, who already has two children of her own:

> Ruth's siblings have been an important influence in her life. Her oldest sister, Mary, is twenty-five and an unmarried mother of two. When asked about her relationship with Mary, Ruth says, "We have a good relationship. Not only is she my oldest sister, but she is also my second mother. As a child she was our mother while our real mother was working. She spanked and chastised us just like my mother. Mary and I have a relationship that I wouldn't trade in for anything. (Williams & Kornblum, 1985, p. 24, as cited in Jarrett, 1995)

The Contexts of Parenting: Genetic and Environmental Contributions

To what extent can the correspondence between parenting styles and the characteristics of adolescents be attributed to parenting per se, and to what extent can this correspondence be attributed to what parents and adolescents have in common to begin with? Families share more than living spaces and meals together. They also share a gene pool. Is reliance on reason and consistency when disciplining, for instance, the *cause* of adolescents' competence and achievement in school? Or might a more complex interplay between parents and adolescents be present, one in which both the parents' and the adolescents' behavior is due to similarities in their genetic environments?

Sandra Scarr (1992, 1993), at the University of Virginia, takes a constructive approach in explaining the interplay of genetic and environmental factors, arguing that adolescents construct their realities from many possible realities that are latent in their environments. The events that make up their daily lives, for instance, can be perceived in quite different ways by different adolescents; consequently, these events will not have the same impact from one adolescent to the next. For instance Matt McGue, Anu Sharma, and Peter Benson (1996) found that measures of adolescent adjustment among adopted siblings—children who were not biologically related yet were reared in the same home—were quite low, indicating that their shared environment contributed little to their adjustment.

Scarr adds that not only do environments not exist for adolescents apart from being constructed by them, but also that the processes that adolescents bring to bear in doing so are themselves influenced by genetic factors, making it impossible to separate environmental and genetic contributions to development. An adolescent's genotype, in other words, will predispose that adolescent to take in certain environmental experiences and not others, even though the latter may be equally present. Such experiences simply will not be as salient for an adolescent with that genotype.

Scarr distinguishes three ways in which genotypes structure environments: passive, evocative, and active.

1. *Passive* Because parents are responsible for both the adolescent's genes and the home environment in which the adolescent grows up, the adolescent's genes and environment will be correlated. For instance, parents who enjoy reading will enjoy things such as talking about books and watching educational programs on television. In this way, the parents' own enjoyment of reading, which is genetically influenced, in turn influences both the adolescent's environment and the adolescent's genotype.

2. *Evocative* In this pattern of influence, genetically influenced behaviors, such as sociability, mood, or intelligence, evoke responses in others that contribute to the adolescent's interpersonal environment and to the adolescent's self-image. It is possible, for instance, that parents' behavior is more similar with siblings who are themselves more similar, such as is the case with identical twins. Genetically influenced traits serve as self-fulfilling prophecies. For instance, children with sunny personalities elicit positive responses in others, which in turn occasion positive moods in the children; fussy children, in contrast, are more likely to experience negative reactions in others, which contribute to their negative moods.

3. *Active* Adolescents select environments that fit their genetically influenced personalities. Thus, the way in which adolescents spend their time, either with others or alone, and what they do will reflect their personalities and talents. Adolescents will sort themselves into different types of environments based on the interests and abilities resulting from different genotypes. This third way in which genetic predispositions structure adolescents' experiences, sometimes called "niche picking," is increasingly likely to occur with age, as children have more opportunities to choose their own activities.

The notion that adolescents create their own environments runs counter to many parents' beliefs concerning the importance of their influence. Yet research examining similarities among siblings differing in degrees of relatedness supports substantial genetic contributions (Plomin & Daniels, 1987). Scarr (1992) points out that the variability among children from the same family is as great as that among children from different families. This observation suggests that family environments have fewer important effects on children than have been supposed, providing, of course, that the family environments are sufficient to support the development of genetically influenced individual differences. In other words, Scarr believes that differences in environments, given that these are "adequate," are not important determinants of differences among children. Some parents, at least, may find comfort in Scarr's words, namely that "children's outcomes do not

How much does the
family environment
affect who the chil-
dren are? If the effect
is strong, siblings
would tend to resem-
ble one another more.

depend on whether parents take children to the ball game or to a museum
so much as they depend on genetic transmission, on plentiful opportunities, and on having a good enough environment that supports children's
development to become themselves" (1992, p. 15).

Support for Scarr's position comes from research examining similarities in the way children perceive their family environments as a function of
the degree to which the children are genetically related to one another.
When identical twins (100% genetic relatedness), fraternal twins (50% relatedness), full siblings (50% relatedness), half siblings (25% relatedness), and
genetically unrelated children (0% relatedness) were asked to evaluate their
family environments along a number of dimensions, such as parental
warmth and the way parents monitor their children's behavior and deal with
conflict, investigators found significant genetic effects for most of their measures. That is, the closer the genetic relatedness among the siblings, the
more similar the siblings' perceptions of their environments. In general, over
25% of the variance of environmental measures was attributable to genetic
similarities among children (Plomin, Reiss, Hetherington, & Howe, 1994).

Yoon-Mi Hur and Thomas Bouchard (1995) also examined identical and fraternal twins' perceptions of their childhood family environments. However, their twins had been separated early in childhood (mean age at separation was 1 year) and grew up in different homes. Even so, these investigators found that identical twins were much more likely than were fraternal twins to share similar perceptions of parental support. With respect to issues of parental control, however, genetic contributions were minimal. Because the twins grew up with different sets of parents and in different homes, these findings suggest a very real biological basis to differences among individuals in the ways in which they perceive, or construct, their surroundings. They suggest, in other words, that children help to create the environments that they experience.

A number of scholars have criticized Scarr's position (Baumrind, 1993; Jackson, 1993). Diana Baumrind (1993) has argued that Scarr has not made clear what makes a family environment "good enough." In the absence of specifying what contributes to a family's environment, Scarr's argument that certain factors (such as parental disciplinary patterns or family income) are not important, loses its force. In fact, Baumrind's point is underscored by Hur and Bouchard's finding that children's perceptions of certain dimensions of the family environment, such as parental support, reflect a biological component, whereas other dimensions, such as parental control, do not. Baumrind also argues that research into genetic and environmental contributions to development is limited by the inadequacies of the instruments currently available for measuring family environment. The research of Baumrind and others on parenting styles clearly underscores parents' contribution to developmental outcomes such as social competence and independence (Baumrind, 1991a; Smetana & Berent, 1993).

In general, parents who are responsive, consistent, willing to listen, and willing to give adolescents a voice in decision making will have healthy relationships with their adolescents. All this may sound good in theory; however, many parents may be at a point in their own lives in which responsiveness, consistency, and a willingness to listen—let alone sharing responsibility—are especially difficult, if not outright problematic. They, too, are facing a crisis—that of middle age.

Whose Identity Crisis? Parents and Middle Age

Middle-aged parents face the downward side of the developmental curves their adolescent children are climbing. Each of the developmental tasks facing adolescents comes up for review again in the middle years. Table 1.1 lists these tasks, along with those of middle age.

Just as puberty marks the beginning of adolescence, physical changes alert parents that they are entering middle age, and many find these changes difficult to accept. Perhaps the first sign of aging for most adults appears when they step on the bathroom scales. Middle age brings an increase in body weight and a change in its distribution. The face becomes thinner, as do legs and arms. But what is lost in the extremities is gained through the middle (Stevens-Long & Commons, 1992). Bob Hope once quipped that "Middle age is when your age begins to show around your middle." Changes such as these are difficult at any age, but the kicker for most parents is the timing: Most adults begin to experience these changes just when their adolescent children are developing beautiful bodies and fantastic physiques.

How might these and other physical changes affect the willingness of parents to listen to or share responsibility for decision making with adolescents? An everyday example such as buying clothes provides some insights. Although bathing suits are merely swimwear to parents of preteens, to parents of adolescents they can raise issues of sexuality or even competition. Adolescents' arguments that suits of the same style are worn by young children go unheard, if parents are alarmed by their adolescent's obvious physical maturity or their own feelings of physical decline and undesirability.

Middle-aged parents face another assault on their egos. The functioning of the reproductive organs begins to decline, marking a period of life known as the **climacteric.** Women experience **menopause,** a cessation of menstrual periods, somewhere between ages 48 and 52. Unlike menarche, menopause is a gradual process that takes many months, and for some women, several years (Masters, Johnson, & Kolodny, 1988). The body also decreases its production of estrogens. As the level of circulating estrogen decreases, the genital tract is affected, sometimes impairing sexual function as a result (Stevens-Long & Commons, 1992).

The climacteric in men is not as noticeable as in women, though it does affect them as well. Middle-aged men are likely to experience a change in sexual functioning. Erections and orgasms take longer to achieve. For both sexes, there may be a slight diminishment of the intensity of orgasm (Masters, Johnson, & Kolodny, 1988). Thus, when their children reach sexual maturity, middle-aged parents face a sexual identity crisis—or at least a serious inventory taking. Changes in sexual function can affect parents' sense of themselves as sexually desirable partners. For increasing numbers of middle-aged adults, these changes come at a time when they face the loss of a marriage partner through divorce and the doubts and anxieties raised by dating. Parents may view their adolescents' dates and romantic involvements with more concern—or perhaps vicarious pleasure—than they would if their own sexual functioning and prowess were not as salient a concern to them.

Similarly, just when adolescents begin to think about future careers, many middle-aged parents begin to review their own careers and question whether the jobs they have been pursuing all these years have been worth the effort they have put into them. Many adults may face the realization that they will never advance beyond their present position. This realization can be especially painful if they see opportunities for their children that offer more promise than the jobs they presently have. Listening to plans about the future can be difficult as parents face hard facts about their own present realities.

Each of these areas of change is a source of stress in the lives of parents and adolescents. The fact that the changes experienced by one generation complement so neatly those experienced by the other almost guarantees that relationships will be more stressful.

Adolescents' Identity Crisis: Gaining a Sense of Self

Many adolescents mistakenly assume, as they begin to get a sense of themselves, that they are unique—completely different and separate from others. The mistake, actually, is in stopping there. They *are* unique, and this highlights their separateness. But their uniqueness is grounded in their most intimate relationships and is only experienced fully when relating to others. Adolescents also share commonalities with others that are as important as their differences—the need to feel good about themselves, to feel a sense of accomplishment, to be loved. Separate? Yes, but only when their sense of connectedness with others gives them the security to explore themselves.

Adolescents' search for the truth about themselves begins when the separate worlds in which they live begin to pull apart. Adolescents begin to see themselves as more than their parents' children, to question where the skills they are acquiring in school will take them, to ask who they will be living with in the future. Erik Erikson (1968) suggests that the search ultimately leads to a sense of "sameness and continuity" that allows adolescents to transcend the differences they experience in their many roles—full-time student, part-time employee, daughter, son, friend, neighbor, and so on.

Gaining a sense of themselves almost seems to require the tools of a magician, or an actor: mirrors, sleight of hand, impressive costumes. Adolescents frequently find themselves playing out roles that are just a bit too big for them or not quite right. They try on these roles because the comfortable ones of childhood no longer fit. Adolescents find themselves looking inward and outward all at once, one eye on the inner self and another on those around them. They are well aware others may be judging them in terms of the cultural images they share, but also in terms of how well the others have achieved precisely what they themselves are attempting to do (Erikson, 1968).

AUTONOMY AND INDIVIDUATION

The drama of gaining a sense of themselves unfolds on a well-known stage: at home as adolescents interact with parents, pressing for greater autonomy. In winning new responsibilities, they discover strengths that are uniquely theirs and that distinguish them from their parents, a process known as individuation.

Autonomy

One of the major issues confronting early adolescents is to become more autonomous. **Autonomy** involves independence and being responsible for one's actions. Adolescents press for greater inclusion in decisions; they ask to be treated as more adult. The number of decisions they make by themselves increases with age from early to late adolescence; decisions they share with parents or that are made by parents alone decrease with age. These trends are more pronounced for males than females (Dornbusch, Ritter, Mont-Reynaud, & Chen, 1990).

Bids for greater autonomy might be expected to occasion some conflict with parents, and they do. Most conflicts are over household routines, such as picking up after oneself, doing homework, and chores. And most of these involve mothers, because they are more immediately involved in maintaining the household than are fathers (Steinberg, 1987a, 1989). Parenting style, especially that of mothers, is particularly important for girls' autonomy. For boys, age is the single most important determinant of increasing independence (Bartle, Anderson, & Sabatelli, 1989).

Autonomy is a much larger issue for early adolescents than for older ones. Arehart and Smith (1990) found that concern with questions of autonomy accounted for nearly half of the variability among early adolescents' answers to a measure of psychosocial maturity. By the end of high school, autonomy issues have been resolved and new issues appear.

Parents can either facilitate or hinder the growth of autonomy (Pardeck & Pardeck, 1990). As adolescents vie for a say in and eventual control over the decisions that affect them, some conflict with parents may be inevitable. (Box 5.2 offers some insight into the potential conflicts between adolescents and parents.) Not all parents react the same to these demands. Some are able to turn over increasing responsibility to their children; others, threatened by bids for greater autonomy, react negatively. The less conflict in the family, the greater the adolescent's movement toward psychosocial maturity (Gavazzi & Sabatelli, 1990). Not all of the difficulty comes from parents. Adolescents contribute to some of the conflict themselves. In order to achieve autonomy, adolescents must go through a psychic housecleaning known as individuation.

Individuation: The Developmental Process

Adolescents must undo one of their major accomplishments as children. They must disassemble and rebuild the psychological structure they have lived in through childhood. They do this by examining their feelings, attitudes, and beliefs, in order to discover which are really theirs and which are their parents'. Because children uncritically assume for themselves their parents' attitudes and ways, this examination process is a necessary step for early adolescents. It may be that the only way children can feel strong enough to step out on their own and explore the world for themselves is to carry some of their parents' strengths along with them. The very internalizations that promote autonomy in childhood are the ones that adolescents must get beyond in order to grow, and this process is termed **individuation** (Josselson, 1980, 1988).

Adolescents accomplish this growth in ordinary ways—by making decisions for themselves and by living with the consequences of these decisions. The major decision all adolescents face is who is going to make the decisions, but because decisions take many different forms, this point is easily missed. Adolescents find themselves arguing about who they can go out with, how tight is too tight for jeans, how late they can stay up, when they

A messy room and a busy phone may be signs of a young adolescent moving toward autonomy rather than of innate sloppiness or irresponsibility.

do their homework, or who gets to say what courses they can take in school. Much of the process is repetitive. Decisions made one day must be renegotiated the next, as the same issues continue to come up in different forms.

Perhaps the process is repetitive because it involves learning in a real life situation instead of in a classroom. In the classroom, principles are stated explicitly, frequently apart from any context, and adolescents must relate these principles to real life situations. Just the opposite occurs when learning outside the classroom. Outside their classes, adolescents learn by doing and by experiencing the consequences. No one is there to help identify which principles operate in that situation. As a result, it is often difficult to separate the elements that remain constant across situations from the situations themselves. Are adolescents really arguing about how loud their music can be, or about who gets to decide how loud is too loud?

There is another reason why adolescents tend to repeat the decision-making process. Frequently what they learn from their decisions has very

Box 5.2   An Interview With Anne Petersen: Adolescents and Their Parents

WHAT IS IMPORTANT FOR PARENTS OF ADOLESCENTS TO KNOW?

The societal view of adolescents is negative. I collect cartoons, and they portray an extreme view of adolescents as having hormone attacks, being difficult, impossible.

This belief in our country that adolescents are difficult and want to be independent is one of the biggest pitfalls for parents. We know that though adolescents want to be autonomous, they need parents. We know that young adolescents are argumentative, sometimes obnoxious. Parents throw in the towel, and that is the worst thing they can do. Adolescents need to know that parental support is there. There have been historical changes in the family, increasing the possibility for kids to be independent with cars and to have more time away from home; all these changes have exacerbated the trend toward independence and separation. Too much freedom is detrimental to adolescents' development.

Parents need to know that when you ask adolescents, especially young adolescents, who is more important to them, they say the parents, even if the parents are reporting conflict. We find, then, that parents are less positive about their adolescents than their adolescents are about them. Adolescents' off-putting behavior—telling parents to get lost because the adolescents are mature—is not really the message they want to send. They are asking for a little more space; they are asking for help in becoming autonomous and interdependent rather than independent.

Research shows that conflicts are about little things, not big things. The conflicts are not about values, but largely about doing dishes, taking out the garbage. They are a way of relieving tensions. Parents ought to be a safe source for venting tensions. If they cease to be a safe source, then young adolescents are really lost; they have no one.

Parents sometimes believe that they need to be their child's buddy, but that's not true. They need to be parents. They need to provide unconditional love, firm guidelines, and strong expectations.

Puberty, with all the change that accompanies it, is a difficult time for boys and girls, especially when they have to change schools. It seems to work slightly differently for boys and girls. In general, boys seem less influenced by what is going on with parents, but basic support is pretty important. If parental support is not there, it is very bad for girls. Those girls who have a lot of family conflict or lack support are the ones who become the most depressed.

---

personal consequences, which they may not be ready to accept. Discovering how to solve an algebraic equation has little bearing on life outside math class; algebra is "safe" knowledge. But discovering that you are the only one who can make decisions for yourself, and that there is no one to blame or praise but yourself, is something else again. Understanding is rarely just an intellectual matter; it also reflects one's emotions and beliefs, and some things can be understood only when one is prepared to let go of old beliefs.

Box 5.2   (*continued*)

HOW WOULD YOU SAY YOUR OWN RESEARCH HAS INFLUENCED THE WAY YOU REAR YOUR CHILDREN?

I think it has changed a lot of things. That my daughter rebelled was a big shock. I remember vividly the day she refused to do something. There was no door banging, but she said she would not do something I had just assumed she would do. I immediately had the stereotypic reaction, "Oh my heavens, what is going on here?" All of a sudden I realized that this was what I had been talking about for a long time. Knowing all the data, why should I be surprised that my kid goes through this too?

It helped a lot to know what could be effective in dealing with this. We had a family conference. What she was saying was, "How about taking my needs into account?" She was upset that we just assumed she would be a part of some activity. It is enlightening to realize that we don't treat an adult, a colleague, or a friend like that. It makes sense to change your behavior toward young adolescents. Well, we worked it out. There are still occasional lapses of communication, and that's where the problems really are. Somebody assumes that somebody else is going to do something, and there is either a conflict of schedules or wishes. But at least saying, "Yes, you are right, you ought to have an increasing role in family decision making" and have a forum within which to do it made a lot of difference to her. She did not have to explode. She could put her two cents in.

When there is a good reason, we change our plans to meet her needs. It is important for us to show that we do not need to be controlling things, that we do respect her views, that she does have a voice. I am sure if you were to ask both our children, they would say they do not have as much say as they would like. That is because we still do believe that we are the parents and there are some things we need to decide.

We believe that it is important to let them see how we are thinking about things and to understand decision-making processes. So, we talk in the family about money and about vacation plans, and we really try to include them—not just out of respect for them to increasingly become a part, but also to let them see how we think about things so they have the benefit of knowing how adults make decisions. That seems to work pretty well.

Source: Adapted from J. Brooks. (1991). [Interview with Anne C. Petersen, Dean of the College of Health and Human Development, Pennsylvania State University]. In J. Brooks, *The process of parenting* (3rd ed.). Mountain View, CA: Mayfield.

Sometimes adolescents, or adults for that matter, cannot allow themselves to understand until they can live with the consequences of that understanding. They may prefer to live with isolated actions, not seeing how one fits with another to form a larger picture (Wapner, 1980).

Even though the daily decisions adolescents make often seem trivial, the process itself never is; it is a way of separating themselves as individuals. The process is also frequently lonely. Rejecting parental attitudes and val-

Box 5.3 The Joys of Parenting Early Adolescents

"Seeing him care for younger children and babies is a great pleasure. He's a great nurturer with small children. He has endless patience."—*Mother*

"He is a talented athlete, and his soccer team got to a championship game. He scored the winning goal, and when he took off with the ball down the field, I was very proud of him. It was a unique feeling of being proud that someone I had helped to create was doing that. He had felt a lot of pressure in the game, so to see how incredibly pleased he was gave me great joy."—*Father*

"Now that they are older, they bring new skills into our lives. I did not learn algebra in school, but to help him with problems now and then, I learned algebra from the book. I am very pleased to be able to help."—*Mother*

"It is gratifying to me to see him learn the rules. He makes sure his homework is done, and he does it on his own steam."—*Mother*

"I like that he does things I did, like play the trumpet. He started at the same age I did and since he took it up, it has rekindled my interest and I started practicing again. This last weekend, we played together. He also brings new interests, too. Because he likes sailing, I have started that and really like it."—*Father*

"She is in that dreamy preteen state where she writes things. She wrote a poem about the difference between being alone and loneliness. She has a real appreciation of time on her own and how nice being alone can be. I like that because I had that at her age."—*Mother*

"It's nice just being able to help them, feeling good because they are being helped out and benefited."—*Father*

"Well, they have their friends over, and we have ping pong, pool, cards, and we stressed having these things available. I enjoy playing all these games with them."—*Father*

ues can often leave adolescents with an empty feeling; they've discarded old ways before developing new ones of their own. Ruthellen Josselson (1980) suggests that emotions help adolescents with this transition. The very intensity of their emotions lets them know there is still someone inside. This function may account for some of the emotional intensity of early adolescence. Older adolescents have become surer of their decisions, and much of the earlier emotional overkill drops out. By late adolescence most have disentangled their needs and ideas from those of their parents and have a sense of being in charge of their lives. They no longer need emotion to fill a psychic void or to convince themselves, or others, that they are in control.

Throughout the individuation process, adolescents attempt to preserve a sense of sameness of their inner selves and of what they mean to others. The identities that emerge must be continuous with their past and also al-

Box 5.3   *(continued)*

"It's nice to see her being able to analyze situations with friends or with her teachers and come to conclusions. She said about one of her teachers, 'Well, she gets excited and she never follows through with what she says, so you know you don't have to take her seriously.'"—*Mother*

"I really enjoy being in the scouts with the boys. Once a month we go on a camping weekend, and I really look forward to that."—*Father*

"I was so impressed and pleased that after the earthquake, he and a friend decided to go door to door and offer to sell drawings they made of Teenage Mutant Ninja Turtles. He raised $150 that he gave for earthquake relief. I was very proud that he thought this up all by himself."—*Father*

"I was very happy one day when I found this note she left on my desk. It said, 'Hello!!! Have a happy day! Don't worry about home, everyone's fine! Do your work the very best you can. But most important, have a fruitful life!!' I saved that note because it made me feel so good."—*Mother*

"He enjoys life. He has a sense of humor. He's like a butterfly enjoying everything; eventually he'll settle in."—*Mother*

"He's very sensitive, and his cousins two years older than he ask his advice about boys. They may not take it, but they ask him even though he's younger."—*Father*

"It's very rewarding to see them in their school activities. My daughter sings in the school chorus, and I enjoy that, and my son is in school plays."—*Father*

"I am very pleased that she is less moody now than she used to be. We used to refer to her lows as 'Puddles of Frustration,' but she's gotten past that now."—*Mother*

Source: Adapted from J. Brooks. (1991). *The process of parenting* (3rd ed.). Mountain View, CA: Mayfield.

low them to project themselves into the future. Adolescents who successfully sort through their own and their parents' attitudes and beliefs can maintain a comfortable closeness with their parents, without fearing a loss of their own individuality. (Box 5.3 describes some of the benefits of parenting early adolescents.) This closeness is an important source of continuity in their lives. Adolescents do not need to discard old relationships or adopt completely new lifestyles in order to be their own person (Mazor & Enright, 1988). Individuation involves both a growing independence from parents, such as in managing daily events or needing less support, and positive feelings about one's independence. The latter, at least for late adolescents, appears to be a better index of individuation than the more concrete changes, as it can predict such things as easier adjustment to college (Rice, Cole, & Lapsley, 1990).

Individuation is the process of distinguishing one's own attitudes and beliefs from those of one's parents. Adolescents who successfully complete this process can maintain a comfortable closeness with their parents and not fear they will lose their newly fledged identity.

Family Interaction and Adolescents' Individuation

The family has a critical role in the personality development of adolescents. But how do families exert their effect? Are parents models for the behaviors adolescents acquire, or do these behaviors develop in the context of interactions among family members?

Individuality and Connectedness in the Family   Harold Grotevant and Catherine Cooper (1986), developmentalists at the University of Minnesota and the University of California, Santa Cruz, identified dimensions of family interaction that contribute to the development of individuation. They used a deceptively simple approach to study family interactions: They asked families to make plans for an imaginary vacation, and analyzed the communication patterns that developed within the family. They looked for patterns that evidenced two qualities they believed to be critical for the development of individuation: individuality and connectedness. **Individuality** is the ability to have and express one's own ideas (*self-assertion*) and to say how one differs from others (*separateness*). **Connectedness** reflects one's openness to others' opinions (*permeability*), and one's respect for their ideas (*mutuality*). Box 5.4 illustrates their approach. These investigators looked for statements that illustrate each of these four factors.

Adolescents in an individuated relationship have a clear sense of themselves as distinct from other people yet feel emotionally connected with them. They have their own ideas, which they can express, and are open to the ideas of the person they are with. In a sense, individuation allows them to respect each person as an individual—including themselves. Equally important, individuated relationships allow adolescents to experience their connectedness with another person and still see how they are different. Research on individuation suggests that adolescents who achieve high levels of individuation can remain close to their parents without feeling a loss of their own distinctiveness. The research also supports the view that parent–adolescent relationships continue to be close as they move toward greater mutuality (Mazor & Enright, 1988; White, Speisman, & Costos, 1983).

Adolescents do not have to have an individuated relationship with both parents. A single relationship in which there are moderate to high degrees of separateness and permeability makes individuation possible. Adolescents who achieve the highest levels of individuation, however, are likely to come from families in which members delight in examining their differences yet experience connectedness with each other.

Adolescents low in individuation typically have families who avoid disagreeing with each other and are so responsive to others' opinions that they cannot form a differing opinion of their own. Families with few disagreements communicate one important message to their members: that it is important to agree. Adolescents from these families must express the family point of view in order to voice anything at all. Doing so reassures others that they agree with them. As an extreme example, when the mother in one family asked where they should go on their vacation, each member responded by repeating the father's suggestion of going back to Spain. When asked for more suggestions by her father, the adolescent daughter could not elaborate and fumbled an "I don't know," indicating her father should offer more suggestions. It was hard for this adolescent to explore issues outside her family's belief system, even when they only involved choices for an imaginary family vacation (Grotevant & Cooper, 1986). Adolescents who can experience their separateness from other members of the family are freer to develop their own point of view. Even so, their explorations take place in an emotional context of connectedness, which provides the security that allows them to examine ideas.

To develop a point of view, adolescents must be able to see how their ideas differ from those of others. Interactions that focus on differences and similarities provide important developmental experiences; they can also involve conflict. Conflict itself isn't necessarily bad. In the context of clarifying a position, it can help adolescents gain a sense of what they believe. For adolescents to have their ideas challenged without experiencing this as criticism, a supportive family atmosphere is important (Powers, Hauser, Schwartz, Noam, & Jacobson, 1983; Shulman, Seiffge-Krenke, & Samat, 1987). In fact, adolescents' experience of support is generally unrelated to conflicts with parents (Barrera, Chassin, & Rogosch, 1993).

Box 5.4   Communication Patterns That Foster Individualism

TANYA: Why don't we visit Grandma and then go someplace exotic like the Everglades?

WILLIE: Do you know how hot it is in florida in August? I vote to skip the family visit this year and go to Acapulco. That's a real vacation.

DAD: I could sure use some time on a beach.

WILLIE: Right, Dad, but you don't want to share it with a crocodile, do you?

TANYA: They're alligators, not crocodiles, Surfer Joe.

MOM: I'd like to see the pyramids in Mexico. We could stop off at Acapulco on the way.

TANYA: Hmm.

DAD: How far inland are they?

MOM: I don't know, but I could call a travel agent.

WILLIE: Get real, Mom. Do you think you can get us to sweat a path through the jungle once we've seen the sands of Acapulco?

TANYA: Willie'd die in the heat there too.

DAD: Maybe we should think of a winter vacation.

TANYA: All right, let's vote on this.

WILLIE: Okay, let's vote.

It would be great if we all had the choices open to this family—sandy beaches, the Everglades, Acapulco, the pyramids of Mexico. In a sense we do. You see, this family is participating in a research project in which they have been asked to make plans for an imaginary two-week vacation, the cost of which is no problem. The researchers, Harold Grotevant and Catherine Cooper, aren't interested in where the family finally decides to go; Grandma might still get lucky. They are studying how members of families interact with one another and how these relationships affect adolescent development.

These investigators identified two dimensions of family interaction, *individuality* and *connectedness,* that contribute to individuation. Two ways of interacting with others, *self-assertion* and *separateness,* contribute to individuality. Similarly, two ways of interacting also contribute to connectedness. These are *permeability* and *mutuality.* Each of these ways of interacting is illustrated below.

INDIVIDUALITY

Self-Assertion   The ability to have one's own ideas and express them. "I'd like to see the pyramids in Mexico."

Ego Development of Parents and Children   Measures of ego development of parents and adolescents find complex relationships between the level of development in parents and that of their children. Stuart Hauser, Emily Borman, Alan Jacobson, Sally Powers, and Gil Noam (1991) found that parents'

Box 5.4   (*continued*)

Separateness   The ability to say how one differs from others.

1. Requests action
   "All right, let's vote on this."

2. Directly disagrees
   "Get real, Mom. Do you think you can get us to sweat a path
   through the jungle once we've seen the sands of Acapulco?"

3. Indirectly disagrees
   "Do you know how hot it is in Florida in August?"

4. Irrelevant comment
   "They're alligators, not crocodiles, Surfer Joe."

CONNECTEDNESS

Permeability   Openness and responsiveness to the opinions of others.

1. Acknowledges
   "Hmm."

2. Requests information or validation
   "How far inland are they?"

3. Agrees with another's ideas
   "I could sure use some time on a beach."

4. Relevant comment
   "Maybe we should think of a winter vacation."

5. Complies with a request
   "Okay, let's vote."

Mutuality   Sensitivity and respect for others' ideas.

1. Indirect suggestion of action
   "Why don't we visit Grandma and then go someplace exotic like the
   Everglades?"

2. Compromise
   "I'd like to see the pyramids in Mexico. We could stop off at Acapulco on the way."

3. States another's feelings
   "Willie'd die in the heat there, too."

4. Answers request for information/validation
   "I don't know, but I could call a travel agent."

Source: Adapted from C. Cooper, H. Grotevant, & S. Condon. (1983). Individuality and connectedness in the family as a context for adolescent identity formation and role-taking skill. In H. D.
Grotevant & C. R. Cooper (Eds.), *Adolescent development in the family.* San Francisco: Jossey-Bass.

ego development, especially that of mothers, predicted ego development in
adolescents, as measured by the coping strategies adolescents used. These
investigators suggest that coping styles in parents, just as in adolescents,
reflect the level of their ego development. By observing and interacting with

Warm and loving relationships within the family help adolescents individuate and develop self-esteem. Without family members who believe in them and stand by them, teenagers may lose faith in themselves and drop out of school long before graduation day.

their parents, adolescents adopt coping styles that reflect the interactional patterns that characterize their family life.

Supporting these observations, research finds that ego development in adolescents relates to the parents' use of cognitively stimulating behaviors and to their supportiveness. Adolescents with the highest levels of ego development are most likely to come from families with a high degree of noncompetitive sharing of perspectives and support. There is little distortion (inaccurate portrayal of another's view or the task) or avoidance (distracting attention from the problem) and little rejection (trying to close off discussion without exploring differences) (Powers et al., 1983).

How might such a family operate when faced with a problem? First, they might not see the problem as having a single solution and are likely to agree to disagree. This approach should not be confused with a dismissal of the problem. Each person thinks carefully about his or her own position and the positions of others. But if they cannot resolve their differences, they are comfortable letting things rest there. They are likely to openly discuss their differences without criticizing each other's remarks. As a result, they aren't defensive with each other. The stress is on clarifying one's position relative to another when differences arise. Members of the family listen a lot to each other, though they are not necessarily swayed from their own ideas. There is also obvious emotional support for each other. Parents are genuinely proud of adolescents for knowing and standing by what they believe (Powers et al., 1983).

We can compare the above family's approach with that of a family in which adolescents are likely to have low ego development. We also see much noncompetitive sharing of perspectives, but there is also high avoidance, distracting attention from the problem. Even though family members may share opinions, they avoid discussing them; they are not able to explore their differences long enough to reach an understanding of each other's position.

Self-Awareness and Support   Other investigators have found similar dimensions of family interaction to be important for the development of individuation. David Bell and Linda Bell (1983) emphasize the importance of self-awareness and support. They find that adolescents with high degrees of self-awareness are more accepting of themselves. Accepting oneself means that one can be aware of needs and motives that one might otherwise feel a need to deny or distort, sometimes by attributing them to others. Thus, self-awareness clears the way for more accurate perceptions of others. Self-aware adolescents are also in a better position to appreciate their own complexity and to acknowledge complexity in others. Insight into themselves and others makes it possible for them to validate the other person's experiences. Others, in turn, are more likely to validate theirs. Being able to communicate that you have heard another person, for example, allows that person to relax and listen to you. This process of mutual validation promotes self-awareness in each person by providing accurate feedback to each (Bell & Bell, 1983).

A negative converse to this bright picture exists for other adolescents. The inability to understand one's own complexities makes it likely that one's approach to others will be simplistic. Adolescents who do not understand their own actions will make inaccurate observations about the reactions of others. Motives unrecognizable in themselves will color their perceptions of others. Neither the adolescents themselves nor those with whom they interact are likely to receive validation through their encounters with each other, further perpetuating this negative cycle.

Family Climate   Bell and Bell believe that supportive—that is, warm and loving—relationships within the family are central to the development of positive self-regard and hence of individuation. It is possible, of course, for families to be supportive and yet not be validating. Such families might be warm and loving, for example, but not comfortable with their differences. Because they are threatening, differences of opinion are avoided. Validating another person merely requires that one be aware of and comfortable with differences between oneself and others, making it possible to listen without the expectations that reflect one's own needs. One can hear what the other is saying more accurately. An accurate reading of another person does not, however, signal agreement, or even liking: A family can be validating yet not supportive.

To test their ideas, Bell and Bell observed adolescent girls and their families interact in a "revealed differences" task, designed to reveal differences in the way members of a family answered various questions (for example, "We fight a lot in our family," or "We really help and support one another"). As family members tried to reach agreement on items on which they had disagreed, a research team coded their exchanges for support and acknowledgment of what each person said.

These investigators found, as had Powers and her associates, that the effect of parental ego development on adolescents' ego development is not direct, but is mediated by a family climate characterized by accurate interpersonal perception. Thus parents' ego development is positively related to an accurate perception of others, which in turn is related to adolescent ego development. It is the family *process,* not a modeling of parental behavior, that promotes ego development in adolescence. The best climate is one in which people accurately read their own and others' actions, in which they are not excessively concerned with others' reactions, and in which there is little covert conflict. Both parental ego development and family comfort with differences facilitate the development of such a climate (Bell & Bell, 1983). However, even with optimal family climates, parents can still wish at times that they had known more about adolescence, as discussed in Box 5.5.

The findings of studies such as these emphasize the need to consider the family system as a whole rather than focus on individuals. Parents' personalities do not directly affect adolescent development; it is the family system that mediates the effect of parental ego development and parental self-regard. However, individual characteristics of parents can contribute to the family climate, which then affects the parents' behavior and the adolescent's personality (Bell & Bell, 1983).

The Family Paradigm

The way a family experiences the world reflects its **family paradigm,** the core beliefs held by members of the family about their environment. A family might believe, for example, that the world is orderly and that one need only persist in order to discover the ground rules that operate in any situation. Other families might see their world as chaotic or even hostile. Thus some families will be optimistic and open to new experiences, whereas others will be pessimistic and retreat into themselves (Constantine, 1987).

One can study family paradigms by observing families as they solve a problem, with the assumption that their approach to the problem will reflect their more general views of the world. Two dimensions that distinguish families are especially important in this context. Families can be distinguished by the degree to which they think through a problem (problem analysis) and the extent to which they work together in coming up with a solution (working together). Families characterized by a high degree of problem analysis look for complexity, revealing their belief that the prob-

Box 5.5   What Parents Wish They Had Known About Adolescence

"They seem to get caught up in fads in junior high. They do certain things . . . to be part of the crowd. I wish I'd known how to handle that. At what point are these fads okay, because it's important to identify with your peer group, and at what point do you say no? If they are really dangerous, then it's easy; but with a lot of them, it's a gray area, and I wish I'd known what to do better."—*Father*

"I wish I had realized that she needed more structure and control. Because she had always been a good student and done her work, I thought I could trust her to manage the school tasks without my checking. But she lost interest in school, and I learned only very gradually that I had to be more of a monitor with her work than I had been in the past."—*Mother*

"I wish I had known more about the mood swings. When the girls became thirteen, they each got moody for a while, and I stopped taking it personally. I just relaxed. The youngest one said, 'Do I have to go through that? Can't I just skip that?' Sure enough, when she became thirteen, she was moody too."—*Mother*

"I wish I'd known how to help the boys get along a little better. They have real fights at times, and while they have a lot of fun together and help each other out, I wish I knew how to cut down on the fighting."—*Father*

"I wish I knew what to expect. They are all so different, and they don't necessarily do what the books say. Sometimes, I'm waiting for a stage; now I'm waiting for adolescent rebellion, and there is none."—*Mother*

"I wish I had known about their indecisiveness. He wants to do this; no, he doesn't. He gets pressure from peers and from what we think is right, and sometimes he goes back and forth. I am more patient about that now."—*Mother*

"I wish I had known that if we had dealt with some behaviors when they were younger, we would not have had a problem from 11 to 14. He was always a little stubborn and hardheaded, wanting to do what he wanted. But right now, I wish we had done something about the stubbornness because it is a problem. He does not take responsibility, and it gets him into trouble at school. Looking back it has always been a problem, but we did not deal with it."—*Mother*

Source: Adapted from J. Brooks. (1991). *The process of parenting* (3rd ed.). Mountain View, CA: Mayfield.

lem need not be simple to be solvable. Families low in problem analysis tend to come up with superficial answers, perhaps reflecting their belief that most problems are insolvable. Similarly, families that work well together pay attention to what each person is doing and coordinate their efforts; those at the other end of this dimension talk little among themselves and come up with individual answers (Reiss, Oliveri, & Curd, 1983).

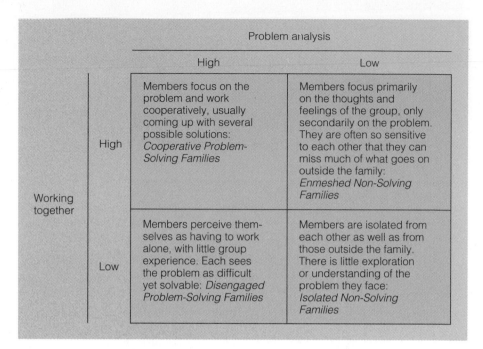

FIGURE 5.1   Family Types Distinguished by the Way They Analyze Problems and Work Together. *Source:* Adapted from D. Reiss, M. E. Oliveri, & K. Curd. (1983). Family paradigm and adolescent social behavior. In H. D. Grotevant & C. R. Cooper (Eds.), *Adolescent development in the family.* San Francisco: Jossey-Bass.

By classifying families according to these two dimensions, we can describe four types of families, each with a distinctive approach to solving problems. David Reiss, Mary Ellen Oliveri, and Karen Curd (1983), developmentalists specializing in family relations, give us descriptions of each type of family (Figure 5.1).

Individuals from various types of families differ in characteristic ways. Autonomy characterizes adolescents from cooperative problem-solving families (those high in both problem analysis and working together) as well as those from isolated non-solving families (those low in both problem analysis and working together), but for different reasons. Members of cooperative problem-solving families explore their surroundings as a team; their approach to problems is optimistic. Members of isolated non-solving families are more pessimistic; they do not approach each other or those outside the family for help even when they face a solvable problem. The high autonomy of adolescents from these families probably reflects their lack of connectedness with other family members. Blind clinical observations of parents and adolescents from each family type confirm these observations. In isolated non-solving families, parents appear worn and confused, and the adolescents depressed and self-destructive. In cooperative problem-solving families, the parents are involved, and the adolescents are assertive and sociable. findings such as these strongly suggest that a family's paradigm has important implications for adolescent social behavior (Reiss, Oliveri, & Curd, 1983).

Reiss, Oliveri, and Curd suggest that the interactions of any family member with those outside the family not only reflect the core beliefs of the family, but also serve to stabilize the family paradigm, that is, to confirm it. The behavior of adolescents, as well as that of other members of the family, functions to maintain the family's view of the world. Thus the high engagement of adolescents from cooperative problem-solving families not only reflects their belief that most problems can be solved; their stance also makes it likely that they will confirm this belief by sticking with problems until they are solved (Reiss, Oliveri, & Curd, 1983).

A family's racial or ethnic background also contributes to the family paradigm by affecting the way it experiences the world. We turn to this next.

Families and Ethnicity

Over the past two decades, the number of ethnic families in the United States has increased dramatically. Twenty percent of all children under the age of 17 belong to an ethnic minority. By the twenty-first century, one-third of all those in school will be Asian American, African American, Hispanic, Native American, or a member of some other minority (G. Miller, 1989). As a group these adolescents have certain problems in common: They experience more poverty, poorer living conditions, inferior education, more unemployment, and higher dropout rates than age-mates from the dominant culture. They are also more likely to experience intergenerational conflict, as they become acculturated into the ways of the majority culture more rapidly than their parents, who frequently remain committed to the traditions of their native culture (Feldman, Mont-Reynaud, & Rosenthal, 1992; Yau & Smetana, 1993). Despite the tensions this can create within the family, adolescents whose parents maintain warm and caring relationships with them weather the stresses of dual-cultural membership (Chiu, Feldman, & Rosenthal, 1992).

Ethnicity is an important factor contributing to the impact of the family on adolescent development. The organization of the family system often takes typically different forms in families with differing cultural backgrounds.

Asian American Families   Less than 1% of adolescents in the United States are Asian and Pacific Islander American, most of whom are of Chinese and Japanese backgrounds, although Vietnamese, Korean, and Filipino groups are growing in number. Asian traditions emphasize the importance of the group rather than the individual, and Asian American adolescents feel strong loyalties to their families. Chinese Americans, as adults, continue to see their parents frequently, two to three times a week (Ying, 1994). Roles in Asian American families are more rigidly defined than in Western families, and relationships are vertically, or hierarchically, arranged, with the father in a position of authority at the top. Family relationships reflect the roles of members more than in individualistic, Western cultures. An aspect of the children's role is to care for their parents. This sense of responsibility to the family characterizes Asian American adolescents (Huang & Ying, 1989; Nagata, 1989). Socialization practices emphasize duty, maintaining control over one's emotions and thoughts, and obedience to authority figures within the family (Nagata, 1989). Chinese American adolescents, for example, indicated, when asked, that they would meet parental expectations rather than satisfy their own desires when these conflicted. However, many of those responding to such questions cited practical reasons for doing so in addition to respect for cultural traditions, saying it would increase the likelihood that they would be given permission to do something else they might want to do (Yau & Smetana, 1993). Even with proportionately higher educational achievements, more Asian and Pacific Islander two-parent families experience poverty (12.4%) than do White families (4.7%); however, the reverse is true for female-headed families. This difference might be attributable to the fact that the earnings of Asian and Pacific Islander males are 87% of those of White males, whereas the earnings of Asian and Pacific Islander females are generally comparable to those of White females (U.S. Bureau of the Census, 1996b).

African American Families Approximately 14% of adolescents in the United States between the ages of 10 and 19 are Black (U.S. Bureau of the Census, 1992). In 1994, 54% of all African American families were maintained by a single parent, nearly all of these by the mother (U.S. Bureau of the Census, 1996b). The median income of Black families with children is approximately 67% that of White families, and usually both parents must be employed for a Black family to have middle-class status (U.S. Bureau of the Census, 1996a). Tremendous diversity exists in income levels, and in associated educational attainment and other indices of well-being, among African Americans. Despite the massive inroads made against discrimination in jobs, schooling, and housing in the 1960s, many forms of covert discrimination still exist. Rates of unemployment are higher and median earnings are lower, for instance, than for White workers (U.S. Bureau of the Census, 1996a).

Family roles are more flexible and are less gender specific than in the dominant culture. Perhaps because of the greater need for African American women to work to help support the family, parents assume responsibilities within the household according to work hours and type of task rather than according to gender-based roles. Parents also show less differentiation in the roles and tasks they assign to children of either sex (Gibbs, 1989). Support from extended family members is also more common than in majority families (Levitt, Guacci-Franco, & Levitt, 1993).

Despite Erik Erikson's (1959) concern that Black adolescents would have difficulty developing a positive identity due to negative images of Blacks in the dominant culture, the self-concept and self-esteem of Black adolescents is as high as, and frequently higher than, that of Whites (Powell, 1985).

Hispanic Families Nearly 8% of U.S. adolescents between the ages of 10 and 19 are Hispanic. Most of these are Mexican American, although large numbers come from Puerto Rican, Cuban, and South and Central American backgrounds (U.S. Bureau of the Census, 1986). For adolescents from Spanish-speaking homes, the sense of being between two cultures is espe-

For bilingual adolescents, intergenerational conflicts over differences between their native culture and the majority culture of their peers are underscored by the different languages spoken in each sphere.

cially strong. Traditionally, Hispanic families are patriarchal, with fathers making the decisions and supporting the family (Webster, 1994), and mothers caring for children and the home. These roles have changed as more Hispanic women find work outside the home. Employment is associated with higher status for the wife and greater decision making in the family (Herrera & DelCampo, 1995). Adolescents are socialized into well-differentiated gender roles (Casas, Wagenheim, Banchero, & Mendoza-Romero, 1994; Ramirez, 1989). As do African American families, Hispanic families enjoy greater extended family support than do majority families (Levitt, Guacci-Franco, & Levitt, 1993). And, as with Asian and Pacific Islander and with Black families, more Hispanic families experience poverty (27%) than non-Hispanic families (11%) (U.S. Bureau of the Census, 1995b).

Native American Families Native Americans include Indians, Eskimos, Aleuts, Alaska Natives, and Metis, or people of mixed ancestry (LaFromboise & Low, 1989). Fewer than 1% of adolescents are Native Americans. Over 500 different native entities are recognized by the federal government. Each has its own customs and traditions, and over 200 Native American languages are spoken today (LaFromboise & Low, 1989).

Native American children frequently experience a cultural shock when they begin school. Many speak another language and have been raised with cultural values that run counter to those of the dominant culture. Often parents are of little assistance, because most have not successfully assimilated themselves. Dropout rates of adolescents are high, averaging 50% in reservation and boarding schools, which 80% of Native American adolescents attend, and running as high as 85% in urban high schools. Rates of alcoholism, illiteracy, poverty, and disease are alarmingly high and attest to the devastation of these minorities through the disruption of family roles and the inability of parents to pass on to their children a vision of the future that includes them (LaFromboise & Low, 1989).

Siblings

Another aspect of the family system that affects adolescent development is its size. Adolescents growing up with sisters and brothers experience a different family life, and are affected differently by it, than those without siblings. Over three-quarters of adolescents have at least one sibling. Most adolescents find that despite the conflicts that inevitably arise, they develop close bonds of affection with siblings. Gene Brody, Zolinda Stoneman, and Kelly McCoy (1994), at the University of Georgia, followed 70 families over a four-year period, assessing the quality of sibling relationships. In general, siblings reported that their relationships with each other improved over time. However, as siblings reached early adolescence, they reported relationships with other children in the family as being more negative, a finding that corroborates that of Larson and associates (1996), who also found adolescents' emotional experiences, when they were with their families, to become more negative by junior high.

The quality of the relationships siblings enjoy with each other is moderated, in part, by the relationships their parents have with other children in the family. This is especially true for their parents' relationships with the older child (Brody, Stoneman, & McCoy, 1994). Gene Brody, Zolinda Stoneman, and Kenneth Gauger (1996) found this "spillover" effect to be especially noticeable when the temperament of the older sibling was "difficult." The quality of each parent's relationship with the older child is only marginally associated with sibling relationships when the older sibling's temperament is "easy," but dramatically so when it is "difficult." Good parental relationships with difficult children appear to buffer those children's relationships with their siblings, perhaps through building better interpersonal skills, or by affecting self-regulatory skills, or simply by creating the expectancy that relationships can be rewarding. Considering only relationships among the siblings themselves, the temperament of the older child rather than that of the younger is most important in determining the quality of the relationship, because older children are better able to dominate a relationship, influencing the form their interactions will take.

Older siblings are models for younger ones. Through their interactions with parents and others, they illustrate expected forms of behavior and family standards. Their achievements influence younger siblings' aspirations and interests. An adolescent girl's interest in sports, for example, will be influenced by having an older sister on the varsity field hockey team. She sees the interest her parents take in her sister's activities and the pride her sister has in her team role. The girl takes it for granted that girls participate in sports and intends to try out for the swimming team herself when she reaches junior high.

Older siblings are also likely to serve as caretakers for younger children in the family. Having to watch out for a younger sister or brother can increase an adolescent's sense of responsibility, usefulness, and competence. If these caretaking activities are too demanding and take time away from schoolwork or friends, however, they can result in frustration, anger, and lowered self-esteem (Hetherington, 1989). Adolescents in single-parent homes are more likely than those from intact families to be given responsibility for watching over younger siblings.

Siblings provide friendship and company for each other. Because they are closer in age to each other than to a parent, they are often more in touch with the problems each faces and can frequently offer better advice than a parent. An older brother can advise a 12-year-old boy that the hazing he is experiencing in the first weeks of junior high will soon end. He knows, because that was his experience a year ago when he started junior high. A parent would be less likely to have this information.

Siblings in stepfamilies experience more conflict than those in intact families. There is more aggression, more rivalry, less warmth, and less involvement with each other. These relationships are more characteristic of stepsiblings than of biological siblings. Relationships in stepfamilies improve with time, but they do not generally reach the level of those in intact families (Hetherington, 1989).

FAMILIES IN TRANSITION

Several major social trends affect the lives of adolescents as we move toward the twenty-first century. Increasing numbers experience divorce, single parenting, and stepparenting, and more live in homes in which both parents are wage earners.

Changing Family Structures

Divorce   Adolescents today are more likely to experience divorce than were their parents or grandparents. Approximately half of all 13-year-olds in 1990 lived for some time in a single-parent family, most of them because of divorce (Proulx & Koulock, 1987; Smith, 1990). What impact does divorce have on adolescents? Simple answers don't exist. Its impact will vary for each adolescent, based on a host of conditions: the family situation prior to the divorce, the adolescent's coping skills, the degree of family conflict, the adolescent's age and gender, the availability of social supports such as

Divorce can be disorienting for adolescents because the environment no longer serves its function of "remaining in place," giving them something from which to assert their independence.

friends and extended family, the amount of time spent with the noncustodial parent, the quality of the relationship with the custodial parent, parental monitoring of activities, whether the divorce involves economic hardship, moving to a new neighborhood or new school, and so on. E. Mavis Hetherington, a developmentalist who has followed numerous families through divorce, remarks that one of the most notable things she has observed is the tremendous diversity in the responses of parents and children (Hetherington, 1989; Hetherington, Hagan, & Anderson, 1989).

Even relatively amicable divorces can be emotionally charged and stressful events. As a consequence, developmentalists have not been surprised to find a number of negative effects associated with its occurrence. Adolescents from divorced homes frequently have lower academic self-concepts than those from intact homes (Smith, 1990). As a group, they are more likely to use substances such as cigarettes, alcohol, or marijuana, and to engage in sexual intercourse at an earlier age (Flewelling & Bauman, 1990; Needle, Su, & Doherty, 1990). They are more likely to use less-mature coping strategies (Irion, Coon, & Blanchard-Fields, 1988). Other, more global measures such as self-concept, self-esteem, social competence, happiness, and maturity have been found to differ for those from divorced homes (Furstenberg, 1988; Wallerstein, 1989; Wallerstein, Corbin, & Lewis, 1988).

Perhaps because these findings support popular stereotypes of children from broken homes, developmentalists have been relatively slow to look beneath surface statistics to determine what factors other than *not* living with a father in the home (the usual custodial arrangement) might be contributing. One of the first studies to follow children of divorce over time discovered a number of conditions contributing to stress, not the least of which is divorce's effects on the parents (Hetherington, Cox, & Cox, 1982). More recent research supports these observations. Recently divorced mothers, for example, report more depression and have poorer parenting skills than mothers in intact families. Difficulties in adjusting among their children can be traced, in part, to the mothers' reactions to the divorce (Forehand, Thomas, Wierson, Brody, & Fauber, 1990). Divorce can be highly damaging to a parent's self-esteem and sense of worth. Many leave a divorce with a sense of failure, not just in the relationship, but as individuals. Most experience depression and increased tension as they adjust to their changed life circumstances. Parents can become preoccupied with their own problems and consequently less responsive to the needs of adolescents who are also adjusting to the divorce.

Perhaps not surprisingly, parenting is less effective initially following a divorce. Fathers become more permissive, perhaps reluctant to spoil their available time on a dispute over discipline, and mothers become more inconsistent, at times ignoring infractions and other times reacting more severely. Each of these changes adds to the level of stress (Hetherington, Cox, & Cox, 1982).

Life evens out within a two- to three-year period following the divorce. Parents and adolescents regain much of their earlier emotional stability, and each is better able to "be there" for the other. Christy Buchanan, Eleanor Maccoby, and Sanford Dornbusch (1992), at Stanford, interviewed over 500 adolescents four years following their parents' divorce. They found that the most important predictors of adolescents' adjustment were their closeness with the parent they were living with and that parent's monitoring of their activities, such as knowing where they were after school, how they spent their time and money, and who their friends were. Similarly, a survey of over 4,000 Scottish adolescents, 13- to 16-years-old, found that psychological distress, when it occurred, was associated with dysfunctional styles of parenting and not with whether adolescents came from single- or two-parent families (Shucksmith, Hendry, & Glendinning, 1995).

Because divorce is more common today than in previous generations, adolescents are less likely to experience any stigma associated with it. Many of their friends have gone through a similar experience, and natural support groups exist in which adolescents can air their feelings and gain perspective on their situation.

Even so, adolescents whose parents are divorced are less likely than peers from intact homes to adopt mature coping strategies, especially when they feel threatened. This is true even though they may recognize that the strategies they use—such as escape, avoidance, confrontation, or self-blame—are not particularly effective. They are also more vulnerable to stress, in that they are not as likely to see themselves as potentially controlling the situation or managing a successful outcome. Perhaps experiencing a divorce, which is an event beyond their control, makes these adolescents less likely to feel in control of other stressful situations. Or it might be that the degree of control they perceive themselves to have in a situation is related to their self-esteem, which is lower in these adolescents (Irion, Coon, & Blanchard-Fields, 1988).

Divorce can also be difficult because it introduces changes in the family just at the time adolescents themselves are in the process of changing. It's hard to push off from something, in other words, when it is moving away from you. Robert Kegan (1982) speaks of three functions that the environment must serve, at any age. The first is *holding on;* the environment needs to support, nourish, and sustain the adolescent. Individuals—such as parents, siblings, and teachers, who make up the adolescent's environment—must "be present" for the adolescent, recognizing and accepting what the adolescent is going through. The second function is *letting go,* or assisting the adolescent in establishing the ways in which she or he differs from others, helping the adolescent find her or his own way. These two functions parallel the dimensions of family interaction referred to earlier as individuality and connectedness. A final function of the environment is *remaining in place* thereby permitting the adolescent to reintegrate aspects of the self that have become differentiated. Kegan notes that "it takes a special wisdom for the family of an adolescent to understand that by remaining in place so that the adolescent can have the family there to ignore and reject, the family is providing something very important, and is still, in a new way, intimately and importantly involved in the child's development" (1982, p. 129). Were the family to "move away," as opposed to remain in place, those aspects of the self that the adolescent has thrown off become lost to the adolescent and cannot be reintegrated into new ways of relating to others.

Marital conflict rather than divorce per se contributes heavily to the stress adolescents experience. Conflict most likely affects adolescents by affecting the quality of parent–child relationships (Fauber, Forehand, Thomas, & Wierson, 1990). Adolescents are more likely to experience problems when their parents divorce relatively late rather than early, when they were children (Needle, Su, & Doherty, 1990; Smith, 1990). Adolescents whose parents divorce late experience more years of marital conflict. A three-year longitudinal study of over 1,000 seventh-, ninth-, and eleventh-graders found that conflict within the family, not divorce, was associated with negative effects such as depression, anxiety, and physical symptoms. Adolescents from intact homes with high levels of conflict showed lower levels of well-being than those in low-conflict divorced homes on all measures that were used (Mechanic & Hansell, 1989). A full 25% of the adolescents reported that their parents' divorce was a positive change. Other studies find even higher agreement among adolescents on the preferability of divorce to their previous conflict-ridden lives (McLaughlin & Whitfield, 1984).

As the conflict surrounding a divorce becomes more openly expressed, some adolescents report experiencing greater feelings of personal control (Proulx & Koulock, 1987). Exposure to conflict need not always be negative; sometimes it is the only way of working through differences. But how sensitive are adolescents to cues, such as conciliatory or angry tones of voice, versus the actual content of what is said in resolving conflict? Kelly Shifflett-

Simpson and Mark Cummings (1996), at West Virginia University, had 5- to 7-year-olds and 9- to 12-year-olds watch videotaped arguments between a couple, systematically varying the endings in terms of emotional tone and content. Thus, an argument might end in a sarcastic apology (I'm *so* sorry I wasn't more sensitive to your needs," said in a negative tone of voice) or a genuine one (the same words spoken in a positive tone of voice). Adolescents are better at discerning what is actually taking place than are children, reacting emotionally to both the content and the emotional tone of the argument. Children, on the other hand, are more literal, responding simply to the verbal content of the message.

Adverse effects of divorce appear to be minimal as adolescents reach early adulthood and can even, for females at least, spur identity development in the occupational and relationship domains (Imbimbo, 1995). Barkley and Procidano (1989) found no difference between late adolescents from divorced and intact families on measures tapping their sense of control, mood, interpersonal dependency, or perceived social supports. In other ways, the increasing divorce rate in society may affect all adolescents. Perhaps the issues facing this generation of adolescents will be to find meaning in relationships and institutions that previous generations accepted as givens. The prevalence of divorce, even when not personally experienced, raises issues of intimacy and family relationships for all adolescents.

Single-Parent Families   Most of the adolescents who live in single-parent families do so because of divorce; most of them live with their mothers (Buchanan, Maccoby, & Dornbusch, 1992). One of the most noticeable differences between these adolescents and those from intact homes is their economic well-being. Approximately half of all families headed by a single female parent live below the poverty level, compared to only 10% of two-parent families (McLanahan & Booth, 1989). For many adolescents, this income level is a dramatic change. One year following a divorce, a single mother's income is likely to have dropped to 67% of the total household income before divorce, whereas the father's income is likely only to drop to 90%. The initially lower earning capacity of most women, along with frequent lack of child support and little state support, contributes to this pattern. On average, single mothers working part-time earn approximately 30% of what married fathers earn, and mothers employed full-time earn 60% as much (McLanahan & Booth, 1989). Economic hardship can contribute to adolescents' distress in intact families as well. In this case, however, it does so primarily by undermining the marital relationship that then affects the way each partner relates to the adolescent (Ge et al., 1992).

Adolescents in single-parent families face the need—some for the first time—to take on part-time jobs to pay for things they previously took for granted. There are advantages and disadvantages in this situation, as in almost any other. On the positive side, adolescents stand to gain in autonomy and independence through being more responsible. Hetherington (1989) finds that adolescents are given greater responsibility, have a greater role in family decision making, and are given more independence than in intact families. Potential disadvantages can result when responsibilities ex-

Adolescents in single-parent families must often take on new roles and responsibilities, such as part-time jobs and additional chores around the house. In return for greater responsibility, however, they gain in autonomy and independence.

ceed adolescents' capabilities or keep them from normal activities, such as schoolwork and social participation.

Many adolescents face additional changes immediately after a divorce. Thirty percent of adolescents move within the first year following a divorce; for many this means adjusting to a new neighborhood and a new school and making new friends. Less-frequent contact with old friends is an additional loss. Frequently, divorced mothers will change their employment within the same time period, adding to the general level of stress within the family. Divorced mothers report lower levels of psychological well-being and more concerns than mothers in two-parent families. Adolescents living with divorced mothers are likely to enjoy the same family support as before, yet they typically have less contact with their neighbors than those living in two-parent families. Most divorced mothers, however, are relatively successful in establishing the social supports they need (McLanahan & Booth, 1989).

On the positive side, relationships between adolescents and mothers often become stronger in the process of coping with these conditions; relationships become closer and less hierarchical. Mothers and daughters especially are likely to find these relationships satisfying, with the exception of early maturing girls, for whom family conflict increases. Adolescents living with their mothers may also develop more liberal attitudes regarding work and gender roles. Daughters living with their divorced mothers report high expectations from their mothers for them to attend college. Divorced mothers may see a need for their daughters to be economically and socially independent, in case of similar circumstances (McLanahan, Astone, & Marks, 1988; Sessa & Steinberg, 1991).

Buchanan, Maccoby, and Dornbusch (1992) compared adjustment in adolescents living either with their mothers, their fathers, or part-time with both. They found, in contrast to previous research (for instance, Hetherington, 1989), that it was relatively unimportant for adolescents to live with the same-sex parent. Boys, in fact, adjusted just as well, if not better, when living with their mothers as with their fathers. Of course, comparisons of this sort are problematic because fathers usually get custody only when the mother has psychological or emotional problems, which in themselves can affect an adolescent's adjustment.

An increasing number of divorced fathers receive custody of their children, although this arrangement is still relatively uncommon. Buchanan, Maccoby, and Dornbusch (1992) found that 19% of the 517 adolescents they interviewed lived with their fathers, in comparison to 70% living with their mothers, and only 10% part-time with both. Perhaps because of the special circumstances under which fathers are likely to be awarded custody, more fathers experienced difficulty. For instance, hostility between parents remained higher when fathers had custody; fathers with custody also worked more hours per week than did mothers with custody, and residential arrangements changed more frequently following the divorce than in the other two types of custody arrangements.

Other things being equal, however, fathers have been found to adjust to their custodial role well. A survey of over 1,000 single fathers found them to be relatively comfortable in their roles. Those who were most comfortable were the ones who had been at it the longest; presumably they had worked out the kinks and developed their own successful routines over the years. Those who were satisfied with their social lives also reported more satisfaction with their roles, as did those who had higher incomes and rated themselves high as a parent (Greif & DeMaris, 1990).

Remarriage and Stepparents   Parents who divorce are likely to remarry and to introduce a stepparent into their children's lives. Close to 20% of children under the age of 18 live with a stepparent, who in most cases is a stepfather. Remarriage usually occurs soon on the heels of the divorce, typically within 3 years. Many stepparents bring a stepsibling or two (residential or weekend) in the process. For adolescents, this series of events comes on top of the changes introduced by puberty, moving to a new type of school, and rapidly changing social relations. Fewer changes would still be enough to disrupt anyone's equilibrium. Yet many families weather the stresses of these new relationships, and some even thrive (Giles-Sims & Crosbie-Burnett, 1989a; Glick, 1989).

We don't have much information about the conditions that facilitate or hinder healthy stepfamily relations (Giles-Sims & Crosbie-Burnett, 1989a).

Yet some general statements can be made. Perhaps the first is to underscore the importance of **role clarity,** the understanding among family members regarding each person's role and how it affects the others (Giles-Sims & Crosbie-Burnett, 1989a; Visher & Visher, 1989). Adolescence introduces its own confusions into roles and issues; for example, child versus adult, dependence, independence, autonomy, and emotional connectedness. The addition of stepparents to this combustible mix creates great potential for human drama. An adolescent who bridles at suggestions from his mother can refuse to even listen to a stepfather. If a 6-foot tall, strapping, 15-year-old male is confused about his role as a "child" to a biological parent, magnify that confusion by an order of 10 when you add a stepfather who is 3 inches shorter, 20 pounds lighter—and an emotional rival.

Adolescents' reactions to stepfathers vary considerably with their gender, frequently improving conditions at home for boys, and just as frequently worsening them for girls (Hetherington, 1989; Needle, Su, & Doherty, 1990). The transition is easiest for boys. Boys in remarriages have been found to differ little in their behavior at home or at school from boys in intact families. Girls remain antagonistic and disruptive. In addition to gender differences, the timing of the remarriage is also important. Boys adjust best in remarriages when their mother remarries prior to adolescence. Adolescents of either sex show behavior problems even in remarriages that have lasted for several years if their mother remarried after they had reached adolescence (Hetherington, 1989).

Ordinary family problems are magnified in stepfamilies. Who makes the decisions? Are stepparents responsible for the children of their spouses? Can they tell them what to do? Discipline them (Fine, 1989)? The most successful families establish clear guidelines for interactions. Families with the most ambiguity in roles are those with a stepmother and at least one child in common (Pasley & Ihenger-Tallman, 1989). The difficulties facing stepmothers are especially acute, because they are likely to oversee the management of the household, a role that can bring them into direct conflict with stepchildren who may resent their presence. For families experiencing problems, support groups and counseling can help establish guidelines for daily living, such as who supervises homework, who disciplines, buys clothes, cleans up, and so on. Mundane matters can easily become explosive unless defused with professional help (Visher & Visher, 1989).

A study of nearly 90 stepfather families with at least one adolescent gives us some answers to questions concerning patterns of decision making and the types of problems different members of the family are likely to experience (Giles-Sims & Crosbie-Burnett, 1989b). Most of the adolescents' problems centered around issues of discipline and authority. Views such as that expressed by the following adolescent were common:

> I resent it when he tries to discipline me, but I realize the bad comes with the good. I *don't* feel he has as much control as my natural father, but in this home it is mostly my mom who disciplines me. We both realize that my stepfather could never take the place of my natural father in my mind and heart. (p. 1071)

Adolescents also said that they would tell other adolescents to think about moving out if they had problems with a stepfather. As one said, "See what things might change, try and get along with him. If it doesn't work out and it is possible, move in with your father, but only as a last resort" (p. 1071).

Mothers' concerns also reflected issues of discipline, but included concerns about financial support and responsibility as well. For stepfathers, as for adolescents, discipline and authority were central concerns (Giles-Sims & Crosbie-Burnett, 1989b). Stepfathers interviewed for the study said things like the following:

> I rarely feel comfortable disciplining . . . maternal instincts are very strong here . . . because early attempts to discipline resulted in her becoming quite defensive about their behavior.
>
>   She is at an age where any authority is threatening to her and she is resentful of my discipline. (p. 1071)

With respect to the major decisions made in these families, the adults felt that the mother had the most power, the stepfather next, and adolescents the least. Adolescents also felt their mothers had the most power, but saw themselves as having more than their stepfathers. Power was distributed more equally with respect to everyday decisions, with no one member having that much more say than the others. Adolescents had their way as often as either adult in these everyday matters. These findings parallel those of other studies which find that stepfathers are less authoritative than fathers in nondivorced families (Hetherington, 1989).

Adolescents themselves may contribute heavily to the success or failure of remarriages (White & Booth, 1985). Giles-Sims and Crosbie-Burnett (1989b) suggest that their ability to do so comes from the relative power they hold in reconstituted families. They note that 12% of the adolescents in their sample had decision-making power equal to or greater than the parents. As the family reorganizes with time, power relationships change. Adolescents in families that had been together longer had less power than in newly constituted ones.

Not all studies find that the age of children in remarriage affects the quality of family life. A comparison of stepfather families with young children, school-age children, or adolescents found marital satisfaction to be unrelated to the age of the child (Kurdek, 1990). The average length of the marriage in this study was 8½ months, a period perhaps not long enough for serious difficulties to develop.

What contributes to the success of reconstituted families? Successful families are those that establish rituals. These can range from everyday routines, such as walking the dog and doing the dishes, to family traditions and celebrations, such as serving breakfast in bed when it's someone's birthday or backpacking on weekends (Whiteside, 1989). Rituals provide for shared experiences and also contribute to role clarity.

Changing Work Roles: Dual-Earner Families

The number of women in the work force has increased substantially over the past several decades. Nearly three-quarters of women between ages 25 and 54 work outside the home (Orthner, 1990). What effect does maternal employment have on adolescents? Research addressing this question has yielded inconsistent findings, suggesting that *whether* mom works is not as important as the *conditions* that are present when she does (Joebgen & Richards, 1990).

Joebgen and Richards (1990), for example, periodically contacted adolescents and parents throughout the day (they wore beepers) to sample their activities and their moods. They found the match between the mother's level of education and her employment to be most predictive of her self-esteem and well-being. This in turn related to well-being in adolescents. Maternal employment per se was not important; what mattered in terms of both her well-being and the adolescent's emotional adjustment was the match between the mother's interests and abilities and the work she did during the day—whether inside or outside the home.

Studies of working mothers and their adolescents find no consistent relationship between maternal employment and such important indicators of adjustment in adolescents as academic achievement, emotional development, or social competence (Armistead, Wierson, & Forehand, 1990; Bird & Kemerait, 1990; Keith, Nelson, Schlabach, & Thompson, 1990). When trends do emerge, they suggest that maternal employment has a more beneficial effect on daughters than on sons (Orthner, 1990), although some research suggests a reversal of this relationship (Paulson, Koman, & Hill, 1990). Similarly, job-related stresses of employed mothers do not seem to spill over to their relationships with their adolescent children or to affect the latter's psychosocial adjustment or to differ significantly from those of working fathers (Schwartzberg & Dytell, 1996). In fact, parent–adolescent relations are most likely to be affected when *both* parents experience work-related stress (Galambos & Maggs, 1990; Galambos, Sears, Almeida, & Kolaric, 1995).

Despite the absence of any consistent negative effects associated with maternal employment, many families have come to expect that dual-income families will suffer as a result of the mother's employment. Galambos and Maggs (1990) quote from an article in *Time* magazine as follows:

> A motif of absence—moral, emotional, and physical—plays through the lives of many children now. . . . To support a family, buy a house and prepare for a child's future education, two incomes become essential. (Morrow, 1988, p. 27)

The effects of mom's joining the work force appear to be more positive than negative. Maternal employment has a liberalizing effect on gender roles in the household. In single-earner families, with the traditional model of fathers as "breadwinners" and mothers as "homemakers," fathers spend more time with their sons than their daughters, while in dual-earner families, they spend equivalent amounts of time with each (Crouter & Crowley, 1990). Even though traditional, single-earner families expect daughters and sons to spend equal amounts of time doing household chores, they assign work in gender-stereotypic ways. Girls, for example, might be expected to clear the table, do dishes, or watch younger siblings; boys might mow the lawn, wash the car, and take out the garbage. In other respects, dual-earner families mirror for daughters the social realities facing employed mothers. Just as the work load of employed mothers increases when they work outside the home (because they continue to be responsible for work within the home), daughters actually do 25% more work in dual-earner homes than in traditional families (Benin & Edwards, 1990).

Maternal employment may affect the mother's sense of well-being more than the children's during adolescence. A study of over 100 families with adolescents between ages 10 and 15 found that parents who were positively invested in their jobs weathered the stresses of adolescence better than those who were not (Silverberg & Steinberg, 1990). As adolescents enter puberty, begin dating, and engage in more activities outside the home, parents face midlife identity issues and frequently a drop in self-esteem. Midlife concerns, self-esteem, and life satisfaction among parents suffer when teens start to date. Parents who are involved in their work roles, however, show increases in self-esteem and life satisfaction and have fewer midlife concerns when their children start to date (Silverberg & Steinberg, 1990).

Maternal employment can relate to well-being in yet another way. As adolescent autonomy increases, conflicts with parents increase, especially with mothers (Smetana, 1988; Steinberg, 1987a). The stability of work roles outside the home, in which established patterns of authority and decision making are not questioned, can buttress parental self-esteem in the face of changing relationships at home.

SUMMARY

A Constructive Interpretation of Relationships

The process of defining oneself, differentiating aspects of the self from others, leads to a renegotiation of the parent–child relationship during adolescence. This relationship is a focus of development during this particular period of life because of the biological changes of puberty and the changes in the way adolescents think and process information.

Changing Relationships With Parents

Psychoanalytic theory expects this change in the parent–child relationship to bring about emotional turmoil and distancing from parents. Large-scale studies of normal adolescents find that even though conflicts increase, adolescents continue to maintain close relationships with parents. These relationships are renegotiated as adolescents press for more mutuality and fuller participation in family decision making.

Several domains of authority exist within a family, and parental authority shifts in only some of them. Conflicts arise when parents and adolescents do not agree about which issues should remain under parental authority and for how long.

Parents and Adolescents

Four styles of parenting have been identified: (1) Authoritative parents are both responsive and demanding; they take their children's ideas into account but are also willing to assert their own authority and to enforce standards of behavior. (2) Authoritarian parents are as demanding as authoritative ones but less responsive; they value obedience over self-reliance. (3) Indulgent parents are responsive to their children but are not demanding; they seldom express expectations for responsible behavior. (4) Neglectful parents are neither responsive nor demanding; they are simply uninvolved in their children's lives. Authoritative parenting fosters competence, self-reliance, and academic achievement.

Authoritative parenting has been shown to be the most effective style of parenting for African American as well as for European American adolescents. Parenting styles are based in a cultural context, however. For example, the Chinese parenting style has been described as authoritarian, but in reality parents and children exercise control over each other in that one goal of parenting is to meet the child's needs. A supportive adult network of relatives and friends can ensure a better outcome for poor children by helping to buffer against the risks that they face.

An adolescent's behavior may be determined as much by parenting style as by similarities in genotype between parents and adolescents, which in turn can influence how an adolescent perceives events and experiences. In fact, environmental and genetic contributions to development interact with each other, and their influence on children's outcome cannot be identified or measured separately.

Most parents face middle age just when adolescents reach puberty. This particular combination of developmental changes and identity crises can heighten the tensions within families with adolescents.

Autonomy and Individuation

Adolescents become more autonomous as they become more independent and responsible for their actions. Frequently these changes bring conflict with parents over household routines, more frequently with mothers than fathers. Parenting style, especially of mothers, is related to girls' autonomy. Age is the best predictor of increased autonomy for boys.

Increased individuation accompanies autonomy as adolescents sort through values and views to discover which ones reflect the way they think. This discovery involves making decisions for themselves and living with the consequences of these.

Individuation gives adolescents a set of attitudes and ways of acting that are genuinely their own; however, they must still put these together into a working whole that reflects an inner sense of self. Family characteristics of individuality and connectedness facilitate the process of identity achievement. Individuality refers to having and expressing ideas of one's own and being able to say how one differs from others. Connectedness reflects one's openness to others' opinions and respect for their ideas. These qualities of family life help adolescents

explore options while feeling emotionally supported even when family disagreements arise.

The quality of adolescents' interactions with their parents, as well as personality characteristics of the parents themselves, are important to ego development in adolescence.

The way a family experiences its world reflects its family paradigm: core beliefs held by family members about their environment. Two dimensions distinguish different family paradigms: the degree to which a family analyzes the problems it faces and the extent to which members of the family work together in solving these problems.

Ethnicity contributes to the impact of the family on development. Adolescent–parent relationships typically take different forms in families with differing cultural backgrounds.

Family size also affects adolescent development. Over three-quarters of adolescents have at least one sibling. Most develop close bonds of affection despite the inevitable conflicts. Older siblings serve as models for younger ones; they are also likely to serve as caretakers. Siblings provide friendship and company for each other.

Families in Transition

Nearly half of all adolescents will experience divorce. The impact of divorce depends on conditions in the adolescent's life, such as age, gender, amount of marital conflict, support from family and friends, and economic stability. The effectiveness of parenting drops in the first several years following divorce, and both parental self-esteem and adolescents' coping strategies suffer. Marital conflict, rather than divorce itself, contributes heavily to the stress adolescents experience, but exposure to conflict need not always be negative.

Most adolescents in single-parent families live with their mothers. Daughters fare better in single-parent families than do sons. With remarriage, daughters experience more problems than before, whereas those of sons eventually lessen. Stepparents, usually stepfathers, report that most difficulties center around issues of authority and discipline. Role clarity facilitates interaction in stepparent families.

The number of women in the work force has increased substantially over the past several decades. The effects of maternal employment on adolescents are mediated by several factors, one of the most important being the mother's satisfaction with her work. Maternal employment may liberalize gender roles in the family and increase a parent's sense of well-being.

KEY TERMS

active listening

you message

I-message

authoritative parents

authoritarian parents

indulgent parents

neglectful parents

climacteric

menopause

autonomy

individuation

individuality

connectedness

family paradigm

role clarity

CHAPTER 6

Adolescents and Their Friends

"Hey, Jenny!" Alisa tossed her books on the table and perched on the chair beside her friend. "I saw Mike today. Think he'll ask you to the rally Friday night?"

"What if he did?" asked Jenny. "I wouldn't be able to go. My parents won't let me date until..."

"Sure, I know—until you're 15. That's what mine said."

"If only! They won't even say. Dad just says 'When we marry off your older sister.' Too bad I don't have an older sister, it might make things easier."

"I do. It doesn't... just makes them nervous."

"What a bummer."

"Uh-huh," agreed Alisa.

"Anyway, Mike's not that hot."

"Forget you!" exclaimed Alisa. "You were so distracted yesterday you put your clothes on over your gym shorts."

"Yeah," smiled Jenny, "but, you know what I mean.... It's just like he's not, well..."

"Yeah, I understand."

"I know you do, kiddo. That's what's so great."

Friends are important at any age, but especially in adolescence when so many things are new. Friends are emotional supports to whom adolescents turn with their concerns, triumphs, secrets, and plans. In larger numbers, they are socialization agents, guiding adolescents into new, more adult roles. And one on one, they are mirrors into whom adolescents look to glimpse the future within.

247

Dramatic hormonal and physiological changes literally transform the emotional and social arenas of adolescents' lives. Ironically, adolescents are least able to turn to their parents in the face of these changes, because relationships with parents are part of the changes. Peers step into the void. The sense of self that develops within the family prepares adolescents for friendships outside it. Self-esteem and peer relationships are discussed in the first section of this chapter.

Distinctive themes distinguish friendships in early adolescence from those in preadolescence. These themes reflect the concerns of each age. Preadolescents are concerned with being accepted by others; adolescents with discovering—and accepting—themselves. A section of the chapter details these differences.

The chapter moves to peer groups: their organization and the functions they serve. Small groups bridge adolescents' first steps outside the family. Larger groups provide a social setting in which adolescents try out more adult social roles. One of the functions of the larger peer group is to facilitate the transition to heterosexual friendships and dating. This section closes with a discussion of dating.

Many parents voice concerns over peer pressure. Even though all of us are influenced by our friends, parents seem particularly distrustful of the influence of friends during adolescence. We look at the attitudes and behaviors adolescents share with their friends, and consider whether these conflict with those shared with parents. In the process, we will take a look at conformity during adolescence.

Although peers exert more influence than parents do in some areas of adolescents' lives, parents continue to influence their children more than friends do in other areas. The chapter closes with a discussion of recent data suggesting that the generation gap is no larger today than it was half a century ago.

FRIENDSHIPS DURING ADOLESCENCE

Adolescents gain a sense of who they are and what their lives are about through seemingly small and insignificant daily encounters with friends and members of their families (Erikson, 1968). They try out new aspects of themselves in the relative safety of close relationships. As a consequence, adolescents are often just as interested in what they discover about themselves as in what they find out about each other. This is especially true for friendships during early adolescence. Different activities with peers serve different functions. Some, such as watching TV together or other noncompetitive activities, simply enhance friendships but do relatively little to help adolescents discover qualities that are unique to them. More competitive activities, such as noncontact sports, help them discover their unique strengths, what they are good at, what they can and cannot do (Zabatany & Hartmann, 1990).

Adolescents experiment with new behaviors as they face a pressing need to discover what is acceptable and what is not. They know, for example, that

they cannot be as dependent as before, but neither are they totally self-reliant. And what about their emotions? Sentimentality is "uncool," but do they have to put a cap on all emotion? Friends provide essential feedback. Adolescents try on new behaviors much as they do clothes on a shopping spree. Which ones fit? Which make them look better? Friends become mirrors in which they can see themselves as they imagine they must look to others. The ability of adolescents to consider the thoughts of others gives early friendships this special reflective quality (Berndt, 1982; Elkind, 1980; Frankel, 1990).

Friends and Self-Esteem

Friendships bear a special burden at first, as significant sources of adolescents' feelings about themselves. Children derive feelings of self-worth from the simple fact that their parents love them; adults additionally derive much of theirs from their work. Adolescents can turn neither to their parents with the simple needs of children, nor feel the strength they will later experience through their jobs and families of their own. Friends help them bridge this difficult passage and make them feel good about themselves. In this respect, having close friends, even if only a few, is better than being popular. The latter, although not to be slighted, may make adolescents feel socially competent, but it does not contribute to self-esteem, as do friends (Hartup, 1993). Friends, especially same-sex friends, affirm adolescents' sense of self.

Whereas young children derive much of their sense of self-worth from their parents, and adults from their work and their children, adolescents receive validation primarily from their friends.

They do this simply by enjoying each other's company, by "being real" with each other. Even quarrels are helpful in this respect, enabling adolescents to discover that their commitment to each other is greater than their differences (Lempers & Clark-Lempers, 1993).

Just as individuals pull in their stomachs and stand a bit straighter when passing a mirror, adolescents see more than their present selves reflected by their friends. By imagining themselves as other than they are, adolescents can rehearse new roles, set goals, and plan ways of attaining them. They can try out ways they would like to be—an ideal self-image. This image includes more than the roles they are refining; it anticipates the adult roles they will soon assume (Bybee, Glick, & Zigler, 1990). We see the importance of the ideal self-image in studies relating it to other measures of adjustment. Adolescents with high ideal self-images are better adjusted: They are more reflective, do better in school, tolerate frustration better, and are more resilient to stress.

How positive adolescents feel about themselves affects the quality of their relationships with others. The quality of their relationships improves, and these improved relationships contribute to even more positive feelings about themselves. Adolescents who feel inadequate and are unsure of themselves find it difficult to believe that others will like them any better than they like themselves. Conversely, adolescents who have positive self-attitudes anticipate positive reactions from others. Not surprisingly, knowing about an adolescent's level of self-esteem tells us a lot about the quality of that person's relationships with others. Adolescents with high self-esteem report having friendships that are more intimate and satisfying than those with low self-esteem (Buhrmester, 1990). Perhaps they're less likely to burden their friends with problems, or maybe they're simply better able to shift their emotional focus away from themselves and onto their friends when they need support. More complex relationships may also be at work. Social competence might contribute to intimacy, which in turn promotes individual well-being, affecting the quality of one's friendships.

Relationships with parents also influence the way adolescents think about themselves (Walker & Greene, 1986). Interactions that communicate support, affection, and encouragement promote self-esteem. Families in which these qualities exist support each other, even when they disagree (see Chapter 5). Adolescents still see their parents as major sources of support (Levitt, Gaucci-Franco, & Levitt, 1993); in fact, relationships with parents become closer with age, with high school seniors reporting greater intimacy with each of their parents than eighth-graders report (Rice & Mulkeen, 1995). Adolescents who are close to their parents report being more satisfied with themselves and having closer relationships with friends than those who are not close to their parents (Raja, McGee, & Stanton, 1992). Adolescents who have a good relationship with their parents are also more likely to seek friends for support, perhaps because they have learned from their families that others can be helpful in solving problems.

It is reasonable to expect that what contributes to successful relationships with parents should also be relevant to relationships with friends. Leslie Gavin and Wyndol Furman (1996) videotaped adolescent girls interacting with their mothers and with their best friends, as they worked on a number of problems together. How well they got along—with their mothers or their best friends—was related to how similar their needs were and to whether at least one of them perceived the other as meeting her needs. Good social skills, such as "sharing power" by cooperating and negotiating when differences arose, also contributed to harmonious relationships with mothers. However, these skills appeared to be less important in relationships with friends, perhaps because, with even minimal social skills, the interests they shared simply because both were adolescents made up the difference.

Adolescents feel happiest and most relaxed when they are with their friends. We turn to patterns of friendships next.

Changes in Friendships With Age

Friendships change with age, taking on themes that characterize the concerns of each age group. Preadolescents want to be understood and accepted by others; adolescents want to understand themselves—and different processes facilitate both of these concerns. Gossip helps preadolescents establish norms and avoid being rejected; self-disclosure helps adolescents define themselves. Friendships reflect these themes in characteristic patterns of interacting.

Preadolescence Preadolescents spend a lot of time comparing themselves to others. In fact, being accepted by others is one of their central concerns. Peer reactions figure heavily in determining preadolescents' levels of self-esteem and self-definition. The cognitive changes discussed in Chapter 4, especially being able to assume the perspective of another, contribute to their awareness of the importance of socially appropriate behavior and the need for "impression management." Fear of rejection and ridicule, and jockeying for position in friendships, characterize relationships among this age group (Parker & Gottman, 1989). Keller and Wood (1989) found that most of the preadolescents they interviewed mentioned trust as the most important issue in their friendships.

Insecurity regarding one's social position is perhaps best reflected in a characteristic mode of interaction: gossiping. Gossiping is important to preadolescents with good reason: It discloses the attitudes and beliefs that are central to the peer group (Parker & Gottman, 1989). This function is vital when we realize that these behaviors are the basis for being accepted or rejected by the group. Listen in on the following conversation as two friends discuss telling lies, something friends are not supposed to do with each other:

Dari:	Barb said that her mom gave her $300 to buy a dress and shoes for the dance, and that the dress, the yellow one she showed us, remember? Well, that that dress cost over $200.
Tracey:	That yellow dress she took out of the closet? It was ripped. I saw it!
Dari:	Yeah. Under the arm. I saw it too.
Tracey:	That wasn't a new dress. There was a stain on it.
Dari:	She told us she bought it for $200. But I think her sister gave it to her, the one who's married.
Tracey:	Yeah. She gives her a lot of clothes.

Continuity and
Diversity in Early
Adolescent
Development

Gossip is a favorite
pastime of preadoles-
cents, and it has a de-
velopmental purpose.
From discussions of
other people's behav-
ior, they learn social
norms to guide their
own behavior.

Notice that in gossiping about Barb, Dari and Tracey affirm the norms of the group; that is, friends don't lie to each other. They also communicate to each other that they adhere to these norms.

Mutual disclosure and affirmation of group norms through gossip allows preadolescents to reaffirm their membership in the group. This is especially important because preadolescents are often insecure about their social status and their general acceptability. Much of the energy that goes into friendship is devoted to solidifying their position and protecting themselves against rejection (Parker & Gottman, 1989).

Gossip serves another important function. It allows preadolescents to explore peer attitudes in areas where they lack clear norms, without actually committing themselves to a position. Because many of the behaviors in question are not common among their peers, gossip frequently involves well-known older adolescents, as in the following example, or even popular figures such as rock musicians and movie stars:

Brian: They say Dale [captain of the varsity football team] uses steroids every football season.

Andy: A lot of athletes do. It helps them build up muscle.

Brian: Steroids are really drugs, you know.

Andy: You think the coach knows?

Brian: Nah. How could he and still let Dale do it? He might lose his job.

Andy: Yeah.

Neither Brian nor Andy directly stated an opinion about using steroids or drugs in general. Yet by the end of the conversation, they had established that athletes who use them have to hide that fact from others and consequently it must be wrong to use them. As demonstrated in this example, gossiping is a low-risk way of determining the attitudes of one's peer group. Neither boy had to reveal a view of his own in order to discover the position taken by the other. Their conversation affords them a way of sampling the reactions and attitudes of peers regarding behaviors that are not yet common to their group (Parker & Gottman, 1989).

Preadolescents are still learning which emotions are appropriate for them and what rules exist for displaying these. By monitoring feedback from peers in social situations, they gain invaluable information regarding each of these aspects of social competence. Even so, their rules for emotional expression are rough at first. Perhaps their most salient guideline is to avoid sentimentality at all costs, especially when with one's friends. The rule of thumb is to be rational, cool, and in control. The Research Focus, "Interviews," looks at a study investigating the rules preadolescents learn about expressing emotions.

Adolescence Adolescents' friendships reflect different concerns, which at this stage take the form of defining who they are and what they are going to be in life. Friends get together to discuss the mix of experiences offered up each day. The remarks of classmates, teachers, and parents and the suc-

Although girls generally find it easier than boys to share their innermost thoughts, disclosure to a close friend is one of the most important ways that all older adolescents learn about themselves.

Research Focus

Interviews: Keeping a Lid on Feelings: Display Rules for Emotional Expression

With Michael Wapner

Sadness, anger, and pain. These are common emotions, yet ones that we frequently hide from others. What factors govern the expression of emotions such as these? Do we learn, with age, to play it cool and hide our feelings? And why would we want to do so? What cultural scripts might we be following?

Janice Zeman and Judy Garber (1996) asked 7-, 9-, and 11-year-olds to listen to four scenarios (involving a party, exchanging gifts, a sporting event, and a favorite possession) that had been found to arouse feelings such as anger or sadness. Then Zeman and Garber asked them to indicate whether they would let another person see how they felt if they were the character in the story. The 9- and 11-year-olds were much less likely to let another see that they were angry or sad than were the 7-year-olds, especially if the other person were a friend. All children said they would express their feelings more openly to a parent, saying that a parent would be more likely to understand or accept their feelings than would a peer.

These investigators incorporated the use of *interviews* into their data collection procedures. Interviews, along with questionnaires, are a type of *survey research*. Surveys rely on self-reports rather than direct observations of behavior, resulting in several important advantages. Researchers can sample a broader range of experience than is permitted by direct observation. Researchers also have access to experiences and behaviors they could not easily observe—attitudes, beliefs, prejudices, and opinions, as well as many private behaviors, such as sexual practices, substance abuse, and family violence.

Interviews provide rich sources of data. Rather than a simple yes or no, they often yield highly personal and complex responses. They are flexible instruments in the hands of a skilled interviewer; the use of *probes* allows the interviewer to follow up on brief responses and gain insights into attitudes and behaviors that would otherwise be missed. The establishment of *rapport*, a comfortable relationship between the subject and the interviewer, increases the likelihood that the interview will reveal information that otherwise might be withheld.

Interviews can reach individuals who might not otherwise respond to a questionnaire. Subjects who cannot read, because they are either too young or illiterate, can nonetheless respond to an interviewer's questions. Also, many subjects who just "wouldn't have the time" to fill out and send back a questionnaire are willing to be interviewed.

Interviews also have a number of disadvantages. Along with questionnaires, they suffer from problems of inaccuracy. Untruthfulness,

cesses and failures of the day are expressed, taken apart, analyzed, and re-analyzed. Friends provide the support—and sometimes the challenge—that adolescents need in order to meet the new and untried, as the following conversation illustrates (Parker & Gottman, 1989):

> *James:* So we're watching the game last night and my dad says, "You need to think about your future." Like, I don't know what I want to do but it doesn't really bother me. [Laughs.]
>
> *Sam:* [Returns laughter.]
>
> *James:* [Laughs again.] It's my life and it bothers my dad more than me that I haven't got my future planned.
>
> *Sam:* My dad's the same. I tell him: "I know I'll be doing *something.*"
>
> *James:* Right, *something!* [Laughs nervously.]
>
> *Sam:* "*Que sera,*" you know?

Research Focus (*continued*)

selective memory, intentional or unintentional withholding of information, and distortion due to social desirability or interviewer bias all potentially contaminate the data. *Social desirability* refers to the tendency of subjects to answer questions in such a way that they "look good" to the interviewer (and to themselves). *Interviewer bias* arises from the many ways in which the interviewer's personality and expectations influence the answers given by the subject. Interviewers can also bias answers by subtly communicating that some answers are better than others—for example, by following certain answers with probes until they conform to expectations and leaving others as they are given.

What do interviews of children and adolescents tell us about their willingness to show emotion? Zeman and Barber *coded* the reasons participants gave as to why they would show or not show their emotions (see Chapter 3, Research Focus, "Coding Descriptive Responses"). The coding categories they used were the anticipated reactions of others—either positive ("She'd understand") or negative ("She'd probably think I was a baby"), concern for others ("I wouldn't want her to feel bad"), desire for help, such as getting a bandage, or to avoid unpleasant consequences, such as having to go to the doctor, and the belief either that they wouldn't be able to control their emotions or that the situation did not merit emotional expression.

How willing are children and adolescents to express anger? Over 90% said they would show their anger in at least one of the situations, and 50% said they would do so in all four of them, most frequently giving as a reason their belief that it would help them in some way or, secondly, that they simply wouldn't be able to hold it in. The willingness to express sadness and pain was similar to that for anger, but the reasons differed somewhat, anticipating positive, supportive reactions from others in the case of sadness and the inability to hide their feelings in the case of pain. Also, older participants were less willing to express sadness and anger than younger ones, and boys were less willing to express sadness and pain.

What about those who said they would not express their anger? The reason most frequently given for not doing so was the expectation that others would react negatively—rejecting, ridiculing, or rebuking them in some way. Essentially the same pattern was found for each of the other two emotions, with the same reasons given. Thus children and adolescents who are less likely to express their emotions expect others to react negatively when they do so. Irrespective of the type of emotion called for, participants indicated they would be more likely to express their feelings when they were alone or with a parent than with a peer. Just how cool is it to express one's anger, sadness, or pain? As Zeman and Garber point out, it all depends on who is watching.

Source: J. Zeman & J. Garber. (1996). Display rules for anger, sadness, and pain: It depends on who is watching. *Child Development, 67,* 957–973.

Exploring uncharted territories in one's life is never easy, as the nervous laughs of the two adolescents above suggest. Yet adolescents are peculiarly well equipped for the task. In many ways, they have reached the pinnacle of thought and can think easily in the abstract, reasoning about the possibilities in their lives and those of their friends (see Chapter 4). Rather than seeing themselves as limited to their present circumstances, they can see their present realities as reflecting a limited sample of the many possible alternatives that exist. Parker and Gottman (1989) note that adolescents are uniquely qualified to help each other through indecisions such as these, and do so with genuine concern, even seeing this as one of the obligations of friendship.

They take this obligation seriously. When adolescents are with their friends, they are most likely to talk about themselves rather than gossip about others. Just as gossip serves the very real needs of preadolescents—

affirming group norms and group membership—self-disclosure serves the needs of adolescents. It is one of the primary means by which they discover themselves. **Self-disclosure** is an intimate sharing or exchange of thoughts, feelings, and otherwise undisclosed aspects of the self with another person. It takes a very different form in adolescence than in childhood or preadolescence. Adolescents respond to disclosures with an honest, almost confrontational examination of the issues raised. They accept these offerings of the self in the spirit in which they are given—as problems to be addressed and solved—whereas self-disclosures among preadolescents are more likely to evoke feelings of solidarity, such as "Me, too" (Parker & Gottman, 1989).

Adolescent friendships reflect considerable emotional development beyond those of preadolescents. Adolescents begin to master the rules for emotional display and feeling that so mystify preadolescents. Adolescents are comfortable expressing a range of emotions, which preadolescents would likely deny. They have moved beyond cool to compassion or any of the many other emotions that might be called for in a situation. They understand that actions can be motivated by several emotions. What remains to refine is an understanding of the potential impact of emotion on their relationships. Many of their conversations are about losing control of an emotion—exploding at someone or just "blowing it"—and the effects this can have (Parker & Gottman, 1989).

FRIENDSHIP PATTERNS

What do adolescents want from their friends? Emotional support, intimacy, and advice. They get these in somewhat different ways depending on their sex. The major activity in girls' friendships is talking. Girls develop close friendships primarily by sharing their feelings. Self-disclosure contributes to emotional closeness in boys as well, but they also develop emotional closeness through sharing experiences, such as sports and other activities (Camarena, Sarigiani, & Petersen, 1990; Frankel, 1990).

Same-sex friendships become more intimate and affectionate with age and become increasingly important as sources of emotional support. Whereas parents are the primary source of support for children, mid-adolescents are as likely to confide in their same-sex friends as in their parents, and late adolescents indicate that friends are more important in this respect than the parents (Furman & Buhrmester, 1992; Levitt, Guacci-Franco, & Levitt, 1993). Not surprisingly, adolescents spend a lot more time with friends than they did as children.

The number of friends also increases in adolescence, especially for girls. The percentage of these friends whom mothers know (40%) remains about the same as in childhood; however, because the circle of friends widens in adolescence, the actual number of friends whom mothers do not know increases substantially (Feiring & Lewis, 1993).

Elizabeth Douvan and Joseph Adelson (1966) interviewed over 2,000 adolescents across the United States, asking them about their friendships. After nearly three decades, these interviews still offer one of the most com-

For girls in their early
and middle teens,
friends are reflections
of themselves. They
tend to pick friends
primarily on the basis
of obvious similarities,
especially of style and
status.

plete and informative studies of how adolescents feel about their friends. These investigators discovered three distinct phases to adolescent friendship, corresponding to early, middle, and late adolescence. These phases reveal characteristic gender differences.

What Girls Want in a Friend

During early adolescence, friendships focus on the activities that bring friends together. Although friendships are more intimate than in childhood, they are less so than they will be in middle or late adolescence (Berndt, 1982; Furman & Buhrmester, 1992). When asked to say what is important in friends, early adolescent girls say less about their personalities than about the things they do together. After listening to these girls talk about their friends, one has the feeling that friendships are not emotionally relevant at this age. If anything, distinct personalities of friends appear to be a disadvantage to the extent that they might interfere with activities. These early friendships are almost always with someone of the same sex (Camarena, Sarigiani, & Petersen, 1990; Lempers & Clark-Lempers, 1993).

Friendships in mid-adolescence focus on security; girls want friends they can trust. Friendships lose their earlier superficial quality and involve emotional sharing and mutuality. Mid-adolescent girls are more aware of their friends' concerns than they were a few years earlier (Berndt, 1982). There is also more concern with personal qualities of friends. Girls are particularly concerned with having a friend in whom they can trust and confide. It is especially important to them that their friends not disclose their secrets to others or talk about them behind their backs (Berndt, 1982). Frankel (1990), for example, finds that the most common stresses in friendships come from not keeping secrets and talking behind a friend's back.

These concerns fall into place when we consider the dramatic physical changes and sexual interests that occur during puberty, which adolescents attempt to understand by sharing their feelings and observations with their friends. finding out that others are going through the same changes assures them that they are normal and that nothing is wrong with the way they feel. In disclosing their feelings, however, they are turning over a part of themselves to their friends, perhaps the part about which they are least secure. Naturally they don't want their confidences divulged to others.

Most girls start to date in mid-adolescence, and friends become especially important in making sense of the emotions they encounter. (Dating is discussed in more detail later in the chapter.) Dating can also be a source of tension among friends. Girls experience more conflict with their friends than boys do when moving into opposite-sex relationships, conflicts frequently centering around fears of disloyalty and competition (Miller, 1990). Relatively few girls develop close friendships with boys at this age, friendships with other girls remaining more important for the majority (Hogue & Steinberg, 1995; Lempers & Clark-Lempers, 1993).

Anxieties about friendships peak in mid-adolescence. The most common anxieties reflect more general insecurities about the changes adolescents are experiencing. They are midway through puberty, renegotiating relationships with their parents, facing a more impersonal and challenging school setting, and beginning to date. These teenagers need the emotional support of friends, and anything that appears to threaten that support causes anxiety.

Friendships in late adolescence focus more on personalities. Some of the earlier intensity is gone, but intimacy continues to grow (Furman & Buhrmester, 1992). Late adolescent girls have more stable identities and better social skills. Being more secure with both themselves and others may make them better able to tolerate individuality in their friends. They no longer need friends to reflect themselves as they did in mid-adolescence. Instead, friends can be appreciated for who *they* are. Self-disclosure is still important, but each friend is able to appreciate the unique qualities the other brings to the relationship (Berndt, 1982; Douvan & Adelson, 1996).

What Boys Want in a Friend

Boys' friendships in early adolescence, just as those of girls, are almost exclusively with others of the same sex. Boys are just as close emotionally with their friends as are girls, but they achieve closeness in somewhat different ways. They spend less time talking about their feelings than do girls and more time sharing activities that cement friendships (Camarena, Sarigiani,

In early and middle adolescence, boys achieve closeness by sharing activities, such as scouting or sports, rather than talking about their feelings, like girls do.

& Petersen, 1990). Even so, when adolescents are asked to evaluate their friendships, girls consistently rate theirs higher in intimacy than do boys (Rice & Mulkeen, 1995).

Elizabeth Douvan and Joseph Adelson found that in mid-adolescence, boys' friendships have many of the same characteristics as do those of girls in early adolescence. Friendships increase in intimacy and affection for boys, as they do for girls, although increases are less pronounced (Furman & Buhrmester, 1992). Boys are looking for someone with whom they can do things. Like girls in early adolescence, they appear to have little interest in the personal characteristics of their friends as long as these do not interfere with the activities they are enjoying together. They have less concern than girls for sharing feelings or being understood. They want someone who is easy to get along with and who enjoys doing the same things they do. Perhaps because they do not self-disclose as much as girls, mid-adolescent boys are not as concerned that friends not betray their confidences. However, they expect their friends not to "squeal" about things they have done together (Bukowski, Newcomb, & Hoza, 1987; Coleman, 1980; Douvan & Adelson, 1966).

Douvan and Adelson did not interview late adolescent boys. However, recent research finds that boys' same-sex friendships in late adolescence continue to be more important than their friendships with girls (Lempers & Clark-Lempers, 1992, 1993).

The friendship patterns described by Douvan and Adelson are as characteristic of adolescents today as they were 30 years ago. They differ only in their timing: Adolescents begin the sequence somewhat earlier today (Bukowski, Newcomb, & Hoza, 1987). The secular trend may be partially responsible for this difference, in that puberty occurs earlier for adolescents today than it did a generation ago, and the social and emotional pressures that puberty brings are certain to be reflected in adolescents' friendships.

Peer Interactions

Are there differences in the ways adolescents of either sex spend time with their friends? Do girls spend more time with a best friend and boys more time in a crowd? Most people would answer yes—and most would be wrong. Even though adolescents of either gender differ in what they say they want in their friendships, actual peer interactions are quite similar for both sexes, popular beliefs notwithstanding.

Stereotypes hold that girls pair off with a best friend and boys get together in large groups. Although these stereotypes are true for the elementary years, peer relations do not show sex differences at all ages. Preschool boys and girls, for example, play in groups of about the same size. Adolescent peer interactions also show surprisingly few consistent sex differences (Montemayor & Van Komer, 1985; Urberg, Degirmencioglu, Tolson, & Halliday-Scher, 1995).

Raymond Montemayor and Roger Van Komer (1985), both at the University of Utah, observed adolescents in natural settings such as shopping malls, schools, parks, and take-out food stands. They found that when adolescents get together, they are most likely to be with one or at most two other friends. Boys are just as likely as girls to pair off with another person. Groups of friends are only slightly larger when adolescents are at school.

Why might boys be more likely to associate in groups in childhood but not in adolescence? The games boys play during elementary school require larger numbers of participants than the activities girls engage in. Such sex-typed playground activities decrease in frequency by adolescence. Nor are they present for preschoolers, accounting for the lack of sex differences in peer interaction at that age as well. Perhaps by adolescence, teenagers of either sex want to spend their time simply socializing rather than engaging in organized activities. This analysis suggests, then, that sex differences in the size of peer groups during middle childhood reflect the number of participants required by organized activities and not a more general orientation to relationships (Montemayor & Van Komer, 1985).

Montemayor and Van Komer noticed one interesting sex difference, however: Boys tend to remain friends longer than girls; their friendships last an average of four and a half years, and those of girls slightly over three years. Douvan and Adelson's data cast some light on these findings. Recall that girls' friendships are more intense than boys' during middle adolescence. They also don't use shared experiences like boys do as an alternate means of establishing intimacy. It may be difficult to maintain the emotional intensity that girls expect for extended periods of time (Montemayor & Van Komer, 1985).

Interracial and Interethnic Friendships

Most friendships among adolescents are with peers of the same race and ethnicity (Hartup, 1993). As a consequence, the sheer number of adolescents at school who share one's racial or ethnic background is likely to be important in forming friendships. When African Americans are a minority within a school, for instance, they are less likely to be members of cliques, or small groups of close friends; similarly, when European Americans are a minority within a school, *they* are the ones less likely to belong to cliques (Urberg, Degirmencioglu, Tolson, & Halliday-Scher, 1995).

Jean Phinney and I (1996) asked Hispanic and European American adolescents whether a student from one ethnic group, who asks to join a club made up exclusively of students from another ethnic group, should be let in. Even though the number of adolescents in favor of including the student did not differ for Hispanic and European American adolescents (nearly 75%), the reasons given for refusing membership—for those who thought the student should not be included—did differ. Hispanic students more frequently mentioned cultural barriers to friendship, whereas European Americans cited rights and rules. It is likely that Hispanics, because of their experience as members of a minority group, were more aware of cultural differences than European Americans, who, for the most part, need only be familiar with their own, the dominant, culture.

Generally, adolescents are likely to have friends who live in the same neighborhood, go to the same school, and share other things in common—including race. Of those who live in integrated neighborhoods and have classes together, a number form interracial friendships. Many adolescents report these friendships to be close, although they do not see these friends with the same frequency outside of school as they do friends of the same race (DuBois & Hirsch, 1990; Hallinan & Teixeira, 1987).

Several conditions affect the formation of friendships between individuals from different races. Classroom climates have been found to affect the sociability of White adolescents toward Black peers. Classrooms where students work together, such as those in which teachers assign students to small working groups, have more cross-race friendships. These friendships are most likely to develop when academic competition is deemphasized and learning per se is emphasized in the classroom (Hallinan & Teixeira, 1987).

When teachers emphasize competitive achievement—whether by preparing the class for tests or stressing grading—they create status hierarchies among students. Because status is often associated with interpersonal attraction, White adolescents are less likely than Blacks to initiate interracial friendships. This is complicated by the fact that Black adolescents tend to be even friendlier to White students in such classrooms. However, Hallinan and Teixeira (1987) point out with respect to "status-leveled" classrooms:

> Though the positive effects of such a climate may be chiefly on whites, that seems to be where it is needed most. It is whites who display the greatest resistance to interracial friendship in the classroom, and it is therefore important to break down their reluctance to socialize across racial barriers. (p. 1370)

Interracial friendships in adolescence are likely only among those who go to the same school and live in the same neighborhood. Close friendships, however, are generally among adolescents with the same racial or ethnic background.

Neighborhood conditions also affect the likelihood of cross-race friendships. Most adolescents who attend integrated schools report having at least one close friend at school of another race, but fewer than one-third of these see the friend outside school. Those who do are more likely to live in integrated neighborhoods and are also less likely to be White. Black adolescents are almost twice as likely as Whites to maintain interracial school friendships outside of school. Blacks have more close neighborhood friends in general than Whites (DuBois & Hirsch, 1990).

Interracial and interethnic friendships face special challenges, not the least of which are differences in the enculturation experiences of adolescents from different backgrounds. **Enculturation** is the acquisition of the norms of one's ethnic group. It differs from acculturation, which is the acquisition of the norms of the larger society. The norms of their group shape adolescents' expectations and reactions to others. The Mexican American culture, for example, stresses group affiliation, interdependence, and cooperation. The African American culture, in contrast, places greater emphasis on individualism and independence. Mexican American adolescents have been brought up in homes with clear hierarchical family relationships and are expected to accept and show respect for authority figures. African American adolescents grow up in more egalitarian homes that permit questioning of authority (Rotheram & Phinney, 1987). We might expect these enculturation experiences to affect the way adolescents from either culture react to social situations, and they do.

Mary Jane Rotheram-Borus and Jean Phinney (1990) showed videotapes of social encounters to African American and Mexican American children and adolescents. The videotapes were of everyday scenes. In one, a student asked a peer for lunch money; in another, a student witnessed a fight; and in another, a student needed materials that another had in order to complete a class assignment.

Clear ethnic differences emerged in reactions to these scenes. The responses of Mexican American adolescents reflected the emphasis their culture places on the group. They were more likely, for example, to say that a peer should share lunch money with someone who had lost theirs, even when the latter was someone they disliked. They also expected others to anticipate their needs (as they would the needs of others) and would wait for others to notice what those needs were. In response to the video in which two peers working at the same table with the supplies that both needed beyond the reach of one and close to the other, Mexican American adolescents saw no problem with the situation, expecting the other person to hand over the supplies. African American adolescents indicated they would be upset and were likely to reach over and get what they needed for themselves. A small difference? Not really. These are just the types of situations that create misunderstandings and lead to hurt feelings among friends.

Another sequence showed a boy being rejected for a team. African American students reported they would get angry or leave; not one of them said they would feel badly. Two-thirds of the Mexican American adolescents said they would feel hurt, but almost none of them would leave, and relatively few said they would be angry. These differences translate easily into the failures of understanding that test friendships. Consider an example in which Eddie, a Hispanic, tries out for football, but gets cut early in the tryouts. He doesn't seem especially angry and doesn't say much about it. His friend Joe, who is African American, thinks Eddie must not care and offers no consolation. Eddie, who has been waiting for his friend to say something, doesn't understand Joe's ostensibly callous attitude and begins to question whether he's really his friend. Joe, assuming that Eddie would react as he would if he minded being cut (by being angry, not silently hurt) has no way to anticipate his friend's growing resentment toward him.

THE PEER GROUP

A Malayan proverb counsels that one should trumpet in a herd of elephants, crow in the company of cocks, and bleat in a flock of goats. This pretty much sums up the behavior of adolescents with their peers. The peer group is one of the most important socializing forces in the lives of adolescents, regulating the pace as well as the particulars of the socialization process. Adolescents who fall behind their friends in social skills are dropped from the group, just as are those who move ahead too quickly. Similarly, those whose tastes and attitudes fail to match the group's are likely to be considered nerdy, geeks, or just "out of it." The cost of bleating when others are crowing can be high.

The peer group assumes special importance in adolescence for a number of reasons. Adolescents are moving toward greater autonomy and independence, and peers provide much needed emotional and social support. Adolescents also learn many social skills with peers that they would not learn from parents or teachers. Peers reward each other with potent reinforcers: acceptance, popularity, and status (Muuss, 1990).

Types of Social Groups

Friendships differ in how exclusive they are, with adolescents frequently having a number of close friends in common. Small groups of such friends are known as **cliques.** A clique can be as large as ten or as small as three, but whatever the size, its members spend much, if not most, of their available time together. These friends are usually the same sex and age, in the same class in school, share the same ethnic background, and live relatively close to each other. Nearly always, one's best friend is in the same clique (Ennett & Bauman, 1996; Urberg, Degirmencioglu, Tolson, & Halliday-Scher, 1995). Similarities in the composition of boys' and girls' cliques are striking. Aaron Hogue and Laurence Steinberg (1995), at Temple University, asked over 6,000 high school students to name their closest friends at school. Sixty-five percent of boys' cliques and 63% of girls' cliques were made up exclusively of same-sex friends, and 85% of boys' and 86% of girls' cliques had no more than one friend of the opposite sex.

Susan Ennett and Karl Bauman (1996), in a study of peer relationships among ninth-graders at five different schools, found that even though cliques are the most common type of social grouping, somewhat less than half of the students (44%) belonged to a clique. What about the other half? Two other types of peer relationships, liaisons and isolates, were also common, each making up about 30% of the students. **Liaisons** are adolescents who are socially active and have friends in a number of cliques but do not themselves belong to any one of these. These students serve the important function of bringing together groups of adolescents who otherwise would have few channels of communication—in a sense, plugging these cliques into the larger social network within the school. **Isolates,** on the other hand, have few friends, either within a clique or outside it, having few links to other adolescents in the social network. (Figure 6.1 illustrates these peer relationships.)

In addition to small groups of friends, larger groups also exist. A **crowd** is larger than a clique and more impersonal. Crowds usually number about 20. Not all the members of a crowd are close friends, but each is someone adolescents feel relatively comfortable with. Crowds usually consist of several of the friends in one's clique along with adolescents from several other cliques. For about half of the adolescents, their best friend is also in the same crowd. It is relatively unlikely for an adolescent to be a member of a crowd without belonging to one of these cliques; however, many adolescents belong to a clique and not to a crowd (Urberg, Degirmencioglu, Tolson, & Halliday-Scher, 1995).

The functions of cliques and crowds differ. Crowd events provide the settings in which adolescents try out new social skills. Clique activities pro-

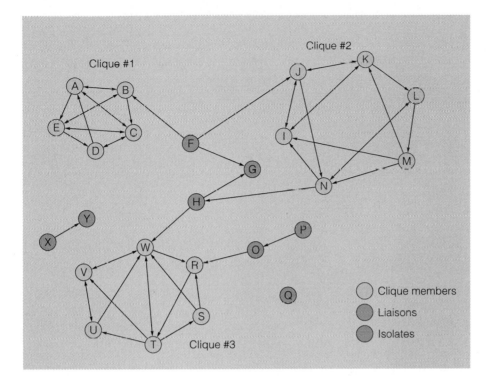

FIGURE 6.1   Adolescent Friendship Patterns: Cliques, Liaisons, and Isolates. *Source:*
S. T. Ennett & K. E. Bauman. (1996). Adolescent social networks: School, demographic, and longitudinal
considerations. *Journal of Adolescent Research, 11,* 194–215.

vide feedback about the success of these skills and advice when skills fall
short. If the crowd has a single purpose, it is to help adolescents move from
same-sex to mixed-sex interactions. Many adolescents need all the help they
can get.

Adolescents spend most of their time talking about crowd activities
when they are with members of their clique, either planning the next event
or rehashing the last one, gathering valuable information from such
"pregame" and "postgame" analyses. The feedback comes from specialists—
other adolescents who know just how difficult a social maneuver can be
and who can recommend something that has worked for them in similar
situations.

If clique activities are coaching sessions, crowd events are the game itself. Adolescents enter the field ready to try out new social moves. Reflecting their specialized nature, crowd and clique activities take place at
different times during the week. Crowd events, just like actual games, occur on weekends, and clique activities, like other coaching sessions, take
place throughout the week.

Developmental changes occur in the structure of peer groups just as
they do with friendships. Both cliques and crowds evolve as adolescents face
different issues; so does the importance of being in a group. Belonging to
groups is most important to early and middle adolescents, and less so for
preadolescents, for whom they are not yet needed, or late adolescents, who

At crowd events, such
as high school foot-
ball games, where var-
ious cliques mingle,
adolescents can prac-
tice new social skills
and new roles with
new people.

no longer need them (Gavin & Fuhrman, 1989). Late adolescents are comfortable with others of the opposite sex, and the crowd disintegrates into
loosely grouped cliques of couples who are "going together." Cliques also
become less important with age. The number of adolescents belonging to a
clique declines from the sixth to the twelfth grades. As the Research Focus,
"Longitudinal Design," discusses, however, the membership of a clique
tends to be stable over time.

All crowds are not created equal. Ask any adolescent. Some are more
prestigious than others. A "leading crowd" exists at most schools. Students

in this crowd are held in high regard by others, sometimes even to the point of envy. Almost always the members of this crowd feel good about themselves as well, having higher levels of self-esteem than students in less-prestigious crowds (Brown & Lohr, 1987). All the students at any school know what it takes to be a member of the leading crowd. For boys, being good at sports is important; for girls, it is being a social leader. Students in the leading crowd are also likely to be leaders in the school and even to have teachers look to them for help with extracurricular activities (Brown & Lohr, 1987).

Other crowds form a loose status hierarchy below the leading crowd. Adolescents receive constant reminders at school of their status. Who they sit with in the cafeteria, who can cut in front of whom in line, which clubs and activities are open or closed to them—all confirm the loose pecking order that reflects the relative prestige of their particular crowd. One might think that the only ones to escape with their self-esteem intact would be those from the leading crowd. However, adolescents from other crowds appear to fare just as well if they like the crowd to which they belong. This suggests that although peer group membership is important for adolescents, it is a sense of belonging rather than the status of the group itself that is critical (Brown & Lohr, 1987).

Popularity

Which adolescents are popular? Research on popularity consistently shows that for boys, being good in sports contributes significantly to popularity, and for girls, being a social leader is important. For both, physical attractiveness is also a significant factor (Coleman, 1961; Williams & White, 1983). In addition, personality characteristics such as being comfortable with oneself, enthusiasm, and friendliness relate to popularity (Coleman, 1980; Sebald, 1981).

Determinants of Popularity   In a classic study of popularity, students at ten different high schools were asked to identify which of their classmates were the most outstanding athletes, social leaders, brains, and so on. For boys at every school, the best athletes were also considered to be the most popular with girls. Athletes were twice as likely to be in the leading crowd as were brains. Perhaps not surprisingly, when boys were asked how they would most like to be remembered, 44% of them said as an athletic star. For girls, being a leader in school activities contributed most to popularity and was the way most of them wanted to be remembered (Coleman, 1961).

This picture has changed little over the years. Williams and White (1983) replicated the earlier study and found that 43% of the adolescent males they interviewed wanted to be thought of as good in sports. Being an athletic star carries as few advantages for adolescent females as it did a generation ago (Kane, 1988). Just like their mothers, the most popular girls are leaders in school activities (Coleman, 1961; Williams & White, 1983). One noticeable change is that adolescent females value good grades more than they did a generation ago (Butcher, 1986).

Even though most adolescents think good looks are important for popularity, physical attractiveness may not be as important as they believe.

Research Focus

Longitudinal Design: Friendship Patterns

How stable are adolescents' friendships? Are the kids that make up an adolescent's closest circle of friends likely to be in that same circle a year later? For that matter, how common is it for adolescents to have a group of intimate friends instead of, say, a single best friend or few close friends at all?

Studies of adolescents' friendships have identified a number of friendship patterns, but until recently we have not known how common or stable each of these patterns was. One friendship pattern is the *clique*. A clique is a small group of intimate friends who are similar in sex, age, ethnicity, and social status. Friends who belong to the same clique spend much of their time together. A second type of friendship pattern is that of the *liaison*. Adolescents who are liaisons have a number of close friendships, but these are with adolescents who belong to several different cliques. Thus, liaisons open channels of communication between cliques, increasing the likelihood that adolescents from different cliques will do things together. A third friendship pattern, that of *isolates,* characterizes adolescents who are not members of a clique and, unlike liaisons, have few friendships in general.

Susan Ennett and Karl Bauman (1996) asked adolescents to name their best friends—first when they were in the ninth grade and a year later when they were in the tenth grade. These investigators used a *longitudinal design.* In this type of research, one studies a single *cohort,* a group of individuals all the same age, and takes several measurements, each at different ages. Ennett and Bauman selected two *times of measurement,* assessing adolescents' friendships in the ninth and tenth grades.

By following the same individuals over time, we can see patterns to development that we might otherwise miss. And because we are comparing the adolescents with themselves at each age, we minimize the problem of having equivalent samples. Are there any problems with this type of research? Unfortunately, the answer is yes. To understand what these problems are, we must define three terms: age changes, time of measurement differences, and confounding.

Age changes are the biological and experiential changes that always accompany aging. They occur in all cultures and at all points in history. We assume that age changes have a biological basis (although we are not always able to identify them) and should therefore be universal; that is, they should occur in all people no matter what their social or cultural background. A good example of an age change is the neural development that continues into adolescence (see Chapter 4) and presumably underlies the development of increasingly abstract thought.

Time of measurement differences reflect social conditions, currents of opinion, and historical events that are present when we make our observations and that can affect attitudes and behavior. When we study age changes by repeatedly

Physical appearance probably contributes to popularity only for those adolescents at either extreme. For those in between—and this would be most adolescents—other factors are more important (Cavior & Dokecki, 1973). Conversely, academic achievement is probably more important than most research has suggested. Part of the difficulty in interpreting the findings on academic achievement may be due to the way questions have been worded. When asked, "How would you like to be remembered?" boys say as an athletic star and girls as a leader in activities (Coleman, 1961). But when asked, "How would you rank the following in importance to you?" most adolescents put getting good grades above being good in sports or being a social leader (Butcher, 1986).

Research Focus (*continued*)

observing the same group of individuals over time, we can mistake time of measurement changes for age changes. It's always possible, for example, that transition from a middle school to a high school setting could disrupt existing friendship patterns.

Confounding occurs when observations reflect systematic differences in more than one variable, with the result that we cannot separate the effects of one from those of the other. Longitudinal research frequently confounds age changes with time of measurement differences, making it impossible to conclusively separate the effects of age from those due to time of measurement. Do changes in friendship patterns over adolescence reflect differences due to age or to disruptions due to transitions from one school setting to another?

Longitudinal research can suffer from other problems as well. It is difficult to keep in touch with individuals over the years. Maintaining elaborate records, and the staff required for this bookkeeping, can be expensive. Longitudinal research is also time-consuming. We must wait while individuals age. And there is no guarantee that we will outlive them. A more serious problem than any of these is the nearly inevitable loss of subjects over time. People move away, die, or for other reasons are not available for study. This loss is called *subject mortality* and is almost always systematically related to age. In other words, the individuals who remain in the study are not necessarily representative of those their age in the general population, because the less healthy and

otherwise less fortunate are the first to leave the sample. (Perhaps adolescents with few friends do not want to be reminded of this and drop out of the study.)

With these cautions in mind, let's go back to Ennett and Bauman's study and see what they found about adolescents' friendships. Consistent with the findings of other studies of friendships, these investigators found that the most frequent type of friendship pattern was the clique, with 44% of adolescents belonging to a clique. Additionally, significant numbers of adolescents were isolates (27%) and liaisons (29%).

What about the stability of these friendship patterns over time? These investigators found that, for any adolescent, both those who were clique members and those who were isolates at the first time of measurement were more likely to have the same status one year later than were those who were liaisons. These findings may not be that surprising, especially when we learn that clique membership itself tends to be stable over a year's time. Also, adolescents who have already experienced difficulty integrating themselves into a social group may not find it that much easier to do so a year later. Liaisons, on the other hand, have already had close friendships in one or more social groups and can more easily move into any one of them, changing their characteristic friendship pattern to that of a clique member.

Source: S. T. Ennett & K. E. Bauman. (1996). Adolescent social networks: School, demographic, and longitudinal considerations. *Journal of Adolescent Research, 11,* 194–215.

The importance of athletic ability, school activities, and academic achievement for popularity also vary from one school to another. Athletic ability tends to have more importance, for example, in rural communities and in schools drawing from lower socioeconomic levels, whereas in urban settings or in communities with more highly educated parents, it is less important (Eitzen, 1975).

Social Competence Several dimensions of **social competence** have been found to be important for popularity among children. Although these dimensions almost surely remain important social skills, we know considerably less about adolescents (Allen, Weissberg, & Hawkins, 1989). The skills involve assessing the situation, responding to it, and adopting a process approach to relationships.

The first component of social competence, assessing the situation, is to see what's going on and adapt one's behavior accordingly (Putallaz, 1983). In a sense, joining a social group involves some of the same skills adolescents learn when driving. One has to judge the speed of the ongoing activity, accelerate, then move into the thick of things. Pulling onto a freeway at 10 miles per hour requires everyone else to slow down to your speed: It doesn't work.

When adolescents "pull into the fast lane" with a remark such as "What are you doing?" they're asking others to stop for them, an unlikely response if they are enjoying themselves. Entry remarks that call attention away from the ongoing activity are likely to be rebuffed. Similarly, remarks about oneself are usually unsuccessful ways of getting a group's attention. Instead, fitting into a group appears to be a matter of figuring out what the group is doing. Those who are better at this are more popular. Simply put, one needs to be able to know what the group is doing in order to join in (Dodge, 1983; Putallaz, 1983).

Figuring out what is going on, however, is not a matter of simply seeing what others are doing. Recall that the constructive approach taken in this text assumes that individuals read meaning into situations, interpreting them in terms of their own expectancies; factors related to one's personality enter into the equation as well. Mary Lynne Courtney and Robert Cohen (1996), at the University of Memphis, showed a videotape to boys who had been rated by their classmates for aggressiveness (see Chapter 1, Research Focus, "An Experiment"). The tape, of two boys playing tag, showed one boy falling down after being tagged by the other. Some of the boys had been told the two were good friends (benign prior information); others had been told they did not like each other (hostile prior information); and still others had been told nothing (neutral condition). Boys who were more aggressive perceived the videotaped sequence differently than those who were less aggressive. The difference was most noticeable when they had least information about the situation (neutral condition), suggesting that aggressive boys are more vigilant in ambiguous situations. In general, more aggressive adolescents are likely to attribute hostile intentions to others more frequently than less aggressive ones (Crick & Dodge, 1996; Waldman, 1996).

The second dimension of social competence is responding appropriately to others' behavior. Those who are popular are distinguished not as much by their own initiation of encounters as by their positive response to the initiations of others. In fact, popular individuals approach others infrequently; but they *are* better at keeping things going, and others appear to have a better time with them (Dodge, 1983).

The third dimension distinguishing social competence is adopting a process approach to relationships. Popular individuals recognize that relationships take time to develop; they wait before entering a group. Apparently, they understand the best way to reach a goal is sometimes an indirect one. For example, instead of directly asking, "What are you doing?" they might ask someone over after school or suggest going to the library to study together (Asher, 1983).

Research with adolescents supports the observation that making friends is a matter of social competence and not luck. Prosocial behaviors, such as sharing and being cooperative, are related to peer acceptance, as is knowing which strategies are appropriate for making friends and which ones aren't (Wentzel & Erdley, 1993). In fact, one of the best correlates of loneliness in mid-adolescence is perceiving oneself as having poor social skills (Inderbitzen-Pisaruk, Clark, & Solano, 1992).

Even in close friendships, social skills are important to the relationship. What form these skills take depends in part on the power adolescents see themselves as wielding compared to that of their friend. Not until about mid-adolescence do same-sex friends see themselves as balanced in power (Furman & Buhrmester, 1992). Power-balanced relationships are important for the types of strategies adolescents use when resolving differences with others; when equally powerful, one can bargain or negotiate; when not, one is reduced to nagging or simply going along with what the other wants (Hartup, 1993).

Dating

Dating is so much a part of the cultural scene one might assume it has always been practiced. Yet it is a relatively recent phenomenon. Prior to the early 1900s, couples dated primarily to determine their suitability for marriage. Before that, girls were given in marriage by their families to suitable partners; young couples had little say over the choices of their prospective mates.

Dating today serves a number of functions, of which the selection of marriage partners is only one. A very important function for adolescents when they first begin to date is simply recreation: Dating is fun—or at least it's supposed to be. Adolescents also report feeling nervous and apprehensive. Dates can have awkward moments. Many adolescents fear rejection and are uncertain as to how to act on a date. Should the boy or the girl open the car door? One girl explained, "You just sort of walk along and if he walks the other way, you know you have to open it yourself." Should the boy help the girl on with her coat? "I act like I'm having problems, and if he doesn't notice, I forget it," suggested one teenager (Place, 1975). Yet despite the uncertainties, most adolescents find dating enjoyable.

When Dating Begins   Adolescents start to date between the ages of 12 and 16. Girls go out on first dates somewhat earlier than boys (they also enter puberty earlier). Most girls start to date by age 14, although age itself is not the only indicator. One can better predict whether an adolescent is dating by knowing whether friends have begun to date than by knowing the adolescent's age or even sexual maturity (Dornbusch et al., 1981). Parents seem especially subject to a form of peer pressure all their own in this respect. As one adolescent girl remarked when she explained how she got her parents to consent to letting her go on a date, "If your girlfriends are not going out, forget it. I just gave examples of who was going out." Another ice-breaker was a strategy learned from childhood:

Joking around with casual acquaintances —other players in a pickup baseball game, for instance—doesn't come easily to every adolescent. For most, however, social competence increases with age and experience.

When they are just beginning to date, most adolescents worry about awkward moments and fear rejection. Once they do date someone regularly, however, the self-consciousness diminishes and they can relax and have fun.

Daughter:	Dad, can I go to the movies with Eddie?
Father:	I don't know; ask Mom.
Daughter:	Mom, Dad said Eddie and I can go to the movies if you say it's okay.
Mother:	Okay, then, you can go.
Daughter:	Dad, Mom said it's okay.

The peer group regulates the pace of socialization into more adult roles. Adolescents who don't begin dating when their friends do may be dropped from their peer groups. Adolescent girls frequently report friction with their friends when they begin moving into opposite-sex relationships. These conflicts often involve concerns of disloyalty and competition. Boys, on the other hand, do not experience the same difficulties (Miller, 1990).

Crushes Even before dating begins, adolescents go through a stage in which they develop crushes. A crush involves an idealized fantasy about another person, and it is rarely reciprocated (Adams-Price & Greene, 1990). The other person remains distant, even if it's someone just two seats away in the same class. The absence of reciprocity and the distance factor in crushes are important features, because they allow adolescents to explore heterosexual role possibilities at a safe distance (Erikson, 1950, 1968).

Multiple Dating Once dating begins, most adolescents practice multiple dating: going out with many different partners. Multiple dating often involves adolescents in superficial relationships in which each partner plays out a well-defined role. Important personality characteristics can be missed in these brief encounters. Characteristics such as loyalty or integrity may never become apparent, because multiple dating involves nonexclusive relationships that limit the commitment between partners. Instead of making it easier for teenagers to meet many different people, multiple dating may bring them up against the same role played out, in somewhat different form, by each. Paradoxically, by dating many different partners, they may have less chance to learn objective ways of assessing the personalities of others than if they got to know one or two people better (Husbands, 1970).

Multiple dating may also reflect a quest for the impossible ideal date—the perfect person who can surely be found if one meets enough people. Many adolescents enter relationships the way they enter a supermarket: with a shopping list in hand. They want someone who is good-looking, intelligent, and has a sense of humor. The problem with looking for someone with specific attributes is that the same characteristics may not fit one's interests and needs in ten years. This approach to finding Mr. Right or Ms. Perfect assumes that relationships are static and do not change with time. But does one stay the same despite one's involvement with another person? The quest for the ideal date assumes that happiness is a function of being with the right person, and that if one is unhappy, one should look for someone else.

Another approach to relationships emphasizes the way they affect the process of personal growth. The relationship becomes a medium for exploring the self and developing one's potential. Well-being is a function of what one brings to the relationship. Other people make one neither happy nor unhappy; satisfaction and happiness reflect a state of self-actualization. How does this relate to dating? The ideal date may be like the unicorn: sought by all but found by none.

ADOLESCENTS, PARENTS, AND PEERS

Conformity

Friends draw adolescents into realms beyond the family that highlight differences between themselves and their parents. These differences become important ways of organizing their individuality; however, they can leave adolescents with feelings of loneliness. Peers provide the emotional support that contributes to feelings of self-worth (O'Brien & Bierman, 1988). Peer expectations for well-defined standards of speech and dress also establish outward behaviors that define the group and establish a sense of belonging among its members. Adolescents consider it a bargain to give up some of their individuality for the security that comes with belonging to a group (Gavin & Furman, 1989).

Conformity peaks in early adolescence when adolescents begin to experience their separateness from their parents. Studies of conformity show that early adolescents are most influenced by others' judgments, sometimes even changing their answers when they are obviously right to conform to those of the group. By mid-adolescence, conformity has already begun to decrease (Gavin & Furman, 1989). Figure 6.2 shows this trend. Although, with respect to age-linked behaviors such as smoking and drinking, adolescents' concerns about what their friends might think may peak somewhat later (Hendry, Glendinning, & Shucksmith, 1996).

Conformity isn't limited to adolescence; it characterizes behavior at every age. Nor is conformity necessarily bad. It is simply a tendency to go along with the standards and norms of one's group. Trends in fashion, food, and recreation are as apparent among 50-year-olds as 15-year-olds. We notice conformity, however, when the norms for one group run counter to those of another, as sometimes occurs with adolescents and their parents. Different behaviors and skills contribute to acceptance more by peers than by adults. These differences increase with age in early adolescence (Allen, Weissberg, & Hawkins, 1989).

Not all adolescents are equally likely to conform to the opinions of others. Those who have high status in their peer group are less likely to show conformity. The same is true for adolescents who have a well-developed sense of themselves. In general, adolescents who have a firm sense of who they are, and are held in high regard by others, are less influenced by others' opinions. The same has been found to be true for adults (Harvey & Rutherford, 1980; Marcia, 1980).

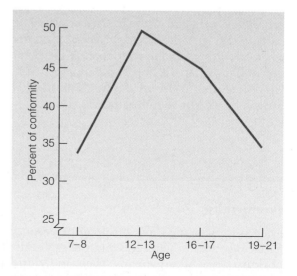

FIGURE 6.2

Changes in Percent of Conformity With Age

Source: P. R. Costanzo. (1970). Conformity development as a function of self-blame. *Journal of Personality and Social Psychology, 14,* 366–374.

Every generation of adolescents creates a culture that seems wholly foreign to older generations. And yet, despite their untraditional tastes, adolescents' values remain surprisingly similar to those of their parents' and grandparents' generations.

Conformity also reflects adolescents' relationships with their parents. Parents who have encouraged adolescents to take part in responsible decision making within the family, who provide reasons when disciplining, and who encourage a verbal give and take with their children—that is, authoritative parents, as discussed in Chapter 5—have adolescents who show the least conformity. Adolescents from these homes have more positive self-concepts and a better developed sense of self. Further, they have learned from childhood to live with the consequences of their decisions, even when these have been as simple as deciding not to clean their rooms and choosing to be grounded instead. They have also learned that even when their parents disagree with them, they still have their emotional support (Cooper, Grotevant, & Condon, 1983).

However, even authoritative parents can worry that peers will have more influence than they on their children's values and activities. Adolescents are beginning to spend more time with their friends than with their families. Perhaps, too, parents realize that the decisions adolescents make can affect their futures in ways decisions rarely do for children. Even so, adolescents report that parents are the best all-around source of support, whether emotional or informational, in the form of advice (Reid, Landesman, Treder, & Jaccard, 1989).

Fashion fads such as shaved heads, black lipstick, and oversized jeans do little for parents' fears that they have lost their children to an alien culture. But even flagrant differences such as these do not mean that parents no longer influence their children's values. If they did not, adolescents would not have to go to such extremes to assert their individuality. Nor do obvious differences in taste, as in music and clothes, reflect a shift in underlying values. This is not to say that adolescents are not influenced by

their peers. They are. But the extent to which they are and the way this occurs cannot be thought of simply as an either-or contest between the values of parents and those of peers.

Values and Peer Pressure

Adolescents experience **peer pressure** as a pressure to think and act like
their friends. The price of belonging to a group is to maintain the ways of
the group. This pressure changes with age. One of the primary functions
of the peer group is to help adolescents gain their footing as they step outside the family. As adolescents become more sure of themselves, pressures
to maintain the norms of the group lessen. Peer pressure is strongest in
early adolescence, when adolescents most need the support of a well-defined
group. Conformity is also greatest then. As adolescents become more sure
of themselves, the peer group becomes less important. As a result, the need
to define group membership through rigidly prescribed standards of dress,
speech, and so on lessens (Clasen & Brown, 1985).

With age, too, adolescents become more comfortable in thinking for
themselves, and arriving at their own decisions. They are less likely to look
to their parents *or* their friends for advice, and when they do seek advice,
they are better able to weigh the opinions of others and arrive at their own
decisions. This confidence reflects a new level of security in their values and
how they arrived at them (Josselson, 1980).

If anything, the values of peers and parents are likely to complement
each other rather than conflict. Friends typically share similar experiences;
they live nearby, come from families of about the same income level, and
are likely to share the same ethnic background. Friends' parents are also important in maintaining the values established by an adolescent's parents,
primarily, it seems, by influencing the behavior of the adolescent's friends.
Socially and academically competent adolescents are likely to seek the company of similar adolescents. These interactions, in turn, often amplify the
initial advantages of each. Anne Fletcher, Nancy Darling, and Laurence
Steinberg, at Temple University, and Sanford Dornbusch, at Stanford University, (1995) studied a large sample of 14- to 18-year-olds, looking in particular at the way adolescents' friends described their parents. In general,
adolescents whose friends described their parents as authoritative had more
positive attitudes toward school and were less likely to use substances such
as alcohol or cigarettes. For boys, authoritative parenting among their
friends' parents was also associated with behavioral measures, such as
greater resistance to conformity and lower levels of misconduct, and for
girls, this parenting style was associated with measures of psychosocial adjustment, such as higher levels of self-reliance and self-esteem.

Of course, some differences between parents and peers can be expected.
And when they occur, the reference group that adolescents turn to will depend on a number of factors, one of which is the type of decision to be
made. Adolescents generally look to their friends for short-term decisions,
such as whether to go to a party or what clothes to buy. They turn to their
parents for decisions about their futures: plans for education or marriage,
or choosing an occupation. Thus parents have more influence over the
larger decisions of life, and friends over the day-to-day particulars of living

it (Frey & Rothlisberger, 1996; Winrre, Hicks, McVey, & Fox, 1988). Among parents, adolescents are more likely to seek, and follow, advice from their mothers than their fathers (Frey & Rothlisberger, 1996; Paterson, Field, & Prayor, 1994).

Important life decisions reflect values, and adolescents are likely to share these with their parents—values about education, relationships, and work. But values as broad as these do not translate easily into the language of daily affairs. They say little about how one spends an afternoon or which movie to see. With respect to actual behaviors such as these, friends have more influence.

Having values in common is not that important to friendship during adolescence. Some similarities are important among friends, certainly, but these are more likely to involve interests and activities such as taste in music and what they enjoy doing, rather than religious beliefs or political views (Kandel, 1978; Tolson & Urberg, 1993).

Most adolescents spend more time talking with their friends than with their parents and are more influenced by their friends about day-to-day decisions. But the background and the values of an adolescent's friends tend to be similar to those of the adolescent's parents.

Deviant Behavior and Peer Pressure

The support of friends remains important with respect to deviant behavior. Adolescents seek out friends who engage in similar activities and, in turn, are influenced by the activities of their friends. In one study of 2,000 adolescents, it was found that after similarities in age, grade in school, sex, and race, friends are most likely to be similar in their use of marijuana. No other single activity or attitude was found to be as likely to be shared by friends as the use of recreational drugs (Kandel, 1978). Similarly, Kathryn Urberg (1992) followed pairs of friends over a two-year period and found that individual friends, and not the social crowd, were the major influence in whether adolescents were likely to smoke.

In part, too, this similarity in the use of recreational drugs reflects adolescents' perceptions of their friends as more deviant than they actually are. Karl Bauman and Lynn Fisher (1986) obtained self-reports from 1,400 seventh-graders whom they followed up in the eighth grade, and another 1,400 ninth-graders whom they surveyed again as tenth-graders. Adolescents were asked to estimate their friends' use of cigarettes, beer, and hard liquor. Then the friends themselves indicated how much they used these substances. The investigators found that adolescents typically overestimated the extent to which their friends engaged in deviant behavior. Adolescents' use of these substances corresponded more closely to their perceptions of what their friends did than with their friends' actual behavior. Adolescents *are* influenced by their friends, but they also appear to select friends based on their perception of similar characteristics—especially as these characteristics relate to deviant behaviors.

Not only is the behavior of adolescents influenced by that of their friends, but so are their feelings. Aaron Hogue and Laurence Steinberg (1995), in a longitudinal study of some 6,000 14- to 18-year-olds, found that adolescents are likely to choose friends whose moods are similar to their own. Furthermore, boys, although not girls, were subsequently influenced by the moods of their friends, their own moods becoming more similar to those of their closest friends over a period of two years.

Actual pressure from friends to misbehave may be relatively slight. A survey of nearly 700 junior high and high school students found little pressure from friends for misconduct—for example, drug or alcohol use or sexual intercourse—and much actual discouragement by friends. Different crowds exert pressure in different areas of adolescents' lives, of course, and the "druggie-toughs" surveyed in this study experienced more pressure for misconduct than did "jock-populars" or "loners" (Clasen & Brown, 1985).

What are adolescents likely to do if approached by a friend to engage in some deviant activity? Adolescents of either sex feel different pressures. Boys are more likely to agree or disagree because of the anticipated outcome; they will say no because they're not interested or they think they might get in trouble. Peer approval and friendship are more important sources of pressure for girls. Girls are more likely to agree even when they anticipate a negative outcome, citing friendship or peer approval as reasons (Pearl, Bryan, & Herzog, 1990; Treboux & Busch-Rossnagel, 1990).

How much influence parents retain with their teenagers when deviant behaviors or conflicting values arise depends in large measure on the quality of the relationship they have with them. For instance, Andrew Fuligni and Jacquelynne Eccles (1993), studying a sample of over 1,700 sixth- and seventh-graders, found that adolescents who perceived themselves as having little opportunity to participate in decision making, and who believed their parents to be overly strict, were less likely than other adolescents to seek advice from their parents and more likely to turn to their peers. They were also more likely to sacrifice significant aspects of their own lives, such as keeping up with schoolwork or developing their talents, in order to be popular with friends.

Parents who are overly permissive or authoritarian are least effective. Adolescents are most likely to listen to parents who have involved them since childhood in decision making in the family and have held them responsible for their actions. These parents are also most likely to give reasons for family rules and to maintain an open dialogue with their children. Adolescents from families such as these, with a strongly developed sense of self, are less likely to be pressured by peers to misbehave.

It is easier for adolescents to listen to their parents' views when they are sure of their own autonomy. The quality of the relationship between adolescents and their parents, not the existence of another reference group, determines whether adolescents will remain close to their parents and seek them out for advice in decisions about their lives (Josselson, 1980).

It should be clear at this point that the relative influence of parents and peers cannot be thought of as a simple tug-of-war with the adolescent in the middle. The values of friends frequently overlap with those of parents, minimizing conflict when it occurs. Parents may occasionally even look to an adolescent's friends to determine what is normative when they are uncertain as to what adolescent behaviors are appropriate, for example, when to wear lipstick or when to get a part-time job. Also, the values of parents and peers influence different types of decisions, leading to less conflict than many parents anticipate. Finally, adolescents vary considerably among themselves in the extent to which they are influenced by the attitudes and behaviors of others, whether these be parents or peers (Conger, 1977).

Are adolescents and parents likely to experience conflict? Probably. Does conflict weaken the relationship? Not necessarily. Conflict can help adolescents restructure and strengthen relationships with parents. Parents are likely to participate in this restructuring process as well. Even as they attempt to get teenagers to agree with them, parents also encourage adolescents to think for themselves and to speak their own minds. Honest exchanges such as these frequently lead to the evolution of joint views shared by both (Youniss & Smollar, 1989).

The Generation Gap: Is It Widening?

Adolescents today live in a culture to which their parents have limited access. This is a relatively recent phenomenon, occurring with the emergence of high schools at the turn of the century. Even just 100 years ago, few adolescents continued their education beyond the eighth grade. In 1882, for example, slightly less than one in a thousand graduated from high school. Most got jobs and worked alongside adults. As a consequence, they shared the same experiences and knowledge as their parents (Youniss & Smollar, 1989).

As more adolescents began to attend high school, they acquired knowledge that their parents didn't have, thereby separating the generations. Even though parents experienced themselves as distanced from their children, they were aware that their children needed schooling in order to acquire the skills they would need to succeed in a changing culture, one that was becoming increasingly industrialized. In effect, parents at the turn of the century experienced the plight of many ethnic groups today. The education that would help their children find a better place in society would also distance their children from them.

High schools today may contribute to a similar sense of unease among parents. By law, all adolescents must attend high school until they reach a certain age. As our society becomes increasingly diverse ethnically and racially, so do the schools that adolescents attend. High school environments enable adolescents from different social classes and ethnic groups to interact more than they would otherwise. Many parents' fears reflect a concern that their values will be replaced by those of another social or ethnic group.

The mass media—radio, television, and movies—also expose adolescents to values that may not be shared by parents. Most adolescents listen to the same music, wear the same clothes, and have the same role models—those provided by television and movies. Is the gap widening?

A study by Bahr (1980) provides us with some answers. Bahr interviewed adolescents from a typical U.S. community. What makes his study especially interesting is that adolescents from this same community were interviewed 50 years before in a similar research effort. As you might expect, there were some differences in the answers of adolescents then and now. But overall, the values of adolescents today are surprisingly similar to those of their grandparents' generation. If anything, Bahr suggests that the generation gap may be smaller now. Teenagers today place more importance on receiving respect for their opinions from parents. They also continue to affirm the importance of time together as a family.

Despite the increasing importance of friends in adolescents' lives, parents continue to remain significant sources of strength and influence. Both parents and peers contribute to adolescents' ability to face changes in yet another area of their lives—school. We will analyze these changes in the next chapter.

SUMMARY

Friendships During Adolescence

Adolescents experiment with new behaviors with their friends, and in doing so, discover new things about themselves. Friends are important sources of self-esteem during adolescence.

Friendships change with age. Those of preadolescents reflect a concern with being accepted. Preadolescents use gossip as a way of affirming group norms and their membership in the group. Adolescent friendships reflect a concern with self-discovery; self-disclosure becomes important to this process.

Friendship Patterns

Patterns of friendship differ with the age and sex of adolescents. Early adolescent girls' friendships focus on the activities that bring friends together. Friendships in mid-adolescence for girls are concerned with the personal qualities of friends more than before. Girls want friends they can confide in and trust. Friendships in late adolescence focus more on personalities. Intimacy continues to grow and more friends are of the opposite sex.

Boys' friendships in early adolescence are also centered around shared activities. By middle adolescence, their friendships are as close emotionally as girls' friendships but involve less discussion of feelings.

Adolescents of both sexes experience greater pressure to grow up faster than adolescents of previous generations.

Despite gender differences in close friendships, peer interactions show many of the same patterns for either sex. Most friendships are with peers of the same race.

Interracial and interethnic friendships form when adolescents live in integrated neighborhoods and attend integrated schools. Classroom climates affect the formation of cross-race friendships, which are likely to develop when students are assigned to small groups to work together in a non-competitive atmosphere. Interracial friendships face challenges posed by different enculturation experiences. Adolescents of different backgrounds can perceive and react to the same situation differently; misinterpretations and hurt feelings can result.

The Peer Group

The peer group regulates the pace of socialization. Adolescents who either fall too far behind or move too far ahead of their friends are dropped from the group.

The most common type of peer group is the clique, a small group of friends. Adolescents not in cliques may be liaisons, who are socially active and have friends in several cliques, or isolates, who have only a few individual friends and are not part of the social network.

Crowds are groups of about 20. Adolescents try out new social skills at crowd events, the most important of which involve the opposite sex. The crowd is primarily important in helping adolescents move from same-sex to opposite-sex relationships, whereas clique activities provide feedback about the success of new social skills.

Cliques and crowds change in importance as adolescents age. They are most important in mid-adolescence and become less so as adolescents begin to form couples who are "going together."

Popularity for boys is closely tied to being good in sports; for girls it is related to being a social leader.

Several dimensions of social competence also contribute to popularity: assessing a situation, responding to it, and adopting a process approach to relationships. Popular individuals are better able to see what is going on in a social situation and adapt their behavior accordingly. They are also more responsive to the overtures of others, and they realize that developing friendships takes time.

Dating can begin anywhere between the ages of 12 and 16. Girls start somewhat earlier than boys. The most important determinant of when they start to date is whether their friends are dating.

Even before dating begins, adolescents go through a stage in which they develop crushes. Once dating begins, most adolescents practice multiple dating, going out with many different partners.

Adolescents, Parents, and Peers

Conformity peaks in early adolescence. Adolescents with high social status and a well-developed sense of self are less likely to conform. Authoritative parenting also gives adolescents skills that help them make decisions for themselves.

The values of peers and parents more frequently complement each other than conflict. Most adolescents have friends with values similar to theirs.

When adolescents seek advice from parents and friends, they are more likely to seek parental advice concerning long-term life decisions and the advice of friends in daily matters. With age, adolescents become more comfortable in making their own decisions.

Peers have an important influence on deviant behaviors. Gender differences exist in response to peer pressure; boys consider the anticipated outcome more, and girls consider peer approval and friendship more.

Despite the importance of the peer culture, adolescents and parents share many basic values.

KEY TERMS

self-disclosure	liaison	social competence
enculturation	isolate	conformity
clique	crowd	peer pressure

CHAPTER 7

Adolescents in the Schools

"Oh, no! Here he comes," I muttered.

"Move over, slime ball. Thanks for the place in line."

The kid was huge and his breath was fogging up my glasses. No food was worth this. I stepped out, and he stepped in line. From what I could see of the steam table, I was ahead on this one.

"Aren't you going to fight him?" nudged Erin

"Sure, Erin. You want me to end up in the tossed salad?"

"This is too much!" she rasped. "The morning has gone from bad to awful—I want out!"

"Me too," I nodded. "But I don't think I could find my way. I got lost three times already today. If I'm late to another class, I'll have detention—and it's still the first week! Four minutes to get to classes! What are they training us for, the track team? I can't even open my locker that fast."

"Some ninth-grader slammed mine shut this morning—just as I popped the combination."

"Welcome to scrubs-ville, Erin."

"If this is what it's going to be like, I'm out of here!" she vowed.

Secondary school is a new experience for early adolescents, one that most will never forget. Adolescents leave behind the comfortable familiarity of elementary school: a classroom they know as well as their living room and a teacher they saw more often than their parents. They also leave the comfortable security of being the oldest and biggest students at school. More opportunities are available to students in secondary school—and more is expected of them.

The number of students attending high schools in the United States has increased dramatically over this century. More than two and a half million students graduate from high school each year (U.S. Department of Education, 1996). A high school education will give them the skills they will need for jobs and college. Courses in computer programming, woodworking and metalworking, conversational French, drafting, journalism, and peer leadership alternate with the basics of math, English, and social studies. In many respects, secondary education is one of our society's biggest success stories. In other respects, it is the focus of national concern and controversy. We look at the successes and failings of our secondary schools in the first section of this chapter.

Not all students have the same interests and not all learn at the same rate. Many schools assign students to academic tracks that reflect their different interests and abilities. Some educators argue that assigning students to academic tracks creates as many problems as it is designed to solve. The practice of tracking and its relationship to academic success are discussed. School variables such as the size of the school and the learning climates of classrooms can also influence adolescents in important ways. We look at these variables in a subsequent section of the chapter.

Some adolescents leave elementary school for a junior high, and others go to a middle school; they spend fifth or sixth, seventh, eighth and sometimes ninth grade here before moving into high school. We consider the research comparing middle schools and junior high schools. Despite obvious differences, these schools have many similarities. Both move at a quicker pace than elementary school. Adolescents move from class to class, with a different teacher in each and sometimes no close friends in any.

In the next section of the chapter, adolescents themselves step into the spotlight. Some achieve and meet the expectations of teachers and parents; others do not. We look first at conditions such as teachers' attitudes and school violence that affect success and failure for all, and then move to a consideration of two extreme populations—the gifted and those with learning disabilities.

Some critics argue that schools are White, middle-class institutions dominated by conventional attitudes. We examine how well schools are meeting the needs of female as well as male students and adolescents from ethnically and racially diverse backgrounds. Research into effective schools raises the question of whether changes that are considered necessary in order to reach alienated minorities are also necessary to effectively teach mainstream adolescents.

SECONDARY SCHOOLS TODAY

The growth of secondary education in this country during the past century has been nothing short of phenomenal. Over the past 100 years, this society has progressed from fewer than 5% of the population completing high school to 87%, with either a diploma or equivalent degree (Youth Indicators, 1996). Quite a success story! Yet the successes of secondary education have been punctuated by crises as well.

As more students attend high school, the diversity of the student population has increased. In years past, the less successful would not have remained in school. The increasing ethnic diversity of our society is also a source of differences among students (Youth Indicators, 1996). Teachers must reach students of widely differing cultural backgrounds, some of whom have limited knowledge of English or of the dominant culture. Many schools face the need to instruct students from two dozen or more cultural backgrounds.

Secondary schools face another crisis: a dramatic increase in the number of students attending school and the need for more teachers and schools to accommodate them. School enrollment declined steadily from the early 1970s through the mid-1980s, as birth rates declined. Beginning in 1985, however, enrollment in kindergarten through the eighth grade began to increase. The number of students in elementary and secondary schools is expected to exceed the record previously set by the baby boomers, with enrollment continuing to increase as we move into the coming century (Youth Indicators, 1996).

Academic Tracking

One of the biggest problems facing high schools is the tremendous diversity of their students. Generations ago, only those who were academically oriented completed high school. Others found jobs and got married. High school was for those with a special interest in, and capacity for, learning. Today, all possible interests, gradations of ability, and goals are present. Can we expect all students to take the same courses? Will some learn so quickly that teachers must move ahead before others have mastered the material? Will slower learners hold the class back? And what about different interests? Should we require all students to take the same courses? If so, what should these be? Can we expect everyone to have an equal interest in math? Auto mechanics? English literature?

Academic tracking is a common solution to problems created by the diverse interests and abilities of students. **Academic tracking** is the practice of offering students several programs of study, with assignment to these based on prior achievement, stated goals, and the evaluations of counselors.

Most high schools offer at least two tracks—college preparatory and noncollege—and many offer other options. Students in different tracks frequently do not take classes together even for the same course. When the same course, such as basic math or English, is required in both tracks, students from different tracks take different sections. Educators assume that multiple tracks allow students to work at different paces and teachers to adjust the content of the courses to match differing interests. These assumptions make tracking seem a reasonable approach for teaching students with very different abilities and interests.

However, tracking may in fact contribute to the problems it was designed to correct. Adolescents from minority groups and low-income families are still more likely to be in noncollege than in college tracks (Page, 1990; Youth Indicators, 1996). Of the students in noncollege tracks, more lose interest in school and drop out than those in college preparatory

Continuity and
Diversity in Early
Adolescent
Development

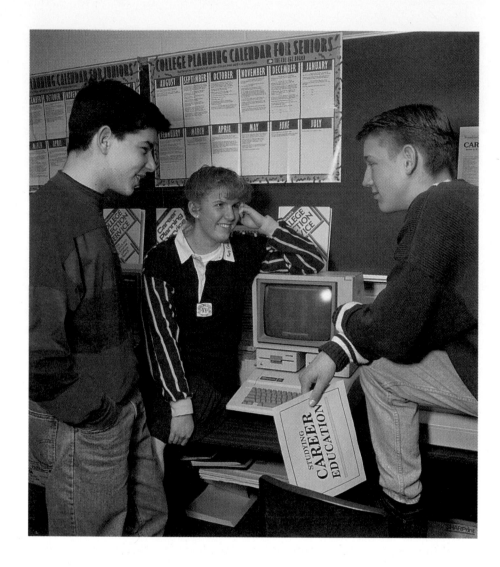

Secondary school students are often divided into vocational and college-bound tracks. The mere assignment to one track or the other can profoundly affect students' performance and teachers' expectations.

tracks. Can assignment to a lower track contribute to a sense of alienation and failure among students? Research suggests that it does (Snow, 1986).

Analysis of a national sample of over 10,000 high school students reveals that those students assigned to a lower track do more poorly and are less likely to graduate from high school (Gamoran & Mare, 1989). These investigators used achievement scores in mathematics and the probability of graduating as indices of student success. Most of the difference in mathematics achievement between students assigned to college and noncollege tracks was accounted for by preexisting differences. At first glance, these data would appear to support the belief that students assigned to each track differ primarily in ability. However, 20% of the difference could be traced to the assignment to tracks. A difference this size is more than the increase in math achievement scores gained by an average student between his or her sophomore and senior years! It is also larger than the difference between the scores of students in noncollege tracks and the scores of high school dropouts. Tracking has an even greater effect on the probability of staying in school than it does on math scores. Over 50% of the difference in graduation rates between students in college and noncollege tracks could be explained by their track assignment (Gamoran & Mare, 1989).

These and similar data strongly suggest that the practice of tracking adversely affects students who are assigned to lower tracks (Oakes, 1985). Tracking makes it more likely that these students will work toward lower goals, proceed at a slower pace, have fewer opportunities to learn, and achieve less than students in higher tracks (Raudenbush, Rowan, & Cheong, 1993). More class time goes to discipline and less to instruction. Even the quality of teaching differs, in addition to what is taught (Page, 1990).

How does tracking contribute to these problems? Reba Page (1990), at the University of California, Riverside, points to the day-to-day experiences of lower-track students, arguing that their courses, rather than training them in job skills, are often watered-down versions of college-preparatory classes. She adds that classroom exercises all too frequently communicate a different set of values, in which luck and guessing, rather than hard work and skill, determine success. Page observed nine lower-track classrooms for six months. A particular lesson that involved a trivia quiz captured the qualities she had come to recognize in much of lower-track instruction. The quiz was presented to students as a "kinda fun" way of improving their listening skills, one in which they needn't "know" the answers, but simply make "a good guess." Students, however, were not given a strategy to use in coming up with a good guess. Nor was the content of the quiz related to their coursework or familiar experiences outside the classroom. Instead, students found themselves participating in a task in which competence had been ruled out and relevance was missing, yet one that they were told would help them in their schoolwork. Disengagement, in the form of problem behavior or lack of apparent motivation, is predictable when effort is unrelated to success and coursework is unrelated to the skills students will need on the job. A vicious cycle is perpetuated when teachers, put off by students' indifference, no longer look for ways of challenging interest and harnessing ability.

One student assigned to the lower track put it this way:

> When you first go to junior high school you do feel something inside—it's like ego. You have been from elementary to junior high, you feel great inside. You say, well, doggone, I'm going to deal with the people here now, I am in junior high school. You get this shirt that says Brown Junior High or whatever the name is and you are proud of that shirt. But then you go up there and the teacher says, "Well, so and so, you're in the basic section, you can't go with the other kids." The devil with the whole thing—you lose something in you—like it just goes out of you. (Schafer, Olexa, & Polk, 1972, p. 47)

Which track students take can have an important influence on the educational and vocational opportunities that are open to then. Some encouraging trends are underway, however: More students are in a college-

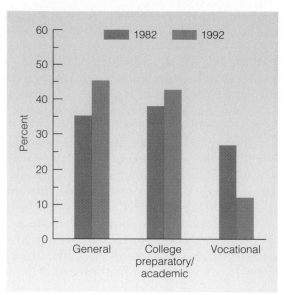

FIGURE 7.1 Percentage
of High School Seniors in
General Education, College-
Preparatory, and Vocational
Tracks. *Source:* Youth Indicators:
*Trends in the Well-Being of American
Youth.* (1996). Washington, DC: U.S.
Government Printing Office.

preparatory track today than in the 1980s, and proportionately fewer are in a noncollege or vocational track than before. Figure 7.1 presents these trends. The trends for minority students are encouraging as well. Whereas the percentage of minority students in college-preparatory tracks is higher for nearly all minorities, significantly more Hispanic students are in college-preparatory tracks than before, and significantly more Black students are completing high school and college than before, as shown in Table 7.1 (Youth Indicators, 1996).

Educators are also trying out alternatives to tracking for dealing with diverse student populations. Alternatives exist. Students of different ability levels can be placed together in small working groups. This approach, known as cooperative learning, gives students recognition for both their individual performance and that of the group. Power relationships subtly shift, placing the responsibility for learning on students rather than the teacher (C. Banks, 1993). Cooperative learning increases achievement in many students and has eased tensions in multicultural classrooms (Slavin, 1985).

Another powerful alternative is the involvement of parents in the educational process. Parents can be involved in a number of ways: instructing students in the classroom, helping them at home, participating in school governance, and becoming involved in community service. James Comer and his colleagues (1985, 1988, 1996), at Yale University, have created a program in which parents, along with teachers, administrators, and staff, are responsible for administering the activities of the school. This program addresses the social and developmental, as well as the educational, needs of students. Comer believes, for instance, that social skills and ties to the community are as important as academic subjects, especially for lower-income students, who often lack these assets. In two inner-city schools using Comer's model, student performance so improved that the schools tied for third and fourth place in the district, with the students testing up to a year above the average for their grade! Attendance also improved dramatically, and behavior problems practically disappeared.

It is easy to understand why such a program could work: Teaching becomes more relevant when academic subjects are translated into the daily concerns of students and their families. In turn, what is learned in the classroom receives the support of parents who are committed to educational programs they help plan.

Despite their proven success, alternatives such as cooperative learning and Comer's model will not be beneficial unless teachers and staff are trained to use them effectively. Cooperative learning, for example, is a relatively complex technique to implement, requiring in-service training. Similarly, parental involvement can be cumbersome and can even increase conflict if parents' and teachers' views of education conflict (C. Banks, 1993).

Another alternative combines assignment to noncollege tracks with actual work experience for which students receive academic credit. This approach also addresses the financial difficulties many low-income students face. Innovative use of computers is a promising alternative for students who are "light-sensitive"—that is, who get most of their information through visual media such as television and spend little time reading (Solomon, 1990).

School Size

The size of schools is known to affect behavior at school—inside and outside class. Adolescents from smaller schools have more positive interactions with each other, fewer discipline problems, less truancy, and fewer dropouts.

TABLE 7.1   **Percentages of High School Seniors Enrolled in General Education, College-Preparatory, and Vocational Tracks, 1982 and 1992**

	General		College Preparatory		Vocational	
	1982	1992	1982	1992	1982	1992
ALL SENIORS						
Females	32.4%	44.2%	38.9%	44.2%	28.7%	11.6%
Males	38.1	46.3	36.8	41.8	25.1	11.9
ETHNICITY						
White	34.8	43.3	40.6	45.7	24.6	11.0
Black	35.1	48.9	33.3	35.6	31.6	15.4
Hispanic	37.4	56.4	24.9	30.6	37.7	13.1
Asian	27.5	40.3	55.9	50.9	16.6	8.8
Native American	55.3	60.8	19.1	22.6	25.6	16.7

Source: Youth Indicators: *Trends in the Well-Being of American Youth.* (1996). Washington, DC: U.S. Government Printing Office.

The critical size for a school is about 500 students. Once that number is reached, further increases don't have much effect (Garbarino, 1980).

Small schools can be more flexible in responding to the needs of adolescents. Bryk and Raudenbush (1988) analyzed data from a national survey of over 1,000 schools. They found that smaller schools can overcome differences related to social class, academic background, and personal factors more readily than large schools. Programs on drug use, multicultural education, and cooperative learning are easier to set in motion and to change in response to student needs. Students in small schools have more opportunity to participate in activities. The particular type of activity is not important—yearbook staffing, hall monitoring, cheerleading, or peer counseling. Each one gives students a sense of belonging and a way of identifying with school (Coleman, 1993).

Although it is not possible to eliminate large schools, it is possible to create smaller "communities for learning" within them. These smaller environments can be just as responsive to students' needs as small schools are (Epstein, 1990).

School Climate

Unique characteristics of schools may be at least as important as their size. The relationship between school input variables—number of students per classroom, computers per student, or books in the library, for example—and school output, in the form of student achievement, is not a simple one. Schools with similar resources can differ markedly in their effectiveness. Process variables that reflect the qualities of a school, such as differences in social and academic climates among schools or differences in their teaching staffs, must also be entered into the equation. Achievement is determined not so much by how many computers are in a classroom or how many books are in the library, but how effectively these resources are integrated into the instruction. Schools that involve parents, either as classroom aides or tutors or as members of governing committees making schoolwide decisions, are more effective, especially in low-income districts where continuity between the home and the classroom needs bridging (C. Banks, 1993). A two-year study of nearly 30 classrooms in nine different schools found that students with a positive sense of school climate not only valued school but felt effective at school; they also had parents who valued education and talked with them about school (Coleman, 1993).

Robert Roeser and Carol Midgley, at the University of Michigan, working with Timothy Urdan at Emory University (1996), looked at levels of achievement in nearly 300 eighth-graders in relation to the psychological environment, or school climate, of the middle schools they attended. These investigators identified two dimensions to a school's climate that were important for achievement. The first of these concerns the way in which a school defines success. Broadly, schools can define success in either of two ways: focusing on **task-mastery goals,** which emphasize individual improvement, mastery of the material, and intellectual development, or focusing on **performance-ability goals,** which emphasize comparisons among students and define achievement in terms of one student's ability

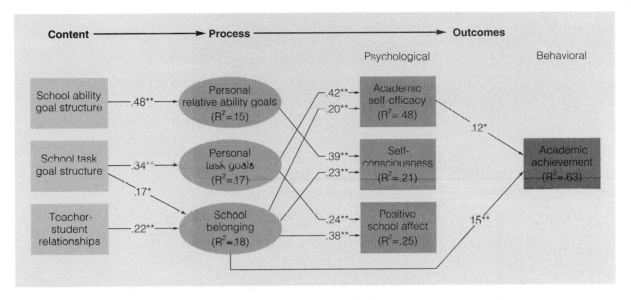

FIGURE 7.2   Predicting Academic Success in Eighth-Graders. *Predictions are based on knowing dimensions of a school's climate and how these are related to the ways students set personal goals and feel about themselves.* Source: Adapted from R. W. Roeser, C. Midgley, & T. C. Urdan. (1996). Perceptions of the school psychological environment and early adolescents' psychological and behavioral functioning in school: The mediating role of goals and belonging. *Journal of Educational Psychology, 88,* 408–422.

relative to that of others, thereby fostering intellectual competition. Do students interpret success in different ways depending on the way their school defines success? If so, students in each type of school should demonstrate differences in their personal goals—such as learning something new versus being the best in the class—and in achievement-related feelings—such as self-efficacy versus self-consciousness, as might result from comparing themselves with what is required by the task or with others. A second dimension to a school's climate concerns the quality of student–teacher relationships. Students who see their teachers as respecting and caring for them would be expected to have positive feelings toward school and have a sense of belonging to school.

As can be seen in Figure 7.2 these dimensions of school climate are related both to the way students set goals for themselves and their sense of belonging to, or engagement in, school. These processes, in turn, are related to how students feel about themselves and their school and, ultimately, to their level of achievement, as measured by their grades at the end of the year.

These investigators point out that many schools attempt to foster achievement with incentives such as honors classes, honor rolls, and other privileges. In reality, such practices may communicate that the school values some of its students more than others and is not willing to support all equally, a perceived climate that can limit the success of many of its students.

Schools that place as much value in educating students in vocational or lower tracks as those in college-preparatory tracks promote higher levels of achievement among all students. Often this requires a redefinition of values among teachers, staff, and parents. Our society has come to define

The most important characteristic of an effective school is teachers who care about their students and have high expectations of them.

intelligence in terms of verbal and mathematical abilities (see Chapter 4), both of which contribute more heavily to performance in college-preparatory tracks. In emphasizing these abilities, we have slighted others such as interpersonal, mechanical, or musical, which are more evenly distributed among students in all tracks.

Teachers' Attitudes

One factor consistently distinguishes effective schools: the beliefs of the teaching staff that all students are capable of learning. Teachers at effective schools have high expectations. They interact with students more, reward them more, and have friendlier classrooms (Teddlie, Kirby, & Stringfield, 1989). Research constantly underscores the potent effect that individual teachers can have on their students (Solomon, Scott, & Duveen, 1996). Expecting the most from students and letting them know when they have succeeded are just as important as the latest in software and the number of books on the shelves. Students in classrooms where progress is monitored and feedback is given as to how well they are doing have higher achievement levels than those not given feedback. New teachers, especially, hold high expectations for their students and most enter the profession for altruistic reasons (Young, 1995). The Research Focus, "Dependent Variables," discusses another issue related to teachers' attitudes, that of the effect of good looks on grades.

School Violence

More important than a school's size or climate or the attitudes of its teachers is its ability to provide an environment in which students feel safe. In the past, safety was simply taken for granted. It no longer can be. Among the top disciplinary problems listed by teachers two generations ago were chewing gum and running in the halls. Today, teachers are concerned about assault, rape, drug abuse, and robbery, as shown in Table 7.2.

Teachers' concerns reflect students' realities. As can be seen in Table 7.3, approximately 30% of ninth-grade males report having been in physical fights at school, 12% said they had been threatened or injured with a weapon, and 46% reported that they had had something stolen or deliberately damaged at school (Centers for Disease Control, 1996c). Differences among ethnic groups and between sexes are large. An even more startling statistic is that 13.6% of ninth-grade males said they had carried a gun to school (Centers for Disease Control, 1996c).

TABLE 7.2   Teachers' Ratings of Top Disciplinary Problems—Then and Now

1940	1990
Talking out of turn	Drug abuse
Chewing gum	Alcohol abuse
Making noise	Pregnancy
Running in the halls	Suicide
Cutting in line	Rape
Dress code violations	Robbery
Littering	Assault

Source: T. Toch. (1993). Violence in schools. *U.S. News & World Report, 115,* 31–37.

TABLE 7.3   Percentage of Adolescents Experiencing Violence While at School

	9th Grade		12th Grade	
	Female	Male	Female	Male
Been in physical fight	12.1%	29.4%	5.6%	15.5%
Had something stolen or damaged	30.2	46.3	21.5	37.5
Been threatened or injured with a weapon	6.8	11.9	4.5	9.0
Carried a weapon such as a gun, knife, or club to school	5.6	14.9	3.1	12.0

Source: Centers for Disease Control. (1996). Youth risk behavior surveillance—United States, 1995. *Morbidity and Mortality Weekly Report.* Washington, DC: U.S. Government Printing Office.

Research Focus

Dependent Variables: Beauty and the Best—Are Looks and Grades Related?

On a scale of 1 to 10, how important are good looks? Many adolescents would answer 10½! Activities such as dating, gaining entrance into social groups, and endless comparisons with cultural 10s can lead many to put physical attractiveness near the top of their lists. But are good looks equally important in everything? Perhaps they help when making an impression on a first date, or in getting noticed to begin with, but surely the value of good looks stops in the classroom, or on the athletic field, or at the tip of one's pencil when taking an exam. Or does it?

Numerous studies report puzzling findings relating physical attractiveness to widely different aspects of personal functioning. Popularity? Naturally. Social competence? Probably. Grade-point average? That may be going too far.

Too far or not, adolescents' grades *are* related to their looks. How is attractiveness related to a student's grades? Do all measures of academic performance pick up this relationship, or only some? And how are we to understand such a relationship?

Richard Lerner and his associates (1990) wanted to know as well. They photographed adolescents and had individuals rate the photos for physical attractiveness on a 5-point scale, with 1 for "very unattractive" and 5 for "very attractive." They also looked at several measures of academic competence: an achievement test (the California Achievement Test, Form C), teacher judgments of classroom performance as reflected in students' overall grade-point averages, adolescents' appraisals of their own abilities, and teachers' appraisals of their abilities. They looked at each measure at three different times over a period ranging from the beginning of the sixth grade to the end of the seventh.

Why did they use more than one measure of academic competence? If the measures don't all show the same relationships, how are we to evaluate which one is more accurate? The answer is that different measures pick up different aspects of behavior. Three criteria distinguish accurate measures: reliability, validity, and sensitivity.

The first consideration with any measure of behavior, or *dependent variable,* is its *reliability:* It should give you the same value each time you use it. If a student takes an intelligence test and retakes it in 3 weeks, one expects the score to be about the same on both occasions. Differences in IQ from one testing to the next reflect factors other than intelligence, that is, *error.* Reliable measures have little error. Second, measures must have *validity.* They must measure what they are designed to measure. Some of the very first intelligence tests were highly reliable but not very valid. Some, for instance, measured how rapidly people could tap their fingers, something that can be measured with little error but that turns out to have little to do with actual intelligence. Third, *sensitivity* is a characteristic of good measures: They are able to detect even small differences where these exist. Current measures of intelligence do more than sort individuals into categories of, say, bright, average, and dull. They offer numerous distinctions within each.

Returning to adolescents' grades and their physical attractiveness, let's consider what Lerner and his associates found. They discovered that students' appearances *are* related to their academic success, but only at the beginning of the school year. This finding suggests that first impressions are important—even in the classroom. At the beginning of the year, before they have much information about a student's ability, teachers' impressions reflect a student's attractiveness. Teachers communicate their expectations to students in subtle ways, and students, in turn, live up to them. Early measures reflect these expectations, both through teachers' impressions, which are present in their grading, and students' self-appraisals, which affect their performance in class and on exams.

With time, differences in ability increasingly contribute to teachers' impressions of students, so that finally neither grade-point averages nor teacher assessments are related to attractiveness. Only by using several response measures could the investigators sort out these many relationships.

Source: R. M. Lerner, M. Delaney, L. E. Hess, J. Jovanovic, & A. von Eye. (1990). Early adolescent physical attractiveness and academic competence. *Journal of Early Adolescence, 10,* 4–20.

TABLE 7.4 Percentage of Adolescents Watching From One to Six or More Hours
of Television a Day

Hours per Day	8th Grade	12th Grade
6 or more	14%	7%
4 to 5	27	18
2 to 3	45	46
1 or less	14	29

Source: National Assessment of Educational Progress (NAEP), 1992 and 1994 Reading Assessments. HTTP ://
www.ed.gov/nces/pubs/96814.htm/

Violence is a more serious problem in urban than in suburban or rural schools; however, no school is immune to its threat. In a survey of high school principals, 64% of those in urban schools reported that violence had increased over the past five years, but so did 54% of suburban principals and 43% of rural ones (Toch, 1993).

Even more disturbing are findings suggesting a new attitude among adolescents concerning conflict—and the value of life. In one survey of high school students, 20% said they thought it was okay to shoot someone "who has stolen something from you," and 8% said it was okay to shoot someone "who had done something to offend or insult you" (Toch, 1993). These students were not embattled inner-city youth—they were from a suburban Southwestern high school!

What are the sources of these attitudes and behaviors? A number of factors suggest themselves. Violence for many begins in the home: 34% of adults responding to a national survey said they had witnessed a man beating his wife or girlfriend (Centers for Disease Control, 1993b), and estimates of various forms of sexual abuse have been as high as one in four girls and one in ten boys (Finkelhor, 1993). These figures cut across ethnic and class lines, affecting all segments of society (see Chapter 12).

Many adolescents, almost 40%, watch three to five hours of television nightly (Table 7.4), hours that are saturated with violence. Before leaving elementary school, children will have watched approximately 8,000 murders and 100,000 violent acts (Toch, 1993). Figures such as these are chilling, given the compelling nature of research demonstrating the effects of viewing aggression (see Bandura, Chapter 2). The ability of television to teach—for good or evil—is well established (Beentjes & van der Voort, 1993).

Connecting copycat acts of violence with ones portrayed in the media is relatively easy because of their uniqueness. But what of the common, ordinary acts of violence in which one person pulls a gun on another—and pulls the trigger? Rather than being seen as the exception, copycat violence can just as easily be seen as supporting research which shows that children will copy acts of violence they have viewed on film, whether inside or outside a research laboratory (Bandura, Ross, & Ross, 1963).

Media modeling of violence is not in itself the cause of the increased violence we are presently experiencing as a society. Also significant are the

To investigate whether violent behavior is learned by imitation, Stanford University researcher Albert Bandura had children watch an adult attacking an inflatable "punching bag" doll in a novel way—hitting it with a mallet, for instance, or pummeling it with balls. He found that most children would attack the doll in the same way when they were put in a room with it.

devastating effects of poverty and discrimination so many adolescents experience, together with very real threats to personal safety both at home and at school. These factors, combined with the accessibility of guns, add up to a national problem. Nearly half of a large survey of tenth-grade males, for instance, said they could get a gun if they wanted to; this figure is substantially higher for inner-city youth where violence is most deadly (*Digest of Education Statistics,* 1993).

Teaching Peace

Even though schools suffer the consequences of these conditions, they are also in a position to change them. Morton Deutsch (1993) argues that schools can encourage values and provide experiences that promote constructive, rather than destructive, means of resolving conflict. Four elements are critical to "teaching peace": cooperative learning, training in conflict resolution, putting controversy to constructive use, and creating conflict resolution centers.

Cooperative Learning Students learn interpersonal skills in cooperative learning classrooms; goals are shared by members of a group, reducing competition. Students are more helpful and caring in these learning environments than in the more traditional, individualistic, and competitive ones.

Conflict Resolution Training   These programs teach students to perceive a conflict as a problem to be solved mutually, one in which all participants can come out ahead, instead of solved competitively, in which some win and others lose. Students also learn to identify potential causes of violence and, knowing its consequences, to discover alternatives (see Chapter 12).

Constructive Controversy   Controversy, in itself, is not undesirable. It can actually stimulate students to think about problems and come up with creative solutions when shown how to do so. One way of doing this is to have students work in small groups in which pairs alternately argue for opposing positions and then reverse their arguments, taking their opponents' position and arguing as earnestly as they can for that. Finally, all work toward reaching a consensus.

Conflict Resolution Centers   Some schools have established mediation programs in which both teachers and students are trained in listening skills and conflict resolution.

ADOLESCENTS AT SCHOOL

Secondary schools challenge students more than elementary schools do. In this section we will look at some of the factors that affect students' performance in school: the relation between television and literacy, patterns of achievement, and gender. Some students fail to meet the challenge and drop out of school.

Preparing for High School: Junior High or Middle School

Educators are still debating the relative merits of middle schools (fifth or sixth through eighth grade) versus junior high schools (seventh through eighth or ninth grades). Two events focus their concerns: Adolescents enter puberty during these years, and they leave one form of school for another. Puberty introduces intellectual, emotional, and psychological changes as well as physical ones. A change in school settings confronts adolescents with a more impersonal environment than the one they have previously known. Will one type of school ease the stresses of puberty more than the other? Also, which arrangement of grades will best facilitate the transition to high school (Epstein, 1990)?

Because of the secular trend, sixth-graders today are physically more like seventh- and eighth-graders than like school children a year behind them. Sixth-graders are also intellectually and emotionally more mature. Most have begun to use formal thought, and patterns of friendship are changing (see Chapter 6). Students at the highest grades in middle school, those in seventh and eighth grades, are still experiencing pubertal changes and just moving into opposite-sex relationships. Middle schools place students going through similar changes in a single setting. Although some educators argue on this basis that sixth-, seventh-, and eighth-graders' needs are best

Whether they graduate to a junior high or a middle school, the transition from elementary school is a big step for young adolescents. No longer do they stay in the same classroom with the same teacher; now they have to find their way around campus and manage their time so that they carry out assignments from several teachers.

met in a middle school, others voice concerns that by placing sixth-graders with older adolescents, they are rushed into more mature forms of behavior. These latter educators want to protect early adolescents from growing up too fast.

In actuality, decisions about middle schools and junior high schools are more likely to be made on the basis of local demographics than educational policy, but because comparisons of these two school settings reveal more similarities than differences, this fact loses much of its importance (Kohut, 1988). Similarities of both types of schools include the curriculum, teaching practices, and extracurricular activities.

Few consistent differences emerge in academic achievement between the two types of schools. Also, attitudes and behaviors among students attending each do not differ consistently. When differences emerge, they usually favor middle schools (Educational Research Service, 1983). Students at middle schools have more positive attitudes about school, and about themselves, their peers, and their teachers, than do junior high students. Teachers' attitudes are more positive, too, in many of the comparisons (Kohut, 1988).

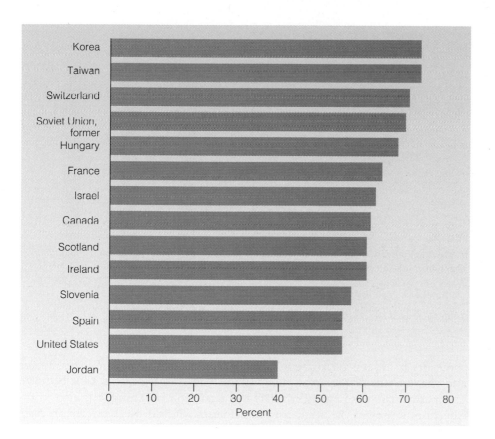

FIGURE 7.3
International Com-
parisons of Correct
Percentages of
13-Year-Olds on a
Math Test. *Source:*
Youth Indicators: *Trends in
the Well-Being of American
Youth.* (1996). Washington,
DC: U.S. Government
Printing Office.

In terms of mathematics proficiency, the average 17-year-old can work
with decimals and fractions, calculate areas of geometric figures such as
rectangles, and work with signed numbers, exponents, and square roots.
Even so, international comparisons of mathematical abilities of 13-year-old
students from 14 countries including Switzerland, the former Soviet Union,
France, and Canada found that U.S. adolescents place 13th in the field of
14, as shown in Figure 7.3, nearly 20 points below the highest scoring participants (Youth Indicators, 1996). Within the United States, students showing greatest improvement on recent national tests in mathematics are
minority youth—African American and Hispanic adolescents (Youth Indicators, 1996). The tremendous diversity due to the sheer numbers of students attending high school and the increasing ethnic variety of the general
population is certainly one factor contributing to the difficulties in meeting common educational goals.

Another factor that may be related to the lower scores of U.S. students
is the greater proportion of time they spend watching television than doing homework. The less television adolescents watch, the better their scores
on a mathematics proficiency test, as shown in Figure 7.4. This relationship,
however, is not easily interpreted. Do adolescents who watch television have
lower scores because they are spending time on television that they could
otherwise spend on activities that would develop those skills? Or is there

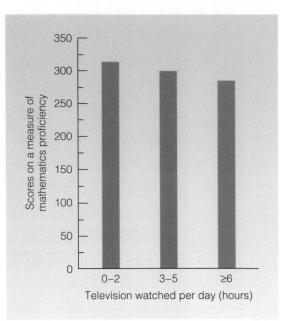

FIGURE 7.4
Mathematics Proficiency
and Hours of Television
Watched per Day. *Source:*
Youth Indicators: *Trends in the
Well-Being of American Youth.*
(1996). Washington, DC: U.S.
Government Printing Office.

some other hidden factor that might account both for their lower scores and the amount of television they watch? The answer may be a bit of both. Test performance is negatively related to television watching, but also to socioeconomic status. In other words, students who do most poorly on tests not only watch more television, but they are also lower in socioeconomic status, a factor in itself that predicts academic success (Youth Indicators, 1996).

Another factor that contributes to skill level among students is the amount of homework they do. Twenty-two percent of eighth-graders, for example, report having no homework assigned on an average day; 35% spend less than an hour, another 30% spend one to two hours, and less than 10% spend more than two hours.

Once in high school, adolescents spend more time on homework than before, but still less time than watching TV. Fewer spend less than 1 hour a day on homework (26%), and almost twice as many spend more than two hours daily. Yet over 45% still watch television two to three hours a day (*Digest of Education Statistics,* 1993; National Assessment of Educational Progress, 1994).

Which adolescents switch off the TV, get involved in school, and do their homework? In the next section, we look at the motivational processes that adolescents bring to the classroom. These can have powerful effects on their levels of achievement.

Academic Achievement

Laurence Steinberg, Bradford Brown, and Sanford Dornbusch (1996) studied over 20,000 adolescents, talking as well with parents and teachers, in an effort to discover why some adolescents succeed in school and others do not. These investigators worked with an ethnically diverse sample, with nearly 40% of the adolescents from African American, Asian American, and Hispanic families, approximately the percentage that will soon characterize the general U.S. population. A number of their findings are alarming; others are encouraging.

One of the more disturbing findings is that many high school students are disengaged from school and simply are not serious about their studies. Over a third said they spend much of their time during the school day "goofing off with their friends." Additionally, a large number of adolescents admitted to cheating on their schoolwork, two-thirds saying that they had cheated on a test and nine out of ten saying they had copied someone else's homework during the past year. On average, these high school students spent only four hours a week doing homework, a figure that is roughly equivalent to the number of hours *per day* spent by students in other industrialized nations. In contrast, one-third reported spending five hours or more a week "partying" with friends. In addition to spending time with friends outside of school, two-thirds of high school students had part-time jobs, many working more than 15 hours a week and many intentionally taking easier classes to reduce their work load while maintaining their grades. Also, many students (40%) reported being involved in some type of school-related activity, usually sports, which took up additional time and often left them too tired to concentrate on their studies (Steinberg, Brown, & Dornbusch, 1996).

Teachers echo these researchers' concerns. In a national survey of secondary school teachers, 38% indicated student apathy as a serious problem, 36% said students came to school unprepared to learn, and 34.5% noted a lack of parental involvement (U.S. Department of Education, 1996).

Steinberg and his colleagues suggest that the problems in secondary education are due not so much to what is taking place in the classroom as to what is going on outside the classroom—at home, with friends, and in the community. This is not to say that the quality of schooling does not matter—it does. But it does point to the importance of the larger context in contributing to the influence schools can have. What contextual factors might be supporting this disengagement from school?

One factor appears to be students' beliefs about how important it is for them to do well in school in order to be successful once they graduate. Steinberg and his associates found that although students believe that future success is related to graduating from high school, they do not relate success to how well they did in their classes. In other words, they believe that having a *diploma* is important, rather than what they have learned. Given this belief, it is not surprising that many put so little work into their classes. In motivational terms, many students appear to be motivated more by the need to avoid failing, or not graduating, than by the need to get something out of their classes.

How might one change this motivational pattern? Several answers were suggested, interestingly, by differences in achievement among adolescents from different ethnic backgrounds. Specifically, Asian American adolescents consistently outperformed European American adolescents, who performed better than African American or Hispanic adolescents. These differences existed even after other factors that are known to relate to academic success, such as family income or parental education, had been controlled for. In

Why are some students
engaged in school and
others unmotivated?
One of the key contex-
tual factors is beliefs
about the future con-
sequences of success
or failure in school.

fact, ethnicity was more importantly related to academic achievement than
any other factor, including affluence. As Steinberg points out, mention of
ethnic differences in academic achievement is a sensitive subject, leading as
it does to questions of differences in native ability. A more probable explanation than native ability, however, is that Asian American students simply
work harder and have more adaptive attitudes toward school. In fact, Steinberg quips, if they really were superior, they would not put in twice as many
hours on homework as other students.

So what is it that contributes to the academic success of Asian American students? We've mentioned one factor—effort. They spend more time
on schoolwork than their peers. Differences in their beliefs, however, are also
important. Steinberg and his associates found that students from different
ethnic backgrounds differed little in their beliefs about school success,
about the importance of getting a good education, but they did differ in
their beliefs about failing in school. When asked, for instance, if they

thought that not doing well in school would interfere with their ability to get a good job, striking differences emerged. Asian American students, more so than any others, believed that not doing well would hurt their chances for later success. Steinberg points out that it is excessive optimism, not pessimism, that is the problem for many African American and Hispanic students: They do not believe that doing poorly in their classes will affect their later success (Steinberg, Brown, & Dornbusch, 1996).

What are the encouraging findings from this research? Perhaps the most important is the power for change that lies within the reach of parents. Most parents value education and want their adolescents to succeed in school. However, not all ways of parenting are equally effective in promoting academic achievement. The most effective parents are accepting (versus rejecting), firm (versus lenient), and encourage autonomy in their children (versus controlling them). This type of parenting is known as *authoritative parenting* (see Chapter 5). Authoritative parenting, in addition to promoting competence, maturity, and academic success, can also offset negative peer influences (Mounts & Steinberg, 1995). Parental expectations, and adolescents' perceptions of these, contribute significantly to academic achievement in both nondisabled and learning-disabled students. In combination with other factors—such as prior achievement, effort, family income, and gender—parental involvement, parental communication, and parental expectations have been found to account for over 70% of the variance in academic achievement (Patrikakou, 1996). The good news is that parents can learn to parent authoritatively.

Another encouraging note, although one that on the face of it might not appear to be so, is that many parents as well as students are disengaged from school (Steinberg, Brown, & Dornbusch, 1996). Many students stated, for instance, that their parents did not know how well or how poorly they were doing in school, and over half reported that they could get Cs in their schoolwork without having their parents mind. Forty percent of parents never attend any of the school programs. The encouraging side to these findings is that when parents become engaged, their children become engaged as well, and academic achievement improves (Comer, 1985, 1996).

Patterns of Achievement

The power of positive thinking is getting some scientific backing. The attitude adolescents take toward their successes and failures is an important determinant of future success. It's not so much whether they fail or succeed—we all experience our share of both; the important thing is what adolescents attribute their failure or success to that determines whether they will persist and eventually achieve. Research distinguishes two quite different patterns of achievement behavior: one defined by a focus on the task and what it takes to master it (a *task-mastery orientation*) and the other by a focus on one's performance or ability (a *performance-ability orientation*). The first approach is adaptive; the second is not (Dweck, 1989; Midgley, Arunkumar, & Urdan, 1996).

Adolescents who are task, or mastery, oriented enjoy situations that challenge them, and work at them even when they are difficult. They even

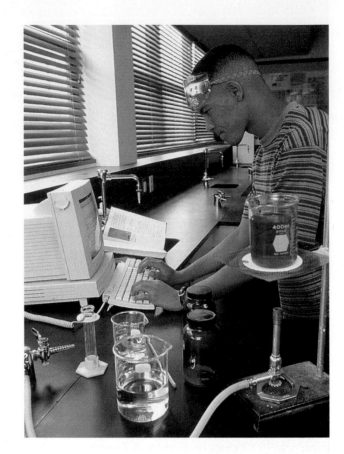

Task-oriented students, who focus on the task to be learned and work to increase their mastery and competence, are more likely to succeed than are students who are primarily concerned with the performance aspects of learning.

take pride in how much effort they have to put into mastering something new. Adolescents who are performance, or ability, oriented avoid challenging situations and show little persistence in the face of difficulty. They view any effort they must expend negatively, because having to try hard puts their ability in question. If at first they don't succeed, they find something else to do (Dweck, 1989).

Performance-oriented adolescents tend not to pursue challenging material unless they're sure they will succeed. They choose situations that will not reveal what they regard as their lack of ability. These students are likely to prefer tasks that are either very easy or very difficult; failure at the first is unlikely, and failure at the second cannot be taken as a measure of their ability. Even above-average students who are performance oriented will avoid situations that involve risk in preference to those they can perform effortlessly and thereby feel smart. In doing so, however, they miss situations that promote further understanding (Covington, 1983; Dweck, 1986).

The difference between students who stick it out and those who give up is basically one of attitude, which researchers term *attribution of outcome*. Adolescents who persist when they experience failure tend to attribute the outcome of their actions to their efforts. Believing they haven't tried hard enough, they increase their efforts. They are task-oriented (Dweck, 1986; Dweck & Reppucci, 1973).

Those who are disrupted by failure, frequently to the point of giving up, are performance oriented. Because they interpret failure to mean that they lack the ability for what they have attempted, they defensively withdraw in the face of it. To believe that failure means that one lacks ability is also to believe that trying harder isn't going to help. Rather than trying harder, these students explain their failure as bad luck, or the task's being too difficult. For them, having to try too hard is dangerous; it's just another way of calling their ability into question.

Carol Midgley, Revathy Arunkumar, and Timothy Urdan (1996) examined the use of *self-handicapping strategies* among African American and European American early adolescents. Such strategies are behaviors—such as not studying until the last minute or partying the night before a test—that could be seen as a cause of poor performance when students do not do well. Like achievement attributions, students may use strategies such as these to explain their performance in achievement situations; however, self-handicapping strategies are put into play before, rather than after, a student experiences success or failure. Thus, instead of explaining why one failed to pass a test that one had actually studied for by saying that one hadn't studied hard enough (attribution of outcome), one might intentionally not study until the night before (self-handicapping strategy), using inadequate time to study as an excuse for failing. Self-handicapping strategies hold the allure of a win–win situation: If one does poorly, those strategies provide an excuse, and if one does well, they make one appear even smarter. The disadvantages to their use are two-edged as well: Not only do they actually handicap students, making failure more likely, they also interfere with the use of adaptive ways of coping with achievement demands.

Given what we know of the ways adolescents interpret failure, we might suspect that some are more likely to self-handicap than others. Midgley and associates found, as suspected, that adolescents who adopt a performance-ability orientation to achievement situations more frequently report using these strategies. Additionally, even though the grade-point averages for African American and European American students did not differ, African American students who adopted a performance-ability orientation were more likely to self-handicap than were European American students. This difference is particularly surprising because African American adolescents were more positive in their self-esteem and certain attitudes toward school than European American adolescents were. Claude Steele (1992, 1995) suggests a possible explanation. Steele argues that African American students face an additional challenge to their ability, which he terms *stereotype threat*. Stereotype threat is the risk of confirming a negative stereotype about one's ethnic group, and hence about oneself, a threat that may increase the use of self-handicapping strategies as a self-defense.

Gender Differences and Achievement

Females frequently respond to success and failure in different ways than do males. Males are likely to attribute their successes to their ability and their failures to lack of effort. What this means, of course, is that males will persist at a problem until, more likely than not, they get it right. Females are more likely to attribute their successes to hard work, luck, or the ease of the task, and their failures to lack of ability, thereby discounting their successes and taking responsibility only for their failures. This interpretation makes females helpless in the face of success; they're not sure how they did it and unsure whether they could do it again. It was luck or an easy grade, they tell themselves, attributing their success to factors other than their own skill. Females are equally helpless in the face of failure. Because they attribute it to their inability, they have little recourse but to give up and try something new (Dweck, 1986, 1989).

Of all adolescents, those who are most likely to show maladaptive achievement behavior are females of high ability. Licht, Linden, Brown, and Sexton (1984) found a gender difference in response to failure *only* among the brightest students: The performance of the most able females was disrupted and that of males was actually facilitated. Bright females are more likely than males of equal ability, or students of either sex of average ability, to avoid challenge, to attribute their failure to inability, and to withdraw in the face of failure (Dweck, 1989).

Similarly, bright females who experience initial confusion at a task are less likely to do well than less capable females. Specifically, the brighter the female, the less likely she is to master a task if she encounters initial problems with it. If she experiences no initial confusion, however, her mastery is directly related to ability. A similar pattern does not exist for males. In fact, males are slightly more likely to master tasks when they experience some initial confusion. This is especially true for those of high ability (Dweck, 1986, 1989).

These motivational patterns frequently become evident only when adolescents enter junior high. Prior to this point, course material may not be sufficiently challenging to prompt defensive withdrawal. Mathematics represents a case in point. Girls do as well in math as boys throughout elementary school. Carol Dweck (1986, 1989) notes that achievement in math takes a new turn in junior high, one that is likely to call into play the gender differences in motivational patterns that we have been discussing. Dweck points out that math, unlike verbal tasks, often requires students to determine which solutions are appropriate to which problems. In verbal tasks they can follow the same approach with new material as with the old. Whether a word is *dog* or *dogmatic,* if it is unfamiliar, the solution is the same: Look it up in the dictionary. New problems in math often require students to adopt a different approach, and they are likely to make errors at first. The initial confusion that results is more likely to interfere with the performance of girls than that of boys.

A study by Byrnes and Takahira (1993) points to the importance of cognitive operations, in addition to motivational processes, in explaining gender differences in mathematics. These investigators focused on high school students' performance on the math section of the Scholastic Aptitude Test (SAT), in which males typically outperform females by over 40 points. Students were given five math problems from the SAT. Prior to taking the test, all students completed a measure testing their knowledge of the concepts that would be needed to solve the problems, and immediately after, they indicated which strategies they had used. Even though males did no better on the test assessing mathematical concepts, they outperformed females on the

Female students, even
gifted ones, are more
likely than male stu-
dents to attribute ini-
tial confusion about a
task to their own in-
ability rather than
to the nature of the
task itself and conse-
quently to withdraw
in the face of failure.

SAT items. Their superiority on these was explained by differences in the
way they put to use what they knew.

Attitudes toward math almost surely are important, and females develop
a less positive attitude toward math with age. In a longitudinal study following females from middle school to high school, Klebanov and Brooks-
Gunn (1992) found that females' attitudes about math became less positive,
even though their grades did not change. These investigators note the importance of socialization in contributing to attitudes toward math, showing
that mothers' attitudes toward their daughters' achievement corresponded
to how well they did in middle school. By high school, females' own attitudes toward math became more important, reflecting sex-role stereotypes in
which math achievement is perceived as masculine. These attitudes may be
changing. Recent trends reveal that females are taking as many math courses
in high school as males (National Center for Education Statistics, 1995) and
that they do at least as well in those courses as do males (Voyer, 1996).

Dweck (1986) cautions that maladaptive motivational approaches can
have cumulative effects. They can lead female adolescents to take fewer math
courses and consequently to become less skilled than males in math. Math
is a "gateway" subject, opening up possibilities in fields such as medicine,
engineering, and most branches of science.

Some adolescents make other decisions in high school that will have
lasting effects: Substantial numbers drop out before they graduate.

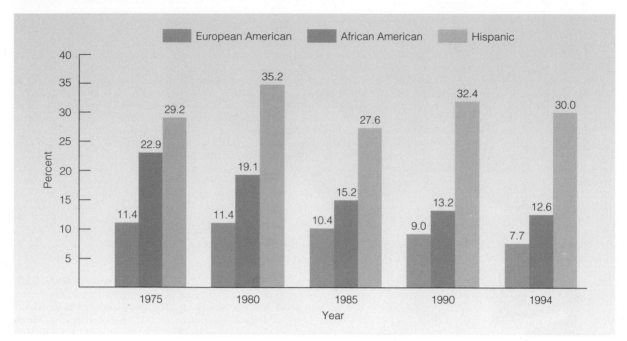

FIGURE 7.5   Percentage of High School Dropouts Ages 16 to 24, 1975 to 1994

Source: Youth Indicators: *Trends in the Well-Being of American Youth.* (1996). Washington, DC: U.S. Government Printing Office.

High School Dropouts

A lower percentage of adolescents drop out of high school today than did 20 years ago. In 1975, 14% of all U.S. high school students dropped out; in 1994, this figure was down to 11.5% (Youth Indicators, 1996). Even larger gains have been made by African American adolescents. In 1994, about 12% dropped out, down from about 23% in 1975. Even so, striking differences exist among minorities. The dropout rate among Hispanic adolescents has remained high, around 30% from 1975 to the present (Figure 7.5). This figure, however, is inflated by Hispanic immigrants born outside the United States. figures for first and second generation Hispanic students were significantly lower, although still higher than those for European American and African American students (National Center for Education Statistics, 1995). The dropout rate for Native Americans averages 50% in reservation schools and reaches a devastating 85% in urban high schools (LaFromboise & Low, 1989). In general, dropout rates among urban students are high, regardless of race (Huelskamp, 1993). Overall, males are more likely than females to drop out. Among Asian Americans, however, females are more likely to drop out, with the exception of Japanese Americans and filipino Americans (Kitano & Daniels, 1988).

Reasons for Dropping Out   A number of conditions both at home and at school predict those who are most likely to drop out. One of the most important is the parents' educational level (Nelson, 1988). Parents serve as models for educational success; adolescents with parents or older siblings who have dropped out of high school are more likely to drop out. The re-

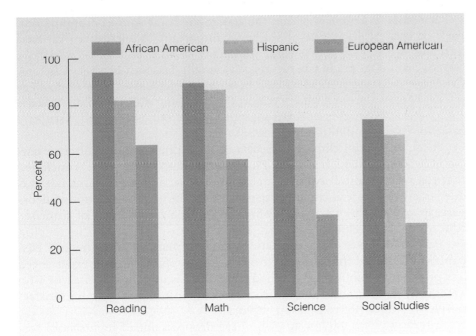

FIGURE 7.6   Percentage of Mothers Placing High Value on Academic Achievement

Source: H. W. Stevenson, C. Chen, & D. H. Uttal. (1990). Beliefs and achievement: A study of black, white, and Hispanic children. *Child Development, 61,* 508–523.

lationship between parental education and socioeconomic status is equally important. Socioeconomic status confers numerous advantages as one moves up the economic ladder. Adolescents from higher income homes have broader cultural experiences, attend better schools, have parents with more time (and skills) to help with homework, and experience lower levels of stress within the family. Not surprisingly, family income level is associated with achievement and staying in school (National Center for Education Statistics, 1995).

Parental attitudes toward education are also important. Interviews of Black and Hispanic mothers revealed that they place a high value on getting good grades—often a higher value than does the dominant culture (Figure 7.6). In addition to the value placed on education in Black and Hispanic families, these differences may reflect an awareness of the greater need for their children to achieve in order to overcome existing social biases (Stevenson, Chen, & Uttal, 1990).

Level of stress within the family is another important predictor of dropping out, as is family composition. Students from stressful homes and those from father-absent homes are more likely to drop out of school (Nelson, 1988). The latter most probably reflects the greater stress experienced in many father-absent homes. On the average, female-headed households have significantly lower incomes than those with both parents present; the stresses that accompany low-income living must be factored in. When they are, family configuration (female-headed households versus two-parent ones) has little bearing on school performance (Entwisle & Alexander, 1990; McLanahan & Booth, 1989).

Students' experiences within the classroom also relate to dropping out. Lack of basic skills is one of the most important. Adolescents who have difficulty with their coursework, who have failed a course, or who have stayed behind a grade are at risk (Connell, Halpern-Felsher, Clifford, Crichlow, & Usinger, 1995). Many of these adolescents are in noncollege tracks, a factor that in itself contributes to dropping out (Gamoran & Mare, 1989). Other predictors of dropping out are low self-esteem and disruptive behavior (Nelson, 1988; Tidwell, 1988).

A school's social climate is associated with dropping out. After reviewing over 700 public high schools, Pitman and Haughwout (1987) concluded that the relationship between a high school's size and its dropout rate was due largely to its social climate. Especially relevant was the amount students participated in school activities, which serves as a rough index of students' educational engagement (Coleman, 1993).

Peer influence is also important. A study of tenth-grade inner-city Hispanic youth found that those at low risk for dropping out had experienced less pressure to join a gang and had fewer friends in gangs than those who were likely to drop out. The low-risk students also reported more satisfaction with school (Reyes & Jason, 1993).

Interviews with adolescents who have dropped out of high school corroborate these findings. When asked why they dropped out, they mentioned poor grades, dislike of school, trouble with teachers, and financial problems. Many mentioned home responsibilities, pregnancy, and marriage. Almost all said they would not recommend dropping out to a friend or sibling (Tidwell, 1988).

Effective Programs Peter Coleman (1993), at Simon Fraser University, contends that dropouts, rather than being a separate problem within the school system, are instead a measure of its quality. Because dropouts are integral to the system, programs that reach them should benefit all students.

At this point, we have some idea what such programs are likely to include. We know, based on Comer's model, described earlier in this chapter, that schools that train students in social skills and establish ties with the community are more successful. So too are those that involve parents in the educational process. Each of these practices makes classroom experiences more relevant to experiences outside the classroom, whether with peers, parents, or the community. Yet instituting changes, especially schoolwide ones, is not easy.

Coleman found, from interviews with several hundred parents, that most of their interactions with schools are not instructionally focused. Yet most parents believe that they could help their children if they were allowed to participate more actively. Coleman points out that because parents' attitudes exert such a strong influence on children's attitudes toward school, reaching out to parents and working collaboratively with them, as in Comer's experimental schools, is one of the most effective ways schools can increase students' commitment.

Among programs designed specifically for dropouts, the most effective are those that simultaneously address the many problems these adolescents face at home as well as at school. Many adolescents, especially those from low-income families, need to work to help support themselves and their families. Innovative work–study programs that combine academic course-work with work in job settings for which students also receive academic credit have been successful, as have those that establish for students the connection between finishing high school and making a living. Almost all at-risk students need individual attention (Bloch, 1989; Nelson, 1988).

One program illustrates many of these points with stunning success. Jefferson County High School in Louisville, Kentucky, has enrolled over 5,000 former dropouts, and in its first four years, it graduated 1,100 of them. A number of features that are especially important for schooling at-risk adolescents distinguish this high school. The school offers an individualized program to every student, ensuring that they complete each unit of coursework with 70% mastery before moving on to the next. The latter requirement guarantees their success at what they attempt next. Students receive hands-on vocational guidance, in which they complete a battery of tests using manipulative materials. After reaching the end of these, they know what jobs they would like and which ones they would be good at. This high school puts as much emphasis on placing students in the right career track as on getting them ready for college (Gross, 1990).

Many dropouts work, and many have children. Because the school allows them to fit their classes into their other schedules, it minimizes the conflicts that might otherwise keep students away from school. Much of the school's flexibility comes from its use of *computer-assisted instruction (CAI)*. CAI makes it possible to respond to, as well as monitor, student progress. As the principal explains, "By advancing students when they get several consecutive questions of one type right and dropping back if a student misses several in a row, the CAI program keeps the problems challenging but well within the students' frustration tolerance" (Gross, 1990). CAI also provides printouts showing a student's trouble spots, so teachers know where to help. CAI centralizes bookkeeping, so that students can pick up where they left off even after an absence—an important plus for students who need to take time off to complete a job or stay home with a sick child.

ADOLESCENTS AT THE EDGE

Two other groups of students have special needs and frequently find themselves out of step with the rest of the class. These adolescents come from all backgrounds. They are the gifted and those with learning disabilities.

Gifted Adolescents

In 1925, Lewis Terman of Stanford University defined the gifted as those who place among the top 2% on a test of intelligence. Seventy years later, the most common criterion for placing students in special educational programs is still a score on an intelligence test: 130 or higher (Horowitz & O'Brien, 1986). The following descriptions come close to what the average person is likely to think of as gifted: the super smart, the ones who ace school, the kids behind the books.

Research Focus

Case Studies: Educating the Gifted Adolescent

By Jan Slater, Director Early Entrance Program, California State University, Los Angeles

The young student and her parents arrived 15 minutes early for the interview. The father carried an inch-thick folder of the awards their daughter Grace had received. This was the opportunity they had been looking for.

After brief introductions, Mr. Xonophon began speaking almost immediately. "Grace hasn't been challenged at school for the last two years, yet they refuse to move her to the next grade. The gifted program is just a lot of busywork. She's so bored she no longer enjoys school."

"Sometimes she comes home in tears," Mrs. Xonophon urged. "She is very unhappy now. Can she enter your program at the university?"

Grace sat almost motionless, looking from parent to parent as they revealed her story. Occasionally she cast an anxious glance at the counselor. When asked how she felt about school, Grace simply nodded her answers.

Somewhat concerned about the young girl's passivity, the counselor gently questioned Grace, hoping she would reveal something of her own personality. The parents, however, continued to answer most of the questions themselves.

Grace's test scores had been high. In fact, they were third highest among the 650 gifted middle-school students last tested. She received straight As in school. On the strength of her academic performance, the counselor conditionally admitted the 13-year-old girl to the Early Entrance Program, a program of radically acceler-

ated education for the precociously gifted. The counselor hoped that she would be able to handle the demands of college classes and eventually show motivation of her own.

The first 10-week quarter went well enough. Grace attended two courses: biology and cultural anthropology. She worked diligently at her classes and appeared each week for her meetings with the program director. Her parents drove her to and from the university each day. She had little free time on campus. Naturally, she developed no more than a passing acquaintance with the other students in the program. She received an A and a B; these grades qualified her for permanent status in the program. She was 13 and a full-time student in college.

At the review meeting with the family, Grace managed to express, although shyly, her desire to remain in the program. She apologized for the B in anthropology. Her father assured the counselor that she would do better now that she understood what college work was like. She planned her courses with her parents and the counselor. The counselor made sure that her three classes would put her on campus 4 days a week and give her several hours between classes. It was critical for Grace to achieve some independence from her parents and begin to relate to her peers in the program.

This picture of Grace is a case study of a gifted adolescent. A *case study* gives an in-depth description of an individual. Usually individuals selected for a case study are atypical in some way. The case study may describe the person's life circumstances, symptoms or special abilities, or the success (or failure) of a treatment program. The writings of Sigmund Freud contain

---

In 1981 Congress passed the Education Consolidation and Improvement Act, which defines giftedness more broadly. The **gifted** and talented are those "who give evidence of high performance capability in areas such as intellectual, creative, artistic, leadership capacity, or specific academic fields, and who require services or activities not ordinarily provided by the school in order to fully develop such capabilities" (Sec. 582).

Howard Gardner (1983) also includes more than traditional measures of intelligence in defining giftedness. Gardner considers seven domains of

Research Focus (*continued*)

many case studies drawn from his clinical work. Erik Erikson used case studies to give us psychological profiles of well-known historical figures such as Martin Luther and Mahatma Gandhi. A case study of a woman suffering from a multiple-personality disorder became the basis of the film *The Three Faces of Eve*.

Case studies are useful because they provide information about conditions that are so unusual they would not otherwise be available for study. Like other forms of naturalistic observation, they provide rich sources for hypotheses that can be checked against other sources of data. They also share the disadvantage of not allowing the investigator to disentangle cause from effect or otherwise isolate the conditions presumed to be responsible for the interesting behavior being described. That type of analysis must await the application of other research procedures. Let's return to the gifted adolescent in our case study and see how successful she has been.

With her first year of college behind her, Grace had developed in measurable ways. At the weekly meetings with the counselor, she admitted that her father had dominated much of her life and that she wished to be free of her parents' ambitions for her. She managed more As and Bs, but became more and more self-critical each time she achieved less than she expected. Like many gifted students, Grace's standards for herself were extremely high. By the end of that first year, both motivation and judgment were more hers than her parents'.

The social aspect of Grace's personality also began to flower. Toward the middle of the first year, she made two friends in the program. The three girls were within a year of each other in age and class level, yet very different in personality. The oldest, a 14-year-old college sophomore, was studious, determined, and rather flatly assertive. Nina provided a standard by which many of the students could measure their achievement. Lindy, on the other hand, was quick and socially vigilant, often sacrificing achievement to amusement and exploration. She easily got Bs and seemed satisfied for the time being. Although Grace remained the shyest, she began to develop a wry sense of humor. Her style of dress evolved from the little girl dresses she originally appeared in to the studied messiness that was standard for adolescents. A little rebellion began to surface.

But only a little. In the following two years, Grace occasionally resisted her parents' and even the counselor's advice, often making very good decisions for herself. She maintained her original friendships and slowly added new ones. Her academic work grew stronger as she matured, yet her standards were never compromised. She planned to enter medical school and had her sights on the best in the country.

Today, Grace is 16 and a junior in college. She is studying for the MCAT, the exam that will play a large part in determining where she will be accepted for medical school. She has progressed from a nearly speechless girl to a quietly confident young woman. Her first friends, Nina and Lindy, have also progressed in their own ways. Nina is planning for her first year in law school. Lindy thinks she might take another year to finish her major in biology, with minors in chemistry and music.

Sources: The 27 gifted adolescents in the 1991 Early Entrance Program at California State University, Los Angeles; compiled by Jan Slater, Director. In P. C. Cozby. (1996). *Methods in behavioral research* (6th ed.). Mountain View, CA: Mayfield.

intelligence: musical, bodily-kinesthetic, logical-mathematical, linguistic, spatial, interpersonal, and intrapersonal (discussed in Chapter 4). Adolescents can be creative in any of these different domains, and for Gardner, creativity is the highest form of functioning. Creativity and giftedness, however, are not neatly related. Many gifted individuals are also highly creative, but many are not. Also, many creative people are not intellectually gifted (Hogan, 1980; Holland, 1961). (The Research Focus, "Case Studies," described a particular gifted adolescent and her educational experience.)

Identifying the Gifted   Perhaps because intelligence reflects our personalities, gifted adolescents fail to fit any stereotype. It is easy to identify those who have large vocabularies, or who top out on standard tests of achievement. But what about the ones who never see things the way others do, have zany senses of humor or vivid imaginations, those who get bored easily or who, when they can't do things perfectly, fail to do them at all? Gifted adolescents are likely to fit any of these descriptions as well.

Barbara Clark (1988), an educator at California State University, Los Angeles, offers the characteristics listed in Box 7.1 as indices of cognitive giftedness. Many of these characteristics would not be taken as signs of unusual talent or intelligence by most of us. Some, in fact, seem to signal just the opposite.

Do gifted adolescents apply their intelligence to advantage in areas of their lives other than academic ones? Research offers a tentative yes. Various studies have found the gifted to be more mature, have better social skills, and to be more self-confident, responsible, and self-controlled than age-mates of average intelligence (Hogan & Weiss, 1974; Hogan, Viernstein, McGinn, Daurio, & Bohannon, 1977). Terman (1925) even noted that his gifted children were slightly more likely to be physically superior to average children, to be heavier at birth, to walk earlier as infants, grow taller, and generally have fewer physical defects. So much for the negative stereotypes of the gifted as bookworms and wimps.

Being gifted does not offer immunity to social and emotional setbacks. In fact, it may make them harder to take. Social injustices can be especially difficult for those concerned with social or political problems, and slights can easily be exaggerated by those who react to life intensely and with passion. Adolescents who sailed through grade school with nothing lower than an A can be devastated when they get their first B. And gifted adolescents—just like others—must cope with emotions and concerns magnified by the changes of puberty.

Educating the Gifted   Educational programs follow one of two alternatives: enrichment or acceleration. The goal of *enrichment* is to provide gifted students with more opportunities and experiences than they would normally get, without moving them to a higher grade. An example would be offering special courses in literature, math, science, or the arts, along with the normal course of studies. *Acceleration* allows gifted students to advance beyond their grade level at a faster than normal rate, that is, skipping grades (Horowitz & O'Brien, 1986). Advocates of enrichment point to the social and emotional needs of gifted students, arguing that these are best met by keeping them with others their age. Although many gifted adolescents are socially and emotionally more advanced than their peers, this argument is especially compelling for late maturers, especially boys.

On the other hand, failure to advance the highly gifted can present as many problems as acceleration. Adolescents who experience little or no intellectual challenge in their classes and feel they are simply "marking time" can face intellectual stagnation, loneliness, and apathy—difficulties as serious as any introduced by moving ahead of their age-mates (Horowitz & O'Brien, 1986).

Box 7.1   Some Characteristics of Gifted Students

Asks many questions.

Has much information on many topics.

Adopts a questioning attitude.

Becomes unusually upset at injustices.

Is interested in social or political problems.

Has better reasons than you do for not doing what you want done.

Refuses to drill on repetitive tasks.

Becomes impatient when can't do an assignment perfectly.

Is a loner.

Is bored and frequently has nothing to do.

Completes part of an assignment and leaves it unfinished for something else.

Continues to work on an assignment when the rest of the class moves on to something else.

Is restless.

Daydreams.

Understands easily.

Likes to solve problems.

Has own ideas as to how things should be done.

Talks a lot.

Enjoys debate.

Enjoys abstract ideas.

Source: B. Clark. (1988). *Growing up gifted* (3rd ed.). New York: Macmillan.

Adolescents With Learning Disabilities

For some students, marking time takes a very different form. They, too, have difficulty maintaining interest in their classes but for reasons very different from those of gifted students. These students have experienced difficulty in school almost from the beginning. Many live with the bewildering sense that something is wrong, though they can't say what. Most feel stupid, though they are not. These adolescents have a **learning disability.**

Estimates of the number of school-age students with learning disabilities range from 2% to over 30%, depending on how learning disabilities are defined (Lovitt, 1989). Of those with learning disabilities, approximately 50% will graduate with a diploma. Another 12% will graduate through certification, and fully 25% of all learning-disabled students will drop out of school (U.S. Department of Education, 1988).

Defining Learning Disabilities   Who are these students, and what special problems do they face? Only recently have experts achieved some consensus in answering these questions. Their answers focus on three defining features of learning disabilities: (1) a discrepancy between expected and actual performance, (2) difficulty with academic tasks that cannot be traced to emotional problems or sensory impairment, and (3) presumed neurological dysfunction.

First, learning-disabled students show a *discrepancy between expected and actual performance.* Students with a learning disability are of average or above-average intelligence but don't perform at the level one would expect based on their intelligence; they frequently fall at least two grade levels behind their peers in academic skills. Second, their *difficulty with academic tasks* cannot be traced to emotional or sensory dysfunction. They may experience difficulty in one or more specific areas (for example, reading or math) or in the general skills needed for many areas, such as being able to pay attention or to monitor their performance (such as remembering which subroutines they have completed in a math problem in order to begin the next). They do not have a learning disability if the source of the difficulty is an emotional problem, problems at home, or a sensory impairment, such as a hearing loss. finally, students with a learning disability are presumed to have some *neurological dysfunction,* because they are of at least average intelligence and their difficulties are not primarily the result of sensory, emotional, or cultural causes (Lovitt, 1989).

Addressing Problems   Learning-disabled adolescents face problems both inside and outside the classroom. In the classroom, problems can range from difficulty paying attention or following class discussions to failure to turn in written assignments. Learning-disabled students have difficulty keeping up with classmates. A national study of 30,000 tenth-graders found that twice as many students with a learning disability placed in the bottom 25% of their class (Owings & Stocking, 1985). Performance for learning-disabled students is likely to be anywhere from two to four grades below grade level in any subject area for junior high students, and up to five to seven grades below grade level for high school students. In addition, most learning-disabled students have poorer study habits, are less likely to do their homework, and, when it comes to demonstrating what they *have* learned, have poorer test-taking skills. Frequently, nonattendance, incomplete assignments, and failure to turn in homework contribute to their failure in a course as much as their scores on tests do (Lovitt, 1989).

The problems of learning-disabled adolescents don't end when they leave the classroom. As a group, they have poorer social skills than other students. They are less likely to pick up on another's mood and respond appropriately, and are less aware of the effect their behavior has on others. Subtle cues can go right by them. The same problems that make it difficult for them to understand what their teachers are saying in class can affect their interactions with friends. They may miss nuances of conversation and respond inappropriately, or miss rule changes in a game and feel they've been taken advantage of when the old rules no longer apply. Frequently they prefer the company of those who are younger, just because they are more compliant.

The learning-disabled are less likely to be involved in extracurricular activities than other students (Spreen, 1988). Perhaps this fact reflects their general disenchantment with school. Or it may reflect a poorer self-image and expectations of failure in these activities as well. Increasing learning-disabled students' involvement in extracurricular activities such as teams, clubs, and music and drama productions might be one of the most important ways of increasing their participation and their motivation to stay in school (Lovitt, 1989).

Schooling the Learning Disabled *Mainstreaming* places learning-disabled adolescents in regular classes. The most common accommodation teachers make is to adjust their grades. Perhaps because so little is done to meet the special needs of the learning-disabled in most classrooms, mainstreaming can introduce special problems of attendance. A growing number of schools that mainstream learning-disabled students provide a *special education consultant* who meets with regular teachers to discuss ways of managing the needs of these students. This procedure allows students to attend classes with their peers while receiving materials designed by someone who has specialized in learning disorders.

The other extreme from mainstreaming places learning-disabled students in *special education classes*. The obvious advantages of such an approach are small classes in which materials can be personalized to the needs of students, and a teacher who is experienced in the special needs of the learning-disabled. A disadvantage is that special education teachers may not be as well versed in many subjects as regular high school teachers. Association with nondisabled students who might serve as positive role models is limited, and teachers may not hold the learning-disabled to the same standards that are required of other students (Lovitt, 1989).

CULTURE AND GENDER IN THE CLASSROOM: EDUCATION FOR ALL

Using materials that capture interest and fire imagination is a goal of education for all students. However, some schools still use materials that exclude half their students from the most exciting adventures.

Gender Stereotypes in Teaching Materials

From Hamlet to Tom Sawyer, most of the characters adolescents read about in classics or see in films are males. School materials also take their readers to high adventure most readily if they are males. These trends begin in elementary school and continue into high school.

Visual Materials One survey of children's textbooks found that males are pictured more often than females and shown in more adventurous roles. Although female characters appear as often as male characters, they still appear in fewer occupations and need rescuing more frequently (Purcell & Stewart, 1990).

Even so, these comparisons represent a giant step away from the sexism that characterized school materials 25 years ago. A similar survey conducted in 1972 found the same trends but differences that were even more exaggerated (Women on Words and Images, 1975).

About 90% of students' time in school is spent with various types of educational materials such as books, films, or class handouts. Surveys indicate that most school materials have been sex-biased and that the use of stereotyped materials influences students' attitudes (Tittle, 1986). Even though many states have introduced regulations to ensure that the portrayal of females and males in textbooks is balanced, many schools do not buy new books until the old ones need replacing.

Materials that show women and men in nontraditional roles or filling roles in proportion to their actual numbers in the work force lead to greater flexibility in sex-role attitudes among students. These findings are consistent across dozens of studies (Michel, 1986; Switzer, 1990). Students who read about females who are doctors or postal carriers and males who are telephone operators or daycare directors are less sex-typed in their approach to occupations in general and in their personal interest in these professions.

Language   A second form of bias occurs through the gender characteristics of language itself. English, for the most part, either ignores females or treats them as exceptions. **Male generic language** uses the pronoun *he* to refer to an individual of either sex and uses words such as *man* or *mankind* to refer to all people. When individuals are identified as female, it is often to call attention to the fact that they are *not* male, such as in terms like *woman doctor* or *sculptress*. These usages suggest not only that doctors and sculptors ordinarily are males, but that when they are females, they are different enough from "regular" doctors and sculptors to require different labels (Lips, 1997).

A formidable array of research shows that male generic language causes people to think of males, not of people in general (Fisk, 1985; Klein, 1985). In one study, seventh-graders completed a story about a student's first day in their class. Some students read a story referring to the new student as "he"; others read stories in which the student could be of either sex. When the subject was referred to as "he," all the males and 80% of the females wrote stories describing the student as a male. When "he or she" or "they" were used, significantly fewer students referred to the new student as a male. Those most affected by the use of inclusive language ("he and she" or "they") were females; whereas 80% wrote stories in which the subject, when referred to as "he," was a male, 21% and 12% wrote about a male when the subject was referred to as "he or she" or "they," respectively (Switzer, 1990). When we realize that teachers are just as susceptible to the influence of male generic language as students, the implications of these findings assume even larger proportions.

Male generic language also affects adolescents' judgments of how competent a woman is in different types of jobs. When students are asked to consider how well a woman might perform a fictional job (for example, a "surmaker"), their evaluations are influenced by the sex of the pronouns used to describe the characters performing the job. Women are thought to be least competent for the job when the surmaker is referred to as "he" and most competent when referred to as "she." Referring to doctors, mechanics, scientists, or artists as "he" has clear implications not only for adolescent females' ability to see themselves in those professions, but also for all students' evaluation of the relative competence of the men and women in those occupations (Lips, 1997).

Multicultural Education

LaRue glanced briefly at his group as Mr. Brooks, his physical science teacher, finished giving the assignment: to study the activity of gases. That shouldn't be too difficult, he thought. But what would he do for his part? He had to think of common examples illustrating the properties of gases. Paulo had an easy part to present to the group; all he had to do was describe their chemical properties. Becky's part would be interesting: identifying the gases that are present in different substances. He could imagine the fun Yinpeng would have with that one. He liked his group. They worked well together, and it was more interesting than working on their own. But what could he contribute? Then he remembered the canned drinks he had put in the freezer—the juices had burst open but the soda hadn't. Of course, gases constrict and liquids expand when cold.

LaRue's physical science class is organized as a **jigsaw classroom.** Students work in small groups that are balanced for ethnic background and ability. Each student in the group contributes a different part of the lesson. The parts fit together, much like the pieces of a jigsaw puzzle: One needs each part to get the whole picture. This approach to classroom learning fosters cooperation among students and promotes better relations among adolescents from different ethnic and racial backgrounds (J. Banks, 1993).

Even in classes that foster cooperative and friendly relations, minority adolescents often face problems that don't exist for those from the dominant culture. They do not always share the cultural perspective, for instance, that is assumed by much of their class material; most textbooks reflect a Eurocentric bias in their portrayal of minorities, often omitting their contributions or presenting them negatively (Garcia, 1993; Hu-DeHart, 1993). Seeing things from a different point of view can make otherwise easy material difficult to understand. Does the westward expansion have the same implications for Native Americans, Hispanics, and African Americans as it does for European American students (Seixas, 1993)? Probably not. Classes that introduce *multicultural perspectives* surmount this difficulty. Asking adolescents to describe the experiences of the pioneers, the American Indians, and the Mexicans turns this problem into an advantage. The introduction of a multicultural perspective enriches all students' understanding of the issues surrounding westward expansion (C. Banks, 1993; Howard, 1993).

Most minority students face instances of prejudice and discrimination on at least some occasions. Interviews with Black adolescents who attended predominantly White high schools revealed a number of ways of coping with their minority status. One way was to be a "model" student. Students who chose this coping style made good grades, studied for college, and participated in school activities. Many also earned the resentment of their Black friends for "acting White." One model student had this to say:

> They . . . prefer to be black, they want to just hang around with the blacks, they don't want nothing to do with the whites. . . . I'm not like that. . . . I attended the ski club and I asked if anyone else wanted to get into it, and you should have seen their faces, it was hysterical. What is this kid talking about, the ski club? It's a bunch of "honkies" gonna be there. (R. Miller, 1989, p. 181)

Learning in a group can be more interesting than learning on one's own. In a jigsaw classroom, students work in small groups that are balanced for both ability and for gender and ethnic or racial background.

Other students coped by forming interracial friendships and becoming members of popular crowds at school. Still others became involved in many different school activities. Not all the Black adolescents preferred attending an integrated school to a predominantly Black school. Some who were bused from inner-city schools to suburban ones made few friends and felt little connection with the school. When asked why they attended, they mentioned getting a better education and more opportunities (R. Miller, 1989).

In the classroom, unfamiliar patterns of communication complicate learning for some minority students. The simple matter of asking questions is a case in point for many African American students. Teachers ask questions in very different ways than do adults in the community (Brice-Heath, 1982). Teachers use questions to stimulate classroom discussions and to focus ongoing behavior. It's common to ask about things the class has already discussed. Adults typically ask questions only when they want information they do *not* have. They rarely use questions as a way of discussing issues or of channeling ongoing behavior into more desirable forms (as a teacher might, by asking a question of a student who is talking with a classmate to get that student to pay attention). Consequently, students may misunderstand questions regarding material the class has already covered ("What is she asking for? We've gone over that"). Effective intervention depends on discovering differences such as these. The solution in this instance is for everyone—teachers, parents, and students—to be made aware of the different rules that regulate language in class and at home (Slaughter-DeFoe, Nakagawa, Takanishi, & Johnson, 1990).

Other problems arise from lack of familiarity in using Standard English, the language used in the classroom. Some minority students—such as Hawaiians, Native Americans, and Eskimos—can understand Standard English well enough, but still not be at ease speaking it in front of classmates if they speak a dialect at home. Using different languages at home and in school limits opportunities to practice the way ESL students need to speak at school and can cause them to be silent for fear of embarrassing themselves. Even written schoolwork becomes problematic for students who have difficulty translating the ideas they frame easily in the intimate language of their home into Standard English. Additional complications arise when corresponding terms are not available in the two languages (Feldman, Stone, & Renderer, 1990).

Overcoming the Differences

The increasing ethnic diversity of our society makes it progressively difficult to characterize students in terms of simple behavioral and motivational profiles. Recognizing the distinctive approaches that characterize different ethnic groups can be a start and can be used to advantage in the classroom. Research on ethnic groups reveals distinct differences along four dimensions of personal interaction: group versus individual orientations, active versus passive coping styles, attitudes toward authority, and expressive versus restrained mannerisms.

Group Versus Individual Orientations   Some cultures, such as Japan and Mexico, stress affiliation, interdependence, and cooperation. Other cultures, such as the United States, stress individual achievement, independence, and competition. Within the United States ethnic differences emerge along this dimension. Chinese, Hispanic, and African American adolescents, for instance, are more group oriented than those from the dominant culture (Rotheram & Phinney, 1987). These adolescents are more attentive to the feelings and expectations of others than their White counterparts are. An Hispanic or an African American adolescent may pay as much attention to the feelings of others as to the demands of the task at hand, an orientation many teachers may not understand or appreciate. However, in learning situations that require students to work together, this orientation will serve these students as well inside the classroom as outside it (Rotheram & Phinney, 1987).

Active Versus Passive Coping Styles   Cultures characterized by active coping styles stress the importance of controlling one's environment and being productive. Those with passive styles place more emphasis on being than on doing. The sense of the present is greater in the latter and of the future in the former. These differences—like those of group versus individual orientation—can translate into either strengths or weaknesses in the classroom. Adolescents with a take charge attitude may find it difficult to wait for others, or to take enough time to explore all the issues. The strength of this approach is the way that it fosters achievement.

The strengths of the passive approach are the freedom it gives students to turn themselves over to the moment and learn what it can teach them. The disadvantages to this coping style are most apparent in classrooms structured according to active coping strategies. Adolescents from cultures with a passive coping style are not likely to ask for help or materials, and if teachers and classmates assume that no help is needed unless asked for, these students will not receive the help they need to keep up (Rotheram & Phinney, 1983).

Attitudes Toward Authority   Clear ethnic differences exist for this dimension. Hispanic and Asian American adolescents, for instance, are likely to have been raised in authoritarian homes (see Chapter 5) and taught to be respectful and not to question those in authority. Certain Native American and many White adolescents have been socialized to make decisions for themselves and are less accepting of authority (Rotheram & Phinney, 1987). It should not be surprising that some students want to be told what to do and do their best work under those conditions, whereas others want to make decisions for themselves and do not fare well with authoritarian teachers.

Expressive Versus Restrained Mannerisms   Interactions in some cultures are informal and open, and in others are ritualized and private. The former is more characteristic of Black and White adolescents, the latter of Asian American adolescents. Black adolescents express their feelings even more openly than Whites; theirs is a high-intensity culture, in which feelings are given more open expression. An Asian American student might easily misread a Black student's expressions of anger as aggression or a White student might regard an Asian American's reaction to an incident as timid simply because each is not familiar with the other's culture.

Adolescents are not very accurate in predicting how those from another culture will react. Differences along each of these dimensions underscore the importance of developing cross-ethnic awareness among adolescents as well as teachers.

Many minority adolescents have difficulty predicting their own experiences as they move from home, to school, to community. As we saw in Chapter 1, Urie Bronfenbrenner (1979) describes the experiences that make up one's reality in terms of overlapping spheres of influence. At the most immediate level, the microsystem, are one's firsthand experiences—interactions at home, in the classroom, and with friends. The mesosystem arises from interactions among the different microsystems of which one is a part. Minority adolescents frequently experience problems with interactions involving the mesosystem. They may see their parents distrust the system, or teachers communicate less respect for their parents than for those of other students.

Adolescents experience the exosystem at the level of their communities. Available housing and the types of schools they attend reflect decisions made at the community level but influence their lives directly. The macrosystem, which consists of the underlying social and political climate,

Minority students from cultures that value the group more than the individual may pay as much attention to the feelings of others as to the task at hand. This orientation can frustrate teachers but it serves the students well in group-learning situations and in the world outside the classroom.

is even further removed from adolescents' daily experiences, yet it impinges on their realities in very real ways. Laws concerning compulsory education, the mainstreaming of students with special needs, and the separation of grades into elementary, junior high, and high schools all illustrate the direct ways the macrosystem can affect the lives of adolescents. A less observable, but no less real, effect of the macrosystem is experienced in the form of beliefs, biases, and stereotypes. The values of the macrosystem can be at odds with those of the home microsystem for adolescents from some minority groups (Spencer, 1985).

John Ogbu (1981, 1992) offers a disturbing analysis of the plight of many minority students. He notes that educational programs have assumed that the problems many minorities experience at school (poor attendance, high dropout rates, low achievement) should be addressed at the level of the microsystem—by improving the home environment or enriching educational experiences. Ogbu suggests that the problem is generated at the macrosystem level and can only be solved by changes introduced at that level. He attributes poor academic performance and high dropout rates among minorities to a "job ceiling," or discrimination in job opportunities, and to their perception that members of their own families have not been rewarded for their achievements.

If all adolescents progressed through the same *social mobility system,* one in which mobility, or social class, reflects their abilities, then the most effective method of intervention for minorities who are failing would be at the microsystem level, reaching into the home or classroom to bring their abilities and skills up to the level of the others. But *do* all members of our society move through the same mobility system? Is there more than one system, similar to academic tracking, but with respect to economic rather than educational opportunities?

If there is more than one mobility system, what factors other than ability and skill determine the system in which individuals participate? Notice that if we have more than one social mobility system, social class is an *effect* rather than a cause, and minority problems must be addressed at another level. Social status among minorities, argues Ogbu, reflects the realities of a job ceiling: a consistent set of social and economic obstacles preventing equal selection based on ability imposed on certain minorities at birth, that is, a society stratified by ethnic and racial castes as well as by class. The problems of minority groups can be resolved only at the macrosystem level, by addressing social ills such as prejudice and discrimination.

SUMMARY

Secondary Schools Today

More adolescents attend high school now than in any previous generation. A hundred years ago, less than 5% of high school–age adolescents graduated from high school; in the 1990s, about 85% will. As more students remain in high school, differences among them have increased. Ethnic diversity is one source of the differences.

Academic tracking is a common solution to diverse interests and abilities among students. But tracking itself contributes to differences in achievement and dropout rates among those assigned to college and noncollege tracks. Powerful alternatives to tracking include forming small cooperative learning groups in the classroom and involving parents in the educational process. Work–study programs and computer-assisted instruction (CAI) offer additional alternatives.

Both the size of a school and its educational climate are related to its success. Research shows that students attending small schools are less likely to drop out; there are also fewer disciplinary problems and less truancy. A school's climate is also determined by the type of goals it has (task, or mastery, and performance, or ability) and by the respect and caring that teachers express toward their students.

Perhaps most important to its success is a school's ability to provide an environment in which students feel safe. Schools suffer from a dramatic increase in violence, which reflects societal attitudes, media modeling, poverty, and discrimination. Schools can promote peace through cooperative learning, training in conflict resolution and constructive controversy, and by establishing conflict resolution centers.

Adolescents at School

Middle schools place fifth- or sixth-, seventh-, and eighth-graders together in a separate school; junior highs place seventh- through eighth- or ninth-graders together. Few consistent differences emerge in comparisons of these two educational settings.

U.S. students lag behind students in many other industrialized countries in mathematics proficiency. The reasons may be the cultural and socioeconomic diversity of the U.S. student population and the greater amount of time students spend watching television rather than doing homework. Spending time with friends, participating in sports, and working are also higher priorities for many U.S. adolescents than school. One reason that school has a low priority for these students is that they do not believe that doing well in high school is related to their future success. Consequently, they are motivated more by the fear of failing than by the desire to learn. Academic achievement is strongly correlated to authoritative parenting in terms of involvement, communication, and expectations.

Achievement motivation patterns distinguish adolescents. Task-oriented adolescents focus on the task and work to increase their mastery. Performance-oriented adolescents focus on their performance and use it as a measure of their ability. Task-oriented adolescents are less likely to be disrupted by initial failure, believing it to result from lack of sufficient effort rather than inability. Performance-oriented adolescents are likely to withdraw in the face of failure and attribute it to an external cause rather than their own lack of effort. Or they may preemptively use self-handicapping strategies to provide an excuse for failing.

Gender differences reveal more adaptive motivational patterns for males. Gender-role stereotypes contribute to the less positive attitudes that affect females' motivation. These differences often do not appear until adolescents enter junior high and encounter work that is challenging enough to prompt defensive withdrawal.

Over the past 20 years, the number of adolescents who drop out of school has decreased for majority and some minority adolescents, while remaining high for others. Even so, more minority students drop out than do those from the dominant culture. Parents' educational level, socioeconomic status, and attitudes toward education are related to dropping out.

School variables that predict dropout rate are a history of difficulty or failure, low self-esteem, assignment to a noncollege track, and behavior problems.

Programs that are effective in helping at-risk students involve parents, provide individualized counseling, and help students meet their financial as well as academic needs, as in work–study programs for which students receive academic credit. Success of a school system's dropout programs is a key measure of the system's quality.

Adolescents at the Edge

Adolescents who score 130 or above on an intelligence test or who have creative, artistic, leadership, or other special talents are defined as gifted. Gifted adolescents fail to fit any stereotype. Educational programs for the gifted offer enrichment, providing them with more experiences than they would ordinarily get, or acceleration, allowing them to advance beyond their grade level.

Adolescents with learning disabilities are of average or above-average intelligence who show a discrepancy between expected and actual performance. They have difficulty in academic tasks that presumably can be traced to a neurological dysfunction. Learning-disabled high school students can fall five to seven grade levels behind classmates in some subject areas and generally have poor study habits and test-taking skills. Social skills are also affected for many.

Mainstreaming places learning-disabled students in regular classes with their classmates. A consulting special education teacher may advise regular teachers on the special needs of these students. At the other extreme, learning-disabled students may be placed in special classes with specially trained teachers. Each of these educational options has different advantages.

Culture and Gender in the Classroom

Some gender-role stereotyping still exists in teaching materials. In textbooks, males are still pictured more frequently than females, appear in more diverse occupations, and need rescuing less frequently. But these differences represent tremendous improvements over the materials in use a generation ago.

The use of male generic language represents another form of bias. Using the masculine pronoun generically predisposes students and their teachers to think of males, not of individuals in general. Their evaluations of the competence of students of either sex for different types of work are thereby skewed.

Jigsaw classrooms, where students work in small groups, each contributing a different part of the lesson, foster cooperation and promote better relations among students from different ethnic backgrounds. Presenting material from several cultural perspectives is helpful to minority students who may not always share the perspective assumed in the textbook or other materials used.

Communication problems arise for some minority students when language is used differently at school and at home. Four distinctive approaches characterize different ethnic and racial groups: group versus individual orientations, active versus passive coping styles, attitudes toward authority, and expressive versus restrained mannerisms. Intervention programs that heighten teacher and student awareness of these differences improve the quality of multicultural education.

Most intervention programs have focused on problems minority students may experience at the level of the microsystem, that is, in the home and the classroom. Problems of poorer achievement and higher dropout rates may have to be addressed at the level of the macrosystem. The assurance of equal opportunity for jobs may be the most effective form of intervention.

KEY TERMS

academic tracking

task-mastery goals

performance-ability goals

gifted

learning disability

male generic language

jigsaw classroom

Part Three

Continuity and Change: Identity Consolidation in Late Adolescence

You have met a number of adolescents so far in this book. Each has illustrated in some way the themes of the text, themes that characterize the experiences of adolescents today: the continuity to their lives, the changes they face, and their cultural diversity.

A strong thread of continuity runs through the lives of adolescents. Despite the dramatic changes that begin with puberty, the achievements of adolescence build on the prior accomplishments of childhood. Issues that focus the experiences of children—such as trust and intimacy in infancy, autonomy in toddlerhood, and competence and mastery during the school years—come up again, in somewhat different form, in adolescence. Adolescents confront the need for trust as they form intimate relationships. Relationships with parents revolve around issues of autonomy and independence. And adolescents' developing sense of self, of identity, reflects as well their sense of mastery and competence in their dealings with the world around them.

Despite this continuity, the concerns of late adolescents and the developmental issues they face are sufficiently different from those of early adolescents to require special attention. What mother would think of her 16-year-old as the same child who, three short years ago, wondered what puberty was all about? What potential employer does not believe that a high school student is more able to shoulder the responsibilities of a job than a middle school student? What teacher does not expect high school students to be capable of more subtle understanding than 11- or 12-year-olds?

In the various domains of development—formulating an identity, attaining sexual maturity, planning for future work or college, and defining values to live by—late adolescents address different issues than do early adolescents. With respect

to achieving a sense of themselves, early adolescents are just beginning to discover the ways they differ from their parents; late adolescents are consolidating these changes into a personal identity. With respect to sexuality, late adolescents are learning to integrate their sexuality into their intimate relationships, whereas early adolescents are still sorting through the significance of pubertal changes for their sense of self.

Differences exist, too, in their extended social worlds. Late adolescents are preparing to leave high school to begin work or enter college, whereas early adolescents are leaving elementary school for a middle school or junior high. Late adolescents are distinguishing values and beliefs unique to them, whereas the beliefs and values of early adolescents are the ones they have acquired from their parents.

Chapter 8 opens Part Three with an examination of identity development in adolescents. Identity gives one a sense of self, and is perhaps one of the most important achievements of adolescence. The next three chapters in Part Three cover separate aspects of identity. Chapter 9 examines sexuality and how adolescents integrate gender roles and sexual experiences into a changing sense of self. Chapter 10 looks at adolescents' ability to envision their future occupational identity. Just as importantly, late adolescents begin to integrate a personal set of values and beliefs into their emergent identity. Chapter 11 looks at the standards adolescents use in making decisions—at their developing ethics and morality.

Chapter 12 examines stress and adolescents' coping strategies. Although all adolescents experience some stress, many must handle extreme stress, whose causes often originate within the home. Some of these adolescents run away; many are abused. Juvenile delinquency, substance abuse, suicide, and psychological disorders such as depression are also discussed in this chapter. Chapter 13 continues to examine the problems of youth, but also looks at the protective factors of adolescence. These factors include families, communities, personal strengths, and love.

Finally, Chapter 14 provides a broad overview of the research methods and issues that have shaped the scientific study of adolescence. Because this presentation relates to the research focus boxes in each chapter, you may wish to read this chapter out of sequence and refer to it often.

CHAPTER 8

Defining the Self
Identity and Intimacy

"Why are you replacing the spark plugs? You just got new ones," whined Francie.

"Because the firing's off and I've tested everything else," snapped Allie as she grabbed the wipe rag. "It's not the distributor; the fuel-injection checks out. Just because my dad said they're new doesn't mean one of them isn't a dud. It's the only possibility I haven't ruled out. You've got to consider all the possibilities, Francie, you can't accept what people tell you."

"What about the possibility that it's 'unnatural' for a cheerleader to know more about engines than most of the guys on the team?"

"Give me that wrench. They were happy enough when I fixed the bus, weren't they? We made the game in time."

"Tell me again why you're doing this?" Francie asked as she examined a broken nail.

"It's the only way I get to have a car. You know my dad, 'If you want to own a car, you'll have to know how it works.'"

"Sounds like Ms. Wright. You missed a fresh class yesterday. She said most history books reflect a point of view. You can't just accept what's written. Did you know that the man who said the British were the first to fire at Lexington was actually a British soldier who was being held as a prisoner by the Colonists?"

"So what's the point?"

"The point is he could have been trying to win their favor so they'd let him go. How come you can think of all the possibilities when it comes to this car of yours but not when it comes to Ms. Wright's class?"

"Dunno. Guess I just don't find history that interesting."

By the time most adolescents are old enough to drive a car (let alone repair one), they have sharpened their sense of themselves through countless exchanges such as the preceding one, in which ambitions and plans mesh with the daily realities of life. **Identity** gives a sense of oneself that transcends any particular moment or circumstance, and establishing one's identity is perhaps among the most important achievements of adolescence. This chapter examines Erikson's original formulation of identity, as well as more recent elaborations of it.

Minority adolescents face an additional task of achieving an ethnic identity, and females, irrespective of cultural or racial background, appear to undertake self-definition in substantially different ways than males do. Intimate relationships are more important in defining the self in females than in males. The variations due to gender and ethnicity have required us to reexamine our view of normal development, and even of maturity itself.

IDENTITY: THE NORMATIVE CRISIS OF ADOLESCENCE

"Normative crisis" sounds like an oxymoron, a combination of contradictory terms like "thunderous silence." Doesn't "normative" refer to a standard, a pattern, something that is predictable and regular? And doesn't "crisis" mean something *out of* the ordinary, something that violates the pattern, that *doesn't* happen every day?

In discussing the concept of "identity crisis," Eric Erikson (1968) noted that, although the phrase later acquired a distinctive meaning, at the time he first coined it, he considered himself to be naming something so familiar as to be taken for granted. He illustrated this point with a story about an old man who vomited each morning but refused to see a doctor. finally, his family convinced him to get a checkup. After examining him, the doctor asked how he was feeling. "fine, just fine" the old man replied. The doctor, impatient with what appeared to be denial of a serious problem, responded, "But your family tells me you vomit every morning!" The old man looked at the doctor in surprise. "Of course I do, doesn't everybody?" he asked.

Erikson's point to this story is that "identity crisis" describes something that all of us have experienced, and have taken for granted, but would have no difficulty recognizing once it is labeled, something that is, despite the upset, quite normative (Erikson, 1968).

Similarly, Erikson used the word *crisis* to refer not to some imminent catastrophe but to a developmental turning point in which the individual must choose one course or another simply because it is no longer possible to continue as before (Erikson, 1968).

Perhaps no term is more closely associated with the writing and thinking of Erik Erikson (see Chapter 2) than *identity*. Erikson was, above all else, a clinician whose concepts reflected real life experiences. In writing about the personality, Erikson noted that "old troubles" return when we are tired

Successfully resolving an identity crisis means finding an adult course that fits one's talents and inclinations and that is fulfilling. These adolescents are learning about adult roles by working part-time in a clinic.

or otherwise defenseless, simply because we are what we *were* as well as what we might want to become or presently may be (Coles, 1970; Erikson, 1954).

Erikson believed that, like his patients, adolescents have to confront "old troubles" in arriving at an identity. Consider Erikson's description of Jill, a young woman he knew:

> I had known Jill before her puberty, when she was rather obese and showed many "oral" traits of voracity and dependency while she also was a tomboy and bitterly envious of her brothers and in rivalry with them. But she was intelligent and always had an air about her (as did her mother) which seemed to promise that things would turn out all right. And, indeed, she straightened out and up, became very attractive, an easy leader in any group, and, to many, a model of young girlhood. As a clinician, I watched and wondered what she would do with that voraciousness and with the rivalry which she had displayed earlier. Could it be that such things are simply absorbed in fortuitous growth?
>
> Then one autumn in her late teens, Jill did not return to college from the ranch out West where she had spent the summer. She had asked her parents to let her stay. Simply out of liberality and confidence, they granted her this moratorium and returned East.
>
> That winter Jill specialized in taking care of newborn colts, and would get up at any time during a winter night to bottle-feed the most needy animals. Having apparently acquired a certain satisfaction within herself, as well as astonished recognition from the cowboys, she returned home and reassumed her place. I felt that she had found and hung on to an opportunity to do actively and for others what she had once demonstrated by overeating:

she had learned to feed needy young mouths. But she did so in a context which, in turning passive into active, also turned a former symptom into a social act.

One might say that she turned "maternal" but it was a maternalism such as cowboys must and do display; and, of course, she did it all in jeans. This brought recognition "from man to man" as well as from man to woman, and beyond that the confirmation of her optimism, that is, her feeling that something could be done that felt like her, was useful and worthwhile, and was in line with an ideological trend where it still made immediate practical sense. (1968, pp. 130–131)

Jill fashioned her identity, as Erikson said we all do, out of old cloth, but she tailored it to the needs of the present. She translated what she *was*— an energetic, intelligent, but envious and dependent child—into a mature personality, capable of responding to her own and others' needs.

Identity Defined

Identity, as Erikson used the term, refers to the sense of self that we achieve through examining and committing ourselves to the roles and pursuits that define an adult in our society. Identity gives us a sense of who we are, of knowing what is "me" and what is "not me." As Jill's story demonstrated, the "me" includes more than the present. Identity allows us to experience a continuity of self over time. We can relate what we have done in the past to what we hope to do in the future, to our ambitions and dreams. Finally, our perception of self includes how others see us, the importance they attach to our values and accomplishments (Patterson, Sochting, & Marcia, 1992).

Jill's story illustrates these aspects of identity. Her new maturity grew out of familiar issues, her "old troubles," that she approached in new ways. Because the "me" that she had been as a child was still recognizable in her more adult concerns, there was a continuity to her experience over time. Lastly, her perception of herself, her confidence and self-esteem, resulted not only from becoming skilled in something she valued, but also from receiving the recognition of the society in which she achieved this, the cowboys she had worked with.

In defining identity, Erikson considered three domains to be of paramount importance: sexuality as expressed in an adult gender role; occupation; and ideology, or religious and political beliefs. Each of these domains will be more closely examined in the chapters that follow. Chapter 9 will consider sexuality and gender roles; Chapter 10 will examine careers and college; and Chapter 11, values and moral development. But for now, we will examine the process of identity formation itself.

The Process of Identity Consolidation

Prior to adolescence, children's identities reflect a simple **identification** with parents: They uncritically take on the behaviors and ways of their mothers and fathers. Adolescents move beyond the identity organizations they had as children by synthesizing elements of their earlier identity into a new whole, one that bears the personal stamp of their own interests, val-

Box 8.1   Parents' Reflections About Late Adolescence

"This may begin earlier, but it goes through adolescence. I had always heard they look for their own independence, their own things to participate in; but until you really experience it with your own, it's hard to deal with it. When you read about independence, it sounds like it's carefully planned out. When it actually happens, all of a sudden they want to do something that they have never done before and which you firmly believe they have no idea how to do. It can be driving for the first time or suddenly announcing they want to go somewhere with friends. I knew it was going to happen; but exactly how to handle it myself and handle it with them so they got a chance to do something new without its being dangerous has been a challenge to me."—*Father*

"I wish that I had known that I had to listen more to them in order to understand what they were experiencing. I sort of assumed that I knew what adolescence was about from my own experience, but things had a different meaning to them. What was important to me was not that important to them, and I wish I had realized that in the beginning."—*Mother*

"I wish that I had got my children involved in more family activities. When they were mostly through adolescence I heard a talk by a child psychiatrist who said that often when teenagers say they don't want to do something with the family, at times you have to insist because they do go along and enjoy the event. I wish I had known that sooner, because I accepted their first 'No,' when I perhaps should have pushed more."—*Mother*

"I wish I had known to be more attentive, to really listen, because kids have a lot of worthwhile things to say and you come to find out they hold a lot of your viewpoints."—*Father*

"I wish I had known it was important to spend time with the children individually. We did things as a family, but the children are so different, and I think I would have understood them better if I had spent time with them alone."—*Mother*

Source: Adapted from J. B. Brooks. (1996). *The process of parenting* (4th ed.). Mountain View, CA: Mayfield

ues, and choices. This process is termed **identity formation,** and involves individuation (see Chapter 5). Individuation gives adolescents a set of attitudes and ways of acting that are genuinely their own; however, they must still put these together into a working whole that reflects an inner sense of self. Although the process begins in early adolescence, adolescents do not consolidate these changes until late adolescence or even early adulthood when choices about jobs, college, and relationships force identity issues to a head. Identity, for Erikson, derives from, as well as directs, the adolescent's commitment to occupational, religious, political, and gender roles and values. Parents contribute to this process too, of course, and, as the quotes in Box 8.1 indicate, hindsight is often better than one's perspective at the time.

Adolescents who achieve a personal identity appreciate their uniqueness even while realizing all they have in common with others. Experience in

One signal of an adolescent's developing sense of self is involvement in a cause—whether against drugs in the neighborhood or for the preservation of an endangered species. Ideology, or commitment to principle, is the name Erik Erikson gave to this domain of identity formation.

making decisions for themselves has given them feedback about their strong and weak points, and they are less dependent on others' judgments in evaluating themselves. They can also become intimate with others without fear of blurring their personal boundaries.

VARIATIONS ON A THEME OF IDENTITY

Although Erikson was the first to describe and elaborate the concept of identity as a normative crisis in adolescence, James Marcia has been largely responsible for generating research on identity formation, primarily by constructing a measure of ego identity, which has made it possible to empirically test many implications of Erikson's writings.

Identity Statuses

Most of the work we do on our identity takes place in adolescence; however, as Marcia notes with a touch of humor, if identity formation were necessary by the end of adolescence, many of us would never become adults.

His point is that achieving a personal identity is not an easy process. Adolescents must be willing to take risks and live with uncertainty.

Some of the uncertainty comes from exploring possibilities and options in life that differ from those chosen by one's parents. Most adolescents expect this exploration to be risky. Few adolescents, however, expect the risks that occur when they must make commitments based on their exploration. Adolescents form their identities both by taking on new ways of being *and* by excluding others. It is every bit as important to let go of their fantasies and commit themselves to a definite course of action as it is to challenge the familiar by exploring possibilities never even considered by their parents or families. Marcia (1980, 1992) refers to these two dimensions of the identity process as exploration and commitment.

Marcia distinguishes four ways by which adolescents arrive at the roles and values that define their identities. Each of these ways, or identity statuses, is defined in terms of the dimensions of commitment and exploration. Adolescents who are committed to life options arrive at them either by exploring and searching for what fits them best or by forgoing exploration and letting themselves be guided by their parents' values. The first alternative results in the ego reorganization that Erikson characterized as identity formation; the second leaves parental identifications unchallenged and unchanged. Adolescents who have searched for life options that fit them best are termed **identity achieved;** those who adopt their parents' values without question are termed **identity foreclosed** (Kroger, 1996; Marcia, 1980).

Similarly, two paths lead to noncommitment. Some adolescents begin to evaluate life options but don't close off certain possibilities because the decisions are too momentous to risk making a mistake; as a result, they remain uncommitted to any path. These adolescents are in **moratorium.** Others remain uncommitted for the opposite reason: failure to see the importance of choosing one option over any other. They are termed **identity diffused.** Even though adolescents in moratorium begin to question parental ways, like foreclosed adolescents they ultimately do not challenge parental identifications: They don't risk making a wrong choice. Identity-diffused adolescents fail to challenge earlier identifications because they lack the sense of urgency that would prompt them to make decisions that would distinguish them as individuals.

Adolescents who open themselves to new possibilities, whether personal beliefs or vocational options, tend to be more tolerant of individual differences and allow others the same freedom for self-definition. Conversely, foreclosed adolescents, who fail to question their lifestyles or to explore religious beliefs or career options, tend to be more authoritarian, living by the rules and believing that others should, too. They hold up the conventional standards they apply to themselves to others.

The process of reorganizing earlier identifications continues into late adolescence—and beyond. Sally Archer (1989a, 1989b) found that among the adolescents she has interviewed, relatively few are in either the moratorium or identity-achieved status by the twelfth grade. Self-definition in areas of occupational choice, religious and political beliefs, and gender roles continues into early adulthood (Kroger, 1988).

Most, if not all, of these football players probably dream of sports scholarships or even going pro. But as they go through the process of identity formation, they will gradually let go of such fantasies and commit themselves to more realistic futures.

Given that we expect adolescents to become more mature with age, to do things such as think for themselves and plan for the future, there is an implicit developmental trend in these statuses. In both moratorium and identity achievement, for instance, adolescents can be seen to engage in thoughtful decision making concerning the direction their lives might take. Identity-achieved adolescents, in addition, pursue their plans, allowing themselves to be defined by their choices. In contrast, there is little evidence of reflective decision making in the foreclosure and diffusion statuses. Although foreclosed adolescents are committed to the goals and beliefs they are pursuing, these do not result from personal exploration, but from holding tight to what they have received from others. finally, identity-diffused adolescents neither explore nor commit themselves to roles that will define them as adults.

Jane Kroger (1996; Kroger & Greene, 1996), at the University of Tromso in Norway, points out that a certain amount of movement from one status to another is to be expected. This movement is not always in the "developmentally correct" direction, however. Developmentalists use the term **regression** to refer to movement from a more complex, differentiated state to

James Marcia's theory of identity statuses suggests that some of these young men are considering a military career because of a family military tradition, that others are motivated by a personal commitment to serve their country, and that still others see military service as a way to postpone deciding what they ultimately want to do with their life.

one that is less so, a move that decreases the adaptiveness of behavior. Kroger (1996) distinguishes several forms of regression with respect to identity statuses. *Regression of disequilibrium* can occur when the way in which an adolescent has made sense of the world is challenged, such as by one's experiences at college or by entering a new situation where new rules apply. This type of regression is a healthy regrouping, one that is most likely to take place in adolescents who are open to their experiences and can tolerate a certain amount of uncertainty. In contrast to this relatively adaptive response to conflict, *regression of rigidification* is a closing off or narrowing of one's perspectives after having begun to explore options. Not only do personality variables, such as a tolerance for ambiguity, influence the form regression can take in the face of conflict, but so do the options that are realistically available to adolescents. A young girl growing up in a small town in which the only women she knows are her mother, her aunt, several teachers, a beautician, and the clerk at the market may dream of going off to college and becoming a social worker, but she may not be able to hold on to her vision, or even be sure that she wants to (Nurmi, Poole, & Kalakoski, 1996).

Even within a status, not all adolescents appear to have addressed the individuation process in similar ways. For instance, although a commitment to life-defining pursuits or values is absent in identity-diffused adolescents, some adolescents ("true diffusions") will remain uncommitted, whereas others ("passive moratoriums") appear likely to enter a period of exploration. Kroger (1995) has suggested that a distinction can be made within the foreclosure status as well, with individuals differing in their openness to change. Those who are willing to accept new challenges, "developmental" foreclosures, eventually move into the moratorium status, and those who are closed, "firm" foreclosures, remain as foreclosures. Kroger, in a two-year longitudinal study, looked for personality differences underlying these two approaches, specifically in adolescents' willingness to experience the anxiety that accompanies the separation from internalized parental figures, underlying personal growth. As anticipated, a greater need for nurturance and security when initially interviewed predicted that "firm" foreclosures would remain in that identity status.

Do adolescents simultaneously address identity issues in each of the different domains? That is, do they consider occupational, ideological, and sexual alternatives at the same point in time? Or do different domains become salient at different points in an adolescent's life (Archer, 1989a)? Can a 17-year-old male be identity-achieved in his occupational plans ("I'll work in construction with my uncle") but foreclosed in his gender role ("I want my wife to stay home with the kids the way Mom did"), diffused in his political beliefs ("I don't see the point in getting too worked up over political issues; after all, what can one person do?") and in moratorium about his religious beliefs ("I don't think of God the way I did as a kid, but I can't dismiss the idea that God is interested in me personally")?

In a two-year follow-up study of late adolescents, Jane Kroger (1988) found that only half the adolescents she studied had a common status in any two domains; another 9% had no domains in common. These data suggest that identity is not "a unitary structure, but . . . a sequence of distinct psychosocial resolutions involved in the definition of self" (1988, p. 60). Kroger's findings are comparable to those of other investigators in suggesting that adolescents do not work simultaneously on all identity domains (Archer, 1989a; Kroger, 1986; Rogow, Marcia, & Slugowski, 1983).

Identity and Personal Expressiveness

Alan Waterman (1992, 1993) has extended Marcia's work on identity statuses by identifying a third dimension to the process of identity formation, in addition to the dimensions of exploration and commitment. Waterman notes that individuals differ not only in how open they are to exploring and to committing to identity options, but also in the passion they invest in this process. Waterman refers to this dimension as personal expressiveness.

The dimension of **personal expressiveness** distinguishes between individuals who look for the most practical options and those who look for options through which they can realize their inner potential, options that allow them to express themselves. Those who seek practical options, even though they may not be fully engaged by what they are doing, are also not

In terms of Alan Waterman's theory of identity formation, is this Peace Corps volunteer more likely to have been motivated by practicality or by a search for self-fulfillment? How might her Peace Corps experience shape her identity, and what kind of work is she likely to move on to?

willing to reopen the process to find a more satisfying identity resolution. Instead, they construct an identity from the most reasonable and attractive options, often resulting in a successful if not personally fulfilling life.

In contrast, those who are personally invested in the process discover their identities by recognizing and then acting on inner potentials that when realized lead to fulfilling lives. They hold to their commitments passionately, are intensely involved in what they are doing, and in fact feel most alive and complete when engaged in these activities.

Identity Styles

Michael Berzonsky (1992) proposes an alternative way of thinking about identity statuses. To use Jane Kroger's (1992) distinction, Berzonsky envisions identity statuses as "organizers" of experience, not as "organizations" of experience. In other words, Berzonsky views identity statuses as an input variable rather than an outcome variable, as a process rather than a structure.

Berzonsky suggests that individuals differ in the way they process information relevant to the self; these differences underlie Marcia's statuses.

Continuity and
Change: Identity
Consolidation in
Late Adolescence

For some young peo-
ple, travel is a way to
learn more about
themselves and the
world. For others,
however, it is a way
to put off making life
decisions.

Some individuals, for instance, actively search for any information that
might be relevant to the problems they face; then they carefully evaluate
this information before making their decisions. Berzonsky refers to this processing style as information oriented. This style characterizes identity-
achieved and moratorium individuals. Others appear to do just the opposite,
putting off decisions and avoiding problems by procrastinating. He calls
this style, which characterizes identity-diffused persons, diffuse/avoidant.
finally, some individuals, when faced with problems, use as information social norms, or the expectations of significant others such as parents. Berzonsky identifies this processing style as normative oriented, and notes that it
characterizes those who are foreclosed. The Research Focus, "Operationalizing Concepts," illustrates the relationships among identity styles and identity statuses.

Janice Streitmatter (1993) has assessed identity statuses and identity
styles in college students and finds substantial relationships between
Berzonsky's identity styles and the four identity statuses. Those using an information orientation are likely to be in the identity-achieved or moratorium statuses. Conversely, normative and diffuse/avoidant orientations are
more likely to be used by identity-foreclosed and identity-diffused students,
the normative orientation more likely by those in the foreclosed status and
the diffused/avoidant orientation more likely by the identity diffused.

Research Focus

Operationalizing Concepts: What Kind of Decision Maker Are You?

By Michael Wapner

Lucky for Henry there was a category for undeclared majors. It had let him postpone that decision for a year and a half. But here it was the end of the first semester of his sophomore year and he was still "undeclared." He had just about finished his general education requirements, and he had taken intro psych, intro soc, intro anthro, and intro poli sci. No way to keep going much longer without choosing a major. But how was a guy to know what he'd want to do three years from now? He'd pretty much narrowed it down to a social science. Or, really, it had been narrowed down for him. He wasn't much good at math or music. He didn't like chemistry or physics. And he couldn't paint or dance. So social science was about all that was left—but which one?

Really, to tell the truth, it wasn't just choosing a major. Henry hated choices in general. He never ate in the cafeteria. Barbara chose the movies they would see and even went shopping with him to pick out his clothes. (Come to think of it, he didn't really *choose* Barbara. They had been fixed up for a blind date and just kept going together.) In fact, he was even at this college because he had delayed so long in deciding that all the other colleges had withdrawn their acceptances.

Although Henry may be an extreme example, he is not unique. His style of dealing with decisions makes him a good candidate for what Michael Berzonsky, at the State University of New York, Cortland, calls a diffuse/avoidant identity orientation.

Berzonsky's social-cognitive model identifies three types of *identity orientation,* or ways an individual approaches (or avoids) the task of constructing and revising a self-identity. These three types are informational, normative, and diffuse/

avoidant. The *informational orientation* is characteristic of individuals who are in an identity-achieved or moratorium identity status, and it is marked by deliberate self-exploration, a personally defined identity, an internal locus of control, problem-focused coping, and an openness to novel ideas, values, and actions. The *normative orientation* is associated with a foreclosed identity status, and it is distinguished by a tendency to be closed to information that would cause one to evaluate central aspects of the self and by conformity to the expectations of others. A *diffuse/avoidant orientation* is associated with a diffuse identity status, a greater likelihood of depression and neurosis, a less particular and pleasant interaction style than that of the other two categories, and a reluctance to deal with problems and decisions.

Berzonsky contends that each identity orientation is characterized by a different strategy of decision making. Information-oriented individuals are most likely to gather as much information as possible, by such means as talking to others or reading up on a subject, before they make a decision. Individuals with diffuse/avoidant orientations, such as Henry, are most likely to procrastinate and engage in defensive avoidance and other self-defeating approaches that are designed to escape decisions more than to make them. (In the research we are currently considering, Berzonsky made no particular predictions regarding the decisional strategies of normatively oriented individuals.)

Having hypothesized these relationships between identity orientation and decisional strategy, Berzonsky and his colleagues undertook extensive research to demonstrate them. However, before data on the question could be gathered, an essential step had to be taken. The concepts under consideration (identity orientation and decisional strategy) had to be *operationally defined.* Because concepts are, by definition, abstract, there are usually a number of different ways of interpreting them. Operationally defining a concept pins it down by expressing it in terms of the methods used to

(*continued*)

Research Focus *(continued)*

measure it. Operationalizing is a very fundamental process employed in all empirical science. Even a seemingly simple concept like "friendliness," in order to be studied, might be operationally defined in terms of a score on a friendliness scale, or a questionnaire filled out by an individual's acquaintances. By operationalizing a concept, investigators define it in a way that others can use and follow and be sure they are studying the same concept.

But not all operational definitions are equally adequate. Suppose, in studying friendliness, we operationally defined a "friendly" person as "anyone who is smiling the first time that person is observed." Although that does fulfill the minimum requirement for an operational definition—that is, it specifies what operation to perform to determine if someone is friendly (observe the person and see if that person is smiling)—it is not likely to be a satisfactory definition. It is likely to be deficient with respect to the two most important criteria for any measure—*reliability* and *validity*—that is, its consistency and the degree to which it measures what we assume it is measuring.

To assess, or operationally define, identity orientation, Michael Berzonsky and Joseph Ferrari employed a questionnaire—the Identity Style Inventory (ISI)—constructed and revised just for this purpose (Berzonsky, 1992). The ISI contains a 10-item informational-style scale with items such as "I've spent a great deal of time thinking seriously about what I should do with my life"; a 10-item diffuse/avoidant scale with items such as "I'm not really thinking about my future now; it's still a long way off"; and a 9-item normative-style scale with items such as "I prefer to deal with situations where I can rely on social norms and standards." Subjects were asked to rate the degree to which statements applied to them.

To assess decisional strategies, Berzonsky and Ferrari used a decision-making questionnaire, in which subjects were asked to rate the extent to which they engage in various decision-making practices. The subscales include: vigilance ("When making decisions I like to collect lots of information"); panic ("I feel as if I'm under tremendous time pressure when making decisions"); and decisional avoidance ("I avoid making decisions").

Were these measures reliable? One way of determining reliability is to give the measure to the same individuals on two separate occasions. The *test–retest reliability*, or consistency in responding to questions from one time to the next, was relatively high. Of equal, if not greater, interest is whether the measure is a valid one. One way to determine a measure's validity is to see how well the measure relates to other measures of the construct. This assessment of validity is known as *construct validity*. In originally constructing the Identity Style Inventory, Berzonsky (1989) selected a number of measures that were known to distinguish individuals in each of the identity statuses, along with a measure of the identity statuses themselves, and administered these to another group of individuals, together with his measure of decision styles. Would the decision-making scores correspond in a meaningful way with those on the other measures? Berzonsky found that they did.

Berzonsky and Ferrari administered the Identity Style Inventory and the decision-making questionnaire to college students. They also administered two scales of procrastination. Are different identity orientations characterized by different strategies of decision making? As expected, students who could be classified as information oriented were likely to use decisional practices in which they gather information, and individuals who could be classified as diffuse/avoidant oriented were more likely to procrastinate and engage in avoidance, excuse making, and other maladaptive behaviors.

Sources: M. D. Berzonsky. (1989). Identity style: Conceptualization and measurement. *Journal of Adolescent Research, 4,* 268–282. M. D. Berzonsky & J. R. Ferrari. (1996). Identity orientation and decisional strategies. *Personality and Individual Differences, 20,* 597–606.

Berzonsky (1993) reports that individuals adopting an information orientation are not only more open to ideas but are more experientially open in general, their openness extending to alternative values, feelings, fantasies, and even things of an aesthetic nature. In contrast, those adopting a normative orientation are closed to information that might challenge beliefs or values central to their self-definition. These styles, by the way, are as likely to be used by adolescents of one sex as the other.

IDENTITY: GENDER AND ETHNICITY

Gender Differences in Identity Formation

Adolescents find answers to the question "Who am I?" by examining the societal roles they see around them, roles they will soon assume. Erikson considered the most central of these roles to be that of a future occupation. Following close on the heels of this decision come decisions about political and religious beliefs, and the expression of an adult gender role (Erikson, 1968). Occupation, political stance, and ideology—all of these characterized males more than females at the time Erikson formulated this concept. Thirty years ago, relatively few females wrestled with issues of occupation and ideology. Ruthellen Josselson writes:

> At this point in his writing, it becomes more apparent that Erikson, like Freud and most other important psychological theorists, is writing about men. Indeed, all Erikson's psychobiographies analyze identity as it develops in men, and most of his case examples are from male patients. All Erikson had to say about women was that much of a woman's identity resides in her choice of the men she wants to be sought by. (1987, p. 22)

Erikson on Gender Differences   *Was* Erikson writing primarily about males? If so, how did he think females formulated an identity? Was it, as Josselson summarizes, through the men in their lives?

Erikson did, in fact, believe that the process of identity formulation differs for males and females—in content, timing, and sequence (Patterson, Sochting, & Marcia, 1992). With respect to the content of identity, he considered interpersonal issues, rather than vocational and ideological ones, to be central for females. He also thought the timing of identity resolution is different for males and females, with females keeping their identity options partially open, rather than resolving them as males do, so that they might better complement a potential mate. Erikson also believed that females resolve identity and intimacy issues more or less concurrently, whereas males resolve these issues sequentially (Patterson, Sochting, & Marcia, 1992).

Why would male and female adolescents go about so fundamental a process in different ways? In partial answer, Erikson referred to a "profound difference...between the sexes in the experience of the ground plan of the human body" that "predisposes" adolescent males and females to work out

their identities in different ways. He believed that women find "their identities in the care suggested in their bodies and in the needs of their issue,
and seem to have taken it for granted that the outer world space belongs
to the men" (1968, p. 274). Males achieve their identities by exploring this
outer world and finding pursuits and beliefs to which they can commit
themselves—an occupation and an ideology.

Erikson asserted that a female finds her identity "whatever her work career" when she "commits herself to the love of a stranger and to the care to
be given to his and her offspring" (1968, p. 265). When asked by young
women whether they can attain an identity before they marry, Erikson answered that "much of a young woman's identity is already defined in her
kind of attractiveness and in the selective nature of her search for the man
(or men) by whom she wishes to be sought" (1968, p. 283). He argued that
she may postpone identity closure with education or a career, but that
"womanhood arrives when attractiveness and experience have succeeded in
selecting what is to be admitted to the welcome of the inner space 'for
keeps'" (1968, p. 283).

Was Erikson right? Do sex differences such as the "ground plan of the
human body," for example a female's sense of "inner space" (the womb), primarily shape the process by which one achieves an identity? Do we see the
same pattern of concerns and commitments among adolescents today as
Erikson saw a generation ago? A number of studies supply us with answers
to these questions.

Research on Gender Differences   Early research on Marcia's identity statuses
found differences in the adaptiveness of different statuses for either sex. The
identity-achieved and moratorium statuses were found to be most adaptive
for males. Both statuses involve a time of soul-searching in which adolescents question and evaluate the options before them. Questioning societal
values and choosing among life options are congruent with cultural expectations for males (for example, self-reliance, decision making, defense of beliefs, risk taking), who are likely to receive more support for pursuing their
identities in this way. Males in these statuses were found to be more self-
assured, have higher self-esteem, be less anxious, perform better under
stress, and be less influenced by others than males in either of the other two
statuses (Bourne, 1978a, 1978b; Marcia, 1980).

Similar research painted a different picture for females. Early work with
identity statuses found that the foreclosure status was as adaptive for females as the achieved status, and that females in the moratorium status
function in many ways like identity-diffused females. Identity-foreclosed females, along with identity-achieved females, were found to enjoy high levels of self-esteem, experience little anxiety, and see themselves as effective
(Marcia, 1980). Marcia assumed that foreclosure was adaptive for females,
even though it did not lead to self-chosen goals, because it reflected cultural
expectations for females.

More recent research, however, finds few differences among male and female adolescents in identity development. In three separate studies, Sally
Archer (1989a) interviewed nearly 300 adolescents in the sixth, eighth, tenth,
and twelfth grades, using a semistructured interview similar to the one de-

Identity achieved females appear to focus on achieving a balance between self-assertion and relatedness. They use strengths drawn from their relationships to fuel their solo efforts.

veloped by Marcia. With few exceptions, she found equivalent numbers of males and females in each of the identity statuses. When gender differences occurred, males were more likely than females to be in the foreclosure status.

Was Erikson right in assuming that the content of identity differs for males and females? Archer (1989a) examined whether different content domains have greater salience for adolescents of one sex than the other by looking separately at vocational choice, religious beliefs, political ideologies, and gender roles. Few differences appeared within any of the domains. When they did, males were more likely to be foreclosed and females to be diffused in their political beliefs, and females were more likely than males to be identity achieved or in moratorium concerning family roles. Overall, Archer concluded from her research as follows:

> The minimal finding of gender differences in the processes, domains, or timing of identity activity in these three studies suggests that the traditional theoretical assumptions . . . should be discarded, or at least reconsidered. . . . Taken together the findings from these studies . . . suggest a similar epigenetic underpinning to the formative period of identity development for males and females. (1989a, p. 136)

Do females keep identity options partially open, as Erikson suggested, resulting in differences in the timing of development? The answer to this question is yes—and no. That is, at least two courses appear to be open to females when it comes to resolving identity issues. One involves a process of self-searching and introspection and is typical of females with continuous careers. It is, in other words, the same process followed by Marcia's identity-achieved and moratorium individuals. The other is the more traditional course described by Erikson, in which females define themselves interpersonally through their husbands and children, gaining a sense of their importance and value largely through their relations with others.

O'Connell (1976) distinguishes the first of these two courses as personal identity and the second as reflected identity. Females who pursue personal identities undergo the most progress in identity development in late adolescence, as do most males. In other words, they do not differ in the timing of their development. Females with reflected identities, however, describe themselves in terms of relational roles until their children start school, and only then begin to develop a personal identity. Contrary to Erikson's assumptions then, a woman's identity does not await confirmation by having children. Instead, having to care for young children appears to require women to postpone work on their personal identity (Patterson, Sochting, & Marcia, 1992).

The sequencing of identity formation appears to be more stepwise for males, with identity serving as a foundation for later intimate relationships (see the section, "Intimacy: The Self Through Relationships"). For females, issues of intimacy and identity are more apt to be resolved concurrently (Patterson, Sochting, & Marcia, 1992).

Recent research by Ruthellen Josselson (1988, 1992), based on narrative accounts of women's lives, reveals the importance that relationships have in giving women a sense of themselves. Josselson's interviews indicate that, rather than defining their identities primarily in terms of individual goals and principles, women also include issues of relatedness and responsibility to others. On the basis of this research, Serena Patterson, Ingrid Sochting, and James Marcia (1992) suggest that, in addition to exploration and commitment, a third dimension, relatedness, is important in defining identity statuses for females.

Is this suggestion contrary to Archer's conclusion that the process of identity formation is more similar than different between adolescents of either sex? Archer (1992) offers a tentative resolution to this apparent contradiction. She points to a remarkable tunnel vision that she noticed in her interviews with adolescents when it came to seeing the implications that commitments in one domain have for another domain. For instance, an adolescent boy might describe his vocational plans in detail as well as his plans for marriage and children, and yet not connect the two. Thus, potential conflicts, such as who would care for the children if his wife also chose a career or whose career would determine where they would live, simply are not anticipated. Those interviewed by Archer who were most likely to make connections between domains were late adolescent females. A sense of relatedness for females, an awareness of themselves in relation to others, may prompt them to integrate identity domains.

Relatedness may also play a more central role in defining the process of exploration in females than in males. For example, a sense of relatedness may cause females to give greater thought to the implications of adopting one lifestyle over another or of setting aside traditional beliefs, each of which would be a potential outcome of exploration. Mary Belenky and her associates, for instance, cite the concern of young college women that, by taking an intellectual stand, they might isolate themselves from others (Belenky, Clinchy, Goldberger, & Tarule, 1986). The very decision to go to college or pursue a career is, for some women, a repudiation of their family's ways, especially for minority females from traditional backgrounds.

In such cases, relationship implications set limits to exploration. However, it is equally possible that the limits may prompt more creative approaches to identity formation given the greater complexities that they introduce to the task for females (Archer, 1985). Patterson, Sochting, and Marcia (1992), in summarizing the findings of Archer and others on this point, note that females face a need to balance competing occupational and interpersonal commitments, involving them in "meta-decisions" across domains. In contrast, males can resolve these more easily as separate issues than females can.

Taken together, the research on gender differences reveals that the *process* of identity formation is comparable for adolescents of either sex. Adolescents who allow themselves to question, explore, and experience the uncertainty of not knowing—to experience a period of crisis—mature in this process. However, the particular content that adolescents address in finding their own way can differ for either gender. Thus similarities in process do not rule out other gender differences.

Contributions of Ethnicity to Identity Development

Because our sense of self reflects an awareness of how others see us, cultural values as well as individual experiences contribute to the development of identity. What happens when the larger society fails to validate these sources of identity? Thirty years ago, Erikson (1968) noted that minorities whose groups are devalued by society risk internalizing the negative views of society and can develop negative identities.

Only relatively recently have social scientists begun to systematically examine the psychological implications of ethnicity and minority status as these contribute to an **ethnic identity** (Phinney, 1990, 1996). Yet the developments that underlie an identity search in majority adolescents are likely to contribute to an awareness of one's ethnicity in minority adolescents. Social networks widen in adolescence, frequently including those from other backgrounds. Intellectual capacities develop, making it possible to view the self from a third-person perspective, heightening one's sense of self. Broader intellectual horizons make it likely that adolescents will recognize the existence of racial and ethnic overtones in local and national issues. All of these factors argue for ethnicity's being a salient factor in adolescent identity development.

The boundaries that define one's group provide members with a feeling of belonging. When boundaries are clear, they allow adolescents to distinguish between their own and other groups, and result in stronger ethnic identity. Some boundaries are maintained from within by the group, others are imposed on the group by the dominant culture. Internal boundaries come about through identifying with others in one's group. Adolescents adopt the values, attitudes, and perspectives of their group. Interactions with those outside the group provide a second type of boundary, through which minority adolescents experience the social opportunities and constraints that exist for members of their group—the relative status and value given them by others. The status of one's group within society is an important component of ethnic identity (Phinney, 1996).

Adolescents' consciousness of their ethnic identity varies with the situations they are in. Rosenthal and Hrynevich (1985) found that adolescents experience a strong ethnic identity when they are with their family or speaking their parents' native language, but feel part of the dominant culture when with others from that culture, such as when they are at school. They also found that the strength of the inner boundary of the ethnic group relates to adolescents' pride in their ethnic identity. Their measure of this strength was the institutional completeness of the community, the extent to which it provides its own schools, markets, churches, and other institutions. This finding may explain why African Americans in segregated schools frequently have higher self-esteem than those in integrated schools (Powell, 1985).

In the process of acculturation, external behaviors of minority adolescents frequently become less distinct from those of the majority culture whereas attitudes and values remain unchanged (see Chapter 1). Doreen Rosenthal and Shirley Feldman (1992) suggest that some components of ethnic identity may be more resistant to change than others because they are more central. Minority adolescents whose behavior closely resembles that of peers from the dominant culture might still have strong ethnic identities in other respects.

These investigators compared first- and second-generation Chinese American and Chinese Australian adolescents on several measures of ethnic identity. As expected, they found that despite differences in knowledge about their culture and in observable behavior between first- and second-generation minorities, the core aspects to their ethnic identities differed little; both first- and second-generation adolescents ascribed the same importance to their ethnic group membership and evaluated their ethnicity equally positively.

William Cross, at Cornell University, distinguishes several steps to the process of forming an ethnic identity. In the *pre-encounter* stage, individuals identify with the dominant culture. They notice differences between themselves and the dominant culture but do not consider them important. The second stage of identity formation, which happens only for minority adolescents, is the *encounter*. Cross traces the emergence of this stage to one or more vivid incidents in which adolescents experience discrimination. These experiences precipitate an awareness of membership in their ethnic group. This stage is a turning point in the development of an ethnic identity in which minority adolescents turn from the ways and values of the dominant culture and take on those of their ethnic group (Cross, 1980, 1987).

In the stage that follows, which Cross called the *immersion* stage, adolescents immerse themselves in the ways of their ethnic group, developing a high degree of awareness and valuation of those ways, along with a devaluation of those of the dominant culture. This stage is frequently characterized by social activism or even militancy. finally, in the *internalization* stage, adolescents become able to appreciate themselves and others as individuals and to recognize differences that don't always correspond to group

membership. Attitudes toward others reflect personal characteristics rather than group membership, as in the previous stage. Ethnic identity is less strident, and attitudes toward the dominant culture are less negative (Cross, 1980, 1987).

This progression parallels a number of other developmental progressions in which development moves from a focus on the self to a focus on the group, to respect for the individual (Aboud, 1987).

Do minority adolescents first internalize the values of the dominant culture and then question these values as they experience their implications before they adopt the values of the minority culture? For ethnic identity—just as for identity achievement in general—a crisis in which one questions the values one had previously accepted may be central to further development. Gordon Parks, an African American photographer, describes such an incident from his boyhood:

> I was only 12 when [a] cousin of mine, Princetta Maxwell, a fair girl with light red hair, came from Kansas City to spend the summer at our house. One day she and I ran, hand in hand, toward the white section of town to meet my mother, who worked there as a domestic. Suddenly three white boys blocked our path. I gripped my cousin's hand and we tried going around them, but they spread out before us.
>
> "Where you going with that nigger, blondie?" one snarled to my cousin.

In the third stage of ethnic identity formation, adolescents immerse themselves in the ways of their ethnic or racial group. Here, three young Native Americans prepare to participate in a pow-wow.

We stopped. The youngest one eased behind me and dropped to his hands and knees, and the other two shoved me backward. Pain shot through my head as it bumped against the sidewalk, and I could hear Princetta screaming as she ran back toward home for help. I caught spit in my face and a kick in the neck. I jumped up and started swinging, only to be beaten down again. Then came a kick in the mouth. Grabbing a foot, I upended its owner, scrambled up and started swinging again. Then suddenly there was help—from another white boy. Waldo Wade was in there swinging his fists alongside mine. The three cowards, outnumbered by the lesser count of two, turned tail and ran.

Waldo's left eye began puffing up as we walked along nursing our bruises. "How'd it all start?" he finally asked.

"They thought Princetta was white." "Idiots," he answered. "Hell, I know'd she was a nigger all the time." Waldo and I had trapped and fished together all our lives, but only through the delicacy of the situation did I resist busting him in his jaw.

That fight was sort of a turning point. (1990, p. 4)

Deborah Plummer (1995, 1996), at Cleveland State University, assessed racial identity attitudes among African American adolescents and found that 14- to 18-year-olds largely endorsed internalization attitudes, having healthy racial identities.

Stages of Ethnic Identity Development Jean Phinney, a psychologist at California State University, Los Angeles, points out that the progression toward an ethnic identity parallels differences among Marcia's (1988) identity statuses. Although Marcia did not initially think of the statuses developmentally, most research suggests that identity achievement is the most mature resolution and diffusion the least, with foreclosure and moratorium as intermediate steps (Josselson, 1982; Orlofsky & Frank, 1986). Phinney (1989, 1993) has proposed a stage model of ethnic identity development that parallels Marcia's analysis of identity.

Three distinct stages to ethnic identity development emerge. Just as with Marcia's identity statuses, it is possible for minority adolescents to avoid exploring the implications of their ethnicity and to remain committed to the values of the dominant culture. Adolescents with an **unexamined ethnic identity** have simply internalized the values and attitudes of the dominant culture, in a way similar to that of foreclosed adolescents, and have little understanding of issues related to their ethnicity. Those in an **ethnic identity search,** or moratorium stage, are involved in exploring the meaning of their ethnicity and may experience a growing conflict between the values of the dominant culture and those of their ethnic group. Adolescents with an **achieved ethnic identity** have a clear sense of their ethnicity that reflects feelings of belonging and emotional identification. They have little defensiveness and show confidence in their ethnicity (Phinney, 1989; Phinney & Rosenthal, 1992). Although different procedures and the use of somewhat different definitions make it difficult to compare findings from one study of ethnic identity development to the next, research suggests that psychosocial adjustment is associated with an achieved, or internalized, ethnic identity (Phinney & Kohatsu, in press; Speight, Vera, & Derrickson, 1996).

Phinney (1989) interviewed tenth-graders from different ethnic back-

TABLE 8.1   Percentage of Minority Adolescents in Stages
of Ethnic Identity Formation

	Unexamined	Search (Moratorium)	Achieved
Asian Americans	57.1%	21.4%	21.4%
Blacks	56.5	21.7	21.7
Hispanics	52.1	26.9	21.7
Total	55.7%	22.9%	21.3%

Source: Adapted from J. Phinney. (1989). Stages of ethnic identity development in minority group adolescents. *Journal of Early Adolescence, 9,* 34–49.

grounds regarding ethnic identity issues. These adolescents were Asian Americans, Blacks, Hispanics, and Whites. The interviews contained questions that tapped their exploration of and commitment to their ethnicity. An exploratory question was "Do you ever talk with your parents or other adults about your ethnic background or what it means to be ———?" Commitment was tapped by questions such as "Some people find these questions about their background pretty confusing and are not sure what they really think about it, but others are pretty clear about their culture and what it means to them. Which is true of you?" Adolescents also completed measures of ego identity, self-evaluation, sense of mastery, social and peer relations, and family relations.

As Phinney expected, stages of ethnic identity development correlated positively with the measure of ego identity. Similar correlations existed for measures of a sense of mastery and peer and family interactions. These findings suggest that the stages are indeed developmental, although we can't say that they increase with age. Slightly less than 50% of the minority adolescents had explored the implications of their minority status by the tenth grade. Even though a direct comparison is not possible because different samples are involved, this percentage is still higher than that for eighth-graders found in a previous study (Phinney & Tarver, 1988).

The stages themselves were independent of any particular minority. As shown in Table 8.1, just about the same percentage of adolescents from the three minorities was in each of the three stages of ethnic identity formation. This latter finding suggests that adolescents from different minorities have the same need to come to terms with the personal implications of minority membership. The important element appears not to be the particular minority group the adolescent is from, but the adolescent's stage of development of an ethnic identity. The one exception to this finding comes from White adolescents, who had no sense of their own ethnicity and saw themselves only as "American." Phinney notes that this ethnocentric attitude is out of touch with our increasingly pluralistic society in which minorities constitute about one-third of those between the ages of 15 and 25.

Somewhat different issues are important for different ethnic groups. Asian American adolescents were more likely to express concerns related to academic achievement, for example, quotas for universities that might exclude them. Black males expressed concern about job discrimination and negative images of Black adolescents, and Black females mentioned standards of beauty that did not include them, for example, long, flowing hair and "creamy" skin. Hispanic adolescents reported most concern with prejudice (Phinney, 1989). Despite these concerns, relatively few minority adolescents appear to have internalized negative attitudes toward their group. Only 20% mentioned negative attitudes during the interview, and these were distributed evenly across identity statuses (Phinney, 1989).

Achieving a Bicultural Identity

How do minority adolescents identify themselves with respect to the two cultures to which they belong? And how do they resolve potential conflicts arising from the differing perspectives and expectations of either culture? How do they arrive at a **bicultural identity?** Do they do so by keeping the two cultures separate? By combining them? Or do they deemphasize the whole issue of ethnicity and culture? Jean Phinney and Mona Devich-Navarro (1997) interviewed African American and Mexican American tenth- and eleventh-graders, asking them questions similar to those just mentioned.

In all, just about 90% of the adolescents who were interviewed thought of themselves as bicultural. However, differences existed among them in the ways in which they integrated the two cultures. One group of adolescents considered themselves to be equally members of their ethnic group and of the wider culture, expressing a strong sense of being American without denying their ethnicity. These adolescents, termed *blended biculturals,* resolved the issues raised by culture either by combining elements of both cultures or deemphasizing differences. An African American adolescent, for instance, said she thought of herself "like half and half . . . to me it is the same thing" (p. 15). Fifty-four percent of African American and 35% of Mexican American adolescents fell into this category.

For other adolescents, their ethnicity was more central to their sense of themselves than was being an American. As one said, "[I am] mostly Black. I am both, but I am more Black" (p. 15). These adolescents often reported thinking of themselves differently depending on where they were or who they were with, such as feeling more American at school and more ethnic at home. However, because they reported feeling at ease in both cultures, Phinney and Devich-Navarro considered them also to have a bicultural identity, referring to them as *alternating biculturals.* Twenty-five percent of African American and 63% of Mexican American adolescents were in this category.

A pivotal factor distinguishing these two groups of biculturals was not so much the importance of their ethnicity, but of their identification with the U.S. culture. Those with a blended bicultural identity were more likely to see the U.S. culture as inclusive, and also as diverse, thus making it possible to see themselves as fitting in. Adolescents whose identity was more situational, the alternating biculturals, had less of a sense of connection with being American.

For a third group of adolescents, the particular situation they were in had little effect on their sense of identity. These adolescents saw themselves primarily in terms of their ethnicity in all situations and did not think of themselves as very American. When cultural issues arose, they dealt with them by keeping the two cultures distinct. As one adolescent said, "I do not see myself as part of America" (p. 16). Phinney and Devich-Navarro referred to these adolescents as *separated.* Seventeen percent of African American and 2% of Mexican American adolescents were in this group.

THE SELF

The search for identity is a central task facing all adolescents. Adolescents are brought face to face with this task by two forces, one from within and the other from without. The first force—puberty—radically alters bodies that have become as comfortable as an old shoe. The shoe begins to pinch when adolescents develop the physiques, feelings, and cognitive capacities of adults. The second force, in the form of psychosocial expectations, confirms these inner changes. Adolescents are expected to be more adult— to start making decisions for themselves, to be responsible, to plan for their futures. But despite this alliance of culture with nature, someone within still asks, "Who am I?"

Self-Concept: Who Am I?

Each of us has a theory about ourself; it helps explain the way we feel, what we like or do not like, what we are good at, and why. Developmentalists call this theory the **self-concept.** Just as with any theory, the self-concept is a way of explaining and interpreting the facts one experiences in daily life, a way of constructing the self (Epstein, 1973).

Adolescents' ability to relate isolated events in terms of more general principles allows them to pull different experiences together into general assumptions about themselves. A boy who backpacks and bikes, plays ball well, and is on the swim team can think of himself as athletic. A friend who belongs to the drama club, is illustrating the class yearbook, and gets As in her art classes can think of herself as artistic. Both adolescents are making generalizations about themselves from specific experiences.

The capacity for self-reflection that comes with adolescence brings with it a concern about personality in general and thoughts about oneself in particular. Adolescents' observations about themselves begin with specific events (for example, being on the swim team or swimming the 100-meter faster than anyone else). These soon take the form of more general beliefs ("I am a good swimmer"). At an even more general level, the adolescent who can say of himself that he is a good swimmer, a strong runner, and a good ball player can integrate these into a sense of himself as athletic. If this adolescent also is a good student and holds down a part-time job, he can formulate even more general self-statements, such as, "I'm competent" and "I'm responsible."

Continuity and
Change: Identity
Consolidation in
Late Adolescence

Adolescents' sense of
self includes who they
have been as well as
who they hope to be.
Formulating their self-
identity requires them
to discover what they
like, what they are
good at, and what
they believe in.

The beliefs adolescents have about themselves determine many of their emotional reactions. Which of these beliefs are central to their sense of self? Adolescents can easily know which are most central by the way they react when these ideas are challenged. An adolescent who values her independence, for example, will find herself in frequent arguments whenever someone tells her that she cannot do something. One who values his competence will resent having anyone tell him he is not able to manage a task.

Because so many of the beliefs about the self in adolescence are recently formulated, they lack experiential support. As a consequence, adolescents' new self-concepts are particularly vulnerable to disconfirming evidence. Perhaps because of this, adolescents spend a lot of time and energy gathering evidence in support of their theories of the self. Events that otherwise might be commonplace take on significance if they support adolescents' beliefs about themselves. Getting a driver's license and going out on a first date are examples of experiences that assume this kind of significance, because they validate important beliefs, such as, "I'm adult" or "I'm attractive"

(Okun & Sasfy, 1977). Many of the self-statements adolescents include in their self-concepts reflect potential more than actual accomplishments. These discrepancies also explain why the theory of self is at first so vulnerable to disconfirming evidence.

To be healthy, self-concepts need to be self-correcting. When they are, adolescents can face new information about themselves openly. When teenagers feel threatened, they tend to close themselves off to defend their beliefs, incapable of seeing the ways in which their experiences fail to confirm these beliefs. But adolescents who feel secure about themselves are able to revise their beliefs in light of their experiences. Remaining open to new views of the self is especially difficult in adolescence because so much changes, and the need to explain these changes is so great.

The self-concept becomes more abstract, more differentiated, and more adaptive during adolescence. Children derive their sense of themselves from concrete, physical characteristics. Adolescents think of themselves in terms of psychological characteristics such as being impulsive, shy, loud, or witty. Children draw their characters in bold strokes—as either good or bad, right or wrong, strong or weak. Adolescents make finer distinctions; they see subtleties and nuance. They understand how a characteristic can be both a strength and a weakness. A 15-year-old might pride himself on his reflectiveness in social situations and his sensitivity with his friends, yet realize that these very same qualities can be his downfall when faced with a taunting classmate, knowing that a less-reflective friend would simply swing a punch at the offender. Self-concepts also become more adaptive as adolescents accumulate more years of decision making. These decisions provide a history of successes and failures. Most have learned that they usually make good decisions, and that even when they make mistakes, they are not devastating.

Self-Esteem: Do I Like Myself?

If the self-concept is a set of beliefs about the self, then **self-esteem** is a measure of how good one feels about these beliefs. A girl who describes herself as athletic, a social leader, witty, short, and friendly does not stop there. She evaluates each of these qualities. "Is it really okay to be as athletic as I am? So I'm witty, but is that as good as being a brain? Am I too short or just tall enough?" The answers she comes up with contribute to her feelings of adequacy and self-worth. Self-esteem is the adolescents' overall positive or negative evaluation of herself or himself (Simmons & Blyth, 1987).

Foundations of Self-Esteem Relationships with parents provide the foundation for self-esteem. When parents are loving, children feel lovable and develop feelings of self-worth. These feelings become established early in life. Infants quickly learn whether the world in which they live will meet their needs; when those around them are responsive, they develop a sense of trust. The establishment of trust in these first, basic relationships permeates all later ones. Self-esteem among adolescents still reflects their interactions with parents (Bolognini, Plancherel, Bettschart, & Halfon, 1996). Adolescents with authoritative parents, who stress self-reliance, shared decision

Box 8.2   Parental Attitudes and Self-Esteem

"I think it's really fun to watch them grow up and mature. It's fun to see them discover things about themselves and their lives. The older ones have boyfriends, and I'm seeing them interact with the boyfriends."—*Mother*

"Sometimes the kids have friends over, and they all start to talk about things. It's nice to see them get along with their siblings as well as their friends. It gives you a good feeling to see them enjoying themselves."—*Father*

"I felt very pleased when my son at sixteen could get a summer job in the city and commute and be responsible for getting there and doing a good job."—*Mother*

"I enjoy that she is following in the family tradition of rowing. I rowed in college, and my brothers did, my father and grandfather did, and she saw a city team and signed up. She does it all on her own and has made a nice group of friends through it."—*Father*

"I like it when they sit around and reminisce about the things they or the family have done in the past. They sit around the table and talk about an outing or a trip we took, saying 'Remember this?' It's always interesting what they remember. This last summer we took a long sightseeing trip, and what stands out in their minds about it is funny. They remember Filene's basement in Boston or a chicken ranch where we stopped to see friends. One father took the scouts on a ski trip. They got stuck in the snow on the highway for hours, and the car almost slid off the road. He said, 'Never again.' I said, 'Don't you realize that because of those things, the boys will probably remember that trip forever. You have given them wonderful memories.'"—*Mother*

"I really enjoy her happiness. She always sees the positive side to a situation. Things might bother her from time to time, but she has a good perspective on things."—*Father*

making, and willingness to listen, have higher feelings of self-worth (Bartle, Anderson, & Sabatelli, 1989; Garber, Robinson, & Valentiner, 1997). Box 8.2 illustrates some of the attitudes parents have about adolescents than can foster self-esteem.

Two especially important sources of self-esteem in adolescence come from interactions with peers and from satisfaction with one's body (Bolognini, Plancherel, Bettschart, & Halfon, 1996; DuBois, Felner, Brand, Phillips, & Lease, 1996). David DuBois (1996), at the University of Missouri, and his associates assessed the contribution of five domains of experience to self-esteem in early adolescents: family, peers, school, body image, and sports/athletics. As can be seen in Figure 8.1, peers and body image are the two largest contributors to global self-esteem.

Ethnicity and Self-Esteem   In general, few differences have been found in global self-esteem between minority and majority adolescents (DuBois et al., 1996; Tashakkori & Thompson, 1991). When we distinguish private aspects of self-esteem, such as pleasure in oneself or pride in one's beliefs, from its

Box 8.2   *(continued)*

"I can't believe that she has had her first boyfriend and it worked out so well. They met at a competition; and he lives some distance away, so they talk on the phone. He has a friend who lives here, and he comes for a visit sometimes and does lots of things with the family. We all like him, and it is nice for her to have a boyfriend like that."—*Mother*

"The joys are seeing them go from a totally disorganized state to a partially motivated, organized state. You can see their adult characteristics emerging."—*Father*

"I enjoy seeing my daughter develop musical ability, seeing her progression from beginning flute to an accomplished player who performs, and seeing how much pleasure she takes in her accomplishment."—*Mother*

"It really gives me a lot of pleasure to see the two of them help each other. They seem to have respect for each other. She is the brain and helps him with school, and he helps her too at times."—*Father*

"I enjoy his maturity. He's so responsible. He tests us, but when we're firm, he accepts that. I'm real proud of him because he looks at the consequences of what he does."—*Father*

"I enjoy his honesty and the relationship he has with his friends. He is real open with his feelings, and his friends look up to him. He's a leader."—*Mother*

"He's not prejudiced. His best friends are of different ethnic groups. People trust him and like him because he's real concerned about people."—*Father*

Source: Adapted from J. B. Brooks. (1996). *The process of parenting* (4th ed.). Mountain View, CA: Mayfield.

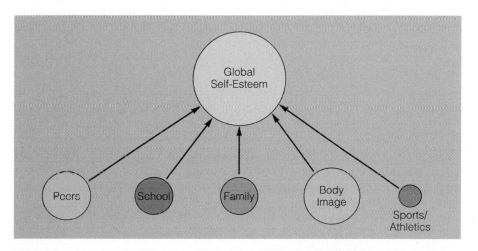

FIGURE 8.1   **Sources of Global Self-Esteem, Indicated by Their Relative Importance**

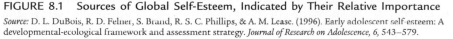

Source: D. L. DuBois, R. D. Felner, S. Brand, R. S. C. Phillips, & A. M. Lease. (1996). Early adolescent self-esteem: A developmental-ecological framework and assessment strategy. *Journal of Research on Adolescence, 6,* 543–579.

more public aspects, such as how intelligent one feels with others or satisfaction with one's physical attributes, different patterns of self-esteem
emerge for minority and majority adolescents. For instance, DuBois and his
associates (1996) found African American adolescents to have significantly
higher self-esteem with respect to peers, body image, and sports/athletics,
but lower self-esteem with respect to school.

The ways in which minority adolescents resolve their relationship with
the majority culture, confronting and coping with issues such as racism and
discrimination, have been found to be associated with differences in self-
esteem. Different ways of resolving this relationship, recall, are represented
by the various stages of ethnic identity, discussed earlier in the chapter.
Thus, pre-encounter adolescents, who have a White cultural orientation,
have been found to have lower self-concept scores and generally show poorer
psychological adjustment than bicultural or internalized adolescents who
have a strong sense of their ethnicity as well as a sense of belonging to the
larger culture (Phinney & Kohatsu, in press).

Gender is an important variable mediating self-esteem in minorities.
Self-esteem among adolescent girls who are African American, Native American, or Asian American has been found to be higher than that for their
male counterparts for public aspects of self-esteem (Martinez & Dukes,
1987). These gender differences may reflect the tendency within the dominant culture to attribute more well defined and frequently less positive
stereotypes to minority males than to minority females (Eagly & Kate, 1987).

Gender and Self-Esteem   A three-year longitudinal study of Swiss 12- to 14-
year-olds found girls to have somewhat poorer self-esteem than boys, most
noticeably so with respect to appearance and athletic ability (Bolognini,
Plancherel, Bettschart, & Halfon, 1996). Essentially the same pattern of differences exists for U.S. adolescents, with boys having higher self-esteem than
girls, especially with respect to body image and sports/athletic ability
(DuBois et al., 1996). Roberta Simmons and Dale Blyth (1987) noticed that
girls are more likely to negatively evaluate the characteristics about themselves they consider to be most important. Figure 8.2 shows that in mid-
adolescence, for example, nearly one-third of all girls who care either "a great
deal" or "pretty much" about their looks are not satisfied with them. Similarly, we see that more than 50% of all ninth-grade girls who are not
satisfied with their weight still care about it very much. Self-esteem has
nowhere to go but down under conditions such as these.

The greater resilience of boys' self-esteem during adolescence shows up
in another respect as well. Their self-esteem is less vulnerable in the face of
change than is that of girls. All adolescents face some transitions in common: puberty, a change in schools, and, with dating, a reordering of their
social world. Some adolescents must also cope with geographic relocations
and with family disruption, when parents change jobs or divorce. Having
time to gradually get used to one change before having to cope with another makes it easier to adjust to such transitions.

The more changes adolescents must cope with simultaneously, the more
likely they are to show the effects of related stress. Grade-point average and

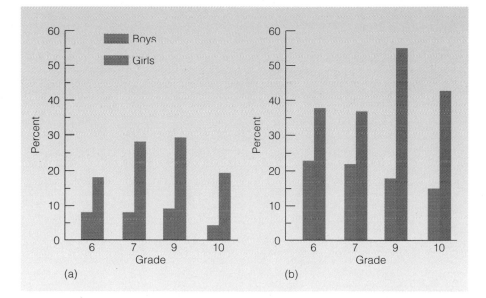

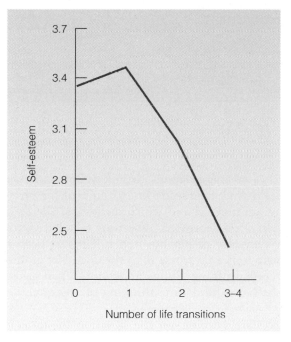

FIGURE 8.2 (above)
**Negative Evaluations of (a)
Appearance and (b) Weight
Among Adolescents Who
Rank These Characteristics
High for Self-Esteem**

Source: R. G. Simmons & D. A.
Blyth. (1987). *Moving into adolescence.*
New York: Aldine de Gruyter.

FIGURE 8.3 (left)
**Drop in Self-Esteem With
Number of Life
Changes for
Adolescent Girls**

Source: R. G. Simmons &
D. A. Blyth. (1987). *Moving into
adolescence.* New York: Aldine
de Gruyter.

participation in school activities drop for both males and females. As shown
in Figure 8.3, as the number of life transitions increases, self-esteem also
drops in girls. A comparable drop in self-esteem does not occur in boys. The
more stability adolescents have in any one area, the better they can cope
with changes in others (Simmons & Blyth, 1987).

Consider a hypothetical 14-year-old girl who is midway through puberty
and just beginning to date. Her parents are recently divorced, and she lives

Self-esteem is the overall positive or negative evaluation of oneself. Opportunities for responsible work help to build self-esteem.

in a new neighborhood. She has so many things to talk about with her friends, but she never gets to see them. She doesn't know which of the physical changes she's experiencing are normal and which are weird. She feels angry all the time—except when she's depressed. When she tells her counselor at school, he tells her it's because of her hormones. The last person she can talk to is her mother, who feels even worse than she does. Her grades have fallen, and she's lost interest in doing things at school. When asked how she feels about herself, she has a hard time thinking of any qualities that she likes.

This adolescent's experiences are extreme, yet the situation she faces is increasingly common for many (see Chapter 5). Under conditions such as these, self-esteem understandably suffers in adolescence.

How do adolescents come up with a sense of themselves that they can live with and like? Puberty forces the issue, but it also sets the stage for new answers. Because of pubertal changes, adolescents find it difficult to think of themselves as they did as children. But they also develop ways of thinking that give them the means to combine aspects of the old self with newly developing ones. Some of these aspects involve others; we turn to intimate relationships next.

INTIMACY: THE SELF THROUGH RELATIONSHIPS

Adolescents of every background have one thing in common: They all will share themselves with others in intimate relationships. Intimacy is often misunderstood. Like many adults, most adolescents associate it with romance, passion, being together, or being so close one can finish the other's sentences. Yet arguments, like romance, can provide the ground for intimate encounters, passion can involve little sharing of feelings, and always being together may signal a relationship that provides little room for being oneself. As for being able to finish another's sentences, this may mean the other has said nothing new for some time. But perhaps the biggest misunder-

Adolescents have to learn to accept themselves before they are ready for an intimate relationship, which requires having the self-confidence to let someone else know them as they really are.

standing with intimacy is that it occurs only in relationships with others. Intimacy begins with oneself and only then can it be extended to others.

What is intimacy? **Intimacy** is a sharing of innermost feelings and thoughts in an atmosphere of caring, trust, and acceptance.

Intimacy With Oneself

Intimacy, when it concerns oneself, means that one is in touch with inner feelings and needs; that is, one possesses self-awareness. Adolescents' capacity for intimacy should develop under the conditions that make it safe for them to know themselves. We discussed some of these conditions in the context of individuation in Chapter 5. Families that allow members to express their ideas, even when they differ from those of others, communicate that it is safe to disagree. Once adolescents have this safety, they are able to examine how they really feel (Grotevant & Cooper, 1986).

Self-acceptance is also important for intimacy. Adolescents who like themselves are free to be themselves without trying to change anything. Self-acceptance and self-awareness go hand in hand. Adolescents who have accepted themselves can be aware of desires and feelings that they otherwise might feel a need to deny or distort. Because a common way of distorting needs is to attribute them to others (that is, projection), self-awareness makes it possible for adolescents to perceive others more accurately as well. In appreciating the complexity of their own feelings, they can realize that the feelings of others are similarly complex and can validate those emotions. Self-acceptance creates a self-perpetuating cycle; having been validated, others are able to hear what these adolescents are saying and, in turn, validate them (Bell & Bell, 1983).

An important ingredient to self-acceptance is liking oneself. Adolescents who like themselves can let others get close enough to see them as they really are. Adolescents who don't like themselves frequently feel ashamed and are unwilling to let others get close. Often they feel it necessary to put up a front to look better, or to use their relationships to prove to themselves that they are acceptable (Masters, Johnson, & Kolodny, 1988). These approaches block intimacy, either by not being open with the other person or by using that person for one's own needs. Adolescents who feel negative about themselves are likely to handle their feelings of depression and anxiety in ways that block self-knowledge, by escaping into alcoholism or drug abuse, seeking distractions such as television, or finding substitutes such as eating. None of these behaviors lends itself to intimacy. Of course, adolescents need not be happy with themselves all the time. As William Masters, Virginia Johnson, and Robert Kolodny (1988) note:

> Generally, we separate what we like from what we don't like and use this process to try to change. If we are honest in our self-appraisals, the intimate knowledge we develop helps us relate to others. At the same time, a person who *never* looks inward (whether out of fear, laziness, or self-hatred) has such distorted self-perceptions that it is unlikely he or she can contribute fully to a relationship with someone else. (p. 318)

The Research Focus, "Path Analysis," describes the relationship between intimacy and identity in adolescence.

Research Focus

Path Analysis: Too Young for Intimacy?

Shelly spends all her time with friends—if not with them at school, then on the phone. Shrieks of laughter and silent smiles punctuate their conversations. It's clear who's "in" and who's not when they're with others. Shelly is 16. Her life revolves around her friends.

Yet some experts would question how close Shelly really is to her friends. These developmentalists argue that adolescents can form intimate relationships only after they have established a stable identity—a task several years beyond this 16-year-old. Erik Erikson assumes that adolescents must resolve the psychosocial crisis of identity before they can become intimate with others, that is, that intimacy is *contingent on* identity. Other theorists, such as Carol Gilligan and Ruthellen Josselson, argue that Erikson's developmental model fits the experience of males better than that of females. These theorists note that females' interpersonal skills prepare them to define themselves through their relationships with others, that is, that intimacy *contributes to* identity. Is the connection between identity and intimacy different for adolescent males and females? How might we tell?

Couldn't we simply measure identity achievement and intimacy in a group of adolescents and see whether those who have a better sense of themselves also have closer relationships with others? Let's say we do and discover that our assumption was correct. Does this finding support Erikson? Gilligan and Josselson? Actually, we have no way of knowing. There is no way to tell from this single correlation which factor is responsible for the other.

Would it help to separate the adolescents by sex and look at the degree to which the two measures are correlated for each? Not really. Even if we found a stronger relationship for one group than the other, we still would not know for that group which quality contributed to, or caused, the other—that is, whether identity is necessary for intimacy to develop, or whether intimacy contributes to the development of identity. All we would know is that adolescents who are high in one attribute are also high in the other, and vice versa.

Path analysis is a statistical procedure that allows developmentalists to infer the direction, or path, of an effect from correlational data. To use this procedure, one must obtain measures for the same variables on more than one occasion. Because causes precede their effects, we need this time difference to trace the direction of the relationship. But how is this procedure any better than a single correlation? We're still measuring

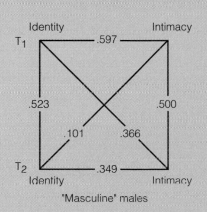

"Masculine" males

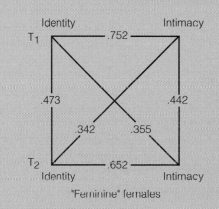

"Feminine" females

(continued)

Research Focus (*continued*)

both factors at the same time, just doing it twice instead of once.

That's true. However, because causes *precede* their effects, we can look for differences in the strength of relationships that differ *only* in which factor precedes the other. If Factor A causes Factor B, these factors should be most strongly correlated when measurements for A precede those for B, that is, between Factor A at Time 1 and Factor B at Time 2. The opposite correlation (Time 1 measures of Factor B with Time 2 measures of Factor A) should be relatively weak. The figure shows these correlations as diagonals stretching from Time 1(T_1) measures at the top to Time 2 (T_2) measures at the bottom.

But let's get back to Shelly. Are her friendships likely to be as intimate as they seem, or is their closeness illusory, awaiting further identity development? Patricia Dyk and Gerald Adams

(1990) conducted the study we have been describing (except their subjects were older than Shelly). These investigators found no simple gender difference in the relationship between identity and intimacy: Identity predicts intimacy for both sexes. However, when factors such as gender typing and empathy are taken into account, different patterns emerge for females and males. In males, and in females high in masculinity, identity predicts intimacy. In highly feminine females the association between identity and intimacy is more fused, suggesting that intimacy and identity develop together as Gilligan and Josselson also suggest. Some of these relationships appear in the figure.

Source: P.H. Dyk & G. R. Adams. (1990). Identity and intimacy: An initial investigation of three theoretical models using cross-lag panel correlations. *Journal of Youth and Adolescence, 19,* 91–110.

Intimacy With Others

Self-disclosure is important to intimacy. Adolescents who are intimates share their thoughts and feelings with each other (Orlofsky, Marcia, & Lesser, 1973; Schiedel & Marcia, 1985). Not everything they share is personal (often it's just gossip), but much of it is. Intimacy takes time to develop, as adolescents learn to trust one another with increasingly personal aspects of themselves. Self-disclosure has to be mutual to be comfortable; one adolescent cannot tell all and the other tell nothing. We tend to shy away from people who tell us everything about themselves the moment we meet them. Choosing to disclose things about oneself is a bit like taking off one's clothes. How undressed one appears depends on how much others are wearing. Someone in a bathing suit has enough on when lounging poolside, but at a dance would look nearly naked.

Adolescents are willing to share their personal experiences when they can trust that others will respect their confidence. Trust takes time to develop and usually requires some testing of the waters. An adolescent may start by sharing things she would not be devastated to hear repeated, such as what she thinks of a particular teacher, and work her way up to her most private thoughts and feelings, for example, what she really thinks of her stepfather, or the details of her relationship with her boyfriend. This kind of trust requires a commitment to a relationship.

Some theorists believe that females define themselves primarily in the course of their relationships but that males must define themselves before they are capable of close relationships. If they hope to build a lasting relationship, young couples need to be willing to accept changes in their partner's self-definition.

INTIMACY AND IDENTITY: DIFFERENT PATHS TO MATURITY?

To what extent are intimacy and identity related? Can adolescents be close to others without knowing themselves well? Can they develop a sense of themselves apart from their intimate relationships with others? Erikson believed that identity is a necessary precursor to intimacy. He wrote that "True engagement with others is the result and the test of firm self-delineation" (1968, p. 167). Intimacy assumes developmental significance for Erikson only after identity has been achieved.

This developmental progression, however, is not typical of females. Josselson (1988) writes that development in females takes place on an "interpersonal track" that is not represented in Erikson's scheme. Erikson wrote, for example, about industry (the crisis preceding that of identity) as the development of competence by learning how things are made and how they work. Competence for females is more likely to take the form of increasingly complex interpersonal skills (Marcia, 1980). These two types of skills set a different stage for the drama that unfolds during adolescence than that envisioned by Erikson. Prior developments prepare females to define themselves *interpersonally* through skills that bring them into relationships with others, whereas the same developments prepare males to define themselves *impersonally* through skills that result in products. As girls move into adolescence, their social networks relate to their self-esteem and

TABLE 8.2   Intimacy Statuses in Late Adolescence

ISOLATE	Relationships consist only of casual acquaintances.
STEREOTYPED	Relationships are shallow and conventional.
PSEUDOINTIMATE	Relationships are similar to those of Stereotyped but have commitment to long-term sexual relationship; these defined through conventional roles rather than self-disclosure.
PREINTIMATE	Close, open relationships characterized by mutuality; ambivalence regarding commitment to long-term sexual relationship.
INTIMATE	Relationships are similar to those of Preintimate but also have commitment to long-term sexual relationship.

Source: D. G. Schiedel & J. E. Marcia. (1985). Ego identity, intimacy, sex role orientation, and gender. *Developmental Psychology, 21,* 149–160.

to their perceived self-competence across a variety of areas, in ways that boys' relationships do not (DuBois et al., 1996; Feiring & Lewis, 1991). In early adulthood, relationships continue to contribute more heavily to identity than does school or occupation (Meeus & Dekovic, 1995).

Erikson viewed intimacy as a characteristic of relationships with others. For females, it is also a process by which they define themselves. Rather than postponing identity consolidation until they find a mate, as Erikson suggested, intimacy affords the means by which female adolescents *achieve* self-definition (Gilligan, 1982; Josselson, 1988; Marcia, 1980). Josselson states:

> Intimacy, or interpersonal development, among women *is* identity and resides not in the choice of a heterosexual partner, but in the development, differentiation, and mastery of ways of being with others (not just men) that meet her standards for taking care, that connect her meaningfully to others, and that locate her in an interpersonal network. (1988, p. 99)

If relationships assume a different developmental significance for females, we should expect to see gender differences in levels of intimacy during adolescence. Don Schiedel and James Marcia (1985), both at Simon Fraser University, classified individuals into intimacy statuses that reflected commitment to and depth of relationships, as shown in Table 8.2. They found significantly more females in the higher intimacy statuses than males. In fact, females were nearly twice as likely as males to be in the highest two statuses. Perhaps because the individuals they studied were in late adolescence or early adulthood, the proportion of females high in intimacy did not increase with age. This proportion did increase for males, however, suggesting that males, as Josselson and Carol Gilligan also imply, are not as prepared for relationships as are females.

But what about the relationship between intimacy and identity mentioned earlier? A number of studies support Erikson's suggestion that intimacy is contingent on achieving identity, but find this relationship to be more characteristic of males than females (Dyk & Adams, 1990; Schiedel & Marcia, 1985). Schiedel and Marcia found, for instance, that for males, those in the highest intimacy categories were most likely to be in the identity-achieved or moratorium status. This trend for females was not significant. Further, they found virtually no males who were high in intimacy but low in identity. Identity and intimacy do not, however, appear to be achieved in succession by females; a full one-third of the females who were high in intimacy were low in identity. These findings support Josselson's contention that for females intimacy *is* a means by which identity is resolved.

Does development take the form of increasing autonomy and separation? Most personality theorists have answered yes. Every now and again a few voices raise alternatives, but until recently, these have not been incorporated into mainstream developmental theory. Revisions may be afoot (Gilligan, 1982; Gilligan, Lyons, & Hanmer, 1989; Josselson, 1987, 1988).

David Bakan (1966) distinguishes two aspects of mature functioning. **Agency** captures qualities of assertiveness, mastery, and distinctiveness, and **communion** reflects qualities of cooperation and union. Bakan considers these two facets of personal functioning to be balanced in the mature person. Developmentalists have traditionally translated these aspects of maturity into a developmental progression moving *from* communion *to* agency, thereby assigning greater maturity to agency. An alternative interpretation of Bakan's view of maturity, but one that equally distorts it, has assigned agency to the masculine personality and communion to the feminine. This approach easily reduces to the first because development in females often falls short of that in males when comparisons use measures that have been standardized with males (for example, Kohlberg's measure of moral development, or the use of rules in games). Most Western cultures implicitly confirm either of these translations through the greater value they place on agentic over communional behaviors. Our society, for example, defines success in terms of individual accomplishment and achievements rather than the quality of a person's relationships.

But is development most accurately thought of as increasing separation and individuation? Ruthellen Josselson (1988) notes that recent research in two areas within psychology—adolescent development and the psychology of women—reveals difficulties in viewing development this way.

Development in Adolescence

Development during adolescence does not require an end to, but rather a modification of, significant relationships with parents. Adolescents achieve a sense of themselves *within* their relationships, not in spite of them (Josselson, 1988). Research with adolescents and their parents such as that of Harold Grotevant and Catherine Cooper (1986) finds that attachment and separation are not opposites but are different aspects of the same process. If the task of adolescence is to break ties with parents, then adolescents either accomplish this task or they don't—they either separate *or* remain attached. If the task is for adolescents to renegotiate relationships with parents to achieve greater mutuality and equality, they can separate as persons *and* remain emotionally connected or attached (Josselson, 1988). Any theory that emphasizes separation as developmentally more advanced gives a distorted view of development in which an autonomous self is accepted as the pinnacle of maturity (Josselson, 1988).

Development in Females

A second challenge to the prevailing view of development as progressive separation and individuation comes from attempts to chart female development. These attempts bring a new awareness of the male bias in much developmental theory. Developmentalists have assumed their theories to be universal, that is, to cover issues fundamental to the whole of human experience. Yet theories are not totally objective representations of human nature; they are interpretations that often reflect the personal experiences of the theorists. And most personality theorists have been males. There is a growing recognition that current theories address experiences that are more common among, or even unique to, males (Adelson & Doehrman, 1980; Bettleheim, 1961; Gilligan, 1982, 1986; Josselson, 1988).

Erikson, for instance, thought of identity as an exploration of issues related to vocation, political views, and religion. When females are interviewed about their identity concerns, one hears about their relationships—not about industry, autonomy, or ideology. Autonomy may well serve the function of a developmental organizer for most males in our society, but relationships serve this function for most females. Josselson adds, "Because women define themselves in a context of relationship, a developmental orientation that equates growth with autonomy will automatically relegate women to lower rungs of development" (1988, p. 99). She notes in support of this point that the cultural myths that exist in our society make it difficult to view the "achievement of adult commitment, fidelity, intimacy, and care [as] meaningful and heroic" (1988, p. 99).

Carol Gilligan (1986) comments that the adolescent girl especially faces a problem in that, as she affirms her connection with her mother, she sees how disconnected they both are from a society in which the male experience defines reality. Gilligan writes:

> The ability to establish connection with others hinges on the ability to render one's story coherent. Given the failure of interpretive schemes to reflect female experience and given the distortion of this experience in common understandings of care and attachment, development for girls in adolescence hinges . . . on the courage to challenge two equations: the equation of human with male and the equation of care with self-sacrifice. Together these equations create a self-perpetuating system that sustains a limited conception of human development and a problematic representation of human relationships. (1986, p. 296)

Dimensions of Relatedness

Ruthellen Josselson points out that social scientists have developed a rich vocabulary for talking about the self, distinguishing among terms such as *self-consciousness, self-awareness, self-control, self-concept,* and *self-esteem,* yet few words to describe the self in relation to others. A single term, *relationship,* serves to describe the many, varied ways we have of interrelating. The paucity of our language has, in turn, contributed to a cultural blindness in which "when we wish to know people, we are therefore more likely to ask about what they do than about how they love. But in fact we would know them better if we knew how they are with others and what they want from them" (Josselson, 1992, p. 2).

TABLE 8.3   Dimensions of Relatedness and Their Pathological Poles

Absence of Dimension	Dimension	Excess of Dimension
Falling	*Holding:* gives a sense of being contained and bounded; provides sense of security. Later takes the form of feeling "supported" by others, of having others who are "there" for us.	Suffocation
Aloneness, loss	*Attachment:* The need to be close to those who are important to us, which the infant expresses by crying in protest when its mother leaves; an essential ingredient of human connection.	Fearful clinging
Inhibition, emotional deadening	*Passionate Experience:* Others become the objects of our desires; ranges from the need to suck in infancy to sexual desire in adolescence and adulthood.	Obsessive love
Annihilation, rejection	*Eye-to-eye Validation:* Lets us see ourselves through the eyes of others and gives us a sense of ourselves in relation to them.	Transparency
Disillusionment, purposelessness	*Idealization and Identification:* Expansion of our sense of ourself by reaching out to and embracing those who are bigger, stronger, grander.	Slavish devotion
Loneliness	*Mutuality and Resonance:* By sharing our experiences with another, we arrive at something jointly created; an expression of our social nature.	Merging
Alienation	*Embeddedness:* A sense of belonging, having a place in the group, experiencing communality.	Overconformity
Indifference	*Tending and Care:* Nurturance that is intentional and deliberate; our capacity to care for others reflects our own need to be needed.	Compulsive caregiving

Source: Adapted from R. Josselson. (1992). *The space between us.* San Francisco: Jossey-Bass.

Josselson (1992) gives us a multifaceted theory of human connection, describing eight dimensions of relatedness. Each of these follows a developmental course, being expressed initially in concrete and literal ways, and only with time symbolically. The dimensions themselves are independent of one another, one not being reducible to the other, and develop more or less simultaneously rather than as stepwise stages. Also, either the absence of each form of relatedness in a person's life or excessive indulgence of it is pathological. Table 8.3 shows the dimensions and their pathological poles. The first four dimensions, holding, attachment, passionate experience, and eye-to-eye validation, are present either from birth or shortly thereafter. The second four do not develop until later. Idealization and embeddedness require that one experience the self apart from others as well as see that self in relation to those others, both of which require a certain cognitive maturity. Similarly, mutuality and tending require the capacity to be responsive to others, which can develop only when the child moves beyond egocentrism.

Although differences
among individuals of
the same sex can be
greater than those be-
tween the sexes, men
and women do char-
acteristically differ in
the way they relate to
other people. Females
pay more attention to
relationships and ex-
pect them to change
over time.

Gender Differences in Relatedness

Josselson (1992) cautions against overstating gender differences in relatedness, pointing out that considerable variability exists among individuals of
the same sex in their expressions of relatedness, but she notes several important differences as well.

Females describe greater complexity to their relationships, catching
more nuance to experience and being able to incorporate contradictory elements, whereas males approach their relationships in more straightforward
and simpler terms. Females tend to view relationships as evolving over time.
In contrast, males see them as more static than dynamic, more as products
that, once arrived at, will remain that way. And finally, individuals of either
sex emphasize different dimensions of relatedness.

Josselson traces these differences to several underlying factors. First,
males tend to fit their relationships into an abstract conceptual system,
whereas for females relationships are more immediate and experiential. For
instance, in their interviews, males would frequently mention being influenced and moved by the works of men whom they had never met, such as
artists and philosophers, yet with whom they had carried on passionate inner dialogues. These intellectual exchanges *felt* relational to them. Females,
in contrast, needed some measure of "affective coloring" before they experienced an exchange as relational.

Josselson locates this abstractness in males within a second factor, one
concerning gender definition. If, as Nancy Chodorow points out, a boy needs

Defining the Self:
Identity and Intimacy

Males, on the other hand, tend to define relationships according to fixed categories and to assume that they'll always remain the same. The difference in the genders' view of relationships may be partly due to differences in identity formation: Males are defined more in terms of what they can do, and females are defined more in terms of how they relate to others.

to separate himself from his mother in order to develop as a male, he achieves masculinity at the *expense* of emotional closeness (see Chapter 2). This distancing has implications for all future relationships, in which "he learn(s) to relate to others across a gulf that both separates him and guards his masculinity" (Josselson, 1992, p. 225). In contrast to the boy, the little girl need not distance herself from the mother but instead learns what it is to be herself within the context of relatedness, comfortable with "the paradox that she is both merged and distinct, both connected and separate" (p. 225).

Having to define oneself as a male this way requires action on the boy's part, that is, separating from the mother, whereas defining oneself as a female does not. A third factor, then, is that males gain a sense of themselves through their actions, through doing, and females through their relationships, through being. Males evaluate themselves in terms of what they can do, their skills and accomplishments, how far they can kick a soccer ball or how many space aliens they can knock out in a video game. Conversely, observes Josselson,

> girls are not liked for being smart or good at soccer, as boys are, but for ill-defined qualities, such as responsiveness to others, self-confidence, playfulness, and charm. And the girl understands, quickly and deeply, that she, too, will be labeled and located in this slippery interpersonal universe. She will be responded to for how she is deemed to *be,* not for what she wills or for her skills. (1992, pp. 226–227)

Because of these factors, gender differences in relatedness are to be expected. For instance, females are more comfortable experiencing mutuality than are males. "For women," says Josselson, ". . . the regulation of closeness and distance, and the shared experience of emotion is the essence of relating" (1992, p. 232). Eye-to-eye validation is also a more significant dimension of relatedness for females, because their sense of self is rooted more deeply in others' responses to them. Passionate experience that is expressly sexual, on the other hand, is more of a driving force in males' relationships. Also, because the way males know themselves is more closely tied to action and doing, identification and idealization are more salient to their relationships than to those of females. Males' ambitions are personalized through identification with figures who are bigger than life, heroes to be idealized and modeled. Females are more apt to draw their strength from those who are close at hand (Josselson, 1992).

A New Definition of Maturity

Josselson (1988) asserts that gender differences in individuals' sense of self are sufficiently great that we must redefine identity to include the concept of self in relation to others. Presently our definition of identity views separation as contributing to the mature individual's experience of self; Josselson argues that our approach to identity must give equivalent weight to a person's relatedness to others. Maturity involves movement toward a greater capacity for relationships. Contributing to this capacity are assertion and autonomy. Josselson turns the tables and makes self-in-relationship the more embracing concept of which autonomy and separateness are components.

Does development move from dependence to autonomy, as traditional theory asserts? Does it involve increasingly articulated ways of relating to others? Adolescents of both genders work out their identities in the context of continuing significant relationships with others, and males as well as females face intimacy as a central issue leading to adulthood. Josselson maintains that each person has a need for separateness *and* attachment, for inclusion *and* exclusion. Each of these creates tensions, but to give in to one and not strive for balance is to forfeit some degree of maturity (Josselson, 1988).

SUMMARY

Identity

Achieving an identity is a central task facing adolescents. Identity gives one a coherent, purposeful sense of self.

There are several ways adolescents arrive at the roles and values that define their identities. Some paths, involving either a personal search or an ad-

herence to old beliefs, lead to commitments. Conversely, other paths can lead to noncommitment—some adolescents not being able to choose among alternatives for fear of closing off important options, and others failing to see the importance of choosing. These paths lead to four identity statuses: identity achievement, foreclosure, moratorium, and identity diffusion. Adolescents may move from one status to another, depending on their willingness to accept new challenges and to experience anxiety.

Even though Erikson believed the search for identity to be a central task facing all adolescents, he assumed that females and males approach it differently. The task for males involves making choices and commitments about an occupation, a set of beliefs, and their sex role. Erikson believed females arrive at their identity by committing themselves to a future mate.

Research shows that gender differences in identity development are minimal. The process and timing of development suggest more similarities than differences.

Ethnic identity development progresses through several stages. Adolescents with an unexamined ethnic identity internalize the values and attitudes of the dominant culture. Those in an ethnic identity search are exploring the meaning of their ethnicity, and those with an achieved ethnic identity have a clear sense of their ethnicity and emotionally identify with their ethnic group. These stages correlate with ego identity statuses. Some bicultural adolescents see themselves as equally members of their ethnic group and the dominant culture; for others, however, one identity or the other predominates according to the situation.

The Self

The self-concept becomes more abstract, differentiated, and adaptive during adolescence. The capacity for self-reflection allows adolescents to think of themselves in terms of psychological characteristics; they appreciate subtlety and nuance. Increased experience in making decisions contributes to more adaptive self-concepts.

Self-esteem reflects the overall positive or negative attitude adolescents have about the self. Relationships with parents and peers and satisfaction with one's body provide the foundations for self-esteem.

Self-esteem varies somewhat with ethnicity and gender. Some aspects of self-esteem are higher among minority adolescents than majority ones; others are not. In general, males have higher self-esteem than females during adolescence.

Intimacy

Intimacy is the sharing of innermost feelings and thoughts in an atmosphere of caring, trust, and acceptance. To be intimate with others, adolescents must first know and accept themselves.

Self-disclosure may provide a vehicle for intimacy with others. Intimacy is often contingent on achieving identity, at least for males. For females, intimacy is often the means by which identity is resolved.

Intimacy and Identity

Development has traditionally been viewed in terms of increasing autonomy and separation from others. Recent research on adolescent–parent relationships and on female development questions this view. Relationships between adolescents and parents show that continuing emotional attachment and increasing autonomy coexist and are different aspects of the same process. For females, relationships with others contribute importantly to their sense of self. New definitions of maturity will need to include movement toward a greater capacity to relate to others, as well as increasing autonomy and separateness.

KEY TERMS

identity	regression	bicultural identity
identification	personal expressiveness	self-concept
identity formation	ethnic identity	self-esteem
identity achieved	unexamined ethnic identity	intimacy
identity foreclosed	ethnic identity search	agency
moratorium	achieved ethnic identity	communion
identity diffused		

CHAPTER 9

The Sexual Self
Close Relationships in Late Adolescence

"Hey, Raffie," Arnie grinned over the locker door. "You a lucky man this morning, or not?"

"Or not," thought Raffie, as he grabbed his books and gave the door a slam.

But he grinned back, "You think you're the only one around here gets lucky?"

"All right!" exclaimed Arnie, giving his friend a "deadarm" and heading for his first class on the run.

Raffie glared at Arnie's back as he disappeared down the hall. What was it with his friends? Did they really have all the sexual adventures they said they had? Was he the only one who was different?

Raffie was 16, and he was worried. Raffie was a virgin.

Now imagine the same scenario between two female adolescents.

"Hey, Rachel," Annie grinned at her friend. "Make anything happen last night, or what?"

"Or what," thought Rachel, but she grabbed her books and grinned back. "You think you're the only 'happening' one around?"

"All right," said Annie, giving her friend an affectionate squeeze. She promised to catch all the details over lunch, then ran off to class.

Rachel stared at her friend as she rushed off. "Am I really that different?" she wondered.

Is the second scene harder to imagine than the first? What does the phrase "getting lucky" communicate about a sexual encounter? Are females and males equally likely to think of sex this way? Would Raffie's father have been as embarrassed in his day by sexual inexperience? Is Rachel likely to be? What are the sexual attitudes and practices of adolescents today, and how do these contribute to teenagers' sense of self?

The topic of sexuality raises questions at any age, but especially during adolescence. Researchers have recently begun to supply us with some answers. In other instances, however, they have only begun to ask the questions. Still, knowing what questions to ask can be the first step to understanding, even if these questions are sometimes very personal. Sexuality looms large in adolescence, in part because it takes exciting new turns and in part because it contributes so heavily to adolescents' sense of themselves.

Ready-made roles, in the form of sex-role stereotypes, await adolescents as they step into adulthood. These gender stereotypes, like ready-made clothes, will fit some adolescents better than others. For still others, they will not fit at all. We will consider stereotypes of masculinity and femininity in the opening section of this chapter, along with the more flexible alternative of androgyny.

Sexuality forms the basis for a new type of emotional intimacy in adolescents' relationships. Adolescent males and females describe their romantic experiences in strikingly similar ways that are also similar to the descriptions of adults. The manner in which sexual feelings are expressed varies with the type of dating relationships adolescents have.

For most adolescents, sexual attraction involves someone of the opposite sex. A small percentage discover they are attracted to those of their own sex. The biological and psychosocial bases of sexual attraction will receive attention in this chapter.

The sexual response cycle is strikingly similar for all individuals, despite differences in gender or sexual orientation. Research reveals four phases of response: excitement, plateau, orgasm, and resolution. We examine similarities in sexual response before discussing myths and misconceptions common among adolescents about their sexual functioning. The chapter ends with a consideration of some consequences of adolescent sexuality: unintended pregnancies and sexually transmitted diseases.

GENDER STEREOTYPES: THE MEANING OF MASCULINE AND FEMININE

Gender-role stereotypes are the cultural expectations concerning which behaviors are appropriate for each sex. These stereotypes play an important role in self-definition as adolescents integrate questions posed by their sexuality into their developing sense of themselves—questions such as "What does it mean to be an adult male or female?" "How much will I have to change the way I think of myself?" "In what ways will I still be the same?"

The Bem Sex-Role Inventory (BSRI) is an instrument that assesses the attitudes of individuals concerning what it is to be masculine and feminine in our society (Box 9.1). A score of 4.9 on either the feminine or the masculine scale is considered average for that scale, indicating a traditionally masculine or feminine gender role. About half of all individuals who take the inventory score at or above this number on one of the scales (Hyde, 1991). Attitudes concerning what is feminine and masculine have changed

Box 9.1   An Inventory of Gender-Role Characteristics

Indicate for each item how each descriptor characterizes you. If it is almost never true of you, place a 1 by the item. If it is almost always descriptive of you, place a 7 by the item. Use numbers between 1 and 7 to reflect differing degrees of descriptiveness.

1. Self-reliant
2. Yielding
3. Helpful
4. Defends own beliefs
5. Cheerful
6. Moody
7. Independent
8. Shy
9. Conscientious
10. Athletic
11. Affectionate
12. Theatrical
13. Assertive
14. Flatterable
15. Happy
16. Strong personality
17. Loyal
18. Unpredictable
19. Forceful
20. Feminine
21. Reliable
22. Analytical
23. Sympathetic
24. Jealous
25. Has leadership abilities
26. Sensitive to the needs of others
27. Truthful
28. Willing to take risks
29. Understanding
30. Secretive

31. Makes decisions easily
32. Compassionate
33. Sincere
34. Self-sufficient
35. Eager to soothe hurt feelings
36. Conceited
37. Dominant
38. Soft-spoken
39. Likable
40. Masculine
41. Warm
42. Solemn
43. Willing to take a stand
44. Tender
45. Friendly
46. Aggressive
47. Gullible
48. Inefficient
49. Acts like a leader
50. Childlike
51. Adaptable
52. Individualistic
53. Does not use harsh language
54. Unsystematic
55. Competitive
56. Loves children
57. Tactful
58. Ambitious
59. Gentle
60. Conventional

To score your answers:
(a) Sum your ratings for numbers 1, 4, 7, 10, 13, 16, 19, 22, 25, 28, 31, 34, 37, 40, 43, 46, 49, 52, 55, and 58. To determine your masculinity score, divide this sum by 20.
(b) Sum your ratings for numbers 2, 5, 8, 11, 14, 17, 20, 23, 26, 29, 32, 35, 38, 41, 44, 47, 50, 53, 56, and 59. To determine your femininity score, divide this sum by 20.
(c) You are androgynous if both your masculinity and your femininity scores are 4.9 or above.

Source: Adapted from S. L. Bem (1974). The measurement of psychological androgyny. *Journal of Consulting and Clinical Psychology, 42,* 155–162.

relatively little since this inventory was constructed a generation ago. In terms of actual behavior, however, such measures may overestimate actual differences (Allen, 1995).

The Masculine Gender Role

Our society expects males to be self-reliant, self-sufficient, able to defend their beliefs, make decisions, take a stand, and be leaders. Few of the qualities that would lead to intimacy and warmth in human relationships are considered to be masculine.

The *masculine* gender stereotype portrays males as the sexual risk takers, the ones to make the moves, to be aggressive, dominant, assertive, and forceful. Qualities that would transform such a role into one that includes sensitivity and caring are notably absent. Because components of gender stereotypes are often polar opposites of each other, qualities such as affection, sensitivity, and tenderness have been relegated to the province of females. The masculine stereotype would lead one to expect males to seek physical satisfaction rather than emotional closeness from their sexual encounters. Linda Kalof (1995), however, found that the emotional intimacy afforded by sexual encounters is as important for adolescent males as it is for females.

The Feminine Gender Role

Females face a different, though equally problematic, set of cultural expectations. In the *feminine* gender stereotype, females are expected to be in touch with their emotions, sensitive to the feelings of others, affectionate, understanding, warm, and tender. Despite the implicit maturity in such an interpersonal stance, in all other respects cultural expectations communicate that females are dependent, passive, and childlike. These latter qualities are particularly disturbing in light of the fact that adolescent females typically assume responsibility for contraception. With respect to sexual encounters, females have traditionally been assumed to be motivated more by a desire for emotional closeness than for physical pleasure. Again, however, Linda Kalof (1995) found gender stereotypes to be more myth than truth for adolescents today. Adolescents of both sexes sought physical pleasure as well as emotional intimacy in their sexual encounters.

Androgyny: A New Alternative

Many individuals score high on both the masculinity and the femininity scales. These individuals are **androgynous.** Adolescents have more latitude in fashioning their gender roles today than they have had in previous generations. Roles that clearly separated the sexes are being reexamined in the light of dual-career marriages, which merge traditional roles of housewife–mother and breadwinner–father. Adolescents of either sex can be assertive and compassionate, self-reliant and sensitive. Androgyny allows adolescents to tailor-make a gender role instead of having to select one off the rack.

But freedom has its price. The very same loosening of gender-role definition, which allows increasing choice and individuality, may bring with it new ambiguities and conflicts. When role definition is rigid and conformity unanimous, everyone knows what to expect from the other and what the other expects. Although that may sound unexciting, it certainly simplifies a relationship, especially in its early stages. On the other hand, the greater

Some adolescents find traditional gender roles comfortable; others want more choices that fit their interests and abilities better. These young women, for instance, have overcome gender stereotyping to join a hockey team.

freedom and flexibility in the social definition of roles, the more that is left to be decided by the individual or negotiated in the heat of a relationship.

Thomas Alfieri and Diane Ruble, both at New York University, and E. Tory Higgins, at Columbia University, (1996) point out that as adolescents begin to integrate sexuality into their identities, one could expect either an increase or a decrease in the flexibility with which they approach gender stereotypes. On the one hand, a decrease in flexibility might occur as they experience the cultural constraints of gender-role expectations at a time when a heightened concern about their sexuality could polarize their attitudes. On the other hand, they are also in a better position to realistically evaluate these gender norms, due to continued intellectual development, making it possible to more flexibly adapt cultural roles to their own needs. Of course, none of these changes occur in a vacuum, and the real life contexts in which adolescents work out their sexuality must also be considered. One of these contexts is the transition in school settings that brings younger adolescents in daily contact with older ones, the transition that occurs as they move into junior high or high school.

Alfieri, Ruble, and Higgins asked fourth- through ninth-graders to indicate whether each of a number of gender-stereotypic adjectives was associated with males, females, or both. A tally of "both" responses was used as their measure of flexibility in gender stereotypes. Additionally, some of the teenagers they studied made the transition to junior high in the seventh

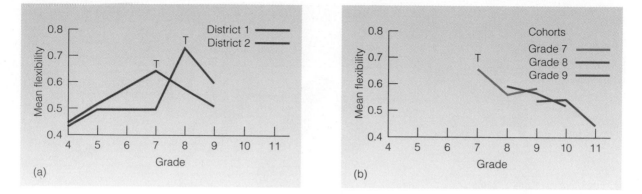

FIGURE 9.1   Gender-Role Flexibility by Grade. *(a) Increases in mean flexibility in gender roles by grade for adolescents entering junior high in the seventh grade (D1) and the eighth grade (D2). T indicates point of entry into junior high. (b) Decreases in mean flexibility in gender roles by grade for three cohort groups of adolescents.* Source: Adapted from T. Alfieri, D. N. Ruble, & E. T. Higgins. (1996). Gender stereotypes during adolescence: Developmental changes and the transition to junior high school. *Developmental Psychology, 32,* 1129–1137.

grade and some in the eighth grade. As can be seen in Figure 9.1, flexibility increases up through the first year of junior high, whether this occurred in the seventh grade or the eighth, but, as these cohort samples were followed over the next two years, flexibility could be seen to dramatically decrease.

Why might gender roles be more flexible early in adolescence than later? These investigators remind us that, as early adolescents enter junior high, their status changes from that of being the oldest and wisest to that of being the youngest and most ignorant. Furthermore, their older schoolmates present them with a broader range of gendered behaviors than they have previously encountered. Faced with new challenges to what they have held to be true, it makes sense for early adolescents to put their beliefs on hold as they survey their new surroundings in order to learn more about gender. Decreases in flexibility are to be expected as they consolidate new beliefs and attitudes, in the face of increasing pressures to adopt more adult gender roles. The irony to these developments is that adolescents' initial flexibility is prompted by entering an environment in which the individuals who populate it hold relatively *in*flexible beliefs about gender.

CONSTRUCTING A SEXUAL IDENTITY

Simone Buzwell and Doreen Rosenthal (1996), at La Trobe University in Australia, note that although sexuality is one of the domains that contribute to adolescents' developing identity, most research on sexuality has not examined its identity implications, but has focused instead on relatively narrow aspects of adolescents' behavior, such as their attitudes regarding sexual practices or condom use. But how do adolescents think of themselves as sexual beings? That is, how do they conceptualize their *sexual selves*? And how does this sense of themselves then relate to their sexual behavior?

TABLE 9.1   Dimensions of the Sexual Self

SEXUAL SELF-ESTEEM: PERCEPTION OF ONE'S WORTH AS A SEXUAL BEING

Feelings about one's sexual activity: "I feel good about my sexual behavior."

Perceptions of one's sexual appeal: "I am confident that males/females find me sexually attractive."

Feelings concerning one's sexual adequacy: "I don't know how to behave with a sexual partner."

Contentment with one's body: "I have a poorly developed body."

SEXUAL SELF-EFFICACY: CONFIDENCE IN ONE'S MASTERY CONCERNING SEXUAL ACTIVITIES

Ability to say no to unwanted sex: "I am confident that I could tell my partner that I do not want to have sex."

Ability to achieve sexual satisfaction: "I am confident that I could ask my partner to provide the type and amount of sexual stimulation I require."

Ability to purchase and use condoms: "I am confident that I could put a condom on an erect penis."

SEXUAL SELF-IMAGE: PERCEPTION OF ONE'S SEXUALITY AND BELIEFS ABOUT ONE'S SEXUAL NEEDS

Perception of arousal: "I have very strong sexual desires."

Perception of openness to sexual experimentation: "I would like to experiment when it comes to sex."

Anxiety in sexual situations: "I would find it hard to relax while having sex."

Commitment to a single sexual partner: "There needs to be commitment before I have sex with someone."

Source: Adapted from S. Buzwell & D. Rosenthal. (1996). Constructing a sexual self: Adolescents' sexual self-perceptions and sexual risk-taking. *Journal of Research on Adolescence, 6,* 489–513.

Buzwell and Rosenthal distinguish several aspects of the sexual self, each of which is thought to contribute to the ways in which adolescents construct a sense of themselves as sexual beings. The constructive perspective, recall, assumes that we actively put together the events to which we respond, and in the process give meaning to experience. This activity of imposing an order on, and thereby gaining a sense of, our world is not limited to what we take to be external to us, but applies equally to our perception of ourselves. With respect to the sexual self, adolescents are likely to construct self-perceptions along at least three dimensions: their perception of their worth as sexual beings (*sexual self-esteem*), the control they perceive themselves to have over their sexual experiences (*sexual self-efficacy*), and their beliefs about their sexual needs (*sexual self image*). These dimensions are presented in Table 9.1.

Working with tenth- through twelfth-graders, these investigators identified five sexual styles, or approaches taken by adolescents in the construction of their sexual selves. Each of these styles represents a different combination of these dimensions of the sexual self. *Sexually naive* adolescents had little confidence in their sexual attractiveness and, with the exception of being able to say no to unwanted sex, felt themselves to have little control over a sexual situation. Perhaps not surprisingly, sexual situations occasioned more anxiety than desire and were attractive only in the context of a committed relationship. These adolescents were the youngest in the sample, and most of them were girls; most also were virgins. A second group of adolescents, the *sexually unassured,* also had low self-esteem and little sense of control in sexual encounters, but were somewhat more interested in exploring their sexuality. They, too, were anxious in sexual situations and most were young. Most of these tended to be boys, and, as with the first group, most were sexually inexperienced. A third group, the *sexually competent,* were confident of themselves, both in terms of their sexual appeal and in their ability to control a sexual situation. These adolescents were less anxious and more interested in exploring their sexuality, though they did so with moderate levels of relationship commitment. The adolescents in this group, made up of both girls and boys, were for the most part in the twelfth grade, and most were sexually experienced.

Adolescents in the two remaining groups were highly confident of their sexual attractiveness and of their ability to take charge of their sexual encounters. The *sexually adventurous* were distinguished by high levels of sexual arousal and interest in sexual exploration, in combination with little anxiety and little relationship commitment. Most of these adolescents were older and were sexually experienced, and a majority were boys. The *sexually driven* were similar to the sexually adventurous with the exception of being unable to say no to sex, whether they considered the partner desirable or not. Most of these adolescents were sexually active boys.

Differences in sexual style are associated not only with sexual experience but with different patterns of sexual behavior. For instance, adolescents with greater confidence in their sexual attractiveness and in their control over sexual encounters take greater risks and have more sexual partners and more one-night stands. Buzwell and Rosenthal emphasize that sexual behavior is closely tied to adolescents' personal constructions of their sexuality. In other words, adolescents' beliefs about themselves as sexual beings, apart from demographic factors such as ethnicity or social class, are associated with differences in their behavior. In fact, these investigators observed striking differences in sexual behaviors among adolescents who, in other respects, had very similar backgrounds.

In general, sexual intimacy is associated with increasing commitment in a relationship. A survey of several hundred college students shows that the percentage of those who engaged in increasingly intimate sexual behaviors increased with the degree of affection and commitment in the relationship. Figure 9.2 shows these trends.

Individuals construct not only their own sexual selves but those of others as well. And in this respect, the blueprints for construction appear to be provided by one's culture, in the form of gender stereotypes. Pamela Regan, at California State University, Los Angeles, and Ellen Berscheid, at the University of Minnesota, (1995) examined some of the beliefs of older adolescents and young adults concerning the causes of sexual desire in others. They found surprising agreement among their respondents, irrespective of their sex. Most believed that thoughts of love or romance caused sexual desire in women, whereas for men, erotic factors were considered important, such as how sexy the woman looked. Often, simply being male was taken as reason in itself (see the Research Focus in Chapter 3, "Coding Descriptive Responses").

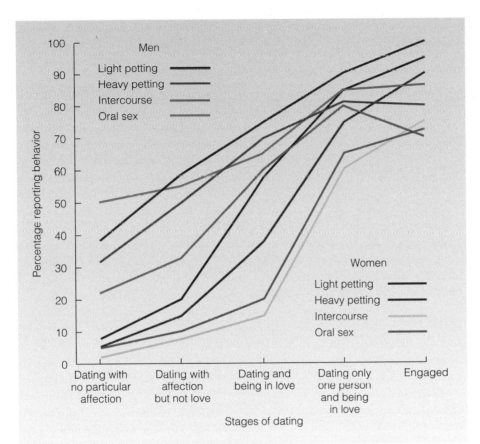

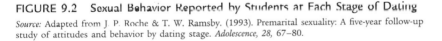

FIGURE 9.2   Sexual Behavior Reported by Students at Each Stage of Dating

Source: Adapted from J. P. Roche & T. W. Ramsby. (1993). Premarital sexuality: A five-year follow-up study of attitudes and behavior by dating stage. *Adolescence, 28,* 67–80.

SEXUALITY AND INTIMACY

Before most adolescents complete work on their sexual identity or their identity in general, they are confronted with the demands of sexual deci-sion making. The setting against which these decisions get played out is that of romance and dating. Catherine Sanderson and Nancy Cantor (1995), at Princeton University, emphasize that what adolescents bring to, and want out of, any dating situation is going to reflect the ways in which they have resolved their own identity issues. Recall, Erik Erikson (1950) believed that one must achieve a sense of one's self before one can share one's self, or be intimate, with another. Adolescents who have a clear sense of themselves as individuals should be more likely to look for emotional intimacy in their dating relationships than adolescents who are still working on identity is-sues. The latter, for whom establishing themselves as separate from others remains an issue, may use the context of dating to discover more about themselves.

Research Focus

Between-Subjects Design: Date Rape

It was well past midnight when Carol Ann slipped into the darkened house.

"Is that you, honey?" her mom called out in a sleepy voice.

"Yeah, Mom," she whispered hoarsely as she hurried to the bathroom.

Safe behind the closed door, she tore off her crumpled clothes, turned on the shower, and let the steaming water scald her skin pink.

She felt so dirty. She still didn't know how she had gotten away. She remembered struggling, punching, fighting back. Ugly bruises reddened on her arms and body as she choked back sobs of rage and humiliation. He had tried to rape her!

It had been their third date. He had been so polite and attentive each time before, never out of line. She hadn't been concerned when he suggested a party at a friend's house and turned down a dark road. What could she have said or done to make him think . . . ? And why did *she* feel so responsible? So terribly ashamed?

Carol Ann's experience is not that unusual. Judith Vicary, Linda Klingaman, and William Harkness (1995), looking at assault and date rape in high school females, found that 15% had experienced date rape over the 4-year period of the study; 60% of acquaintance rapes among college students occur in a dating situation (Koss, Dinero, Seibel, & Cox, 1988). What kind of male violates the consent of his date? Is it one whose sex drive is so strong that once aroused, he cannot stop himself? Or does date rape first start in the mind—with an attitude?

Rape myths are stereotyped perceptions of rapists and victims that minimize rape as a crime by shifting blame to the victim. As the term implies, they represent myth, not fact. Are males who endorse such statements more accepting of violations of consent on a date? Would they be more likely to answer yes than no? Several of these myths appear below:

- If a girl engages in necking or petting and she lets things get out of hand, it is her fault if her partner forces sex on her.

- Any healthy woman can successfully resist a rapist if she really wants to.

- In the majority of rapes, the victim is promiscuous or has a bad reputation.

- A woman who is stuck up and thinks she is too good to talk to guys on the street deserves to be taught a lesson.

- When women go around braless, or wearing short skirts and tight tops, they are just asking for trouble.

- Many women have an unconscious desire to be raped, and may then unconsciously set up a situation in which they are likely to be attacked.

- If a woman gets drunk at a party and has intercourse with a man she's just met there, she should be considered fair game to other males at the party who want to have sex with her too, whether she wants to or not.

These differences should extend to sexual activity as well. Adolescents with intimacy goals should place greater importance on emotional interdependence and open communication in a relationship, whereas those with identity goals should focus more on self-reliance and sexual pleasure. These investigators assessed ego identity status in late adolescents, along with a measure of their desire for commitment in a sexual relationship and found, as expected, that those with higher identity scores indicated less willingness to engage in sexual relations outside of a committed relationship and a greater desire for intimacy in their dating relationships. These relationships

Research Focus *(continued)*

Are beliefs such as these more likely to be held by certain people than by others? What other attitudes are they related to? Do they predict attitudes toward other intimate behaviors such as kissing, necking, petting, or even holding hands? Do attitudes about violations of consent depend on the level of assumed intimacy in the relationship? How could we find out?

Leslie Margolin, Melody Miller, and Patricia Moran (1989) found answers to these and similar questions by having male and female students read a description of a dating situation in which a male tried to kiss a female while they were at a movie together; when she refused, he kissed her anyway. Some of the students read that John and Mary were on a first date, others that they had been going together for 2 years, and others that they were married. Can you identify the independent variable in this experiment? If you said something like "level of intimacy," you were right. The other variable—gender—is a classification variable. (See Chapter 1, Research Focus, "An Experiment," and Chapter 4, Research Focus, "Correlational Research," for definitions of terms.)

These investigators used a *between-subjects design*. In this type of experiment, each subject experiences only one level of the independent variable. Remember that some of the students read that John and Mary were on a first date, others that they were going together, and still others that they were married. When subjects are randomly assigned to one and only one level of an independent variable, it is a between-subjects design. Why might this matter? Why might we care whether they experienced more than one experimental condition?

A major advantage to this type of design is

that investigators need not worry that subjects' responses will reflect the effects of another condition that may still be present. In other words, what if subjects assigned to the "first date" condition had just previously read of a similar incident involving a couple who was married? Could we safely assume that these subjects would be able to separate their reactions to each situation? In a between-subjects design, one need not worry about such matters. Also, because subjects can be assigned at random to conditions, investigators can be reasonably confident that groups do not initially differ until they impose different treatments. Both assumptions involve the issue of internal validity. (See Chapter 12, Research Focus, "Internal and External Validity.") To the extent that guarantees exist in experimental research, between-subject designs offer high guarantees of internal validity.

What did these investigators discover about attitudes toward violations of consent? They found that acceptance of rape myths *is* related to acceptance of violations of consent, regardless of level of intimacy. They also found that males are more accepting of rape myths than are females. Consequently, they were not surprised to find that males also were more supportive of John's right to violate Mary's consent to be kissed.

Sources: Adapted from M. P. Koss, T. E. Dinero, C. A. Seibel, & S. L. Cox. (1988). Stranger and acquaintance rape: Are there differences in the victim's experience? *Psychology of Women Quarterly, 12,* 1–24. L. Margolin, M. Miller, & P. B. Moran (1989). When a kiss is not just a kiss: Relating violations of consent in kissing to rape myth acceptance. *Sex Roles, 20,* 231–243. J. R. Vicary, L. R. Klingaman, & W. L. Harkness. (1995). Risk factors associated with date rape and sexual assault of adolescent girls. *Journal of Adolescence, 18,* 289–306.

---

tended to last longer as well. Conversely, those still working on their identity were likely to engage in casual dating and to have more sexual partners. (The Research Focus, "Between-Subjects Design," examines an alarming form of sexuality in a dating situation—that of date rape.)

Phrases such as "teenage romance" and "adolescent crush" suggest that adolescents' romantic feelings differ from those of adults. But do they? Roger Levesque (1993) asked 300 high school students who were currently involved in a dating relationship to indicate how satisfied they were with their relationship and what made it satisfying to them.

Box 9.2 Lee's Styles of Loving

Eros, or romantic love, is intense, romantic, and passionate. These lovers report being immediately attracted to each other, feeling a physical chemistry, and becoming quickly involved. They delight in the way the other looks, smells, and feels—for example, "I love the way his hair smells" or "I just can't take my eyes off her when she's in the room."

Storge, or companionate love, is based on friendship. These individuals slip into love, often surprising themselves at how their friendship has blossomed into romantic involvement—for example, "It is hard to say exactly when we went from being friends to being romantically involved." At the base of their relationship is a deep, caring friendship.

Ludus, or game-playing love, is characterized by charm and a lack of commitment. Love is a sport to be played with skill; commitment and intimacy only get in the way. Ludic lovers are often involved in several relationships at the same time—for example, "I have sometimes had to keep two of my girlfriends from finding out about each other."

Mania, or possessive love, is obsessive and insecure. These lovers have difficulty concentrating on anything other than the object of their love. Both insecure and jealous, they are consumed with self-doubt and fear of rejection, frequently reporting, "When she doesn't pay attention to me, I feel sick all over."

Pragma, or pragmatic love, is rational, patient, and practical. These individuals look for someone with a background similar to theirs, who will fit in with their family and future career plans, and make a good mate and parent—for example, "Before getting very involved with someone, I try to figure out what our children would be like, if we were to have any."

Agape, or selfless love, is long-suffering and nondemanding, always putting the needs of the other ahead of one's own—for example, "I can't be happy unless I put her happiness above my own."

Sources: J. A. Lee. (1973). *The colors of love.* Ontario, Canada: New Press; J. A. Lee. (1988). Love styles. In R. J. Sternberg & M. L. Barnes (Eds.), *The psychology of love.* New Haven, CT: Yale University Press.

Levesque found a surprising correspondence among adolescents and adults in what contributes to satisfaction. Factors that are important at any age, it seems, are passion, communication, commitment, emotional support, and togetherness (Ammons & Stinnett, 1980; Assh & Byers, 1990; Hendrick & Hendrick, 1991; Hendrick, Hendrick, & Adler, 1988).

Several surprising differences emerged as well. Unlike adults, adolescents' satisfaction with a relationship is not diminished when they experience trouble or conflict, such as upsets, hurt feelings, and jealousies. In fact, tolerance in these matters relates positively to satisfaction with the partner. Of far greater importance to adolescents than the absence of conflict for relationship satisfaction are positive feelings such as exhilaration, growth, tolerance, appreciation, and specialness. Table 9.2 gives examples of each of these components.

TABLE 9.2   Components of Satisfying Love Relationships in Adolescents

Love Components	Description
Exhilaration	Feeling "crazy" about each other, the happy, giddy side of the relationship: "He makes me come alive."
Growth	Encouraging independence, growth, self-actualization, interest in partner and each other as individuals and as a couple: "I am pleased when she pursues her own interests."
Toleration	Willingness to change for partner, to compromise and to accept faults of partner and relationship: "I am patient with him."
Appreciation	Respect, approval, admiration: "I think he has good ideas."
Specialness	Uniqueness, idealism, belief in relationship's differentness: "I feel that she was meant for me."

Source: Adapted from R. J. R. Levesque. (1993). The romantic experience of adolescents in satisfying love relationships. *Journal of Youth and Adolescence, 22,* 219–251.

Attempts to discover what is important to adolescents, or adults, in a loving relationship have been complicated by the fact that not everyone defines love in the same way. For some it is a wild, passionate roller coaster ride. For others it is a quiet, companionate walk together. And for still others, love is a game, often involving more than two players (Hendrick & Hendrick, 1986; Lee, 1988). John Lee (1973, 1988) has described six styles of loving. These styles appear in Box 9.2.

SEXUAL ORIENTATION

One of the central tasks of adolescence involves achieving a personal identity, and a major component of this is one's sexual identity. Although children label themselves as being one sex or the other from the earliest years on, sexual orientation does not become firmly established until adolescence. It is then that sexual experimentation embellishes and confirms, or disconfirms, these earlier labels. Late adolescence brings the additional task of infusing relationships with emotional intimacy.

Sexual orientation refers to the attraction individuals feel for members of the same or the other sex. Those with a **heterosexual** orientation are attracted to people of the opposite sex, those with a **homosexual** orientation are attracted to members of their own sex, and **bisexually** oriented people are attracted to individuals of both sexes. *Gay* and *straight* are terms commonly used to refer to people who are homosexuals and heterosexuals, respectively; *lesbian* is a term used to refer to homosexual women.

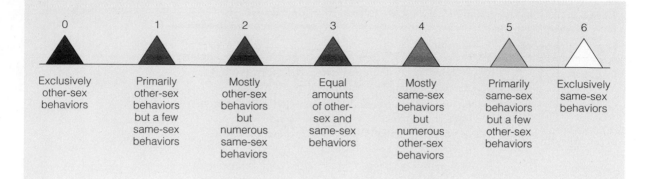

FIGURE 9.3
Kinsey's Continuum
of Sexual Orientation

Source: Adapted from A. C.
Kinsey, W. B. Pomeroy, &
C. E. Martin. (1948). *Sexual
behavior in the human male.*
Philadelphia: Saunders.

How many adolescents share each of these orientations? Simple answers are not forthcoming, for a number of reasons. Rather than discrete categories into which individuals neatly sort themselves, sexual orientations are more like segments along a continuum, as shown in Figure 9.3. It is not always clear where one orientation leaves off and another begins. For instance, surveys reveal that 13% of all females have had sex with another female to the point of orgasm, yet only 1% to 3% of females consider themselves to be lesbian. Similarly, from 20% to 37% of adolescent and adult males have had sex to the point of orgasm with another male, yet only 4% are exclusively gay throughout their lives (Kinsey, Pomeroy, & Martin, 1948; Kinsey, Pomeroy, Martin, & Gebhard, 1953; Strong & DeVault, 1997).

This last statistic introduces yet another factor that contributes to the fuzziness of these categories. Sexual attraction can change during one's lifetime. For instance, Alfred Kinsey found that 10% of the males he interviewed were predominantly homosexual for three or more years; however, only 4% remained so throughout their lifetime.

An additional complication is that sexuality cannot be reduced simply to behavior; it includes attraction and desire as well. One could, in other words, be celibate throughout one's life and still be straight or gay (Strong & DeVault, 1997).

Homosexuality

How is one to think of homosexuality, if having homosexual experiences does not necessarily mean that one is homosexual? In general, homosexuals are individuals who, for some extended period of their lives, are more attracted sexually to individuals of their own sex than to those of the opposite sex. This definition underscores several points. first, sexual attraction is as important in defining sexual orientation as actual behavior; and second, an isolated sexual experience does not mean one is homosexual: Sexual orientation reflects a prolonged sexual preference. Furthermore, many individuals are neither exclusively heterosexual nor exclusively homosexual.

Establishing a sexual identity is difficult for most adolescents, but especially so for those who wonder whether or not they're homosexual. Being different is never easy, especially when it places one in a group that is viewed negatively by many segments of society. Fear and denial can prolong the

Too few gay adolescents are like the young men and women in this group. Most have no one with whom to share concerns and questions about their developing sexual identity, and they must cope by themselves with the social prejudices against homosexuality.

process of establishing a sexual identity. Angela Pattatucci and Dean Hamer (1995), at the National Cancer Institute, however, found that many lesbians were aware of their attraction to other females very early in adolescence, and that bisexual females were also, though on the average a bit later.

For adolescents of either sex, awareness that they are gay often develops only gradually. Many gay adolescents report having felt vaguely different during childhood, but without a sense of what that might mean. These feelings assume sexual significance with puberty and homosexual attractions. Even then, a period of confusion may follow. Even those who are predominantly attracted to people of their own sex may alternately consider themselves to be straight, gay, or bisexual. In part, the confusion may reflect the fact that many report being attracted to individuals of both sexes from early adolescence on (Pattatucci & Hamer, 1995). One study of 75 gay men found that most had noticed being attracted to someone of the same sex by about the age of 10, but had not necessarily considered themselves homosexual. Some did not do so until their twenties or even their thirties (Hamer, Hu, Magnuson, Hu, & Pattatucci, 1993). Recall, this confusion may also reflect the difficulty gay teenagers experience in identifying themselves as members of a group considered to be deviant by society (Strong & De-Vault, 1997).

Research Focus

Matched-Subjects Design: Sexual Orientation of Children Raised in Lesbian Families

How much, if at all, do parents influence the sexual orientation of their children? How likely is it that a child's sexual orientation will be affected by observing the gender roles of parents? Are sexual preferences learned through exposure to parents who model various behaviors? Are they acquired through a process of identifying with the same-sex parent? Or, do sexual preferences reflect, in large measure, a roll of the genetic dice?

Recent research with gay men with either monozygotic or dizygotic twin brothers (Bailey & Pillard, 1991), and with lesbian women with twin sisters (Bailey, Pillard, Neale, & Agyei, 1993), finds that monozygotic twins are significantly more likely to also be homosexual themselves than are dizygotic twins. This finding indicates a genetic link to homosexuality in that monozygotic twins have identical genetic makeups, developing as they do from the same fertilized ovum, whereas dizygotic twins develop from two separate ova and are no more similar genetically than any other two siblings. One's genetic makeup, then, can be argued to significantly influence one's sexual orientation.

Social-cognitive theory, on the other hand, argues that modeling of gender roles by the same-sex parent, along with the parents' differential reinforcement of appropriately masculine or feminine behaviors, are important determinants of gender development. Accordingly, family environment, as provided by the sexual orientation of parents, should be an important influence on the sexual orientation of children.

Previous research on the development of sexual orientation in children has been limited to heterosexual families. Critical comparisons of the sexual preferences of adult children raised by homosexual versus heterosexual parents have been lacking. Susan Golombok and Fiona Tasker (1996) corrected this deficiency by investigating the sexual preferences of children raised in lesbian families and by comparing these with the preferences of children raised in heterosexual families.

Golombok and Tasker contacted 27 lesbian mothers and 27 heterosexual mothers when their children were approximately 9 years old. The children were contacted again 14 years later, when they were approximately 23 years old, to determine the influence of being raised by a lesbian mother. Simple? Yes, as long as one controls for other variables that might relate to sexual orientation, such as the presence or absence of a father in the home, mother's age, and social class. Golombok and Tasker made sure that children in each of the two types of families were raised in homes in which the fathers were absent, the homes differing only in the sexual orientation of their mothers. Thus the lesbian mothers were *matched* with control mothers who differed only in sexual orientation. (As one might expect, most of these mothers had at least one relationship [heterosexual] during the time the children were living at home, just as most of the lesbian mothers had at least one lesbian relationship.)

To match subjects along some variable, one first needs to rank the subjects in each sample

Gay, lesbian, and bisexual adolescents face a number of additional problems. Academic performance frequently deteriorates, and for many substance abuse is a problem. Significantly more gay than straight adolescents attempt suicide, some studies reporting close to one-third of gay males having done so (Coleman & Ramefedi, 1989). Tracie Hammelman (1993) examined suicidal tendencies in gay and lesbian youth and found almost half had thought about suicide at one point or another, and a third had actually made a suicide attempt, most during adolescence, and most mentioned sexual orientation as a reason contributing to the attempt. Not all research paints such a bleak picture, however. Willie Edwards (1996), at East Texas State University, found the late adolescent gay males whom he studied to be well adjusted

Research Focus (*continued*)

according to the matching variable—say, social class—and then draw pairs of subjects from the two samples that are from the same or approximately the same income bracket. Using this procedure, one can be sure that the two groups will be equivalent regarding the matching variable. If social class is related to sexual orientation, it will be equated for the two groups. Any differences between groups in sexual orientation cannot be due to social class.

Matching carries an additional advantage: It reduces the amount of unexplained variability in the groups. This variability is termed *random error.* By reducing random error, one can more easily see the effects of the variable of interest. Another way of describing this advantage is to say that matched designs are more *sensitive* than those in which each subject is randomly assigned. The sensitivity of a design refers to its ability to detect a difference due to the treatment variable if such a difference exists.

Matching sounds like such a good idea that one has to wonder why investigators don't use this method all the time. Yet, like other procedures, it has its disadvantages. The most serious drawback is a statistical one concerning the degrees of freedom used when determining the significance of the tests that evaluate the research outcome.

In designs that do not match subjects, the degrees of freedom reflect the number of *subjects;* in matched-subjects designs, they reflect the number of *pairs.* Matching cuts the degrees of freedom in half. This means that one must obtain a larger difference for it to reach statistical significance. The irony to this disadvantage is that matching is most advantageous when one is

using few subjects, because it increases the sensitivity of the design. But this is the very condition under which one can least afford to lose degrees of freedom. Before one matches, one needs to be sure that the matching variable is highly correlated with the measure one is using. Only in this way will it effectively reduce unexplained variability and pay for the loss in degrees of freedom.

Matched designs are slightly more *time-consuming* to conduct than are those involving simple random assignment of subjects. One must first administer the matching variable, then rank subjects before they can be assigned to conditions. Extra *expense* may also be involved. A more serious disadvantage than either of these is the threat to *external validity* that occurs when subjects who can't be matched must be discarded. Any loss of subjects can affect the representativeness of the sample and the ability to generalize to the population from which it was drawn.

What does Golombok and Tasker's matched design tell us about the influence of lesbian mothers on the sexual orientation of their children? Although children from lesbian families more frequently explored same-sex relationships, by far most of the children of lesbian families identified themselves as heterosexual.

Sources: J. M. Bailey & R. C. Pillard. (1991). A genetic study of male sexual orientation. *Archives of General Psychiatry, 48,* 1089–1096; J. M. Bailey, R. C. Pillard, M. C. Neale, & Y. Agyei. (1993). Heritable factors influence sexual orientation in women. *Archives of General Psychiatry, 50,* 217–223; S. Golombok & F. Tasker. (1996). Do parents influence the sexual orientation of their children? Findings from a longitudinal study of lesbian families. *Developmental Psychology, 32,* 3–11.

and comfortable with their sexual orientation. Even so, most had not revealed their sexual orientation to others. Similarly, Heidi Wayment and Anne Peplau (1995) found that, at least among women, psychological well-being was related to support from their social network, and that lesbians and heterosexuals reported similar amounts of support. Additionally, being in a relationship, and not their sexual orientation, predicted their sense of well-being.

Biological and Psychosocial Bases of Sexual Attraction

What determines one's sexual orientation? Are we born straight or gay? Can sexual attraction be traced to formative experiences, such as the type of family one is raised in or a first sexual encounter? We will look first at recent biological explanations and then at psychological ones.

Biological Factors J. Michael Bailey and Richard Pillard (1991) interviewed gay and bisexual men with twin brothers. Twins can be of two types. Identical (monozygotic) twins share the same genetic makeup, having developed from the same cell (zygote). Fraternal (dizygotic) twins develop from separate cells and are no more similar genetically than other siblings. If there is a genetic contribution to sexual orientation, more identical twin brothers should both be homosexual than fraternal twin brothers. This study also included an additional, third group of gay and bisexual men; these men had adoptive brothers, that is, with no shared genetic background. It was expected that the co-incidence of homosexuality would be lowest in this third group.

Bailey and Pillard found that over 50% of the identical twins whose brothers were homosexual were themselves homosexual, whereas only 22% of the fraternal twin brothers were, and even fewer, 11%, of the adoptive brothers.

A similar study of sexual orientation in females revealed comparable findings. Forty-eight percent of monozygotic twin sisters of gay women were also lesbian, in contrast to only 16% of dizygotic twin sisters, and 6% of adoptive sisters (Bailey, Pillard, Neale, & Agvei, 1993). Similarly, Pattatucci and Hamer (1995) found higher rates of nonheterosexuality among female relatives of lesbians. Their data, however, did not allow them to distinguish the contribution of genetic influences from those that could arise simply from being influenced by similarities in their environments. However, Susan Golombok and Fiona Tasker (1996), at City University, London, found that, by far, the majority of children brought up in lesbian families nonetheless considered themselves to be heterosexual and did not differ in sexual orientation from children brought up by heterosexual single mothers, where there also was no father in the home.

Overall, these findings strongly suggest a genetic component to sexual orientation. Additional research suggests that the path of genetic transmission, at least for males, is likely to be through the mother. A higher percentage of maternal uncles of gay men, and cousins who are sons of maternal aunts, are gay than the base rate of homosexuals in the population. Higher rates are not found for paternally related males. Furthermore, a particular site along the X chromosome of the 23rd pair of chromosomes (the pair determining one's sex) has been implicated through research on genetic mapping. The X chromosome is received from the mother (Hamer et al., 1993).

Such research should not be taken to mean that all genetic contributions to sexual orientation will relate to the X chromosome or take any single form. It is likely, given the complexity of our genetic makeup, that many avenues of transmission are possible.

Nor is the precise means by which genes might influence sexual orientation known. One possibility is through the hormones that are present in differing amounts in males and females. However, studies of gay males and lesbians and of heterosexuals do not find expected differences in the levels of circulating hormones (Money, 1988).

Hormones might also affect prenatal brain development. One study found that a node of the hypothalamus, which is related to sexual behavior, is smaller in gay males than in heterosexual males (LeVay, 1991). However, because the gay males in this study had all died of AIDS, differences in hypothalamic size might have been due to the disease, or even to their behavior. Additionally, because the researcher analyzing the brain tissues was not blind to the sexual orientation of the subjects, this knowledge could have influenced the observations (see the Research Focus, "Bias and Blind Controls" in Chapter 3).

It is also possible that individuals may be genetically predisposed to homosexuality but nonetheless develop a heterosexual orientation because of the presence or absence of other contributing factors.

Psychological Factors Sexual orientation develops within a psychosocial environment. Freud assumed that children are initially bisexual and only gradually develop heterosexual interests. He traced the development of these interests to the child's resolution of the Oedipal or Electra complex in early childhood (see Chapter 2). Other theorists have suggested that homosexuality in males is due to a domineering, overprotective mother and a passive father (Bieber, 1962). However, one would expect such family influences to affect siblings, and the incidence of homosexuality among brothers of gay males is no higher than in the population at large, with the exception of twins, as discussed above. The Research Focus, "Matched-Subjects Design," on pages 390–391, describes a study of children in lesbian families, which again showed that children's sexual orientation is not determined by that of their parents.

Similarly, lesbianism has been traced to traumatic early sexual experiences that turned these women away from males as objects of sexual desire. However, estimates of the frequency of such experiences are considerably higher than the incidence of homosexuality among females (see Chapter 12).

The most immediate context in which sexual behavior can be studied is the very private world of the human sexual response. Like much else related to adolescent sexual functioning, our understanding has been late to develop, and myths and misconceptions consequently abound.

SEXUAL FUNCTIONING: FACT AND FICTION

The Sexual Response Cycle

Sputnik had orbited the earth and Neil Armstrong had one foot on the moon before scientists began to unravel the complexities of the human sexual response. In 1966, two scientists, William Masters and Virginia Johnson, published their signal research on sexual physiology. Like Alfred Kinsey before them, they braved a critical social climate—and took one step forward for humankind. Their study of sexual physiology differed from previous research in an important respect: They studied actual sexual encounters between men and women. Their research reflects over 10,000 sexual episodes between more than 300 men and 300 women under conditions of controlled observation.

Masters and Johnson's research revealed a sexual response cycle consisting of four phases: excitement, plateau, orgasm, and resolution. Two processes underlie the changes of each phase: vasocongestion and myotonia. *Vasocongestion* is an accumulation of blood in the vessels serving the erogenous zones (areas of the body that are particularly sensitive to sexual arousal), and *myotonia* is an increase in muscular tension. The tension is more like a building up of energy in the muscles rather than a state of feeling tense. At each phase of the cycle, striking similarities exist in the response of females and males.

Excitement   Vasocongestion is responsible for the first signs of *excitement,* or sexual arousal, in both males and females. In males it causes blood to pour into the spongy tissues in the shaft of the penis, making it erect. Masters, Johnson, and Kolodny (1988) note that because an erection is caused by an increase in fluid pressure, it is essentially a "hydraulic event." Vaginal lubrication, one of the first signs of sexual arousal in females, occurs when blood vessels in the pelvic area swell with blood, pressing fluids into the tissues surrounding the vagina (Lips, 1997). In both sexes, the nipples harden and muscular tension increases throughout the body (myotonia).

Plateau   Continued vasocongestion during the *plateau* phase causes the erection in males to become harder. Drops of lubricating fluid, secreted by the Cowper's glands, appear at the opening of the glans. Because this fluid frequently contains live sperm, withdrawal prior to ejaculation, a birth control practice common among teenagers, is not an effective means of preventing pregnancy. In females, continued vasocongestion causes the walls of the vagina to swell, creating an *orgasmic platform,* which constricts the size of the vagina, making penis size relatively unimportant for stimulation. Because females require more pelvic congestion than males to reach orgasm, the plateau stage lasts longer in females (Williams, 1983).

Orgasm   The sensations of *orgasm* result from rhythmic muscular contractions and discharge of tensions resulting from vasocongestion and myotonia. Orgasms can vary in intensity from one time to the next, depending on a host of factors, including mood, fatigue, and so on. Despite similarities in its physiological bases for both sexes, orgasm tends to be a more consistently uniform phenomenon in males than in females (Masters & Johnson, 1966). However, individuals of both sexes describe their experience of orgasm in similar ways. Box 9.3 presents some of these descriptions.

Resolution   In the *resolution* phase, following ejaculation, the penis becomes flaccid, and males experience a *refractory period,* lasting anywhere from several minutes to several hours, during which stimulation will not produce an erection. Resolution lasts much longer in females, because vasocongestion in the pelvic area dissipates slowly, and they can experience *multiple orgasms.*

Box 9.3   Descriptions of the Experience of Orgasm

Research finds that trained judges can't tell which written descriptions of orgasm are given by females and which by males. Can you? (See answers below.)

1. "Like a mild explosion, it left me warm and relaxed after a searing heat that started in my genitals and raced to my toes and head."

2. "Suddenly, after the tension built and built, I was soaring in the sky, going up, up, up, feeling the cool air rushing by. My insides were tingling and my skin was cool. My heart was racing in a good way, and breathing was a job."

3. "Throbbing is the best word to say what it is like. The throbbing starts as a faint vibration, then builds up in wave after wave where time seems to stand still."

4. "When I come it's either like an avalanche of pleasure, tumbling through me, or like a refreshing snack—momentarily satisfying, but then I'm ready for more."

5. "My orgasms feel like pulsating bursts of energy starting in my pelvic area and then engulfing my whole body. Sometimes I feel like I'm in freefall, and sometimes I feel like my body's an entire orchestra playing a grand crescendo."

6. "An orgasm feels like a dive, magnified many times over. First I feel my muscles tensing, then there's a leap into a cool lake, a sense of suspension and holding my breath, and then my whole body feels relaxed and tingling."

7. "Exhilaration is the best word I can find. I feel all pumped up and then, instead of exploding, I am one big wave of happiness and whooshing feeling."

8. "Some orgasms feel incredibly intense and earth-shattering, but other times orgasms feel like small, compact, self-contained moments."

9. "I feel like a cork popping out of a champagne bottle."

10. "There is a warm rush from my toes to my head, with a strong, pulsing rhythm. Then everything settles down like a pink sunset."

1. M   2. F   3. M   4. F   5. F   6. M   7. F   8. M   9. F   10. M

Source: Adapted from W. H. Masters, V. E. Johnson, & R. C. Kolodny. (1988). *Human sexuality* (3rd ed.). Glenview, IL: Scott, Foresman.

Myths and Misconceptions

Despite today's relatively open attitudes toward sex, considerable ignorance and myth surround sexual functioning. Interviews with adolescents found that many are surprisingly ignorant about even the basics. A 16-year-old girl remarked, "I wasn't ready for it being so *real*. Because in movies they don't get sweaty and—you know—all this awkward stuff. Like maybe not being that easy to get it in, him not finding quite the right place, it kind of hurting" (Aitken & Chaplin, 1990, p. 24). Most of the boys who had intercourse said they had trouble even finding the vagina. One boy commented, "I wish

Interviews with adolescents reveal that many are surprisingly ignorant about even the basics of sexual intimacy and its consequences.

sex came with instructions. All the time I was thinking about doing it, I was worrying, *How* do you do it?" (p. 24). A surprising number of boys feared there was something wrong with them because they did not know the way a male's body functions sexually. A few, for example, thought that they suffered from impotence when they lost an erection, and many, because they did not know how long it normally takes a male to reach orgasm, believed they were premature ejaculators (Aitken & Chaplin, 1990).

Ignorance concerning sexual functioning is by no means limited to adolescents. Many of their parents are surprisingly uninformed, too. Countless adults cannot accurately name the parts of their own genitals or those of the opposite sex. Masters, Johnson, and Kolodny (1988) noted that "While we cannot imagine a person unable to distinguish between eyes, nose, mouth, and chin, many men and women have no idea of the locations of the female urethra, clitoris, or hymen" (p. 53).

Bigger Is Better   For adolescent boys, concern about the size of their penis is at the top of the list. Many boys don't know what size is normal and are sure theirs is too small. This concern is fueled by large variations from one boy to the next in the timing and rate of growth. Comparisons are inevitable, and as Masters, Johnson, and Kolodny (1988) point out, a boy's penis almost always looks shorter to him than someone else's simply because his visual perspective (in looking down) foreshortens it.

Size assumes added importance as a result of the common misconception that penis size is related to sexual adequacy—which is simply untrue. The orgasmic platform corrects for differences in circumference of the penis, and because there are few nerve endings in the upper vagina, length is unimportant. Though one penis can differ noticeably from another in size when flaccid, this difference all but disappears when erect. Masters, Johnson, and Kolodny (1988), in fact, refer to an erection as "the great equalizer."

A common concern among adolescent girls concerns their breasts. Many notice that one breast is slightly larger than the other. Girls may wonder if it's normal for one breast to be smaller than the other (it is), and what they can do about it (nothing short of cosmetic surgery). Boys face a similar concern when they notice that one testicle is higher than the other, which is also quite normal.

Capacity for Sexual Pleasure   Perhaps the most pervasive cultural myth among adolescents is that males experience more sexual pleasure than females. The fact that females take longer to reach orgasm may contribute to this myth. Once they reach orgasm, however, their capacity to achieve additional orgasms exceeds that of males. Similarities in the phases of the sexual response cycle in either sex, and in the way individuals describe orgasm, suggest similarities in the pleasure each experiences.

Need for Orgasm   A related misconception is that only males need to reach orgasm. Considerable discomfort can result from reaching the plateau phase and not experiencing orgasm. Both males and females experience this discomfort, the result of blood vessels remaining engorged in the pelvic and genital areas. This vasocongestion underlies orgasm in both sexes, and failure to release the accumulated blood and the muscular tension produces discomfort in both males and females.

Intercourse During Menstruation   Numerous cultural taboos exist regarding intercourse during menstruation (Delaney, Lupton, & Toth, 1977). Some cultures even isolate menstruating females, fearing that they might contaminate the things with which they come into contact, whether these be people, animals, food, or plants. What dangers might befall a male? Misconceptions range from fears of infection to impotence and loss of virility. There is no factual basis for any of these fears (Delaney, Lupton, & Toth, 1977).

Current attitudes concerning menstruation are less negative than in previous generations, but reference to it as "the curse" is still common. Cultural messages—for example, advertisements and commercials for pads and tampons—communicate in subtle ways that menstruation is an untidy and unsanitary condition, to be cleaned up by using "sanitary napkins." Similarly, advertisements for tampons communicate that if a female handles things properly, she can go about her business almost as if she were "normal" (Lips, 1997; Masters, Johnson, & Kolodny, 1988).

Even though attitudes toward menstruation are changing, negative attitudes are likely to persist as long as we have a sexually polarized society in which the attributes of one sex are valued more than those of the other. Gloria Steinem once observed that if men menstruated, cultural views of the menstrual cycle almost surely would be different; in all probability we would see the cycle as a psychobiological advantage. Imagine thinking of the menstrual cycle in terms of peaks of heightened energy and productivity that rise from a baseline of normal competence and energy.

Intact Hymen and Virginity Another common misconception is that the presence of a hymen indicates virginity. The hymen is actually likely to tear in most girls during childhood with active play or curious exploration (see Chapter 3). Some girls are not even born with a hymen, and in others intercourse only stretches the hymen and does not rupture it (Masters, Johnson, & Kolodny, 1988).

TEENAGE PREGNANCIES AND PARENTING

Teenage Mothers

More than half the teenagers who become pregnant choose childbirth over abortion, and more than 95% keep their infants. What do we know of these mothers?

Kristen Sommer and her associates (1993) compared pregnant adolescents and adults on a number of measures assessing their readiness for parenting. They found that, in general, teenage mothers were less ready for parenting and experienced more stress in this role than adults. Adult mothers, for instance, knew more about infants, such as when a baby is able to hold a bottle or say its first words, and were more responsive and adaptive to their infants' needs. Katherine Nitz (1995), at the University of Maryland School of Medicine, and her associates, also found adolescent mothers to be stressed. When these young mothers were asked who they turned to for support, advice, and help when needed, most mentioned their own mothers. Friends were also important sources of support.

A study of unmarried teenagers who agreed to interviews 1, 3, 5, and 17 years after giving birth provides important longitudinal information about adolescent mothers who choose to keep their infants. Furstenberg, Brooks-Gunn, and Morgan (1987) found that a majority of the teenage mothers they interviewed finished high school and were regularly employed; though periodically on welfare, most supported themselves and their families. Most also had families no larger than those of their classmates who had children later. The vast majority coped.

Teenage Fathers

There are fewer teenage fathers than teenage mothers because nearly half of the fathers involved in teenage pregnancies are at least 20 years old (Sonenstein, 1986).

What do we know of the fathers who are teenagers? Contrary to stereotypes casting them as exploitive or uncaring, most remain psychologically involved with the mother through the pregnancy and for some time following the child's birth (Strong & DeVault, 1997). Most teenage fathers have less education and lower incomes than do those who postpone parenting, and many find it difficult to provide support for the mother and infant. Many are themselves children of unmarried mothers and grew up in homes without a father present. But most teenage fathers indicate a willingness to learn to be fathers (Strong & DeVault, 1997).

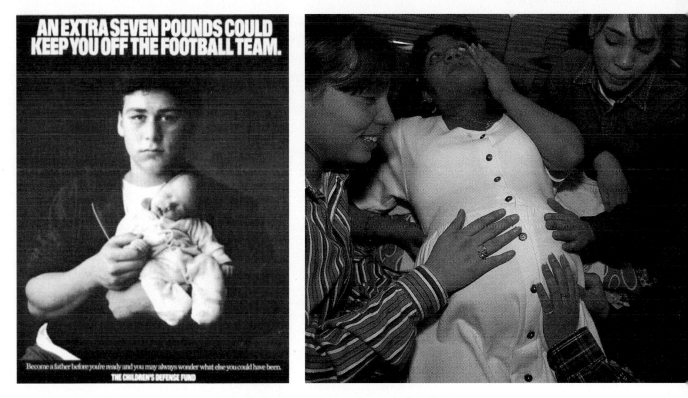

Teenage pregnancies are due partly to a lack of information and partly to a denial of personal responsibility. Adolescents need help in learning how to make decisions about their sexual behaviors, especially those that could alter the course of their lives.

Presently, there are few programs to help teenage fathers learn to be better fathers. Those in existence stress the importance of finishing high school and getting a job. Many provide job training as well as parenting classes, enabling teenage fathers to provide financial as well as emotional support.

Adolescents and Abortion

Approximately 42% of teenage pregnancies end in abortion (Strong & DeVault, 1997). What conditions affect an adolescent's decision to abort a pregnancy? Adolescents who say they intended to become pregnant are more likely to have the baby. The issue of intentionality, however, is not a simple one to evaluate. Girls review their intentions only when they discover they are pregnant; for most, conception was unintended, and carrying the baby to term is the decision that reflects intending to be pregnant.

Reasoning such as this makes it sound as if adolescents use abortion as an alternative to contraception. Yet studies following teenagers who have aborted a pregnancy suggest that this is not the case. Adolescents who have aborted one pregnancy are even less likely than those who give birth to have a second pregnancy within two years of the first. Repeat abortions are relatively infrequent among teenagers. Approximately 12% of 15- to 17-year-olds who have had an abortion have another, compared to 22% of 18- to 19-year-olds (Hayes, 1987).

Box 9.4 Unintended Pregnancy: Personal Decisions About Abortion, Adoption, and Keeping the Baby

Many factors influence an adolescent girl's decision when faced with an unintended pregnancy. Family, friends, and personal beliefs are all important, as the following examples illustrate.

STEPHANIE

Stephanie hadn't been careless—the contraceptive device she'd used had failed. "I want a baby in what I think is a healthy circumstance," she said. "I don't have a husband. I don't have a man who really wants this child. Russ will see me through an abortion, but he's walking out of my life when it's over."

After the abortion: "I felt abandoned. I wanted a lot of hugging and to know that somebody cared." The father had offered to accompany her to the clinic where she had her abortion and to spend the weekend with her, but he didn't behave lovingly. "Russ couldn't deal with the experience and was quite cruel, really. I suppose he was frightened, but that didn't make it any easier for me. He stayed with me, but when I wanted to be held, he said, "Don't hug me; we're just friends." Considering I'd just gone through an abortion in order not to have this person's child, I thought that was a ludicrous thing to say."

LAURA

After eight pregnancy tests and eight personal denials, Laura's father confronted her by asking if she was pregnant. She answered, scared, "Yes."

"My father gave me an ultimatum: to have an abortion or leave the family. I chose to leave.

"Knowing I had to leave the house I went to the crisis pregnancy center. They took care of me.

"I am currently at home again with my 3-month-old boy. I am now engaged and looking forward to having my own family soon."

Family background variables and peer influences also affect the decision to abort or to carry a baby to term. Teenagers from middle-class homes are more likely to abort an unintended pregnancy than those living at the poverty level. White adolescents are also more likely to terminate a pregnancy than are Black adolescents (Centers for Disease Control, 1997). These relationships are difficult to interpret because, as noted earlier, race and socioeconomic status are clearly related. Personal variables such as religious beliefs and parents' attitudes also play a role in a teenage girl's decision to carry a baby to term or to abort. Girls who have strong religious beliefs are less likely to abort a pregnancy, as are those whose parents disapprove of abortion. Peers influence an adolescent's decision, too. Girls with friends who are single teenage parents are more likely to carry the pregnancy to term; those whose friends view abortion positively (and are perhaps less likely themselves to be single parents) are more likely to terminate a pregnancy (Hayes, 1987). Box 9.4 gives a close-up view of decision making prompted by unintended pregnancy.

Box 9.4   (*continued*)

SUSAN

Susan was a freshman in college and was very caught up in her new academic and social activities. Bill (another student) and she had been dating for about three months when one evening she decided to "take a chance" because she had just finished her menstrual period. When her next period was two weeks overdue, she had a pregnancy test. It was positive.

When Bill first learned of the pregnancy, he became distant, but he did agree to help pay for an abortion. Soon, however, he withdrew completely and had no further contact with Susan. The hardest time for Susan was before the abortion when she found herself crying frequently. She talked a lot with her close girlfriends, who comforted her. After the abortion, she felt that she had made the best decision, but she occasionally wondered how she would feel in future years.

KAREN

Karen chose not to have an abortion, but to give her baby up for adoption. When the Bakerfields arrived at the hospital and walked down the corridor, Karen held out her baby to them. The baby was wearing a T-shirt with the inscription, "I love my Mommy and Daddy!" Then the Bakerfields and Karen prayed together, and Karen formally relinquished her child to their care.

"I was so happy to give life to someone else to start a family," Karen said. "That excited me. It still excites me." Karen has told her story to a number of high school audiences, and generally they are puzzled about her decision. What Karen tries to communicate is that love motivated her.

"I never had a father, really, growing up," she said. "By giving my baby to the Bakerfields, I gave her a father. She needed that."

Source: Adapted from P. M. Insel & W. T. Roth. 1998. *Core concepts in health* (8th ed.). Mountain View, CA: Mayfield.

Complicating decisions about abortion for many teenagers is the fact that many do not realize at first that they are pregnant. Young adolescents especially are likely to have irregular menstrual cycles, making it difficult to determine when they have missed a period. Still others may attempt to deny they are pregnant until it is no longer possible to hide from the truth. The difficulties adolescents experience in finding out where to go for health services and arranging transportation compound these problems. As a result, teenagers are less likely to have an abortion in early pregnancy than are women who are young adults (Hayes, 1987).

The issues surrounding abortion are magnified as the result of delay, because the timing of an abortion has both health and moral consequences. Early abortions carry less risk to the adolescent. Similarly, issues concerning the taking of a life are less clear-cut before the fetus becomes viable, or even earlier in the pregnancy, before the appearance of signs, such as brainwave activity, that are used at the other end of the age spectrum in decisions to terminate life support.

Furstenberg, Brooks-Gunn, and Morgan (1987) note that other countries such as England, Sweden, and the Netherlands have rates of adolescent sexuality similar to those in the United States, yet they have lower pregnancy rates. One reason, they suggest, is that these countries have identified teenage *pregnancy,* not teenage sexuality, as a social problem. They offer programs that teach teenagers to assume responsibility for their sexuality, and more teenagers in these countries practice contraception effectively. As a consequence, one sees far fewer instances of teenage parenting or abortion.

Better access to clinics, more information, and promotion of contraceptive use in the media are important steps to be taken here at home. Yet teenage pregnancies are likely to remain a problem, especially among minority adolescents who live with poverty and discrimination. The likelihood of future success for most minority adolescents is much lower than for nonminority age-mates. The temptation to compromise future options, which may appear doubtful at best, for the immediate gain of sexual conquest can be hard to resist.

SEXUALLY TRANSMITTED DISEASES

Quite another consequence of teenage sexuality threatens the health of increasing numbers of adolescents. Many **sexually transmitted diseases (STDs)** have reached epidemic proportions. STDs affect approximately 3 million adolescents each year (Strong & DeVault, 1997). Because many STDs are asymptomatic and because many adolescents do not seek treatment, the actual number of adolescents affected is almost surely greater than estimated.

A sexually transmitted disease is an infection that is spread through sexual contact. Some STDs, such as syphilis and HIV infection, can also be acquired through blood transfusions, and a few, at least theoretically, by contact with contaminated toilet seats and bedsheets. They range in seriousness from irritating itches to life-threatening infections. Some are reaching epidemic levels among adolescents. The most serious STDs are HIV infection, syphilis, and gonorrhea. Less serious infections range from genital herpes, for which there is no known cure, to pests such as pubic lice, which can be treated with a prescription shampoo. Figure 9.4 shows the incidence of the five most common STDs.

Some Common STDs

Chlamydia   **Chlamydia** is a common STD in the United States. It is caused by an organism that acts both like a bacterium and a virus (Strong & DeVault, 1997). Many individuals experience no initial symptoms; approximately 80% of females are asymptomatic, as are 30% to 50% of males. Those who do have symptoms experience urethral itching, painful urination, and usually notice a discharge. Adolescents can easily dismiss each of these. However, the consequences of doing so are serious, especially for females.

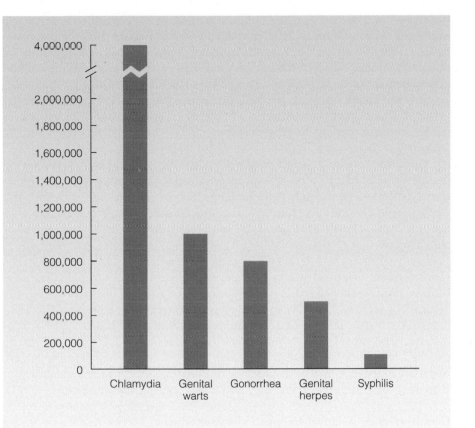

**FIGURE 9.4
Estimated Annual
STD Cases in the
United States**

Source: B. Strong & C. De-Vault. (1997). *Human sexuality* (2nd ed.). Mountain View, CA: Mayfield.

The infection can spread through the reproductive tract, causing pelvic inflammatory disease (PID). Inflammation of the tiny tubules of the tract leaves scar tissue and increases the risk of ectopic pregnancy (a pregnancy occurring outside the uterus) and sterility in both sexes. Abdominal pain, a symptom of pelvic inflammatory disease, should be treated promptly (Brookman, 1988).

Gonorrhea   The next most common STD is **gonorrhea,** a bacterial infection. Gonorrhea can be transmitted by just about any form of sexual contact: intercourse, oral-genital sex, or even kissing. From 10% to 40% of males and 50% to 80% of females experience either no symptoms or very mild ones. In males, the most noticeable symptom is a watery discharge from the penis; females also may notice a discharge, and both may experience pain when urinating. Left untreated, the disease spreads through the reproductive system, leaving scar tissue that can block the tubules and cause infertility. Untreated cases of gonorrhea can also affect the joints, causing a type of arthritis, and the heart, affecting the valves.

Early adolescent females may run a special risk because the immature cervix is especially vulnerable to infection by the bacterium causing gonorrhea. Early coital activity also appears to delay cervical development, as does the use of oral contraceptives. Thus early adolescent females who are using oral contraceptives are at greater risk of infection than those using other forms of birth control. Because the long-term consequences of infection for females include a higher risk of cervical cancer, those who have ever had gonorrhea should routinely get Pap smears (Brookman, 1988).

Prompt treatment with penicillin can cure the infection completely. Recently, the gonorrhea rate among adolescents has decreased but still varies considerably according to ethnicity and race (Centers for Disease Control, 1996b).

Adolescents who discover they have gonorrhea should notify any sexual partner who is likely to have been infected or to have passed on the infection (symptoms are usually noticeable within two to ten days of infection). They should also refrain from sexual contact until a checkup indicates that the infection is gone. Both steps are important in preventing the spread of this disease.

Genital Warts **Genital warts** (sometimes called HPV for their cause, the human papilloma virus) are painless, dry, light-colored outgrowths on the genitals or rectum. Until recently they were not thought to pose a threat to health. Yet because the presence of warts is associated with other STDs, adolescents who notice them should seek treatment and at the same time be checked for other infections. Data also suggest that when left untreated, warts are associated with a higher risk of cervical cancer in females although they may only be a contributing, and not a causal, factor (Franco, 1991).

Genital Herpes **Genital herpes** infections, caused by the herpes virus, are usually spread by sexual contact. However, the virus can also be spread by hand, after touching an infected area, and can survive for several hours on surfaces such as toilet seats, sauna benches, towels, and in tap water (Strong & DeVault, 1997). Clusters of itching or burning blisters appear, usually on the genitals but also in the rectum, on the cervix, or in the urethra, accompanied by slight fever, headache, and body soreness. The blisters break after several days, leaving small wet sores that dry up in a week or two. Even though the blisters eventually disappear, the virus remains dormant in the body, and outbreaks can recur at any time. No cure presently exists for herpes, although medication can diminish the unpleasantness of the symptoms when they first occur and decrease the frequency of recurrences.

Persons with genital herpes are contagious when the blisters appear. Recent data suggest that a partner can be infected even when there are no blisters, although this form of transmission is not as common. The incidence of genital herpes has increased dramatically since the mid-1960s. With approximately 40 million people in the United States already infected and 200,000 to 500,000 more infected each year, genital herpes has reached epidemic proportions. Because females with herpes may be at risk of developing cervical cancer, even those who have had only a single herpes outbreak should have a Pap smear twice a year. Cervical cancer can be successfully treated when detected early (Hatcher et al., 1990; Srong & DeVault, 1997).

Syphilis Sexual contact is the most common way **syphilis** is transmitted, although this bacterial infection can also be transmitted through contaminated blood transfusions or passed from an infected pregnant woman to her fetus. Symptoms first occur from two to four weeks following infection. In the *primary stage* of the disease, small, usually painless sores appear on the genitals, rectum, fingers, mouth, or nipples. These typically heal within several weeks, and unsuspecting adolescents may believe that whatever they had is gone.

If not treated, syphilis progresses to a *secondary stage* marked by symptoms including a rash, fever, headache, and sore throat. These symptoms are easily mistaken for flu, especially as they can come and go for several months. During this time highly infectious open sores develop around the genitals and anus. Once these symptoms disappear, the disease enters a *latent stage*. Although adolescents in the latent stage can no longer infect others, the disease continues its course within their bodies. Many who have syphilis remain in this stage and experience no further complications. Others move into a *tertiary stage* in which damage to the heart, eyes, brain, and spinal cord can occur, and blindness, insanity, paralysis, and death can result (Strong & DeVault, 1997).

Despite its highly destructive nature, syphilis is easily treated with penicillin in the primary and secondary stages, and even in later stages is responsive to larger doses over longer periods. The number of cases in 1995 was lower than it has been in over 30 years, with 69% of counties in the United States not reporting any cases. Of youth affected, however, the vast majority are minority adolescents (Centers for Disease Control, 1996b).

Pubic Lice   Frequently known as crabs, **pubic lice** are pests that are usually transmitted sexually but can also be transmitted via bedsheets or clothing. Lice live in the pubic hair, causing severe itching as they draw the blood on which they live. Bedding used by an infested person can remain infected for up to a week. A prescription shampoo (marketed as Kwell) kills the lice, but because eggs that drop onto bedding and clothing can survive for five or six days, clean sheets and clothing are important to prevent a recurrence.

Risks and Precautions

Many adolescents mistakenly believe that other people get sexually transmitted diseases—not them. Well-dressed, neatly groomed teenagers assume they could never get anything like syphilis or gonorrhea, much less AIDS. Assumptions such as these couldn't be further from the truth. STDs are presently as American as apple pie and country music. The facts are simple: Most diseases have reached epidemic proportions, and some, such as gonorrhea, are especially rife among adolescents. Adolescents who are sexually active are likely at some point to get a sexually transmitted disease.

Knowing the Risks   One need not be promiscuous to run the risk of contracting an STD. Even adolescents who practice serial monogamy, limiting themselves to one sexual partner before becoming active with another, expose themselves to the sexual history of their partner—as well as the sexual history of each of their partner's partners, and so on. Like standing in a hall of mirrors, the regression is infinite. Because many diseases have no symptoms following the initial infection, adolescents who are infected, even if well intentioned, can pass the disease unknowingly to future partners.

Taking Precautions   Symptoms such as a discharge or the appearance of sores should receive immediate medical attention. Most STDs can be treated with a single shot of penicillin if caught before complications develop. Honesty is important, and partners need to be informed so they can get treatment, too. Routine medical checkups are especially advisable for sexually active females because they are not as likely as males to experience symptoms, and the health complications that arise when infections are left untreated can be considerable.

Adolescents who are sexually active should wash their genitals before and after intercourse and should always use a condom. A condom is important even when another form of contraception is used, because it offers protection against STDs as well as pregnancy. Females and males can both assume responsibility here. But as simple as this precaution is, it is still likely to be neglected. Many females feel they can only engage in sex if they are swept away in a moment of passion; pulling a condom out of a purse implies advance planning. Males may fear that stopping to put on a condom can break the mood. However, using a condom is the most effective precaution against STDs.

Although even late adolescents report good intentions about using a condom, only half said they had used one the last time they had engaged in sex (Sanderson & Cantor, 1995). A national survey of high school students found a similar percentage, approximately half, reported using a condom when they had last had sex. Seventeen percent of sexually active students reported using birth control pills, with use of these being greater among White than among Black and Hispanic adolescents and increasing with age from the ninth to the twelfth grades (Centers for Disease Control, 1996b). Not only ethnicity and age but also gender affect contraceptive strategy use. Sherrine De Bro, Susan Campbell, and Anne Peplau (1994) found that, among college students, females and males use different strategies in persuading a sexual partner to use a condom, males most frequently using seduction whereas females report they are more likely to withhold sex.

Difficulties to Confront   Precautions that are relatively simple for an adult may be next to impossible for an adolescent. Many adolescents feel invulnerable to infection and may not take precautions. Others may be too frightened or embarrassed if symptoms do appear to get medical attention. Early adolescents frequently avoid seeking treatment, assuming the problem will go away by itself. Many are afraid their parents will discover their secret problem, and many more don't know how to get treatment or where to go, especially if they do not want their parents to find out. In addition, most don't have enough money to pay for a doctor's visit or for prescription medication. Transportation can be a problem, too, especially for those living in rural areas (Klerman, 1988).

Shame, fear, or anger may prevent adolescents from informing a partner about their own symptoms. And partners who are told may likewise do nothing for the same reasons. Even adolescents who seek treatment will not necessarily comply with the directions they have been given, especially early adolescents who do not yet have an adult's concern about the future. They may fail to take medication as prescribed or discontinue use when symptoms first disappear; they may fail to abstain from sex or to return for a

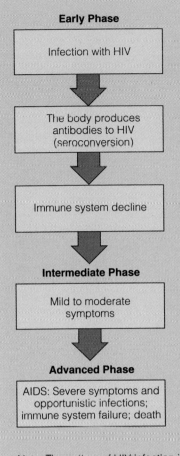

Early Phase

Infection with HIV

HIV is transmitted through intimate contact with body fluids—blood, blood products, semen, or vaginal secretions. The primary means of transmission are sexual contact, direct exposure to blood through injecting drug use or trans-fusions (prior to 1985), and from an infected mother to her child during pregnancy, childbirth, or breastfeeding.

The body produces antibodies to HIV (seroconversion)

Antibodies usually appear 2 to 12 weeks after the initial infection, a process known as seroconversion. Once antibodies appear, an infected person tests positive if given an HIV-antibody test. About 30 percent of people experience flulike symptoms during this period, lasting for a few days to a few weeks.

Immune system decline

Though the individual has no symptoms, the virus is infecting and destroying cells of the immune system. Many people remain asymptomatic for 3 to 10 or more years. About half of all people infected with HIV develop AIDS within 10 years.

Intermediate Phase

Mild to moderate symptoms

Once the immune system is damaged, many people begin to experience symptoms such as skin rashes, fatigue, weight loss, night sweats, and so on. When the damage is more severe, people are vulnerable to opportunistic infections. Treatments may allow recovery, but infections often recur.

Advanced Phase

AIDS: Severe symptoms and opportunistic infections; immune system failure; death

People are diagnosed with AIDS if they develop one of the conditions defined as a marker for AIDS or if their CD4 lymphocyte count drops below 200/mm^3. Chronic or recurrent illnesses continue until the immune system fails and death results.

Note: The pattern of HIV infection is different for every patient and not everyone infected with HIV will go through all these stages.

checkup to make sure they are clear of the infection (Brookman, 1988). Clearly, for preventive programs to be effective, these need to address more than the misinformation and lack of information that currently exists among adolescents.

HIV Infection and AIDS

HIV infection is the most recent STD and the most life threatening. HIV (human immunodeficiency virus) is a virus that attacks the immune system, causing it to break down. This in turn leaves the body defenseless against infection, eventually resulting in death. HIV infection progresses through several stages, the last of which is **AIDS** (acquired immune deficiency syndrome). The virus is almost always transmitted by sexual contact but can also be transmitted by contaminated needles shared by intravenous drug users or by blood transfusions from an infected person. As with syphilis, HIV infection can be passed from an infected pregnant woman to her unborn child. Figure 9.5 shows the progressive course of HIV infection.

FIGURE 9.5
The Progressive Course of HIV Infection. *Sources:* Adapted from R. Schwartz. (1992). *AIDS medical guide.* San Francisco: San Francisco AIDS Foundation; and Centers for Disease Control. (1991). *HIV infection and AIDS: Are you at risk?*

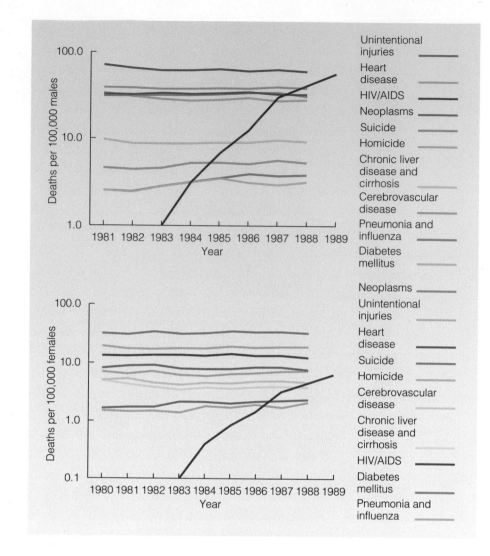

FIGURE 9.6
Leading Causes of
Death Among U.S.
Males and Females,
Ages 25 to 44, 1980
to 1989. *Source:* Centers
for Disease Control.
(1991b). Mortality
attributable to HIV infec-
tion/AIDS—United States,
1981–1990. *Morbidity and
Mortality Weekly Report, 40,*
41–44.

The virus works by attacking cells within the immune system known as T cells, cells that trap invading cells that would otherwise cause infection. As the number of healthy T cells decreases, the body is less able to ward off infection. The most recent classification system (Centers for Disease Control, 1992a) distinguishes early, intermediate, and late phases of the disease in terms of the number of T cells per milliliter of blood. In the *early phase* (also known as HIV infection), the T cell count is at least 500, enough to fight off infections and remain free of disease-related symptoms. In the *intermediate phase* (HIV-related disease), the T cell count drops to between 200 and 500, and the person experiences one or more symptoms related to the disease. In the *advanced phase* (AIDS), the T cell count drops to under 200, the immune system is no longer able to ward off infection, and the person experiences severe symptoms. Death occurs when the immune system fails.

HIV infection has spread at an alarming rate since first identified in the early 1980s (Figure 9.6). A survey conducted by the Centers for Disease Con-

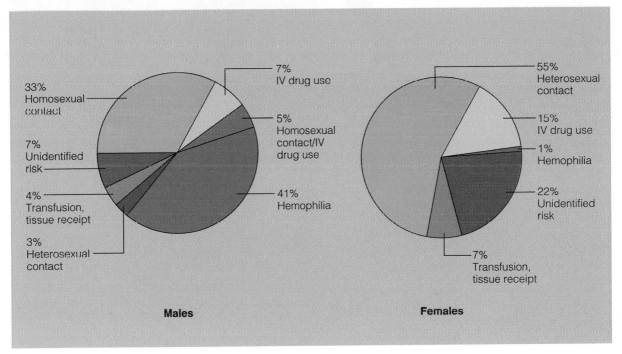

Males

33% Homosexual contact

7% Unidentified risk

4% Transfusion, tissue receipt

3% Heterosexual contact

7% IV drug use

5% Homosexual contact/IV drug use

41% Hemophilia

Females

55% Heterosexual contact

15% IV drug use

1% Hemophilia

22% Unidentified risk

7% Transfusion, tissue receipt

trol (1991b) of nearly 1,500 randomly selected individuals 18 or older, in which actual blood samples were drawn, found that 0.4% of those tested were infected with the virus. In other words, among any group of a thousand people, we can expect that about four will be infected.

Is this a large or a small number? How are we to evaluate figures such as these? Are adolescents that much at risk?

Initially, HIV infection was largely limited to homosexual and bisexual males and to intravenous drug users; these groups still account for the greatest numbers of those infected. However, HIV infection is now increasing most rapidly among females, adolescents, and heterosexual young adults (Centers for Disease Control, 1993c; Strong & DeVault, 1997).

The numbers of adolescents and young adults, 13 to 24 years old, with AIDS increased by 77% between 1990 and 1992 (Strong & DeVault, 1997). Figure 9.7 shows the incidence of AIDS cases among 13- to 19-year-olds up until 1996. This represents only a percentage of those actually infected with HIV. Once infected, most individuals do not show any symptoms for several years; this is especially true for adolescents (Hein, 1989). As long as those who are infected remain sexually active, any of their partners can be infected with the disease, which they, in turn, can pass on to others. At present, we do not know the actual numbers of adolescents who are infected. However, given the relatively long incubation period, up to eight years, and statistics showing that among adults who have the disease 20% are in their twenties, it is likely that significant numbers of those with AIDS were infected as adolescents (Hein & Futterman, 1991).

Because the incidence of AIDS is fast increasing, it is particularly important that teenagers know the risks and avoid this fatal disease. What steps can adolescents take to protect themselves from HIV infection? The

FIGURE 9.7
Comparison of Distribution of AIDS Cases Among U.S. Males and Females, Ages 13 to 19, through June 1996

Source: Centers for Disease Control. (1996, June). *HIV/AIDS Surveillance Report, 8,* Table 7.

HIV infection is increasing rapidly among adolescents because they, like Krista, who contracted the disease in her teens, do not believe they are at risk and do not have safe sex.

first step is simply a mental one, but it is as important as any that follow because adolescents are unlikely to take additional steps unless they begin with the realization that *anyone* can get AIDS, including themselves. Realizing they are at risk is not an easy step for many. Nancy Leland and Richard Barth (1993) asked 1,000 high school students how likely they thought it was for them to "get AIDS." Most adolescents did not think they were likely to be infected, as many as a third indicating there was "no chance."

For those who can narrow this mental distance, a number of practices can significantly reduce the risk of sexually transmitted HIV infection. The only completely effective one is abstinence. This alternative is included in almost all sex education classes, yet has not been that effective in reducing sexual activity, perhaps because it is presented as an all or nothing choice. However, many adolescents who would find it difficult to "save themselves for marriage" can nonetheless pledge abstinence for shorter periods of time. This approach deserves encouragement, especially among early adolescents who are notoriously ill-informed and unlikely to use any protection (Roper, Peterson, & Curran, 1993; Strong & DeVault, 1997).

For sexually active adolescents, the following precautions can significantly reduce the risk of exposure to HIV infection.

1. *Avoid the exchange of body fluids.* Although HIV is most highly concentrated in blood and semen, it has also been found in other body fluids, for example, vaginal and pre-ejaculatory secretions. For infection to occur, the virus must enter the body through a break in the skin, usually a cut, tear, or sore, and from there reach the bloodstream. Vaginal intercourse,

anal intercourse, and oral-genital sex all carry risk of exposure. Even inter-course without ejaculation carries some risk of infection because the virus can be present in pre-ejaculatory and vaginal secretions. Male homosexuals run the highest risk of infection because the lining of the rectum tears eas-ily during anal intercourse, allowing the virus in the semen of an infected partner to enter the body. The lining of the vagina is less likely to tear dur-ing intercourse. However, any cuts or sores in the genitals of either partner expose that person to the virus if the other is infected. Similarly, sores or cuts in the mouth provide exposure to the virus during oral-genital contact (Masters, Johnson, & Kolodny, 1988).

2. *Use a latex condom.* If one engages in intercourse, the use of a con-dom decreases the risk of infection because the virus cannot pass through the latex walls. Even so, using a condom is no guarantee that sex is ever completely safe; a tear in the condom or the escape of semen due to im-proper condom use can expose the partner to infection. The effectiveness of condoms is also dependent on their being consistently used (Roper, Pe-terson, & Curran, 1993). Most adolescents who report using condoms do so only intermittently.

Beliefs play an important role in determining usage. Adolescents who believe condoms are effective are more likely to use them (Hingson, Strunin, Berlin, & Heeren, 1990). Similarly, those who believe themselves to be at greater risk are more likely to use condoms. One survey of condom use asked men to self-identify as either straight, homosexual, or bisexual. Among those identifying themselves as straight yet reporting at least one occurrence of anal sex with men, 64% said they never used condoms; in com-parison, only 16% of those who considered themselves homosexual or bi-sexual said they never used condoms (Centers for Disease Control, 1993a).

3. *Use a spermicide.* Combining a spermicide that contains nonoxynol-9 with use of a condom offers more protection than a condom alone. Nonoxynol-9 has been found to kill HIV. Spermicide alone, however, is not as effective as with a condom.

4. *Be discriminating.* Certain practices and lifestyles increase the risk of infection. Individuals who have had numerous sexual partners and those who have used drugs intravenously are more likely to have been infected.

It is also possible to avoid infection by having an exclusive sexual rela-tionship with a noninfected partner. Of course, both partners must be free of the virus at the outset. A blood test can establish whether an individual is free of the virus; those who are infected with the virus have antibodies in their blood. Because it takes several months for antibodies to develop, a blood test done too soon after the last sexual contact is not conclusive.

How likely are adolescents to follow or even understand any of these precautions? A randomly sampled survey of 1,773 adolescents aged 16 through 19 found that adolescents who have the most sexual partners (more than ten a year) are least likely to use a condom, yet these adolescents have the highest risk of infection (Hingson, Strunin, Berlin, & Heeren, 1990).

All the factors that make it difficult for adolescents to use contracep-tives in general apply equally to the precautions they must take against HIV infection. Massive misinformation among adolescents complicates the problem. One study found that 30% of teenagers living in San Francisco believed that AIDS could be cured. Another 25% thought they could be infected with HIV by casual physical contact such as a handshake or sharing personal items (DeClemente, Zorn, & Temoshok, 1987).

Cultural beliefs can also compound the problems of general misinformation. For instance, one study of working-class Latino males found that most believe they can tell whether a woman is infected simply by her appearance or her social class. Few understand that individuals infected with HIV can be symptom-free and appear healthy. Many also believe that casual contact, such as sharing personal items, can lead to infection (Forrest, Austin, Valdes, Fuentes, & Wilson, 1993).

More than misinformation is at work with adolescents. Almost surely adolescents' cognitive immaturity sets limits on their ability to understand the seriousness of the disease or the precautions that need to be taken (Peterson & Murphy, 1990). So, too, does adolescents' sense that they are invulnerable.

SUMMARY

Gender Stereotypes

Well-defined gender roles exist for both male and female adolescents. The gender-role stereotype for males emphasizes independence, action, and self-reliance but little emotional sensitivity. The gender-role stereotype for females emphasizes interpersonal sensitivity but little assertive action. These stereotypes have been found to be more myth than reality, however. An androgynous role, combining both male and female personality characteristics, represents an alternative to the stereotypes. Nevertheless, flexibility with regard to gender roles decreases after adolescents enter junior high school, where they are influenced by older adolescents, who tend to be less flexible in their beliefs about gender roles.

Constructing a Sexual Identity

The sexual self-perception of adolescents is constructed from the dimensions of sexual self-esteem, sexual self-efficacy, and sexual self-image. Five sexual styles are characteristic of adolescents: sexually naive (mostly young females), sexually unassured (mostly young males), sexually competent (mostly males and females in twelfth grade), sexually adventurous (mostly older males), and sexually driven (mostly sexually active males). Demographic factors play little part in adolescents' sexual behaviors. Construction of one's sexual self depends to a large degree on the gender stereotypes of one's culture.

Sexuality and Intimacy

Adolescents who have achieved a sense of themselves are more likely to look for emotional intimacy and are less willing to engage in sexual relations outside of a committed relationship. In contrast, those with identity goals use dating to discover more about themselves and are more likely to engage in casual dating and have more sexual partners.

Factors that are important to adolescents' satisfaction with relationships are similar to ones important for adults: passion, communication, commitment, emotional support, and togetherness. As the degree of affection and commitment increases, adolescents are more accepting of increasingly intimate sexual behaviors.

Sexual Orientation

Sexual orientation refers to the attraction individuals feel for members of the same or the other sex. Adolescents who are homosexual are, for some extended period of their lives, more attracted sexually to individuals of their own sex than to those of the opposite sex. Gay, lesbian, and bisexual adolescents are more likely to experience problems associated with their sexual orientation and may be at greater risk for suicide than are straight adolescents. Research comparing co-incidence of homosexuality among identical and fraternal twins and adoptive siblings suggests a genetic component to sexual orientation.

Sexual Functioning

The sexual response cycle consists of four phases: excitement, plateau, orgasm, and resolution. Similarities in the sexual response for each gender exist for all phases. Two processes, vasocongestion and myotonia, underlie the changes that occur in each phase.

Adolescents have numerous misconceptions about sexual functioning. Many are not aware that the size of the male's penis is not important in sexual functioning, or that females have the same capacity for sexual pleasure as males. Adolescents frequently do not know that individuals of either sex experience discomfort if orgasm does not follow the plateau phase. Adolescents as well as adults fail to distinguish cultural taboos from physical reasons for not engaging in intercourse during menstruation.

Teenage Pregnancies and Parenting

Over 95% of adolescent females who give birth keep their babies. Most unmarried teenage mothers finish high school, are regularly employed, and have no more children than their later-childbearing classmates do. Teenage fathers, though generally willing to be involved, often find it difficult to take on the responsibilities of parenthood.

Approximately 40% of teenage pregnancies end in abortion. Decisions to abort or carry the pregnancy to term are related to whether the pregnancy was intended, socioeconomic status, race, and personal as well as parents' and friends' attitudes.

Sexually Transmitted Diseases

STDs are on the rise among adolescents. Some of these have reached epidemic proportions, and many do not have well-defined symptoms. If treated promptly, most STDs do not have serious health consequences. If left untreated, some can cause sterility and serious complications—even death.

Chlamydia is the most common STD in the United States. It can affect the reproductive system and cause pelvic inflammatory disease in females. Gonorrhea results from a bacterial infection and has reached epidemic proportions among adolescents. Many individuals experience no symptoms. If not treated, the disease can cause infertility and other medical problems. Genital herpes is caused by the herpes virus. The incidence of this disease has increased markedly over the past generation, as has genital warts. Syphilis is a bacterial infection that progresses through three stages. If not treated, it can result in serious medical complications and even death. Pubic lice, which can cause severe itching, are easily killed by medicated shampoo.

Risks and Precautions

Sexually active adolescents have difficulty realizing that they run a high risk of contracting STDs. Many do not take precautions to prevent these diseases or get treatment when symptoms do appear because of ignorance, shame, or a sense of invulnerability. Preventive programs must change adolescents' personal and cultural beliefs and dispel myths as well as provide information on safe sex practices.

Human immunodeficiency virus (HIV) attacks the immune system. The disease progresses through three stages, the last of which is AIDS. There is no known cure for the disease; individuals die when the immune system fails. Prevention of HIV infection includes avoiding exchange of body fluids, using condoms and spermicides, and being discriminating in sexual relationships.

KEY TERMS

gender-role stereotypes	agape	genital warts
androgynous	heterosexual	genital herpes
eros	homosexual	syphilis
storge	bisexual	pubic lice
ludus	sexually transmitted disease (STD)	HIV infection
mania	chlamydia	AIDS
pragma	gonorrhea	

CHAPTER 10

Careers and College

Kip leaned on the horn and cursed his friend's ability to sleep through an alarm. "Late one more time and you'll be docked in pay," Mr. Perkins had said.

Sam flew out the door with a sandwich in his mouth and a sweater half over his head.

"Climb in," shouted Kip, as he threw the car in gear and spun away from the curb.

"Gi-yugh," spat Sam, "I got jelly on this sweater."

"Don't worry, no one will notice."

"Not on the outside, fool. It's inside the sleeve!" griped Sam.

"Serves you right," Kip said. "You're the only one I know eats in his clothes—and I mean inside 'em."

"So what was I supposed to do with the sandwich while I was putting on the sweater?"

Sam changed the subject. "How much longer on this shift?"

"It's a killer, isn't it? Sometimes I wonder if these wheels are worth it," Kip replied.

"Can you see doing this the rest of your life?" Sam asked from under the sweater, turning the sleeve inside out for repairs.

"I'm already tired of working and I've just started," answered Kip, as he wheeled into the last parking space and switched off the ignition. "Let's go. Sooner begun, sooner done, or something like that, as my dad says."

"You wonder how they do it," Sam replied. "Year after year at the same old job. Is this what it's gonna be like for the next fifty years?"

What it's like for the next fifty years, give or take ten for most people, will depend on a number of things, many of which get sorted out in adolescence. This chapter opens with a look at adolescents in the workplace. Increasing numbers of adolescents work while still in high school. Others start full-time jobs after graduating, and still others will work while they go to college. For those who never finish high school, occupational choices are more limited. We will consider students, dropouts, and work in the opening section of the chapter.

Why do individuals choose one type of work and not another? Explanations for vocational choice differ. Social-cognitive theory looks at environmental variables that influence career decisions—such as parents' occupations and the salience of models in different occupations. The developmental theories of Eli Ginzburg and Donald Super identify stages of occupational choice. Ginzburg, for example, believes that realistic decisions occur fairly late in the process, and Super links occupational choice to the development of the self-concept. Finally, Holland identifies different personality types that are suited to different types of work.

What happens to young workers once they are on the job? Many need additional training beyond high school. Business and industry increasingly find that they must pick up the tab for the education of their newest workers, often having to train them in basic skills such as reading and math. Ironically, many of the nation's newest full-time workers must continue their education on the job. Adolescents in the work force is the subject of the next section.

Many factors affect adolescents' decisions about the type of work they will do. Not least among these are gender and ethnicity. Some adolescents never even consider certain jobs because they rarely see individuals of their gender or race in them. Even when adolescents do consider a wide variety of jobs, the opportunity structure all too frequently reflects inequities associated with gender, race, and socioeconomic level. Gender and ethnicity are considered as they relate to occupational choice in adolescence. Intervention programs aimed at changing belief structures about career opportunities have been effective in helping adolescents realistically evaluate the opportunities available to them.

Many adolescents will go off to college instead of beginning work. They too will face new experiences; these can change the way they think about themselves, even the way they think about knowledge itself. Is it possible to discover truth? Or does truth, like beauty, exist only in the mind of the beholder? Some adolescents attempt to discover absolute truths in their classes; others view truth as relative. Still others achieve ways of reconciling the alternative truths of relativism. This progression takes different forms in male and female adolescents, and we will chart changes in knowing separately for each.

Real life problem solving is not as straightforward as logicians would have us believe. For instance, adolescents, like everyone else, think most efficiently and in more sophisticated ways in areas that interest them, and problems arising in the context of one's culture are solved more efficiently than similar problems that do not utilize culturally specific knowledge. Cultural knowledge is a form of expertise in which natives think like experts and strangers like novices.

The chapter moves to a discussion of the ways in which knowledge is put to work in daily settings, whether on the job or pursuing a degree. Facts can become easily compartmentalized; adolescents can miss the connection between what they have learned and their other experiences. Psychologists speak of compartmentalized facts as "inert" knowledge. Unlike inert metals or gases, inert knowledge has few uses. We'll consider several ways of addressing this problem.

Next the subject of creativity is discussed. What qualities distinguish creative adolescents from those who don't express their creativity? Can it be cultivated in all adolescents? The final section of the chapter addresses the way adolescents think through practical problems in daily settings. As with other aspects of reasoning, success increases with age.

ADOLESCENTS AT WORK

Part-Time Employment

Most high school students have part-time jobs. A representative sample of adolescents in one urban school district, for instance, found that 52% of ninth-graders and 64% of twelfth-graders were employed. Furthermore, the number of hours worked a week increases with age, with ninth-graders working an average of 11 hours a week and twelfth-graders working nearly 21 hours a week (Mortimer, Finch, Ryu, Shanahan, & Call, 1996). Even more adolescents would be working if only they could find jobs. The unemployment rate for 16- to 19-year-olds seeking but unable to find work is approximately 25%. Not all adolescents are equally affected by unemployment, however. For minority adolescents, the percentage is much higher. Recent unemployment among White adolescents was 14.5%, for example, but comparable figures among Black and Hispanic adolescents were 35.7% and 24%. Unemployment of Black adolescents of either sex is more than double that of Whites, and unemployment of Hispanics is nearly 50% greater than that of Whites their age. These differences persist into early adulthood, as can be seen from Figure 10.1 (Youth Indicators, 1996).

Spending Patterns   Adolescents with jobs spend their money in different ways than they will as adult workers. Most of what they earn they spend on personal items such as clothes, CDs, and entertainment (Figure 10.2). Because over half of those who work earn more than $50 a week, adolescents can engage in a fair amount of conspicuous consumption. The price of clothes is high if one buys designer labels—and many adolescents do. Popular name-brand athletic shoes once topped the line at $50 to $70, but are now outstripped in price by footgear such as "airs" that go for well over $100. One might imagine that at those prices, few adolescents would buy name-brand athletic shoes. But increasing numbers of adolescents choose to work in order to spend money on personal items such as these. Jeans, a staple wardrobe item for most adolescents, are also expensive, many starting at $50 a pair and working their way up, depending on extras such as

Continuity and
Change: Identity
Consolidation in
Late Adolescence

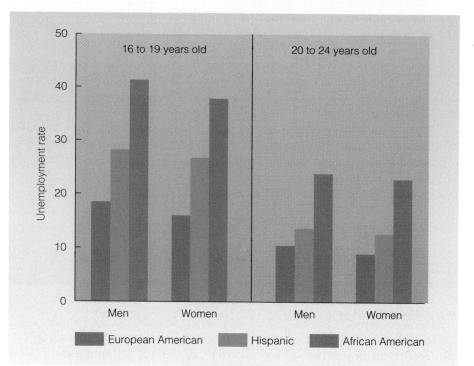

FIGURE 10.1
Unemployment
Among White,
Hispanic, and Black
Youth. *Source:* U.S.
Department of Labor, Bu-
reau of Labor Statistics,
Employment and earnings
(January issues); and labor
force statistics derived from
the *Current population survey:
A data book,* Vol. 1, Bulletin
2096. In Youth Indicators:
*Trends in the Well-Being of
American Youth.* (1993).
Washington, DC: U.S. Gov-
ernment Printing Office.

FIGURE 10.2   How
High School Seniors
Spend Their Money

Source: University of
Michigan, Institute for
Social Research, *Monitoring
the future, 1992.* In Youth
Indicators: *Trends in the
Well-Being of American
Youth.* (1996). Washington,
DC: U.S. Government
Printing Office.

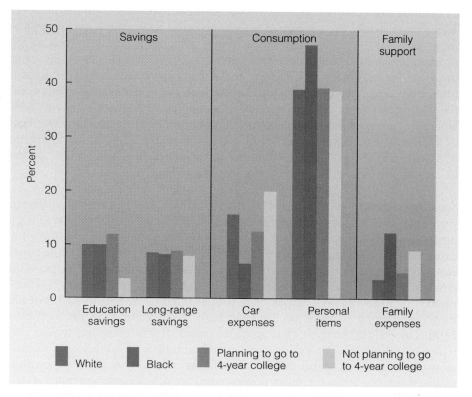

acid-washes, type of cut, and so on. The cost of an outfit can add up, and we haven't even gotten above the belt in this example.

Adolescents put much of the money they earn toward entertainment. A simple date, such as a movie and hamburger afterward, can cost $20 or more: $12 to $15 for tickets, another $5 or $6 at the concession stand, and a whopping $5 to $10 more for hamburgers and drinks afterward—and this doesn't include the cost of the round-trip gas. Special events, such as rock concerts, can be four to five times as expensive. Even though most adolescents go to concerts infrequently, they go to other events, such as school dances or get-togethers after games, regularly—and these all add up. Just spending an evening with a friend or two can be expensive. When adolescents get together, they eat. Two or three adolescents can kill several 2-liter bottles of cola in a night and munch through several bags of chips at $3 a bag.

The above expenses can be minor compared to those for a car. Car expenses are a significant item for many adolescents as Figure 10.2 shows. A sizable number of adolescents—25%—spend from half to all they make on their cars.

A number of adolescents save some of their money for either upcoming education or other long-term plans. High school seniors who are planning to attend a four-year college are, predictably, more likely to put more of their money into savings for education than those without plans for college. Figure 10.2 shows that a fairly large number of Black adolescents contribute to their families' expenses. Nearly 18% of the Black adolescents who work report putting anywhere from half of what they earn to all of it toward their families' expenses. The comparable figure for White adolescents is just over 6% (Youth Indicators, 1996).

Disadvantages of Part-Time Employment   Some researchers question whether part-time employment exposes adolescents to an unrealistic standard of living. They point out that most teenagers are allowed to spend what they earn as discretionary income; as we have seen, only a few contribute to family expenses. As a result, few adolescents are prepared for the realities that confront employed adults, such as the costs of housing, food, transportation, and health care. Figure 10.3 presents a comparison of spending patterns of people under 25 to overall spending patterns.

Laurence Steinberg, Suzanne Fegley, and Sanford Dornbusch (1993) surveyed 1,800 high school sophomores and juniors concerning part-time employment. By following these students over a year's time, they could look for differences that existed prior to their part-time employment, as well as compare adolescents who worked with those who did not. These investigators found that adolescents who work are less invested in school than their peers, even before beginning to work, and that working contributes to their disengagement from school, especially if they work more than 20 hours a week. Conversely, adolescents who work moderate hours and then quit their jobs show improved performance in school.

Jaylen Mortimer and associates (1996) also found that low work hours were associated with better performance in school. However, grades for these students were not only higher than for those working more hours, they were

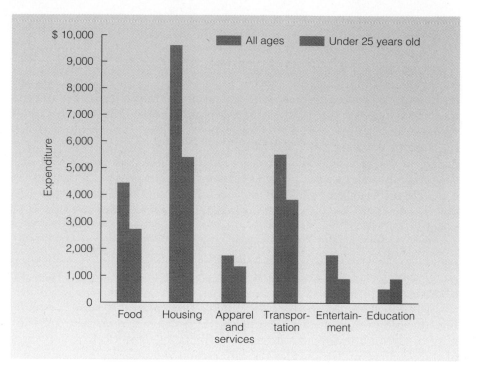

FIGURE 10.3   Spending Patterns of People 25 Years of Age and Under
Compared to All People

Source: U.S. Department of Labor, Bureau of Labor Statistics, *Consumer expenditure survey:
Integrated study,* unpublished data. In Youth Indicators: *Trends in the Well-Being of American Youth.* (1996). Washington, DC: U.S. Government Printing Office.

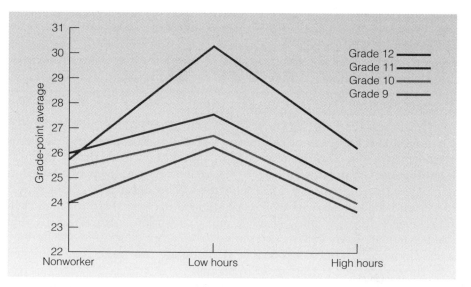

FIGURE 10.4   Grade-Point Average by Work Hours, Grades 9 to 12

Source: J. T. Mortimer, M. D. Finch, S. Ryu, M. J. Shanahan, & K. T. Call. (1996). The effects of work intensity on adolescent mental health, achievement, and behavioral adjustment: New evidence from a prospective study. *Child Development, 67,* 1243–1261.

More high school students work today than a generation ago. But their jobs are usually for minimum wage and provide few opportunities to move up to more responsible and challenging positions.

also higher than for classmates who did not work at all (Figure 10.4). It is possible that employment fosters work habits and personal discipline that carry over to their studies. Or, conversely, it may be that students who work accommodate for the demands on their time by taking less rigorous classes (Steinberg, Fegley, & Dornbusch, 1993). Mortimer and associates (1996), who also studied a large representative sample, did not find evidence of working students taking easier classes, however. Clearly, simple answers concerning the relationship of part-time employment to success in school are not forthcoming.

Nor, for that matter, is the relationship any clearer between part-time employment and measures of mental health. Although part-time employment is consistently related to increased use of alcohol (Mortimer et al., 1996; Steinberg, Fegley, & Dornbusch, 1993), evidence of its relationship to other criteria of mental health is not that consistent. Whereas Steinberg, Fegley, and Dornbusch found adolescents who do not work to be better adjusted than those who do—having higher self-esteem, greater self-reliance, and less delinquency—Mortimer and associates found no difference in self-esteem or in other measures of adjustment.

The types of jobs adolescents fill, in addition to the hours they work, also need to be considered. In this respect, at least, a clearer picture emerges. Most adolescents are employed in high-turnover positions, with little pay, little authority, and relatively little opportunity for advancement. The work is often simple and repetitive and requires little skill or training. Such jobs

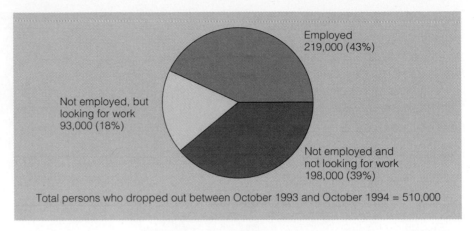

Employed
219,000 (43%)

Not employed, but
looking for work
93,000 (18%)

Not employed and
not looking for work
198,000 (39%)

Total persons who dropped out between October 1993 and October 1994 = 510,000

FIGURE 10.5   Employment Status of High School Dropouts.   *Source:* U.S. Department of
Labor, Bureau of Labor Statistics, *Employment of school-age youth, graduates, and dropouts.* In Youth Indicators: *Trends
in the Well-Being of American Youth.* (1996). Washington, DC: U.S. Government Printing Office.

are associated with negative consequences for workers, whether adolescents
or adults (Mortimer, Finch, Shanahan, & Ryu, 1992).

When adolescents perceive their work as contributing to skills they
could later use, however, part-time employment has been found to be associated with a number of measures of well-being (Mortimer, Finch, Shanahan, & Ryu, 1992). Holding a job can help adolescents develop a sense of
responsibility and give them a feeling of being productive. Work can also
develop general skills, ranging from interpersonal ones, such as getting
along with co-workers, to personal ones, such as managing time. Some
jobs may help adolescents discover where their interests lie, even if by
exclusion—they may discover, for example, that they would not enjoy the
same work in a full-time capacity.

For some adolescents, such a discovery is a luxury. Adolescents who
drop out of high school find it difficult to obtain work even under the best
of circumstances. Many cannot afford to be choosy. We turn to this group
of workers next.

Dropouts and Employment

Adolescents who drop out of high school are more than twice as likely to
be unemployed as those who graduate (U.S. Bureau of the Census, 1994).
Because future jobs will require even more education and preparation,
dropouts will find it harder to compete for these jobs than in the past. Figure 10.5 shows the proportions of dropouts who are employed or unemployed. Differences do not end there, however. Even when employed, high
school dropouts are less satisfied with their working conditions, see less opportunity for promotion, and experience less security and permanence in
their jobs (Youth Indicators, 1996). Given the importance of finishing high
school, one looks for programs that have been successful in working with
adolescents at risk of dropping out. Several successful programs share four
features, referred to as the four Cs: cash, concern, computers, and coalitions.

Schools that are effective in reaching potential dropouts, such as teenage parents, communicate to students that they care. These schools usually support teacher involvement by reducing class work loads so that teachers can have more time to interact with students.

Cash High schools that are effective in keeping at risk adolescents in school establish the connection between having a diploma and earning money. Although the actual amount of money earned by high school graduates versus dropouts is not always large, the likelihood of *having* a job is significantly greater if one has a diploma. Successful programs offering work opportunities that provide on-the-job experience have been particularly successful. Most also give intensive training in basic skills, increasing the likelihood of success both at school and on the job. Many programs also prepare students to take the GED, a test that, when passed, gives them the equivalent of a high school diploma.

Concern Effective programs usually have lower student–teacher ratios, smaller campuses, and an atmosphere that communicates the message that any student who wants to can be successful. Teachers have more time to interact with students. Many schools also provide infant care for adolescent mothers returning to school.

Computers   Many dropouts have a history of school failure and are demoralized by the time they reach high school. Effective programs integrate computers into their instructional programs, using them for individualized instruction in basic skills. Remedial programs in reading and math help break self-defeating cycles in which students avoid work at which they feel inadequate, causing them to fall even further behind.

Coalitions   Successful schools often involve individuals from the community, such as civic leaders and local businesses and industry, in their programs. Students learn about resources in the community. Parents are an important part of any coalition, and these programs involve parents in the students' progress (see Chapter 7). Frequently, too, counseling for emotional problems is available to students who need it.

Successful programs increase the motivation of the students enrolled in them. They also help students set realistic goals, or, as Bloch says, narrow "the gap between fantasy and reality." These two benefits are almost surely related. Students' motivation to do well in their courses will increase as they see the relationship between their own success and what they need for specific jobs. More generally, these programs have an impact on students' self-esteem; when one likes oneself, one does not have to have fantasy-level aspirations about a job—reality does quite well (Bloch, 1989).

CHOOSING A VOCATION

At-risk students face one problem in common with other students. Almost all adolescents have difficulty discovering the type of work for which they are best suited or would enjoy most. We look first at social-cognitive theory for an explanation of how adolescents select the type of work they will engage in for most of their adult lives, and then at the theories of Eli Ginzburg, Donald Super, and John Holland.

Social-Cognitive Theory

Why do individuals choose the occupations they do? Social-cognitive theory, which emphasizes the role of observational learning and modeling, focuses on complex interactions between the inborn talents, the environmental conditions in which these are played out (for example, demographic trends affecting the availability of jobs or social policies regulating equal employment opportunities), the unique learning histories of each person, and the skills with which individuals approach their work (Mitchell & Krumboltz, 1990).

Adolescents observe themselves and note how well their skills, interests, and values match the requirements of the situation. These observations have consequences for the types of work they think they might be good at. They are also related to what they are interested in and what they value (Mitchell & Krumboltz, 1990). Let's take a look at how social-cognitive theory puts these various factors together in explaining career choices.

Consider the case of a fictitious adolescent, Carlos, age 17. Carlos grew up in a quiet, ethnically mixed neighborhood; his mother is native-born and his father came to this country as a young boy. Both parents are hardworking; his father is a contractor and his mother a daycare worker. Carlos was quiet in elementary school and received little attention from his predominantly European American teachers. He often heard his father say that "White teachers think Mexican kids aren't that smart." He began to perceive his teachers as different from himself, and he emotionally shut down when interacting with them. Nothing in elementary school disproved what he had learned from his father.

In junior high, Carlos's English teacher noticed that his creative stories were well written and that he had an unusually large vocabulary for his age. She displayed his work in the classroom. Carlos felt proud, and his classmates often asked him for help. Carlos began to think that not all teachers are alike—some think he is smart.

Carlos tells himself that he might not tell stories as well as his grandma, but he knows he's better than the other kids in his class. Carlos enjoys writing and wonders if he's good enough to get paid for doing it for a living. He also questions whether he would enjoy it more than being a contractor. When he has worked for his father, he has always felt competent. He wonders which occupation would be best for him and decides to take some creative writing courses and talk to his father about a summer job.

Environmental events such as higher interest rates on loans (and a drop-off in construction) and a TV writer's strike can affect vocational decision making. Even though social-cognitive theory emphasizes individual learning experiences, many of which are planned (such as taking a writing course), it acknowledges the impact of unplanned events like an economic recession and its effect on the construction industry, or a screen writer's strike and national awareness of the importance of writers (Mitchell & Krumboltz, 1990).

Critique of Social-Cognitive Theory   A strength of social-cognitive theory is its use of learning principles to explain individual choices, yet doing so without portraying individuals as automatons. Social-cognitive theory recognizes that people actively attempt to understand the consequences of their actions and use this understanding in ways that change their environments to better meet their needs (Mitchell & Krumboltz, 1990). Mitchell and Krumboltz (1990) point out that, unlike theories of vocational selection that analyze sociological forces and economic conditions, social-cognitive theory explains the way individuals incorporate such conditions into their decision making. Economic recessions and depressions, demographic changes that affect the size of one's cohort group and consequent competition for jobs, and technological changes that affect the workplace all have an impact on career decision making.

A shortcoming of the social-cognitive approach is that it does not give us a model of normative behavior at different points in the life cycle, nor does it relate decision making to developmental changes in such important aspects of the self as identity and self-concept (Brown, 1990). For a developmental approach to vocational choice, we turn to the theories of Ginzburg and Super.

Vocational development can be viewed as a progressive narrowing of choices in the search for the best fit between one's goals and self-concept and the opportunities that actually exist.

Ginzburg: Vocational Stages

Eli Ginzburg and his colleagues (1972) view vocational development as a progressive narrowing of choices that at first reflect only fantasy but with age come to be based on reality. Like other stage theorists, Ginzburg assumes that all individuals move through the same sequence and that the process is largely irreversible, because one is unable to relive the choices made at earlier points in life. Compromises are made at each step along the way. Choosing a career is an adaptive process in which individuals continually seek the best fit between their own goals and the opportunities that actually exist. The process unfolds over three stages: fantasy, tentative, and realistic.

Three Vocational Stages   The **fantasy stage** lasts through childhood. During this time, children imagine themselves in the roles of those with whom they identify. These figures can be as real as parents, teachers, even ballerinas or sports heroes, or as fantastic as the cartoon characters they see on television. This stage involves no real assessment of what one might be good at or what the actual requirements of an occupation might be. Children respond to visible aspects of jobs—uniforms, firetrucks, and ballet slippers. Ginzburg (1990) notes that the 5-year-old son of a banker may say he wants to be a policeman when he grows up, but it is unlikely it will turn out that way. To the young, the uniform and activities of a policeman are understandable in a way that those of a banker are not.

In the **tentative stage** (from about age 11 to age 17), career thoughts begin to reflect personal aspects such as interests, abilities, and values. At first, only their *interests* focus adolescents' thoughts about careers. One adolescent may plan to be a jockey because she loves horses, or another a musician because he is interested in jazz. With time, adolescents become aware that their interests change, and, more importantly, that they may not match their *capabilities*. A boy who lives for basketball may fail to make the team at school, or a girl who wants to be a jockey may find that at 12 she is already larger than most professional jockeys. In other words, adolescents discover that interest alone is not enough. Somewhere around 15 or 16, adolescents begin to think of work in terms of what they *value*. They question how important it is to make a lot of money, whether their work will contribute to society, or how much they value free time, independence, or security. As they think through the things that are important to them, they let certain choices slide in favor of others that better fit their values and abilities.

Adolescents enter the **realistic stage** when they *explore* the tentative choices they have been considering. For college students this means taking courses in a specific field. Some will find these courses interesting and challenging and will go on to major in that field, whereas others may find they are not sufficiently interesting or challenging and look for another field in which to concentrate. Similarly, students who start to work after high school will find out whether the jobs remain interesting or whether they need to look for different ones.

Adolescents soon pull together, or *crystallize,* the many factors bearing upon a career choice: the required training, their own interests and talents, and the actual opportunities that exist. This integration results in commitment to a particular vocational path. College students will complete the required courses in their major; adolescents working at a job will finish the training programs needed for advancement. finally, individuals *specialize* within their field. Students preparing to teach, for instance, will decide whether to do so at the elementary or the secondary level; an auto mechanic will decide whether to specialize in foreign or domestic cars.

Critique of Ginzburg's Theory   Developmental data support Ginzburg's distinctions between fantasy, tentative, and realistic bases for thinking about work. We know, for example, that young children understand their world in terms of its visible and tangible properties long before they appreciate its more abstract qualities (Flavell, Green, & Flavell, 1986). The fantasy stage illustrates the concrete nature of early thought (see Chapter 4). Similarly, in early adolescence, individuals begin to think of themselves in terms of their psychological characteristics—interests, abilities, and values—as in Ginzburg's tentative stage. finally, the commitment to an occupation that occurs in Ginzburg's realistic stage is an integral part of the identity formation process of late adolescence.

A weakness of Ginzburg's theory is his failure to give an explanation for movement from one stage to the next. He does not, in other words, explain the process responsible for developmental change. An example of such a process in another well-known stage theory, that of Piaget, is the cycle of assimilation and accommodation that accounts for the growth of thought from one stage to the next (see Chapter 4). The process responsible for change in Ginzburg's theory remains unclear.

Also, Ginzburg based his theory on data collected exclusively with males. Although it is true, as John Holland (1987) points out, that basing a theory on observations only of men does not invalidate the theory or even mean it can't be used to make statements about women, limiting one's sample to men raises the strong possibility that interesting data may have been missed that might permit a better description of the career plans of women, and perhaps of some men.

Super: Careers and the Self-Concept

Donald Super (1981, 1990) thinks of vocation in terms of self-perception. People choose occupations that are consistent with the way they see themselves, that reflect their interests, values, and strengths. But self-concepts change with age, and Super's is a developmental theory. Only with adolescence, for instance, do individuals even begin to think of themselves in terms of their personalities (for example, "I'm quiet and enjoy reading" or "I like people and get along with them well"). Prior to that time, they think of themselves primarily in terms of physical characteristics. People continue to discover things about themselves well into adulthood, as they sample new experiences and integrate the information these bring into their sense of themselves. Generally, the self-concept becomes more complex and better defined with age.

Choosing an occupation means finding a match between the self-perceptions that make up one's self-concept and the actual requirements of the jobs one is considering, a process that in some ways is like reaching for a brass ring on a carousel—both you and the ring are moving, but not at the same speed or necessarily in the same direction. Adolescents' views of different occupations and of work itself change as they age, as do their self-concepts. An adolescent may have only the vaguest idea of what a psychologist does after speaking with one at school. She may think that all psychologists work in schools testing students. Several years later, that same adolescent may have discovered that some psychologists counsel people with personal problems, that others work in industry, and even others work in laboratories collecting and analyzing data. Meanwhile this adolescent's sense of herself may have changed from someone who wanted to help others to someone who is more interested in ideas than in people. How suitable she sees psychology as an occupation depends on how her perceptions of the discipline have evolved as she has changed.

Five Vocational Stages   Super describes five stages of vocational development. In the **growth stage,** which lasts until about age 14, adolescents discover more about themselves than about an occupation. Super feels that the major developmental task in this stage is simply to develop a realistic self-concept (1990). At the same time adolescents are also developing a feeling for what work involves. They may find, for example, that they have to cut into their free time in order to do well in their courses.

In the **exploration stage,** which can last through one's mid-twenties, adolescents begin to make choices that relate to their future work. Choosing courses in school is part of this process. Should they take algebra, drafting, or bookkeeping? An even earlier step comes when adolescents realize they must think about their futures. Once they realize this, a realization that includes a sense of themselves as self-supporting, they can explore different opportunities in earnest. Super identifies three substages in the exploration period. Adolescents move from plans that reflect only their interests (what they would *like* to be), to those that reflect a growing awareness of their abilities (and how well these match their interests), to a realistic appraisal that includes the availability and accessibility of certain jobs.

For Super, choosing a vocation is not the end of the process; it is only the beginning. In the **establishment stage,** which typically lasts through early adulthood, individuals settle into their work. Even if they change jobs, they are likely to find the same form of work in another setting or office.

The years of middle adulthood, from about 45 to 65, are devoted to maintaining one's occupational position, the **maintenance stage.** Super speaks of the developmental task in these years as "holding one's own against competition," whether in the form of others who are involved in the same type of work, or maintaining the same level and quality of the work as in the past. Finally, the **decline stage,** which occurs in late adulthood, involves retirement for most workers and the need to find other roles through which to express themselves.

Critique of Super's Theory   Super's theory is one of the most widely cited and influential theories of vocational development. It is also one of the most interesting psychologically, in that it traces vocational development through the life cycle by relating it to changes in the self-concept and the roles one fills at different ages. Super's theory enjoys considerable research support (Osipow, 1983).

The process Super uses to account for development is similar to the homeostatic or equilibrium model in other organismic theories, such as Piaget's. A match between self-perceptions and the requirements of one's work results in vocational stability; this stability is maintained until changes in self-perceptions or work requirements create a mismatch. Mismatches produce instability and the need to repeat elements of the larger cycle until individuals find another type of work that suits them (Super, 1990).

Holland: Personality Types and Work

Picasso once said, "When I work I relax; doing nothing or entertaining visitors makes me tired." Picasso illustrates Holland's explanation for vocational success: His personality type corresponded to the type of work he did. John Holland (1985a) classifies individuals into one of six types. Different work environments either complement or oppose the qualities that make up any type. As an artist, Picasso excelled; as a banker, he would have been a flop.

Six Personality Types   **Realistic personality types** are practical and down to earth. They prefer problems that can be explicitly defined and that yield to an orderly approach, as opposed to those that require abstract or creative approaches. Their interpersonal skills are weak, and they like work that does not involve them with people. These types prefer occupations such as mechanic, farmer, construction worker, engineer, or surveyor.

Investigative personality types are as curious as realistic types are practical. They delight in situations that call for a creative or analytic approach. They are thinkers rather than doers, and their approach is intellectual and abstract. They enjoy being by themselves and getting caught up in their own world of ideas. Investigative types make good scientists, doctors, computer programmers, and writers.

Artistic personality types are original, imaginative, and creative. They prefer situations that are relatively unstructured and allow them to express their creative talents and do well in occupations such as painter, author, or musician.

Social personality types are understanding, friendly, and people oriented. They have the verbal and interpersonal skills that allow them to work well with others. They are comfortable with their own and others' feelings, often approaching problems in terms of feelings rather than seeking an intellectual solution. They make good counselors, ministers, teachers, and social workers.

Enterprising personality types are gregarious and dominant. They have strong interpersonal skills and enjoy work that brings them into contact with others in ways that allow them to express their assertiveness. fields such as real estate, management, law, or sales suit their ambitious temperament.

Conventional personality types are efficient and tidy. They like well-defined tasks in which their conscientious approach is likely to bring success. They are followers—of rules and authority figures—and seek out highly structured environments in which they need not be leaders themselves. Occupations for which they are suited include banking, accounting, and secretarial services.

Holland believes these personality types reflect different learning histories and inborn talents that together shape patterns of success, resulting in preferred approaches to problems or tasks.

Critique of Holland's Theory   Perhaps the strongest features of Holland's theory are its usefulness and the extent to which it has stimulated research in the field of vocational choice. The Strong-Campbell Interest Inventory (Campbell, 1974) and the Vocational Preference Inventory (Holland, 1985b), both based on Holland's typology, are widely used measures of vocational preference (Donnay & Borgen, 1996). Holland himself considers the usefulness of a theory to be one of its most important features.

However, Holland's theory has not given sufficient consideration to social context variables such as gender and ethnicity. Holland predicts that personality types influence the work one chooses, yet for many adolescents vocational choices are limited by variables such as sex, ethnicity, and socioeconomic level. For instance, African American and Hispanic men are overrepresented (considering their actual numbers relative to other groups)

in low level realistic jobs and underrepresented in all other types of jobs. All women, regardless of their ethnic background, are overrepresented in conventional and social jobs, and African American and Hispanic women are particularly overrepresented in low-level realistic types of work (Arbona, 1989).

Despite the realities of the work world, however, Jennifer Ryan, Terence Tracey, and James Rounds (1996), at the University of Illinois, nonetheless found the interests of African American and White high school students to be highly similar when assessed with Holland's Vocational Preference Inventory. As for gender, Holland's model was found to fit the interests of high school females somewhat better than males. With college students, though, gender differences do emerge, with females expressing more confidence on the realistic and social themes and males on the enterprising, investigative, and conventional (Betz, Harmon, & Borgen, 1996).

Ryan, Tracey, and Rounds's research is important in another respect, as well. The career interests of these minority adolescents did not differ from those of Whites. Because minority students are likely to experience barriers in pursuing their occupational objectives, it is important for school counselors to help students identify the source of the difficulties they are experiencing and to suggest possible ways of dealing with them. Differences in the levels of occupation they actually attain underscore the need for approaches to career counseling developed especially for minority students (Arbona, 1989).

Why do some people pursue a career in nursing and others in hospital administration? A combination of gender, ethnicity, socioeconomic level, and personality type seem to influence most adolescents' vocational choices.

JOINING THE WORK FORCE

Job Availability

What kinds of jobs await youths who are about to join the work force? Some of the fastest growing jobs are in health-related occupations (for example, home health aides), technical occupations (for example, systems analysts and computer scientists), service occupations (for example, child-care workers), and in the professions (Bureau of Labor Statistics, 1996). Figure 10.6 presents projections of the fastest growing and fastest declining occupations. These figures may be somewhat deceptive, however, because the fastest growing jobs are not necessarily the most *numerous* jobs. There are far more cashiers, janitors and cleaners, waiters, and nurses than there are systems analysts and computer scientists.

In many respects, the picture is a bright one for youth entering the work force. The number of 16- to 24-year-olds looking for jobs is smaller than it was a generation ago, reducing competition for jobs. And for some types of work, such as service and retail jobs, there are more jobs than there are entry-level workers to fill them (U.S. Bureau of the Census, 1994; Bureau of Labor Statistics, 1996). Even though some of the fastest growing occupations are also ones that require more education, such as professional and technical jobs, more youths are going to college than previously, gaining the skills they will need for these jobs.

Those for whom the picture is not so bright are unskilled workers, who will be looking for work in an increasingly automated, technological workplace. Even though most adolescents will replace workers in existing jobs, the qualifications for these jobs will increase as technology and foreign trade affect the workplace. Twenty years ago, an auto mechanic had to master only 5,000 pages of service manuals to work on any car on the road, compared to today, when 465,000 pages of service manuals exist for the hundreds of models sold in this country. Equally demanding changes are taking place in service sector jobs:

> The secretary who once pecked away at a manual typewriter must now master a word processor, a computer and telecommunications equipment. Even the cashier at the 7-Eleven store has to know how to sell money orders and do minor maintenance jobs on the Slurpee and Big Gulp machines. ("The forgotten half," 1989, p. 46)

The newly created jobs will require more skill than did jobs in the past. Peter Coleman (1993) estimates that approximately 40% of new jobs will require more than 16 years of preparation and training. The greatest challenge facing our nation is to meet the needs of adolescents who will *not* be college graduates (Glover & Marshall, 1993; Hoyt, 1988).

Although unemployment among young workers is down, this decrease is not uniform across all adolescents, and many minority youth face significantly higher rates of unemployment than the White majority. Among

FIGURE 10.6 Occupations With the Fastest Growth and Decline, 1994–2005 ▶

Source: Bureau of Labor Statistics. (1996). U.S. Department of Labor, Washington, DC: U.S. Government Printing Office.

Fastest Growing Occupations

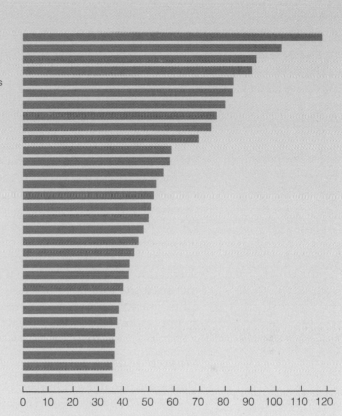

Personal and home care aides
Home health aides
Systems analysts
Computer engineers
Physical and corrective therapy assistants and aides
Electronic pagination systems workers
Physical therapists
Residential counselors
Human services workers
Manicurists
Medical assistants
Paralegals
Medical records technicians
Teachers, special education
Amusement and recreation attendants
Correction officers
Operations research analysts
Guards
Speech-language pathologists and audiologists
Detectives, except public
Surgical technologists
Dental hygienists
Adjustment clerks
Teacher aides and educational assistants
Data processing equipment repairers
Nursery and greenhouse managers
Securities and financial services sales workers
Bill and account collectors
Respiratory therapists
Pest controllers and assistants
Emergency medical technicians

0 10 20 30 40 50 60 70 80 90 100 110 120

Percent increase

Fastest Declining Occupations

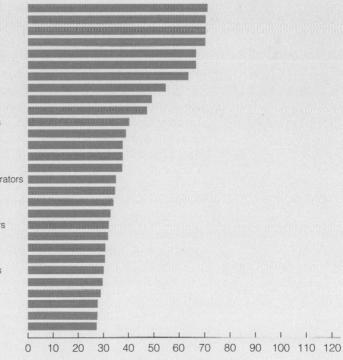

Typesetting and composing machine operators
Directory assistance operators
Station installers and repairers, telephone
Central office operators
Billing, posting, and calculating machine operators
Data entry keyers, composing
Shoe sewing machine operators and tenders
Peripheral EDP equipment operators
Cooks, private household
Motion picture projectionists
Rail yard engineers, dinkey operators, and hostlers
Central office and PBX installers and repairers
Computer operators, except peripheral equipment
Statement clerks
Housekeepers and butlers
Drilling/boring machine tool setters and set-up operators
Fitters, structural metal, precision
Mining, quarrying and tunneling occupations
Typists and word processors
Photoengraving and lithographic machine operators
Boiler operators and tenders, low pressure
Railroad brake, signal, and switch operators
Lathe and turning machine tool setters
Cement and gluing machine operators and tenders
EKG technicians
Machine tool cutting operators, metal and plastic
Paste-up workers
Shoe and leather workers and repairers, precision
Bank tellers

0 10 20 30 40 50 60 70 80 90 100 110 120

Percent decrease

inner-city minority youth, unemployment can reach staggering proportions, exceeding 70% in some inner-city areas (Panel on High-Risk Youth, 1993). These inner-city youth face not only joblessness, but also poverty, poorly equipped schools, increased drug use, and high rates of violent crime. Furthermore, many businesses have left the cities, making employment even less accessible. Job-training programs have offered one of the few opportunities to change the life circumstances of these youth, but federal funding for these has recently been cut. For these youth to begin to realize the promise of the talents within them, they need programs to help not only with jobs, but with the host of conditions that attend joblessness, both at the individual and community level. At present, some of the most successful attempts to turn conditions around come not from federally sponsored programs but from individual efforts. Ervin "Magic" Johnson, for instance, has built a number of upscale movie theaters in low-income, high-crime neighborhoods. These theaters have not only contributed jobs but have also increased the volume of business for surrounding bookstores and eating establishments, as moviegoers browse before or after a show. Perhaps equally as important, these theaters have contributed to a sense of community.

Women and Work

Discrimination in Employment   Most women of working age are employed —80% in their mid-twenties to mid-forties, and just below 70% in their mid-fifties to mid-sixties (U.S. Bureau of the Census, 1993). Even though more female adolescents today plan to work in top-level jobs than ever before (Davey & Stoppard, 1993), sex segregation in the work force is still widespread. More females than males hold low-status, low-paying clerical, sales, and service jobs; the vast majority of high-paying professional jobs are held by males (U.S. Bureau of the Census, 1993). Table 10.1 shows the median weekly earnings for each of six occupational categories and the percentages of males and females employed in each of them.

Although the numbers of males and females graduating from college are about equal, college education will not guarantee equivalent pay. Even among adolescents, the median annual income for males exceeds that for females. Males aged 15 to 19 make nearly $1,200 more than females their age. This difference increases to $3,100 for 25- to 29-year-olds, and reaches a stunning difference of $8,348 over all ages (Youth Indicators, 1996).

Sex discrimination in the work force takes shape primarily in the different types of jobs held by individuals of either sex. The terms *pink collar* and *blue collar* refer to occupations that are female- or male-dominated. Females are more likely to work in service occupations—clerical and salesclerk positions or child care—and males as craftsmen, machine operators, technicians, farmers, or laborers.

The trends are changing, however. Occupational planning among high school seniors is not as sex-typed as in previous years. Gerstein, Lichtman, and Barokas (1988) compared the occupational plans of a national sample of 28,000 high school seniors in 1980 with a comparable sample in 1972 and found that the number of adolescent females planning for a profession had substantially increased, whereas the number of males had decreased slightly (Table 10.2). Nearly 30% of the females indicated an intention to en-

TABLE 10.1   Occupations and Median Weekly Earnings of Males and Females, 1992

Occupational Categories	Male		Female	
	% of Total Employed	Median Weekly Earnings	% of Total Employed	Median Weekly Earnings
Managerial and professional (e.g., business executives, doctors, nurses, lawyers, teachers, engineers)	52.7%	$777	47.3%	$562
Technical, sales, and administrative support (e.g., health technicians, sales representatives, sales clerks, bank tellers, teacher aides)	36.1	519	63.9	365
Service (e.g., child-care workers, police officers, firefighters, food service workers, janitors, hairdressers)	40.9	330	59.1	248
Precision production, craft, and repair (e.g., mechanics, construction workers, carpenters)	91.4	503	8.6	336
Operators, fabricators, laborers (e.g., machine operators, truck drivers, bus drivers, freight handlers)	75.0	393	25.0	279
Farming, forestry, fishing (e.g., farmers, loggers, fishers)	84.1	269	15.9	223

Source: U.S. Bureau of the Census. (1993). *Statistical abstract of the United States. 1993* (113th ed.). Washington, DC: U.S. Government Printing Office.

ter a profession such as accountant, artist, nurse, or social worker (Professional 1 category). The 30% figure is considerably higher than in prior years and is slightly higher than that for male adolescents. The percentage of adolescent females planning to become lawyers, college professors, doctors, dentists, or scientists (Professional 2) nearly doubled over the same time period and is equal to that for males. In all, nearly half of female high school seniors planned for professional occupations.

Table 10.2 also shows a large decrease in the percentage of females planning to become teachers, secretaries, and salesclerks, and those planning to enter service jobs—all of which are traditionally female-dominated occupations. The percentage of high school females planning for professional occupations or thinking of entering male-dominant occupations increased from just over half in 1972 to over two-thirds in 1980 (Gerstein, Lichtman, & Barokas, 1988).

Advancement Opportunities   Despite statistics such as these, females will find it difficult to get the jobs they want. Kenneth Hoyt (1989), at Kansas State University's Manhattan campus, notes that the upward mobility of entrants to the labor force will be limited by the large numbers of baby boomers already there (see Chapter 1). Hoyt (1988) points out that 75% of those who will be working in the year 2000 presently hold jobs. Shifts in patterns of employment are not likely until these baby boomers reach retirement age. The relatively large numbers of middle-aged boomers also cuts

TABLE 10.2   Occupational Plans in 1972 and 1980 for All Seniors—Males and Females

Plan	All Seniors (%)*			Males (%)			Females (%)		
	1972	1980	Percentage Difference	1972	1980	Percentage Difference	1972	1980	Percentage Difference
Professional 2 (e.g., attorney, physician, scientist)	11.9	13.5	+1.6	16.6	13.3	−3.3	7.8	13.7	+ 5.9
Professional 1 (e.g., accountant, architect, artist, engineer, nurse, social worker)	19.8	27.6	+7.8	19.1	25.4	+6.3	20.5	29.4	+ 8.9
Technical	6.0	9.3	+3.3	7.8	11.6	+3.8	4.5	7.0	+ 2.5
Teacher	11.5	3.8	−7.7	6.7	1.6	−5.1	15.7	5.6	−10.1
Manager/Proprietor	4.4	10.9	+6.5	7.0	13.2	+6.2	2.1	8.8	+ 6.7
Craftsman/Operator	13.2	9.5	−3.7	24.9	16.9	−8.0	3.1	2.0	− 0.9
Clerical/Sales	18.2	12.3	−5.9	3.1	3.9	+0.8	31.3	19.2	−12.1
Service	8.1	5.3	−2.8	4.7	3.2	−1.5	11.1	7.0	− 4.1
Farmer/Laborer	3.5	3.2	−0.3	6.8	5.8	−1.0	0.7	0.7	0.0
Military	1.7	2.4	+0.7	3.1	3.6	+0.5	0.6	1.3	+ 0.7
Housewife	1.5	2.4	+0.9	0.1	0.1	0.0	2.7	4.1	+ 1.4

*Percentages based on number of responding to this question. Excludes missing data.

Source: Adapted from M. Gerstein, M. Lichtman, & J. U. Barokas. (1988). Occupational plans of adolescent women compared to men: A cross-sectional examination. *Career Development Quarterly, 36,* 222–230.

down on advancement opportunities for youth who are starting work now, because they will still be in the work force when the latter are ready to move up to more advanced positions (Fullerton, 1987).

More females are employed today than previously, and the number of attractive new jobs (that is, those requiring more skill and offering better pay) is relatively small. By far the largest number of available jobs are low paying and offer little opportunity for advancement. The upshot is a situation in which relatively stiff competition exists. Under similar conditions in the past, we have seen the privileged group, in this case European American males, close ranks to protect its interests. Unless effective social initiatives continue, external barriers to advancement for females in the year 2000 may be worse than today (Subich, 1989).

The problem for females is not so much getting work as it is getting *quality* work (Subich, 1989). Females still have difficulty entering certain occupational areas and getting jobs from which they can advance. Until recently, career counselors focused primarily on external barriers to equal employment—active or passive discrimination. Such barriers will continue until eradicated by social movements; however, internal barriers in the form of self-limiting expectations are also present. Subich comments that an immediate advantage to focusing on these barriers is to place the forces of change in the hands of the individual. Change through broad social movements such as legislation will of course remain important (Subich, 1989).

Even though more female adolescents today aspire to high-level jobs than in previous generations, they will still have to battle many assumptions about women's ability to make hard decisions and close multi-million-dollar deals.

Self-Limiting Expectations   One of the primary internal barriers adolescent females face when they begin a job is the value they assign to their work. Studies find that females place less value on their work than do males (Major & Forcey, 1985). As a consequence, females expect to be paid less—and are. An office worker who sees the importance to a company of maintaining files and records (invoices, shipments, and so on) will value the work he or she does and expect to be paid accordingly. This person might argue, with reason, that the company's income depends on how effectively records are kept. Those who consider their work to be important are likely to show initiative and creativity—important for pay increases and advancement to higher positions. Most, if not all, of the self-limiting expectations females have are learned (Major & Forcey, 1985).

A number of factors distinguish females who expect to pursue nontraditional occupations (the ones that also pay more) from those who stay in traditional types of work. The influence of significant others, including role models, is important. So, too, is the anticipated cost of education (Davey & Stoppard, 1993). Information about the availability of jobs and the many types of jobs that exist is also vitally important. But for such information to have an effect, adolescent females must see it as relevant to their own career plans—that is, that *they* can be a botanist, beautician, electrician, ship loader, teacher, or business owner (Subich, 1989).

Many of the problems women face in the work force are shared by minorities. We turn to a consideration of minorities in the work force next.

Minorities and Work

Whitney Young, a prominent African American leader, once remarked, "The trouble is that blacks are so visible. You hire one secretary and it looks like a whole lot of integration." As Young reminds us, we are still at the "token" stage with respect to the full range of job opportunities open to minority adolescents. One African American or Hispanic in the office may look like a lot of integration, but that token minority person is usually a secretary, not the boss.

TABLE 10.3   Percentage Breakdown by Occupational Category
for Black and White Workers

Occupational Categories	Median Weekly Wage	Blacks	Whites
Managerial and professional	$670	18.6%	30.6%
Technical, sales, and administrative support	442	26.5	30.7
Service	289	22.5	10.6
Precision production, craft, and repair	420	9.0	12.2
Operators, fabricators, and laborers	336	21.6	13.0
Farming, forestry, and fishing	246	1.9	3.0

Source: U.S. Bureau of the Census. (1993). *Statistical abstract of the United States: 1993* (113th ed.). Washington, DC: U.S. Government Printing Office.

Minority youth start out with career aspirations as high as those of youth from the dominant culture. But they encounter numerous social, cultural, and personal barriers to success. Despite the landmark legislation in the 1960s and 1970s that paved the way for equity in employment, progress has been slow. At least one expert in the field has concluded that "minority persons in the labor force are worse off today than they were in 1968" (Hoyt, 1989, p. 208). Hoyt (1989) grimly adds that the picture is not likely to get better in the near future; upward mobility in the work force will continue to be limited for minorities. Table 10.3 shows the percentages of Blacks and Whites employed in different types of occupations, along with the median weekly earnings in each. We find many more White workers in the two highest paid categories (managerial and professional; technical, sales, and administrative support) and, if we exclude the infrequent category of "farming, forestry, and fishing," more Black workers are in the two lowest paid categories (service; operators, fabricators, and laborers).

Poverty   The high incidence of poverty among minority adolescents is a common link among the factors that affect their eventual employment; among the most important factors are staying in school, receiving quality education, and making informed decisions about their futures. The rate of poverty can be four times as high among minorities as among Whites (Panel on High-Risk Youth, 1993). Poverty in relation to education is much like oil in relation to water—the two don't mix. Low-income students are nearly four times as likely to drop out of high school as their upper-income counterparts (Wetzel, 1987), and those who remain in school are more likely to be tracked in noncollege-preparatory and vocational courses (see Chapter 7).

Poverty is also related to lower academic performance. Low-income students are not as likely to achieve at the same levels as middle-income and upper-income students (Wetzel, 1987), nor are the educational programs they receive of the same quality as those provided to middle- and upper-income youth. Poverty is unevenly distributed, tending to be centralized in urban and inner-city schools, where minority students make up most of the student body. In 23 of the 25 largest cities in the United States, for example, minorities make up most of the students (Hoyt, 1989).

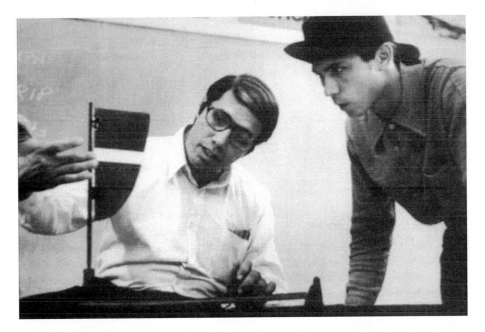

The film *Stand and Deliver* is the story of a high school math teacher in East Los Angeles who dared to believe in his students and to demand that they believe in themselves. Motivated by his high expectations and his refusal to give up on them, these adolescents not only stayed in school but also passed the advanced placement exam in calculus.

Programs   Some programs are more important to occupational success than others. Math and science courses provide a gateway to many of the higher level jobs. Preparation in both of these areas is generally poorer among minority students (Hall & Post-Kammer, 1987). African American students, for instance, take fewer math courses and do more poorly in them than European American students (Reyes & Stanic, 1985). They also have less actual experience with science either inside the classroom (for example, watching chicks hatch, growing a plant from seed, studying an ant colony) or outside it (such as trips to museums and science fairs) and, not surprisingly, can think of fewer uses for science (Kahle, 1982). Almost two-and-a-half times as many White as Black males in college major in math or science (Trent, 1983). With the exception of Asian Americans, all minorities are underrepresented in science, math, and engineering (Brooks, 1990; Hall & Post-Kammer, 1987), and these are the fields preparing students for the high-level jobs of the future (Arbona, 1989; Hall & Post-Kammer, 1987).

Planning   Many minority adolescents simply don't know about the many types of career options that exist and are unaware of the financial aid that is potentially available to them. Most also do not receive adequate help with career planning. Many students choose their courses with little knowledge of the requirements they'll need for different types of jobs. Even more immediately, few know what courses they will need if they want to go to college or what courses will best prepare them for trade or technical schools. In one study, when students were asked who had been the most help to them in planning their programs, most said either their friends or their parents—not counselors and teachers (Boyer, 1983). Because parents and friends of minority parents are less likely to have attended college themselves, these students are not likely to receive the information they need.

Preparation   Many of the newly created jobs will require some postsecondary education. On an encouraging note, significantly more minority high school students are entering college than a generation ago and more are completing college. Among African American youth, for instance, more than four times the number of individuals completed four years of college in 1995 than in 1960 (*Digest of Education Statistics,* 1996).

Positions   Most minority youth are all too aware of the barriers to equal employment, and both Blacks and Hispanics adjust their expectations accordingly. Thus Hispanic students have just as high career *aspirations* as do Whites, but lower expectations of achieving them (Arbona, 1989). Similarly, Black students are aware of the existence of barriers (Howell, Frese, & Sollie, 1984). Perhaps no statistic speaks more clearly to this issue than unemployment rates: Unemployment among Blacks who graduated from high school in 1986 was higher than among Whites who dropped out of school (Wetzel, 1987).

INTERVENTION PROGRAMS: STRATEGIES FOR CHANGE

Adolescent females, minority students, and the counselors who work with them need to increase their awareness of the problems, and opportunities, these youth face in making career decisions.

Counselors as Change Agents

Because the opportunity structure for minority adolescents, and for females, is not the same as that for White, middle-class males (see Chapter 7), counselors may have to become active "change agents" in order to effectively prepare students for jobs (Brooks, 1990; Ogbu, 1992). Linda Brooks (1990) suggests that counselors leave their offices and meet with parents, teachers, and local businesses to combat the inequities that minority youth face. Many minority adolescents are not as well prepared as their nonminority counterparts for the careers that have traditionally been held by White males. Many have fallen below competitive levels in basic skills such as reading and math. Counselors may need to act as student advocates, working with teachers and schools to develop effective intervention programs that prepare minority youth for the full range of careers open to others.

An example of one such program is currently under way at California State University, Los Angeles (Wapner, 1990). The university established a contractual agreement with a local, predominantly Hispanic, junior high school. All students who participate in a precollege program in the sciences are guaranteed admittance to the university. Junior high school teachers,

> **Box 10.1   Myths That Interfere With Adaptive Career Decision Making**
>
> - "I have to know exactly what I want to do before I can act."
> - "Choosing a career involves making just one decision."
> - "If I change my mind once I've picked a career, I'm a failure."
> - "If I can only be good in nursing [construction, management, and so on], then I will be content."
> - "Work satisfies all of a person's needs."
> - "If I work hard enough, I can be successful at anything."
> - "How good I am at my job determines my worth as a person."
>
> *Source:* L. K. Mitchell & J. D. Krumboltz. (1987). The effects of cognitive restructuring and decision-making training on career indecision. *Journal of Counseling and Development, 66,* 171–174.

counselors, university professors, and administrators meet with students and parents to familiarize them with the program. Students receive tutoring in basic math and reading skills while taking science courses in junior high and, later, high school. Programs such as this one have been started at a number of universities across the country (Kammer, Fouad, & Williams, 1988).

Before counselors can assume the role of active change agents, many need to face their own biases. A counselor who accepts a talented minority girl's statement that she is interested in working with children as an aide or a helper in a classroom or playground, without suggesting other career opportunities that also involve helping people (such as medicine, psychology, social work), reveals an insensitivity to the existence of very real gender or culturally based conflicts (Brooks, 1990).

Would it be too intrusive to direct this student to consider other career options? Brooks argues that counselors *must* begin directing minority and female students' attention to areas other than the role-traditional ones in which they express an initial interest. Those who have doubts as to the appropriateness of such actions should consider what the same counselor would be likely to do if a talented White male student expressed interest in becoming a teacher's aid or helper (Brooks, 1990).

Irrational Beliefs and Maladaptive Myths

Students frequently approach career decisions with maladaptive beliefs and myths (Krumboltz, 1991; Luzzo, Funk, & Strang, 1996). These can be about themselves ("I'm not very smart"), a profession ("You have to be self-confident to be a nurse"), or the conditions that lead to satisfaction with a career ("I wouldn't be happy in a profession unless I made a lot of money at it"). Box 10.1 identifies types of myths that keep many people from trying interesting careers.

Research Focus

Factorial Designs: Career Indecision—Don't Push Me; I'm Still Thinking

The way she described it, she felt like a diver, her toes on the edge of the high board and the pool a blue square beneath her. People were climbing up the ladder, crowding behind her, telling her to jump. But she'd forgotten how to swim.

The counselor had heard it before. He met so many students throughout the year, mostly juniors and some seniors. All were panicked at the thought of jumping off—graduating and beginning a career. What makes it hard for some individuals to make career decisions while others find it relatively easy? Is there anything to be done to help those who have difficulty deciding on a career?

Career indecision is associated with numerous maladaptive beliefs and myths. Students believe that they have to be "absolutely certain" before they can do anything, that "planning for a career involves just one decision," that their parents will "never understand" if they don't become a teacher, social worker, carpenter, brain surgeon, and so on. Do these myths interfere with adaptive decision making? Or does the problem lie in the decision-making steps themselves? Most career counselors assume the latter, and train students in the skills they need to make career decisions. Although the most common inter-

vention approach to career counseling, this type of decision-making training has had only modest success.

An alternative approach, cognitive restructuring, addresses the irrational beliefs students have about career decisions. This method confronts students with their irrational beliefs and thus enables them to replace these with adaptive ones. Lynda Mitchell and John Krumboltz compared the effectiveness of cognitive restructuring and decision-making training as methods of dealing with career indecision. They included a third condition, in addition to cognitive restructuring and decision-making training, in which students received no career counseling—that is, a *no-treatment control.*

These investigators used a factorial design that included, in addition to counseling conditions, the sex of the students as a variable. In a *factorial design,* two or more independent variables, or factors, are completely *crossed* so that each level of one variable is combined with each level of all the other variables. This design appears in schematic form in the next column. Factorial designs provide information about the effect of each independent variable alone, called a *main effect,* and information about the effect of a variable when another variable is present, called an *interaction.*

An interaction exists when the effect of a variable changes when a second variable is present. We might find, for instance, that both types of counseling are equally effective for female stu-

Intervention Techniques   One approach to counseling students with career indecision, known as *cognitive restructuring,* recommends confronting them with their irrational beliefs. Confrontation can result in cognitive restructuring, making more adaptive decision making possible. A female, for instance, may think that her parents "would have nothing to do with her" if she didn't become an elementary school teacher. Because she has little interest in teaching, she finds it difficult to plan for college or think about a career.

Intervention in the form of cognitive restructuring would encourage her to look at the evidence supporting the belief that her parents would sever their relationship if she did not become a teacher (she might find little to support this belief). A counselor might then give her the assignment of talking to her parents about her future. She discovers they are concerned only

Research Focus *(continued)*

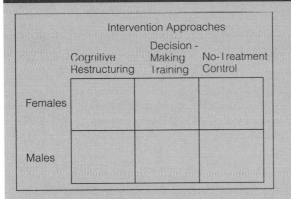

	Intervention Approaches		
	Cognitive Restructuring	Decision - Making Training	No-Treatment Control
Females			
Males			

dents, but for males, one type works better than the other. The existence of an interaction means that we must qualify what we say about a variable. Is decision-making training just as effective as cognitive restructuring? It depends. If the students being counseled are females, then it is. But if males are being counseled, then it is not.

Going back to Mitchell and Krumboltz's experiment, let's see what they did and what they found. Students in the cognitive restructuring condition participated in a five-week program in which they identified maladaptive beliefs and their effect on behavior and completed actual assignments requiring them to test the accuracy of these beliefs. Students in the decision-making training condition also participated in a five-week program in which they learned decision-making skills: defining the problem, clarifying their objectives, then generating and systemati-

cally eliminating alternative solutions, and, finally, committing themselves to a course of action. Students in the control condition received no treatment.

How effective were the programs? Cognitive restructuring helped to reduce anxiety about career decisions more so than did decision-making training. This was true even though students' maladaptive attitudes did not change significantly. Because anxiety is almost always associated with career indecision, its reduction through cognitive restructuring is important. A one-month follow-up revealed that the cognitive restructuring group continued to explore career possibilities more than the other groups. A scale designed to assess decision-making skills revealed that all groups had good skills and did not differ in this respect. This latter finding is especially important, because career decision counseling often focuses on decision-making skills—something at which most students are already quite good. Finally, the type of intervention program interacted with the gender of the students. Males who received training in decision-making skills used these skills less than did the females who were trained in them, or than students of either sex who were trained in cognitive restructuring.

Sources: P. C. Cozby. (1997). *Methods in behavioral research* (6th ed.). Mountain View, CA: Mayfield. L. K. Mitchell & J. D. Krumboltz. (1987). The effects of cognitive restructuring and decision-making training on career indecision. *Journal of Counseling and Development, 66,* 171–174.

that she will be able to support herself in a secure job. She is also assigned the task of interviewing five women in different professions and asking them the most satisfying and frustrating aspects of their work. She finds that accounting, career guidance, and being a teacher (surprise!) are all attractive alternatives. She decides to apply to college. Lynda Mitchell and John Krumboltz (1987) report that cognitive restructuring helps reduce students' anxiety when thinking about career planning, consequently making it easier for them to think about their futures. The Research Focus, "Factorial Designs," discusses career planning and cognitive restructuring.

A related approach, termed *attributional retraining*, focuses students' attention on the way they explain career-related outcomes. Do they attribute career outcomes to conditions for which they are responsible and over which they have control, conditions that will yield to their efforts? Or do they see career outcomes as being influenced more by circumstances beyond their control, where their efforts will do little to change the situation? The former beliefs are adaptive, whereas the latter are not (Luzzo & Ward, 1995).

Darrell Luzzo, at Auburn University, and Tammy James and Marilyn Luna, at the University of North Alabama, (1996) showed students with maladaptive beliefs an attributional retraining video containing adaptive attributional statements such as the following:

> I realized as I was growing up that anything worthwhile in terms of my career was going to take effort and hard work. I pretty much took control over my career decisions. I've worked hard . . . and it has helped me. If I hadn't taken the time and put forth the effort that I did, I wouldn't be doing as well as I am now. (p. 417)

After attributional retraining, these students were significantly more likely to believe that they had control over career decisions, and that the more work they put into these, the more successful they would be. Furthermore, a six-week follow-up showed these differences to persist over time.

At present we need much more information about the effectiveness of the many programs that exist to help minority youth and adolescent females combat the internal and external barriers they face in attaining career goals. What is clear so far is that most teachers, parents, counselors, and students need to expand their thinking beyond role-traditional careers for minorities and females.

ADOLESCENTS AND COLLEGE: THINKING ABOUT IDEAS

With age, adolescents get better at solving life's problems. Is this simply because they can bring more experiences to bear on any decision? Or do their experiences contribute to new ways of thinking, ways that allow them to see that what they presently face often has much in common with problems they solved in the past?

New Solutions to Old Problems: Structural Analytical Thinking

What form might thinking take if it were to move beyond the formal thinking that emerges in early adolescence? Remember, formal thought enables adolescents to stretch their minds beyond a physical world defined by their senses to a world of possibilities that exists first and foremost in their minds, a process that enables them to think of all the possible forms a problem could assume. Formal thought is thought that generates a system, a set of all possible alternatives.

Commons and Richards (1982) suggest a way of thinking that allows individuals to relate two or more systems. Just as formal thinking generates a single system, **structural analytical thinking** identifies parallels between several systems by noting relations that are common to each.

Does structural analytical thinking sound like something only philosophers and metaphysicians engage in? Don't be too quick to say yes. You have already used this way of thinking yourself when reading Chapter 4. Piaget himself has provided us with an example of structural analytical thought: He had to think in a structural analytical way to envision the characteristics of formal thinking. Piaget had to see, in other words, how each of several quite different problems required the same operations for their solution. Whether determining what form life might take on a newly discovered planet or which combination of chemicals produces a yellow liquid, one must isolate the relevant variables, generate all the possible combinations, and systematically test each combination. To see each problem as a reflection of formal thinking, one must think at a structural analytical level.

Structural analytical thinking has a distinct advantage over formal thinking: It gives one a perspective from which to view the problems one is attempting to solve. Unlike formal thinking, which is limited to solving problems within the systems that define them, structural analytical thinking makes it possible to mentally step outside any particular system and consider another approach.

Propositional and Dialectical Reasoning   Stepping outside a system and seeing things from another perspective touches all areas of adolescents' lives, not just the intellectual. Not every adolescent (or even every adult) can do this; it requires reasoning in a new way. Klaus Riegel (1973) distinguishes this reasoning, which he terms dialectical reasoning, from the propositional reasoning that develops with formal thinking. Both types of reasoning start with a set of premises, or assumptions that are accepted as true. As these assumptions are put to the test, in the course of thinking through numerous life problems, they are either supported or refuted.

In **propositional reasoning,** these premises are never questioned, even though any number of situations may reveal them as wrong. In dialectical reasoning, the premises are put into question if, over time, actions based on them are not supported. What does it mean to question our most basic assumptions? We must be able, if only for the moment, to assume another perspective, another view of reality. We must be able to move beyond our worldview to frame questions about the assumptions that underlie it. **Dialectical reasoning** provides a means by which we can gain a perspective on the system we use to define our world.

Formal and Structural Analytical Thinking Compared   Consider two adolescent females as each realizes that even though her parents have always told her that she was free to do or be whatever she wanted, they do not accept her plans for her life. Each has introduced to her parents a young man she intends to marry and has found that they do not approve of her choice.

Connie is upset and confused. She can think of only two explanations for her parents' reaction. Either she is wrong or her parents are wrong. Either her parents *are* willing to accept the choices she makes, but this choice is so outrageous that no parent could support it, or her parents have been living a lie—it's not all right with them for her to be anything she wants to be if that means being different from them. She reacts with hurt and anger and can think of nothing to say to them or to her fiancé.

Although a job can help older adolescents develop structural analytical thinking and dialectical reasoning, the college experience provides more systematic opportunities for cognitive growth. These students will be prepared for a wider array of career possibilities than their counterparts who start working full-time right after high school.

Janice recognizes her hurt and anger at her parents and begins to think about the differences in their values and hers. She recognizes that people's values influence their actions, but that in acting, people change events, and these changes frequently lead to new awareness and new values. Her parents' affirmation of her freedom to be herself has allowed her to be the person she is—a person who is quite different from them. Janice knows that because her parents have valued her, they valued her freedom to make her own decisions, and that because of this freedom she has had experiences they never had. She realizes that these experiences have changed her view of the world and allow her to see things in others that her parents are not able to recognize. Although Janice is sad that her parents cannot appreciate the qualities in her fiancé that she values, she is grateful she had the opportunity they gave her to be herself (Basseches, 1984).

Connie and Janice have each dealt with a painful situation in different ways. Connie's approach reflects formal thinking. She believes there are a set of truths that are described by a point of view. She can evaluate situations and events from this point of view, but has no way of reconciling differences that may challenge it. Thus, either she or her parents must be wrong. Janice can step outside her beliefs and see how they have evolved from those of her parents. Her ability to see evolution and change as a natural part of people and relationships may help her find ways to re-establish a new relationship with her parents. We have discussed the ability to move from one perspective to another, noting differences and finding relationships between them, as an intellectual feat—that is, as structural analytical thinking. Yet more than intellect may be involved. The ability to stand back from one's own way of thinking while viewing that of others may reflect one's personality as much as one's intellect. There's a risk in letting one's beliefs be put to the test in this way. We examine the implications of this very personal stance on knowledge in the next section.

How College Changes the Way Adolescents Think

William Perry (1970), of Harvard University, identified important changes during the college years in the way adolescents think about ideas. These changes reflect their beliefs about the nature of truth as much as their ability to think in general. Perry conducted his observations among college men. However, individuals in any setting should experience similar changes if they let their experiences challenge their ideas. Perry identified three major forms of thought: dualism, relativism, and commitment to relativism.

Dualism: Looking for Answers   **Dualistic thinking** is the belief that problems are simply solved by finding the right answer, that is, by discovering the truth. Dualistic thinkers have not yet encountered differences of perspective or belief that are so great they could not be bridged by a single set of answers. They operate, in other words, within a single frame of reference. For them learning is mostly a matter of acquiring the facts; it does not require evaluation of the facts. Adolescents who function at this level tend to view ideas, and people, as right or wrong, as good or bad. Ideas that are familiar—that can be assimilated into their belief system—are accepted as legitimate; those that violate their beliefs are regarded as illegitimate, or at the very least, suspect (Perry, 1970).

Adolescents who function at this level have rarely experienced ways of life that are different from their own. To them, issues are straightforward, and problems yield to discipline and hard work. The following is an adolescent's description of life in his hometown:

> Well I come, I came here from a small town. Midwest, where, well, ah, everyone believed the same things. Everyone's Methodist and everyone's Republican. So, ah, there just wasn't any . . . well that's not quite true . . . there are some Catholics, two families, and I guess they, I heard they were Democrats, but they weren't really, didn't seem to be in town really, I guess. (Perry, 1970, p. 70)

One of the central experiences of adolescence is the discovery that others have points of view different from one's own. This discovery is pivotal in moving out of the first of Perry's levels. Here is what the same adolescent had to say about diversity:

> So in my dorm I, we've been-ah a number of discussions, where, there'll be, well, there's quite a variety in our dorm, Catholic, Protestant, and the rest of them, and a Chinese boy whose parents-ah follow the teachings of Confucianism. He isn't, but his folks are.... And a couple of guys are complete-ah agnostics, agnostics. Of course, some people are quite disturbing, they say they're atheists. But they don't go very far, they say they're atheists, but they're not. And then there are, one fellow who is a deist. And by discussing it-ah, it's the, the sort of thing that, that really-ah awakens you. (1970, p. 70)

Relativism: Losing Oneself to Ideas   Perry points out that the steps from dualism to relativism require courage. It's an uncomfortable journey. Instead of accepting simple answers, adolescents must learn to rely on their own judgment and risk their own ideas. Students know that this process is difficult. As one student said, "Every now and again you do, do . . . do meet p-people who just give up and try and find 'answers' . . . I mean . . . it's hopeless" (1970, p. 107).

Relativistic thinking compares ideas instead of looking for the single one that is right. Relativistic thinkers become aware that what they had accepted as facts are actually interpretations that make sense within some frame of reference, whether a theory presented in a class or the perspective offered by the culture. They also know that more than one frame of reference exists, and that each represents a legitimate point of view. From Perry's description of these characteristics, it sounds as if students are moving from formal thought, in which they are operating within a single frame of reference, to structural analytic thought, in which they can compare several worldviews or frames of reference. The development of dialectical reasoning may be pivotal to this change, as this would allow students to evaluate their assumptions as they go along.

One student had this to say about the change to relativistic thought:

> I think the main thing that was interesting this year was questioning basic assumptions.... It was interesting in anthropology, particularly, which I didn't go into very deeply, but what I saw as the very basic differences, things that never occurred to me to question before, I don't know whether I'm questioning them now, but at least I know that it's possible to question. (1970, p. 117)

Students experience a new freedom in these discoveries: a freedom to see that they can decide for themselves which ideas are best rather than try to discover what has made most sense to someone else. Learning becomes personally relevant, as they shift their focus from the facts they have been amassing to the process of thinking itself. Relativistic thinking carries a distinct advantage: Students can discover *themselves* in addition to the concepts and theories they are studying. Looking back on this discovery, one student remembered his first year in college as follows:

I remember my first Christmas vacation home from college. Nobody could say anything about the world that I didn't say was just an hypothesis. My Dad and I argued all the time. He'd say something was an established scientific fact, like gravity or the world being round, or anything else that most people believe, and I would answer that a "fact" is just an hypothesis that hasn't been disproved yet. I know I must have been a pain in the butt to everybody but I had discovered relativism. I "knew" that what people believed to be true, including scientists, was what fit their experience. And since different people had different experiences—and even the same people had new experiences—nothing was true for everybody for all time. I'm a little embarrassed now when I think back to how I must have sounded, but I sure thought that I had found the philosophical answer to everything (Wapner, 1990)

Commitment to Relativism: Finding Oneself   Erik Erikson (1959) has said that one's sense of identity requires a feeling that what "I" know is also what "I" value. Relativism challenges this equation as students cut themselves adrift from the moorings of ideas and values they once accepted as absolutes. The danger of relativism is the potential loss of identity that adolescents face. If knowledge reflects different contexts, adolescents will experience discontinuity in what they believe and value as they move from one context to the next.

The pathway out of this maze is choice. Adolescents move beyond relativism by making commitments, becoming agents, choosing, investing themselves, and affirming their experiences. Perry notes that choice and **commitment in relativism** create meaning that would not otherwise exist in a relativistic world; reason alone offers little basis for commitment to any particular worldview. Paradoxically, intellectual development lies in going beyond reason, in taking a position despite one's knowledge that reason alone does not justify this position over others. This step, in a very real sense, involves an act of faith, just as the previous one involved courage. Adolescents move from first defining themselves through individual commitments, such as a career or a mate, to the realization that commitment has come to characterize a way of living.

Gender Differences in Intellectual Development

Does the above description fit the intellectual journey of college women as well as men? We simply don't know. Perry included a small number of women in his sample, but he referred only to interviews with males in validating his scheme of intellectual development. Although the females he interviewed conformed to this progression, he may have missed other progressions that better describe intellectual transitions in college women. More recently Mary Belenky, Blythe Clinchy, Nancy Goldberger, and Jill Tarule (1986) conducted a similar study with women.

Unlike Perry, these investigators did not interview a homogeneous sample of students in a university setting. One third of their sample was composed of mothers facing the real life challenges of parenting. Belenky and her associates point out that it is easiest to see a sequence such as the one Perry observed when the sample is homogeneous and the context in which

Many female adolescents maintain a surface conformity, becoming polite listeners and spectators. Rather than asserting their abilities, many experience intellectual loneliness and become silently alienated from the learning process.

development takes place does not vary. Only future research will tell us if females move through a similar intellectual progression. Meanwhile, the comparisons Belenky and her colleagues provide with Perry's data are indeed interesting.

They note, first, that females do not think in ways neatly described by Perry's categories. Differences emerge from the very beginning. Let's look again at the first step males take. Belenky and her associates note that the adolescent male, once he discovers the multiplicity of truth,

> foresees his own future as an authority and stakes his claim to the intellectual terrain. . . . [His] perception of the multiplicity of truth becomes a tool in the process of his separation and differentiation from others. His opinion distinguishes him from all others and he lets them know it. (1986, p. 64)

Adolescent females take a different first step. Those who begin the intellectual journey move from subjective knowledge (realizing that truth is relative) to procedural knowledge (assuming responsibility for what they know) to constructive knowledge (being aware that knowledge is constructed by each knower). Not all complete this journey.

Subjective Knowledge: Agreeable Dissent   Adolescent females with **subjective knowledge** appreciate that the multiplicity of truth frees them from traditional authority; but they are cautious about embracing an intellectual position. Unlike males, who have been rewarded for testing the status quo, females have been rewarded for being quiet, predictable, and agreeable. Speaking up, taking a stand, or disagreeing with others runs counter to all they have learned. Female adolescents repeatedly express concern that, in taking an intellectual stand, they will isolate themselves from others. Thus their relationships constrain them from forming and defending ideas that would distinguish or separate them from other people. They experience few expectations about, and get little support for, this type of intellectual risk taking (Belenky, Clinchy, Goldberger, & Tarule, 1986).

Rather than speaking out, many maintain a surface conformity while they covertly examine issues. "They become the polite listeners, the spectators who watch and listen but do not act" (Belenky, Clinchy, Goldberger, & Tarule, 1986, p. 66). Belenky and her associates note the intellectual loneliness of these female adolescents:

> The tragedy is that [they] still their public voice and are reluctant to share their private world; ultimately this hinders them from finding mentors who might support their intellectual and emotional growth. [They] can be silently alienated . . . , knowing somehow that their conformity is a lie and does not reveal the inner truth or potential they have recently come to value. (p. 67)

In speaking up, males lay claim to an intellectual terrain that has been staked out for centuries as theirs. There are few equivalent intellectual domains for females, and few means are identified for their use in defining one. Instead of reason—the ultimate analytic tool—females have been told their strength lies in intuition, which in relation to reason is like a divining rod compared to a surveyor's level. Instead of mapping out ideas, many learn to wait for the gentle tug of mind in an otherwise silent trek across an uncharted terrain.

In becoming skilled listeners of themselves and others, some women come to see the contradictions of their stance. Their observations make it possible for them to develop the more critical thought that characterizes the next step they take. (The Research Focus, "Theory-Guided Research," explores the issue of sexism in our language.)

Procedural Knowledge: Stepping Out Intellectually   Women who step out intellectually—with **procedural knowledge**—assume responsibility for discovering things for themselves. Some do this by mastering the facts in an area, whether it be political economics, nursing, or managing a home. Others adopt a more subjective approach to what they are learning, approaching ideas for what they have to say about their lives. The understanding these women gain is more intimate and personal than that of the first group. Only the first approach is characteristic of Perry's males. For those who adopt it, doubting becomes an important way of putting ideas on trial, and bull sessions provide a forum in which individuals attack each other's position to hone the cutting edge of their logic. Belenky and her associates (1986) note that

> women find it hard to see doubting as a "game"; they tend to take it personally. Teachers and fathers and boyfriends assure them that arguments are not between *persons* but between *positions,* but the women continue to fear that someone may get hurt. (p. 105)

Research Focus

Theory-Guided Research: How Sexist Is Our Language?

Masculine words such as *he* and *man* have been used generically in English for centuries to refer to individuals of either sex. In contrast, when comparable words such as *she* or *woman* are used, the listener knows that the person being referred to is female. But how generic are those masculine words? Are listeners equally likely to think of a woman as a man when they hear "he"? Or do they do a quick semantic shuffle and mentally note that the word could also refer to females?

The question is an interesting one, but the answer has been difficult to obtain. It's hard to observe quick semantic shuffles, especially when these are mental. In this case, theory suggests a way to get some answers. Sik Hung Ng used the concepts of proactive inhibition and release from proactive inhibition, concepts derived from a theory of learning and memory, to determine how words are linguistically coded in memory.

We know that words are coded both for their specific meaning and for category membership. Thus the word *poodle* would be coded in terms of the animal's specific characteristics (for example, curly hair, intelligence, pointed snout), but also in terms of the category "dog." This is true for "man" as well. *Man* would be coded in terms of specific characteristics (such as adult, human), and also in terms of the category "male." But are words such as *he* and *man* assimilated just as easily into the feminine category as the masculine one? Linguistically speaking, that is, are they truly generic?

The concept of proactive inhibition suggests a way of finding out. *Proactive inhibition* refers to interference caused by prior learning when remembering new material. The interference is greatest when the old and new material are similar. In other words, one's ability to learn something new is inversely related to how much similar material one has previously learned. Proactive inhibition tells us that memory for a new word will not be as good if one has already memorized other words from the same category (that is, if the new word shares the same linguistic category) than if the word is different from others one has memorized (be-

---

Conversations for females serve the function of bull sessions for males. Belenky and her associates give an example of a young Ethiopian college student who explained in one such conversation with an American friend why her country had adopted communism. They note the following:

> These young women did not engage in metaphysical debate. They did not argue about abstractions or attack or defend positions. No one tried to prove anything or to convert anyone. The Ethiopian articulated her reality, and the American tried to understand it. They did not discuss communism in general, impersonal terms, but in terms of its origins and consequences among a particular group of real people. (p. 114)

Though more advanced than subjective knowledge, procedural knowledge operates within a system of knowledge that cannot examine itself. Females who think in either of these ways

> can criticize a system, but only in the system's terms, only according to the system's standards. Women at this position may be liberals or conservatives, but they cannot be radicals. If, for example, they are feminists, they want

Research Focus (*continued*)

longs to a different linguistic category). *Release from proactive inhibition* occurs when the new word is from a different category; the release takes the form of better memory for the distinctive than the similar item. These twin concepts provide a means for discovering the linguistic category of any word. If the linguistic code for *his* and *man* is truly a masculine one, these words will not be remembered as easily following a list of other masculine words (proactive inhibition) as after a list of feminine ones (release from proactive inhibition).

Adolescents were randomly assigned to one of two conditions in which they listened to pairs of feminine words (queen-Linda, nun-Mary, girl-Iris, mom-Ruth) or masculine ones (king-Ivan, son-Lewis, boy-Ross, dad-Mike). After each list, they heard two additional pairs (man-Robin and his-Chris). Unlike the names in the masculine or feminine list, both Robin and Chris are unisex names. Will *man* and *his* be as easy to remember after the list of masculine pairs as after the feminine? If so, these words are genuinely generic.

Theory tells us that we first need to check for a buildup of proactive inhibition over the initial list of pairs, that is, to look for poorer recall of the last words than the first ones. As expected, this occurred. Next, we need to determine whether proactive inhibition continued for the generic words when they followed the masculine list, and whether release from proactive inhibition occurred following the feminine list. Both of these occurred as well.

These findings tell us that the words *man* and *his* are coded as masculine words in memory and are not truly generic. The author notes that if they are generic, then their usage in sentences such as the following should not appear incongruous: "Throughout most of history, men have always breast-fed their babies." But sentences such as these do jar and prompt a rereading to discover what is amiss.

The problem adolescents face is not one of having to make sense of incongruities such as the preceding example. The more serious problem occurs when they experience no incongruity—when language so structures experience that half of *human*kind can be excluded.

Source: S. H. Ng. (1990). Androcentric coding of *man* and *his* in memory by language users. *Journal of Experimental Social Psychology, 26,* 455–464.

---

equal opportunities for women within the capitalistic structure; they do not question the premises of the structure. When these women speak of "beating the system," they do not mean violating its expectations but rather exceeding them. (Belenky, Clinchy, Goldberger, & Tarule, 1986, p. 127)

For females to move beyond these forms of knowing, they need more than formal thought.

Constructive Knowledge: Examining the Self   Females who move into **constructive knowledge** report a period of self-examination in which they experience being out of touch with parts of themselves. "During the transition into a new way of knowing, there is an impetus to allow the self back into the process of knowing, to confront the pieces of the self that may be experienced as fragmented and contradictory" (Belenky, Clinchy, Goldberger, & Tarule, 1986, p. 136). These females ask themselves questions such as "Who am I?" and "How will I approach life?"

Questions such as these echo the concerns of Perry's young males who experienced the need for commitment in their relativistic thought. Belenky and her associates note that these females experience a "heightened consciousness and sense of choice" about the ways they examine their world and who they will become. They become aware of the fact that given a different perspective or even a different point in time, they could come up with different answers to the same questions (Belenky, Clinchy, Goldberger, & Tarule, 1986). This awareness leads to the central truth of constructed knowledge: that knowledge is constructed and hence relative, and the knower is an intrinsic part of the process. This position allows these females to examine a set of beliefs from a perspective outside that system. Something like structural analytical thinking almost surely is present at this point.

In addition to their general approach to knowledge, how much adolescents know about the subject they are studying affects how they think about it and how much they will remember of what they learn. We turn to research on expert knowledge next.

ADOLESCENTS AS EXPERTS

Experts and Novices

On the subject of expert knowledge, research supports the age-old observation that the rich get richer. The more adolescents know in a given area, the easier it is for them to learn even more. A classic study supports this observation. Chess masters and novices briefly saw boards from chess games in progress and attempted to reproduce what they had seen. The masters could reproduce the entire board of play easily; novices could not. However, when each viewed boards with pieces placed at random, the masters were no better than the novices (de Groot, 1965). The masters were only better when they could bring their knowledge to bear on the situation. Are chess masters uniquely gifted? And do adolescents ever function like experts?

They do—inside the classroom and out. Just as chess masters can remember more of the board in play, adolescents who are *experts* in a subject have better memory for what they've read on the subject than do novices. In fact, how much adolescents will remember of what they read is much more closely related to their background knowledge about the material than their ability (S. Lee, 1990).

Chi (1985), at the University of Pittsburgh, found that students who know a lot about a subject organize information differently than those who do not. Specifically, students with expert knowledge are more likely to organize what they know according to high-level, abstract categories. Those who know less not only have fewer facts at their disposal but also organize them less efficiently. Consider a science class in which students have just completed a section on desert ecology. The teacher has asked them to name all the insectivores. The more knowledgeable students will have classified life forms in a way that allows them to pull out this information, abstractly according to functions, such as eating habits. Less knowledgeable students

distinguish organisms in terms of their immediately obvious features, such as size or shape (Boster & Johnson, 1989).

Deane Schiano and her colleagues (1989) classified high school students according to their skill in an area and compared the strategies each type of student used in solving problems. These investigators looked for differences between skilled and unskilled adolescents in the way they organized information and used strategies. This research, just as Chi's, found that more knowledgeable students organize information in higher-level categories, an approach which in turn allows them to adopt more efficient strategies when solving problems. Adolescents who are unskilled sort problems on the basis of perceptual similarities. Skilled students look for similarities in the relationships among problems. Students who are skilled are better able to abstract prototypes of the problems involved; less skilled adolescents are limited to visual comparisons of the alternatives at hand (Schiano, Cooper, Glaser, & Zhang, 1989).

Jill Larkin, at Carnegie-Mellon University, studied the way expert and novice college students approach problems. Once again, Larkin (1985) found that students of either type tend to adopt different approaches. Those who know more—the experts—approach problems in terms of general principles that reflect what they know of the elements involved. In organic chemistry, for example, one must be able to say what reactions will result when two or more chemicals are combined under different conditions. The number of potential outcomes under different conditions can be quite large.

Research supports the observation that the rich get richer, at least with respect to increasing expert knowledge. Students who know a lot about a subject organize information about it differently and make better use of it than do students who know less.

Larkin finds that students who are knowledgeable rely little on memorized combinations. Instead, they abstract properties of the chemicals that would affect their combination with other elements and use these properties to predict possible reactions. Similarly, expert students in physics solve problems by first classifying them according to general principles and then applying specific equations appropriate to that domain of problem. Novices, lacking the knowledge that would allow them to classify problems in this way, apply formulas that are suggested by specific expressions in the problems and often end up pursuing the wrong course. Larkin's observations confirm those of Chi and others who find that experts organize information into more abstract categories, which in turn allows them to apply more efficient strategies (Larkin, 1985).

Expert knowledge offers a way of explaining the noticeable differences in thought that often characterize adolescents. Some parallels exist between this approach and Piaget's stage theory of intellectual development. Both experts and formal thinkers are systematic in their approach to a problem. Experts define a domain of knowledge in terms of abstract categories—for example, eating habits—and classify specific instances accordingly. Does this sound like formal thought? Both approaches require a high degree of abstraction in defining the parameters of the domain and then a systematic ordering of particular instances within that domain.

Knowledge of One's Culture: Everybody's an Expert

We have seen that what adolescents know can affect how easily they can learn even more. The examples of expertise considered thus far have involved academic knowledge, the type gained in the classroom. All adolescents are experts in one other area: their own culture. This expertise makes it easy to assimilate information that is consistent with what they know based on their experiences. Information that is inconsistent is not easy to learn, because they must change the way they understand things in order to accommodate a new perspective. Consequently, it is difficult to learn concepts and facts that violate one's cultural perspective or are incongruent with one's experiences.

Anderson Franklin, at the City University of New York, put these observations to the test in a simple experiment. Franklin (1985) assumed that Black adolescents would have an advantage over White adolescents in remembering words common to the African American culture but not common outside it. Franklin interviewed 75 urban Black teenagers to obtain commonly used slang terms. He constructed lists of categories of words using the terms they supplied, together with words common to both Blacks and Whites.

As shown in Figure 10.7, Black adolescents remember more words than do White adolescents. In fact, if one did not know how the list of words had been derived, one might assume that Black adolescents have better memories than do Whites. Based on similar comparisons, some investigators have assumed that Whites are more intelligent than Blacks and other minorities because they score higher on measures common to intelligence tests. In doing so, these investigators have failed to take into account that minorities may not be familiar with all the items included in the tests (see

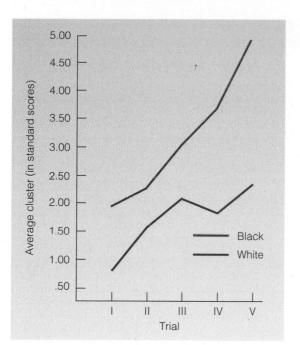

FIGURE 10.7
**Clustered Recall of Words
by Black and White Adolescents.** *Source:* A. J. Franklin.
(1985). The social context and so
cialization variables as factors in
thinking and learning. In S. F. Chipman, J. W. Segal, & R. Glaser (Eds.),
Thinking and learning skills (Vol. 2).
Hillsdale, NJ: Erlbaum.

Chapter 4). Franklin noticed that Black adolescents were also better at re-
calling items that were equally familiar to the White students. Blacks were
more likely to categorize items into related clusters, a strategy that vastly
improves memory when it is used. The presence of unfamiliar items may
have led the White adolescents to believe that the words were unrelated. Familiarity with all the words, which was the case only for the Black adolescents, had allowed them to see that the words could be easily categorized
(Franklin, 1985).

PUTTING KNOWLEDGE TO WORK

Active Knowledge

Aside from the fact that some students are experts in a particular subject
and some are not, important differences still remain in the amount of
knowledge adolescents bring to a subject. Just as with experts, the more they
know, the easier it is for them to learn even more. Differences in what adolescents know can affect their ability to understand, remember, and put new
information to use. How much they know will also determine the types of
strategies they use in learning new material.

Consider an example from a high school health class in which students
are learning about the cardiovascular system. The teacher has just told them
that arteries are thick and elastic and veins are thin. Students who know
nothing else about either type of blood vessel may have difficulty remembering which is thin and which is thick unless they do something to hold
on to these facts. Most will rely on rote memorization. Students with some
knowledge of arteries and veins—who know, for example, that arteries carry

Box 10.2   Applying Strategies in Problem Solving

The same strategy applies to the solution of each of the problems below.

MILITARY CAMPAIGN

A general wishes to capture a fortress located in the center of a country. There are many roads radiating outward from the fortress. All have been mined so that while small groups of men can pass over the roads safely, a large force will detonate the mines. A full-scale direct attack is therefore impossible. The general's solution is to divide his army into small groups, send each group to the head of a different road, and have the groups converge simultaneously on the fortress. (Gick & Holyoak, 1980)

INOPERABLE TUMOR

Suppose you are a doctor faced with a patient who had a malignant tumor in his stomach. It is impossible to operate on the patient, but unless the tumor is destroyed the patient will die. There is a kind of ray that may be used to destroy the tumor. If the rays reach the tumor all at once and with sufficiently high intensity, the tumor will be destroyed. At lower intensities the rays are harmless to healthy tissue, but they will not affect the tumor either. What type of procedure might be used to destroy the tumor with the rays, and at the same time avoid destroying the healthy tissue? (Duncker, 1945)

Sources: Adapted from K. Duncker. (1945). On problem solving. *Psychological Monographs, 58* (Whole No. 270). M. L. Gick & K. J. Holyoak. (1980). Analogical problem solving. *Cognitive Psychology, 12,* 306–355.

blood away from the heart and veins carry it back—may be able to relate that information to the need for arteries to be elastic, to expand and contract with each pulse of blood (Bransford, Stein, Shelton, & Owings, 1981).

But what about those students who do not know anything about the cardiovascular system? Is it possible for them to learn material without blindly memorizing facts? The answer depends a lot on the techniques teachers use. Simple presentations of facts are more likely to result in memorization, whereas class experiences that require students to put information to use generate the type of learning that results in understanding.

Let's say the teacher in the above example gives the class the task of designing an artificial artery. As students consider possible materials from which to construct the artery, they are likely to encounter the issue of whether the materials should be rigid or elastic, thick or thin, and so on. The teacher might feed relevant information into the discussion as decisions are being made, indicating, for example, that the heart pumps blood in spurts, that considerable pressure occurs, or that blood travels uphill from the heart to the head as well as laterally and downhill. Students will arrive at the need for elasticity themselves. They will see its function in accommodating surges of blood and as a constricting value that closes after each surge, preventing blood from flowing back to the heart (Bransford, Stein, Shelton, & Owings, 1981; Bransford, Vye, Adams, & Perfetto, 1989).

Inert Knowledge

Having access to background knowledge has a potent effect on how and what one learns and remembers. Yet some adolescents fail to use the information they possess.

What adolescents know all too often exists as **inert knowledge:** facts and concepts they can recite but not use. Is this because the information they learn in school is so exotic it is irrelevant to the daily problems they face? Not always. More to the point, inert knowledge refers to the inability to draw on knowledge in just those situations in which it is potentially useful (Whitehead, 1929).

Why might adolescents be unable to use what they know? The ways in which they acquire information can make access to it difficult. Facts that have been memorized do not transfer readily to new situations. Gick and Holyoak (1980) presented students with a problem of an inoperable tumor, to be solved using the same strategy they'd just memorized concerning a military campaign. As shown in Box 10.2, the same strategy can be used to solve two completely different problems, yet even though the tumor problem directly followed the military one, 80% of the students didn't realize the military solution could be used as a strategy to destroy the tumor. When given a hint that the military tactics were applicable to the second situation, 90% solved the problem.

Adolescents frequently have difficulty overlooking content-specific details to see underlying commonalities among problems. Memory seems to be triggered more by the content of what one is doing than by the procedures one is carrying out. Some courses lead to better transfer than others. Students do better, for instance, in applying what they have learned in algebra to their physics problems than vice versa (Bassok & Holyoak, 1989). One of the things they appear to learn in algebra is to disregard the content and focus on the procedure. When the procedure one is following becomes the content (by focusing on it), spontaneous transfer to problems with a similar procedure is likely. Miriam Bassok (1990) found that high school students could interchange solutions to physics and algebra problems (Box 10.3), but only when everything about the problems was the same. When seemingly small changes were made, students needed many hints before they thought to apply a previously learned solution.

Thinking as Problem Solving

Bransford and his colleagues (1989) suggest that we think of learning as problem solving and thinking, rather than as simply remembering. They make the point that problems of learning, such as inert knowledge, do not reflect either a poor memory or limitations to one's ability to learn; they are simply failures to apply the proper strategies when facing a new problem. The task becomes one of knowing what it means to understand something. These authors suggest a five-step approach for overcoming some of the difficulties that lead to inert knowledge. The names of these five steps are combined to form the acronym **IDEAL.**

Basic to this approach is learning to *identify* when a problem exists, that is, to recognize when one does not understand something just read or heard.

Box 10.3   Finding Commonalities Among Problems

PHYSICS

What is the acceleration (increase in speed each second) of a train if its speed increased uniformly from 15 miles per second at the beginning of the 1st second to 45 miles per second at the end of the 12th second?

ALGEBRA

Every typist goes through a warm-up period during which his/her typing rate constantly increases until reaching a typical typing rate. Jane starts typing at a rate of 40 words per minute, and after 12 minutes reaches her typical typing rate of 58 words per minute. What is the constant increase in her typing rate during her warm-up period?

Sample protocols of students:

Student 1:   This is pretty similar to the things we did with a straight line in physics. Maybe I can use something from that.

   Experimenter: How is it similar?

   Because it's just like her going faster, she's not moving in a straight line; it's just how many words she types. So it's just like meters per second. Acceleration equals . . . I'm using the acceleration formula. Her acceleration would be 8⅓ words per minute.

Student 2:   Subtract the initial words per minute from the final words per minute to get 18. Divide that by the number of minutes to get 1.5. So you get 1.5 words per minute.

Source: Adapted from M. Bassok. (1990). Transfer of domain-specific problem-solving procedures. *Journal of Experimental Psychology: Learning, Memory, and Cognition, 16,* 522–533.

The next step is to *define* the problem. Why didn't I understand? Was it a momentary lapse in attention? Or was it because I didn't have some relevant information? One can *explore* alternative solutions to the problem. One might reread the passage or get additional information. In either case, one must *act,* and then *look* to see if these actions have improved comprehension. Notice that learning becomes an active rather than a passive process (Bransford, Vye, Adams, & Perfetto, 1989). Procedures that increase one's engagement with the material decrease the likelihood that what one learns will become inert.

Many of the problems of inert knowledge can be resolved by teaching thinking skills. Even so, individuals of some ages may not find it easy to think about their thinking. Remember that this ability develops during adolescence. Adolescents almost surely will find it easier than young children to search their memories or monitor their learning. Each of these activities is more abstract than simply putting information to use. Both involve getting information about information or knowing what one knows, and formal thought is necessary in either case.

If inert knowledge is the failure to see the relationship between what one knows and the problems one faces, creativity is just the opposite. Creativity allows us to put knowledge together in novel and unexpected ways.

CREATIVITY

Characteristics of Creativity

Creative adolescents have a high *tolerance for ambiguity*. Ambiguity exists whenever one is uncertain regarding a course of action or the meaning of an event. Creative adolescents enjoy the risks that come with uncertainty, even when it involves a certain amount of disorder. They welcome people and ideas that are different. Instead of closing themselves or others off when faced with uncertainty, they remain open-minded.

John Dacey (1989b) studied creativity by having individuals write a story about a simple picture, instructing them to try to create a story no one else would. Nearly three-quarters of the more than 1,000 stories were the same; creative stories, however, were highly dissimilar. They revealed a restless imagination and a disdain for following the rules by telling an ordinary story. Rules are the antithesis of ambiguity. When there are rules, one knows what to do. Creative adolescents enjoy *stimulus freedom*. They can bend the rules when the rules interfere with their creative ideas, and they do *not* assume that rules must exist unless they are in evidence. Less-creative age-mates may even make up rules in ambiguous situations to reduce their fear of being wrong. Dacey considers the fear of being wrong to be the most powerful inhibitor of creativity (1989b).

Not seeing rules where none exist is a necessary condition for creativity. The solution to the problem shown in Figure 10.8 depends on it. One must be able to leave the field of the rectangle described by the dots. Adolescents who have been coloring outside the lines since kindergarten have no trouble eventually coming up with a solution (Dacey, 1989b). The ability to leave the field is analogous to the ability of structural analytical thinkers to mentally step outside the logical system they are using in order to gain a new perspective on it.

Creative adolescents are both *analytic* and *intuitive*. They combine intuitive leaps of imagination with careful analyses of outcomes compared to

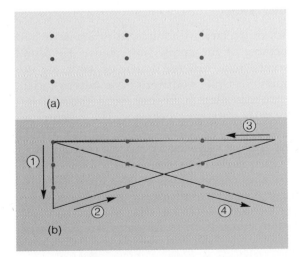

FIGURE 10.8
The Nine-Dot Problem
(a) Connect the nine dots in this figure with four straight lines, without taking the pen or pencil off the page. (b) Solution.

Creative adolescents are both reflective and spontaneous. They are less likely to conform to accepted practice and more likely to try new ways of doing things than their less creative peers. These two teenagers in the Bronx used their spray cans to transform a crumbling concrete wall next to an empty lot.

their expectations. Another characteristic is *open-mindedness*. Creative adolescents are less likely to prejudge new situations or try to fit unfamiliar information into comfortable categories. finally, they are both *reflective* and *spontaneous*. They can deliberate on the spontaneous flashes that come to them (Dacey, 1989b).

Origins of Creativity in Adolescents

Dacey (1989a) compared families with a creative adolescent or a creative parent with those in which no member of the family was creative. He found that parents of creative adolescents frequently use a style of parenting not previously identified (see Chapter 5). Unlike authoritative, authoritarian, and permissive parents, these parents show high interest in their adolescents' activities yet set very few rules governing behavior. The mean number of rules in noncreative families is six, whereas creative families average one rule! Rather than rules, parents provide strong models through their own behavior and use family discussions to establish behavioral expectations. Like authoritative parents, they expect adolescents to make decisions for themselves. These parents give frequent feedback on their children's behavior but rarely punish. Their teenagers comment that their parents' disappointment in them is a stronger motivation to do well than any system of punishment or rewards.

Humor is an important element in creative families. Jokes and kidding around are common. When asked what they value, members of creative families rank humor higher than those of other families, often placing it well above characteristics such as popularity or high intelligence. Creative adolescents rank getting high grades or having a high IQ moderately low.

Dacey (1989a) notes that many creative adolescents experience more trauma in life than average children. He suggests that the need to cope with trauma stimulates creative approaches. Creative adolescents see themselves as working harder than their peers. This quality contradicts the stereotype of the creative individual who spontaneously generates novel ideas and approaches. Spontaneity is there, but creative people follow up in a deliberate and disciplined way.

ADOLESCENT DECISION MAKING

Intellectual changes during adolescence have very real implications for daily living. How effective do adolescents perceive themselves to be? What are they willing to attempt? How motivated are they to pursue different goals? How successful will they be? The answers to these and similar questions reflect their burgeoning intellectual skills. The Research Focus, "Ethics," looks at adolescent decision making, using the example of choosing a college.

Personal Effectiveness

Feelings of personal effectiveness reflect how much control adolescents feel they have in a situation, which stems directly from their ability to predict the outcome. The ability to predict is an intellectual skill. "If I tell Gina that the junior she has a crush on asked me out, she'll flirt with my boyfriend." Or, "if I work all the different types of algebra problems in this chapter, I'll be able to pass the test on it." Adolescents who know the consequences their actions will have are in a better position to control what happens to them by doing or not doing certain things. Predicting outcomes involves the same type of analytic thinking (if . . . then . . .) adolescents use in the classroom: inductive and deductive reasoning.

Adolescents can think about outcomes of their actions probabilistically, a development that accompanies formal thought. They also realize that events can have more than one cause (for example, "Gina might also flirt with my boyfriend because she thinks he's cute") and that the same event can contribute to different outcomes (for example, "Gina might even spend more time with me . . ."). In addition to intellectual skills, how much adolescents believe in themselves also affects their approach to any situation; in this case, by the type of outcomes they anticipate. Those who perceive themselves as effective anticipate positive outcomes. They mentally rehearse adaptive solutions, which help them find their way through problems more effectively (Bandura, 1989; Zimmerman, Bandura, & Martinez-Pons, 1992).

The type of outcome adolescents anticipate also affects their motivation to engage in an activity. In other words, the goals they set reflect their appraisal of their ability to meet them. Those who doubt themselves are likely

Research Focus

Ethics: How Do Adolescents Feel When Making a Big Decision?

For many adolescents, the first major life decision they will make is about college. More specifically, for increasing numbers of adolescents, this decision concerns *which* college they will attend. At first blush, a decision such as this may sound relatively easy. But think, for a moment, of all that can be involved. The college one chooses can influence not only the type of work one pursues in life but, more immediately, other aspects of one's life as well, such as where one lives, the friendships one maintains, and even the extent to which one goes into debt. How do adolescents feel when making such a life-framing decision? In order to find out, one must ask adolescents to talk about how they feel about a potentially difficult, and often personal, process.

What ethical concerns guide such research? The overriding principle governing any research with humans is to protect the *dignity and welfare* of the subjects who participate in the research. Investigators inform the subjects in their study that their participation is *voluntary* and can be discontinued at any point. They also inform them of anything that could affect their willingness to participate. Once individuals agree to serve as subjects, investigators assume responsibility for protecting them from *physical or psychological distress*. After the data have been collected, the investigators *debrief* the subjects, informing them about the nature of the study and removing any misconceptions that may have arisen. If investigators suspect any undesirable consequences, they have the responsibility to correct them. Any information gained about participants is *confidential*.

Let's look at some research that illustrates these principles. Kathleen Galotti and Steven Kozberg (1996), at Carleton College, asked high school juniors and seniors to describe, in writing, the process of making a decision about college and how they felt about it. Students initially wrote answers to these questions in the spring of their junior year and twice again as seniors. Prior to beginning the research, however, the investigators obtained written parental consent for students who were less than 18 years old as well as the consent of the students themselves. Notice that in order for participation to be voluntary, participants had to know what it was they were agreeing to. Accordingly, students and parents were informed that the research was about individuals' college decision making. A second, and related, aspect of voluntary participation is the right of participants to discontinue the research at any point. In fact, a number of the students who completed several of the measures for this study dropped out before the research was finished.

How do high school students feel about the process of choosing a college? In general, these students gave themselves good marks for the way they handled the decision-making process but agreed that the process itself is stressful and at times even overwhelming. As one student put it,

Choosing what you're going to do for a living and going to college are really big decisions that are going to affect the rest of your life and if you don't choose what's best then you have screwed up your life! . . . It's a rather confusing and bewildering decision. There are many colleges to choose from and they all seem alike. The brochures for colleges tend to seem similar to any other college brochure. It's one of the first large decisions in a person's life and it can affect the rest of life. That prospect is daunting. (Galotti & Kozberg, 1996, pp. 11–12)

Source: K. M. Galotti & S. F. Kozberg. (1996). Adolescents' experience of a life-framing decision. *Journal of Youth and Adolescence, 25,* 3–16.

to give up when they face some difficulty; adolescents who believe in themselves work harder. Belief in self has other effects as well; it can determine how much stress one can tolerate. Those who think they can cope with something do not anticipate all the possible negative outcomes that others with self-doubts imagine. As a consequence, they don't have to deal with the negative emotional side effects such fantasies may produce (Bandura, 1989).

Bandura points out that, at times, inaccurate self-assessments can actually *help* adolescents when making decisions. Optimistic evaluations of competence—if not too far off the mark—can help for all the reasons just reviewed. A less optimistic, if truer, judgment can be self-limiting, failing to motivate adolescents to stretch beyond their present performance.

Feelings of competence or incompetence can be general or quite specific. Are some adolescents more likely than others to react to failure with general feelings of inadequacy? Poole and Evans (1988) had adolescents rate their competence in several life skill areas (such as use of time, setting goals, making choices, social awareness). In general, adolescents view themselves as being competent at the things they value, though not always as much as they might desire. Important gender differences exist in self-perceptions. Females view themselves as less competent than males overall and as competent in fewer areas, even though an objective measure that all adolescents completed showed females doing slightly better (Poole & Evans, 1988). Do female adolescents' lower ratings of themselves limit their actual competence in any way? At the very least, we might expect their lower ratings to affect the goals they set for themselves.

Dealing With Everyday Problems

Most of the thinking adolescents do is directed at solving the problems of life—*their* lives. Most of these take the form of daily hassles, that is, interpersonal problems such as an argument with parents or a misunderstanding with friends. Several skills help adolescents negotiate successful resolutions to interpersonal problems. Not unexpectedly, older adolescents are better at these than younger ones (Berg, 1989; Mann, Harmoni, & Power, 1989).

Any of three general strategies can be attempted when a problem arises. Adolescents can alter their behavior so that it better fits their environment, they can attempt to change the environment so that it better fits their behavior, or they can select another environment (Sternberg, 1985). A number of additional steps are important. The first is simply to plan to take action. Also helpful is to get more information and to change one's perception of the problem. Sometimes redefining the problem, looking at it in a different way, is all that is needed to emotionally defuse it.

Each of these steps underscores the importance of flexibility when faced with a problem, and flexibility increases with age. When asked, "What does a good decision maker do when making a decision?" older adolescents are more likely to mention generating options, and they are better at doing this themselves. They are also more likely to take into consideration the consequences of following any of the options and to check the advice or information they get (Mann, Harmoni, & Power, 1989).

Cynthia Berg (1989) asked adolescents to evaluate the effectiveness of the above strategies when faced with a problem such as the following:

The demands of school and homework are relatively inflexible compared to the negotiated settlements that can be reached with friends and parents.

Your parents have become more strict in what time you must be home at night. On Friday and Saturday nights you have to be home by 12:00. You and your friends want to go out to a movie on Friday night that will not be over until 12:30, so you won't be home until 1:00. You find out from the movie theater that the movie will be showing at the theater for one more week. Rate how good each of the answers is in allowing you to see the movie and be home by 12:00. [The curfew for fifth-, eighth-, and eleventh-graders was 9:30, 10:30, and 12:00, respectively.]

Ask your friends if they have a strict time that they must be home at night. (Get more information)

Decide that seeing the movie is really not worth causing problems with your parents. (Redefine the problem)

Wait to see the movie on Saturday afternoon. (Alter behavior)

Persuade your parents that the new rule is not fair. (Change the environment)

Spend Friday night at the house of a friend who does not have to be home so early. (Pick another environment)

Plan how you could both see a movie and be home by 12:00. (Plan a course of action) (p. 618)

Older adolescents choose more effective strategies than younger ones, and females do so more than males. As obstacles are introduced or removed, less-effective problem solvers are likely to radically alter their approach. The best problem solvers change their strategies relatively little. This difference suggests that interpersonal problem solving is a skill that, once learned, adolescents can apply across a variety of settings. Supporting this interpretation is Berg's finding that using strategies effectively is related to adolescents' own evaluations of their practical intelligence, as well as that of their teachers' and parents', and to their actual achievement (in the form of grades and achievement test scores).

The effectiveness of strategies varies with the setting in which problems arise. Adolescents believe, for example, that the problems they encounter at school (for example, getting into a special class, resolving a grade discrepancy) are best handled either by redefining their perception of the problem or by simply selecting another environment. An adolescent who receives a C on an essay that she feels deserves a B might think the teacher is biased against her. Most adolescents in high school realize that the best way to resolve grade discrepancies is to find out what the teacher wanted (that is, redefine the problem from an interpersonal one to an academic one) or try to get another teacher next time (select another environment).

When problems arise outside of school, planning and getting more information are seen as most effective. Opting for different approaches in either setting itself reveals knowledge of effective strategies. School settings are relatively inflexible compared to the environments where one can negotiate settlements, such as with friends or parents. Older adolescents are more likely to realize this difference than younger ones (Berg, 1989).

In all, whether it be thinking through academic arguments and abstract ideas or facing everyday decisions, adolescents use increasingly sophisticated strategies.

SUMMARY

Adolescents at Work

Most high school students have part-time jobs, and more want to work than can find jobs. Unemployment among minority adolescents is higher than among majority youth. Most adolescents spend their money on personal items such as clothes, entertainment, and cars. Smaller numbers save for education or other long-term plans. Students who work part-time spend less time on schoolwork and with families, but they develop a sense of responsibility and feel productive

High school dropouts are more than twice as likely to be unemployed as graduates. Programs that are successful in preventing at-risk students from dropping out communicate the importance of having a degree for making money. These programs create an atmosphere of caring and involvement, provide individualized instruction through computerized programs, and involve the community and parents.

Choosing a Vocation

Social-cognitive theory emphasizes the interrelationships among inborn abilities, one's particular environment and unique learning history, and each person's skills in explaining vocational choices.

Developmental theories trace occupational choices over stages. Ginzburg views vocational development as a progressive narrowing of choices that at first reflect only fantasy, then tentative career choices, and, with increasing age, realistic choices.

Super assumes that people choose occupations that reflect the way they see themselves. Because the self-concept changes with age, so will occupational plans. In the growth stage, adolescents develop a realistic self-concept; in the exploration stage, they begin to make choices related to future work. Individuals settle into their work as early adults in the establishment stage, maintaining their occupational position through middle adulthood in the maintenance stage. The decline stage involves retirement.

Holland classifies individuals into six personality types; different work environments either complement or oppose the qualities that make up any type. Realistic types prefer orderly, structured work. Investigative types prefer work that involves analytic skills. Artistic types do best in unstructured situations that let them express their creativity. Social types have good interpersonal skills. Enterprising types enjoy work that brings them into contact with others in ways in which they can express their assertiveness. Conventional types prefer to work under the direction of others.

Joining the Work Force

Most of the fastest growing occupations are in the fields of health, technology, and child care and education; many of these jobs require more skills than in the past. These are not necessarily the most numerous jobs, however, and many of the latter do not require more skills than previously. Employment opportunities of any kind for inner-city minority youth are scarce, however.

More female adolescents plan to work in professional jobs than before. Sex segregation still exists in the work force, and advancement opportunities for females are limited. Female adolescents also have internal barriers to advancement that take the form of lower expectations for pay and lower valuation of their work; these barriers are learned.

Minority adolescents face problems similar to those of females; in addition, poverty contributes heavily to the problems they face. Minority adolescents' career aspirations are as high as those of majority adolescents, but their lower expectations reflect social barriers to equal employment opportunities.

Intervention Programs

Because of inequities in the opportunity structure for minority adolescents and females, counselors may need to become active change agents to prepare these students for the full range of jobs that exists. Effective intervention programs work with local businesses, parents, and teachers as well as the students. Counselors often must first address their own biases.

Students frequently approach career decisions with maladaptive beliefs and myths. Intervention programs based on cognitive restructuring and on attributional retraining effectively address these as the first step to vocational counseling.

Adolescents and College

Some developmentalists believe a new form of thinking develops in late adolescence. Structural analytical thinking builds on the achievements of formal thought and allows adolescents to find parallels among different views of a problem.

Dialectical reasoning is necessary for structural analytical thought, just as propositional reasoning is necessary for formal thought. In propositional reasoning, the premises are not questioned even when they are not supported. In dialectical reasoning, one questions the premises if, over the course of time, actions based on them are not supported.

William Perry has identified three major forms of thought in college men: (1) Dualistic thinkers approach problems in a straightforward manner and look for the right answer. They operate within a single frame of reference that allows them to view ideas as either right or wrong. (2) Relativistic thinkers are aware that what they previously accepted as facts are actually interpretations that make sense within a given frame of reference. They are aware that more than one frame of reference exists and that each represents a legitimate point of view. (3) Relativists who commit themselves to a point of view create new meaning through anchoring their beliefs in a committed style of life.

Female adolescents do not think in ways captured by Perry's intellectual progressions: (1) Subjective knowers covertly examine issues while maintaining a surface conformity to traditional ideas. (2) Procedural knowers own the responsibility of discovering things for themselves, but their thought is limited by the confines of formal thinking. (3) Constructive knowers are aware that knowledge is constructed and hence relative, and that the knower is an intrinsic part of the process. They can examine their beliefs using structural analytical thought.

Adolescents as Experts

Adolescents who know a lot about a subject organize information more efficiently and use more abstract, high-level categories than novices. This approach allows them to use more efficient strategies when solving problems.

A form of expertise that does not involve academic learning comes from knowledge of one's culture. All adolescents are experts in their own culture. This expertise makes it easy for them to assimilate information consistent with cultural experiences but difficult to learn material that runs counter to their experiences.

Putting Knowledge to Work

Even adolescents who are not experts can remember material more easily if they have had to put the information to some use when learning it than if they have simply memorized it. Frequently students are unable to draw on knowledge in situations in which it is potentially useful. Such information exists as inert knowledge.

Approaching learning as problem solving prompts adolescents to adopt study skills that allow them the best use of what they have learned. IDEAL is an acronym for a set of thinking skills that teaches students to identify problem areas and adopt an active approach.

Creativity

Creative adolescents are distinguished by their tolerance of ambiguity. They can remain open-minded in the face of uncertainty. They can bend the rules when they interfere with their creative approach and do not assume any rules unless they are evident. Creative adolescents are most likely to come from families with a creative parent or older sibling. Their parents show high interest in their activities and set few rules governing their behavior. Humor is an important element in creative families.

Adolescent Decision Making

Adolescents' intellectual skills contribute to their sense of personal effectiveness. The control they feel in situations stems directly from their ability to predict outcomes, which involves the same types of analytic thinking used in the classroom.

Most of the intellectual skills put to use outside the classroom are directed at solving interpersonal problems. Adolescents get better at this with age.

KEY TERMS

fantasy stage

tentative stage

realistic stage

growth stage

exploration stage

establishment stage

maintenance stage

decline stage

realistic personality types

investigative personality types

artistic personality types

social personality types

enterprising personality types

conventional personality types

structural analytical thinking

propositional reasoning

dialectical reasoning

dualistic thinking

relativistic thinking

commitment in relativism

subjective knowledge

procedural knowledge

constructive knowledge

inert knowledge

IDEAL

CHAPTER 11

Facing the Future
Values in Transition

White-lipped and shaking, Sarah replaced the receiver with exaggerated care, as if each movement could restore order to her world.

"So what's the word? Are you or aren't you?" asked Gina in a voice tight with urgency.

"I'm not," replied her friend.

"So, then, what's the problem?"

"I'm not sure," began Sarah, "but until now I don't think any of this has been real to me."

"You mean," interrupted Gina, "that a minute ago you weren't afraid you might be pregnant?"

"Hey, I was. I just didn't feel anything. But when I heard that the test was negative, I felt empty . . . sad . . . and happy and angry . . . all at once. It's strange. When I thought I might be pregnant, I felt nothing, but now that I know I'm not, I have all these feelings."

Gina looked at her friend with concern. "How could you have taken care of a baby?"

"I sure can't imagine myself as a mother," agreed Sarah, with a wry look on her face.

"You would've had to forget about plans for college and working with abused children."

"That's a laugh!" Sarah answered bitterly. "How can I put those two parts of myself together—the one that thought about giving the baby away or even getting an abortion and the other that wants to help children whose parents hurt them?"

"You have a responsibility to yourself as well," offered Gina.

"Sure, but how do I balance that against my responsibility to someone else? Would it have been responsible to give the baby away if I couldn't have taken care of it properly? Or was it wrong to have even thought of it?"

The parents of today's teenagers aren't as different as their children sometimes think. Their attitudes are quite similar with regard to life goals, the value of an education, and roles for women.

"Was Eddie any help in thinking about this?" asked Gina.

"We were both too numb to think very clearly," answered Sarah. "But the few times we talked, we seemed to be discussing different problems altogether."

"I can relate to that!" snapped Gina. "At times J.J. doesn't even seem to speak the same language."

"Eddie talked about whether the fetus was a person, and whether it had the same rights that we had. It sounded so impersonal. All I could think of was whether I could take care of it and still take care of myself," Sarah replied quietly, as she broke another toothpick and absently added it to the pile in front of her.

Many adolescents find themselves face to face with problems like Sarah's and Eddie's. In this chapter, we will look at the standards adolescents use in making decisions—decisions that increasingly affect others as well as themselves. Changing roles, untrodden rights, and uncharted responsibilities create a compelling need for a system of values to guide decisions. Beliefs that have worked all through childhood come up again for review in adolescence. Many will withstand close scrutiny; others will not. All will be tested against a developing system of values as adolescents face the challenge of defining themselves.

Self-definition means that adolescents must distinguish values and beliefs that are unique to them from those they acquired from their parents.

Many begin by scrutinizing their families' values to see which ones they will accept for themselves. Some adolescents forgo this process and continue to live by standards set by others. The development of values is an integral part of one's identity.

What criteria distinguish moral concerns from social convention? From religious beliefs? Some developmentalists consider early experiences within the family to be pivotal to later moral development, while others stress the importance of interactions with peers. Do females and males approach moral issues differently? Are there progressions in religious development as there are in moral development? Developmentalists, as well as the families they study, frequently arrive at different answers to questions such as these. Their answers will structure our discussion of moral development.

THE VALUES OF ADOLESCENTS

The values of adolescents have changed little in the last ten years. Looking to the future, most adolescents indicate that experiencing success in their work, providing better opportunities for their children, and maintaining strong friendships are most important. Conversely, having lots of money is not that important. Many translate these values into action. Nearly 30% of high school seniors participate in some type of volunteer work on a monthly basis, and 10% to 15% do so on a weekly basis (Youth Indicators, 1996).

Most adolescents hold attitudes that are in substantial agreement with those of their parents. Close to 90% of adolescents and their parents have similar attitudes concerning the value of an education, and nearly 75% agree with parents on big questions such as what to do with one's life. Similarly, high agreement exists concerning religion, racial issues, and certain conventional behaviors, such as how to dress. As Figure 11.1 shows, agreement in each of these areas between adolescents and parents has increased since the mid-1970s (Youth Indicators, 1996).

More similarities than differences also exist in the values held by adolescent females and males. In comparison to adolescents a decade ago, adolescent females in 1994 were just as likely as males to say that being successful in one's work was "very important," and just as many males said that providing better opportunities for their children and having strong friendships was "very important," as shown in Figure 11.2. Differences appear only when it comes to having children and making money: Among high school seniors, females are more likely than males to indicate that having children is important, and males are more likely to place a higher value on having a lot of money. In other respects, the values of each are remarkably similar (Youth Indicators, 1996).

Values and Identity

Adolescents' values shape their sense of themselves. Erik Erikson believed values are an important component of our identity. A sense of identity allows us to make countless daily decisions, to take ourselves for granted, as

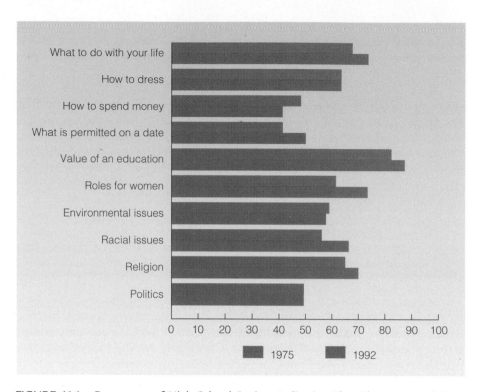

FIGURE 11.1   Percentage of High School Seniors Indicating That They Agree With Their Parents on Selected Topics, 1975 and 1992. *Sources:* University of Michigan, Institute for Social Research, *Monitoring the future,* various years. Youth Indicators: *Trends in the Well-Being of American Youth.* (1996). Washington, DC: U.S. Government Printing Office.

Ruthellen Josselson (1987) puts it. Like much of the way we function, our identity remains largely unavailable for inspection—until we hit a snag.

Developmental snags await us all. They take the form of age-related changes in the expectations that we and others hold up to ourselves. Erikson (1956, 1968) refers to these changes as psychosocial crises. Crises arise when physical maturation, together with changing personal and cultural expectations, lead individuals to re-examine their sense of who they are and what they are about. "Taking oneself for granted," because it flows from one's identity, is precisely what most adolescents find hardest to do: Most of them are continually revising their sense of themselves (see discussion of identity statuses in Chapter 8).

Prior to adolescence, the elements that contribute to identity are ascribed (Josselson, 1987). For example, children have few choices in such matters as where they live, go to school, worship, and so on. Adolescents can begin to explore possibilities that differ from those chosen by their parents. Some will continue to live out the patterns established by their parents. This is still a choice, although adolescents who follow this path may not be aware of making a decision as such. The decision facing *all* adolescents is whether they will decide things for themselves or live with decisions made by others. Being aware that one has choices, and considering the various possibilities, can make adolescents uncomfortably aware of themselves. Erikson considers this discomfort to be central to one's experience of cri-

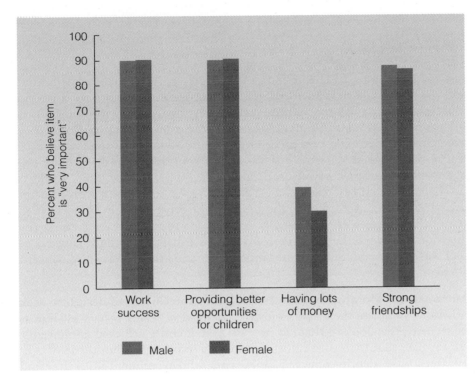

FIGURE 11.2   Percentage of Female and Male High School Seniors Who Believe That Certain Life Values Are "Very Important," 1994. *Sources:* U.S. Department of Education, National Center for Education Statistics, "National Longitudinal Study" First Followup study, "High School and Beyond" Second Followup survey, and "National Education Longitudinal Study," Second and Third Followup surveys. Youth Indicators: *Trends in the Well-Being of American Youth.* (1996). Washington, DC: U.S. Government Printing Office.

sis. By crisis he does not mean that adolescents' lives are in pieces, but simply that until identity decisions are firmly behind them, they cannot "take themselves for granted."

Because identity reflects one's values, the stance toward values taken by adolescents in each of the identity statuses described in Chapter 8 will differ.

Identity Achievement   Adolescents who have begun to discover the ways in which they differ from their families are more tolerant of differences in others than those who have not experienced a period of crisis. Openness in examining one's own beliefs goes hand in hand with accepting different beliefs in others. Perhaps because of the high value that identity-achieved adolescents place on discovering themselves, even at the risk of displeasing others, they are unwilling to hold others to conventional standards of right or wrong (Marcia, 1988).

Does this description sound too good to be true? Keep in mind that conscientious and principled behavior is not necessarily what most adults label as "good." Adolescents in search of themselves are likely to question and experiment. They may dress flamboyantly, act outrageously, and generally adopt a "show me" attitude. They may not follow in their parents' footsteps or be ready to settle down when others their age have already found their way. The positive side to this picture is that these adolescents develop a sense of who they are and translate that image into effective strategies for

living, including close relationships with others. The independence they
achieve reflects an internal struggle, one that frees them for change, not an
external one in which they must sever ties with others.

Identity Foreclosure Identity-foreclosed adolescents are more rule-bound
and authoritarian than identity-achieved adolescents. They have a strong
sense of duty and feel that others, just as they, should obey the rules. Their
respect for rules and tradition is reflected in the conventional standards they
hold for their own and others' behavior. These adolescents tend to be critical of those whose behavior or ideas differ from their own or who are unconventional in other ways (Josselson, 1987).

Foreclosed adolescents derive their feelings of self-esteem from the approval of others. Accordingly, the opinions of others remain important to
them; these adolescents are highly sensitive to social cues concerning the
appropriateness of their behavior. Actions or beliefs that might cause conflict will be rejected. Security, not independence, is their overriding concern
(Marcia, 1980).

Moratorium Moratorium adolescents, like foreclosed adolescents, seek
others to complete themselves. However, instead of seeing others as sources
of security, they look to them as models. Like identity-achieved adolescents,
they realize that their own values are not any more right than those of others, but unlike identity-achieved adolescents, who experiment until they find
their own way, moratorium adolescents set out on a "kind of crusade, determined to discover what is 'really right'" (Josselson, 1987). Josselson points
out that theirs is an impossible quest, made all the harder because they hold
back from experiences that would define them, always leaving a back door
open through which to escape if they make a wrong choice. Josselson writes:

> Often, we unconsciously arrange for someone to function as a kind of sav-
> ings bank. We deposit our old self in them for safekeeping, trusting them to
> hold it for us if we decide to come back to claim it. Many of the moratorium
> women spoke of this process. In describing the ways in which they thought
> their parents expected them to be, they were describing old selves, ways they
> used to be. They could, then, have the luxury of experiencing their growth as
> an external battle, between themselves and their parents, rather than inside
> themselves. In addition, they knew that their parents were holding the old
> selves for them, just in case they ever decided to return, which is exactly what
> many of them did. (1987, p. 138)

Perhaps because moratorium adolescents live with so much indecision
themselves, they are tolerant of differences in others. Their ability to question, and to tolerate the uncertainty of not having all the answers, a characteristic they share with identity-achieved adolescents, allows them to
transcend the thinking of the group and move beyond social convention.
Adolescents who have not examined their values—foreclosed adolescents—
are more likely to live lives of conformity and be bound by the expectations
of others (Josselson, 1987; Marcia, 1980).

Identity Diffusion Identity-diffused adolescents, rather than confront issues head-on, tend to avoid them (Berzonsky, 1992; Berzonsky & Ferrari,
1996). These adolescents are, in large measure, defined by the absence of

Identity-achieved and moratorium adolescents do not automatically define themselves according to convention, and they are tolerant of others who are unconventional.

strong commitments of their own and by their dismissal of the importance of commitment in others. Their actions, rather than reflecting beliefs or values, are likely to reflect the demands of the situation or the moment. These adolescents are neither rule-bound and authoritarian as are foreclosed adolescents nor truly tolerant as are identity-achieved and moratorium adolescents. Tolerance of differences in both of the latter implies a tension arising out of these differences that is not present in diffused adolescents, because others' ways do not conflict with clear-cut beliefs of their own.

A Developing Morality

Adolescents and children differ in important ways with respect to a developing morality. Adolescents evaluate others' actions in terms of internalized standards; children do not. Adolescents take the intentions of others into

When they were younger, these skateboarders probably enjoyed the thrill of skateboarding where they weren't supposed to if they knew they wouldn't be caught. Now, because their moral reasoning is more mature, they are more likely to limit their skateboarding to legal sites.

consideration; children judge actions in terms of their consequences. Adolescents can question values; children adopt a fixed standard of right and wrong. How are we to understand these developmental changes?

Answers differ, depending on who is speaking. In the sections that follow, we will consider four approaches to the development of morality: Social-cognitive theory, derives from the environmental model; Kohlberg's and Gilligan's approaches, as does Freud's, reflect the assumptions of the organismic model.

SOCIAL-COGNITIVE THEORY AND MORAL DEVELOPMENT

Why do adolescents internalize the standards of their communities? Why do they become law-abiding citizens? Social-cognitive theorists look to principles of learning for explanations.

Internalizing Standards

Those who adopt the social-cognitive approach assume that rewards and punishments regulate behavior. These incentives are initially effective in young children only when other people, such as parents and teachers, are around to administer them. As children imitate adult models, they also tell themselves when they have been good or bad, administering their own rewards and punishments (Mischel & Mischel, 1976).

Community standards determine which behaviors are to be rewarded and which ones punished. In learning the consequences of their behavior, children also acquire the standards of the group. These internalized controls tend to be concrete at first. Children learn specific actions and their consequences; they learn to say thank you, for example, or not to interrupt. In time they also acquire the principles behind these actions. Being polite, for instance, can take the form of a thank you or considering others' feelings by not interrupting. Thus, social-cognitive theory offers an explanation for internalizing the standards of one's community.

Considering Intentions

How does social-cognitive theory explain age-related changes in moral thought? Children at first do not take the intentions of others into consideration; they judge actions in terms of their consequences. This literal focus is one of the facts that any theory of moral development must address. Social-cognitive theorists point out that the experiences of children make this type of reasoning likely. Adults rarely give children reasons for doing things, often simply relying on physical restraints. Because physical rewards and punishments are common with young children, they are more likely to attend to the rewards or punishments that follow what they do than to the reasons that directed their actions (Mischel & Mischel, 1976).

Parental reactions to damage and messes probably contribute to children's literal focus. Most parents become more upset over big messes than small ones, even though both can be equally unintentional. Consider a child who, keeping out of his mother's way as she fixes dinner, attempts to pour himself a glass of milk. His grip slips as he positions the milk carton, and he watches, transfixed, as a stream of milk sends the cup scudding, flooding the countertop with milk. Is this mother likely to comment on his thoughtfulness at not disturbing her? Probably not. This child, like most, will be scolded for making a mess. It makes sense that children fail to understand that intentions can enter into one's evaluation of a situation when their intentions are so imperfectly considered.

Continuity and
Change: Identity
Consolidation in
Late Adolescence

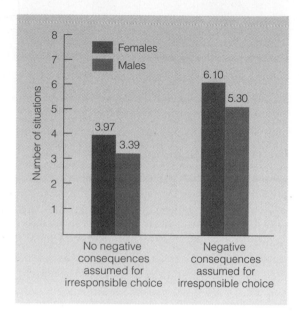

FIGURE 11.3
Mean Number of Situations in Which Adolescents Choose to Act Responsibly

Source: M. E. Ford, K. R. Wentzel, D. Wood, E. Stevens, & G. A. Siesfeld. (1989). Processes associated with integrative social competence: Emotional and contextual influences on adolescent social responsibility. *Journal of Adolescent Research, 4,* 405–425.

Questioning Values

Social-cognitive theory also explains the questioning of values that occurs in adolescence. Parents and teachers expect adolescents to start thinking for themselves, to evaluate ideas on their merit instead of accepting the endorsement of authorities. Social-cognitive theorists argue that we subtly reward adolescents for questioning the very ideas we taught them to uncritically accept as children. Similarly, learning experiences explain the relativistic form of thought that emerges in many adolescents as they near their twenties. Exposure to new values challenges them to consider their own values as one of a number of possible belief systems.

Acting Morally

How likely are adolescents to act in ways that reflect their moral understanding? In part, it depends on the incentives. *Incentives* are the rewards and punishments for acting in particular ways. Martin Ford and his associates (1989) asked adolescents to indicate how they would respond in a situation involving conflict (for example, giving a friend exam questions versus abiding by the school's honor code) if they could be sure that nothing bad would happen to them if they acted irresponsibly, and then to imagine what they would do if there were negative social consequences (such as getting grounded, peer disapproval). As expected, adolescents were considerably more likely to choose the socially responsible alternative when there would be negative consequences for not doing so; the results are shown in Figure 11.3. The emotions motivating their choice reflected both external consequences, like fear of negative sanctions, and internalized ones, such as anticipated guilt and empathic concern. Choices were more likely to be motivated by self-interest or concern with peer approval when negative consequences were not anticipated (Ford, Wentzel, Wood, Stevens, & Siesfeld, 1989).

Factors other than incentives also affect the likelihood of action. Adolescents are more likely to imitate the actions of prestigious people than of those whom they don't regard as important. Models who are nurturant are also more likely to be imitated, perhaps because we like them more than less-nurturant people and want to be like them. Models who are similar to us in one or more ways are also likely to be imitated, again perhaps because we can imagine being like them (Mischel & Mischel, 1976).

Critique of Social-Cognitive Theory

How well does this approach explain particular forms of moral behavior? We can look at how well it explains two forms of behavior: cheating at school and shoplifting.

Cheating   Cheating in most students is motivated by the fear of failing or the need for approval. However, whether adolescents with those motives will actually cheat is influenced by situational variables such as the normative behavior of classmates, incentives either for being honest or for cheating, the amount of risk involved, and characteristics of models for honesty and dishonesty.

Both personality and situational variables explain cheating in preadolescents. In one experiment, students worked at unsolvable problems that could be finished only if they cheated. Some worked for a tangible prize and others just for recognition. The likelihood of cheating was related both to the students' personalities and to the incentives they were working for. Both self-esteem and need for approval predicted cheating. Students with high self-esteem and low approval needs were least likely to cheat. Those with equally high self-esteem but high need for approval were as likely to cheat as those with low self-esteem. Regardless of personal motives, students working for a tangible prize were more likely to cheat (Lobel & Levanon, 1988). Cultural differences have also been found in what students consider to be cheating. Even so, the similarities seem to be greater than the differences, with all students, irrespective of their nationality, understanding that cheating involves, in one way or another, a shirking of their responsibilities to their studies (Evans, Craig, & Mietzel, 1993; Waugh, Godfrey, Evans, & Craig, 1995).

High school students report that they frequently cheat even though they consider it wrong to do so. Social-cognitive theory reminds us that what people do is not necessarily what they believe is right. Students report, however, that they engage in less serious forms of cheating, such as copying someone's homework, more frequently than serious ones, such as cheating on exams (McLaughlin & Ross, 1989). Similarly, studies find that about 30% of college students admit to cheating on exams (Lanza-Kaduce & Klug,

1986; Ward, 1986), and over 50% admit to plagiarizing, even though most said they thought it was unethical (Hale, 1987).

Among college students, cheating becomes more likely as the school term progresses and as students become more concerned with their grades, that is, as the incentives increase (Gardner, Roper, Gonzalez, & Simpson, 1988). These same investigators found that students with low exam grades are also more likely to cheat than are those who are doing better in their courses, although not all surveys find a relationship between students' overall grade-point averages and cheating (Houston, 1986).

Situational factors, such as sheer opportunity, are also important. Gardner and his colleagues (1988) found that, on the average, students cheated on half the questions they answered when completing a study guide assignment. When allowed to correct their own midterms, not knowing that scores had already been recorded, almost 30% of another group of students cheated (Ward, 1986). Houston (1986) similarly found that conditions such as the size of the room and student-to-proctor ratios predicted amount of cheating.

Shoplifting   Other forms of deviant behavior similarly lend themselves to explanations through social-cognitive principles. Some research has found, for example, that shoplifting is more likely when conditions of unemployment and low income make incentives more desirable and when individuals believe that their need justifies their actions (Ray & Briar, 1988; Turner & Cashdan, 1988). Whether rationalizations such as need or unemployment make it possible for individuals to engage in deviant behavior without guilt appears to depend on whether they believe these motives apply to the situation at hand. Survey data regarding both cheating and shoplifting suggest that students can engage in these behaviors with less guilt if they believe there are extenuating circumstances (Agnew & Peters, 1986). Similarly, Lucia Lo (1994) found that shoplifting was more likely among adolescents who did not regard it as morally wrong. However, she found shoplifting to be motivated more by thrill seeking than by need.

The frequency with which one engages in deviant behavior may alter one's perceptions of the deterrents that exist. A comparison of expert and novice shoplifters, for instance, found that novices are deterred by feelings of guilt, fear, and the possibility of getting caught. Experts, on the other hand, report being deterred primarily by strategic problems, such as whether an item is too big to conceal. Then again, those who engage in these activities to the point of becoming experts may experience little guilt to begin with (Weaver & Carroll, 1985).

Little mention has been made about conscience in this discussion. Social-cognitive theory suggests that many internalized controls are not necessarily related to moral values or to conscience; they simply reflect conditioning. Adolescents become helpful or law-abiding in order to avoid the anxiety they associate with doing otherwise. Conscience, when it does apply to behavior, is merely the set of standards one internalizes with the learning process (Seiber, 1980). For social-cognitive theorists, there is no inner voice other than the echo of the voices around them.

KOHLBERG AND MORAL DEVELOPMENT: MORALITY AS JUSTICE

What makes one moral? Is it simply that one internalizes the standards of one's community? Is it ever possible for individuals to function at a higher level than the society in which they live? Where does a sense of justice come from if it is not present in the social order? Lawrence Kohlberg's theory of moral reasoning addresses these questions.

Kohlberg's (1976, 1984) theory bases its assumptions about moral development on the organismic model, stressing the importance of the inner forces that organize development. The most important of these forces is a sense of justice, which underlies the highest forms of moral thought.

Kohlberg's theory traces moral reasoning over a number of discrete stages. Movement from one stage to the next is prompted by the need to resolve conflict. This conflict arises when one realizes that others view things differently. Individuals gain insight into the perspectives of others through increases in role-taking skills. As they become able to put themselves in the place of another, they can see things as that person does. Cognitive maturity—the ability to think about and balance the competing demands produced by examining several perspectives—also contributes to moral development. Kohlberg assumes that one's level of cognitive development places limits on the sophistication of moral thinking (Kohlberg, 1976, 1984).

Kohlberg traces moral development over three levels of moral reasoning, with two stages at each level. The levels reflect the stance adolescents take in relation to the standards of their community. Not all standards reflect moral issues. Some standards exist as laws, others simply as conventions or customary ways of behaving. It is the law, for example, that one not take another person's life; it is customary that one not giggle when hearing of another's death. Both of these reflect a common value—the sacredness of life. But only when adolescents reach the postconventional level of moral reasoning do they distinguish social convention, whether codified as laws or customs, from the values these conventions reflect. And only then, according to Kohlberg, can they distinguish conventional concerns from moral ones. Box 11.1 presents Kohlberg's levels of moral development and corresponding stages of moral reasoning.

Children at the level of **preconventional moral reasoning** want only to satisfy their needs and not get punished while doing so. At this level, they have not internalized the standards of their community even though they know what these standards are. They abide by the rules only when someone else is around. The "rule enforcers," and not the rules, constrain their actions. In the absence of the former, anything goes as long as you don't get caught (Kohlberg, 1984).

By adolescence, most adopt the standards of their community and reach the level of **conventional moral reasoning.** Simply observing the behavior of individuals at the first of Kohlberg's two levels does not reveal underlying differences. Kohlberg stresses the importance of the motives behind actions, not just the actions themselves, when evaluating moral conduct.

Box 11.1   Kohlberg's Stages of Moral Reasoning

PRECONVENTIONAL LEVEL OF MORAL REASONING

Stage 1: Obedience

Perspective	Only one's own
Motive	To satisfy one's needs; avoid punishment
Standards	The rules of others
Criteria	Consequences

Stage 2: Instrumental

Perspective	One's own and a second person's
Motive	To satisfy one's needs and those of the other
Standards	The rules of others
Criteria	Fairness

CONVENTIONAL LEVEL OF MORAL REASONING

Stage 3: Conformist or "Good Boy, Nice Girl"

Perspective	A third person's
Motive	To receive approval from others
Standards	Internalized rules
Criteria	Living up to expectations

Stage 4: Social Accord or "Law and Order"

Perspective	The community's
Motive	To uphold the law
Standards	Rules codified as laws
Criteria	Compliance with the law

POSTCONVENTIONAL LEVEL OF MORAL REASONING

Stage 5: Social Contract

Perspective	Society's, as seen by someone from another society
Motive	To maintain the social order
Standards	Laws as agreements among those governed
Criteria	Justice

Stage 6: Universal Principles

Perspective	Any society's as seen by humankind
Motive	To ensure human rights for all
Standards	Personal principles
Criteria	Universal moral values

Those at the conventional level want to live up to the standards of their group and are not motivated simply by the desire to avoid punishment. These standards have become their own; they are no longer other people's rules. In one sense, though, their behavior still lacks internal control, because the standards they live by are set by others rather than by themselves.

Box 11.2   Rachel's Dilemma

Rachel didn't know what to do. Elsie looked so whacked out she could hardly put one foot in front of the other. Was it lack of sleep? (Elsie *did* party a lot.) Or was she actually on something? They had experimented with marijuana together, and Rachel suspected that Elsie had tried other drugs. Elsie had once started to talk about her friends and the parties they went to. It sounded like they did a lot of drugs. Elsie had gotten nervous when Rachel asked her about this. She'd changed the subject, and Rachel never heard any more about it. Elsie no longer wanted to get together with Rachel and their old friends, even referring to them as "small time" once. Rachel could see even from here that Elsie's eyes looked funny, like she was having a hard time focusing, even though it was only second-period gym class. She was perspiring, too, and the air conditioning was on. Should she tell her counselor that she thought Elsie was on drugs? Elsie and she had once promised each other they would never betray their confidence about smoking marijuana. And if she reported Elsie, her parents would almost surely find out that she also had experimented with drugs. She could forget about that lifeguard job this summer. They'd never let her out of their sight. Then again, drugs could kill.

Only at the level of **postconventional moral reasoning** do adolescents and young adults develop genuine inner controls over behavior; the principles by which they live are self-derived standards rather than the conventions of their community. Motives, as well, reflect a sense of obligation to live within a code that is determined by one's principles. Thus, Kohlberg distinguishes levels of moral development in terms of both a progressive internalization of standards for behavior and motives for living according to these standards (Hoffman, 1980; Kohlberg, 1984).

Preconventional Moral Reasoning

Stage 1: Obedience   Individuals at this stage (usually children) assume that everyone sees things as they do, not realizing that their view of a situation is just one of several possible perspectives. Consequently, they experience little or no conflict in their interactions with others. Their actions reflect only a need to satisfy their own desires, without getting punished for doing so. Stage 1 morality is not reflective; individuals do not take motives and intentions into consideration (they do not understand others' feelings and points of view easily). They judge behavior simply in terms of its consequences. Actions that are rewarded must have been good; those that were punished, bad. Read the dilemma presented in Box 11.2 before continuing, then consider how a Stage 1 adolescent might respond to this situation.

What should Rachel do? Kohlberg reminds us that it is the reasoning rather than the answer itself that reveals the stage at which an adolescent is functioning. Adolescents at Stage 1 might not report Elsie to the school counselor, fearing that the counselor would discover that they, too, had used drugs and that punishment would result. Conversely, they might report her, fearing that they would be punished if they didn't. There is nothing in this reasoning to indicate conflict over which course of action is *right;* decisions are based on the potential impact the actions have for oneself.

Stage 2: Instrumental, or Considering Intentions   As adolescents become better able to put themselves in the place of another person, they can see things as the other person would. Adopting the other's perspective gives them two points of view, and, in turn, the likelihood that they will experience conflict. Which perspective is right? They can understand the reasons for the other person's actions and know that the other can understand theirs—that each of them can consider the intentions of the other. Adolescents who reason at this level don't have to rely on others' reactions to evaluate behavior. They can look at the motives behind an action. Even though fairness is central to reasoning at this stage, morality is still preconventional because adolescents consider only the actions and intentions of those they are with and not the rules or laws of the group, whether the school or community.

What would Rachel do? First consider the reasoning that would lead a Stage 2 adolescent to believe Rachel should not report Elsie. This adolescent knows it's the rule to report anyone using drugs. However, Elsie and Rachel had made an agreement never to tell on each other. It's only fair for Rachel to live up to that promise. Besides, if she reported Elsie, she'd almost surely get caught herself. Best to let everyone take care of themselves in this case. The reasoning that might lead an adolescent to say that Rachel should report Elsie is similarly self-serving. Rachel might be rewarded in some way for reporting her friend; even if the authorities found out that she, too, had experimented with drugs, they would not punish her as severely as if she didn't indicate her respect for the rules by reporting those who she knew were breaking them.

Conventional Moral Reasoning: Internalizing Standards

Stage 3: Conformist, or "Good Boy, Nice Girl"   The self-reflection that comes with formal thought makes it possible for adolescents to see themselves as they imagine others would. This third-person perspective forms the basis for taking the norms of their group, in the form of concern with what others think of them, into consideration, and here adolescents move into conventional reasoning. This concern about the opinions of others adds a new dimension to morality: the need to live up to the expectations of others. Kohlberg believes that Stage 3 reasoning is dominant during adolescence, and even common in adulthood (Kohlberg, 1984). The prevalence of Stage 3 reasoning helps to explain adolescents' sensitivity to the approval of peers. Rather than thinking through a situation in terms of the claims of those involved, adolescents are likely to be swayed by the opinions of their friends.

How would Stage 3 adolescents reason about Rachel's dilemma? Reasoning that leads to not reporting Elsie would focus on loyalty among friends—how would she look turning in a friend? Reasoning that leads to reporting her would focus on what her teachers and parents would think of her for *not* reporting Elsie. The decision turns on which reference group the adolescent considers: that of friends and peers or that of teachers and parents.

Stage 4: Social Accord, or "Law and Order"   As the ability to think more abstractly increases, adolescents begin to see themselves as members of an invisible but nonetheless real community. As such, they realize the need to evaluate actions by the community's standards. Kohlberg believes that reasoning at the fourth stage is frequently the highest that most people reach.

Rachel's dilemma takes on new proportions for adolescents at Stage 4. On the one hand, friendship demands that she not betray Elsie to the authorities; her duty is to be loyal to her friend. On the other hand, Rachel has a duty to live within the law and to see that others do as well. After all, if everyone "did their own thing," the system would break down. Stage 4 reasoning is usually adequate for most situations. It breaks down, however, when laws conflict with human values. When this occurs, adolescents must develop a way to see their society in relation to the needs of others.

Postconventional Moral Reasoning: Questioning Values

Stage 5: Social Contract   Kohlberg believes that adolescents move into Stage 5 only when they have been exposed to other value systems, usually in late adolescence. Individuals who come to respect others' ways of life find it difficult to continue seeing their own as more valid. Once adolescents recognize that their society's conventions are in some sense arbitrary, they are forced to look beyond the conventions themselves to the function they serve. When they do, they discover that laws derive their importance because they represent agreements among people who live together, not because they are right in and of themselves. Members of a society enter into a contract with others in the society in which they agree to live within its laws, forgoing some individual freedoms, for the mutual benefit of all.

Stage 5 adolescents might reason that Rachel should not report Elsie because the way she has chosen to live her life reflects her values, and values are relative. They might add that Rachel is obliged to act in a way that protects each person's rights, including Elsie's, and might remind us that Rachel and Elsie had entered into a contractual agreement concerning their use of drugs. Reasons for reporting Elsie would stress that, as members of society, Rachel and Elsie have implicitly agreed to keep the laws of their community and that these laws must be upheld for the greater good of all.

Stage 6: Universal Principles   This stage provides adolescents with yet another perspective: seeing past the mutual agreements shared by members of a society to the values these agreements reflect. The social contracts we enter into reflect underlying values such as truth, justice, honor, and the value of life itself. The step that adolescents take in order to gain a perspective on their society removes them from the claims of time and circumstance. Kohlberg asserts that all societies throughout history have recognized these values—that they are, in fact, universal ethical principles. Those who reason at this final stage understand that societal conventions are imperfect reflections of these values and, consequently, individuals must look beyond conventions, and even laws, to their own principles when arriving at moral decisions (Kohlberg, 1984).

Why might Rachel not report Elsie to the counselor? Stage 6 reasoning stresses the honor among friends that would require Rachel to keep her

In the course of moral development, adolescents come to see themselves not only as members of the community but also as able to challenge community decisions that they feel are wrong. These high school students are attending a school board meeting to protest the dropping of a class.

word with Elsie. Conversely, those who reason that Rachel should report Elsie would be likely to mention the value of Elsie's life, which is threatened by her use of drugs. They might add that even if they were in Elsie's place, they would expect to be turned in by anyone else who opposes the use of life-threatening drugs. This last reason illustrates a point that Kohlberg makes about Stage 6 individuals. He describes them as able to imagine themselves in the place of every other person in a situation and to impartially evaluate the rights of each. The image of the Stage 6 person is that of the blindfolded figure of Justice who weighs the claims of each without knowing which person has made which claim. This ability is truly an idealized form of role-taking, and very few people function at this level (Kohlberg, 1984).

Critique of Kohlberg's Theory

Kohlberg's is a developmental theory, and, as such, one would expect older individuals to reason at higher stages than younger ones. Rosemary Jadack, Janet Shibley Hyde, Colleen Moore, and Mary Keller (1995), at the University of Wisconsin, Madison, asked students differing in age to consider dilemmas concerning sexual behavior in which a character must decide whether to tell a partner about the presence of a sexually transmitted disease. These investigators found that older college students (mean age 22 years) generally reasoned at a higher level, as assessed by a scoring system designed for use with Kohlberg's dilemmas, than did younger students (mean age 18 years). Younger students focused more on the likelihood of simply acquiring the disease, whereas older students introduced issues of responsibility and accountability.

Implicit in the assumption of developmental change is the expectation that reasoning can be characterized, at any point, as being at one stage or another. However, reasoning about different situations has often been found to be at several adjacent stages (Jadack, Hyde, Moore, & Keller, 1995; Wark & Krebs, 1996).

Do most adolescents and adults reason at Stages 3 and 4, as Kohlberg asserts? Snarey (1985) reviewed nearly 50 studies that had used Kohlberg's scale and found that 75% of the individuals who were interviewed reasoned entirely at the conventional level or at a combination of conventional and preconventional levels. Less than 10% functioned at higher levels. Similarly, Schweder, Mahapatra, and Miller (1987) reported that only 15% of the children and adults they interviewed treated conventional rules (such as those governing table manners or forms of greeting) as if they could be changed. These data suggest that most people do not distinguish moral issues from social conventions.

Joan Miller and David Bersoff (1989) of Yale University question this conclusion. They find that adults and children alike consider the usefulness of social conventions before deciding whether they could be changed. Nearly 80% thought it wrong to violate conventions that are useful (those that maintain order, such as using properly marked exits), but less than 15% felt it wrong to violate ones with little usefulness (such as standards of dress). Rules with little utility were accepted only for private settings. Violating the same restrictions in a public setting was not considered wrong, whereas violating a moral rule was considered wrong irrespective of the setting—and by individuals of all ages (Miller & Bersoff, 1989).

Both morals and conventions set forth rules for behavior, however, each relates rules to behavior in different ways. Elliot Turiel (1983), a psychologist at the University of California, Berkeley, maintains that even very young children distinguish moral rules from conventional ones. Conventional rules reflect accepted ways of doing things. As these change, so do the rules. Standards of dress and speech reflect these flexible relationships. The rules relating moral concerns to behavior are inflexible. Moral rules reflect a concern for the well-being of others and do not change with climates of opinion.

Charles Helwig, Carolyn Hildebrandt, and Elliot Turiel (1995) interviewed first-, third-, and fifth-graders and found that nearly all the children agreed that moral acts such as pushing someone down would not be all right even in the context of a game that legitimized such actions. The youngest children, however, were less clear about acts leading to psychological harm, such as name calling as part of a game. Similarly, Larry Nucci, Cleanice Camino, and Clary Sapiro (1996), interviewing 9- and 15-year-olds in Brazil, found that children as well as adolescents distinguished moral from conventional issues, agreeing that if there were no rules against doing so, it would be all right not to wear a school uniform, but not to hit or steal. These data indicate that even children distinguish moral from conventional concerns; Kohlberg assumes that one makes this distinction only with the fifth stage of reasoning.

If even children can distinguish moral issues, how can we explain the developmental progression that Kohlberg has noted? Martin Hoffman (1980) answers that we socialize children in either of two very different ways: One way stresses being obedient and following the rules; the other emphasizes altruism and a concern for others. Hoffman points out that it is possible for young children to comply with both sets of demands because the behaviors called for by either usually apply in different settings. However, older children frequently experience conflict between the demands for living by the rules and their prosocial concerns. Hoffman suggests that the emergence of truly moral concerns in adolescence is actually a resurgence of earlier prosocial ones that had been channeled into conventional behavior in middle childhood in the course of acquiring society's norms (Hoffman, 1980, 1988).

Kohlberg's theory, despite the debate it has occasioned, enjoys wide support. His theory has an intrinsic elegance. Each of the six stages is a logical extension of the preceding one, and the progression is systematically related to new role-taking skills and cognitive maturity. But there may be another reason to account for the popularity of this theory. Kohlberg has given us a sympathetic view of human nature. He accounts for our ability to control our behavior in terms of the development of an inner sense of justice, rather than the "carrot and stick" approach of social-cognitive theory.

Carol Gilligan questions whether justice is the highest arbiter of moral issues. She finds that an ethic of care, rather than a morality of justice, is more characteristic of females. She points out that Kohlberg developed his theory based on interviews with only males. Like many developmentalists before him, Kohlberg equated the male perspective with development in general (see Chapter 2).

GILLIGAN: AN ETHIC OF CARE

Carol Gilligan (1982, 1988a, 1988b, 1989a, 1989b), of Harvard University, gives a fresh perspective on moral development, one that balances male-oriented theories such as Kohlberg's and Freud's with insights gained from interviews with females. Gilligan finds that most females think of morality more personally than males do; they adopt an **ethic of care.** They speak of morality in terms of their responsibilities to others rather than as the rights of individuals. Their moral decisions are based on compassion as well as reason, and they stress care for others as well as fairness.

Gilligan traces these approaches to differences in the way females and males define themselves in relation to others. Whereas males tend to view themselves as separate from others, females see themselves in terms of their relationships with others. These themes of separation and connectedness translate into different approaches to morality. The assumption that one is separate from others highlights the need for rules to regulate the actions of each person with respect to the other; the assumption that one is connected to others emphasizes the responsibility each has to the other (Gilligan, 1982).

Because females define themselves in relation to others and males define themselves as separate from others, the course of their moral development is different, according to psychologist Carol Gilligan.

Gender differences also exist in the way individuals think of responsibility (see Chapter 2). Males tend to think of responsibility as *not* doing something that would infringe on the rights of others, such as not hurting them. Females think of responsibility in terms of *meeting* the needs of others, that is, as something to be done. Both males and females are concerned with not hurting others, yet each sex thinks of this in a different way. Gilligan points out that, given differences such as these, attempts to chart moral development as a single sequence are bound to give us only half the picture.

Gilligan traces moral development in females through three levels, each of which reflects a different resolution to the conflict between responsibility to self and responsibility to others. Movement from one level to the next occurs in two transitional periods. At the first level, the primary concern is with oneself. Transition to the next level occurs when one sees caring only for oneself as selfish and at odds with responsibility to others. At the second level, females equate morality with goodness and self-sacrifice—caring for others. Transition to the third level occurs when they experience problems in their relationships that result from excluding themselves from their own care. At the third level, they equate morality with care for both themselves and others.

Level 1: Caring for Self (Survival)

The primary concerns at this level of moral development are pragmatic: What's best for me? The motivation is survival. Actions are guided by self-interest and self-preservation. Gilligan says of this perspective that "the woman focuses on taking care of herself because she feels that she is all alone. From this perspective, *should* is undifferentiated from *would*, and other people influence the decision only through their power to affect its consequences" (1982, p. 75). Gilligan notes that the issue of "rightness" is considered only when one's own needs are in conflict and force the individual to consider which need is more important. Otherwise there is little conflict over making the right decision.

Why might individuals function at this level? Gilligan believes that a preoccupation with one's needs reflects feelings of helplessness and powerlessness. These feelings have their origin in being emotionally cut off, or *disconnected,* from others. The young women she interviewed who were at this level had frequently experienced disappointing relationships in which they had been hurt by others. These women often chose to hold themselves apart from others rather than experience further pain. Feeling alone and cut off from others, they were left with the sense that they had to look to their own needs, because no one else would (Gilligan, 1982).

This first level is similar to Kohlberg's preconventional level of moral reasoning. In neither level do individuals consider others except for their possible reactions to what they do, that is, except as potential consequences for their actions. Conflict is also absent in both levels and self-interest, rather than the need to make the right decision, dictates what one does.

Transition: From Selfishness to Responsibility

Individuals begin to move beyond the first level when they experience a discrepancy between the way they are and the way they feel they ought to be, that is, between self-concern and responsible concern for others. A certain amount of self-worth is needed in order to move through this transitional phase. One must feel sufficiently good about oneself in order to see oneself as having the capacity for good and to be included in the social group (Gilligan, 1982).

Level 2: Caring for Others (Goodness)

Gilligan assumes that females move to a second level of moral development when they internalize social conventions. The progression is similar to that described by Kohlberg for movement from preconventional to conventional reasoning. Gilligan notes that in the first level,

> morality is a matter of sanctions imposed by a society of which one is more subject than citizen, [and in the second] moral judgment relies on shared norms and expectations. The woman at this point validates her claim to social membership through the adoption of societal values. Consensual judgment about goodness becomes the overriding concern as survival is now seen to depend on acceptance by others. (1982, p. 79)

Transition: From Conformity to Choice

The equation of morality with conventional feminine goodness is a step toward repairing the failed relationships that led to a preoccupation with the self at the first level. But this equation creates a second imbalance that itself is in need of repair. Conventional images of feminine goodness center around the care of others. They also involve self-sacrifice. Females at the second level of morality purchase membership in the larger community at the cost of caring for themselves. The price of membership is costly and introduces tensions that, for some, will prompt movement to the third level. These individuals realize that excluding themselves from their own care creates as many problems as excluding others had done previously; in other words, goodness results in as much hurt as selfishness (Gilligan, 1986). This realization is an important step in moving to an ethic of care that includes themselves as well as others. Gilligan, like Kohlberg before her, believes that many females do not take this step and do not develop beyond conventional forms of thought.

Level 3: Caring for Self and Others (Truth)

To move into the third level, females must move beyond the conventional wisdom that tells them to put the needs of others above their own. In doing so, they must reformulate their definition of care to include themselves as well as others. As females reconsider their relationships with others, they once again must consider their own needs. Questions such as "Is this selfish?" again arise. Because these occur in the context of relationships with others, they also prompt a re-examination of the concept of responsibility.

When one moves beyond conventional forms of wisdom, one finds there is no one to turn to for answers but oneself. Females at this level cannot rely on what others might think; they must exercise their own judgment. This judgment requires that they be honest with themselves. Being responsible for themselves, as well as for others, means they must know what their needs actually are. As Gilligan asserts, "The criterion for judgment thus shifts from goodness to truth when the morality of action is assessed not on the basis of its appearance in the eyes of others, but in terms of the realities of its intention and consequence" (1982, p. 83). The bottom line is simple: To care for oneself, one must first be honest with oneself and acknowledge the reasons behind one's actions.

Individuals at this level adopt an inclusive perspective that gives equal weight to their responsibility to themselves and to others. Care extends to all. To exclude the self would introduce pain that could otherwise be avoided, and their commitment to minimizing pain requires a new balance of concern for self with responsibility for others.

Although Gilligan and Kohlberg document developmental sequences that parallel each other in many respects, a critical difference separates these two accounts. Kohlberg believes that his sequence is a path universally trodden by all individuals as they move into adulthood. He assumes that this sequence takes the form it does because it reflects developments in cognitive maturity that have a strong biological component (see the discussion of Piaget in Chapter 2). Gilligan is not equally convinced that the sequence she documents in adolescent girls and young women is developmentally necessary. She does not believe the sequence to be "rooted in childhood," as does Kohlberg. She suggests, instead, that it is a response to a crisis, and that the crisis is adolescence itself (Gilligan, 1989a).

Gilligan proposes that leaving childhood is problematic for girls in ways that it is not for boys. The problem lies with the culture each enters. Adolescence introduces the expectation that children will assume the conventions of their society, whether these be adult gender roles, the knowledge that forms the basis of cultural wisdom, or behaviors that fit prescribed definitions of "goodness" and "rightness." Why should this expectation present more problems for girls?

Gilligan's answer is powerful. The most visible figures populating the landscape of adulthood are males—whether plumbers, politicians, poets, or philosophers—and their collective experiences form its norms. Girls risk losing themselves as they relax the intimate bonds of childhood to embrace a larger world of experience. Gilligan writes:

> As the river of a girl's life flows into the sea of Western culture, she is in danger of drowning or disappearing. To take on the problem of her appearance, which is the problem of her development, and to connect her life with history on a cultural scale, she must enter—and by entering disrupt—a tradition in which "human" has for the most part meant male. Thus a struggle often breaks out in girls' lives at the edge of adolescence. (1989b, p. 4)

The problem is pervasive because it is woven into the very fabric of cultural thought. Even formal education, Gilligan suggests, presents a challenge to female identity: "In learning to think in the terms of the disciplines and thus to bring her thoughts and feelings into line with the traditions of Western culture, . . . she also learn[s] to dismiss her own experience" (1989b, p. 2).

Gilligan traces the crisis of connection for girls to their ability to find a "voice" with which to speak and a context in which they will be heard. The culture they are entering has not been equally responsive to the voices of women and men, "or at least has not been up to the present. The wind of tradition blowing through women is a chill wind, because it brings a message of exclusion. . . . The message to women is: keep quiet and notice the absence of women and say nothing" (Gilligan, 1989a, p. 26).

Critique of Gilligan's Theory

What evidence is there for gender differences in moral concerns? D. Kay Johnston (1988) asked 11- and 15-year-olds to generate solutions to two of Aesop's fables involving moral issues. Specifically, she wanted to know whether gender differences exist in the spontaneous use of justice and care orientations and whether both orientations are available to adolescents of each sex. The two fables appear in Box 11.3. Boys were much more likely to spontaneously adopt a justice than a care approach to both of the fables. Girls, however, were fairly evenly divided in their adoption of either approach. Judgments about the best solution showed that boys still strongly

Box 11.3 Two Moral Orientations to Fable Dilemmas

THE PORCUPINE AND THE MOLES

It was growing cold, and a porcupine was looking for a home. He found a most desirable cave but saw it was occupied by a family of moles.

"Would you mind if I shared your home for the winter?" the porcupine asked the moles.

The generous moles consented and the porcupine moved in. But the cave was small and every time the moles moved around they were scratched by the porcupine's sharp quills. The moles endured this discomfort as long as they could. Then at last they gathered courage to approach their visitor. "Pray leave," they said, "and let us have our cave to ourselves once again."

"Oh no!" said the porcupine. "This place suits me very well."

THE DOG IN THE MANGER

A dog, looking for a comfortable place to nap, came upon the empty stall of an ox. There it was quiet and cool and the hay was soft. The dog, who was very tired, curled up on the hay and was soon fast asleep.

A few hours later the ox lumbered in from the fields. He had worked hard and was looking forward to his dinner of hay. His heavy steps woke the dog who jumped up in a great temper. As the ox came near the stall the dog snapped angrily, as if to bite him. Again and again the ox tried to reach his food, but each time he tried the dog stopped him.

Examples of Care Orientation

- Wrap the porcupine in a towel.
- If there's enough hay, split it.

Examples of Justice Orientation

- The porcupine has to go. It's the moles' house.
- It's a question of ownership and nobody else has the right to it.

Source: D. K. Johnston. (1988). Adolescents' solutions to dilemmas in fables: Two moral orientations—two problem solving strategies. In C. Gilligan, J. V. Ward, & J. M. Taylor (Eds.), *Mapping the moral domain.* Cambridge, MA: Harvard University Press.

preferred (three to one) a justice solution to one of the fables; girls strongly favored a care solution as best to both of the fables.

Judy Daniels, Michael D'Andrea, and Ronald Heck (1995) replicated Johnston's experiment with adolescents in Hawaii and found no difference in the solutions spontaneously offered by girls and boys. Furthermore, when asked for the best solution to the dilemmas, all adolescents offered a care approach. Differences between their findings and those of Johnston might reflect cultural differences, or simply changes in gender roles with time. In individualistic cultures such as the mainland United States, the rights of individuals tend to be emphasized, whereas in traditionally collectivistic cultures such as Hawaii, the good of the collective, or group, is emphasized (Markus & Kitayama, 1991).

Young people, male and female, with a justice orientation are more likely to protest inadequate funding for AIDS research, whereas those with a care orientation are more likely to express their concern by providing a helping hand to people with AIDS.

It is also possible that differences between these studies may be due to changes in gender roles (Sochting, Skoe, & Marcia, 1994). Rosemary Jadack and her associates (1995) found that females and males differed little in the extent to which they adopted a care or a justice orientation in reasoning about real life types of dilemmas. In fact, individuals of either sex frequently used reasoning characteristic of both approaches, suggesting that these are not competing perspectives. Similarly, Gillian Wark and Dennis Krebs (1996) found that, although females did mention more care-based reasons than males, the difference was small and occurred only when they were reasoning about certain types of problems.

Comparison of Gilligan's and Kohlberg's Approaches

Some dilemmas may yield themselves more easily than others to a care perspective. Many of Kohlberg's dilemmas, for instance, are relatively impersonal. Onlookers are asked to think about courses of action that might be taken by people they have never met. Is reasoning under such conditions more likely to be abstract and to stress justice rather than care for others? Lonky, Roodin, and Rybasch (1988) compared the reasoning of people who were asked to respond to dilemmas from the position of someone actually experiencing the dilemma versus those who read about a dilemma as experienced by someone else. They found that when people are asked to imagine the dilemma as their own, they are more likely to adopt a care orientation. Evaluating dilemmas as experienced by someone else favors the adoption of a justice orientation. These data suggest that both orientations are available to each sex, and that which guides reasoning will depend on how the situation is presented.

Gilligan views the developmental sequence that she catalogues as complementing that of Kohlberg's, not as an alternative (Gilligan & Attanucci, 1988). She points out, however, that the care orientation would have been missed had she and others not studied females as systematically as Kohlberg studied males.

FREUD: MORALITY AND THE SUPEREGO

Freud's theory of moral development derives from his more general theory of personality development. Like other organismic theorists, Freud looked to sources within the organism to explain certain developmental changes. Freud assumed that the strong biological forces he identified must be balanced by equally strong social constraints that develop only with age.

Freud believed that responsibility for moral behavior resides with the **superego,** the last of the three facets of the personality to develop (see Chapter 2). The superego embraces the cultural standards of right and wrong that make up the *conscience*. Prior to the development of the conscience (at about age 5), Freud assumed that children are governed only by the desire to win parental affections and the fear of being rejected for wrongdoing. Like social-cognitive theorists and Kohlberg, Freud believed that an internalized code or ethic is not present in early childhood.

Freud (1925b) assumed that the libido—the life force within each individual—seeks genital expression in childhood, and that the object of the child's sexual desires is the very person who is closest in so many other ways. For the boy, this is the mother; for the girl, it will become the father. Sexual desire for the parent of the opposite sex makes the parent of the same sex a rival. The emotional triangle that results creates unbearable anxiety in the child. Freud believed that children repress their sexual desires to reduce the anxiety they experience, and identify with the same-sex parent. **Identification** is the process by which the child internalizes or appropriates the values and behaviors of the parent. These values form the superego and serve as the basis for an internalized set of standards for behavior.

Freud assumed the situation differed for male and female children. Freud reasoned that girls are not as motivated as boys to resolve Oedipal tensions, because they have already suffered an incalculable loss: They were not born with a penis. Rather than fearing castration (castration anxiety), they long for a penis (penis envy). Because girls literally have less to lose than boys, they do not experience the same anxiety that motivates boys to identify with the same-sex parent. Also, the figure with whom the girl identifies, the mother, is not as powerful or threatening as the father. As a consequence, Freud believed that girls' superegos are not as strong or as demanding as those of boys.

The final step in moral development occurs in adolescence when puberty threatens the surface tranquility achieved through repression and identification. New sexual desires assail the fragile bulwark the child has erected against Oedipal turmoil. Freud assumed that adolescents' only defense against the onslaught of their own sexuality, and the incestuous threat this poses, is to emotionally distance themselves from their parents. In doing so, they have to toss out the parental figures they had internalized in childhood. Adolescence becomes a time for reworking the parental standards that have been uncritically accepted as part of these figures (Josselson, 1980, 1987).

Critique of Freud's Theory

Freud's theory of personality development and his assumptions about moral development are widely accepted. His theory influences vast numbers of clinical practitioners and is taught in college courses around the world. Many of his concepts—such as the unconscious, projection, and repression—have entered the popular vocabulary. Nevertheless, the bulk of support for this theory comes from clinical evidence based on small numbers of individuals and is often heavily interpreted (Hoffman, 1980).

Carol Tavris and Carole Wade (1984) point to the absence of systematic, objective support for Freud's twin concepts of castration anxiety and penis envy, concepts that are central to his explanation of moral development in males and females, respectively. Regarding the concept of penis envy, they note that females as well as males value the male role more highly, but point out that males have enjoyed more power, greater opportunities, and more privileges than females. Do females envy males for their penis? Or do they desire the social advantages that go with having one?

Freud believed that the absence of castration anxiety in females and the presence, in its stead, of penis envy resulted in a weaker superego in females and differences in their moral behavior. Freud wrote:

> I cannot evade the notion (though I hesitate to give it expression) that for women the level of what is ethically normal is different from what it is in men. Their superego is never so inexorable, so impersonal, so independent of its emotional origins as we require it to be in men. Character traits which critics of every epoch have brought up against women—that they show less sense of justice than men, that they are less ready to submit it to the great exigencies of life, that they are more often influenced in their judgment by feelings of affection or hostility—all these would be amply accounted for by the modification in the formation of their super-ego which we have inferred. (1925b, pp. 257–258)

These assumptions concerning the basis for gender differences in moral behavior have not received empirical support. Research on the internalization of moral standards does not find males to have stronger superegos than females. Nor do differences in behavior, when they occur, favor males. They are, if anything, as likely to favor females (Ford, Wentzel, Wood, Stevens, & Siesfeld, 1989; Lobel & Levanon, 1988).

Research has similarly failed to support other of Freud's assumptions related to the development of morality. For instance, adolescence is not a period of emotional turmoil for most teenagers. Also, large surveys of normal adolescents do not find they are preoccupied with sex or with controlling their impulses. Nor do most adolescents have weak egos, nor have they cut emotional ties with their parents (see Chapter 5).

Internalizing Standards   How does Freud explain the facts that other theories of moral development have addressed? Like social-cognitive theorists (as well as Kohlberg and Gilligan for conventional standards of morality), Freud assumes that individuals acquire their values and their sense of right and wrong by internalizing society's norms. The conditions that prompt children to internalize parental standards differ for each theory, however. Freud traces internalization to resolution of the Oedipal complex and identification with the parent of the same sex. Social-cognitive theory speaks of the child's ability to reinforce itself, rather than having to receive praise or punishment at the hands of others. Both theories must address the central problem with internalization as an explanation for moral conduct: If one's culture is the ultimate source of moral authority in an individual's life, how does a person ever reach a level higher than that which characterizes the society? Gilligan and Kohlberg both view the internalization of social conventions as an intermediate step in moral development. Gilligan believes that females take this step when they experience a discrepancy between their self-concern and concern for others. Kohlberg traces this step to increases in cognitive maturity.

Considering Intentions   For Freud, the emergence of the superego explains the child's shift from evaluating behavior in terms of its consequences to the motives that underlie it. Social-cognitive theorists, in contrast, explain this shift in terms of the social-learning experiences of the child, but frequently fail to take into consideration the child's own motives and intentions or the expectation that adolescents will begin to think for themselves. Kohlberg attributes this shift to new levels of cognitive maturity and role-taking skills. Gilligan's analysis of morality begins with individuals who have already made this transition.

Questioning Values   And how might Freud explain the flexibility that characterizes the moral thought that develops in some with late adolescence? Rather than refer to changing social expectations, increasing cognitive maturity, or the need to repair relationships, psychoanalytic thought attributes flexibility in moral judgments to the work of the ego in balancing the demands of the id and superego. Individuals who remain relatively inflexible are those dominated by a threatening superego. The ability to evaluate a situation, to develop coping strategies, and to delay gratification of one's impulses are all functions of the ego and characterize mature moral functioning.

ADOLESCENTS' RELIGIOUS BELIEFS

Do adolescents think of God the same way children do? Or do the intellectual developments that occur in adolescence affect their views of God and religion just as they affect their views of so many other things? James Fowler (1981, 1991) suggests that they do. He identifies stages of religious belief that parallel the stages of moral development discussed earlier.

Children's views of God reflect the concrete nature of the way they think in general. To them, God is someone with a human form who sits celestially enthroned above them. They accept the teachings and stories of their religion literally and do not question them, other than to try to fit them into their current ways of understanding such as wondering how God can be everywhere at the same time (Fowler, 1981, 1991).

The ability to think abstractly that comes with adolescence also transforms their religious beliefs. More abstract qualities of God can be appreciated, such as righteousness, compassion, and mercy, and more sophisticated reasoning about religious practices is possible (Helwig, 1995). Just as adolescents begin to question other sources of authority in their lives, they begin to question religious beliefs. "If God is all-powerful, why is there suffering and evil in the world?" The answers adolescents arrive at reflect an increasingly personalized faith much as Kohlberg's final stages of postconventional morality reflect commitment to personally arrived at principles (Fowler, 1981, 1991). The Research Focus, "Within-Subjects Design," explores issues of forgiveness and justice.

Even so, religious beliefs reflect more than adolescents' ability to think in certain ways. The processes of exploration and commitment that are central to identity formation also contribute to differences in religiosity. The

Research Focus

Within-Subjects Design: Forgiveness

"Forget it, kiddo. It's cool."

Tiffany couldn't believe what she heard. She knew how important that car was to Jenny, even if the old clunker *was* older than either of them. When she had asked to borrow it, she hadn't expected to dent the rear fender. Nor did she have the money to repair it. Volvo parts were pricey even for old models. At best, she had hoped to work out a "just solution"—like $3 a week for the next three years! But after a few tense discussions, Jenny had forgiven her—told her she didn't have to worry about paying for the damages.

We know a lot about the development of justice in adolescents. But we know very little about forgiveness. Justice is a consideration of competing claims among individuals; it weighs them and makes a decision in favor of one or the other. Forgiveness is a decision to release a person from a claim that justice would honor.

How are forgiveness and justice related? Is forgiveness just a special case of justice, one in which the injured person turns over any claims for retribution? If forgiveness *is* different, does it develop with age and social understanding as does justice? Are these different moralities? To the extent that certain religions, such as Christianity, emphasize the importance of forgiving, will forgiveness be related to the practice of one's faith?

Robert Enright, Maria Santos, and Radhi Al-Mabuk (1989) presented individuals of several ages with situations in which justice or forgiveness were called for. One of these described the dilemma of a man whose wife is dying of cancer. The man unsuccessfully attempts to persuade a druggist who has patented an expensive drug to sell him enough at a reduced price to save his wife's life. The druggist refuses, pointing out that it is through the sale of the drug that he makes his livelihood. In the justice scenario, individuals consider the competing claims of life versus private property. In the forgiveness scenario, the druggist anticipates that the man will try to steal the drug and hides it. The wife dies. Individuals answer questions that reflect stages of forgiveness by the husband ranging from vengeful retribution to unconditional forgiveness based on a principle of love. The degree of religiousness for each individual was also measured.

These investigators used a *within-subjects design,* in which each subject experienced all of the experimental conditions, that is, both the justice and the forgiveness scenarios. This design can be compared with a between-subjects design in which each subject would experience only one condition. (See Chapter 9, Research Focus, "Between-Subjects Design.") Within-subjects designs are *economical,* requiring fewer subjects because the same subjects react to all conditions. They are also *sensitive.* A design is sensitive to the extent that it can pick up, or detect, differences resulting from the experimental treatment. Within-subjects designs are sensitive because they use the same subjects in all conditions, thus reducing variability due to individual differences.

Despite these important advantages, this type of design has several serious disadvantages. One runs the risk of *carryover effects,* in which the effect of one treatment is still present when the next is given. In this example, subjects who read the forgiveness scenario first (in which the wife dies) may respond to the justice scenario with the feelings they had when earlier reading that the wife died. Carryover effects are not necessarily symmetrical for each of the orders in which different subjects read different scenarios; reading the justice scenario first might have no effect on subse-

(continued)

ability to think abstractly may make it possible for adolescents to entertain questions such as why God would tolerate suffering, but this ability alone is not enough to determine that they will.

Acceptance of religious tenets has been viewed by some as a means of controlling the ultimate risks of life, risks such as those introduced by disease

Research Focus (*continued*)

quent measures of forgiveness. In addition to carryover effects, there can be *order effects* with this design. These reflect systematic changes in performance over time due to factors such as practice, fatigue, boredom, and so on. Both carryover and order effects introduce the potential for *confounding*. Confounding exists when the difference between treatments can be explained in more than one way, that is, when an experiment lacks internal validity. (See Chapter 12, Research Focus, "Internal and External Validity.")

Enright, Santos, and Al-Mabuk *counterbalanced* the order in which subjects experienced the justice and forgiveness scenarios. Counterbalancing presents each condition an equal number of times in each order, thus balancing any effects due to order equally across conditions.

What did they find? First, reasoning about forgiveness, just as about justice, becomes more mature with age. Adolescents find it easiest to be forgiving when they know it's expected of them (expectational forgiveness). Children are likely to say they can forgive only if they first get back what they lost (restitutional forgiveness). Adults are likely to forgive because it is required by their religion, or to defer to a higher authority (lawful forgiveness). Their forgiveness, like that of adolescents, however, is conditional. With the latter, it depends on encouragement from others, mainly friends, and with the former, from a religious authority. Relatively few instances of *unconditional*, or principled, forgiveness (based on a principle of loving others) were found, and all of these occurred among adults.

In many ways, reasoning about forgiveness parallels Kohlberg's stages of moral reasoning about justice. Those who can forgive only after first punishing the offender or otherwise recouping their losses (the lowest stages of forgiveness) are also likely to reason at Kohlberg's lowest (preconventional) level of moral reasoning. The conditional forgiveness of adolescents and early adults reflects the conventional level of moral reasoning described by Kohlberg; both depend on social supports. Unconditional forgiveness, the highest stage, reflects a principled (Kohlberg's postconventional) reasoning that emphasizes the importance of loving others. These parallels suggest the contribution of similar role-taking skills for each type of reasoning. In addition, religious beliefs and practices appear to contribute to reasoning about forgiveness. Adolescents who practiced their faith, for example, attending church and Bible study groups, had more mature approaches to forgiveness. Among a sample of college students and parents, religiosity has been found to be unrelated to forgiveness when the offense has been committed by someone close, such as a family member or friend. However, when the offense has been committed by a more distant person, such as an employer or a general "other," those who indicated they practiced their religion were more likely to forgive (Subkoviak et al., 1995).

Research on forgiveness suggests that if adolescents are to learn to forgive, they need the support of friends who encourage them to adopt forgiveness as part of their approach to resolving interpersonal conflicts. Why forgive in the first place? Often other strategies of conflict resolution are equally appropriate. Many times, however, these leave the injured person with residual anger and resentment. The decision to release another from obligation, however, can free the person who has been injured from these feelings and open the way to restoring the relationship.

Sources: R. D. Enright, M. J. Santos, & R. Al-Mabuk. (1989). The adolescent as forgiver. *Journal of Adolescence, 12,* 95–110. M. J. Subkoviak, R. D. Enright, C. Wu, E. A. Gassin, S. Freedman, L. M. Olson, & I. Sarinopoulos. (1995). Measuring interpersonal forgiveness in late adolescence and middle adulthood. *Journal of Adolescence, 18,* 641–655.

and natural disaster (Malinowski, 1925). From this perspective, those who reject religious beliefs become the risk takers. However, as we have seen with other aspects of identity exploration, a determination of what is risky cannot be made in any simple way without reference to the particular contexts of an individual's life. In this respect, risk taking in religious beliefs, just as in the vocational and social domains of identity, takes the form of daring the unknown. Thus, it would be equally risky for an adolescent whose par-

TABLE 11.1   Religious Practices and Beliefs Among High School Seniors,
1976 to 1994

Religious Activity and Level of Interest	Percentage of Seniors		
	1976	1984	1994
FREQUENCY OF ATTENDING RELIGIOUS SERVICES			
Weekly	40.7	37.7	32.3
1–2 times a month	16.3	16.2	16.5
Rarely	32.0	35.8	36.8
Never	11.0	10.2	14.3
IMPORTANCE OF RELIGION IN LIFE			
Very important	28.8	29.7	29.6
Pretty important	30.5	32.6	28.6
A little	27.8	26.7	26.4
Not important	12.9	11.0	15.4

Source: University of Michigan, Institute for Social Research, *Monitoring the future,* various years. In Youth Indicators: *Trends in the Well-Being of American Youth.* (1996). Washington, DC: U.S. Government Printing Office.

ents are avowed atheists to explore a belief in God as it would for an adolescent coming from a deeply religious background to reject those religious beliefs.

The very same willingness to consider the unfamiliar, whether in terms of a career or a lifestyle, is also at the heart of religiosity. Will adolescents give themselves the freedom to explore their religion? Some will, others will not. Adolescents can remain committed to traditional religious beliefs without ever examining them. These adolescents can be said to be foreclosed in their religiosity. Conversely, adolescents can explore their beliefs, asking questions to which they do not have simple or familiar answers, and be identity-achieved (Markstrom-Adams, Hofstra, & Dougher, 1994; Markstrom-Adams & Smith, 1996).

One cannot distinguish either type of adolescent simply by looking at their beliefs. It is not so much a question of *what* adolescents believe as it is the *process* by which they have gotten to these beliefs. Just as with the broader process of identity formation, the beliefs one ends up with can remain essentially unchanged. It is the believer who has changed. One index of religious exploration, for instance, is switching one's church affiliation due to dissatisfaction with its teachings. Individuals who switch have been found to be more actively involved in their religion subsequent to switching than those whose beliefs have remained unexamined (Hoge, Johnson, & Luidens, 1995).

Importance of Religion

How important is religion in the lives of adolescents? Nearly 30% of high school seniors in a recent survey indicated that religion is very important in their lives, and another 30% said it was pretty important. Thirty-two per-

Continuity and
Change: Identity
Consolidation in
Late Adolescence

In a few years, be-
cause cognitive devel-
opment affects all
aspects of life, these
adolescents may start
to question some of
the religious beliefs
they accept today.

cent attended religious services weekly, and another 16% attended at least once or twice a month (Youth Indicators, 1996). Table 11.1 illustrates that religious beliefs are an important aspect of adolescents' lives.

Are adolescents today as religious as adolescents have been in previous generations? In terms of attending religious services, one might think not. Surveys show that fewer adolescents attended religious services on a weekly basis in 1994 than in the mid-1970s. Even so, the importance of religion in adolescents' lives has not changed. Just as many adolescents in 1994 as in 1976 (29%) reported that religion was very important to them. Another 30% reported that religion was "pretty important" to them. In all, nearly 60% of the adolescents who were surveyed indicated that religion was either very important or pretty important in their lives. Given these figures, more research on religious beliefs and practices is needed for a fuller understanding of adolescent development.

We have considered in this chapter the ways in which adolescents' values relate to their identity and to a developing system of moral and religious beliefs. In the next chapter, we will look at the crisis of values in adolescents' lives—at alienation, delinquency, violence, and substance abuse.

SUMMARY

The Values of Adolescents
The values of adolescents have changed little over the past 10 years. Today, most adolescents indicate that work, family life, and friendship are most important to them, much as they did a generation ago. Most adolescents hold attitudes about values that substantially agree with those of their parents. Also, more similarities than differences exist in the values held by adolescent females and males.

The way adolescents approach both their own and others' values reflects identity issues. Identity-achieved and moratorium adolescents have explored issues for themselves and are tolerant of similar explorations and differences in others. Foreclosed adolescents tend to be more rule-bound and authoritarian than identity-achieved or moratorium adolescents. They are more likely to be critical of those who are different from them.

Social-Cognitive Theory and Moral Development

Social-cognitive theory assumes that children eventually internalize controls that initially are effective only when enforced by others. In doing so, children acquire their community's standards. Age-related changes in moral thought are explained by referring to the experiences that make different forms of thought most likely at different ages. Research on variables predicting cheating and shoplifting support social-cognitive theory.

Kohlberg and Moral Development: Morality as Justice

At the preconventional level of moral reasoning, individuals lack internalized standards of right and wrong; their motives are only to satisfy their needs without getting into trouble. At the conventional level of moral reasoning, individuals have internalized the standards of their community and are motivated to live according to the standards of their group. At the postconventional level of moral reasoning, individuals live according to self-derived principles rather than the conventions of their community.

Higher levels of reasoning increase with age. Although some studies find that many individuals reason at adjacent stages about different situations, critics of Kohlberg's theory argue that individuals can usually distinguish conventional from moral issues even as children.

Gilligan: An Ethic of Care

Gilligan asserts that most females think of morality more personally than do males. She finds that an ethic of care characterizes females' approach to moral decisions; this ethic emphasizes compassion and a sense of responsibility to others in contrast to the justice orientation of Kohlberg, which emphasizes reliance on rules and reason.

Gilligan traces gender differences in moral reasoning to differences in ways of viewing the self. Females define themselves in relation to others; from this comes a sense of responsibility of each to the other. Males define themselves as separate from others; the assumption of separateness highlights the need for rules to regulate the actions of each with respect to the other.

Gilligan traces moral development in females through three levels, each reflecting a different resolution to their conflict between responsibilities to themselves and to others. In Level 1 the primary concern is care for oneself. Females soon see this as selfish and move to Level 2, in which they equate morality with care of others. Only as they encounter problems that result from excluding themselves as legitimate recipients of their own care do females move on to Level 3, in which they equate morality with care both of themselves and of others.

Research finds that while a care orientation is not necessarily the approach adopted by all women, it is somewhat more characteristic of women than men. Studies find that both women and men share concerns about justice and care and that individuals frequently use both orientations in thinking through a dilemma.

Freud: Morality and the Superego

Freud placed the responsibility for moral behavior in the superego, an aspect of the personality that embraces cultural standards of right and wrong. The superego develops when the young child identifies with the same-sex parent. Freud assumed the superego of females to be weaker than that of males because they are not as motivated to resolve Oedipal tensions and identify with a less-threatening parental figure.

Despite the usefulness of Freud's theory to clinicians, his assumptions concerning gender differences in moral development have not been supported by research.

Adolescents' Religious Beliefs

The intellectual changes that occur in adolescence make it possible for adolescents to view God in new ways and to question beliefs they once accepted uncritically. As with identity status, processes of exploration and commitment determine the form beliefs will take. For nearly 60% of adolescents, religion remains very to moderately important in their lives.

KEY TERMS

preconventional moral reasoning

conventional moral reasoning

postconventional moral reasoning

ethic of care

superego

identification

CHAPTER 12

The Problems of Youth

"No, don't! . . ." Abbie bolted upright in a sweat. She sat in the dark, the dream swirled around her, its sharp pain softening with each panting breath.

"Too much!" she cried, slipping her feet over the side of the bed and starting for the bathroom.

As her foot hit the dresser, she hissed angrily, "Why isn't anything where it's supposed to be?" Then, blindly feeling for the light switch and finding nothing, she remembered where she was. This wasn't her room. She was in her stepsister's bedroom at her father's house. Her mom had thrown her out. She had forgotten the reason for the fight; they had thrown things, said things.

As the heavy reality of her world closed in on her, she slipped to the floor sobbing—the angry words, fists, and ashtrays flying, her friends so far away, her father nervous, on edge, his wife distant and formal—and no place to call her own. She suddenly felt that she could bear none of it anymore.

Adolescents face many pressures. Abbie is one of those with more than her share. Most adolescents will cope in one fashion or another; Abbie may, too. Relatively few will fail to cope. In this chapter we will address the problems of those for whom coping has become the ultimate test: the alienated and abused, delinquents, adolescents with emotional disorders, the drug abusers, the severely depressed, the suicidal, and those who become schizophrenic.

Calvin and Hobbes

by Bill Watterson

Part of the appeal of the *Calvin and Hobbes* cartoons for adults is nostalgia for the innocence of childhood. (CALVIN AND HOBBES © 1991 Watterson. Distributed by Universal Press Syndicate. Reprinted with permission. All rights reserved.)

ALIENATION AND THE FAILURE TO COPE

Some of the most common stressors in adolescence reflect the absence rather than the presence of something. Adolescents frequently feel cut off from themselves and others, emotionally distanced from their world, observers rather than participants in their own reality. Feelings of **alienation**—a sense of estrangement and loss—can be common in adolescence. These feelings are to be expected, given the many changes adolescents experience; however, when alienation becomes the predominant focus of an adolescent's experience, he or she is in trouble.

The most interesting times in life are those characterized by innovation and change, yet both are stressful and bring the potential for crisis and dislocation (Wapner, 1990). Adolescents live in very interesting times; they face enormous changes. Each change introduces a new realm of experience; each also represents a loss. Many adolescents experience sadness at the passing of their childhood. The success of cartoonists such as Bill Watterson comes in part from restoring the Hobbes to the Calvin in each of us. Many adolescents also feel cut off from themselves as well as their parents, as they struggle to define their values and goals.

Feelings of cultural estrangement can also contribute to feelings of alienation. Adolescents are expected to assume more adult ways but are not given the same privileges as adults nor the same freedom to define the standards by which they will live. Many feel disenfranchised and powerless—pressured to conform to customs of dress, speech, and behavior that are not their own.

Change leaves adolescents with more questions than answers. What are they to hold on to? To let go of? What really matters? Does anything matter if everything can be questioned? When nothing matters, adolescents feel

Most runaway adolescents were physically mistreated at home; although life on the street may offer companionship with other homeless youth who understand their experiences, the conditions are seldom any safer or healthier.

they have lost everything they have valued. Though most adolescents at times feel alienated, only a few act out their feelings of separateness, powerlessness, and isolation. As the Research Focus, "Statistical Tests of Significance," indicates, the way that adolescents act out differs from culture to culture.

Loss is central to alienation, and it is always the loss of something important. Reactions to this loss can range from hostility to sadness to indifference—from anger to a defensive "What does it matter anyway?" The alienated who cannot replace their loss with the sense of a competent self, linked to a social order that gives meaning to their lives, surround the void without filling it.

Runaways

For some adolescents, the loss is of something they never had. Approximately 1.5 million adolescents run away from home before they reach the age of 18 (Farber, 1987). Some run away in the hopes of finding excitement, independence, or their own maturity, but most are running *from* something—frequently from neglect or abuse. Until recently, the number of abused runaways was thought to be quite small, no more than about

Research Focus

Statistical Tests of Significance: What Do a *Huai Haizi,* a *Warui Ko,* and a Bad Kid Have in Common?

None of the students seemed to notice the chatter of birds outside the classroom window, or other signs of spring in Taipei, as they bent over their desks, completing the questionnaire. These Chinese adolescents had been asked to think of someone they knew who was a *huai haizi,* a "bad kid," and to describe what kind of person that was. In another classroom nearly a thousand miles away, Japanese students were asked to describe a *warui ko* (bad kid), as were yet other students, American adolescents in Minneapolis, who were similarly asked to describe a "bad kid."

How comparable were the descriptions of these adolescents? To what extent do perceptions of deviance reflect the social values of one's culture? Are the behaviors that American teenagers think of as bad similarly bad in other cultures?

David Crystal and Harold Stevenson, at the University of Michigan, set out to get answers to

such questions by asking Chinese, Japanese, and American eleventh-graders what a "bad kid" meant to them. After coding their responses to the open-ended questions (see Research Focus in Chapter 3, "Coding Descriptive Responses") into 12 types of behavior, they found that 40% of the Chinese students mentioned society-related behaviors, such as "rebels against society," "makes trouble for society," or "is a member of a street gang," whereas only 29% of the American adolescents described a bad kid this way, and even fewer Japanese students did (14%). Other interesting differences emerged. The most frequently mentioned behaviors by Japanese students (84%) made reference to disruptions of interpersonal harmony, such as "hurting other people's feelings," "being argumentative and starting fights," and "speaking badly of other people"; only 50% and 53% of Chinese and American adolescents, respectively, mentioned such behaviors. American adolescents, on the other hand, were most likely to mention behaviors related to self-control, 38% referring to being "weak-willed," "childish," or "immature"; in contrast, only 24% of Chinese and Japanese students did so.

What are we to make of these differences?

5%. Studies of runaways, however, suggest that most have been abused or neglected (Morrow & Sorell, 1989). Table 12.1 shows the types of problems reported by adolescents in runaway and homeless youth centers: 62% of the females and 46% of the males had experienced some form of physical or sexual abuse, or parental neglect. Abuse in general is more frequent among adolescents than is widely known; 24% of all fatalities resulting from abuse are of adolescents, for example, and 41% of serious injuries resulting from abuse involve those between ages 12 and 17 (Farber, 1987).

Despite the uniqueness of individuals when looked full in the face, the profile of runaways is disturbingly similar: low self-esteem, depression, poor interpersonal skills, insecurity, anxiousness, impulsiveness, and little sense of control over life's events. Most do poorly in school, and many run into trouble with the law. Almost all experience conflict within their families, and for a majority this includes abuse. One-quarter have attempted suicide. With an average age of 15, runaways can be from any socioeconomic level; there is little difference in the numbers from blue-collar and white-collar homes.

Research Focus (*continued*)

Can we conclude that adolescents from each of these cultures differ in what they consider to be bad? How different must their answers be in order to support this conclusion? After all, each adolescent is an individual, and one can always expect slight variances simply as a result of individual differences. Unexplained variability, such as individual differences, that is not due to the variable being investigated is termed *random error.* (See Chapter 9, Research Focus, "Ethics.")

To determine whether a difference between two groups is due to random error or whether it reflects the variable being studied, one uses a *test of significance.* Common tests are chi-square, t-tests, and F-tests. If the value obtained is larger than a tabled value for the same number of subjects, one can reject the assumption that random error was responsible and attribute the difference to the independent variable. Probability theory tells us that the likelihood that random error is responsible for the difference decreases with increases in the number of subjects in each group. The number of subjects is reflected in the *degrees of freedom.* With larger degrees of freedom, one needs a smaller difference to reject the assumption that random error was responsible.

Crystal and Stevenson's statistical tests comparing differences in the frequencies with which adolescents from the three cultures mentioned different types of behaviors were significant. Chinese students were significantly more likely to mention society-related behavior than American or Japanese students; Japanese students were significantly more likely to mention interpersonal behavior than were Chinese or American students; and American students were significantly more likely to mention self-control than were Chinese or Japanese students.

Bad kids—unlike roses, which, the poets tell us, would still be a rose by any other name—do not differ in name only. Each culture has its own profile of social values and, although there is considerable overlap from one culture to the next, what is considered to be "bad" differs to the extent that the most prominent values in a culture, but not necessarily those in another, are violated.

Source: D. S. Crystal & H. W. Stevenson. (1995). What is a bad kid? Answers of adolescents and their mothers in three cultures. Journal of Research on Adolescence, 5, 71–91.

Running away is clearly not the answer to their problems. It is equally clear that these adolescents are unable to face their problems and come up with any reasonable solution at the moment. Running away is almost never well planned. Two-thirds, for example, leave home with less than a dollar in their pocket. Many stay with friends or relatives, some seek out youth shelters, and others are homeless. Most return within the first week, and 40% the same day. Nearly 90% will run away again in the future (Farber, 1987).

Home life for most runaways is chaotic. The problems from which they are running (and to which almost all will return) have usually existed for years, yet the solutions remain as distant as ever. The dynamics of family life that would offer an answer to the problems are the very same ones that foster personal development in family members. Thus, most runaways lack a sense of who they are or what they can become, in large part because the development of their sense of self and of their potential has not been supported within their families. Runaways are in need of programs that give them the interpersonal skills they did not develop within their families: skills in communicating thoughts and feelings, negotiating conflict, and in making responsible decisions (see Chapter 5).

TABLE 12.1   Problems Reported by Adolescents in Runaway
and Homeless Youth Centers

Type of Problem	Total	Female	Male
FAMILY PROBLEMS*			
Emotional conflict at home	41%	43%	39%
Parent too strict	21	24	18
Parental physical abuse	20	23	18
Parental neglect	20	19	21
Parent drug or alcohol problems	18	19	17
Family mental health problems	11	12	11
Parental domestic violence	10	10	10
Parental unemployment	9	9	9
Wants to live with other parent	6	7	6
Parental sexual abuse	7	9	2
Physical or sexual abuse by other family member	5	6	3
Physical or sexual abuse by nonfamily member	4	5	2
No parent figure	4	4	5
Parent is homosexual	1	2	1
None of the above	16	13	19
INDIVIDUAL PROBLEMS*			
Poor self-image	49%	51%	46%
Depressed	43	48	36
School attendance or truancy	33	33	33
Bad grades	31	30	33
In trouble with justice system	19	13	27
Drug abuse	15	13	17
Alcohol abuse	13	13	13
Possibly suicidal	12	15	8
Cannot get along with teachers	13	10	17
Learning disability	7	5	10
Custody change	5	5	5
Pregnant or suspects pregnancy	4	7	0
Other health problems or handicap	4	4	4
Homosexual or sexual identity issue	2	2	3
Prostitution	1	2	1
Venereal disease	1	1	0
None of the above	19	19	20

*Because multiple responses are permitted, totals exceed 100%.

Source: K. Maguire, A. L. Pastore, & T. J. Flanagan (Eds.),. (1993). *Sourcebook of criminal justice statistics 1992.* U.S. Department of Justice, Bureau of Justice Statistics. Washington, DC: U.S. Government Printing Office.

Edward Farber (1987) notes that many more services are available to abused youth than to runaways; society tends to see the former as victims and the latter as merely unruly. Yet in a study of runaways, Farber and his associates found these adolescents had experienced the same amount of violence as had a similar group of adolescents identified as abused. Seventy-eight percent of the runaway adolescents studied had been physically mistreated within the past year (Farber, Kinast, McCoard, & Faulkner, 1984). Although estimates vary from one study to the next, most likely 25% of runaways have been sexually abused at home. Rather than being the problem itself, running away is a symptom of other problems. One cannot expect such troubled adolescents to return home without first addressing the problems of family conflict and violence they would face upon their return.

Abuse and Neglect

The actual number of adolescents who are abused is unknown; however, some estimates place this figure at nearly half of all reported cases of abuse of children 18 or under (Doueck, Ishisaka, & Greenaway, 1988). Cases of adolescent abuse and neglect are likely to follow one of three patterns: a continuation of earlier child abuse, a change in the type of punishment used by parents, and neglect related to the onset of adolescence (Doueck, Ishisaka, & Greenaway, 1988).

Continuation of Earlier Abuse   The abuse some adolescents experience continues a pattern of earlier child abuse within the family. The following fictional case study illustrates this type of abuse:

> Mr. and Mrs. B have been married 15 years. Mrs. B is 34 years old and Mr. B is 38. They have 4 children: Tom, 14; Richard, 12; Sheila, 9; and Laura, 5. Mr. B works on and off at odd jobs doing maintenance and/or janitorial work. He is currently unemployed. His relationship with his wife and family has been a stormy one. Periodically he physically assaults her or beats one of the children. After particularly violent episodes, he leaves the house and is not heard from for several days. They live in a small, two-bedroom home in a rural county and seldom see relatives or friends. Both Mr. B and Mrs. B have been in alcohol treatment centers on at least two separate occasions. The children have few friends at school, spending most of their time alone. Tom is in a special class for behavior problem children. Richard and Sheila are in special education programs. Recently, Tom was picked up by the police for shoplifting. He has run away several times over the past 2 years and was expelled from school for vandalism. (Doueck, Ishisaka, & Greenaway, 1988, p. 136)

Tom comes from a family with many long-standing problems: violence between parents, alcoholism, financial instability, few social supports, and physical isolation from others. The abuse he presently suffers is not much different from that experienced when he was younger or the abuse currently experienced by his younger brother and sisters and reflects the inadequate coping skills of the parents and the generally dysfunctional nature of the family.

Abusive Punishment A second type of abuse, a change in the type of punishment used, is illustrated in this second fictional case study:

> John is a 16-year-old boy who appears physically strong and socially confident.... When he dressed down for physical education, his teacher noticed bruises on John's back, arms, and legs.... The teacher reported the incident to protective services. During an interview with the parents, the protective services worker was told by John's father, a 39-year-old contractor, that John had always been a problem child who needed guidance and correction. Frequently, the correction consisted of a "good spanking like my father did to me!" John's mother supported these practices and said that lately they weren't working because John was still misbehaving: smoking, staying out at night, using drugs, shoplifting, hanging out with the wrong crowd, and disobeying his father. She stated that, most recently, John got into an argument with his father over the length of John's hair. A fist fight ensued between John and his father, who used a strap in an attempt to "knock some sense into the child!" (Doueck, Ishisaka, & Greenaway, 1988, p. 137)

In this second type of abuse, parents who have used physical punishment since childhood have increased the intensity of the punishment in an attempt to control adolescent misbehavior. Families in which this form of mistreatment occurs are typified by controlling, rigid parents who become even more controlling, to the point of abuse, when faced with adolescent bids for greater autonomy and independence and the loss of their own control (Doueck, Ishisaka, & Greenaway, 1988).

Neglect Precipitated by Adolescence A third type of mistreatment is brought about by the onset of adolescence itself. An example is illustrated by the following fictional case account:

> Lois is a 14-year-old girl who lives with her divorced father, age 41. Her parents divorced when she was 9, with her mother leaving town. Lois's father described Lois as his sole means of emotional support during the early years of his divorce. [Following a serious illness] he quit his job . . . and changed careers. Lately he has been spending two nights a week outside the home. During these nights away, he leaves money for Lois to "buy whatever she needs." He states, "Now that she is 14, she is capable of caring for herself." The family situation came to the attention of the local mental health agency when Lois called their hotline and said that she was all alone in the world and was going to commit suicide." (Doueck, Ishisaka, & Greenaway, 1988, p. 137)

In this type of neglect, the parent mistakenly concludes that because the child has reached adolescence, she is able to be on her own and care for herself. The parent's conduct appears to be related to midlife concerns of his own.

Each of the three examples illustrates common factors related to child or adolescent abuse and neglect. Most abusive parents have had inadequate parenting models themselves and have inadequate parenting skills (Kelly & Grace, 1990). They appear to be less able to deal with stress, more depressed, passive, and withdrawn. Long-term unemployment of the father, alcoholism in either parent, and social isolation are also common (Moeller & Bachmann, 1993).

TABLE 12.2 Males and Females Sexually Abused
by Different Types of Offenders

| | Victim | |
Offender	Male	Female
Biological father	26.2%	37.8%
Stepfather	16.2	22.5
Biological mother	10.0	5.0
Stepmother	2.3	0.6
Other relative	5.4	13.4
Nonrelative	11.5	10.3
Other (e.g., daycare)	28.5	10.3

Source: K. C. Faller. (1989). Characteristics of a clinical sample of sexually
abused children: How boy and girl victims differ. *Child Abuse and Neglect, 13,*
281–291.

Physical and emotional abuse of adolescents is not limited to low-income families. A study of nearly 700 predominantly White women revealed that abuse had occurred at all income levels, although multiple forms of abuse (for example, both physical and emotional abuse or physical and sexual abuse) were more common in lower-income families (Moeller & Bachmann, 1993). Also, rates of abuse appear not to have changed substantially with time. The ages of the subjects in this particular study ranged from 16 to 76, a span of 60 years, and younger subjects reported no more abuse than older ones.

Sexual Abuse

Recent epidemiological studies indicate that sexual abuse is not as rare as was once thought. Some studies estimate that one of every four girls and one of every ten boys has suffered some form of sexual abuse (Finkelhor, 1993). Contrary to current social prejudices, sexual abuse appears to be as common at higher socioeconomic levels as lower ones. For instance, even though the *reported* incidence is greater for lower-income homes, community surveys find sexual abuse to be equally represented in higher-income families, suggesting the operation of class-biased stereotypes among health care professionals. Also, in no racial or ethnic subgroup is sexual abuse uncommon (Finkelhor, 1993).

The risk for sexual abuse increases sharply in preadolescence (Finkelhor & Baron, 1986). Two characteristics of families are associated with increased risk of sexual abuse: inadequate supervision of children's activities and the presence of physical or psychological abuse or neglect (Finkelhor, 1993).

Most victims of sexual abuse are female. Eight times out of ten the abuser is a male. Almost as often the abuser is a member of the immediate family or a relative. Table 12.2 shows the percentages of sexual abuse committed by individuals in various relationships to the victim. Despite figures showing greater overall incidence of abuse by biological fathers than step-fathers, stepfathers are disproportionately (because their numbers are lower) more likely to sexually abuse daughters in the family (Gordon, 1989; Habenicht & Futcher, 1990). In a majority of cases, the abuse starts early. In over 300 confirmed abuse victims, more than 50% were sexually abused before they were 6 years old. Less than 20% first became victims as adolescents (Faller, 1989).

Criteria for Sexual Abuse Criteria for distinguishing abusive sexual contact from exploratory behavior between young siblings or playmates stress the exploitive nature of the contact. Exploitation exists when one of the members is considerably older than the other or uses force or threats. Finkelhor and Hotaling (1984) recommend the following criteria for determining abuse:

1. If the victim is under 13 and the perpetrator is five or more years older, or the victim is age 13 to 16 and the perpetrator is ten or more years older, sexual contact is abusive.
2. If force, threat, deceit, or exploiting a position of unequal authority occurs, the sexual contact is abusive at any age.

Consequences of Sexual Abuse As the severity of the abuse increases (from fondling to sexual intercourse), negative consequences become more likely. These include depression, lowered self-esteem, and a number of overt behaviors such as running away, truancy, attempted suicide and other self-injurious behavior, eating disorders, use of alcohol and drugs, and promiscuity (Irving, 1993; Morrow & Sorell, 1989). Long-term physical and psychological consequences also persist into adulthood. Table 12.3 presents the consequences to women who were abused during childhood.

Ways that sexually abused victims cope with the inner pain tend to discredit their disclosures when they finally make them. At either extreme are adolescents who act out their conflict and those who hide all evidence of conflict. Neither the angry, delinquent adolescent nor the "well-adjusted" teenager is likely to be believed (Habenicht & Futcher, 1990). The secrecy, accommodation, delayed disclosure, and the all-too-common retraction that characterize most incest victims detract from the believability of their account. Why did she wait so long to say anything? If what she has said is really true, why does she sound so unconvincing? Why does she now tell us none of this ever happened?

Most female adolescent incest victims feel responsible for holding the family together (believing that everything would unravel if they said anything) and frequently feel responsible for the incest as well (part of the exploitive nature of the relationship). As a group they are detached, shy, withdrawn, and self-sufficient (unwilling to trust themselves or their needs to another). They also are more confident and report feeling more intelligent than age-mates; these latter qualities may reflect their premature entrance into adulthood and their assessment of how well they have deceived friends and family (Habenicht & Futcher, 1990).

TABLE 12.3   Long-Term Physical and Psychological Consequences for Female
Victims of Childhood Abuse (Physical, Emotional, and/or Sexual)

	Percentages for Women Reporting Childhood Abuse	Percentages for Women Reporting No Abuse
SELF-PERCEIVED CHARACTERISTICS OF PHYSICAL HEALTH		
Frequent feelings of fatigue	45.4	27.0
Obesity	30.1	15.3
Severe PMS	19.4	11.0
Frequent gynecologic problems	15.2	4.6
Excessive drug use	5.4	0.3
Alcoholic	2.5	0.0
Satisfied with physical health	62.3	71.4
Frequent headaches	27.6	19.8
Trouble sleeping	26.5	17.5
Frequent vaginal infections	14.7	9.7
Frequent stomachaches	12.1	8.8
Often miss work due to illness	5.6	2.0
Underweight	4.8	4.6
Drug overdose	1.4	0.0
SELF-PERCEIVED CHARACTERISTICS OF PSYCHOLOGICAL HEALTH		
Generally optimistic	59.7	74.0
Satisfied with emotional health	47.1	61.7
Calm	9.2	30.2
Get along well with others	85.9	92.5
Depressed feelings	45.1	22.1
Anxious	43.9	28.6
Lack of confidence	34.4	14.9
Dissatisfaction with sexual life	31.8	15.6
Often lonely	29.1	15.6
Extreme tension	25.9	8.1
Frequent emotional outbursts	19.7	6.2
Generally pessimistic	17.5	7.1
Frequent nightmares	10.4	2.9
Thoughts of hurting self	9.6	1.0
Victim of a crime	6.2	1.0
Suicide attempts	4.5	0.7
Thoughts of hurting others	6.2	3.9
Frequent conflicts	4.2	1.6
Learning problems	3.7	0.7
Accident prone	2.3	4.5

Source: P. P. Moeller & G. A. Bachmann. (1993). The combined effects of physical, sexual, and emotional abuse during childhood: Long-term health consequences for women. *Child Abuse and Neglect, 17,* 623–640.

JUVENILE DELINQUENCY

Juvenile delinquency involves illegal actions committed by a minor; in most states a minor is a person below the age of 18. The actions can be as serious as homicide or as relatively trivial as shoplifting. Some actions are illegal at any age; others are illegal only when engaged in by adolescents. A few distinctions should help unravel some of the knottier problems in defining delinquency.

Status offenses are behaviors that are illegal when engaged in by minors but perfectly legal for adults. Running away and truancy are status offenses. Adults are free to choose where and with whom they will live and when they will leave. There's no such thing as a 40-year-old runaway—not legally, at least. Similarly, once adolescents reach the legal age set by their state, they are no longer considered truant even though they may not attend school.

Index offenses are behaviors that are criminal at any age: homicide, rape, robbery, burglary, auto theft, petty larceny, use and sale of illegal drugs, prostitution, disorderly conduct, and so on. These illegal actions vary

TABLE 12.4   Delinquent Activities High School Seniors Say They Have Engaged in During the Past 12 Months

Delinquent Activity	Class of 1980	Class of 1992
Argued or had a fight with a parent	86.8%	90.7%
Taken something belonging to someone else worth under $50	33.1	32.6
Taken something from a store without paying for it	30.8	30.4
Gone into a house or building where not supposed to be	25.1	26.0
Gotten into trouble with police because of an act committed	22.4	22.2
Taken part in a fight where a group of friends were against another group	17.6	21.3
Gotten into a serious fight at school or work	15.8	18.9
Damaged school property on purpose	13.2	14.7
Hurt someone badly enough to need bandages or a doctor	11.7	12.8
Taken something belonging to someone else worth over $50	6.6	10.5
Taken part of a car without permission of the owner	7.1	6.1
Damaged property at work on purpose	7.0	6.0
Taken a car that didn't belong to a family member without permission of the owner	4.8	6.0
Used a knife or gun or some other weapon (like a club) to get something from a person	2.9	4.3
Hit an instructor or supervisor	3.2	3.3
Set fire to someone's property on purpose	1.5	2.8

Source: Adapted from K. Maguire, A. L. Pastore, & T. J. Flanagan (Eds.). (1993). *Sourcebook of criminal justice statistics 1992.* U.S. Department of Justice, Bureau of Justice Statistics. Washington, DC: U.S. Government Printing Office.

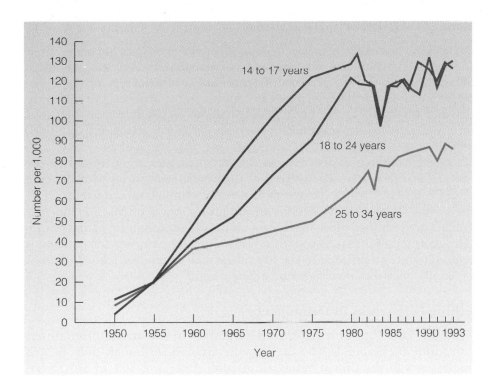

FIGURE 12.1 Arrest
Rates, 1950 to 1993

Source: Youth Indicators:
*Trends in the Well-Being of
American Youth.* (1996).
Washington, DC: U.S. Gov-
ernment Printing Office.

in their seriousness and in whether they involve property or violence to others. Table 12.4 gives the percentages of adolescents reporting different types
of delinquent activities, in 1980 and in 1992. These figures show little
change since 1980. The most dramatic increases in delinquency occurred between 1950 and 1980. Figure 12.1 shows this trend. The number of adolescents below the age of 18 arrested annually increased sixfold from 1955 to
1993. A similar increase occurred for 18- to 24-year-olds (Youth Indicators,
1996).

Age Differences in Delinquency

The type of delinquent acts adolescents engage in varies with their age.
Many minor forms of delinquency—such as running away, violating cur-
fews, smoking marijuana, drinking alcohol, petty theft, or vandalism—begin in early adolescence but decrease by adulthood. More serious types of
crimes—like auto theft, burglary, and larceny—peak at about age 16, and
robbery at about 17 (Federal Bureau of Investigation, 1987). Violent offenses—homicide, rape, aggravated assault—are more common in adulthood than in adolescence (Youth Indicators, 1988).

There is little evidence to suggest that minor forms of delinquency predict a shift to more serious crimes later on, even for multiple offenders. The
pattern instead suggests a small subgroup of delinquents who start early
and account for a relatively high proportion of criminal activity (Henggeler,
1989). In addition to age differences in delinquency, there are large differences due to gender, race, and social class.

Gender Differences in Delinquency

Females are less likely to engage in delinquent activities than are males. Even so, the delinquency rate for females has risen sharply over the past three decades. The size of the gender difference varies with the type of crime. Females are almost as likely as males to commit status offenses, but males are two and a half times more likely than females to engage in minor theft, and four and a half times more likely to commit robbery (Huizinga & Elliott, 1987).

Gender differences also exist in the way delinquents are treated by the juvenile justice system. The severity of the punishment varies with the type of offense. Males receive harsher treatment for criminal offenses than do females, but females receive harsher treatment for status offenses. Frequently females are punished more harshly for status offenses than for actual crimes (Henggeler, 1989). This last point reflects a greater tendency for parents to refer daughters than sons to the juvenile justice system for status offenses, especially ones that involve sexual acting-out.

Ethnic Differences in Delinquency

Relatively large differences exist in the numbers of adolescents from different ethnic backgrounds who are actually arrested. Although only 15% of adolescents in the United States are African American, 30% to 50% of arrests are of Black youth (Krisberg, Schwartz, Fishman, Eisiloits, Guttman, & Joe, 1987, reported in Henggeler, 1989). One study in California found that nearly 70% of Black adolescents were arrested before reaching early adulthood compared to 30% of White adolescents (Tillman, 1986). Even more disturbing is the statistic that an African American male born in California in 1988 is three times more likely to be murdered than to be admitted to the University of California ("Blacks in college," 1990). Despite these statistics, the most rapidly increasing incarcerated group is Hispanic youth (Henggeler, 1989).

Self-report comparisons for Black and White adolescents fail to reveal the differences in delinquent activities that would be expected given the arrest figures. In fact, self-reports of delinquent activities among Black and White adolescents are very similar. This fact strongly suggests that the differences in arrest rates reflect racial biases within the justice system. Some studies find that African American adolescents are seven times more likely than European American adolescents to be arrested for the same type of crime (Henggeler, 1989).

Delinquency and Social Class

The effects of ethnicity and social class are difficult to separate. Arrest rates for minority adolescents are higher than those for nonminority youth, as are arrests of adolescents from lower-income versus middle-income homes. Disproportionate numbers of minority youth come from lower-income homes, and factors common to poverty are related to delinquency apart from ethnic status. Unemployment, poorer academic and vocational preparation, and fewer social and family resources are just a few of these factors.

Middle- and lower-income youth are equally likely to commit status offenses and minor delinquent acts, such as vandalism. Adolescents from lower-income homes are more likely, however, to commit violent crimes or major crimes against property, such as auto theft or burglary.

In addition, much middle-income (nonminority) delinquency is never reported; families are able to intervene, and youth authorities are more willing to release offenders to their parents' custody.

Even so, some types of delinquent activity vary with social class. Middle-income youth are less likely to commit violent crimes (such as aggravated assault, rape, robbery) or crimes against property (for example, auto theft, burglary) than are lower-income youth. Status offenses and minor delinquent acts such as creating a public nuisance, drunkenness, and disorderly conduct are as common among middle-income as lower-income adolescents.

The Face of Delinquency

Are there common characteristics of adolescents who engage in delinquent activities? Is delinquency a social problem? A personal decision? A bit of both? Are there typical patterns to delinquent adolescents' interactions at school, with peers, or parents? Questions such as these raise a host of complex issues.

Most delinquency is never reported; much of it is simply never observed. When it is, observers may turn a blind eye to avoid retaliation, as may the victims themselves when victims are involved. A 1991 survey revealed that nearly 1.2 million crimes involving violence against adolescents were not reported (U.S. Department of Justice, 1991). Of the delinquents who reach the attention of the police, over one-third do not go to court. Many offenders are let go with a warning, others are released to parents, others may be held in temporary custody, still others may be referred to welfare or other social agencies.

One self-report study of delinquency found that of 2,000 12- to 18-year-olds surveyed, 93% had engaged in at least one act of delinquency during the past year that, if detected, could have resulted in being processed by the juvenile justice system. Eighty-eight percent of the adolescents had committed status offenses (for example, truancy, use of alcohol). Although as many as 82% admitted to committing criminal offenses (such as petty theft, use of drugs, vandalism), only 9% had engaged in serious delinquent acts such as robbery (LeBlanc, 1983). A more recent study of largely middle-class 13- to 17-year-olds confirms these trends (Simons, Robertson, & Downs, 1989).

Rather than label any adolescent who has engaged in delinquency a delinquent, only those repeatedly brought to the system's attention by police or parents, or those who engage in activities that would be regarded as criminal at any age, are considered to be delinquents. Problems still remain in separating cause from effect. Do poor peer relations, for example, contribute to delinquency, or is a delinquent who is impulsive and aggressive likely to have poor relationships with others? The answer may involve a combination of factors.

1. *Academic Skills* Delinquents characteristically fall behind their peers in achievement at school. In schools having more than one track, they are less likely to be in the academic track, are more likely to drop out, and less likely to be involved in school activities. Many are learning-disabled, falling two or more grades behind their peers, and many have poor verbal skills (Perlmutter, 1987; Quay, 1987).

2. *Self-Esteem* Delinquents typically have low self-esteem and poor self-images. They are less apt than their peers to see themselves as competent and successful (Arbuthnut, Gordon, & Jurkovic, 1987). Lack of success in school and in other areas of their lives—family relations, for instance—probably contributes to the relationship between low self-esteem and delinquency (Henggeler, 1989). Delinquent activities can also enhance self-esteem, especially for those in lower-income groups, if the acts receive peer approval (Rosenberg, Schooler, & Schoenbach, 1989).

3. *Family Relations* Delinquents come from homes characterized by violence, and many are victims of child abuse, neglect, or both. Poor communication, excessively harsh punishment, and parental strife are common (Cernkovich & Giordano, 1987; Henggeler, 1989; Huesmann, Lefkowitz, Eron, & Walder, 1984). Parental rejection, experienced as a lack of warmth, affection, or love, is consistently related to delinquency (Simons, Robertson, & Downs, 1989).

1. *Social Skills*   Delinquents are more aggressive than their peers and more likely to rely on physical than verbal means to settle disagreements (Goldstein, Sprafkin, Gershaw, & Klein, 1980). Among a group of fifth-graders followed to the end of high school, aggression toward peers significantly predicted juvenile delinquency (Kupersmidt & Coie, 1990). The same study found that children who were rejected by their peers were also more likely to have had some police contact or problems with school, such as truancy, suspension, or dropping out. A number of studies suggest that delinquents have poorer problem-solving skills than peers, although Hains and Ryan (1983) have suggested that this difference may reflect a failure to see the need to consider alternative solutions rather than a lack of ability to generate them.

5. *Self-Control*   Delinquents are more impulsive and less likely to rely on internalized constraints for behavior than their peers. They tend to evaluate situations in terms of their needs and evaluate their actions in terms of how likely they are to get away with something. Many express little guilt for their actions, and some appear to believe they are being punished not for what they did, but because they got caught (Arbuthnut, Gordon, & Jurkovic, 1987). As individuals, delinquent adolescents can cause considerable harm to others and themselves. As a group, their presence in a community can be disastrous.

Gangs

The number of gangs has risen dramatically over the past generation. In 1960, for instance, 58 cities reported the presence of gangs. In 1992, this figure had increased to 769 cities (Klein, 1995). The implications of this presence are considerable, both for adolescents and for the communities they live in.

Membership in a gang is associated with higher rates of criminal activity (Huff, 1996). Thornberry, Krohn, Lizotte, and Chard-Wierschem (1993) found that rates of delinquency were approximately four to five times higher for gang members. Because these investigators followed the same adolescents over several years, they could compare rates of delinquency for these adolescents prior to joining a gang with rates when they were members of a gang. The researchers found these adolescents did not have higher rates of delinquency than other adolescents prior to becoming gang members; furthermore, once they left the gang, their rates typically dropped. Only when they were in a gang did they have a high rate of delinquency.

Not only the number but also the nature of gangs has changed over the past generation. In previous generations gangs arose from the spontaneous associations of neighborhood males, and gang activities were primarily oriented toward defending the neighborhood territory or turf. Membership was almost exclusively limited to males and to those of the same ethnic group. Rumbles with rival gangs defined the territories of each and gave status to gang members. The leader of the gang carried a gun, but most members did not (Kratcoski & Kratcoski, 1986). Today, gang members have sophisticated weapons and use them freely. As one former gang member from Detroit remarked,

Research Focus

Internal and External Validity: *Cholas* and Gang Girls

With Michael Wapner

In Los Angeles County alone there are more than 600 gangs with approximately 100,000 members. Gangs, once restricted to low-income inner-city neighborhoods, now stretch into surrounding suburban neighborhoods and schools. Mexican American adolescents make up an increasing number of gang members in the suburbs surrounding Los Angeles, with females composing a significant subgroup in all Mexican American gangs.

Mary Harris (1994), of Bloomsburg University, sought to understand the world of gang members, specifically that of Mexican American gang girls, or *cholas,* from *their* perspective. Accordingly, Harris interviewed 21 current and former gang girls in suburbs of Los Angeles, sometimes individually and at other times in groups, asking what motivated them to join a gang and how they felt about their gang activities. She conducted these interviews in different settings—in parks or street corners, neighborhood centers, the barrio, and their homes.

As a science, psychology has developed many powerful and subtle research techniques to ensure, as much as possible, the validity of its con-clusions. Some of these techniques have been presented in the Research Focuses, like this one, distributed throughout the book. However, sometimes the most sophisticated techniques cannot deliver as dramatic and moving a look at living human experience as can a straightforward approach, such as simply approaching individuals, in the daily contexts of their lives, and asking them to them recount their experiences.

Harris found a strong cohesion and an unwavering loyalty to the gang. When asked their reasons for joining, for instance, these girls spoke of their sense of belonging, as well as their need for group support:

> *Benita: All it really is that you want to be a Chola because you see the other girls that want to be a Chola and it looks as if they have fun and everything. You want to put the make-up on like them too. (Harris, 1994, p. 293)*
> *Reselda: You can belong as long as you can back up your s—— and don't rat on your own homegirls or back away. If you don't back them up and you run we'll jump that girl out because she ain't going to take care of nothing. All she wants is our backup and our support but she ain't going to give us none of hers, so what's the use of her being around. She has to be able to hold up the hood. (Harris, 1994, pp. 292–293)*

These girls also spoke of their gang as a family; and for many, loyalty to the gang came first. Most gang members derived their status, self-esteem, identity, and sense of belonging from the

When I grew up we had it out with our hands. Maybe we'd steal a car and go for a ride. Now they steal a car and rip somebody off or shoot somebody. I'm afraid to walk down the street at night. I've never seen it like this. (Kratcoski & Kratcoski, 1986)

Also, as the Research Focus, "Internal and External Validity," points out, the number of females in gangs has grown significantly. Gangs are still formed from neighborhood associations, and gang activities still involve defense of turf, but gangs are more likely to be linked with organized crime than in the past, and making money, primarily through the sale of narcotics, is one of their major activities. Joseph Sheley and his colleagues (1995), at Tulane University, point out that gang activity tends to be more or less specialized in, or limited to, one or two types of criminal activities regularly committed. These investigators surveyed adolescent males in correctional facilities in four states, asking them if they had been members of a gang and what types of activities their gang had been involved in. They

Research Focus (*continued*)

gang, which substituted for often weak support from family and the absence of any real connections to school:

> *Reselda: I used to hate my dad because of what he did to my mom. I grew up with this hatred and anger. . . . A lot of them do come from families that are messed up. A lot of girls, like they ain't got backup in their families. If they get into a gang they got more backup. They've got more girls to really hang around with. . . . They ain't got too much love in the family. So they don't care what's going on. If their family don't care, she don't care. Nothing's going right in her house so what should she care about what's going on out there.* (Harris, 1994, p. 294)

As powerful and as clearly worthwhile as research such as this is, there can be problems. Harris conducted her interviews in the girls' homes and neighborhood settings, even at times having several members of a gang present for a single interview. An advantage to conducting interviews in this way is that the girls were most likely to be comfortable, and hence candid, when in familiar settings or with their friends. A problem, however, is that one cannot be sure that what they said about their experiences was not influenced by the presence of other members of the gang or even by their knowledge that, though alone with Harris, their remarks might be overheard. It is possible, in other words, that they may have been less willing to admit to conflicts about belonging to a gang or to other feelings

under such conditions. In short, there was more than one possible explanation for some of the findings. When research does not provide an unambiguous answer to the question it was designed to address, we say that it lacks *internal validity*.

A second type of validity is *external validity*. Does the answer we get apply only to the people we have observed, or can we generalize the findings to others? Just how representative are the findings? Can we assume that we have an accurate picture of the life of female gang members all over Los Angeles? California? The United States? This is the problem of external validity. The impression we get of gang life can be totally valid *for these girls* (a question of internal validity) and yet be largely invalid for other gangs (a question of external validity). External validity can also be affected by the very conditions that are necessary to achieve internal validity. Were Harris to have attempted to experimentally control for some of the factors that might affect the way gang girls responded in these interviews—such as by conducting individual interviews on a university campus—she might have obtained data that were unrepresentative of the way these girls would normally have responded, or might not even have been able to interview any gang girls at all!

Source: M. G. Harris. (1994). Cholas, Mexican-American girls, and gangs. *Sex Roles, 30,* 289–301.

found that over 40% of the gangs could be categorized in terms of the criminal activities in which they engaged. For 20% of these gangs, this specialty was armed drug selling. Another 16% were involved in some other single activity, and another 4% were involved in some combination of two activities. Among the 22% of respondents who indicated their gangs had regularly been involved in three types of activities, it was found, on closer inspection, that most of these activities were related to the sale and use of drugs, thus supporting the notion that gangs are specialized in the activities in which they engage. The implications of these findings, beyond their obvious link of gangs to criminal activities, is that gangs are more than just youth from a neighborhood who band together for social or defensive purposes (Sheley, Zhang, Brody, & Wright, 1995).

If the purpose of gangs has shifted from defending turf to developing criminal enterprises, then what types of functions do gangs serve in the lives of their members, and how have these changed over the past generation? Judy Evans and Jerome Taylor (1995), at the University of Pittsburgh,

Today's gangs are more likely to be linked to organized crime and the sale of drugs than in the past.

interviewed members of early gangs (46 to 55 years old) and contemporary gang members (15 to 20 years old), asking them why they belonged to a gang and what their role was in the gang. For both early and contemporary gang members, the most frequently given reason for gang membership was social (for example, "I see my homies every day"). Social reasons, however, were far more important for early gang members than contemporary ones, who also indicated career and economic ("It's how I make my money") reasons for belonging to a gang, as shown in Table 12.5.

A second difference to emerge between early and contemporary gang members is in the nature of the violence they engage in. For early gang members, violence took the form of fighting, with 56% saying this had something to do with their role in the gang. In stark contrast, none of the contemporary gang members said that fighting had anything to do with what they did as a gang member. Rather, violence for these gang members took the form of shooting, with 26% indicating this as their role within the gang. By way of contrast, none of the early gang members indicated shooting as an activity they engaged in, as shown in Table 12.6.

Table 12.6 also reveals another striking difference between early and contemporary gangs. The former had virtually no involvement in drug-related activities, whereas 93% of the activities of contemporary gang members are drug related, 13% being involved in scouting, 53% in dealing, and 27% in shooting. The corresponding percentage for each of these drug-related activities for earlier gang members is 0% (Evans & Taylor, 1995).

TABLE 12.5   Reasons for Staying in Gangs, as Reported by Members
of Early and Contemporary Gangs

Reason	Early Gangs (n = 18)		Contemporary Gangs (n = 30)	
	n	Percentage	n	Percentage
Career	0	0%	9	30%
Economic	2	11	7	23
Political	2	11	2	7
Social	14	78	12	40

Source: J. P. Evans & J. Taylor. (1995). Understanding violence in contemporary and earlier gangs: An exploratory
application of the theory of reasoned action. *Journal of Black Psychology, 21,* 71–81.

TABLE 12.6   Distribution of Roles Reported by Members
of Early and Contemporary Gangs

Reason	Early Gangs (n = 18)		Contemporary Gangs (n = 30)	
	n	Percentage	n	Percentage
Fighting	10	56%	0	0%
Scouting	0	0	4	13
Dealing	0	0	16	53
Robbing	4	22	2	7
Shooting	0	0	8	27
None of the above	4	22	0	0

Source: J. P. Evans & J. Taylor. (1995). Understanding violence in contemporary and earlier gangs: An exploratory
application of the theory of reasoned action. *Journal of Black Psychology, 21,* 71–81.

A final, and important, difference concerns the relative loyalty of gang
members to family or their gang. Fully 100% of the early gang members said
that, if they had to choose, they would protect their families before protecting their gang. Eighty percent of contemporary gang members, however,
said they would protect their gangs before protecting their families.

C. Ronald Huff, at Ohio State University, and Kenneth Trump at Tri-
City Task Force, (1996) note that gang activities are not limited to the streets
but permeate the school system as well. Huff (1996), based on interviews of
gang members from three metropolitan areas, reports that over half of the
gang members interviewed admitted that members of their gangs had assaulted teachers, and approximately 70% indicated that gang members had
assaulted students. Furthermore, over 80% said members of their gangs had
taken guns to school, with nearly as many taking knives onto school campuses. Over 60% said their gangs had sold drugs at school.

What attractions do gangs hold for their members? It has been suggested that gangs serve as surrogate families, offering an intense intimacy,
emotional support, protection, and a feeling of belonging (Henggeler, 1989;
Vigil, 1988). Research has found, for instance, that parents of gang members do not monitor their children's activities closely, and families are less

Continuity and
Change: Identity
Consolidation in
Late Adolescence

Do violent scenes in
the movies and on
television desensitize
adolescents to vio-
lence or make them
more likely to act
violently?

cohesive (Henggeler, 1989). Parental absence, either in the form of long
work hours, a single parent, or simple neglect, is also more common. In general, positive role models are less in evidence. Gang membership is also believed to confer a sense of identity, something especially important in
adolescence. Members dress alike and adopt unique identifying behaviors
they share with their gang, even being tattooed with gang insignia. The violence, too, can be an attraction, providing feelings of power and excitement
to members.

Jean-Marie Lyon, Scott Henggeler, and James Hall (1992) found only
partial support for the above assumptions. In a study comparing gang and
nongang members on a number of measures, these investigators found no
difference between the two groups in measures of family relations such as
parental acceptance or in peer relationships such as emotional bonding in
friendships. In fact, friendships among gang members were more aggressive
and less mature than those of nonmembers. The constant need of gang
members to prove themselves to maintain their status within the gang also
argues against emotional intimacy.

Youth and Violence

Violence is not restricted to inner-city youth or gangs; it extends to the suburbs and middle-income families. Across all ethnic groups, homicide is the
second leading cause of injury-related deaths in children and adolescents;
teenagers are two and a half times more likely to be victims of a violent
crime than is someone 20 years or older (Hammond & Yung, 1993). Minority males are most at risk: Native Americans are more than twice as likely
to die violently as White males their age, Hispanic males are three to four

times more likely, and African American males are nine times more likely than their White counterparts to die violently. In the ten-year period from 1978 to 1988, homicide accounted for over 40% of the deaths of African American males aged 15 to 24 (Hammond & Yung, 1993).

Patterns emerge in the midst of this violence. Blacks are most likely to be killed at home, by a friend or an acquaintance, and be killed by a gun. Hispanics are more likely to be killed on the street, and to die from a stabbing. Across all ethnic groups, the most commonly given reason for violent crimes such as these is retaliation or revenge (Hammond & Yung, 1993).

In examining factors related to assaultive violence among African American adolescents, W. Rodney Hammond and Betty Yung, at Wright State University, summarize a number of contributing misperceptions and myths. Those who are most aggressive, for instance, are more likely to interpret accidents as intentional and malicious. They are also more likely to endorse aggression as a means of settling disputes. A survey of inner-city adolescents (Price, Desmond, & Smith, 1991) revealed that African American adolescents tend to believe that Blacks are most likely to be shot by the police, and for this reason, that limiting ownership of guns would be unfair to them. Blacks believe they are safer with a gun in the house; they do not know that Blacks who are shot are most likely to be shot by a friend or acquaintance in their own homes (Hammond & Yung, 1993).

Adolescents in all segments of society risk becoming desensitized to violence. Evening programs on television are saturated with murders, rapes, kidnappings, and petty thuggery, and box office stars offer images of buffed and bare-chested bodybuilders with semi-automatic weapons. Both television programs and movies model graphic acts of violence as well as provide violent role models with whom adolescents can identify. Much popular music, whether rock or rap, provides an undercurrent of violent imagery, both in lyrics such as those found in gangsta rap and in the sensational behavior of the artists (Leland, 1993). An anecdote offers an interesting, if chilling, example of the way in which television and the movies contribute to our images of violence. A niece reported she had recently been in a bank when it was held up by two armed men. She noted that on hearing "Everyone down," people knew immediately what to do—lie face down on the floor, not crouch or kneel, and not look at the robbers' faces—because they had all seen this on the screen. However, after the robbers left, no one knew what to do—the TV and movie cameras always cut to the getaway and chase.

Some have argued that recent media attention to inner-city violence, in particular that associated with gangs, may reflect a subtle racism within society, confirming the dominant society's preconceptions of minority youth. Comparable treatment of youth who make it out of the inner city, by studying hard, getting good grades, and holding down jobs or going on to college, is harder to find (Horowitz, 1993).

Social factors contributing to violence cannot be discounted. The poverty and hopelessness confronting inner-city youth, their daily exposure to community and family violence, and the reality of job discrimination and racism for minority adolescents are powerfully related to violence. In the end, however, some adolescents choose violence and others do not. Most who engage in violent crimes have law-abiding siblings with whom they have eaten at the same family table and shared relatives, friends, and life experiences (Horowitz, 1993; Kennedy & Baron, 1993; Witkin, 1991).

Among social factors contributing to violence, the most important, in all probability, is the accessibility of firearms. Not only handguns, but sophisticated semi-automatic weapons are readily available to those who would have them. The most frequently used weapon in the United States is a gun. Studies tracking the relationship of gun regulations to patterns of violent crime find them to be predictably related. A six-year study conducted in Seattle and Vancouver, for instance, found that as gun regulations became more restrictive, the risk of injury or death by guns decreased (Garland & Zigler, 1993; Sloan et al., 1988).

ADOLESCENTS AND DRUGS

As Ferris Bueller says, "Life moves pretty fast. If you don't stop and look around once in a while, you could miss it." He's right. If anything, it's faster now than ever before: instant banking, e-mail, faxing, 24-hour markets, fast foods, and five-lane expressways. Stimulants, tranquilizers, sedatives, and alcohol fit neatly into the pace of our lives—they instantaneously pick us up, settle us down, mellow us out, or just blur the edges.

Today's adolescents expect fast results, and drugs are part of society's response to that expectation. Millions of people in the United States find it impossible to get started in the morning without coffee or a cigarette, or to relax in the evening without a drink. Millions more take medication for pain, pills to sleep, laxatives to correct faulty diets, pills to suppress appetites, and vitamin supplements when they fail to eat enough. Adolescents see quick pick-me-ups and instant remedies modeled everywhere around them. It is little wonder that by their senior year in high school, 80% of adolescents have tried alcohol, 71% have ever tried a cigarette, 42% have used marijuana or hashish, and 16% have used some other illegal drug (Centers for Disease Control, 1996c). Figure 12.2 shows the number of high school seniors reporting use of various drugs.

Adolescents try drugs for many reasons, of course; the prevalence of drugs in society is just one of them. Adolescence itself is a time of experimentation, and many adolescents explore substances as well as roles and ideas. Part of the attraction of legal drugs such as cigarettes and alcohol is that they are used by adults; and when adolescents use them, they feel more adult. Also, advertisements make their use look glamorous. Many adolescents experience peer pressure to use substances and countless other adolescents use substances to boost low self-esteem, dull pain, feel more confident, or compensate for poor social skills. Like any quick remedy, the promise far exceeds the payoff, and with some substances, even casual experimentation carries substantial risk.

Our discussion of drugs follows their pattern of use by adolescents. We will look first at alcohol, cigarettes, and marijuana, the three most com-

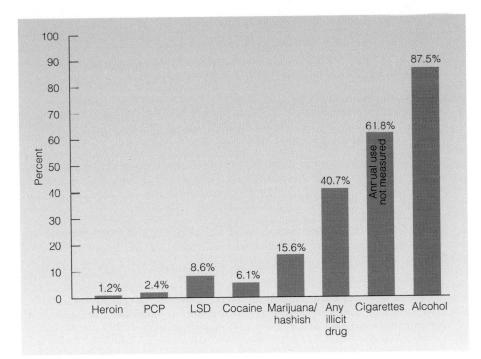

FIGURE 12.2   High School Seniors Reporting Having Ever Used Selected Drugs

Source: Youth Indicators: *Trends in the Well-Being of American Youth.* (1993). Washington, DC: U.S. Government
Printing Office.

monly used substances. From there we will consider the use of stimulants,
depressants, hallucinogens, and narcotics. Finally, we will look at the increasing use of steroids (*DMS-IV,* American Psychiatric Association, 1994).

What Is Dependence?

Drug addiction and **drug dependence** are interchangeable terms. Both refer to a physical dependence on a substance. Not all drugs lead to dependence; one could take an aspirin a day for months or years with no such
effect (although there might be others). The drug must be *psychoactive:* one
that is self-administered, that alters one's mood, and comes to control behavior in such a way that one is no longer free *not* to use it (Surgeon General's Report, 1988). Dependence on a drug always involves developing a
tolerance for it; the body requires increased amounts of the drug to achieve
the same effect. Dependence also results in withdrawal symptoms whenever
use is discontinued. Drug dependence can interfere with school, work, and
relationships (*DSM-IV,* American Psychiatric Association, 1994). The criteria
for drug dependence appear in Box 12.1.

Alcohol

Alcohol is usually the first drug adolescents try; most do so before they reach
high school. Many people do not think of alcohol as a drug, because its use
is so embedded in the context of everyday life, but it is a powerful central

Box 12.1   Criteria for Drug Dependence

Drug dependence is present when at least three of the following seven criteria are present:

1. Development of tolerance so that more of the substance is needed to achieve the same effect.

2. Physical and/or cognitive withdrawal symptoms if use of the substance is discontinued.

3. Use of the substance in larger amounts or over a longer period than was intended.

4. A persistent desire or unsuccessful attempts to cut down or control substance use.

5. Significant amounts of time devoted to obtaining and using the substance and recovering from its use.

6. Giving up or reducing important social, occupational, or recreational activities because of substance use.

7. Continuing to use the substance in spite of knowing that it contributes to a psychological or physical problem (such as cocaine-induced depression or an ulcer aggravated by alcohol).

Source: Adapted from *Diagnostic and statistical manual of mental disorders* (4th ed.). (1994). Washington, DC: American Psychiatric Association.

nervous system (CNS) depressant. Its effect on the nervous system is to restrain inhibitions, making the person feel more spontaneous. Many people become more talkative, confident, and socially at ease after they have had a drink.

Alcohol's effect on the central nervous system is in direct relation to its concentration in the blood. As the blood-alcohol level rises, activities controlled by the CNS are increasingly affected. Movements become uncoordinated, thoughts disorganized, reactions slowed, and mood frequently turns negative. Even small amounts of alcohol may be enough to affect complex activities requiring coordination and judgment. Continued use of alcohol leads to dependence (Insel & Roth, 1998).

Despite, or perhaps because of, its powerful effects, most high school seniors have tried alcohol; 52% use it with some regularity. Even though the number of adolescents who drink daily is low, 33% engage in periodic episodes of heavy drinking, in which they are likely to have five or more drinks in a row at least once in a two-week period. These episodes are more frequent among males, largely due to the frequency with which they drink beer (Centers for Disease Control, 1996c). Not all adolescents are equally at risk for abusing alcohol. Hispanic adolescents, and particularly Dominican adolescents, are especially at risk (Bettes, Dusenbury, Kerner, James-Ortiz, & Botvin, 1990). Conversely, Black high school seniors have been found to have lower frequencies of alcohol use than White classmates (Benson & Donahue, 1989).

The abuse of alcohol is associated with numerous complications. Alcohol is absorbed into all tissues of the body, affecting everything from the central nervous system, to internal organs, to the skeletal muscles. Excessive use of alcohol can damage the liver, produce gastritis, affect kidney functioning, lead to sensory disturbances; it can cause blackouts, memory loss, coma—and ultimately even death (Insel & Roth, 1998). Its destruction to the bodies of chronic abusers is paralleled by the destruction it causes in the lives of those around them. Approximately one and a half million people are injured each year by drunk drivers, and hundreds of thousands die in alcohol-related deaths. Tougher legislation and organizations such as Students Against Driving Drunk (Box 12.2) have increased adolescents' awareness of the hazards of combining alcohol and driving.

Cigarettes

Most adolescents who smoke start before they reach high school, usually somewhere between the sixth and ninth grades. By the time adolescents reach their senior year in high school, over 71% will have tried cigarettes, more than a third smoking at least once a month, and 16% reporting frequent cigarette use (Centers for Disease Control, 1996c). Longitudinal data confirm that smoking is a difficult habit to break, even among adolescents. Over 50% of the adolescents who smoke half a pack or more a day said they had tried to quit and had not been able to. Nearly 75% of those who smoked in high school on a daily basis were still doing so ten years later, although only 5% thought they would continue when they began (Johnston, O'Malley, & Bachman, 1989). These figures are not surprising, given the withdrawal symptoms adolescents experience when attempting to stop: irritability, nervousness, anxiousness, impatience, difficulty concentrating, increased appetite, and weight gain (Insel & Roth, 1998).

The psychoactive agent in cigarettes is *nicotine,* which is both a stimulant and a depressant. Smokers feel both more alert and more relaxed when they smoke. These pleasures come with a heavy price tag. Smoking increases heart rate and blood pressure and carries an increased risk of heart disease. It also increases the risk of respiratory disorders such as emphysema and chronic bronchitis, and increases the risk of lung cancer.

Pregnant adolescents who smoke jeopardize the health of their babies as well as their own health. Smoking during pregnancy is associated with prematurity, low birth weight, spontaneous abortion, and perinatal problems. The latter complications are especially disturbing, because females are just as likely to smoke in high school and early adulthood as are males (Centers for Disease Control, 1996c).

Most adolescents are aware of the hazards of smoking. Over 60% of the seniors sampled by Johnston, O'Malley, & Bachman (1989) believed that smoking carries serious risks. Almost all adolescents (92%) said their parents would disapprove if they smoked a pack or more a day, and 75% said their friends would. Perhaps because of this increased awareness, the number of adolescents who smoke has declined considerably since the late 1970s, from just under 30% to 18%.

Box 12.2 Students Against Driving Drunk (SADD)

Students Against Driving Drunk (SADD) is designed to improve adolescents' knowledge about alcohol in order to save their lives—and the lives of others. The program has three components.

1. It provides a series of lessons that present the facts about drinking and driving, permitting students to make informed decisions.

2. It mobilizes students to help each other, through peer pressure, to face up to the potential dangers of mixing driving with alcohol or drugs.

3. It promotes a dialogue between adolescents and their parents through the SADD Contract. Under this agreement, both students and their parents pledge to contact each other should they ever find themselves in a potential DUI (driving under the influence) situation.

CONTRACT FOR LIFE

A Contract for Life
Between Parent and Teenager
The SADD Drinking-Driver Contract

Teenager   I agree to call you for advice and/or transportation at any hour, from any place, if I am ever in a situation where I have been drinking or a friend or date who is driving me has been drinking.

_____
Signature

Parent   I agree to come and get you at any hour, any place, no questions asked and no argument at that time, or I will pay for a taxi to bring you home safely. I expect we would discuss this issue at a later time.

I agree to seek safe, sober transportation home if I am ever in a situation where I have had too much to drink or a friend who is driving me has had too much to drink.

_____
Signature

_____
Date

S.A.D.D. does not condone drinking by those below the legal drinking age. S.A.D.D. encourages all young people to obey the laws of their state, including laws relating to the legal drinking age.

Distributed by S.A.D.D., "Students Against Driving Drunk"

Adolescents who become smokers do not differ from nonsmokers in their beliefs about the negative effects of smoking; they differ only in holding more positive attitudes about smoking.

Not all adolescents who experiment with smoking go on to become smokers. Many factors tip the balance. Important among these are adolescents' attitudes about the effects of smoking. Adolescents who become smokers do not differ from nonsmokers in their beliefs about the *negative* effects of smoking; they differ only in their more *positive* attitudes about smoking (Gerber & Newman, 1989). Findings such as these point to the need for educational programs directed at the positive fantasies adolescents have about smoking; adolescents who smoke, for example, associate smoking with having fun, being independent, and being sociable. These programs assume special significance, given the relationship between smoking and the use of other drugs. The drug next most likely to be tried if one drinks and smokes is marijuana.

Marijuana

Marijuana comes from the *Cannabis sativa* plant, which contains the psychoactive substance THC (delta-9-tetrahydrocannabinol). This substance produces a high characterized by feelings of relaxation and peacefulness, a sense of heightened awareness of one's surroundings and of the increased significance of things. Marijuana can distort perception, affect memory, slow reaction time, and impair motor coordination, especially for unfamiliar or complex tasks. The only physical effects are an increase in heart rate, reddening of the eyes, and dryness of the mouth. Because marijuana affects perception, reaction time, and coordination, it impairs one's ability to drive. Yet adolescents under the influence of marijuana experience heightened confidence in their abilities and are likely to take greater risks while driving, despite their impaired functioning (Insel & Roth, 1998).

Long-term heavy use of marijuana carries a number of potential health risks. Marijuana has been found to affect the reproductive system in males reducing both the number and motility of sperm, and in females shortening the phase of the menstrual cycle in which conception can occur. The smoke from marijuana causes irritation of the bronchia and can lead to chronic bronchitis. Marijuana smoke also contains considerably more tar than does smoke from even high-tar cigarettes, and 70% more benzopyrene, a known carcinogen (Matuschka, 1985).

Of all illicit drugs, marijuana is the most frequently used by adolescents, with 42% of high school seniors reporting they have used it. Marijuana is also one of the first illicit drugs an adolescent is likely to try (Centers for Disease Control, 1996; Johnston, O'Malley, & Bachman, 1989).

The use of marijuana has declined substantially over the past two decades. The number of those reporting ever using it dropped from 60.3% in 1980 to 43.7% in 1989 (Youth Indicators, 1991). Adolescents are more aware of the potentially harmful effects of using marijuana than they have been in the past. Johnston, O'Malley, and Bachman (1989) found that over 90% thought their parents would highly disapprove of occasional marijuana use, and 67% felt that their friends would disapprove of their even experimenting with marijuana.

Many parents fear that marijuana will lead to the use of other illicit drugs. This view of marijuana as a gateway drug is unfounded. Actual gateway drugs are those used by parents themselves: alcohol and cigarettes. The use of cigarettes and alcohol are closely associated, and both predict the use of marijuana and other drugs. In one survey, nearly 75% of the adolescents who considered themselves smokers also drank alcohol, whereas less than 25% of those who were not smokers drank alcohol. Similarly, almost 50% of the smokers also used marijuana, compared with 5% of nonsmokers (National Institute on Drug Abuse, 1985).

Denise Kandel (1975, 1985) proposes a five-stage model to explain initiation into illicit drug use. In the first stage, adolescents do not use any drugs; those who become substance users start by using beer or wine in the second stage. This step is followed by the use of cigarettes, hard liquor, or both in a third stage. In the fourth stage marijuana is used, and in the fifth adolescents try other illicit drugs. Yamaguchi and Kandel (1984) followed tenth- and eleventh-graders over a ten-year period to identify the order in which they began to use drugs. They found that among those who had tried alcohol and cigarettes, 70% of the males and 55% of the females used alcohol first. Of those using cigarettes and marijuana, 67% of the males and 72% of the females started with cigarettes.

Although adolescents continue to try illegal drugs, use among high school seniors has dropped in recent years. Drug education programs are at least partially responsible for having made adolescents more cautious about using drugs.

Stimulants

Stimulants excite the central nervous system; they boost energy, elevate mood, and depress appetite. Depending on the dosage, they can produce feelings of increased well-being and euphoria, or aggression, paranoia, and delusions. Because they increase heart rate, high doses can cause extreme tachycardia (very rapid heartbeat), cardiac collapse, and death (Insel & Roth, 1998). Stimulants include amphetamines, cocaine, and the crystal form of cocaine known as crack. The most widely used stimulants, however, can be purchased in supermarkets in the form of cola soft drinks, coffee, tea, and cigarettes.

Amphetamines   Approximately 20% of adolescents have tried some form of **amphetamine.** Known as speed, uppers, bennies, meth, or dex, these stimulants most frequently come in the form of pills. The use of amphetamines has also declined. At the same time, there has been a doubling in the use of over-the-counter stay-awake pills containing caffeine (Johnston, O'Malley, & Bachman, 1989).

Cocaine   **Cocaine** comes from the coca plant grown in South America. Cocaine (coke, blow, toot, snow, or lady) produces feelings of euphoria and a sense of mastery. It is usually inhaled but can also be injected or smoked as crack. Recent use of cocaine among high school seniors has dropped dramatically. Despite a spreading of the drug to new communities, this decline is most likely the result of media coverage of the hazards associated with its use. Adolescents have become increasingly aware that even one-time use can kill. Many adolescents appear to have been motivated not to even try cocaine, and many of those who have used it have stopped. Of the 7% of adolescents who said they had ever tried cocaine, less than half had used it in the past month (Centers for Disease Control, 1996c).

Depressants

Substances called **depressants** reduce or lower the activity of the central nervous system. Alcohol is the most common of these; other depressants used by adolescents include inhalants, barbiturates, and tranquilizers. These substances decrease anxiety and produce a sense of euphoria. Because they depress the activity of vital centers in the nervous system, their use can be dangerous or even fatal in higher doses. Barbiturates, for example, are especially dangerous when combined with alcohol (Insel & Roth, 1998).

Inhalants   Inhaling fumes from substances such as glue, gasoline, paint thinner, lighter fluid, nail polish remover, and other solvents can produce feelings of mild intoxication and elation. The use of **inhalants** can also result in disorientation, nausea, pulmonary crisis, psychosis, and even coma. Inhalants are especially toxic substances that can damage numerous tissues within the body, including those of the brain, kidneys, liver, and bone marrow. Perhaps because inhalants are readily accessible (many are found around the house), they are among the first substances to be tried by many adolescents. One-fifth of adolescents surveyed nationally said they had ever used inhalants (Centers for Disease Control, 1996c).

Barbiturates   Street names for barbiturates include yellow jackets (Nembutal), reds (Seconal), and tueys (Tuinal). Literally thousands of different types of barbiturates are manufactured for medical use; many of these end up on the street. **Barbiturates** give adolescents a sense of euphoria and lessened inhibitions; their use can also result in intense mood swings, paranoia, and suicidal thoughts. Almost all barbiturates are highly addictive. Their use has been declining (Johnston, O'Malley, & Bachman, 1989; Kaufman, Shaffer, & Burglass, 1985).

Quaaludes   Commonly known as ludes, **Quaaludes** produce effects similar to those of barbiturates, though they are not actually barbiturates. Their addictive potential is high. The use of this drug by adolescents has been steadily declining (Johnston, O'Malley, & Bachman, 1989).

Tranquilizers   **Tranquilizers** include such drugs as Valium, Librium, Equanil, and Miltown. They decrease anxiety and increase feelings of well-being and relaxation; they can also produce psychological and physiological dependence. As with other depressants, their use has declined (Johnston, O'Malley, & Bachman, 1989).

Narcotics

Narcotics include heroin, morphine, and opium. *Heroin* is a derivative of *morphine*, which itself is derived from opium; *opium* comes from the seeds of poppies. Heroin produces its most intense effects when injected into the bloodstream ("mainlining"), although it can also be injected under the skin ("popped") or sniffed. Users report an intense initial euphoria followed by a more prolonged period of calm and well-being that lasts for several hours. Weakness, sweating, nausea, and vomiting are also common among users. Relatively few adolescents try heroin; 1.2% of high school seniors surveyed had ever tried it (Youth Indicators, 1993).

All narcotics are highly addictive, and tolerance develops rapidly. The extreme pleasure experienced initially by users lessens with continued use, making it necessary for them to increase the dosage to obtain the same effect. The risk of an overdose increases as the dosage is increased. This risk is even greater than might be imagined, because the difference between a dose that would produce a high and a lethal dose is often relatively small.

Narcotics are actually not as toxic to the body as alcohol and barbiturates; however, their use carries greater secondary risk. Because heroin is almost always injected, infection from shared contaminated needles is a major risk. Hepatitis, tetanus, and AIDS are associated with the practice of sharing unsterilized needles. Users can also inject an air bubble into their vein, which can be fatal. Once dependence is established, the cost of the drug can run as high as several hundred dollars a day, a habit that for most can only be supported by crime.

Hallucinogens

The experience obtained from using hallucinogens is unlike that from using any other substances. **Hallucinogens** primarily affect thought and perception. One person described the experience as follows: "Closing my eyes, I saw millions of color droplets, like rain, like a shower of stars, all different colors" (Goode, 1984). It is common for adolescents to experience ordinary objects as fascinating, time as slowing, emotions as magnified, and the sense of self as profoundly changed. *LSD* and *mescaline* are common hallucinogens. Marijuana can also produce hallucinogenic effects.

Anabolic Steroids

Anabolic steroids are synthetic male hormones widely used by athletes to improve their muscular development and athletic performance. (*Anabolic* is the term for a metabolic process that builds up tissue.) An estimated half a million adolescent athletes use anabolic steroids. Considerable controversy surrounds their use because steroids have a number of negative side effects. Anabolic steroids increase aggressiveness and hostility, cause liver damage, raise blood pressure, and are associated with the development of several types of cancer. The only effects that adolescents may notice immediately arc a slight change in their mood; they become more irritable and aggressive. However, the lure of enhanced performance and the "body beautiful" may seduce many to use steroids and disregard the potential hazards of their long-term use.

Most adolescents will experiment with at least some drugs before they reach adulthood. A positive note is that most will not abuse them. However, even casual experimentation with some substances carries substantial risks. How best can society protect adolescents from the potential hazards of experimentation? Is the most effective approach to bombard them with information concerning the dangers of drugs such that they never take that first sip, puff, or pop? Given the pleasurable effects of drugs and the powerful pressures to use them, as well as the excitement of daring the forbidden, scare programs are not likely to keep most adolescents from experimenting. Candid discussions that acknowledge the pleasurable effects of drugs as well as their potential for abuse promise a better safeguard for adolescents. Establishing trust through open communication makes it possible for adolescents to approach adults when they need information, or even help.

DEPRESSION

Emotions color experience and give meaning to life. For most individuals they are anchored in reality, tethered to the situations that prompt them. Some individuals are pulled past reality to an inner world of thoughts and feelings that bear little resemblance to the situations that occasion them. These individuals suffer from **affective disorders,** disturbances that affect their mood. Mood is an enduring emotional state that varies along a continuum of depression to elation (*DSM-IV,* American Psychiatric Association, 1994). Individuals who suffer from affective disorders live much of their lives at the extremes of this continuum.

Three Depressive Disorders

From time to time everyone feels sad. Those who live with **depression** feel a crushing weight of hopelessness and despair. They may have any of three major forms of depression. Adolescents with *major depressive disorder* experience severe periods of depression lasting several weeks or more. These are accompanied by some or all of the following symptoms: difficulty concentrating, loss of pleasure, slowed speech and movements, and vegetative signs such as sleepiness, loss of appetite, and weight changes. Adolescents suffering from *dysthymia* have a less severe form of depression but one that generally lasts much longer. The third form, *adjustment disorder with depressed mood,* is brought on by stress and is relatively brief (Petersen et al., 1993).

Feelings of sadness, loneliness, and despair become common by midadolescence. Nearly half of all adolescents report experiencing some of the

Nearly half of all adolescents report experiencing some of the symptoms that characterize depression: sadness, crying spells, pessimism, and feelings of unworthiness.

symptoms that characterize depression—sadness, crying spells, pessimism, and feelings of unworthiness. Even so, the prevalence of major depressive disorder among adolescents is considerably lower—about 10%—with three quarters of those affected being female (McFarlane, Bellissimo, Norman, & Lange, 1994).

Adolescents who suffer from depression share with adult depressives feelings of low self-esteem, pervasive sadness, hopelessness, and helplessness (Craighead & Green, 1989). A self-defeating cycle exists in which low self-esteem contributes to depression, which in turn fuels negative feelings about the self (Rosenberg, Schooler, & Schoenbach, 1989). More females than males experience depression. A change in the sex ratio of those suffering from depression occurs during puberty (Rutter, 1986). This change could reflect hormonal influences or may reflect identification with culturally defined gender roles. The female gender role includes more socially undesirable characteristics than does the male gender role. This difference could easily affect the self-esteem of adolescent females as they identify with the culturally defined role. Craighead and Green (1989) found differences in self-esteem to account for approximately half of the variability in depression among normal adolescents.

Masked Depression

Depression is often masked in early adolescence Several symptoms signal *masked depression,* the most frequent being fatigue, poor concentration, and hypochondriasis (excessive concern with illness or health). Continual fatigue can reflect inner struggles with feelings that adolescents cannot put to rest or talk about with others. Similarly, difficulties in concentration can result from concerns they do not yet feel secure enough to articulate, and preoccupations with their health, or a seeming lack of it, may reflect fears of inadequacy or incompetence.

Each of these symptoms can be mistakenly interpreted as a natural part of adolescence. Fatigue is expected, given the accelerated growth of puberty and the demands of school, friends, and family. Similarly, poor concentration can easily be mistaken for problems with schoolwork ranging from boredom to being overwhelmed, and excessive concern with one's body is natural, given the changes that take place during puberty. Treatments that take into consideration the underlying source of an adolescent's depression will be more effective in combating these symptoms than those that are directed at the symptoms themselves: the fatigue, poor concentration, or excessive concern with health (Weiner, 1980).

Irving Weiner (1980) suggests that adolescents may not be able to admit feelings of inadequacy and still accomplish the developmental tasks they face—achieving emotional independence, finding a sense of self, developing heterosexual relationships, and so on. Any one of these would be difficult under the best of conditions, and can be impossible with feelings of inadequacy. Early adolescents may also be more caught up in *doing* things than in reflecting about them. In either case, depression, or attempts to keep it at bay, are likely to at first assume a physical form in early adolescence.

SUICIDE

An alarming number of adolescents report thinking about suicide. In a national survey of high school students in 1995, 24% said that they had thought seriously about attempting suicide at some point during the past year, 18% indicating they had even made specific plans (Centers for Disease Control, 1996c). By comparison, the percentage who actually attempt suicide is relatively low, 8.7%, and still fewer actually commit suicide. However, adolescence stands out as a time in life that is especially hazardous with respect to suicide. Suicide is the third leading cause of death among 15- to 19-year-olds, being responsible for 14% of all deaths in that age group (National Center for Health Statistics, 1991). The number of suicide attempts peaks between ages 15 and 24 (Schuckit & Schuckit, 1989).

The rate of suicide for 15- to 19-year-olds has more than tripled over the past three decades (National Center for Health Statistics, 1991). Approximately every 90 minutes a young person completes a suicide (Bolton, 1989). Startling as these figures are, they probably underestimate the actual

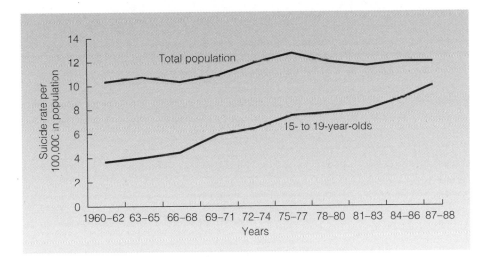

FIGURE 12.3   Suicide Rates per 100,000 in Population
for Total Population and for 15- to 19-Year-Olds

Source: A. F. Garland & E. Zigler. (1993). Adolescent suicide prevention: Current
research and social policy implications. *American Psychologist, 48,* 169–182.

number of deaths by suicide because they don't include the many deaths
recorded as accidents (for example, single-person car crashes, drownings,
overdoses), which in many cases are misclassified suicides. The picture dark-
ens further with the addition of attempted suicides. For every completed
suicide, anywhere from 8 to 20 more adolescents unsuccessfully attempt it;
of these, up to 10 percent will later succeed (*Report of the Secretary's Task Force
on Youth Suicide,* 1989).

Though startling in themselves, these figures assume a more ominous
note when compared with suicide rates for other age groups. Figure 12.3
shows that the overall rate of suicide for the total population has changed
little over this same time period, whereas that for young persons has increased substantially.

Gender and Ethnic Differences

Males are more likely than females to complete a suicide, despite the fact
that females attempt suicide twice as often as males (Centers for Disease
Control, 1996c). In part, this difference can be traced to the different methods chosen by males and females. Males are most likely to use a gun or attempt to hang themselves, both of which are more immediately lethal than
ingesting harmful substances, the method most commonly used by females
(Garland & Zigler, 1993). Among completed suicides, for both sexes, using
a gun is the most frequent method. Although at first glance these gender
differences would seem to suggest less ambivalence about dying among
males, other factors are probably more important. Males, in general, are
more impulsive and violent than females, qualities that are reflected in the
methods they choose. Impulsivity may be a critical factor in most suicides,

TABLE 12.7   Percentages of Black, Hispanic, and White High School Students
Reporting Suicidal Thoughts and Behavior

Ethnicity	Suicidal Thoughts	Made Suicide Plans	One or More Suicide Attempts	Attempt(s) Requiring Medical Attention
Black	20.0	14.2	9.5	3.2
Hispanic	25.0	19.5	13.4	4.8
White	24.9	18.0	7.6	2.4

Note: Questions asked whether students had seriously thought about attempting suicide at any time in the past year, whether they had made a specific plan, how many attempts they had made, and whether any of these required treatment by a doctor or nurse.

Source: Centers for Disease Control. (1996c). Youth Risk Behavior Surveillance—United States, 1996. *Morbidity and Mortality Weekly Report, 45*, No. 55-4. Washington, DC: U.S. Government Printing Office.

and males, because they are likely to choose a violent method, will be successful more frequently (Garland & Zigler, 1993). Also, females may be able to seek out and use interpersonal supports more easily than males, who typically find it more difficult to reveal neediness or ask for help (Garland & Zigler, 1993).

Ethnic differences exist as well in suicidal thoughts and behavior. Table 12.7 summarizes the responses of high school students to questions concerning suicide. Black students reported fewer suicidal thoughts or attempts than either White or Hispanic students (Centers for Disease Control, 1996c). Among all ethnic groups, the rate of suicide is highest for Native Americans. However, large differences exist between different tribes. The rate of suicide among Navajos, for instance, is close to that nationally, whereas the rate among Apaches is more than three times as high (Garland & Zigler, 1993). As a rule, tribes that are more traditional tend to have lower suicide rates, perhaps because they provide a greater sense of community and their members experience more support (Wyche, Obolensky, & Glood, 1990).

Suicide used to be most common among older White males with mental health problems. Currently, the rate of suicide in that segment of the population is decreasing, while increasing among the young, many of whom do not have the same history of problems. As a consequence, previous prevention and treatment approaches may not be useful in identifying potential youth suicides.

Prevention is just one link in a chain beginning with detection. A report of the Secretary's Task Force on Youth Suicide observes that the rate at which adolescents are committing suicide is unprecedented, but concludes that we know less about youth suicide than most other health problems. Past research on suicide has focused on the relation between suicide and mental disorders. The extent to which we can extend this relationship in any simple fashion to youth suicide remains to be seen (*Report of the Secretary's Task Force on Youth Suicide,* 1989).

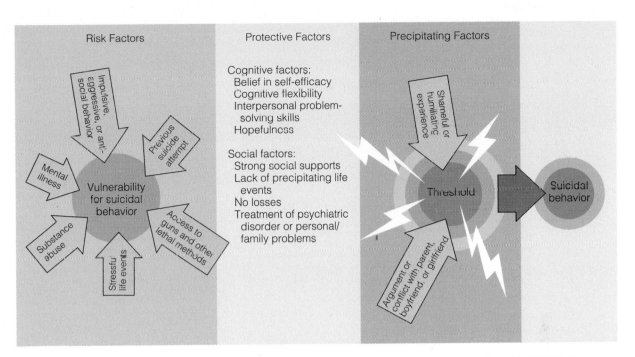

FIGURE 12.4
Factors Contributing to Suicide

Source: Adapted from S. J. Blumenthal & D. J. Kupfer. (1988). Overview of early detection and treatment strategies for suicidal behavior in young people. *Journal of Youth and Adolescence, 17,* 1–23.

Warning Signs

Although every case of suicide is unique, a number of common warning signs exist. These include sudden changes in behavior, changes in patterns of sleeping or eating, loss of interest in usual activities or withdrawal from others, experiencing a humiliating event, feelings of guilt or hopelessness, an inability to concentrate, talk of suicide, or giving away one's most important possessions (Blumenthal & Kupfer, 1988). The presence of any one of these is a cause for concern; the presence of several is a clear signal that an adolescent is in danger.

Risk Factors

A variety of factors are associated with an increased risk of suicide. Most of these characterize the person at risk, although some, such as substance abuse or exposure to suicidal behavior, can also involve elements of the family or the larger culture. Even though most suicides are associated with one or more of these risk factors, about one-third of youth suicides are associated with no risk factors at all; these youths come from loving and supportive homes.

Blumenthal and Kupfer (1988) classify risk factors into potentially overlapping domains. As the overlap among domains increases, so does the risk of suicide, as illustrated in Figure 12.4. According to this approach,

> the breakup of a relationship might be a final humiliating experience that triggers a depressive episode in a young person with a family history of affective disorder. Such an individual may also have poor social supports, which interact with the other identified risk factors to increase the individual's vulnerability for suicide. (Blumenthal & Kupfer, 1988, p. 4)

Box 12.3   A Poem Written by a 15-Year-Old Boy Two Years Before Committing Suicide

TO SANTA CLAUS AND LITTLE SISTERS

Once . . . he wrote a poem.
And called it "Chops."
Because that was the name of
   his dog, and that's what it was
   all about.
And the teacher gave him an "A"
And a gold star.
And his mother hung it on the
   kitchen door, and read it to
   all his aunts . . .
Once . . . he wrote another poem.
And he called it "Question Marked
   Innocence."
Because that was the name of
   his grief and that's what it
   was all about.
And the professor gave him an "A"
And a strange and steady look.
And his mother never hung it
   on the kitchen door, because
   he never let her see it . . .

Once, at 3 a.m. . . . he tried another
   poem . . .
And he called it absolutely nothing,
   because that's what it was all
   about.
And he gave himself an "A"
And a slash on each damp wrist,
And hung it on the bathroom
   door because he couldn't reach
   the kitchen.

Sources: A. Russell Lee, M.D., Director of
Family Therapy Training, Pacific Medical
Center, San Francisco, California, and Con-
tra Costa, California, Mental Health Ser-
vices; and Charlotte P. Ross, Executive
Director, Suicide Prevention and Crisis
Center, San Mateo County, Burlingame,
California.

Cognitive factors that help to protect adolescents from the threat of suicide are feelings of self-efficacy, problem-solving skills, and hopefulness.
Similarly, social factors decreasing the risk of suicide are the presence of
strong social supports, the lack of precipitating life events, and getting treatment or help for personal or family problems.

Mental Illness   Mental illness plays a significant role in almost all adolescent suicides (Garland & Zigler, 1993). Several diagnostic categories in particular are especially implicated; suicide is particularly high for those with
affective disorders and schizophrenia (Blumenthal & Kupfer, 1988; Garland
& Zigler, 1993). Antisocial behavior is also closely linked to suicidal behavior. The Secretary's Task Force notes that "antisocial behavior and depressive symptoms appear to be a particularly lethal combination" (*Report of the
Secretary's Task Force on Youth Suicide,* 1989, p. 20).

Prior Attempt   Perhaps one of the most serious risk factors for suicide is
having made a prior attempt. Anywhere from 50% to 80% of all actual suicides by adolescents have been preceded by a previous attempt (Shafii, Carrigan, Whittinghill, & Derrick, 1985). Suicidal remarks or other warning
signs among such adolescents assume added significance.

A common cultural stereotype of adolescent suicide attempts holds that
these are shallow and impulsive bids for attention. Neither assumption is

true. Adolescents who are suicidal are in personal pain and have usually sought a number of solutions to their present problems. Suicidal adolescents usually attempt to communicate their distress in a number of ways, and thoughts of suicide are often a last resort (Weiner, 1980). The poem in Box 12.3 is a poignant illustration of this point.

Personality Traits   Three personality characteristics are especially linked to suicide: aggression, impulsiveness, and a sense of hopelessness, the most significant characteristic (*Report of the Secretary's Task Force on Youth Suicide*, 1989).

Substance Abuse   Abuse of alcohol or other substances, either by adolescents themselves or by someone in their families, is associated with increased risk of suicide (Windle, Miller-Tutzauer, & Domenico, 1992). Thirty percent to 40% of adolescents who attempt suicide have parents who abuse alcohol (*Report of the Secretary's Task Force on Youth Suicide*, 1989). Many adolescents who attempt suicide get drunk first, perhaps to muster the courage they need. Although alcohol dulls psychological pain, it is a depressant and may contribute to suicidal impulses. As a substance that can be easily abused, it can also interfere with long-term constructive approaches to problem solutions. The combined effects of alcohol and other substances, such as barbiturates, amphetamines, and cocaine, can be especially deadly.

Other forms of substance abuse are also significantly related to suicide. Death rates among adolescents who are heavy drug users are anywhere from two to eight times higher than among those their age in the general population. Approximately half of these deaths are estimated to be suicides.

Psychosocial Circumstances   Adolescents who attempt or commit suicide commonly experience more life stress, more losses, and more changes within the family than those who do not. Frequently a humiliating event precipitates the suicide attempt, such as a crisis or an interpersonal problem involving parents or peers. Family life is more likely to be chaotic, relationships with parents are frequently problematic, and parental strife is more common. Suicidal adolescents generally have fewer social supports and personal resources while facing these added stresses (Blumenthal & Kupfer, 1988).

Lethal Means   The availability of lethal methods, particularly firearms, appears to be a factor affecting suicide rates. The increase in the rate at which adolescents commit suicide by shooting themselves has risen three times faster than the rates for other methods. This increase has paralleled the increased availability of guns to teenagers, both in their own homes (Brent et al., 1988) and in society in general (Garland & Zigler, 1993). Because firearms are the most frequent means in the United States by which adolescents commit suicide, the importance of determining the impact of gun control legislation cannot be overestimated. Guns account for the majority of suicides—among females as well as males (*Report of the Secretary's Task Force on Youth Suicide*, 1989).

Biochemical Imbalance   Evidence suggests involvement of brain neurotransmitters (chemicals involved in communication between one nerve cell and another) in suicidal behavior. The two neurotransmitters involved are serotonin and dopamine. Specifically, investigators find lower levels of the byproducts of these neurotransmitters (5-hydroxyindoleacetic acid, or 5-HIAA, and homovanillic acid, or HVA) in the cerebrospinal fluid (*Report of the Secretary's Task Force on Youth Suicide,* 1989).

Exposure to Suicidal Behavior   Coverage of a suicide by the news media has been shown to affect local suicide rates, especially among adolescents. Also, adolescents who have a friend or family member who has attempted or committed suicide are more likely to attempt suicide (Garland & Zigler, 1993).

Counseling and Prevention

In some adolescents, suicidal behavior may be a desperate attempt to effect a change in someone they love, such as an alcoholic parent, rather than a true wish to die, as is more likely in older suicide victims (Weiner, 1980). Tragically, the intellectual changes that make it possible for adolescents to reflect on their lives also make it possible for them to imagine the reactions of others to their deaths. Elkind (1978) warns that the personal fable, the belief that one is different from others and somehow invulnerable to the dangers others face, may prevent adolescents from realizing the consequences of their actions—that they will not be around to see how much others actually cared for them.

Communicating With Suicidal Adolescents   Weiner (1980) stresses the pivotal place of communication in the lives of suicidal adolescents. Adolescents who are genuinely listened to following an attempt are less likely to engage in further suicidal behavior. Conversely, callous or angry reactions or even indifference from those they love can prompt further suicidal attempts. Caring, open, and supportive efforts to address problems on the part of those closest to the adolescent are vital. Yet important as these efforts are, they should never replace professional help.

Frequently those adolescents communicate with their peers. Frequently, too, peers are uninformed concerning warning signs of suicidal intent. Only half of one sample of adolescents knew, for instance, that remarks about wanting to die, seeming worried, or having problems in school or with a relationship might be related to suicidal behavior. Fewer than 20% knew that adolescents who are suicidal are likely to threaten they will kill themselves. Even more alarming was the finding that over 40% of these adolescents believed that such behaviors were *not* likely to be related to suicide (Norton, Durlak, & Richards, 1989).

What advice is there to give to those who fear that an adolescent close to them may be suicidal? Suicidal adolescents communicate their pain to those to whom they are closest. It is important to pick up on these signals. One should not be afraid to openly ask the adolescent if she or he has thought of self-destructive behavior. Listening to what the adolescent has to say can be painful, but it is vitally important. Attempting to deny the reality of the adolescent's pain through false assurances that everything will

Adolescents who are alienated, delinquent, suicidal, or mentally ill follow a different developmental path than most. But all adolescents share the need to be listened to and supported by those who are closest to them.

be okay only communicates that one has not heard the pain or the hopelessness. Serious thoughts of suicide require professional attention. Loving concern, though important in its own right, is not a substitute. Professional help should be obtained immediately.

Prevention Programs   The most effective programs help suicidal adolescents face truths in their lives and have these work for them. Sometimes the truth can be as simple as learning how to say something and then make it happen. The approaches that work best are brief, crisis-oriented, and give adolescents skills they can apply in their ongoing relationships (Kerfoot, Harrington, & Dyer, 1995).

To be effective, programs must reach the adolescents who need them. Many adolescents who attempt suicide do not show up for therapy, or they drop out before they complete it. One study found that 20% did not keep any of the appointments they made, another 19% dropped out during the initial assessment sessions, and nearly one-third more discontinued the program before they finished (Trautman & Rotheram, 1986; Trautman, 1993). Given the chaotic home lives of many of these adolescents, completing anything, even breakfast, can be an accomplishment. One program found it helpful to give adolescents who had been hospitalized for a suicide attempt a token that would give them readmission to the hospital on a "no questions asked" basis, should circumstances become intolerable (Cotgrove, Zirinksy, Black, & Weston, 1995).

The most effective treatments are highly structured programs that train adolescents in skills they can apply at home and in school. Most also teach adolescents to attribute their successes to their own efforts; they aim at getting them to a place where they can say, "I did that and I did it well."

Usually counselors help adolescents identify problem areas and generate alternative solutions. When adolescents can think of alternative solutions to conflicts and predict the effects of acting one way or another, they can cope more effectively. Even if the other person reacts negatively, being able to predict a response puts adolescents less "at the effect of" the other person. If adolescents can also anticipate their own feelings about negative reactions, they are in an even better place to control these feelings. In a sense, conflict management is a bit like surfing: You need to stay just behind the crest of the wave to keep it from crashing down on you.

Family Therapy Because many suicide attempts are precipitated by conflict with a parent, treatment that includes the family will almost always be the most effective. This type of therapy shifts the focus from the adolescent to family interactions that preceded the suicide attempt. Improving communication within the family is usually an important element to intervention programs (Kerfoot, Harrington, & Dyer, 1995).

SCHIZOPHRENIA

Schizophrenia is a disorder that permeates all aspects of functioning, frequently making it impossible for the person to relate to others. Emotions are frequently inappropriate or blunted, and behavior is often bizarre. Disturbances of thought and perception are common and involve delusions and hallucinations, especially auditory ones (*DSM-IV,* 1994).

Schizophrenia is most likely to occur first in adolescence or early adulthood. Frequently its appearance can be missed and mistaken for other conditions. Two quite different types of onset are especially likely in adolescence, and each is easily misinterpreted as something else. In one type, adolescents withdraw from others, lose interest in ordinary activities, and show other symptoms characteristic of depression, including changes in mood and suicidal thoughts. In the other type, adolescents show disturbances primarily of behavior rather than mood, such as increased family conflict, fighting at school, truancy, doing poorly in coursework, lying, and stealing. Gender differences exist as well. Females tend to become increasingly shy, withdrawn, and inhibited, and males to be more aggressive, irritable, and defiant.

Certain characteristics of schizophrenia are not found in depression or antisocial disorders. The most distinguishing is a disturbance of thought that is reflected in loosely associated and shifting ideas. The following passage illustrates this characteristic. In response to the question, "What did you think of the whole Watergate affair?" the individual answered:

> You know I didn't tune in on that, I felt so bad about it. I said, Boy, I'm not going to know what's going on in this. But it seemed to get so murky, and everybody's reports were so negative. Huh, I thought, I don't want any part of this, and I don't care who was in on it, and all I could figure out was Artie had something to do with it. Artie was trying to flush the bathroom toilet of the White House or something. She was trying to do something fairly simple. The tour guests stuck or something. She got blamed because the water overflowed, went down in the basement, down, to the kitchen. They had a, they were going to have to repaint and restore the White House room, the enormous living room. And then it was at this reunion they were having. And it's just such a mess and I just thought, well, I'm just going to pretend like I don't even know what's going on. So I came downstairs and 'cause I pretended like I didn't know what was going on, I slipped on the floor of the kitchen, cracking my toe, when I was teaching some kids how to do some double dives. (*DSM-IIIR*, American Psychiatric Association, 1987)

In summarizing the findings of several research projects, Weiner (1980) notes that about one-quarter of the adolescents who were initially hospitalized for schizophrenia recover, and another quarter improve with occasional relapses. The other half were permanently hospitalized. Studies of adult schizophrenics show that about one-third recover, one-third experience some remission, and one-third remain hospitalized. Discoveries concerning the role of brain biochemistry promise further success in treating this disorder.

The atypical developmental paths taken by adolescents who are alienated, delinquent, suicidal, and mentally ill differ from those followed by most. Yet all share a need to be listened to and supported by those closest to them. The problems of most adolescents discussed in this chapter are sufficiently complex to warrant a multifaceted treatment approach—counseling, skill training, crisis intervention, in some cases hospitalization, and in all cases the support of someone who cares.

SUMMARY

Alienation and the Failure to Cope

Feelings of alienation are common in adolescence. These can be triggered by pubertal changes, identity issues, and feelings of cultural estrangement.

Many alienated adolescents are runaways. These youths are frequently abused or neglected. As a group they suffer from low self-esteem, depression, poor interpersonal skills, insecurity, anxiousness, impulsiveness, and lack of a sense of personal control over their lives. Home life for most is chaotic and characterized by violence.

Three home life patterns distinguish adolescents who are abused and neglected. The abuse may be a continuation of abusive patterns that started in childhood, it may reflect a change in the type of discipline used when they reach adolescence, or it may be occasioned by the onset of adolescence itself. Abusive parents are likely to have had inadequate parenting models and have inadequate parenting skills.

Most adolescents who are sexually abused are female. Most of the perpetrators are males, and most are members of the immediate family or are relatives. Most sexual abuse starts in childhood.

Juvenile Delinquency

Juvenile delinquency involves illegal behavior committed by a minor. Status offenses are behaviors that are illegal when engaged in by minors but legal for adults. Index offenses are behaviors that are criminal at any age.

The incidence of adolescents committing either type of offense has increased in the past 40 years. The type of delinquent act varies with age. There is little evidence suggesting that minor forms of delinquency predict a later shift to more serious crime. The pattern instead suggests a small subgroup of delinquents who start early and account for a relatively large proportion of criminal activity.

Gender, ethnic, and social class differences exist in delinquency. Females are nearly twice as likely as males to commit status offenses, and males are more likely to commit index offenses. Large ethnic differences exist, but these are difficult to separate from social class differences and racial bias within the juvenile justice system.

Adolescents who become delinquent usually experience problems in school, have low self-esteem, come from homes characterized by violence and abuse, have poor social skills, are more aggressive with peers, and are more impulsive.

Juvenile gangs have changed over the past generation. They are more likely to be linked to organized crime than in the past and are associated with more violent crimes and the sale of narcotics. The threat of violence is not limited to gang members. Teenagers are two and a half times more likely to be victims of violent crime than those 20 years or older. Homicide is the second leading cause of injury-related deaths in children and adolescents. Those most at risk are minority males.

Adolescents and Drugs

Physical drug dependence occurs with psychoactive substances when they control behavior so that the individual cannot easily discontinue their use. Dependence on a drug involves developing a tolerance for it such that increased amounts are necessary to achieve the same effect, resulting in withdrawal when use is discontinued. Adolescents are likely to first try alcohol, then cigarettes, and then marijuana.

Alcohol depresses the activity of the central nervous system; it loosens inhibitions and makes individuals feel more spontaneous. As blood-alcohol level rises, activities controlled by the central nervous system are increasingly affected. Most high school seniors have tried alcohol and nearly 52% do so with some regularity.

Cigarettes contain nicotine, which is both a stimulant and a depressant. Most adolescents who smoke start before they reach high school. Sixteen percent of high school students smoke cigarettes frequently. Most adolescents who start to smoke have tried unsuccessfully to stop. The use of cigarettes and alcohol is associated with the use of other, illicit substances.

Marijuana is a mild hallucinogen that affects thought, perception, reaction time, and coordination. Long-term heavy use carries a number of potential health risks. Of all illicit drugs, marijuana is the most frequently used by adolescents.

Stimulants excite the central nervous system, boost energy, elevate mood, and depress appetite. They include amphetamines, cocaine, and the crystal form of cocaine known as crack. Serious health hazards attend their use.

Depressants reduce or lower the activity of the central nervous system. Alcohol is the most common depressant; others include inhalants, barbiturates, and tranquilizers. The use of each of these by adolescents has declined in recent years.

Narcotics include heroin, morphine, and opium. Heroin is a derivative of morphine, which is derived from opium, which comes from the seeds of poppies. Tolerance develops rapidly with narcotics; the risk of an overdose increases correspondingly. Other serious risks attend the use of narcotics. Hallucinogens primarily affect thought and perception. LSD, mescaline, and marijuana are common hallucinogens.

Anabolic steroids are synthetic hormones that improve muscular development and athletic performance. They are widely used by athletes. Steroids increase aggressiveness and hostility, and their use is associated with numerous health risks.

Most adolescents will experiment with some drugs before they reach adulthood; most will also not use them frequently. Even casual experimentation with some substances carries substantial risks. Candid discussions that acknowledge the pleasurable effects of drugs as well as their potential dangers promise to be the most effective ways of providing help to adolescents.

Depression

Depression is an affective disorder that can take a number of forms. Adolescents with major depressive disorder suffer episodes of debilitating depression that can last for several weeks or more. Those with dysthymia experience less severe but longer-lasting symptoms. Those with adjustment disorder with depressed mood experience brief bouts of depression brought on by stress. Adolescents who suffer from depression have feelings of low self-esteem, sadness, hopelessness, and helplessness. Depression can be masked by physical symptoms in early adolescence.

Suicide

The rate of suicide among adolescents has nearly tripled over the past three decades. Males are more likely than females to complete a suicide. Suicide is the third most common cause of death among those 15 to 19 years old.

Warnings signs include sudden changes in behavior, changes in sleeping or eating patterns, loss of interest in usual activities or withdrawal from others, experiencing a humiliating event, feelings of guilt or hopelessness, inability to concentrate, talk of suicide, or giving away important possessions.

Factors that place adolescents at risk of suicide are mental illness, substance abuse, life stresses and chaotic family lives, biochemical imbalances, the availability of lethal means, and prior suicide attempts.

The most effective treatment programs work with the family as well as the suicidal adolescent.

Schizophrenia

Schizophrenia is a disorder characterized by disturbances of thought, perception, and emotion. It is most likely to occur first in adolescence or early adulthood. Warning signs include becoming shy and withdrawn or aggressive.

The most distinguishing feature to schizophrenia is a disturbance of thought that takes the form of loosely associated and shifting ideas. Approximately one-quarter of adolescents who have been hospitalized for schizophrenia recover and another quarter improve with relapses.

KEY TERMS

alienation

juvenile delinquency

status offenses

index offenses

drug dependence

marijuana

stimulants

amphetamine

cocaine

depressants

inhalants

barbiturates

Quaaludes

tranquilizers

narcotics

hallucinogens

anabolic steroids

affective disorders

depression

schizophrenia

CHAPTER 13

Protective Factors in Adolescence
Meeting the Challenges and Making It Work

What is it that we—as parents, teachers, employers, and members of the community—want of adolescents? What is the cultural agenda awaiting adolescents as they move into adulthood? Do we simply want them to settle down, do well at school, and get to work on time? Or do expectations run deeper than that? What does it take, in other words, for us to consider them "grown up"?

Robert Kegan (1994), at Harvard University, says that it takes a lot. Kegan asserts that we do not simply expect adolescents to change how they behave. We expect them to change how they *know,* to change the way they understand, or give meaning to, their experiences. Such a change requires adolescents to let go of their current grasp of the way things are, a grasp that includes the way they know themselves.

Consider Sylvia, for instance. Sylvia is 15 and she is having a bad day. She has cut her afternoon classes to go to the mall with her friends. Glancing up from the cosmetics counter where they've been trying on lipsticks, she looks into the face of her mother, who is looking back at her. Her flushed excuse of a short day at school doesn't change the set to her mother's mouth or the look in her eyes, a mixture of hurt and anger.

For her part, Sylvia's mother is wondering why she has bothered for the past five months to pick her daughter up from school when she can so obviously get where she wants to go on her own. Where is the child who used to hold her hand so sweetly whenever they'd leave the house? Not that she wants that in a 15-year-old. No, and as much as she values independence and planning in her children, Sylvia's mother does not feel like congratulating her daughter on the way she has planned her afternoon or gotten to the mall on her own. Not on your life! In fact, she feels like saying, "It's

One of the major steps in growing up is developing a relationship with one's parents that is mutual and reciprocal.

time you started taking your schooling more seriously, sister! You've got a future to think about. You're not a kid anymore. And how do you think I feel knowing you would have met me in the parking lot lying about where you'd been all afternoon!" (Kegan, 1994).

Sylvia's mother was disappointed in her. She expected so much more of her daughter than this. But just what is it that parents expect of their teenagers? Is it simply that they behave better than Sylvia did? Is it that we don't want them to cut class, lie about where they've been, or in other ways deceive us? The answer to that, of course, is yes, but it is also no. What we really want of adolescents has more to do with the reasons behind their actions. We want them to do what they do for the right reasons. Kegan points out, however, that reasons have to do with the way we understand the world. And for Sylvia to behave differently, and do so for the right reasons, she would have to understand her world, understand both herself and others, differently.

Sylvia has organized her meaning of self largely in terms of her relationship with her parents. If asked to recount what happened this day, Sylvia would probably talk more about her mother than herself, saying things such as, "No matter what I do, she's always checking up on me. She

CHAPTER 13   **557**

Protective Factors
in Adolescence:
Meeting the
Challenges and
Making It Work

doesn't care how I feel. Sometimes I think she'd rather have a robot than a real daughter."

What are we to make of Sylvia? Is she simply a "bad" teenager? An adolescent with no sense of values and headed for trouble? Actually, if you knew a little more about her, you would find her to be quite the opposite, to be affectionate and loving, helpful and polite, and genuinely so in all of these things. If asked, for instance, about her favorite memories, she would most likely talk about the family holidays, the times when they are all together, the big meals, noisy evenings, and quiet mornings with leftovers for breakfast instead of cereal.

The problem is not as simple as sorting the good kids from the bad kids. If it were, we would all have an easier time of it. Sylvia is, with a few notable exceptions, a good kid. This does not mean that skipping school or lying to her mother is acceptable or that her mother should let it pass with no consequences. In important ways, however, Sylvia's problem is larger than what happened at the mall. Her problem has to do with how she understands herself.

Sylvia has difficulty separating herself from her parents, separating the way she sees things from the way she sees them. For instance, in order for her to see her mother differently, to take her mother's feelings into account, she must come to see herself differently, to distinguish the way she is feeling at the moment from her larger sense of who she is, from her sense of self. Only then will she be able to coordinate her own needs with the needs of others. When adolescents can recognize the needs of others as well as their own, and with this, appreciate the obligations each has toward the other, they can step into relationships characterized by reciprocity and mutuality (Kegan, 1982). And this is what most of us mean by being "grown up." Mutuality means that one not only does the right things but does them for the right reasons.

A developmental step of this magnitude, even though we expect it of all adolescents, is not an easy one to take. In order for adolescents to move toward greater mutuality in their relationships, to become full members in the adult community, they need the support of that community (Zeldin & Price, 1995). To change the way they know themselves and understand their world, they must let go of themselves enough to grow into new ways of being.

For adolescents to do something as risky as letting go, someone else needs to be there to hold on. In order to "grow up," in other words, adolescents need to experience not only the challenge to grow but the support that makes this possible. The supports that "hold" adolescents as they take these steps toward greater maturity assume a number of forms. Adolescents are held, for instance, by their families. They are also held by their communities—by such things as schools and teachers, activities and clubs, parks, libraries, recreation centers, and places of worship. Adolescents are also sustained, as they construct a new understanding of themselves and their world, by the strengths within them, such as their temperament, attitudes, and spirituality.

Adolescents need all the support they can get. Not only do they face the normative, developmental tasks of adolescence, each of which presses for a

Research Focus

Confidentiality: Troubled Relationships—"You Sound Just Like Your Mother!"

"There you go again, just like your mother," he shouted, "always changing the subject when things get hot."

"And what if I do," she objected. "Mom and Dad have been married for 19 years—I could do a lot worse."

"And fighting for 18 of them—probably because he never gets a chance to finish a sentence. She keeps changing the subject before he can make his point."

"That's a cheap shot! Maybe we should stop seeing each other until this blows over."

"There you go again. Do you think that not seeing each other is going to settle anything? C'mon, stop avoiding things and talk to me."

Does this teenager fight the way her parents do? Do we inherit patterns of coping from our parents, passing them on from one generation to the next along with the shape of our noses and the color of our eyes? Do parents who deal with conflicts by avoiding them, for instance, have adolescents who use the same approach with *their* boyfriends or girlfriends? How might we find out?

This is a sensitive area of research. To obtain data, investigators must ask adolescents to answer difficult questions about their own and their parents' relationships. Often the answers aren't pretty: petty quarrels, verbal aggression, family violence, failed relationships. These are matters most of us would like to forget, and nearly all of us, if we *do* tell others, want to be sure the information will be held in confidence. How do investigators treat issues of confidentiality? More generally, what ethical considerations guide their treatment of subjects?

The American Psychological Association, like most professional organizations, provides guidelines governing the ethical conduct of research with human subjects. The overriding concern is to respect the dignity and welfare of those who participate in the research. Other considerations follow from this concern. Subjects are informed, for instance, that their participation is voluntary and that they are free to leave at any time. They are also assured that their answers will be held in confidence.

new understanding of some aspect of their lives (see Chapter 1), but they must also cope with numerous daily stressors, such as academic pressures, conflict with parents and peers, and for many, poverty, divorce, and the threat of violence. We will examine stress and coping in adolescents before turning our attention to the supports that "hold" adolescents as they meet the challenges of personal growth.

STRESS AND COPING

Bones mend and cuts heal, but worries fray the edges of the mind. Sometimes it's all one can do to keep from unraveling totally. Adolescence offers no immunity to life's stresses; in fact, the body's response to stress is remarkably similar at all ages. The only thing that changes is the way individuals cope with stress as they grow older. The Research Focus, "Confidentiality," explores the issue of conflict and coping strategies across generations.

Research Focus (*continued*)

How can an investigator keep answers confidential and still make public the findings of the research? The key to this problem is *anonymity*. Investigators code the information subjects give them to prevent the identification of individuals. A common procedure gives subjects numbers to use instead of their names. If an investigator anticipates the need to disclose information, she or he must inform subjects in advance so that they can decide whether to participate under those conditions.

What conditions might cause an investigator to disclose confidential information? Information suggesting that a subject may be dangerous to himself or herself or to others is sufficient cause to violate confidentiality. Threatened suicide or attacks against others are examples. In other instances, investigators may be forced by the courts to reveal information concerning illegal activities. Research on gangs or delinquent activities serve as examples.

Barclay Martin (1990) looked for similarities in the ways adolescents and their parents resolve conflict. Late adolescents responded to questionnaires on the frequency of overt conflict between their parents, on the ways their parents were

most likely to resolve conflicts, and on the way they resolved conflicts with their own boyfriend or girlfriend. Martin protected his subjects' confidentiality by assigning each subject a code number to use instead of a name.

As expected, Martin found that conflict styles are similar across generations, especially when avoidant styles are used. Martin suggests that because the latter approaches do not deal with conflicts directly, needs and feelings will persist. Also, adolescents don't have the chance to learn the skills that will enable them to cope with conflicts when they arise in their own relationships.

Martin also suggests that adolescents may select partners who are similar to their parents in the way they resolve conflicts—for example, those who also use avoidant styles—either because this style is familiar and comfortable or for deeper psychodynamic reasons. In either case, they are more likely as a couple to perpetuate the difficulties in the relationship experienced by their parents than if they were to select a partner who approached conflict more directly.

Source: B. Martin. (1990). The transmission of relationship difficulties from one generation to the next. *Journal of Youth and Adolescence, 13,* 181–199.

What Is Stress?

Hans Selye (1982), a pioneer in stress research, defines **stress** as the body's specific and nonspecific responses to a demand or event. Depending on the event, the specific response can differ widely: shivering when cold, perspiring when hot, heart pounding when in danger. Selye labels the nonspecific response the **general adaptation syndrome, or GAS.** This response consists of three stages. In the *alarm reaction,* initial shock is followed by a mobilization of defenses. Mobilization is possible for only so long, and symptoms such as nervous tension, headache, and irritability soon develop. In the *adaptation* phase, the body accommodates to the additional demands, and stress symptoms diminish or even disappear. These reappear in the final stage of *exhaustion* as the body loses its ability to accommodate further.

Selye refers to the chemical messengers that organize behavior as messengers "of peace" and "of war." The former coordinate behavioral responses when we are not stressed. The latter ready the body for fight or flight when stressed (Selye, 1982). Adolescents have the option of interpreting many situations in ways that would make either reaction possible. Consider an example in which someone bumps into a boy's locker, knocking it shut. The adolescent can either swing around ready for a fight, or he can simply ignore the incident. If he chooses to fight, chemical messengers will flood his body with adrenaline, pump blood into his muscles, stop his stomach from digesting his lunch, and heighten his awareness to all incoming stimuli. His blood pressure and heart rate will soar. These adaptations prepare him for a fight if one should occur, but they are also, to use Selye's words, "biologically suicidal" when called upon too frequently.

Adolescents can also ignore potential stressors. In the above example, doing so would allow other chemical messengers to coordinate the adolescent's reactions, permitting him to reopen the locker, continue a conversation with a friend, and get on with digesting his lunch. The quality of life is determined not simply by the presence or absence of stressors, but by the way adolescents interpret and cope with them. In other words, it's not *what* happens, but *how* one reacts to what happens that ultimately matters, illustrating again the way in which we construct meaning.

How Adolescents Cope With Stress

The above example highlights the distinction between stress and coping. A stressor is an event; **coping** is what one does about it. Adolescents can cope in either of two general ways. Problem-focused coping attempts to change the stressful situation; this approach is primarily offensive. Emotion-focused coping is directed at minimizing the impact of the stress and is primarily defensive. When adolescents cope in the first of these two ways, they are likely to look for additional information or come up with an alternative, less stressful approach to the problem. The process is an active one in which they evaluate information, make decisions, and confront the problem. Emotion-focused coping is *re*active rather than active. The focus, as the term suggests, is on minimizing the emotional damage of stress, not on changing the stressor. This approach more frequently takes the form of defensive measures such as wishful thinking, denial, or disengaging from the situation.

The ways adolescents cope reflect more general aspects of their personalities. For example, Thomas Reischl and Barton Hirsch (1989) found that highly social students seem to cope in ways that utilize their social skills; they seek help from friends, maintain relationships, and continue social activities like studying and eating together. Students who are academically oriented cope in academic ways, such as taking classes they enjoy, taking less difficult courses, and keeping up with their schoolwork. Each type copes effectively but differently.

Coping reactions can also be thought of as a continuum, with repression and denial at one extreme and hypersensitivity at the other (Krohne & Rogner, 1982). Responses in the middle range of this continuum are the most adaptive; those at either extreme are usually maladaptive. Adolescents who repress or deny their problems will usually fail to process or deal with negative information. In contrast, those who are hypersensitive will typically focus only on the negative. Neither approach is adaptive, because adolescents need to be not only aware of situations that are potentially threatening but also able to see means of resolving them. Michael Berzonsky (1993,

1996) distinguishes individuals in terms of their openness to information, whether in coping with stressors or resolving identity issues (see Chapter 8). Those who seek out experiences that are relevant to the decisions or problems they face (information oriented) are most likely to adopt a problem-focus approach to coping. Conversely, those who are relatively closed to new information, relying instead on the standards of others (normative oriented), are more likely to use emotion-focused approaches, as are individuals who procrastinate and do nothing when faced with stress (avoidant oriented).

Ways of coping have also been found to differ somewhat by gender. Susan Phelps and Patricia Jarvis (1994) found that female high school students were more likely than males to use emotion-focused coping strategies, such as seeking the support of others (either to discover what they had done in similar circumstances or to talk about their feelings), finding strength in their religion, looking for the good in what happened, or venting their emotions. Males, on the other hand, were more likely to use avoidant strategies, such as humor or disengaging from the situation through the use of alcohol or drugs. In other respects, the genders coped in similar ways.

Many of the stressors adolescents face occur daily. Those at school take a number of forms, in addition to the expected pressures of grades. Among the most common are aggression (whether actual or threatened), fear of

Adolescents who live in gang-ridden neighborhoods experience a high degree of stress. Some try to cope by looking for solutions to the problem; others try to minimize the emotional damage by joining a gang themselves or by emotionally withdrawing.

theft, and racial tensions. Seventy percent of the students in one survey (Armacost, 1989) said they feared their belongings would be stolen. Nearly 70% mentioned stresses related to the academic track they were in at school, with those in the highest tracks experiencing the most stress. Additional stressors take the form of conflicts with parents and peers, and dating anxieties (Adwere-Boamah & Curtis, 1993; Kohn & Milrose, 1993; Phelps & Jarvis, 1994). Adolescent girls are more likely to mention interpersonal issues, and boys concern with their grades; but more similarities than differences exist in what is experienced as stressful by most adolescents.

The concerns of adolescents remain relatively similar across racial and socioeconomic groups and over time and across cultures (Violato & Kwok, 1995). For instance, Joseph Adwere-Boamah and Deborah Curtis (1993) found that a predominantly low-income sample of African American and Hispanic students ranked the same concerns as most and least serious as did a sample containing mainly European American students who were surveyed five years earlier. For all these junior and senior high school students, the most important concerns were career, grades, and future schooling, and the least important were problems relating to drugs, cigarettes, or alcohol. The fact that low-income minority students place career goals and grades as their highest concerns underscores the importance of specific interventions in school counseling programs, which make clear to minority students all the academic and career paths that are available (see Chapter 10). Despite these similarities in the experience of stress, some important differences exist as well. For instance, many of the situations that nonminority adolescents might find stressful, such as having to take care of younger brothers and sisters, were not perceived as stressful by the minority adolescents. Cultural expectations about extended families and child-care responsibilities rendered these situations normative rather than stressful. On the other hand, adolescents in immigrant families acquire the ways of their new culture more rapidly than their parents do, creating intercultural tensions in addition to the intergenerational tensions that all adolescents experience. (Szapocznik & Kurtines, 1993; Zetlin, 1993).

Positive as well as negative events can be stressful. Being elected class president, making the debating team or the cheerleading squad, or getting the job one applied for are all stressful even though each is desirable. Stress exists whenever adolescents must respond to new demands and events, and both positive and negative events can require adolescents to adapt in new ways.

Learning Effective Coping Strategies

Coping with stress, like most of the activities adolescents engage in, requires skill; therefore, some are better at it than others. Luckily, as with other skills, adolescents can be taught to cope with stress. Meichenbaum's **stress-inoculation training** program teaches adolescents ways to cognitively restructure stressful situations, making them less stressful and improving the chances of coping successfully (Cameron & Meichenbaum, 1982; Meichenbaum, 1988; Meichenbaum & Deffenbacher, 1988). Three elements make up this program. Adolescents learn to identify and appraise stressful situations, anticipate their own reactions, and manage the resulting emotions.

CHAPTER 13   **563**

Protective Factors
in Adolescence:
Meeting the
Challenges and
Making It Work

Appraising the Situation   Misinterpretations easily arise from personal blind spots that can cause adolescents to overestimate or underestimate potential stressors. Overestimates can turn what could have been a harmless episode into an interpersonal disaster, whereas underestimates can expose adolescents to potential harm. Only by appraising a situation correctly can adolescents predict the most likely set of events. Accurate prediction, in turn, puts them in a place where they can better influence the course of events. Appraisal becomes more accurate as adolescents learn to think of alternative interpretations for situations.

Adolescents can learn to challenge self-defeating interpretations. This learning requires adolescents to put their new intellectual skills to use: thinking of all the possibilities in a situation, thinking logically, and thinking abstractly by analyzing a situation in terms of its underlying elements. (These features of thought are discussed in detail in Chapter 4.) As adolescents bring new intellectual capacities to bear on problems, they're better able to revise their reading of ongoing situations and react appropriately. Frequently the most appropriate step is to get more information to find out which interpretation is the most reasonable. Sometimes this step can be as simple as asking the other person, "Did you really mean . . . ?" (Hains & Szyjakowski, 1990).

Adolescents (like individuals of all ages) are likely to make an **attributional error** in which they overestimate the importance of *dispositional stressors* (presumed traits such as aggressiveness or anger) and underestimate the importance of *situational stressors* (such as tensions due to relationships or threats of personal violence). A girl who is dissatisfied with her boyfriend because she sees him as aggressive and angry (dispositional stressors) may think there is little possibility of improving their relationship. By tracing his anger to situational factors—strife at home or hazing at school, for example—it becomes possible for her to think of ways to improve their relationship (McAdams, 1990).

Adolescents frequently commit a second error when they notice only information that confirms their appraisal of a situation, or *confirmatory information*. An adolescent who expects a teacher to be unsympathetic or overly demanding is likely to act in a hostile way toward that teacher, provoking a reaction that confirms the expectation. Cameron and Meichenbaum (1982) recommend that adolescents look for, and even generate, behavior that disconfirms predisposing expectations. The above adolescent might, for example, thank the teacher in advance for her attention and time, thus creating a positive atmosphere in which she will be more likely to listen to the problem sympathetically.

Responding to the Situation   Sometimes the response can be as simple as getting information or advice, or suggesting a talk with a friend. At other times the most effective action can be *no* action, like not shooting back an angry reply to a friend or parent. In most cases, skills related to assertiveness, communication, negotiation, and compromise are involved. Even adolescents who have these skills don't always think to use them. Under the stress of the moment they may not use an approach that has worked for them in the past, or they may fail to recognize which skills are called for. Sometimes, too, adolescents fail to respond effectively, because other, less adaptive responses are more dominant. Nonassertive adolescents might fail to speak up, for instance, simply because of concerns that inhibit assertive action.

The most effective responses are those that prevent stressful situations from occurring. Individuals create, as well as respond to, their environments. This fact makes preventive actions possible. Adolescents can pick up on social cues that bring out the best in others. Adolescents who develop these skills are more likely to bring out friendly, helpful behavior in others and less likely to cause the hostile or aggressive behaviors that typify stressful interactions.

Managing Emotions   Even after successfully handling a stressful encounter, adolescents must still deal with the emotions caused by the situation. Adolescents differ widely in how quickly they get over feelings of anger or frustration. Although not as much is known about this aspect of coping as the others, mentally rehearsing one's successes or failures will either facilitate or interfere with the process of "unwinding" (Cameron & Meichenbaum, 1982; Meichenbaum & Deffenbacher, 1988). Adolescents who have been trained in a stress-inoculation program involving the above three components (appraising, responding, and managing) have lower anxiety, less anger, and higher self-esteem (Hains & Szyjakowski, 1990).

Most research with adolescents has focused on the problems they face or on the ways in which they have been deficient in responding to these. A neglected area of study is that of healthy adolescents who not only cope but who make the world better in some way for others as well (Moore & Glei, 1995). Who are these adolescents and what do we know about them?

BEYOND COPING: CARING AND PROSOCIAL BEHAVIOR

Daniel Hart, at Rutgers University, and Suzanne Fegley, at Temple University (1995), were interested in how adolescents who are distinguished by remarkable caring and prosocial behavior understand their world and themselves. These investigators studied a group of urban minority adolescents, African American and Hispanic, in an economically distressed Northeastern city. These adolescents were remarkable in one way or another for their involvement in such things as volunteer work or unusual family responsibilities.[1] A comparison group of adolescents was matched for age, gender, ethnicity, and neighborhood. The latter adolescents were also well adjusted, attended school regularly, and many of them were also involved in volunteer activities, but not to the same degree. All adolescents were interviewed and completed a number of personality measures.

These investigators found, as anticipated, that the caring adolescents understood themselves quite differently than did the comparison adolescents. They were more likely to describe themselves in terms of their values and ideals. Also, their parents contributed more heavily to their sense of themselves than was the case for the comparisons, for whom best friends

---

[1]The sample was arrived at by contacting social agencies, church leaders, schools, and youth groups.

CHAPTER 13   **565**

Protective Factors
in Adolescence:
Meeting the
Challenges and
Making It Work

Adolescents who
distinguish themselves
for community service
and other kinds of
prosocial behavior
are likely to have expe-
rienced caring rela-
tionships with their
parents or other
adults.

contributed most heavily. Differences between the caring and comparison
adolescents, however, did not appear to be due to any single factor, such as
overall maturity or sophistication of thought. The former did not, for instance, use more advanced moral reasoning or have more complex or sophisticated perceptions of others. Also, because these adolescents were not
followed over time, one cannot say for sure whether the ways in which these
remarkable teenagers saw themselves were responsible for the care they extended to others or whether their involvement in the care of others drew
them away from friends, thus causing them to see themselves less in terms
of their peers and more in terms of idealized figures.

P. Lindsay Chase-Lansdale, Lauren Wakschlag, and Jeanne Brooks-Gunn
(1995) point to the importance of the family for the development of caring. The experience of being loved appears to be essential if one is to develop as a caring person. The research on attachment, beginning in infancy
but extending throughout the lifespan (Ainsworth, 1985; Ainsworth, Blehar,
Waters, & Wall, 1978; Bowlby, 1982), underscores the importance of the
caregivers' sensitivity to the needs of the child and responsiveness in meeting these for healthy development. Children cared for in this way not only

develop a sense of trust in their world but come to believe that others are trustworthy, and perhaps most importantly of all, come to believe that *they* are worthy of being cared for in this way (Erikson, 1968).

Not all adolescents are born into homes in which they will receive this type of care from their parents. What sort of chances do these adolescents have of developing into competent, caring adults? The research of Emily Werner and her colleagues (Werner, 1989; Werner & Smith, 1982, 1992) indicates that the chances are good—as long as there is at least one caring person in that young person's life, someone such as a grandparent, an aunt or uncle, or a sibling to love him or her (see Chapter 2).

PROTECTIVE FACTORS IN ADOLESCENCE

Adolescents are supported, or "held," by many protective factors in their environment. Each of these factors—whether aspects of their homes, schools, or communities—helps adolescents to redefine themselves, to change the way they know themselves, so that the self they bring to their encounters with others will be one that is capable of mutuality and one that can continue to grow.

Families

One of the most important supports in adolescents' lives is their relationships within the family, especially with parents. These relationships can be characterized in terms of two broad dimensions: care and support, sometimes referred to as *responsiveness,* and discipline and monitoring of adolescents' activities, or *demandingness* (see Chapter 5). Each of these dimensions of families has been found to be related to healthy development.

Longitudinal research confirms the contribution of responsiveness. Kristin Moore and Dana Glei (1995) followed a nationally representative sample of children from the ages of 7 through 11 to the ages of 18 to 22, interviewing both children and parents. These investigators found that adolescents who experienced fewer family disruptions, such as marital conflict or divorce, and who had warm and emotionally satisfying relationships with their parents in childhood were more likely to have a greater sense of well-being in adolescence and to avoid serious risk taking, such as dropping out, using cigarettes or other drugs, or engaging in delinquent behavior. Similar findings from an even larger study of over 30,000 adolescents confirm the importance of caring and a feeling of connectedness within the family as significant protective factors contributing to the well-being of adolescents, even when other family variables such as socioeconomic status and single- versus two-parent family structure were controlled for (Resnick, Harris, & Blum, 1993).

Robin Jarrett (1995), at Loyola University, summarizes a number of family characteristics—illustrating the dimensions of responsiveness and demandingness—that enhance the development of youth. Although these strategies are ones that have been found effective specifically in counteracting the eroding effects of poverty among African American families, their

CHAPTER 13 **567**

Protective Factors
in Adolescence:
Meeting the
Challenges and
Making It Work

wisdom cuts across income level and ethnicity, making them applicable in varying degrees to all families.

One of the first characteristics to emerge from the welter of research reviewed by Jarrett, a characteristic illustrating the dimension of responsiveness, involved the use of *supportive adult network structures.* These networks took the form of additional adults who could be called on to provide care. Adults, such as grandparents, godparents, or neighbors, provided resources that otherwise would not be available to these adolescents. The following excerpt illustrates this type of support:

> [Aunt] Ann . . . paid for [Ben's] class ring, his senior pictures, and his cap and gown. Ann did not see this as unusual behavior as it was exactly what Jean [her sister] had done for her a long time ago. She also pointed out that she had been helping to pay nominal school fees for Jean's children for several years. (Zollar, 1985, p. 79, as cited in Jarrett, 1995)

The Research Focus, "Randomized Versus Quasi-Experimental Designs," describes another kind of supportive adult network, an intergenerational mentoring program.

These successful families also made use of *supportive institutions within the community,* such as churches and schools. Churches were found not only to undergird these families spiritually but also to offer activities for youth in which they could form friendships and develop new skills. Church beliefs also foster self-respect, personal discipline, and a concern for others (Jarrett, 1995; Moore & Glei, 1995). Parental use of schools similarly took a number of forms. Parents collaborated with school personnel, attending parent–teacher meetings, serving on committees, and maintaining close contact with their children's teachers. But parents were also willing to confront school personnel in order to ensure that their children received the attention they needed. As one mother explained, "This lady tells me that the principal doesn't have time to look at everybody's case. So I told that lady, 'that may be the case but this is one that he's going to look at.' . . . I was going to the Board of Education and everywhere I could think of to see that Marie could go ahead and graduate" (Clark, 1983, p. 41, as cited in Jarrett, 1995).

The strategies identified by Jarrett also illustrate the second dimension of family interaction: demandingness. For instance, Jarrett found parents to *monitor* their adolescents' activities and friendships, setting limits on whom they could associate with, what they could do, and when they were to get home. "Chaperonage" figured centrally in this monitoring, beginning in childhood as parents accompanied their children as they went into the neighborhood and taking a particularly inventive form in adolescence by having a younger sibling tag along on dates and other activities. Other research, as well, finds that adolescents whose parents monitor their activities by asking where they are going and who they will be with have fewer problem behaviors (Blyth & Leffert, 1995; Buchanan, Maccoby, & Dornbusch, 1992).

Demandingness was also evident in parental expectations that adolescents assume *responsibility for helping with the family's needs,* whether economic or domestic. Thus adolescents might be expected to have a part-time job to contribute to the family budget, do chores around the house, or help with

Research Focus

Randomized Versus Quasi-Experimental Designs: What's in a Name? Communication Across the Ages

Joey was beginning to like his name. He liked the soft way it sounded when Mrs. Thomas spoke to him, even though this was usually when they were talking about his homework. Funny, a year ago he would never have thought of doing homework, or going to a museum with his class, or even to school basketball games. But he did now, and his mom did too, every now and then, when Mrs. Thomas called her. For that matter, a year ago he would never have thought he'd even know anyone as old as Mrs. Thomas. She must be at least 60, he thought, as he watched her coming into the room with a pencil and another piece of pie.

Joey lives in a low-income, high-crime neighborhood in Philadelphia. His sixth-grade class is part of an intergenerational mentoring program in which older members of the community, such as Mrs. Thomas, volunteer time with students, doing things such as helping with homework or school projects, going to games or cultural events, and taking part in community service activities. The purpose of the program is to increase the protective factors in the lives of high-risk children. By working with these students, mentors serve as friends and role models, as well as advocates and challengers, helping to build the self-esteem, confidence, and skills they need to stay drug-free.

In addition to mentoring, this unique program includes three other components. It also involves students in community service, offers classroom-based instruction in life skills, and includes a workshop for parents. The community service aspect of the program enables these students to see how they can help others, giving them a sense of personal and social responsibility and contributing to their self-esteem. In contrast, the classroom instruction teaches skills applicable to students' real life problems within their families and with their friends and with peer pressure. Finally, the workshop for parents helps the students' parents develop more effective par-

enting skills and more positive ways of interacting within the family. Essential to the success of the program are the teachers and school personnel who have been trained in its implementation and evaluation.

Programs like this are expensive—not only in money, but also in a community's investment of its limited reserves of passion and hope. How might one determine whether an intergenerational mentoring program such as this one is effective? Leonard LoSciuto, Amy Rajala, Tara Townsend, and Andrea Taylor (1996), at Temple University, employed a *randomized pretest-posttest control group design*. Three sixth-grade classes per school were randomly selected from all of the sixth-grade classes in schools that were willing to participate in the study (almost all of them). Within each school, each class was randomly assigned to one of three conditions:

1. Students received the complete program of mentoring, community service, instruction in life skills, and parent workshops.
2. Students received everything but mentoring.
3. Students received no intervention at all. They were the control condition.

At the beginning of the academic year, prior to starting the intervention program, all the students were pretested on a variety of measures assessing their knowledge, attitudes, and behavior related to the program goals. All students were tested again with a series of posttests at the end of the academic year. This type of experimental design, because it randomly assigns subjects to conditions and uses a separate control comparison (see Research Focus in Chapter 1, "An Experiment"), in addition to the comparison between pretest and posttest performance, has high internal validity (see Research Focus in Chapter 12, "Internal and External Validity"). This internal validity enables the investigators to conclude that the changes they observe are actually due to the program and not to some other factor.

Because the students are randomly assigned to conditions and each student has the same chance as any other of being assigned to each group, one can be reasonably certain that the three groups do not differ in any systematic way at the outset of the program. Additionally, pretesting students before they begin the inter-

Research Focus (*continued*)

vention program makes it possible to determine whether equivalence has, in fact, been achieved.

Pretesting offers other advantages as well. Pretests allow investigators to assess the extent to which individuals *change* over time. Thus, if some students are responsive to the treatment whereas others are not, pretesting may suggest clues, which can be followed up in subsequent research, as to why some are more responsive than others. Pretesting is also useful when subjects drop out of the program, as is common for lengthy programs. Loss of subjects in this manner is known as *subject mortality* and is a potential source of bias if it is systematically related to the experimental conditions. For instance, poorer students might be least responsive to the demands of mentoring and community service and most likely to drop out, leaving proportionately more of the better students in the intervention group. In this way, even interventions that have no effect may appear to result in improved performance. By inspecting the pretests of students who drop out, however, one can determine whether they differ from the ones who remain in the program. Pretesting also has a disadvantage. It can sensitize subjects to the purpose of the investigation, making it possible for them to figure out what is expected of them and potentially affecting the way they respond to the experimental treatment.

Many intervention programs are not able to randomly assign subjects to experimental and control conditions. Research about such programs is termed *quasi-experimental* because it relies only on comparisons of pretest and posttest performance. A number of problems exist with quasi-experimental designs. Because there is no control condition, we don't know how to interpret the findings. Suppose, for instance, posttest scores are no better than pretest scores. Can we conclude that the program is ineffective? Not necessarily. It's always possible that performance could have declined during that time and that only because of the program did scores remain the same. Similarly, increases in performance on the posttest do not lend themselves to a simple interpretation. Several potential *confounds* exist. These can be due to maturation, testing, history, instrument decay, or statistical regression.

Maturation reflects any systematic changes that occur over time. These can be long term,

such as the developmental changes in intelligence discussed in Chapters 4 and 10, or short term, such as changes due to fatigue, boredom, or practice. *Testing* reflects any changes that occur due to familiarity with the tests. Because pretests usually involve the same type of questions as posttests and frequently measure knowledge about the same subject matter, testing effects are likely. *History* refers to events that occur between testings that can affect the behavior being measured. For example, at the same time as the intervention program, television might run a series of public service spots featuring famous athletes who warn kids against the use of drugs. *Instrument decay* reflects changes in the measures used; these are especially likely when people are the "instruments"; for example, counselors or teachers can become more practiced over time, or they may change their standards in other ways. *Statistical regression* can occur when students are selected for a program because they are atypical, that is, because their scores are either especially low or high. Because no two tests can ever be perfectly correlated, most scores will change somewhat. Students who are selected because of especially low scores will look like they have improved due to the program, but because they were at the bottom of the distribution, their scores could *only* go up. By the same token, students with especially high scores on a pretest would show a drop in performance on the posttest. In each case scores "drift," or regress, toward the mean of the distribution, because that is where most scores are to be found.

None of these confounds, however, threaten the validity of the research of LoSciuto and his colleagues about the intergenerational mentoring program. These investigators found that students who received all four components of the program were likely to do best. They were more likely to react appropriately when offered drugs, were absent from school less, and had more positive attitudes toward school, community service, and their own futures. There is also some indication that mentoring resulted in increased feelings of self-worth and well-being and reduced sadness and loneliness.

Source: L. LoSciuto, A. K. Rajala, T. N. Townsend, & A. S. Taylor. (1996). An outcome evaluation of Across Ages: An intergenerational mentoring approach to drug prevention. *Journal of Adolescent Research, 11,* 116–129.

Continuity and
Change: Identity
Consolidation in
Late Adolescence

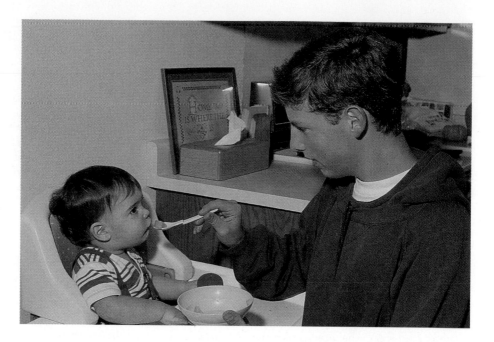

Being expected to
help with family
needs, such as caring
for younger siblings,
gives adolescents a
sense of competence,
an important factor in
healthy development.

younger siblings or an elderly grandparent. Such responsibilities not only contribute to family cohesion but also foster individual competencies and give a feeling of mastery (Jarrett, 1995).

Earlier in the text (Chapter 5), we discussed several aspects to family interactions that contribute to healthy personality development, specifically, to the development of individuation in adolescence. Harold Grotevant and Catherine Cooper (1986) identified two such dimensions of interaction: *connectedness* and *individuality*. The first of these reflects the degree of emotional support within the family, support that takes the form of openness to others' opinions (permeability) and respect for their ideas (mutuality). The dimension of connectedness is similar to the dimension of responsiveness that we mentioned earlier in the chapter. The second dimension—individuality—reflects the ability to function as an individual within this supportive context, to see how one differs from others and to express one's own ideas. There is a paradox to these findings, namely, that it is necessary to be held in order to be set free. Or, said another way, it is necessary to be supported by one's family in order to find oneself as an individual.

In a sense, these findings should not come as a surprise. Mary Ainsworth (1978, 1985) observed much the same thing in her studies of attachment in infants and toddlers. Infants whose mothers were sensitive and responsive to their needs—qualities, by the way, that are similar to the permeability and mutuality that comprise connectedness—were those who as toddlers were the most independent and curious. These were the ones who would be likely to disappear around a corner to explore, knowing that Mom or Dad would be there in a moment if they should call out. That, after all, is what they had learned: that it's safe to venture out on your own, because your parents will be there when you need them. To be held, or supported, by one's family does not create dependency in children. It frees them to develop as individuals.

CHAPTER 13 **571**

Protective Factors
in Adolescence:
Meeting the
Challenges and
Making It Work

Communities

Dale Blyth and Nancy Leffert (1995), at the Search Institute in Minneapolis, compared over 100 communities in terms of the experiences of the adolescents living in them, to discover the ways in which communities support their youth. They defined the health of these communities in terms of the relative absence of problem behaviors in their youth. They found that although the communities were quite similar in terms of their demographic makeup, they differed considerably in the number of problem behaviors engaged in by youth and in the support their youth experienced.

As we saw earlier in the discussion, the healthiest communities were those in which adolescents were more likely to be "plugged in" to institutions within the community. Adolescents in these communities experienced their schools as caring and supportive, were more likely to attend religious services, and to participate in activities within the community. According to Blyth and Leffert, the strong relationship between active participation in religious and other community-based activities and the overall health of the community suggests that such extracurricular activities "may not be *extras*" after all. Their observation mirrors Robin Jarrett's finding about the way that successful families use institutions within their communities.

Blyth and Leffert note, too, that the adolescents who profit most from living in healthy communities are the ones who are most in need of support and who have the fewest personal resources. Even though similar findings have emerged from comparisons of adolescents from widely differing types of communities, such as inner-city versus suburban youth, Blyth and Leffert point out that they also hold true for communities that, on the surface, have few visible differences.

Personal Strengths: Temperament, Competence, and Religion

The personal qualities that adolescents possess also serve as protective factors, qualities such as temperament and outlook on life, intelligence, competence, attitudes about self-efficacy, and religious beliefs. Adolescents with easy temperaments—that is, those who react positively to new situations and who are sociable and moderate in their activity level—are more likely to ride out the stresses of daily living. Not only does their positive approach equip them to deal with problems better, but their engaging ways endear them to others, thus enabling them to recruit the support they need. Possessing at least average intelligence, being able to communicate well with others, and believing that they are in control of, rather than simply reacting to, the circumstances affecting their life (known also as having an internal locus of control) also serve as important protective factors (Chase-Lansdale, Wakschlag, & Brooks-Gunn, 1995; Lau & Lau, 1996; Werner, 1989).

Religious beliefs also are an important factor contributing to healthy development (Brody, Stoneman, & Flor, 1996; Donahue & Benson, 1995). For instance, Loyd Wright, Christopher Frost and Stephen Wisecarver (1993) found that adolescents who attend church frequently and for whom their religion gives their life meaning are also the least likely to suffer from depression. Similarly, Kristin Moore and Dana Glei (1995) found that

Attending church and having spiritual values are among the protective factors that help adolescents weather the stresses of growing up.

greater religiosity contributes to a sense of well-being in adolescents, and Jarrett (1995), reviewing numerous research studies, found attendance at church and spiritual values to contribute to healthy development, even in the face of the multiple risks associated with poverty. Emily Werner and Ruth Smith (1982, 1992) also noted the importance of a strong religious faith to the healthy development of resilient individuals from infancy to middle adulthood.

Love

Finally, one cannot overestimate the importance of being loved. Even though this is a truth we all live with, it is encouraging to see it find empirical support. Chase-Lansdale, Wakschlag, and Brooks-Gunn (1995) emphasize that just one caring relationship in an adolescent's life can make the difference between developing in a healthy or unhealthy way, even in the face of family conflict, poverty, parental psychopathology, and other formidable factors. Similarly, Emily Werner and Ruth Smith (1982, 1992) found that the essential ingredient to healthy development in each of the individuals they studied, who were at risk for one or more reasons, was a "basic, trusting relationship" with someone who cared for them.

Perhaps Urie Bronfenbrenner (1990) summed it all up best when he said what adolescents need most is someone who finds them "somehow special, especially wonderful, and especially precious" (p. 31).

SUMMARY

A central difference between adolescents and adults is how they understand themselves. When adolescents can recognize the needs of others as well as their own and appreciate their obligations to others, they can have "grown up" relationships. In order to "grow up," adolescents need not only to be challenged but to be supported by their families, their communities, and the strengths within themselves.

Stress and Coping

Stress is the body's nonspecific response to any demand. This response, which Selye terms the general adaptation syndrome, has three phases: an alarm reaction, adaptation, and exhaustion. Many situations can be interpreted in ways that increase or reduce their stress potential.

The ways adolescents cope with stress can be problem focused or emotion focused, reflecting their personalities and differing by gender. Common stressors are aggression, fear of theft, and racial tensions. Other stressors are related to schoolwork, parents, peers, and dating. The concerns of adolescents are much the same regardless of racial or socioeconomic group or gender, and they can be positive as well as negative.

Several skills promote effective coping. These can be learned. Stress-inoculation training teaches adolescents to appraise stress situations accurately. Attributional errors, errors that overestimate the importance of dispositional stressors and underestimate the importance of situational stressors, and errors arising from a tendency to notice only confirming information frequently lead to inaccurate appraisals and less than optimal coping strategies. The ways adolescents respond to stress can reduce it or increase it. Skills related to assertiveness, communication, negotiation, and compromise are most effective. Adolescents can also learn to anticipate and manage the emotions prompted by stress.

Beyond Coping: Caring and Prosocial Behavior

Prosocial adolescents are more likely than their peers to describe themselves in terms of their values and ideals, and their sense of themselves is more likely to come from their parents than from their peers. The experience of being loved, of having their needs met by someone in their life, appears to be essential for adolescents to develop into caring people.

Protective Factors in Adolescence

From their families and their communities, adolescents need a combination of care (responsiveness) and discipline (demandingness). Responsiveness can be expressed not only by immediate family members but also by adult network structures and by community institutions. Demandingness is expressed through monitoring adolescents' activities and expecting them to help out with the family's needs. Family interactions that promote both connectedness and individuality also contribute to healthy personality development.

Communities with the fewest problem behaviors among their youth are those where the adolescents experience their schools as caring and supportive and are likely to attend religious services and participate in other community activities. In addition to characteristics of the family and the community, the personal qualities of adolescents themselves are also protective factors. Their temperament, intelligence, competence, sense of self-efficacy, and religious beliefs can help protect them against the stresses of daily life. Finally, research into protective factors in adolescence shows that just one caring relationship in an adolescent's life can make the difference between developing in a healthy or an unhealthy way.

KEY TERMS

stress

general adaptation syndrome (GAS)

coping

stress-inoculation training

attributional error

CHAPTER 14

Studying Adolescence
Research Methods and Issues

Even the best minds can arrive at the wrong conclusions unless they base them on sound observations. For instance, Robert Solso and Homer Johnson (1994) note that medieval scholars believed that a shaft of wheat, if left undisturbed in an open box for several days, would actually turn into mice. If these scholars had only taken the time to observe a few boxes with lids on them, they could have avoided making a mistake such as this. It's possible, of course, that they *did* and still concluded that wheat turned into mice—mice, after all, are very good at gnawing their way into things. Clearly, observation alone carries no guarantees.

The opening section of this chapter introduces a number of research strategies. Research strategies differ in terms of the numbers of individuals studied and the degree of control the investigator exerts. A number of different strategies will be examined in terms of their relative effectiveness.

Developmental research, in which age is a variable, faces the need to separate the effects of age from variables that may vary with age. Three research designs—cross-sectional, longitudinal, and sequential—are compared for their effectiveness in achieving this end.

The chapter moves to a discussion of response measures and research issues, including internal versus external validity, operationalizing concepts, sampling, and ethics.

The last section of the chapter compares the relative advantages and disadvantages of between-subjects, within-subjects, matched-subjects, and factorial designs.

Additionally, the Research Focuses that appear in each of the preceding chapters of the book present the different types of research that developmentalists employ in studying adolescents. Each box introduces a particular research problem concerning adolescents, then analyzes the research procedures that were used. Together, these boxes illustrate distinctions that are basic to an understanding of the methodology used by developmentalists.

RESEARCH STRATEGIES

Research strategies are procedures that scientists follow to safeguard against making faulty observations. Our discussion of these procedures will be organized in terms of two dimensions: (1) the number of subjects that are studied and (2) the degree of control the investigator has over conditions that could affect the observations. With respect to the first of these dimensions, strategies differ markedly. Researchers can limit their observations to a single individual, as in research involving case studies, or they can collect observations from as many as hundreds or even thousands of people in survey research. Differences are equally large with respect to the degree of control. At one extreme is naturalistic observation in which researchers record behavior in natural, everyday surroundings. At the other extreme are experiments in which behavior is observed under the controlled and often highly artificial conditions of the laboratory. Between these extremes lie correlational research and quasi-experiments. Clearly, we are talking about very different procedures in each case. Each type of research carries a particular set of advantages, and each has its own problems.

Number of Subjects

Case Studies   In a **case study,** the investigator studies a single case extensively in order to arrive at a picture of the individual. The case is usually a person, although sometimes it might be a new program in a school, such as a jigsaw classroom (see Chapter 7), or even a school or work setting itself if it is unique in some way. Many clinical observations reflect the case study method. This method presents a detailed picture of the person. Freud, for example, saw many of his patients daily. The richness of the observations this method supplies is, in fact, one of its advantages. For instance, the case study of Grace, the highly gifted 13-year-old who was admitted to college (see Chapter 7, Research Focus, "Case Studies"), was based on extensive interviews with both Grace and her parents and weekly meetings with the director of the gifted program she participated in. Additional input came from sources such as Grace's grades in her college courses and observations of her developing relationships with peers. This strategy is useful, as the case study of Grace illustrates, for studying cases or conditions that are highly unusual and can't be studied in large numbers. One can gain insights through case studies leading to hypotheses that can be tested using other types of research.

Disadvantages to this approach concern the *generalizability* of the findings and the *objectivity* of the observations. How confident can we be that observations collected from a single individual are representative of others?

Interviews and other self-report measures give researchers access to information that cannot be easily observed. Roberta Simmons, shown here interviewing a young adolescent, used this technique in her research into adolescent development. With Dale Blyth and other colleagues, she provided important insights into the social and academic effects of early and late maturation.

This objection becomes especially critical when the individual is atypical. The concern, in fact, has been raised with respect to Freud's theory of psychosexual development (see Chapter 2). How reasonable is it to formulate a general theory of development based on the study of limited numbers of individuals, most or even all of whom suffered from psychological problems important enough to warrant psychoanalysis? Also, because the developmentalist collecting the observations works closely with the individual or program being observed, there is always the danger of losing one's objectivity and reading more into the behavior than is actually there.

Surveys   *Surveys* allow one to study large numbers of people through **self-report** measures supplied by *interviews* or *questionnaires*. In self-reports, the subjects supply the information about themselves; the investigator does not observe their behavior directly. A distinct strength of this approach is the opportunity it provides to study behavior that could not be observed easily otherwise. For instance, Zeman and Garber (1996) asked children and adolescents whether they would reveal emotions, such as anger, sadness, and pain, under different circumstances (see Chapter 6, Research Focus, "Interviews"). The interview format allowed these investigators to study something that would have been difficult, if not impossible, to directly observe—a gamut of emotions, and none of them pleasant. Similarly, information about adolescents' sexual attitudes or practices is obtained almost exclusively through surveys. So, too, is most information about drug use. A weakness to relying on individuals' reports about themselves is the opportunity for distortion, either through deliberately changing information or by failing to remember events as they actually happened. Memory is significantly better for pleasant events than for unpleasant ones.

Degree of Control

Research strategies also differ in the *degree of control* the investigator has over conditions that could affect the observations. Procedures vary from those that exercise no control, such as archival research or naturalistic observations, to those with a high degree of control over extraneous conditions—experiments. Between these extremes lie quasi-experimental designs and correlational procedures.

Archival Research   **Archival research** uses data that already exist to answer questions posed by the investigator. Archival data exist in many forms, the most extensive source being the census. What percentage of adolescents live with a single parent? How many work at part-time jobs? What percentage of adolescents finish high school, go on to college, and so forth? To obtain answers to questions such as these, developmentalists can use census data and need not collect their own. Because census data are collected from large groups of individuals, they have the additional advantage of being representative of the population.

Other archival sources exist in the form of public records, such as birth certificates, marriage license applications, and applications for housing or welfare. One investigator checked marriage license applications for place of residence to identify changes in patterns of cohabitation prior to marriage and found that 53% of the couples gave the same address in 1980 in comparison to only 13% in 1970 (Gwartney-Gibbs, 1986).

Numerous public and private organizations maintain extensive archives; hospitals, housing and welfare agencies, newspapers, and libraries are just a few examples. What diseases are most common among adolescents? Records maintained by local health agencies provide answers. Are males more prone to accidents than females? Hospital emergency room records indicate that they are. Do more adolescents live in poverty today than 20 years ago? State and federal welfare agencies supply answers. For more on archival research, see Chapter 1, Research Focus, "Archival Research."

Naturalistic Observation   Perhaps the purest form of research is to directly observe subjects in their natural settings. Developmentalists using **naturalistic observation** as an approach do not disrupt the natural flow of events; they simply watch and record behavior. Dian Fossey's research on the mountain gorilla of central Africa is perhaps the most widely known example of this type of research. Pure though it may be, this research is often extremely difficult to carry out. Fossey's research illustrates this point well. Mountain gorillas live in the rain forest, making it impossible to observe them from a distance. Yet if she attempted to get closer, the gorillas would notice her and either flee or attack. Her solution was to become a *participant observer,* observing their behavior by moving among them as just another member of the group. How does one do this? For Fossey this meant acting like a gorilla until they accepted her as one. Fossey describes beating her chest, vocalizing like a gorilla, and sitting for hours chewing on wild celery. The gorillas eventually accepted her, making it possible for her to live among them and observe their behavior.

Naturalistic observation is most helpful when the investigator does not know much about the domain being studied. As Fossey's research illustrates, naturalistic observation allows one to discover patterns in the observed behavior. These patterns frequently suggest hypotheses that can be tested with other forms of research. Although it gives richly detailed descriptions of behavior, naturalistic observation does not offer explanations for why the behavior occurs. Developmentalists arrive at explanations only when they can rule out competing alternatives. To do this, they must be able to control extraneous conditions that could affect the behavior. Only experiments provide this type of control.

Erikson's Psychohistorical Approach   Erik Erikson developed a unique style of research that combined the tools of clinical analysis with those of fieldwork. His insights into human development reflected the psychoanalytic training he had received in working with Sigmund and Anna Freud. Erikson applied these skills to an analysis of the relationship between the individual and the group. His observations of individuals from different groups—whether American teenagers or the Sioux and Yurok—convinced him that human development takes place within a social community. His willingness to study individuals in their natural communities contributed to his insights concerning the psychosocial nature of human development. This approach is discussed in Chapter 2, Research Focus, "Erikson's Psychohistorical Approach."

Quasi-Experimental Designs   **Quasi-experimental designs** work with existing groups, introduce a treatment, and look to see whether differences follow. This type of research differs from archival research and naturalistic observation in that the researcher intervenes in, or steps into, the flow of behavior. These designs differ from experiments in that investigators do not randomly assign subjects to the groups. Instead, they work with intact groups. Examples are groups of students in different academic tracks; social groups such as the populars, the brains, the jocks; and so on. Quasi-experimental research is common in applied settings in which developmentalists may want to observe the effects of a treatment but don't have control over all the conditions that might affect their observations.

The disadvantage to quasi-experimental designs is that one can't be sure that differences actually reflect the treatment. They may reflect differences that were present in the groups before the treatment was introduced. These disadvantages are discussed in Chapter 13, Research Focus, "Randomized

Versus Quasi-Experimental Designs." The presence of alternative explanations for observed differences is known as **confounding.** Other potential confounds exist in quasi-experimental research. *Maturation* refers to systematic changes over time, apart from those due specifically to the treatment under study.

Another type of confound common to quasi-experimental research is a **testing effect.** The performance of adolescents enrolled in special programs, for instance, may improve simply because they have been tested so often that they are better at taking tests than others whose performance is not being monitored so closely. Testing effects include both specific and general knowledge. For instance, pretests might include the same types of questions, covering the same information, as those included on tests given at the conclusion of the program. Adolescents enrolled in such programs would then be more familiar with these items and do better on tests including them. Also general test-taking skills are acquired with frequent test taking. Students learn, for instance, whether to guess, how to manage their time, and how to stay on top of anxiety that might otherwise interfere with their performance.

Similarly, a **history effect** refers to confounding resulting from events that occur during the time in which adolescents are enrolled in a program to be evaluated and that can affect the behavior being measured. For instance, network channels might run a series of public service spots featuring well-known personalities who promote the value of a particular activity, such as staying in school or avoiding the use of drugs.

Statistical regression is yet another confound that can occur. This confound enters the picture when participants are selected because of their initial differences, either because they are behind or ahead of others in their group. For instance, students selected for a special program are more likely to have low scores on initial measures of their performance. When these students are retested at the conclusion of the program, the scores for most will be higher, but not necessarily because they have profited from the program. When they are tested at the end of the program, most scores will change somewhat simply because the two tests are not perfectly correlated. This change is to be expected because no tests ever are perfectly correlated. But for students who were initially at the bottom of the distribution, test scores can only go up. Because such a change is expected by those administering such programs, it is usually not questioned.

However, if one were to place another group of students who initially scored at the top of the distribution in such a program, their second test scores would drop, and for the same reason. Just as with the other students, there is only one direction in which their test scores could change, and for these students that would be down. In each case, scores on the second test drift toward the mean of the distribution, because this is where most of the scores are. In other words, to the extent that performance on the first test is unrelated to performance on the second test, chance influences the score a student gets. What score would a student be most likely to draw by chance? A score that occurs most frequently in the distribution—in other words, a score that is close to the mean, where most of the scores lie.

To assess the relation between body image distortion and eating disorders, J. Kevin
Thompson and his colleagues set up an experimental laboratory situation. They created
an adjustable light beam apparatus that subjects adjust to what they believe is the width
of their cheeks, waist, hips, and thighs. The estimated width divided by the actual width
gives a ratio that represents the amount of body image distortion.

Experiments   **Experiments** start with equivalent groups of subjects and
treat each group differently. If the groups differ at the conclusion of the experiment, we can assume the difference is due to the way they were treated.
To be confident about this assumption, we need to be sure that the groups
are comparable at the outset. Given the myriad ways in which adolescents
differ from each other, such an assumption might seem an impossible
requirement.

Is it? Do investigators have a way of ensuring initial equivalence among
their groups? The key to the solution is that the groups need not be identical, only equivalent. Rather than requiring that subjects be the same in
each of the groups, an admittedly impossible requirement, we need only require that they not differ in any *systematic* way. They will, of course, differ
in countless respects, but if each person has the same chance of being assigned to each group, and if enough people are assigned to each group, differences among people will soon be balanced across the groups. **Random
assignment**—assigning subjects in such a way that each has the same
chance as every other of being assigned to any condition—distributes individual differences more or less evenly across the groups.

Let's say we want to determine the influence of a television model on
adolescents' choice of reading materials. Specifically, we want to see whether
adolescents will choose magazines that are described as appropriate to their
gender and avoid those that are described as inappropriate. We can pretest
a variety of magazines and select those for our experiment that appeal

equally to either sex. In one part of the experiment, twenty 15-year-old girls will be randomly assigned to either of two groups. Each group is shown one of two videotapes in which the model describes several magazines. One videotape describes the magazines as appropriate for males; the other describes the same magazines as appropriate for females.

We could then have the girls wait for the next part of the experiment in another room with those magazines plus others on a table. We would record the amount of time they spent looking at the target magazines. Let's say we found that the girls spent more time looking at the magazines that were identified as appropriate for them. Because the only difference between the groups was the way the magazines were described, we could assume that the televised sequences had affected their behavior.

We said that an experiment treats two or more groups of individuals differently and looks for measured differences in their behavior. The treatment assigned to either group is called the **independent variable.** The independent variable in this experiment is the televised sequence viewed by each group. The measure of the effect of the independent variable is called the **dependent variable.** In a sense, the way individuals react "depends" on how they are treated. The dependent variable in this experiment is magazine choice. Which magazine the girls chose to look at depended on the way they had been treated.

We see the experimental approach illustrated in the research described in Chapter 1, Research Focus, "An Experiment." Mary Lynne Courtney and Robert Cohen (1996) wanted to determine whether adolescents who had been told that two boys at play were either friends, enemies, or told nothing, would perceive the boys' actions differently. Adolescents were randomly assigned to groups, differing in what they were told about the boys.

Because subjects had been assigned to groups at random, giving each subject the same chance as every other of being assigned to one of the three groups, these investigators could be confident that the three groups were equivalent. When enough subjects are assigned to groups in this way, the likelihood of any systematic differences between groups is very low, and any resulting differences in perceptions of the boys' play between subjects in the three groups can be attributed to the information they were given.

Correlational Research   The experimental approach described above is often difficult to achieve in developmental research. Age is not a variable that can be manipulated. Individuals come to the laboratory with one age or another; they can't be assigned one. Instead of working with an independent variable, one that can be assigned at random to different groups, **correlational research** works with **classification variables.** Developmentalists classify individuals according to age, or some other variable, and then see whether that variable is related to other differences. The use of classification variables is illustrated in Chapter 4, Research Focus, "Correlational Research." Table 14.1 presents the ways in which experimental research differs from nonexperimental research.

Let's say we want to know whether adolescents become more conscious of the sex-appropriateness of their behavior with age. We could show a group of 10-year-olds, a group of 15-year-olds, and a group of 20-year-olds

TABLE 14.1   Comparison of Nonexperimental and Experimental
Research Strategies

	Nonexperimental	Experimental
Control	Nonmanipulative	Manipulative
Subjects	Not randomly assigned to conditions	Randomly assigned to conditions
Variables	Classification variables	Independent variables
Conclusions	X co varies with Y	X causes Y

video materials similar to those described above. Assume for the moment that we find that sex-appropriate choices of magazines increase with age. Is this because adolescents become more aware of the sex-appropriateness of their behavior with age? They may, in fact, but this is just one of several alternative conclusions.

These adolescents already differ in at least one respect: their age. They probably differ in other ways, too. Their age may be related to another condition that is causing the relationship we noticed. An author of several books on methodology (Underwood, 1957) tells of a teacher in a private boys' school who observed that the best students all had very good vocabularies. This teacher suggested to a colleague that the school should require all students to take a course in developing their vocabularies. After a moment's thought, the colleague answered that he had noticed a relationship between the height of these students and the length of their trousers, but he doubted whether the school could increase their height by lengthening their pants.

We also have no way of knowing, in this hypothetical study of ours, if the relationship we observed is due to age itself. All we observed was a difference that corresponded to age. This difference could be an age change, something we would see in anyone the same age, regardless of their culture or the historical period in which they lived; or it could be either of two alternatives that are frequently confused with age in developmental research: cohort differences and time of measurement effects.

ISSUES AND DESIGNS IN DEVELOPMENTAL RESEARCH

Developmentalists face the central problem of separating genuine age changes from changes due to cohort differences or time of measurement differences (Schaie, 1965).

Age changes are the biological and experimental changes that always accompany aging; these occur in all cultures and all points in history. We assume that age changes have a biological basis (although we are not always able to identify it); therefore, these changes should be universal—that is, they should occur in all people no matter what their social or cultural background. A good example of an age change is the loss of high frequency tones in hearing. If we notice that adolescents in all cultures become more aware of the sex-appropriateness of their behavior with age, we might be willing to say this awareness is a genuine age change. Even so, the difference could reflect either of two alternatives: cohort differences and time of measurement differences.

The only way we can observe age changes is to observe individuals of different chronological ages. The problem is that people who differ in chronological age also differ in other ways, namely, in their social and historical backgrounds. These differences don't always have to affect the way they respond to the measures we are taking, but they might. People of the same age belong to the same *cohort* group. Cohorts are more likely to have similar cultural experiences than people of different ages. Adolescents today live in relatively plentiful times, usually grow up in urban or suburban settings, and can remember no wars. Adolescents born in 1930 grew up in the shadow of the Depression and lived with World War II. Differences such as these appear in all sorts of attitudes and behaviors and can easily be confused with age changes and are termed **cohort differences.**

If we return now to our hypothetical study, we can see how changing gender and work roles might lead to behavior that is less sex-stereotyped than before, with the consequence that older adolescents, who are further removed from these changes, may show more stereotyped behavior.

It is always possible, of course, to test a single group of 10-year-olds and then wait until they reach 15 and test them again, then wait and retest them again at 20. We wouldn't have any cohort differences, but we could have **time of measurement differences.** These differences reflect social conditions, currents of opinion, and historical events that are present when we make our observations and can affect attitudes and behavior. When we study age changes by repeatedly observing the same group of individuals over time, we can mistake time of measurement changes for age changes. It's always possible, for example, that researchers today are more aware of sexist attitudes and more likely to notice adolescents who label some things as appropriate only for one sex.

Developmentalists need to distinguish differences due to cohort effects and time of measurement from genuine age changes. We can evaluate the adequacy of three common developmental designs by their ability to do just this.

Cross-Sectional Designs

The **cross-sectional design** (discussed in Chapter 4, Research Focus, "Cross-Sectional and Sequential Designs") is one of the most common designs in developmental research. This design calls for testing several groups of individuals, each of a different age, at the same time. Going back to our hypothetical study, we would measure sex-appropriate choices for adolescents at each of three ages: 10, 15, and 20. There is but a single time of measurement in this design, but several cohort groups (Figure 14.1).

It is difficult to interpret cross-sectional data, because differences between the groups can reflect either age changes or cohort differences. Until fairly recently, however, we were unaware of this weakness in the design and

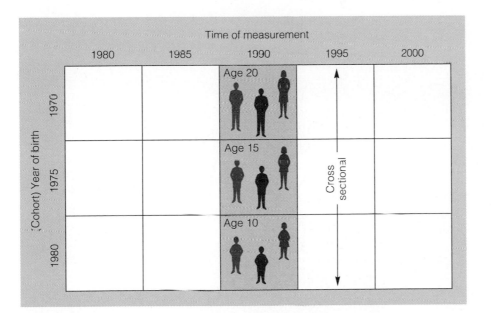

FIGURE 14.1
Cross-Sectional
Design

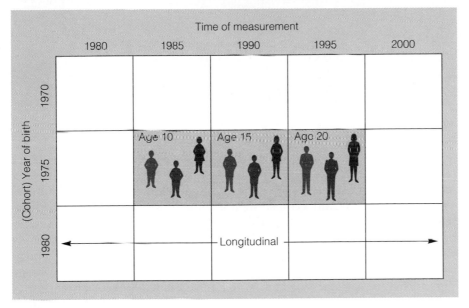

FIGURE 14.2
Longitudinal Design

Source: Adapted from
J. Stevens-Long &
M. Commons. (1992).
*Adult life: Developmental
processes* (4th ed.). Mountain
View, CA: Mayfield.

used it regularly, mainly because it simplified data collection. We can obtain
information about developmental differences relatively quickly, certainly in
a matter of days as opposed to decades. The relative strengths and weaknesses of this design receive attention in the Research Focus.

Longitudinal Designs

The longitudinal design studies a single cohort group of individuals over
time, repeatedly observing its members as they age. Thus we have a single
cohort group but several times of measurement. We illustrated this design

How does intelligence change with age? Are personality traits constant over time? Do sibling relationships go through predictable changes at various stages of the life cycle? To answer these kinds of developmental questions, researchers use longitudinal studies of the same individuals, such as this brother and sister, over a number of years.

(Figure 14.2) when we sampled a group of 10-year-olds, tested them, then retested them when they reached 15, and again at 20. By following the same individuals over time, we can see patterns to development that we might miss with cross-sections. And because we are comparing individuals with themselves at each age, we minimize the problem of having equivalent samples.

This design, too, is seriously flawed, however, because it confounds age changes and time of measurement differences. It is impossible, in other words, to separate the effects of age from those due to time of measurement. This difficulty is discussed in Chapter 6, Research Focus, "Longitudinal Design." The design suffers from other problems as well. Longitudinal research is very expensive because a large research staff is needed to maintain the elaborate records that must be kept to stay in touch with the individuals and maintain information about them over the years. Longitudinal research is also time-consuming. We must wait while individuals age—and there is no guarantee that we'll outlive them.

A more serious problem than either of these is the nearly inevitable loss of individuals with time. People move away, die, or for other reasons are not available for study. This loss is called **subject mortality** and is almost always systematically related to age. Thus, the individuals who remain are not representative of those their age in the population, because the less healthy and otherwise less fortunate are generally the first to leave the sample.

Each of these designs has its own problems of interpretation, which we can see by looking at some of the research on age-related changes in intelligence. Cross-sectional studies for many years charted a marked decline in intellectual functioning after about age 30. Warner Schaie (1965), a researcher at the University of Southern California, cautions that most of this decline actually reflects cohort or generational differences. Our society has changed significantly within our lifetimes, and individuals today have different experiences than those born 20 or 30 years ago. Longitudinal research supports Schaie's argument. When we track the intellectual functioning of an individual over time, we fail to see real decline until advanced old age.

Sequential Designs

A third design, the **sequential design** (discussed in Chapter 4, Research Focus, "Cross-Sectional and Sequential Designs") is the most successful in isolating age changes from cohort and time of measurement differences. This design tests several different cohort groups at several different times. In a way, the sequential design is a number of longitudinal studies, each starting with a different age group, as shown in Figure 14.3.

Let's suppose we want to see whether intelligence changes with age. By looking at the blocks that form the diagonals in Figure 14.3, we can com-

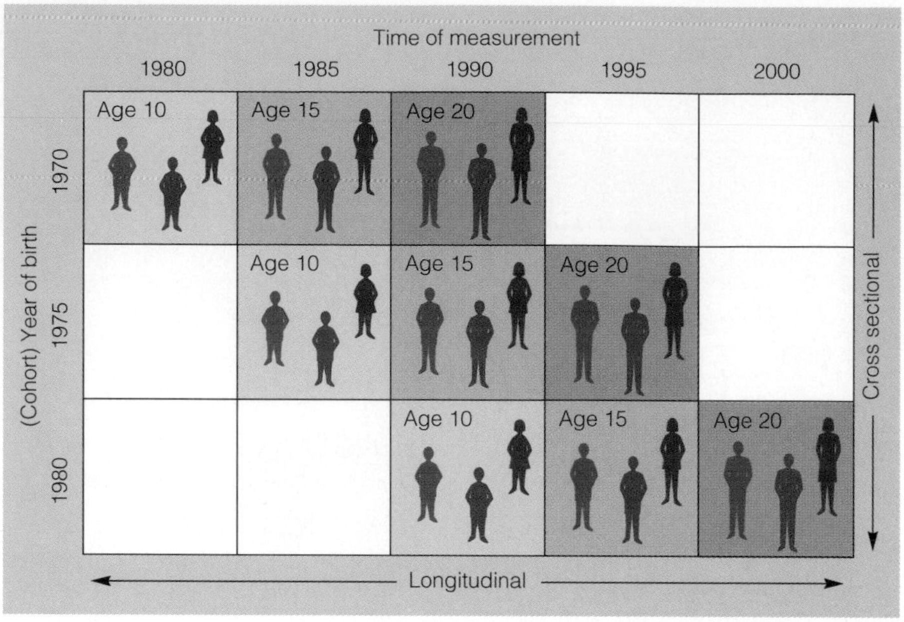

FIGURE 14.3
Sequential Design

Source: Adapted from
J. Stevens-Long &
M. Commons. (1992).
*Adult life: Developmental
processes* (4th ed.). Mountain
View, CA: Mayfield.

pare 10-year-olds with 15-year-olds and 20-year-olds. The means for each of those diagonals will reflect age differences in intellectual functioning as well as cohort differences and time of measurement differences.

By taking an average of the scores for the blocks in the top row, we get a mean for the 1970 cohort. By averaging the scores for the blocks in the middle row, we get a mean for the 1975 cohort. And by averaging the scores for the blocks in the bottom row, we get a mean for the 1980 cohort. Differences among these three means provide an estimate of the amount of variability in intellectual functioning that is contributed by cohorts.

We can also estimate the effect of time of measurement. We can compare performance measured in 1985 (the blocks in the second column), for example, with performance measured in 1995 (the blocks in the fourth column). Thus, by using appropriate statistical techniques, we can isolate cohort and time of measurement effects and subtract these out; differences that remain reflect age changes.

Sequential designs signal an increasing sophistication in developmental research. Many problems of observation and data collection remain, of course, but we are still able to arrive at interesting observations about adolescents.

Path Analysis

Path analysis (discussed in Chapter 8, Research Focus, "Path Analysis") is a statistical procedure that allows one to infer the path, or direction of effect in a relationship between variables representing correlational data. For path analysis, one must have measures for the same variables taken at two separate times. Because causes precede their effects in time, we can use this time difference to trace the direction of the relationship. Specifically, path analysis looks for differences in the strength of relationships according to which factor precedes the other. If television viewing is a cause of poor grades, for instance, the factors should be most highly correlated when the measure of television viewing precedes the measure for grades, that is, the correlation between television viewing at Time 1 and grades at Time 2. The opposite correlation, between grades at Time 1 and television viewing at Time 2, should be relatively weak. By using path analysis, developmentalists can look for causal relationships between classification variables.

RESPONSE MEASURES IN DEVELOPMENTAL RESEARCH

Dependent Variables

All research is based on observation. Dependent variables (discussed in Chapter 7, Research Focus, "Dependent Variables") are the measures researchers use in making these observations. The dependent variable is always some aspect of a person's behavior, feelings, or thoughts. Developmentalists attempt to trace behavior to its causes. Does watching violence on television cause children to be more aggressive? Or get poorer grades? In each case, aggressiveness or grades is the dependent variable. Each is a measure of the effect of the independent variable watching violence on television.

What qualities does one look for in a dependent variable? First, the variable should be **reliable;** random variation should create little difference in a person's score from one occasion to the next. Second, the variable should be **valid.** The validity of a measure refers to whether it measures what it was designed to measure. Early intelligence tests, for instance, often included highly reliable but not very valid measures of intelligence, such as reaction time or speed of finger tapping. Finally, the variable should be **sensitive;** it should pick up even small differences.

Types of Response Measures

Dependent variables differ in the degree to which they measure behavior directly; in decreasing order, these measures involve direct observations, self-reports, and projective measures.

Direct Observation   Observing behavior directly has a number of advantages. **Direct observation** of an adolescent's behavior eliminates potential bias from factors such as selective memory or intentional distortions. Observers are trained to identify different types of behaviors and code them for frequency, context, and their consequences. A disadvantage to direct observation is that it takes a greater amount of time than measures relying on self-report.

What's happening in this picture? Is the scene one of tension and danger? Or of calm and relaxation? In the Thematic Apperception Test and other types of projective measures, subjects project their thoughts and feelings in stories they make up to describe ambiguous pictures such as this one.

Self-Reports   Both questionnaires and interviews provide self-report measures of adolescents' behaviors, attitudes, and feelings. The Research Focus, "Questionnaires," in Chapter 5 describes the use of questionnaires to obtain information about the relationship between adolescents' experience of "flow," or their immersion in an ongoing activity, and their relationship with their parents. Something such as flow is not as easily observed as it is reported. Subjective states such as flow are difficult to observe, so most of our information relies on self-report data. Self-report measures can tap feelings and states through questionnaires or interviews (see Chapter 6, Research Focus, "Interviews"). A disadvantage to self-report data is the possibility of distortion, when subjects deliberately change information (as they might to questions such as, "How many times have you used an illicit substance in the past year?") or when adolescents fail to remember or report events the way they actually occurred, as mentioned in discussing surveys.

Projective Measures   **Projective measures** consist of ambiguous stimuli to which subjects are asked to respond. Common projective measures are the Rorschach inkblot test and the Thematic Apperception Test (TAT). In the Rorschach test, individuals identify what they see in a series of inkblots. In the TAT, they are asked to tell a story about characters in pictures. Because the pictures themselves are unclear, it is assumed that subjects must project themselves into the situation they are describing and, in doing so, actually tell about their own thoughts and feelings. The Research Focus, "Projective Measures," in Chapter 2 describes the use of the TAT to investigate gender differences in aggression. Projective measures have the advantage of tapping feelings and thoughts of which even the individual may be unaware. They suffer from the disadvantage of having relatively low reliability and validity.

RESEARCH ISSUES

Internal and External Validity

Research is a way of asking and getting answers to questions. Thinking of it this way, we can evaluate just how good research is by the quality of the answers it gives us. Are these answers clear and unambiguous? Or can they be interpreted more than one way? Research that provides unambiguous answers to the questions it was designed to address has **internal validity.** Research in which competing explanations cannot be ruled out is confounded. Confounding exists when extraneous variables are not controlled.

A second criterion exists for evaluating any research study: How representative are its findings? Do they apply to other groups of adolescents than those who were studied? Research has **external validity** when its findings can be generalized to other populations and contexts. Frequently the conditions that are necessary to ensure internal validity conflict with those that promote external validity. Internal validity is easiest to achieve in laboratory experiments, in which the investigator has control over the conditions that can affect the observation. However, a laboratory setting is the very type of situation in which subjects are most likely to be on their best behavior—acting any way other than the way they normally would. On the other hand, external validity is virtually guaranteed for research conducted in natural settings, in which the investigator intervenes little in ongoing behavior. Yet these are the conditions that are rife with extraneous variables that can threaten the internal validity of one's observations. The Research Focus, "Internal and External Validity," in Chapter 12 provides examples of this continuing tension in developmental research.

Theory-Guided Research

Ideas for research come from many sources. One rich source is developmental theory, such as that of Erikson, Gilligan, Piaget, or Freud. Theories summarize specific facts under more general concepts that organize our understanding of development. Theories also make it possible to anticipate changes that would be congruent with the theory, even though they may never have been observed. The Research Focus, "Theory-guided Research," in Chapter 10 provides an interesting example of theory-guided research.

Operationalizing Concepts

Operationalizing a concept defines it in terms of the methods that are used to measure it, that is, in terms of a set of operations that anyone can follow. **Operational definitions** make it possible to empirically investigate even abstract concepts, such as the growth of autonomy, popularity, or identity in adolescents. Operational definitions also make it possible for investigators working independently in different parts of the country to be sure they are studying the same concept, as long as they are using the same instrument or set of procedures to measure it. The Research Focus, "Operationalizing Concepts," in Chapter 8 presents an example of a successful attempt to operationalize a difficult concept.

Sampling

Most studies actually work with relatively small numbers of adolescents; yet each generalizes its findings to all adolescents, or to subgroups—for example, early adolescent females, or college-bound late adolescents, or late adolescent minority males. How can an investigator who observes or interviews a limited number of adolescents hope to generalize the findings from that study to adolescents in general? The answer comes from the way the investigator samples the subjects that are actually studied from the larger population (discussed in Chapter 5, Research Focus, "Sampling"). The **population** is the entire group of adolescents in which one is interested. The **sample** is a subgroup drawn from this population. If the sample is drawn at random from the population, we can be reasonably confident that it will be representative of that population. When randomly sampled, each adolescent has the same chance of being chosen as every other adolescent. Consequently, as the size of the sample grows, it increasingly approximates the characteristics of the population from which it was drawn.

Bias and Blind Controls

Adolescents differ among themselves in countless ways. These individual differences are reflected in all types of research. Specifically, variability in subjects' responses that is not due to the variable being investigated is termed *random error*. Error obscures the effect of a variable. Despite this unwanted effect, there is no way to eliminate its presence from an investigation. As long as adolescents differ in individual ways, we will have random error. Investigators arrange their conditions of observation to minimize the presence of random error.

Bias, like error, reflects variations in subjects' responses that are not due to the variable being investigated. However, the similarity between bias and error ends here. **Bias** occurs when the source of variation is *differentially* present in one condition and not the other. These distinctions are discussed in Chapter 3, Research Focus, "Bias and Blind Controls." Unlike error, which simply makes the effect of a variable more difficult to detect, bias actually distorts the effect of a variable. Investigators have only one option when facing the possibility of bias: to eliminate it. Bias threatens an investigation's internal validity.

Bias exists in many forms. The extraneous conditions that threaten the internal validity of quasi-experimental designs all reflect different types of bias. The Research Focus, "Bias and Blind Controls," in Chapter 3 illustrates another common source of bias: experimenter expectancies that can influence their observations. **Double-blind controls** eliminate the possibility of this source of bias by controlling for the experimenter's knowledge of which condition a subject is experiencing. The experimenter is blind with respect to the condition each subject is in. As a result, expectations cannot bias observations.

Tests of Significance

Will adolescents get a better grade in a course if they keep a log of the date, hour, and time spent studying each time they read their textbook or study for the course? One could assign students at random to two groups within the course. The experimental group is told they are part of a study on how adolescents learn and is given instructions on how to keep the log. The other group, the control, is merely told that they are part of a study examining how adolescents learn. Will the simple act of keeping a log improve the grade of students in the experimental group? How can we tell? How much better would these students have to do in the course to support this conclusion? Remember, too, that each student is an individual, and each will learn at a slightly different rate due to individual differences. Individual differences contribute heavily to random error.

To determine whether a difference between groups is due to random error or whether it reflects the variable being studied, one uses a **test of significance** (discussed in Chapter 12, Research Focus, "Statistical Tests of Significance"). Common tests are chi-square, t-tests, and F-tests. If the value that is obtained is larger than a tabled value for the same number of subjects, we can rule out random error as responsible for the difference and attribute it to the independent variable, in this case, whether students kept a

Behaviorist John Watson's experiments in the 1910s to condition phobic reactions in "Little Albert" would not have met the guidelines for ethical research later drawn up by the American Psychological Association. After Watson had transferred Little Albert's conditioned fear of white rats to several other objects, including human hair and Santa Claus masks, he simply sent the 3-year-old home with his artificially created fears intact. (Courtesy of Professor Benjamin Harris)

log. The likelihood of random error being responsible for the difference decreases with increases in the number of subjects in each group. The number of subjects is reflected in the **degrees of freedom.** With larger degrees of freedom, one needs a smaller difference to reject the assumption that random error was responsible.

Ethics

What ethical concerns guide research? Like most professional organizations, the American Psychological Association provides guidelines governing the ethical conduct of research with human subjects (see Research Focus, "Ethics," in Chapter 10 and Research Focus, "Confidentiality," in Chapter 13). The overriding principle governing any research with human participants is to protect the *dignity and welfare* of the subjects who participate in the research. Other considerations follow from this concern. Participants are told, for instance, that their participation is *voluntary* and that they are free to leave at any point. They are also informed of anything in the research that could affect their willingness to participate.

Once participants agree to serve as subjects, investigators assume responsibility for protecting them from physical or psychological distress. After the data have been collected, the investigators debrief subjects, informing them about the nature of the study and removing any misconceptions that may have arisen. If investigators suspect any undesirable consequences, they have the responsibility for correcting these. Any information gained about participants is confidential.

RESEARCH DESIGNS

Between-Subjects Designs

In a **between-subjects research design,** each subject experiences only one level of the independent variable. The Research Focus, "Between-Subjects Design," in Chapter 9 describes an experiment in which subjects read a description of a dating situation in which a male tried to kiss a female while they were at a movie together and, when she refused, kissed her anyway. Some of the subjects read that it was a first date; others read that they were married. The independent variable here is the couple's level of intimacy. Thus, some students experienced one level of the independent variable (first date), and other students experienced another level (married).

Why might we care whether subjects experience no more than one experimental condition? A major advantage to their not doing so is that investigators need not worry that subjects' responses will reflect the effects of any other condition that may still be present. What if subjects assigned to the "first date" condition had just previously read of a similar incident involving a couple who was married? Could we safely assume that these subjects would be able to separate their reactions to each situation? In a between-subjects design, one need not worry about such matters.

There is a second advantage to this design. Because subjects can be assigned at random to conditions, investigators can be reasonably confident that groups don't initially differ before they experience the different treatments. Both advantages address the issue of internal validity (discussed in Chapter 12, Research Focus, "Internal and External Validity"). Between-subjects designs are high in internal validity.

Within-Subjects Designs

In a **within-subjects research design,** each subject experiences all of the experimental conditions. This design can be compared to the between-subjects design above, in which each subject would experience only one condition. Within-subjects designs are *economical;* they require fewer subjects because the same subjects react to all conditions. They are also *sensitive.* A design is sensitive to the extent that it can pick up, or detect, differences due to the experimental treatment when these exist. Within-subjects designs are sensitive because they use the same subjects in all conditions, thus reducing variability due to individual differences. The Research focus, "Within-Subjects Design," in Chapter 11 demonstrates this research design.

Despite these advantages, this type of design has a number of serious disadvantages. **Carryover effects** can occur in which the effect of one treatment is still present when the next is given. In addition to carryover effects, there can be **order effects** with this design. These reflect systematic changes in performance over time due to factors such as practice, fatigue, boredom, and so on. Both carryover and order effects introduce the potential for confounding, in that the difference between treatments can be explained in more than one way.

Matched-Subjects Designs

The Research Focus, "Matched-Subjects Design," in Chapter 9 describes research in which subjects in each of two groups were *matched* for a number of variables, such as absence of father in the home, mother's age, and social class. To match subjects along some variable, one first needs to rank the subjects in each sample according to the matching variable—for example, from oldest to youngest—and then draw pairs of subjects that are the same or approximately the same age from the two samples. Using this procedure, one can be sure that the two groups will be equivalent with regard to the matching variable. If age is related to the independent variable, age is then equated for the two groups; that is, any differences between the groups cannot be due to age.

A **matched-subjects research design** carries an additional advantage. It reduces random error, or the amount of variability between groups that does not result from the independent variable. By reducing random error, one can more easily see the effects of the independent variable. Another way of describing this advantage is to say that matched designs are more sensitive than those in which each subject is randomly assigned to a condition.

Given the importance of these advantages, one might wonder why investigators don't routinely match subjects in all their experiments. Yet like other procedures, matching has its disadvantages. The most serious of these is a statistical one, concerning the degrees of freedom used when determining the significance of the tests that evaluate the research outcome. In designs that do not match, the degrees of freedom reflect the number of *subjects*. In matched-subjects designs, they reflect the number of *pairs*. Matching cuts the degrees of freedom in half. This means that one must obtain a larger difference for this to reach statistical significance. The irony to this disadvantage is that matching is most advantageous when one is using few subjects, because it increases the sensitivity of the design. But these are the very conditions under which one can least afford to lose degrees of freedom. Investigators should determine that the matching variable is highly correlated with the measure they are using before matching. Only in this way will matching effectively reduce unexplained variability and pay for the loss in degrees of freedom.

A second disadvantage is less serious. Matching designs are somewhat more time-consuming to conduct than are those involving simple random assignment of subjects. One must first administer the matching variable and then rank subjects before they can be assigned to conditions. Extra expense may also be involved. A more serious disadvantage than either of these is the threat to *external validity* that occurs when subjects who cannot be matched must be discarded. Any loss of subjects can affect the representativeness of the sample and the ability to generalize to the population from which it was drawn. finally, investigators run the risk of *sensitizing* subjects to the treatment by first pretesting them along a matching variable. Subjects who are sensitized become aware of the treatment in ways that other subjects are not. Because they are sensitized to a variable, subjects may respond to it in ways they might not, had their awareness not been initially raised.

Factorial Designs

In a **factorial design** two or more independent variables, or factors, are completely *crossed,* so that each level of one variable is combined with each level of all the other variables. Factorial designs provide information about the effect of each of the independent variables alone, called a **main effect,** and information about the effect of a variable when another variable is present, called an **interaction.** An interaction exists when the effect of a variable changes when a second variable is present.

The Research Focus, "Factorial Designs," in Chapter 10 describes an experiment testing the effectiveness of two types of career counseling with male and female college students. To illustrate an interaction, we might find that both types of counseling are equally effective for females, but that one type works better than the other for males. The existence of an interaction means that we must qualify what we say about a variable. Is Type X counseling effective? It depends. If the students being counseled are females, then it is. But if males are being counseled, then it is not.

SUMMARY

Research Strategies

Research strategies are procedures that social scientists follow to avoid making faulty observations. The strategies can be broadly distinguished in terms of two dimensions: the number of subjects studied and the degree of control the investigator has over conditions that could affect the observations.

In terms of number of subjects, research can follow a single case, as in a case study, or can embrace large numbers of subjects, as in surveys. Case studies have the advantage of giving richly detailed data that can lead to hypotheses for future research but suffer from problems of generalizability and objectivity. Surveys, which rely on self-report measures obtained through either interviews or questionnaires, allow investigators to study behavior that is not open to direct observation, but carry the risk of distortion.

In terms of degree of control, both archival research, which utilizes existing records, and naturalistic observation, which involves observation of behavior as it occurs in a natural setting, involve no control by the investigator over conditions that might affect the observations, thereby reducing the chance that participants are responding to the particular procedure an investigator has chosen to use rather than the variables the investigator is interested in. Erikson's psychohistorical approach applies clinical skills in a fieldwork setting. These designs do not allow the investigator to make causal inferences concerning the relationships observed.

Quasi-experimental designs involve more intervention, or control, than the previous methods, but less than experiments. Potential confounds in quasi-experimental designs are maturation, testing and history effects, and statistical regression.

Experiments offer the greatest control over possible confounds. In an experiment, the experimenter randomly assigns subjects to groups, which are then exposed to different treatments. Random assignment, by distributing individual differences across groups, ensures that the groups are initially equivalent and allows the investigator to attribute any observed differences to the way the groups are treated.

Developmental Research

Developmental research, in which age is a variable, faces problems of confounding. Longitudinal designs, in which a single cohort is repeatedly tested at different times of measurement, reveals patterns of developmental change but is time-consuming, expensive, and potentially confounds age changes with time of measurement differences. Cross-sectional research, in which several age cohorts are tested at a single time of measurement, takes less time to complete but may miss developmental patterns and potentially confounds age changes with cohort differences. Sequential designs, in which several cohorts are each tested at several times of measurement, allow investigators to estimate time of measurement and cohort effects and to isolate these from age changes.

Response Measures

The advantages and disadvantages of a number of response measures were considered: direct observation, self-reports, and projective measures.

Research Issues

Research is internally valid to the extent that it provides an unambiguous answer to the questions it was designed to address. External validity exists when the findings of a particular study can be generalized to other populations and contexts.

Concepts can be operationally defined by defining them in terms of the operations that are used in their measurement. Operational definitions make it possible for investigators working in different laboratories to study the same concept.

Research Designs

In a between-subjects research design, each subject experiences only one level of the independent variable. In a within-subjects research design, each subject experiences all of the experimental conditions. The latter design is economical and sensitive but runs the risk of carryover and order effects. Matched-subjects designs reduce variability due to individual differences by matching subjects along a third variable, but also reduce degrees of freedom by half, risk sensitizing subjects to the intent of the study by pretesting them, and jeopardize external validity by not including subjects who cannot be matched. Factorial designs combine two or more independent variables and provide information about interactions.

KEY TERMS

case study	age changes	operational definition
self-report	cohort differences	population
archival research	time of measurement differences	sample
naturalistic observation	cross-sectional designs	bias
quasi-experimental designs	longitudinal designs	double-blind controls
confounding	subject mortality	test of significance
testing effect	sequential designs	degrees of freedom
history effect	path analysis	between-subjects design
statistical regression	reliability	within-subjects design
experiment	validity	carryover effects
random assignment	sensitivity	order effects
independent variable	direct observation	matched-subjects design
dependent variable	projective measures	factorial design
correlational research	internal validity	main effect
classification variable	external validity	interaction

Glossary

academic tracking The assignment of students to one of several courses of study in high school on the basis of criteria such as academic interests and goals, past achievement, and ability.

accommodation Piaget's term for the process by which cognitive structures are altered to fit new events or experiences.

acculturation A socialization process by which members of a minority adopt the customs of the dominant group, while maintaining a separate cultural identity.

achieved ethnic identity The final stage in ethnic identity formation; a clear sense of one's ethnicity that reflects feelings of belonging and emotional identification.

active listening A way of listening that reflects the message and feelings back to the speaker.

affective disorders Disorders whose primary symptoms reflect a disturbance of mood, such as depression.

agape In Lee's typology of styles of love, selfless, long-suffering, and nondemanding love.

age changes Biological and experiential changes that accompany aging, irrespective of cultural or historical context.

agency An aspect of mature functioning characterized by assertiveness, mastery, and distinctiveness; the complement of communion.

AIDS Acquired immune deficiency syndrome: a sexually transmitted disease resulting from a virus that attacks the immune system; can also be transmitted through contaminated blood transfusions or from an infected pregnant woman to her fetus.

alienation Indifference where devotion or attachment formerly existed; estrangement.

amphetamine A central nervous system stimulant; sometimes known as speed.

anabolic steroids Synthetic hormones widely used by athletes to improve muscular development and performance.

androgens Male sex hormones.

androgynous Characterizing a personality in which there are both masculine and feminine attributes.

anorexia An eating disorder characterized by severely limiting the intake of food; most common in females.

archival research The use of existing data, such as public records, to provide answers to research questions.

artistic personality types In Holland's typology of vocational interests, individuals who prefer work requiring imagination and creativity.

assimilation Piaget's term for the process by which new events and experiences are adjusted to fit existing cognitive structures.

asynchrony Differences in the timing of pubertal changes within an adolescent, or from one adolescent to the next.

attributional error An overestimation of the importance of dispositional stressors or an underestimation of the importance of situational ones.

authoritarian parenting Parenting that stresses obedience, respect for authority, and traditional values.

authoritative parenting Parenting that stresses self-reliance and independence; parents are consistent, maintain an open dialogue, and give reasons when disciplining.

autonomy Being independent and responsible for one's actions.

axioms The unquestioned assumptions that form the basis of a theory.

barbiturates Central nervous system depressants; most are highly addictive.

between-subjects design A research design in which each subject experiences only one level of the independent variable or one experimental condition.

bias Distortion of the effect of a variable due to research design or researcher expectations.

bicultural identity The process by which minority adolescents identify themselves with respect to the two cultures to which they belong.

bisexuality Sexual attraction toward individuals of both sexes.

bulimia An eating disorder characterized by binging and then purging; most common in females.

carryover effects In within-subjects research designs, the effects of previous conditions that persist when subsequent conditions are given.

case study Intensive observation of a single subject, such as an individual or a program.

centration Piaget's term for the tendency to focus on one aspect of an object to the exclusion of others; thought to characterize preoperational thinking.

cervix The opening to the uterus.

child labor laws Laws that specify minimum ages for various types of work.

chlamydia A sexually transmitted disease, caused by a bacterium, that can affect the reproductive tract, possibly leading to pelvic inflammatory disease.

circumcision Surgical removal of the prepuce covering the glans of the penis.

classification variable A variable, such as age, that cannot be manipulated, as can an independent variable.

climacteric Gradual decline in functioning of the reproductive organs in middle age.

clique A peer group made up of one's best friends, usually including no more than five or six members.

clitoris That part of the external genitals in females that is the primary source of sexual stimulation.

cocaine A stimulant from the coca plant; also known as crack when in crystallized form.

cohort A group of people born during the same historical period or undergoing the same historical influences.

cohort differences Experiential differences between groups of people born at different periods in time; these differences can be confounded with age changes.

commitment in relativism The third of Perry's three forms of thought: committing oneself to a point of view from which one can derive meaning.

communion An aspect of mature functioning characterized by cooperation and union; the complement of agency.

compulsory education laws Legislation making school attendance mandatory for children and adolescents until they graduate or reach a minimum age.

concrete operational thought Piaget's third stage of intellectual development, thought to characterize middle childhood, during which knowledge is gained through mental operations.

conformity The tendency to go along with the standards and norms of one's group.

confounding The presence of factors other than the variable that can account for observed differences.

connectedness A quality of family interactions thought to be important for individuation; it reflects openness to and respect for others' opinions.

conscience That part of the personality that is concerned with issues of right and wrong; Freud believed the conscience to be part of the super ego.

conservation The realization that something remains the same despite changes in its appearance.

constructive knowledge The third of Belenky and associates' three forms of thought in females: an awareness that knowledge is constructed; the ability to examine one's beliefs.

constructive perspective The view that perception is an active, constructive process in which individuals interpret and give meaning to their experiences.

contextual perspective The view that development is influenced by one's ethnicity and culture.

continuity–discontinuity issue Disagreement as to whether the same set of laws is sufficient to explain behavior at all developmental levels and for all species (continuity assumption) or whether lawful relationships change with age and across species (discontinuity assumption).

conventional moral reasoning Kohlberg's second level of moral reasoning, in which moral thinking is guided by internalized social standards.

conventional personality types In Holland's typology of vocational interests, individuals who prefer highly structured environments and well-defined tasks.

coping Strategies for managing stressful situations that tax personal resources.

correlational research A procedure in which subjects are assigned to groups on the basis of pre-existing characteristics.

Cowper's glands Glands in males that secrete a lubricating fluid that facilitates passage of sperm through the urethra.

cross-sectional design A research design in which several age cohorts are compared at a single time of measurement.

crowd A peer group, averaging 20 members and formed from several cliques of the same age group.

crystallized intelligence The specific knowledge and skills acquired through schooling and acculturation.

cultural assimilation A socialization process by which members of a minority lose their distinctive characteristics as they assume the customs and beliefs of the dominant group.

cultural pluralism The coexistence of minority and majority groups within a society such that each participates fully in its political and economic systems while retaining cultural diversity.

decline stage Super's fifth stage of vocational development, in which one retires.

deductive reasoning Reasoning from the general to the particular.

degrees of freedom The number of scores in a set that are free to vary given certain constraints, such as a known mean.

dependent variable The measure of the effect of the independent variable in an experiment.

depressants Substances that reduce or lower the activity of the central nervous system.

depression An affective disorder that may take any of three major forms, all of which are characterized by a disturbance of mood; the three forms are major depressive disorder, dysthymia, and adjustment disorder with depressed mood.

development The orderly set of changes that occur over the lifespan.

developmental contextualism The position that development must be studied in real life settings, thereby facilitating the integration of research with applied policies and programs.

developmental tasks Age-related norms that reflect social expectations for normal development.

dialectical reasoning Reasoning that questions the premises on which it is based when tests of the premises are not supported.

differentiation A process by which one distinguishes or perceives differences not previously recognized.

diffuse/avoidant orientation A style of information processing characterized by procrastinating and avoiding decisions.

direct observation A response measure in which behavior is observed and recorded as it occurs.

double-blind control Research procedure in which neither the researcher nor the subjects know which subjects have been assigned to which experimental condition.

drug dependence Physical dependence on a substance, such that one develops a tolerance and experiences withdrawal when use is discontinued; also known as drug addiction.

dualistic thinking The first of Perry's three forms of thought: the belief that truth is independent of one's frame of reference.

early adolescence That period of adolescence between the ages of about 11 to 15, marked by the onset of puberty, changing gender roles, more autonomous relationships with parents, and more mature relationships with peers.

ego The executive aspect of the personality in Freudian theory, which seeks to satisfy impulses in socially acceptable ways.

egocentrism The failure to realize that one's perspective is not shared by others.

emergence The appearance of new structures or functions that cannot be reduced to earlier and simpler forms.

encoding The process by which information is transferred from one form to another in memory.

enculturation Acquiring the norms of one's social group.

endocrine system The system of the body that includes the glands that produce hormones and those parts of the nervous system that activate, inhibit, and control hormone production.

enterprising personality types In Holland's typology of vocational interests, individuals who prefer work involving interpersonal skills and assertiveness, such as management, law, or sales.

epididymis A mass of coiled tubes near the top of each testis that receives the sperm produced by the testes.

epigenesis The emergence of new complexities in development that cannot be predicted from, or reduced to, earlier forms.

epigenetic principle Erikson's assumption that an internal ground plan governs the timing or period of ascendence for each new development.

equilibration Piaget's term for the balance between assimilation and accommodation that is responsible for the growth of thought.

eros In Lee's typology of styles of love, intense, romantic, passionate love.

establishment stage Super's third stage of vocational development, in which one settles into one's work.

estrogens Female sex hormones.

ethic of care Gilligan's description of a morality based on responsiveness to and care for others;

complements Kohlberg's morality based on individual rights and justice.

ethnic identity An awareness of belonging to an ethnic group that shapes one's thoughts, feelings, and behavior.

ethnic identity search The intermediate stage in ethnic identity formation; exploration of the meaning of one's ethnicity.

exosystem Contexts occurring at the level of the community, such as types of schools and housing.

experiment A research procedure in which subjects are randomly assigned to groups which are then treated differently.

exploration stage Super's second stage of vocational development, in which one begins to make choices related to future work.

external validity The generalizability of research conclusions to other populations and contexts.

factorial design An experiment in which two or more independent variables, or factors, are completely crossed, so that each level of one variable is combined with each level of all the other variables.

fallopian tubes The tubes that feed into either side of the uterus from the ovaries; also called oviducts.

family paradigm The core beliefs held by members of the family about their environment.

fantasy stage Ginzburg's first stage of vocational development, characterized by focus on highly visible aspects of vocations and no assessment of personal qualifications.

female circumcision The excision of the clitoris, the primary source of sexual stimulation, and of the inner labia and sewing shut most of the outer labia in girls.

fluid intelligence Reasoning and problem-solving skills acquired independently from formal education.

formal operational thought Piaget's fourth stage of intellectual development, thought to characterize adolescence and adulthood, during which mental operations are extended to include thoughts in addition to concrete objects.

gender differences Culturally determined differences in masculinity and femininity.

gender-role stereotypes The cultural expectations concerning behaviors that are appropriate for each sex.

general adaptation syndrome (GAS) A three-stage response to a stressor in which the body mobilizes its defenses (alarm reaction), accommodates to the additional demands imposed by the stressor (adaptation), and finally loses the ability to further accommodate (exhaustion).

genital herpes A sexually transmitted disease characterized by recurring outbreaks of itching or burning blisters; caused by a virus that remains dormant in the body.

genital warts A sexually transmitted disease caused by the human papilloma virus.

gifted Characteristic of individuals who place above a predetermined cut off point on intelligence scales or who demonstrate special talents in diverse areas.

glans The part of the clitoris or penis that is most sensitive to stimulation.

gonads The sex glands; the ovaries in females and the testes in males.

gonorrhea A sexually transmitted disease caused by a bacterium.

growth The result of a metabolic process in which proteins are broken down and used to make new cells.

growth spurt A period of rapid growth which often occurs during puberty.

growth stage Super's first stage of vocational development characterized by little discovery about vocations.

guided participation Rogoff's term for the shared activity of a novice and one who is more skilled in which both participate to decrease the distance between their respective contributions to the activity.

habituation Decreased responsiveness to a stimulus with repeated exposure to it.

hallucinogens Psychoactive substances that can produce altered states of awareness, for example, a distorted sense of time, hallucinations.

heterosexuality Sexual preference for individuals of the other sex.

history effect Events extraneous to a research project that can affect the behavior being measured and confound the research results.

HIV infection Impairment of the immune system by the human immunodeficiency virus (HIV), leading to AIDS (acquired immune deficiency syndrome).

homosexuality Sexual preference for individuals of the same sex.

hormones Chemical messengers that are secreted directly into the bloodstream and are regulated by the endocrine system.

hypothalamus A center within the brain that regulates hormonal activity and regulatory activities such as eating, drinking, and body temperature.

I-message A message that tells the listener how his or her actions make one feel.

id The primitive aspect of the personality in Freudian theory, which seeks immediate gratification of biological impulses.

IDEAL The acronym for a five-step approach to overcoming problems of learning.

identification The child's uncritical incorporation of parental ways and beliefs.

identity The part of one's personality of which one is aware and is able to see as a meaningful and coherent whole.

identity achievement The resolution of conflict over identity through the personal formulation of occupational goals and religious and political commitments.

identity diffusion A failure to develop a strong sense of self coupled with a failure to experience much discomfort or conflict over the issues of identity resolution.

identity foreclosure A resolution of the problem of identity through the assumption of traditional, conventional, or parentally chosen goals and values without the experience of crisis or conflict over identity issues.

identity formation In adolescence, a synthesizing of elements of one's earlier identity into a new whole; involves individuation.

imaginary audience The experience of being the focus of attention; assumed to be due both to adolescents' ability to think about thought in others and to their confusing the concerns of others with their preoccupation with themselves.

independent variable The variable that is manipulated in an experiment, by randomly assigning subjects to levels of it.

index offenses Behaviors that are criminal at any age, such as homicide or burglary.

individuality A quality of family interactions thought to be important for individuation, reflecting the ability to express one's ideas and say how one differs from others.

individuation The process of distinguishing one's attitudes and beliefs from those of one's parents.

inductive reasoning Reasoning from the particular to the general.

indulgent parents A style of parenting characterized by warmth and nurturance (high responsiveness) but little supervision (low demandingness).

inert knowledge Facts and concepts that one can recite but not use.

information orientation A style of information processing characterized by actively searching for and evaluating information.

inhalants Central nervous system depressants; obtained by inhaling fumes from substances such as glue, gasoline, paint thinner, and other solvents.

intelligence The ability to profit from experience and adapt to one's surroundings; measured by intelligence tests.

interaction An interaction exists when the effect of a variable changes when another variable is present.

internal validity The extent to which a research study unambiguously answers the questions it was designed to address.

intimacy The ability to share oneself with another; characterized by self-disclosure and mutuality.

investigative personality types In Holland's typology of vocational interests, individuals who prefer work requiring intellectual curiosity, best suited for careers in science and math.

isolate A term for adolescents who have few friends, either within a clique or outside it, and who have few links to other adolescents in the social network.

jigsaw classroom A classroom organized into small, ethnically balanced working groups in which each student contributes a different part of the lesson.

juvenile delinquency Illegal actions committed by a minor.

juvenile justice Legislation instituting separate legal proceedings for juveniles and adults.

late adolescence That period of adolescence between the ages of about 16 to 19 that is organized around the central task of achieving an identity, in which adolescents integrate their sexuality into their relationships, prepare for a vocation, and fashion a personal set of beliefs.

laws Relationships that are derived from axioms and that can be proven to be true or false.

learning disability Difficulty with academic tasks that is not due to emotional or sensory problems and presumably reflects neurological dysfunction.

liaison A term for adolescents who have friends in several cliques but do not themselves belong to any one of these.

libido The psychic energy Freud assumed is expressed through different body zones and motivates much of behavior.

lifespan perspective The view that development is characterized by continuity as well as change throughout life.

longitudinal design A research design in which a single cohort group is followed over time, tested at several times of measurement.

long-term memory A relatively permanent memory of unlimited capacity, in which information is organized according to meaning.

ludus In Lee's typology of styles of love, game playing, uncommitted love.

macrosystem The underlying social and political climate at the level of society.

main effect In a factorial research design, the effect of each independent variable alone.

maintenance stage Super's fourth stage of vocational development, in which one maintains one's occupational skills and position.

male generic language Use of the pronoun *he* to refer to an individual of either sex, and use of words such as *man* or *mankind* to refer to all people.

mania In Lee's typology of styles of love, possessive, obsessive, insecure love.

marijuana A mild hallucinogen from the plant *Cannabis sativa;* the psychoactive substance is THC.

masturbation Self-stimulation of the genitals.

matched-subjects design A research design in which groups are initially equated by matching subjects according to a variable that correlates highly with the dependent variable.

menarche The occurrence of a girl's first menstrual period.

menopause A cessation of menstrual periods in middle age.

mental operations Piaget's term for actions that can be carried out in one's head and then reversed or undone.

mesosystem Social contexts involving interactions of several microsystems, such as when parents meet teachers.

metamemory The awareness of one's memory and of those factors that affect it.

microsystem One's immediate social contexts, involving firsthand experiences, such as interactions at home or in the classroom.

minority A social group, distinguished by physical or cultural characteristics, that often receives differential treatment.

model A set of assumptions about reality in general and about human nature in particular from which theories proceed.

moratorium The experience of conflict over the issues of identity formation prior to the establishment of firm goals or long-term commitments.

narcotics Highly addictive opiates, such as opium and its derivatives, morphine and heroin.

naturalistic observation The observation and recording of subjects' behavior in their natural setting.

nature–nurture controversy The controversy concerning the primary source of development: nature (heredity) or nurture (environment).

negative reinforcement An event that increases the frequency of the behavior on which its removal is made contingent.

neglectful parents A style of parenting characterized by little warmth or nurturance (low responsiveness) and little supervision (low demandingness).

nocturnal emission A spontaneous ejaculation of seminal fluid during sleep; sometimes called a wet dream.

normative orientation A style of information processing characterized by reliance on social norms and the expectations of relatives and friends.

obesity An eating disorder in which one is 20% above the mean (average) weight for one's height.

object permanence Piaget's term for the infant's recognition that objects exist even when they cannot be seen.

observational learning A form of learning through which one acquires new behaviors by observing others.

Oedipal complex A Freudian concept in which the young boy is sexually attracted to his mother, and the young girl to her father.

operant Skinner's term for actions that do not have identifiable stimuli eliciting them, that can be brought under the control of a reinforcing event.

operant conditioning A simple form of learning in which the probability of a behavior is affected by its consequences.

operational definition The definition of a concept in terms of the procedures used to measure it.

order effects In within-subjects research designs, systematic changes in performance over time due to factors such as practice and fatigue.

ovaries Structures within the female reproductive system flanking the uterus that house the immature eggs and produce female sex hormones.

ovum (plural **ova**) The female sex cell, also called the egg; the male equivalent is sperm.

path analysis A statistical procedure that indicates the direction, or path, of effect with correlated variables.

peer group A group of individuals of the same age; a social group that regulates the pace of socialization.

peer pressure Experienced pressure to think and act like one's friends.

penis The part of the external genitals in males that is the primary source of sexual stimulation.

performance-mastery goals Goals that emphasize comparisons among students, defining achievement in terms of one student's ability relative to that of others; to be contrasted with task-mastery goals.

performance orientation A motivational pattern in which students focus on their own performance, using it as a way of assessing their ability.

permissive parenting Parenting that uses little punishment, is accepting, makes few demands for responsibility, and exercises little control.

personal expressiveness A dimension of identity formation that distinguishes between seeking practical from personally fulfilling options.

personal fable The feeling of being special; thought to derive from the imaginary audience.

pituitary An endocrine gland located beneath the hypothalamus that is part of a feedback system regulating the hormonal control of puberty.

population The entire group of individuals in which an investigator is interested.

positive reinforcement An event that increases the frequency of the behavior on which its occurrence is made contingent.

postconventional moral reasoning Kohlberg's third level of moral reasoning, in which moral thinking is guided by self-derived principles.

pragma In Lee's typology of styles of love, pragmatic, rational, patient, and practical love.

preconventional moral reasoning Kohlberg's first level of moral reasoning, characterized by the absence of internalized standards.

preoperational thought Piaget's second stage of intellectual development, thought to characterize toddlerhood and early childhood, during which experience is represented symbolically.

prepuce A thin skin covering the glans of the clitoris or penis.

primary sex characteristics Sex differences in the reproductive system that develop during puberty.

procedural knowledge The second of Belenky and associates' three forms of thought in females: independent thought that is nonetheless limited to a single frame of reference.

projective measure Ambiguous stimuli, such as inkblots or uncaptioned pictures, that subjects are asked to describe; in doing so, they may reveal subconscious feelings and thoughts.

propositional reasoning Reasoning from a set of premises that themselves are not questioned even when not supported by tests derived from them.

prostate gland A structure at the base of the urethra in males that is involved in producing semen.

protective factors Conditions present in individuals, families, communities, or society that promote healthy development.

pseudostupidity The inability to see the obvious by making a simple task more complicated than it is; thought to derive from the ability to think hypothetically and consider a problem from all possible perspectives.

puberty Growth processes, including the skeletal growth spurt and maturation of the reproductive system, that begin in early adolescence and transform children into physically and sexually mature adults.

pubic lice Pests that are usually transmitted sexually; sometimes called crabs.

quaaludes Central nervous system depressants with effects similar to barbiturates; potentially addictive.

quasi-experimental design A research design in which subjects are not randomly assigned to conditions, but preexisting groups are used, causing problems of confounding.

random assignment The assignment of subjects to groups in such a way that each subject has an equal chance of being assigned to any condition.

realistic personality types In Holland's typology of vocational interests, individuals who prefer situations that are explicitly defined and require few interpersonal skills; suited for work as farmer, mechanic, computer programmer.

realistic stage Ginzburg's third stage of vocational development, characterized by exploration of and commitment to a vocational path.

reductionism Explaining complex behaviors by reducing them to their simpler components.

reflective abstraction A process of thought in Piagetian theory in which aspects of behavior become abstracted so that they can be applied in other contexts.

regression Movement from a more complex, differentiated state to one that is less so, which decreases the adaptiveness of behavior.

rehearsal A control process used to prolong items in short-term memory by repeating them.

relativistic thinking The second of Perry's three forms of thought: awareness of more than one frame of reference by which ideas can be evaluated.

reliability The extent to which the same observations are obtained each time a measure is used.

repression A Freudian defense mechanism that operates by relegating distressful thoughts and feelings to the unconscious.

respondent conditioning A simple form of learning in which simple behaviors are brought under the control of environmental stimuli that are associated with biologically significant events.

reverse Piaget's term for the ability to mentally undo or reverse an action in one's head.

risk factors Conditions present in individuals, families, communities, or society that place adolescents at risk for developmental problems.

role clarity An understanding among family members about each one's role.

sample A subgroup drawn from the population that is the subject of research.

schemes Piaget's term for the precursors of concepts; ways of representing experience through one's actions.

schizophrenia A psychotic disorder characterized by disturbances of thought and perception.

scrotum The sac that hangs just beneath the penis and houses the testes.

secondary sex characteristics Differences between females and males in body structure and appearance, other than differences in the reproductive system; include differences in skeletal structure, hair distribution, and skin texture.

secular trend The earlier onset of puberty, faster growth, and larger size reached by adolescents today than in the past.

self-concept The individual's awareness of the self as a person; a theory about the self that explains personal experience.

self-disclosure The sharing or exchange of personal information; considered a primary basis for the development of intimacy.

self-esteem The individual's overall positive or negative evaluation of herself or himself.

self-report Information supplied by research subjects themselves, usually in response to interview or survey questions.

semen A milky white fluid in which sperm are suspended.

seminal vesicles Structures within the male reproductive system in which sperm are stored.

sensitivity The extent to which the dependent variable can pick up very small differences due to the independent variable.

sensorimotor thought Piaget's first stage of intellectual development, assumed to characterize infancy, during which knowledge is based on perception and reflexes.

sensory memory A brief memory, usually lasting for less than a second, that preserves information during processing.

sequential design A research design in which several different cohort groups are tested at several times of measurement; essentially, a number of longitudinal studies, each starting with a different age group.

sex differences Biological and physiological differences distinguishing the sexes.

sexual dimorphism The physical differences that distinguish adult females and males.

sexually transmitted disease (STD) An infection that is spread through sexual contact.

shaft The part of the clitoris or penis that becomes erect during sexual stimulation.

short-term memory A brief memory, limited in capacity to about seven items.

smegma A thick secretion that collects around the glans and under the prepuce.

social competence Accurately assessing and maintaining a social encounter.

social personality types In Holland's typology of vocational interests, individuals who prefer work involving them with people, such as counseling or teaching.

social understanding Assumed to develop gradually with the ability to assume another's perspective and eventually to coordinate one's own with others' perspectives.

sperm The male sex cell; the female equivalent is the ovum.

spermarche A boy's first ejaculation of seminal fluid.

stage A level of development that is assumed to be qualitatively different from the earlier level from which it evolves. Stages are assumed to occur in a fixed sequence and to occur universally within a species.

statistical regression A potential confound in quasi-experimental research in which extreme pretest scores drift toward the mean of the posttest distribution.

status offenses Behaviors that are illegal when engaged in by minors but legal for adults, such as truancy and drinking alcohol.

stimulants Substances that excite the central nervous system.

storage In Lee's typology of styles of love, companionate love based on friendship.

stress The body's specific and nonspecific responses to a demand or stimulus that disrupts its balance.

stress-inoculation training A coping strategy that teaches ways to cognitively restructure stressful situations by identifying the stressful elements, anticipating one's reactions, and managing the emotions they occasion.

structural analytical thinking A stage of cognitive development characterized by the ability to relate two or more systems of thought.

subject mortality In longitudinal studies, the loss of subjects over time.

subjective knowledge The first of Belenky and associates' three forms of thought in females: covert examination of issues while maintaining a surface conformity to traditional ideas.

superego The aspect of the personality in Freudian theory that represents the internalized standards and values of society.

syphilis A sexually transmitted disease, caused by a bacterium, that can also be transmitted through blood transfusions or from a pregnant woman to her fetus; progresses over several stages.

task orientation A motivational pattern in which students focus on the task they are learning and work to increase their mastery and competence.

task-mastery goals Goals that emphasize individual improvement, mastery of the material, and intellectual development; to be contrasted with performance-mastery goals.

tentative stage Ginzburg's second stage of vocational development, in which vocational choice is directed more by interests than capacities.

test of significance Use of a statistical table to determine whether a difference in scores between experimental groups is due to random error or to the effects of the independent variable.

testes Structures within the male reproductive system contained in the scrotum that produce sperm and male sex hormones.

testing effect Knowledge and skills acquired by taking similar tests over the course of a research project; a potential confound in research.

theory A set of testable statements derived from the axioms of a model.

time of measurement differences Differences due to social conditions, currents of opinion, and historical events that can affect observations in longitudinal research; such differences are confounded with age changes.

tranquilizers Central nervous system depressants; potentially addictive.

unexamined ethnic identity The initial stage in ethnic identity formation; a lack of awareness of the issues related to one's ethnicity; a simple internalization of the values of the dominant culture.

urethra The urinary canal, leading from the bladder to the urethral opening.

uterus A muscular enclosure at the top of the vagina that holds the fetus during pregnancy.

vagina The muscular tube in females leading from the labia at its opening to the uterus.

validity The extent to which the dependent variable measures what it was designed to measure.

vas deferens Long coiled tubes that carry sperm to the seminal vesicles, where they are stored.

WAIS-R An intelligence scale for adults that is individually administered.

within-subjects design A research design in which each subject experiences all levels of the independent variable.

you-message A message communicating what you think of another person.

youth An age group spanning the years from early adolescence to early adulthood.

zone of proximal development Vygotsky's term for the distance separating a novice's performance from what that performance might optimally be; for individuals to profit from working with those who are more skilled, their performance must already approximate that of the other person.

REFERENCES

Aboud, F. E. (1987). The development of ethnic self-identification and attitudes. In J. S. Phinney & M. J. Rotheram (Eds.), *Children's ethnic socialization,* Beverly Hills, CA: Sage.

Adams-Price, C., & Greene, A. L. (1990). Secondary attachments and adolescent self-concept. *Sex Roles, 22,* 187–198.

Adelson, J., & Doehrman, M. J. (1980). The psychodynamic approach to adolescence. In J. Adelson (Ed.), *Handbook of adolescence.* New York: Wiley.

Adwere-Boamah, J., & Curtis, D. A. (1993). A confirmatory factor analysis of a four-factor model of adolescent concerns revisited. *Journal of Youth and Adolescence, 22,* 297–312.

Agnew, R., & Peters, A. A. (1986). The techniques of neutralization: An analysis of predisposing and situational factors. *Criminal Justice and Behavior, 13,* 81–97.

Aiken, L. R. (1987). *Assessment of intellectual functioning.* Boston: Allyn & Bacon.

Ainsworth, M. (1985). Attachments across the lifespan. *Bulletin of the New York Academy of Medicine, 61,* 791–812.

Ainsworth, M., Bleher, M. C., Waters, E., & Wall, S. (1978). *Patterns of attachment: A psychological study of the strange situation.* Hillsdale, NJ: Erlbaum.

Aitken, D., & Chaplin, J. (1990). Sex miseducation. *Family Therapy Networker, 14,* 24–25.

Alfieri, T., Ruble, D. N., & Higgins, E. T. (1996). Gender stereotypes during adolescence: Developmental changes and the transition to junior high school. *Developmental Psychology, 32,* 1129–1137.

Allen, B. P. (1995). Gender stereotypes are not accurate: A replication of Martin (1987) using diagnostic vs. self-report and behavioral criteria. *Sex Roles, 32,* 583–600.

Allen, J. P., Weissberg, R. P., & Hawkins, J. A. (1989). The relation between values and social competence in early adolescence. *Developmental Psychology, 25,* 458–464.

Ammons, P., & Stinnett, N. (1980). The vital marriage: A closer look. *Family Relations, 29,* 37–42.

Anastasi, A. (1988). *Psychological testing* (6th ed.). New York: Macmillan.

Ansuini, C. G., Fiddler-Woite, J., & Woite R. S. (1996). The source, accuracy, and impact of initial sexuality information on lifetime wellness. *Adolescence, 31,* 283–289.

Apter, D., & Volko, R. (1977). Serum pregnenolone, progesterone, 17-hydroxyprogesterone, testosterone and 5 alpha. *Journal of Clinical Endocrinology and Metabolism, 45,* 1039–1048.

Arbona, C. (1989). Hispanic employment and the Holland typology of work. *Career Development Quarterly, 37,* 257–268.

Arbuthnut, J., Gordon, D. A., & Jurkovic, G. J. (1987). Personality. In H. C. Quay (Ed.), *Handbook of juvenile delinquency.* New York: Wiley.

Archer, S. L. (1985). Career and/or family: The identity process for adolescent girls. *Youth and Society, 16,* 289–314.

Archer, S. L. (1989a). Gender differences in identity development: Issues of process, domain, and timing. *Journal of Adolescence, 12,* 117–138.

Archer, S. L. (1989b). The status of identity: Reflections on the need for intervention. *Journal of Adolescence, 12,* 345–359.

Archer, S. L. (1992). A feminist's approach to identity research. In G. R. Adams, T. P. Gullotta, & R. Montemayor (Eds.), *Adolescent identity formation.* Newbury Park, CA: Sage.

Archart, D. M., & Smith, P. H. (1990). Identity in adolescence: Influences of dysfunction and psychosocial task issues. *Journal of Youth and Adolescence, 19,* 63–72.

Arey, L. B. (1956). *Developmental anatomy.* Philadelphia: Saunders.

Aries, P. (1962). *Centuries of childhood.* New York: Knopf.

Armacost, R. L. (1989). Perceptions of stressors by high school students. *Journal of Adolescent Research, 4,* 443–461.

Armistead, L., Wierson, M., & Forehand, R. (1990). Adolescents and maternal employment: Is it harmful for a young adolescent to have an employed mother? *Journal of Early Adolescence, 10,* 260–278.

Arnett, J. J., & Taber, S. (1994). Adolescence

terminable and interminable: When does adolescence end? *Journal of Youth and Adolescence, 23,* 517–537.

Artman, L., & Cahan, S. (1993). Schooling and the development of transitive inference. *Developmental Psychology, 29,* 753–759.

Asher, S. R. (1983). Social competence and peer status: Recent advances and future directions. *Child Development, 54,* 1427–1434.

Assh, S. D., & Byers, E. S. (1990). Effects of behavioral exchanges and cognitions on the relationship satisfaction of dating and married persons. *Canadian Journal of Behavioral Science, 22,* 223–235.

Auslander, B. A., & Dunham, R. M. (1996). Bulimia and the diffusion status of ego identity formation: Similarities of the empirical descriptors of self and parent. *Journal of Adolescence, 19,* 333–338.

Bahr, H. M. (1980). Changes in family life in Middletown, 1924–77. *Public Opinion Quarterly, 44,* 35–52.

Bailey, J. M., & Pillard, R. C. (1991). A genetic study of male sexual orientation. *Archives of General Psychiatry, 48,* 1089–1096.

Bailey, J. M., Pillard, R. C., Neale, M. C., & Agyei, Y. (1993). Heritable factors influence sexual orientation in women. *Archives of General Psychiatry, 50,* 217–223.

Bakan, D. (1966). *The duality of human existence.* Boston: Beacon Press.

Bakan, D. (1971). Adolescence in America: From idea to social fact. *Daedalus, 100,* 979–995.

Bandura, A. (1977). *Social learning theory.* Morristown, NJ: General Learning Press.

Bandura, A. (1980). Self-referent thought: A developmental analysis of self-efficacy. In J. H. Flavell & L. D. Ross (Eds.), *Cognitive social development: Frontiers and possible futures.* New York: Cambridge University Press.

Bandura, A. (1989). Regulation of cognitive processes through perceived self-efficacy. *Developmental Psychology, 25,* 729–735.

Bandura, A., Ross, D., & Ross, S. A. (1963). Imitation of film-mediated aggressive models. *Journal of Abnormal and Social Psychology, 66,* 3–11.

Banks, C. A. McGee. (1993). Restructuring schools for equity: What we have learned in two decades. *Phi Delta Kappan, 75,* 42–48.

Banks, J. A. (1993). Multicultural education: Development, dimensions, and challenges. *Phi Delta Kappan, 75,* 22–28.

Bardwick, J. M., & Douvan, E. (1971). Ambivalence: The socialization of women. In V. Gornick & B. K. Moran (Eds.), *Women in sexist society.* New York: Basic Books.

Barkley, T. J., & Procidano, M. E. (1989). College-age children of divorce: Are effects evident in early adulthood? *Journal of College Student Psychotherapy, 4,* 77–87.

Baron, J. B., & Sternberg, R. J. (1987). *Teaching thinking skills: Theory and practice.* New York: Freeman.

Barrera, M., Jr., Chassin, L., & Rogosch, F. (1993). Effects of social support and conflict on adolescent children of alcoholic and nonalcoholic fathers. *Journal of Personality and Social Psychology, 64,* 602–612.

Barth, R. P., Fetro, J. V., Leland, N., & Volkan, K. (1992). Preventing adolescent pregnancy with social and cognitive skills. *Journal of Adolescent Research, 7,* 208–232.

Bartle, S. E., Anderson, S. A., & Sabatelli, R. M. (1989). A model of parenting style, adolescent individuation and adolescent self-esteem: Preliminary findings. *Journal of Adolescent Research, 4,* 283–298.

Basseches, M. (1984). *Dialectical thinking and adult development.* Norwood, NJ: Ablex.

Bassok, M. (1990). Transfer of domain-specific problem-solving procedures. *Journal of Experimental Psychology: Learning, Memory, and Cognition, 16,* 522–533.

Bassok, M., & Holyoak, K. J. (1989). Interdomain transfer between isomorphic topics in algebra and physics. *Journal of Experimental Psychology: Learning, Memory, and Cognition, 15,* 153–166.

Bauman, K. E., & Fisher, L. A. (1986). On the measurement of friend behavior in research on friend influence and selection: Findings from longitudinal studies of adolescent smoking and drinking. *Journal of Youth and Adolescence, 15,* 345–353.

Baumeister, L. M., Flores, E., & Marin, B. V. (1995). Sex information given to Latina adolescents by parents. *Health Education Research, 10,* 233–239.

Baumrind, D. (1967). Child care practices anteceding three patterns of pre-school behavior. *Genetic Psychology Monographs, 75,* 43–88.

Baumrind, D. (1971). Current patterns of parental authority. *Developmental Psychology Monographs, 4,* 1–103.

Baumrind, D. (1986). Sex differences in moral reasoning: Response to Walker's (1984) conclusion that there are none. *Child Development, 57,* 511–521.

Baumrind, D. (1991a). The influence of parenting style on adolescent competence and substance use. *Journal of Early Adolescence, 11,* 56–95.

Baumrind, D. (1991b). Effective parenting during

the early adolescent transition. In P. A. Cowan & E. M. Heatherington (Eds.), *Family transitions* (pp. 111–164). Hillsdale, NJ: Erlbaum.

Baumrind, D. (1993). The average expectable environment is not good enough: A response to Scarr. *Child Development, 64,* 1199–1217.

Beentjes, J. W. J., & van der Boort, T. S. A. (1993). Television viewing versus reading: Mental effort, retention, and inferential learning. *Communication Education, 42,* 191–205.

Belenky, M. F., Clinchy, B. M., Goldberger, N. R., & Tarule, J. M. (1986). *Women's ways of knowing.* New York: Basic Books.

Bell, D. C., & Bell, L. G. (1983). Parental validation and support in the development of adolescent daughters. In H. D. Grotevant & C. R. Cooper (Eds.), *Adolescent development in the family.* San Francisco: Jossey-Bass.

Bem, S. L. (1974). The measurement of psychological androgyny. *Journal of Consulting and Clinical Psychology, 42,* 155–162.

Benbow, C. P., & Stanley, J. C. (1980). Sex differences in mathematical ability: Fact or artifact? *Science, 210,* 1262–1264.

Benbow, C. P., & Stanley, J. C. (1982). Consequences in high school and college of sex differences in mathematical reasoning ability: A longitudinal perspective. *American Educational Research Journal, 19,* 598–622.

Benbow, C. P., & Stanley, J. C. (1983). Sex differences in mathematical reasoning ability: More facts. *Science, 222,* 1029–1031.

Benda, B. B., & DiBlasio, F. A. (1994). An integration of theory: Adolescent sexual contacts. *Journal of Youth and Adolescence, 23,* 403–420.

Benin, M. H., & Edwards, D. A. (1990). Adolescents' chores: The difference between dual- and single-earner families. *Journal of Marriage and the Family, 52,* 361–373.

Benson, P. L., & Donohue, M. J. (1989). Ten-year trends in at-risk behaviors: A national study of black adolescents. *Journal of Adolescent Research, 4,* 125–139.

Berg, C. (1989). Knowledge of strategies of dealing with everyday problems from childhood through adolescence. *Developmental Psychology, 25,* 607–618.

Berman, A. L., & Jobes, D. A. (1991). *Adolescent suicide: Assessment and intervention.* Washington, DC: American Psychological Association.

Berndt, T. J. (1982). The features and effects of friendships in early adolescence. *Child Development, 53,* 1447–1461.

Berzonsky, M. D. (1989). Identity style: Conceptualization and measurement. *Journal of Adolescent Research, 4,* 268–282.

Berzonsky, M. D. (1992). A process perspective on identity and stress management. In G. R. Adams, T. P. Gullotta, & R. Montemayor (Eds.), *Adolescent identity formation.* Newbury Park, CA: Sage.

Berzonsky, M. D. (1993). Identity style, gender, and social cognitive reasoning. *Journal of Adolescent Research, 8,* 289–296.

Berzonsky, M. D. & Ferrari, J. R. (1996). Identity orientation and decisional strategies. *Personality and Individual Differences, 20,* 597–606.

Betancourt, H., & Lopez, S. R. (1993). The study of culture, ethnicity, and race in American psychology. *American Psychologist, 48,* 629–637.

Bettelheim, B. (1961). The problem of generations. In E. Erikson (Ed.), *The challenge of youth.* New York: Doubleday.

Bettes, B. A., Dusenbury, L., Kerner, J., James-Ortiz, S., & Botvin, G. J. (1990). Ethnicity and psychosocial factors in alcohol and tobacco use in adolescence. *Child Development, 61,* 557–565.

Betz, N. E., Harmon, L. W., & Borgen, F. H. (1996). The relationships of self-efficacy for the Holland themes to gender, occupational group membership, and vocational interests. *Journal of Counseling Psychology, 43,* 90–98.

Bieber, I. (1962). *Homosexuality: A psychoanalytic study.* New York: Basic Books.

Bird, G. W., & Kemerait, L. N. (1990). Stress among early adolescents in two-earner families. *Journal of Early Adolescence, 1,* 344–365.

Bjorklund, D. F. (1989). *Children's thinking.* Pacific Grove, CA: Brooks/Cole.

"Blacks in college: Trend reverses." (1990, April 17). *Los Angeles Times.*

Bloch, D. P. (1989). Using career information with dropouts and at-risk youth. *Career Development Quarterly, 38,* 160–171.

Block, J. H. (1978). Another look at sex differentiation in the socialization behaviors of mothers and fathers. In J. Sherman & F. Denmark (Eds.), *Psychology of women: Future directions of research.* New York: Psychological Dimensions.

Blos, P. (1967). The second individuation process of adolescence. In R. S. Eissler et al. (Eds.), *Psychoanalytic study of the child* (Vol. 22). New York: International Universities Press.

Blos, P. (1979). *The adolescent passage.* New York: International Universities Press.

Blumenthal, S. J., & Kupfer, D. J. (1988). Overview of early detection and treatment strategies for suicidal behavior in young people. *Journal of Youth and Adolescence, 17,* 1–23.

Blyth, D. A., & Leffert, N. (1995). Communities as contexts for adolescent development: An empirical analysis. *Journal of Adolescent Research, 10,* 64–87.

Bolognini, M., Plancherel, B., Bettschart, W., & Halfon, O. (1996). Self-esteem and mental health in early adolescence: Development and gender differences. *Journal of Adolescence, 19,* 233–245.

Bolton, I. M. (1989). Perspectives of youth on preventive intervention strategies. *Report of the Secretary's Task Force on Youth Suicide* (Vol. 3). Washington, DC: U.S. Government Printing Office.

Bosma, H. A., Jackson, S. E., Zijsling, D. H., Zani, B., Cicognani, E., Xerri, M. L., Honess, T. M., & Charman, L. (1996). Who has the final say? Decisions on adolescent behavior within the family. *Journal of Adolescence, 19,* 277–291.

Boster, J. S., & Johnson, J. C. (1989). Form or function: A comparison of expert and novice judgments of similarity among fish. *American Anthropologist, 91,* 866–889.

Bourne, E. (1978a). The state of research on ego identity: A review and appraisal. Part I. *Journal of Youth and Adolescence, 7,* 223–257.

Bourne, E. (1978b). The state of research on ego identity: A review and appraisal. Part II. *Journal of Youth and Adolescence, 7,* 371–392.

Bowlby, J. (1982). *Attachment: Attachment and loss* (Vol. 1). New York: Basic Books.

Boyer, E. (1983). *High school: A report on secondary education in America.* New York: Harper & Row.

Boyes, M. C., & Chandler, M. (1992). Cognitive development, epistemic doubt, and identity formation in adolescence. *Journal of Youth and Adolescence, 21,* 277–304.

Bransford, J. D., Stein, B. S., Shelton, T. S., & Owings, R. A. (1981). Cognition and adaptation: The importance of learning to learn. In J. Harvey (Ed.), *Cognition, social behavior and the environment.* Hillsdale, NJ: Erlbaum.

Bransford, J. D., Vye, N. J., Adams, L. T., & Perfetto, G. A. (1989). Learning skills and the acquisition of knowledge. In A. Lesgold & R. Glaser (Eds.), *Foundations for a psychology of education.* Hillsdale, NJ: Erlbaum.

Brent, D. A., Perper, J. A., Goldstein, C. E., Kolko, D. J., Allan, M. J., Allman, C. J., & Zelenak, J. P. (1988). Risk factors for adolescent suicide: A comparison of adolescent suicide victims with suicidal in-patients. *Archives of General Psychiatry, 45,* 581–588.

Brice-Heath, S. (1982). Questioning at home and at school: A comparative study. In G. Spindler (Ed.), *The school achievement of minority children: New perspectives.* Hillsdale, NJ: Erlbaum.

Brody, G. H., Stoneman, Z., & Flor, D. (1996). Parental religiosity, family processes, and youth competence in rural, two-parent African American families. *Developmental Psychology, 32,* 696–706.

Brody, G. H., Stoneman, Z., & Gauger, K. (1996). Parent–child relationships, family problem-solving behavior, and sibling relationship quality: The moderating role of sibling temperaments. *Child Development, 67,* 1289–1300.

Brody, G. H., Stoneman, Z., & McCoy, J. K. (1994). Forecasting sibling relationships in early adolescence from child temperaments and family processes in middle childhood. *Child Development, 65,* 771–784.

Bronfenbrenner, U. (1979a). Contexts of child rearing. *American Psychologist, 34,* 844–850.

Bronfenbrenner, U. (1979b). *The ecology of human development.* Cambridge, MA: Harvard University Press.

Bronfenbrenner, U. (1990). Discovering what families need. In D. Blankenhorn, S. Bayme, & J. B. Elshtian (Eds.), *Rebuilding the nest* (pp. 27–38). Milwaukee, WI: Family Service American.

Bronfenbrenner, U. (1994). Ecological models of human development. *International Encyclopedia of Education* (Vol. 3, 2nd ed., pp. 1643–1647).

Brookman, R. R. (1988). Sexually transmitted diseases. In M. D. Levine & E. R. McArney (Eds.), *Early adolescent transitions.* Lexington, MA: D.C. Heath.

Brooks, J. B. (1991). *The process of parenting.* Mountain View, CA: Mayfield.

Brooks, L. (1990). Counseling special groups: Women and ethnic minorities. In D. Brown, L. Brooks, & Associates (Eds.), *Career choice and development.* San Francisco: Jossey-Bass.

Brooks-Gunn, J. (1991). Consequences of maturational timing variations in adolescent girls. In R. M. Lerner, A. C. Petersen, & J. Brooks-Gunn (Eds.), *Encyclopedia of adolescence* (Vol. 2, pp. 614–618). New York: Garland.

Brooks-Gunn, J., Newman, D. L., Holderness, C., & Warren, M. P. (1994). The experience of breast development and girls' stories about the purchase of a bra. *Journal of Youth and Adolescence, 23,* 539–565.

Brooks-Gunn, J., & Ruble, D. N. (1982). The development of menstrual-related beliefs and behaviors during early adolescence. *Child Development, 53,* 1557–1566.

Brooks-Gunn, J., & Ruble, D. N. (1983). The experience of menarche from a developmental perspective. In J. Brooks-Gunn & A. C. Petersen (Eds.), *Girls at puberty.* New York: Plenum Press.

Brooks-Gunn, J., & Ruble, D. N. (1986). Men's and women's attitudes and beliefs about the menstrual cycle. *Sex Roles, 14,* 287–299.

Brooks-Gunn, J., & Warren, M. P. (1985). Measuring physical status and timing in early adolescence: A developmental perspective. *Journal of Youth and Adolescence, 14,* 163–189.

Brown, A. L., & DeLoache, J. S. (1978). Skills, plans, and self-regulation. In R. S. Siegler (Ed.), *Children's thinking: What develops?* Hillsdale, NJ: Erlbaum.

Brown, B. B., & Lohr, M. J. (1987). Peer group affiliation and adolescent self-esteem: An integration of ego-identity and symbolic-interaction theories. *Journal of Personality and Social Psychology, 52,* 47–55.

Brown, D. (1990). Summary, comparison, and critique of major theories. In D. Brown, L. Brooks, & Associates (Eds.), *Career choice and development.* San Francisco: Jossey-Bass.

Bryk, A. S., & Raudenbush, S. W. (1988). Toward a more appropriate conceptualization of research on school effects: A three-level hierarchical linear model. *American Journal of Education, 97,* 65–108.

Buchanan, C. M., Maccoby, E. E., & Dornbusch, S. M. (1992). Adolescents and their families after divorce. Three residential arrangements compared. *Journal of Research on Adolescence, 2,* 261–291.

Buhrmester, D. (1990). Intimacy of friendship, interpersonal competence, and adjustment during preadolescence and adolescence. *Child Development, 61,* 1101–1111.

Bukowski, W. M., Newcomb, A. F., & Hoza, B. (1987). Friendship conceptions among early adolescents: A longitudinal study of stability and change. *Journal of Early Adolescence, 7,* 143–152.

Butcher, J. (1986). Longitudinal analysis of adolescent girls' aspirations at school and perceptions of popularity. *Adolescence, 21,* 133–143.

Buzwell, S., & Rosenthal, D. (1996). Constructing a sexual self: Adolescents' sexual self-perceptions and sexual risk-taking. *Journal of Research on Adolescence, 6,* 489–513.

Bybee, J., Glick, M., & Zigler, E. (1990). Differences across gender, grade level, and academic track in the content of the ideal self-image. *Sex Roles, 22,* 349–358.

Byrnes, J. P., & Takahira, S. (1993). Explaining gender differences on SAT-math items. *Developmental Psychology, 29,* 805–810.

Camarena, P. M., Sarigiani, P. A., & Petersen, A. C. (1990). Gender-specific pathways to intimacy in early adolescence. *Journal of Youth and Adolescence, 19,* 19–32.

Cameron, R., & Meichenbaum, D. (1982). The nature of effective coping and the treatment of stress related problems: A cognitive-behavioral perspective. In L. Goldberger & S. Breznitz (Eds.), *Handbook of stress.* New York: Free Press.

Campbell, D. (1974). *The Strong-Campbell interest inventory.* Palo Alto, CA: Stanford University Press.

Campione, J. C., & Brown, A. L. (1978). Toward a theory of intelligence: Contributions from research with retarded children. *Intelligence, 2,* 279–304.

Capaldi, D. M. (1996). The reliability of retrospective report for timing first sexual intercourse for adolescent males. *Journal of Adolescent Research, 11,* 375–387.

Casas, J. M., Wagenheim, B. R., Banchero, R., & Mendoza-Romero, J. (1994). Hispanic masculinity: Myth or psychological schema meriting clinical consideration? *Hispanic Journal of Behavioral Sciences, 16,* 315–331.

Cavior, N., & Dokecki, P. R. (1973). Physical attractiveness, perceived attitude similarity, and academic achievement as contributors to interpersonal attraction among adolescents. *Developmental Psychology, 9,* 44–54.

Cech, D., & Martin, S. (1995). *Functional movement development across the life span.* Philadelphia: Saunders.

Centers for Disease Control. (1991). Mortality attributable to HIV infection/AIDS—United States, 1981–1990. *Morbidity and Mortality Weekly Report, 40,* 41–44.

Centers for Disease Control. (1992). 1993 revised classification system for HIV infection and expanded surveillance case definition for AIDS among adolescents and adults. *Morbidity and Mortality Weekly Report, 41,* 1–19.

Centers for Disease Control. (1993a). Condom use and sexual identity among men who have sex with men—Dallas, 1991. *Morbidity and Mortality Weekly Report, 42,* 7–17.

Centers for Disease Control. (1993b). Emergency department response to domestic violence—California, 1992. *Morbidity and Mortality Weekly Report, 42,* 617–619.

Centers for Disease Control. (1993c). *HIV/AIDS Surveillance Report, 5* (3).

Centers for Disease Control. (1996a). CDC surveillance summaries, September 27, 1996. *Morbidity and Mortality Weekly Report, 45* (No. SS-4).

Centers for Disease Control. (1996b). *Sexually transmitted disease surveillance, 1995.* U.S. Department of Health and Human Services, Public Health Service. Atlanta: Author.

Centers for Disease Control. (1996c). Youth risk behavior surveillance—United States, 1995. *Morbidity and Mortality Weekly Report, 45* (No. SS-4), 1–86.

Centers for Disease Control. (1997). Abortion surveillance. *Morbidity and Mortality Weekly Report,* January 3.

Cernkovich, S. A., & Giordano, P. C. (1987). Family relationships and delinquency. *Sociological Quarterly, 20,* 131–145.

Chao, R. K. (1994). Beyond parental control and authoritarian parenting style: Understanding Chinese parenting through the cultural notion of training. *Child Development, 65,* 1111–1119.

Chase-Lansdale, P. L., Wakschlag, L. S., & Brooks-Gunn, J. (1995). A psychological perspective on the development of caring in children and youth: The role of the family. *Journal of Adolescence, 18,* 515–556.

Cheek, D. B. (1974). Body composition, hormones, nutrition, and adolescent growth. In M. M. Grumbach, G. D. Grave, & F. E. Mayer (Eds.), *Control of the onset of puberty.* New York: Wiley.

Chi, M. T. H. (1985). Interactive roles of knowledge and strategies in the development of organized sorting and recall. In S. F. Chipman, J. W. Segal, & R. Glaser (Eds.), *Thinking and learning skills* (Vol. 2). Hillsdale, NJ: Erlbaum.

Chiu, M. L., Feldman, S. S., & Rosenthal, D. A. (1992). The influence of immigration on parental behavior and adolescent distress in Chinese families residing in two Western nations. *Journal of Research on Adolescence, 2,* 205–239.

Chodorow, N. (1978). *The reproduction of mothering.* Los Angeles: University of California Press.

Chomsky, N. (1957). *Syntactic structures.* The Hague: Mouton.

Clark, B. (1988). *Growing up gifted* (3rd ed.). New York: Macmillan.

Clasen, D. R., & Brown, B. B. (1985). The multidimensionality of peer pressure in adolescence. *Journal of Youth and Adolescence, 14,* 451–468.

Clausen, J. A. (1975). The social meaning of differential physical and sexual maturation. In S. E. Dragastin & G. H. Elder (Eds.), *Adolescence in the life cycle.* New York: Wiley.

Coleman, E., & Ramefedi, G. (1989). Gay, lesbian, and bisexual adolescents: A critical challenge to counselors. *Journal of Counseling and Development, 68,* 36–40.

Coleman, J. C. (1980). Friendship and the peer group in adolescence. In J. Adelson (Ed.), *Handbook of adolescence.* New York: Wiley.

Coleman, J. S. (1961). *The adolescent society.* New York: Free Press.

Coleman, J. S. (Chairman). (1974). *Youth: Transition to adulthood. Report on the panel for youth, President's Science Advisory Committee.* Chicago: University of Chicago Press.

Coleman, P. (1993). Testing the school system: Dropouts, accountability, and social policy. *Curriculum Inquiry, 23,* 329–342.

Coles, Robert. (1970). *Erik Erikson: The growth of his work.* Boston: Little, Brown.

Comer, J. P. (1985). The Yale–New Haven Primary Prevention Project: A follow-up study. *Journal of the American Academy of Child Psychiatry, 24,* 154–160.

Comer, J. P. (1988). Educating poor minority children. *Scientific American, 259,* 42–48.

Comer, J. P., Haynes, N. M., Joyner, E. T., & Ben-Avie, M. (Eds.). (1996). *Rallying the whole village: The Comer process for reforming education.* New York: Teachers College Press.

Commons, M. L., & Richards, F. A. (1982). A general model of stage theory. In M. L. Commons, F. A. Richards, & S. Armon (Eds.), *Beyond formal operations: Late adolescent and adult cognitive development.* New York: Praeger.

Condry J. C., & Ross, D. F. (1985). Sex and aggression: The influence of gender label on the perception of aggression in children. *Child Development, 56,* 225–233.

Conger, J. J. (1977). *Adolescence and youth.* New York: Harper & Row.

Connell, J. P., Halpern-Felsher, B. L., Clifford, E., Crichlow, W., & Usinger, P. (1995). Hanging in there: Behavioral, psychological, and contextual factors affecting whether African American adolescents stay in high school. *Journal of Adolescent Research, 10,* 41–63.

Constantine, L. L. (1987). Adolescent process and family organization: A model of development as a function of family paradigm. *Journal of Adolescent Research, 2,* 349–366.

Constantinople, A. (1973). Masculinity-femininity: An exception to a famous dictum? *Psychological Bulletin, 80,* 389–407.

Cook, W. L. (1993). Interdependence and the interpersonal sense of control: An analysis of family relationships. *Journal of Personality and Social Psychology, 64,* 587–601.

Cooper, C. R., Grotevant, H. D., & Condon, S. M. (1983). Individuality and connectedness in the family as a context for adolescent identity formation and role-taking skill. In H. D. Grotevant & C. R. Cooper (Eds.), *Adolescent development in the family.* San Francisco: Jossey-Bass.

Costanzo, P. R. (1970). Conformity development as a function of self-blame. *Journal of Personality and Social Psychology, 14,* 366–374.

Cotgrove, A., Zirinsky, L., Black, D., & Weston, D. (1995). Secondary prevention of attempted suicide in adolescence. *Journal of Adolescence, 18,* 569–577.

Cotman, C. W., & McGaugh, J. L. (1980). *Behavioral neuroscience.* San Francisco: Academic Press.

Courtney, M. L., & Cohen, R. (1996). Behavior segmentation by boys as a function of aggressiveness and prior information. *Child Development, 67,* 1034–1047.

Covington, M. V. (1983). Strategic thinking and the fear of failure. In S. F. Chipman, J. Segal, & R. Glaser (Eds.), *Thinking and learning skills: Current research and open questions* (Vol. 2). Hillsdale, NJ: Erlbaum.

Cozby, P. C. (1993). *Methods in behavioral research* (5th ed.). Mountain View, CA: Mayfield.

Cozby, P. C. (1997). *Methods in behavioral research* (6th ed.). Mountain View, CA: Mayfield.

Craighead, L. W., & Green, B. J. (1989). Relationship between depressed mood and sex-typed personality characteristics in adolescents. *Journal of Youth and Adolescence, 18,* 467–474.

Crick, N. R., & Dodge, K. A. (1996). Social information-processing mechanisms in reactive and proactive aggression. *Child Development, 67,* 993–1002.

Cross, W. E., Jr. (1980). Models of psychological nigrescence: A literature review. In R. L. Jones (Ed.), *Black psychology.* New York: Harper & Row.

Cross, W. E., Jr. (1987). A two-factor theory of black identity: Implications for the study of identity development in minority children. In J. S. Phinney & M. J. Rotheram (Eds.), *Children's ethnic socialization.* Beverly Hills: Sage.

Crouter, A. C., & Crowley, M. S. (1990). School-age children's time alone with fathers in single- and dual-earner families: Implications for the father–child relationship. *Journal of Early Adolescence, 10,* 296–312.

Crystal, D. S., & Stevenson, H. W. (1995). What is a bad kid? Answers of adolescents and their mothers in three cultures. *Journal of Research on Adolescence, 5,* 71–91.

Csikszentmihalyi, M. (1990). *Flow: The psychology of optimal experience.* New York: Harper & Row.

Cutler, G. B., Jr., Comite, F., Rivier, J., Vale, W. W., Loriaux, D. L., & Crowley, W. F., Jr. (1983). Pituitary desensitization with a long-acting luteinizing-hormone-releasing hormone analog. In J. Brooks-Gunn & A. C. Petersen (Eds.), *Girls at puberty.* New York: Plenum Press.

Dacey, J. S. (1989a). Discriminating characteristics of the families of highly creative adolescents. *Journal of Creative Behavior, 23,* 263–271.

Dacey, J. S. (1989b). *Fundamentals of creative thinking.* Lexington, MA: D. C. Heath.

Daniel, W., Jr. (1983). Pubertal changes in adolescence. In J. Brooks-Gunn & A. C. Petersen (Eds.), *Girls at puberty.* New York: Plenum Press.

Daniels, J., D'Andrea, M., & Heck, R. (1995). Moral development and Hawaiian youths: Does gender make a difference? *Journal of Counseling and Development, 74,* 90–93.

Darling, C. A., & Hicks, M. W. (1982). Parental influence on adolescent sexuality: Implications for parents as educators. *Journal of Youth and Adolescence, 11,* 231–245.

Davey, F. H., & Stoppard, J. M. (1993). Some factors affecting the occupational expectations of female adolescents. *Journal of Vocational Behavior, 43,* 235–250.

deAnda, D., Becerra, R. M., & Fielder, E. P. (1988). Sexuality, pregnancy, and motherhood among Mexican-American adolescents. *Journal of Adolescent Research, 3,* 403–412.

De Bro, S. C., Campbell, S. M., & Peplau, L. A. (1994). Influencing a partner to use a condom: A college student perspective. *Psychology of Women Quarterly, 18,* 165–182.

de Gaston, J. F., Jensen, L., Weed, S. E., & Tanas, R. (1994). Teacher philosophy and program implementation and the impact on sex education outcomes. *Journal of Research and Development in Education, 27,* 265–270.

de Groot, A. D. (1965). *Thought and choice in chess.* The Hague: Mouton.

Delaney, J., Lupton, M. J., & Toth, E. (1977). *The curse: A cultural history of menstruation.* New York: New American Library.

Deutsch, M. (1993). Educating for a peaceful world. *American Psychologist, 48,* 510–517.

DiBlasio, F. A., & Benda, B. B. (1992). Gender differences in theories of adolescent sexual activity. *Sex Roles, 27,* 221–236.

DiClemente, R. J., Zorn, J., & Temoshok, L. (1987). The association of gender, ethnicity, and length of residence in the Bay Area to adolescents' knowledge and attitudes about acquired immune deficiency syndrome. *Journal of Applied Social Psychology, 17,* 216–230.

Digest of Education Statistics. (1993). U.S. Department of Education. Washington, DC: U.S. Government Printing Office.

Dillard, A. (1974). *Pilgrim at Tinker Creek.* New York: Harper's Magazine Press.

Dodge, K. A. (1983). Behavioral antecedents of peer social status. *Child Development, 54,* 1386–1399.

Donahue, M. J., & Benson, P. L. (1995). Religion and the well-being of adolescents. *Journal of Social Issues, 51,* 145–160.

Donnay, D. A. C., & Borgen, F. H. (1996). Validity, structure, and content of the 1994 Strong Interest Inventory. *Journal of Counseling Psychology, 43,* 275–291.

Dornbusch, S. M., Carlsmith, L., Gross, R. T., Martin, J. A., Jenning, D., Rosenberg, A., & Duke, D. (1981). Sexual development, age, and dating: A comparison of biological and sociological influences upon the set of behaviors. *Child Development, 52,* 179–185.

Dornbusch, S. M., Ritter, P. L., Leiderman, P. H., Roberts, D. F., & Fraleigh, M. J. (1987). The relation of parenting style to adolescent school performance. *Child Development, 58,* 1244–1257.

Dornbusch, S. M., Ritter, P. L., Mont-Reynaud, R., & Chen, Z. (1990). Family decision making and academic performance in a diverse high school population. *Journal of Adolescent Research, 5,* 143–160.

Doueck, H. J., Ishisaka, A. H., & Greenaway, K. D. (1988). The role of normative development in adolescent abuse and neglect. *Family Relations, 37,* 135–139.

Douvan, E., & Adelson, J. (1966). *The adolescent experience.* New York: Wiley.

Dovidio, J., & Gaertner, S. (1986). *Prejudice, discrimination, and racism.* Orlando, FL: Academic Press.

Drumm, P., & Jackson, D. W. (1996). Developmental changes in questioning strategies during adolescence. *Journal of Adolescent Research, 11,* 285–305.

DSM-IIIR: Diagnostic and statistical manual of mental disorders (3rd ed., rev.) (1987). Washington, DC: American Psychiatric Association.

DSM-IV: Diagnostic and statistical manual of mental disorders (4th ed.) (1994). Washington, DC: American Psychiatric Association.

DuBois, D. L., Felner, R. D., Brand, S., Phillips, R. S. C., & Lease, A. M. (1996). Early adolescent self-esteem: A developmental-ecological framework and assessment strategy. *Journal of Research on Adolescence, 6,* 543–579.

DuBois, D. L., & Hirsch, B. J. (1990). School and neighborhood friendship patterns of Blacks and Whites in early adolescence. *Child Development, 61,* 524–536.

Duke-Duncan, P. (1991). Body image. In R. M. Lerner, A. C. Petersen, & J. Brooks-Gunn (Eds.). *Encyclopedia of adolescence* (Vol. 2, pp. 90–94). New York: Garland

Duncker, K. (1945). On problem solving. *Psychological Monographs, 58* (whole no. 270).

Dweck, C. S. (1986). Motivational processes affecting learning. *American Psychologist, 41,* 1040–1048.

Dweck, C. S. (1989). Motivation. In A. Lesgold & R. Glaser (Eds.), *Foundations for a psychology of education.* Hillsdale, NJ: Erlbaum.

Dweck, C. S., & Reppucci, N. D. (1973). Learned helplessness and reinforcement responsibility in children. *Journal of Personality and Social Psychology, 25,* 109–116.

Dyk, P. H., & Adams, G. R. (1990). Identity and intimacy: An initial investigation of three theoretical models using cross-lag panel correlations. *Journal of Youth and Adolescence, 19,* 91–110.

Eagly, A. H., & Kate, M. E. (1987). Are stereotypes of nationalities applied to both women and men? *Journal of Personality and Social Psychology, 53,* 451–462.

Eccles, J. E., Buchanan, C. M., Midgley, C., Fuligni, A. J., & Flanagan, C. (1991). Individuation reconsidered: Autonomy and control during early adolescence. *Journal of Social Issues, 47,* 53–68.

Educational Research Service. (1983). *Organization of the middle grades: A summary of research.* Arlington, VA: Author.

Edwards, W. J. (1996). Operating within the mainstream: Coping and adjustment among a sample of homosexual youths. *Deviant Behavior, 17,* 229–251.

Eisenman, R. (1994). Conservative sexual values: Effects of an abstinence program on student attitudes. *Journal of Sex Education and Therapy, 20,* 75–78.

Eisert, D. C., & Kahle, L. R. (1986). The development of social attributions: An integration of probability and logic. *Human Development, 29,* 61–81.

Eitzen, D. S. (1975). Athletics in the status systems of male adolescents: A replication of Coleman's *The adolescent society. Adolescence, 10,* 267–276.

Elkind, D. (1967). Egocentrism in adolescence. *Child Development, 38,* 1025–1034.

Elkind, D. (1976). Understanding the young adolescent. *Adolescence, 13,* 127–134.

Elkind, D. (1978). *A sympathetic understanding of the*

child: Birth to sixteen (2nd ed.). Boston: Allyn & Bacon.

Elkind, D. (1980). Strategic interactions in early adolescence. In J. Adelson (Ed.), *Handbook of adolescence.* New York: Wiley.

Elkind, D. (1984). *All grown up and no place to go: Teenagers in crisis.* Reading, MA: Addison-Wesley.

Elkind, D. (1985). Egocentrism redux: Reply to D. Lapsley and M. Murphy's Developmental Review paper. *Developmental Review, 5,* 218–226.

Emshoff, J., Avery, E., Raduka, G., Anderson, D. J., & Calvert, C. (1996). Findings from Super Stars: A health promotion program for families to enhance multiple protective factors. *Journal of Adolescent Research, 11,* 68–96.

Ennett, S. T., & Bauman, K. E. (1996). Adolescent social networks: School, demographic, and longitudinal considerations. *Journal of Adolescent Research, 11,* 194–215.

Enright, R. D., Santos, M. J., & Al-Mabuk, R. 1989. The adolescent as a forgiver. *Journal of Adolescence, 12,* 95–110.

Entwisle, D. R., & Alexander, K. L. (1990). Beginning school math competence: Minority and majority comparisons. *Child Development, 61,* 454–471.

Epstein, J. (1990). What matters in the middle grades—Grade span or practices? *Phi Delta Kappan, 71,* 438–444.

Epstein, S. (1973). The self-concept revisited, or a theory of a theory. *American Psychologist, 28,* 405–416.

Erikson, E. H. (1950). *Childhood and society.* New York: Norton.

Erikson, E. H. (1954). Problems of infancy and early childhood. In G. Murphy & A. J. Bachrach (Eds.), *An outline of abnormal psychology.* New York: Modern Library.

Erikson, E. H. (1956). The problem of ego identity. *Journal of the American Psychoanalytic Association, 4,* 56–121.

Erikson, E. H. (1959). Identity and the life cycle: Selected papers. *Psychological Issues Monograph, Series 1, No. 1.* New York: International Universities Press.

Erikson, E. H. (1963). *Childhood and society* (2nd ed.). New York: Norton.

Erikson, E. H. (1968). *Identity, youth and crisis.* New York: Norton.

Evans, E. D., Craig, D., & Mietzel, G. (1993). Adolescents' cognitions and attributions for academic cheating: A cross-national study. *The Journal of Psychology, 127,* 585–602.

Evans, J. P., & Taylor, J. (1995). Understanding violence in contemporary and earlier gangs: An ex-

ploratory application of the theory of reasoned action. *Journal of Black Psychology, 21,* 71–81.

Fairburn, C. G., & Cooper, P. J. (1982). Self-induced vomiting and bulimia nervosa: An undetected problem. *British Medical Journal, 284,* 1153–1155.

Faller, K. C. (1989). Characteristics of a clinical sample of sexually abused children: How boy and girl victims differ. *Child Abuse and Neglect, 13,* 281–291.

Farber, E. (1987). The adolescent who runs. In B. S. Brown & A. R. Mills (Eds.), *Youth at high risk.* (DHHS Publication No. ADM 87–1537). Washington, DC: U.S. Government Printing Office.

Farber, E., Kinast, C., McCoard, W., & Faulkner, D. (1984). Violence in families of adolescent runaways. *Child Abuse and Neglect, 8,* 295–299.

Fauber, R., Forehand, R., Thomas, A. M., & Wierson, M. (1990). A mediational model of the impact of marital conflict on adolescent adjustment in intact and divorced families. *Child Development, 61,* 1112–1123.

Faust, M. S. (1983). Alternative constructions of adolescent growth. In J. Brooks-Gunn & A. C. Petersen (Eds.), *Girls at puberty.* New York: Plenum Press.

Federal Bureau of Investigation. (1987). *Uniform crime reports.* Washington, DC: U.S. Department of Justice.

Feiring, C., & Lewis, M. (1991). The transition from middle childhood to early adolescence: Sex differences in the social network and perceived self-competence. *Sex Roles, 24,* 489–509.

Feiring, C., & Lewis, M. (1993). Do mothers know their teenagers' friends? Implications for individuation in early adolescence. *Journal of Youth and Adolescence, 22,* 337–354.

Feldman, C. F., Stone, A., & Renderer, B. (1990). Stage, transfer, and academic achievement in dialect-speaking Hawaiian adolescents. *Child Development, 61,* 472–484.

Feldman, S. S., Mont-Reynaud, R., & Rosenthal, D. A. (1992). When East moves West: The acculturation of values of Chinese adolescents in the U.S. and Australia. *Journal of Research on Adolescence, 2,* 147–173.

Fine, M. A. (1989). A social science perspective on stepfamily law: Suggestions for legal reform. *Family Relations, 38,* 53–58.

Finkelhor, D. (1993). Epidemiological factors in the clinical identification of child sexual abuse. *Child Abuse and Neglect, 17,* 67–70.

Finkelhor, D., & Baron, L. (1986). High-risk children. In D. Finkelhor et al. (Eds.), *Sourcebook on child sexual abuse* (pp. 60–88). Beverly Hills, CA: Sage.

Finkelhor, D. H., & Hotaling, G. T. (1984). Sexual abuse in the national incidence study of child abuse and neglect: An appraisal. *Child Abuse and Neglect, 8,* 23–33.

Fisk, W. R. (1985). Responses to "neutral" pronoun presentations and the development of sex-biased responding. *Developmental Psychology, 21,* 481–485.

Flavell, J. H. (1963). *The developmental psychology of Jean Piaget.* Princeton, NJ: Van Nostrand.

Flavell, J. H., Green, F. L., & Flavell, E. R. (1986). Development of knowledge about the appearance-reality distinction. *Monographs of the Society for Research in Child Development, 51* (Serial No. 212).

Flavell, J. H., Miller, P. H., & Miller, S. A. (1993). *Cognitive development* (3rd ed.). Englewood Cliffs, NJ: Prentice-Hall.

Fletcher, A. C., Darling, N. E., Steinberg, L., & Dornbusch, S. M. (1995). The company they keep: Relation of adolescents' adjustment and behavior to their friends' perceptions of authoritative parenting in the social network. *Developmental Psychology, 31,* 300–310.

Flewelling, R. L., & Bauman, K. E. (1990). Family structure as a predictor of initial substance use and sexual intercourse in early adolescence. *Journal of Marriage and the Family, 52,* 171–181.

Ford, M. E., Wentzel, K. R., Wood, D., Stevens, E., & Siesfeld, G. A. (1989). Processes associated with integrative social competence: Emotional and contextual influences on adolescent social responsibility. *Journal of Adolescent Research, 4,* 405–425.

Forehand, R., Thomas, A. M., Wierson, M., Brody, G., & Fauber, R. (1990). Role of maternal functioning and parenting skills in adolescent functioning following parental divorce. *Journal of Abnormal Psychology, 99,* 278–283.

The forgotten half. (1989, June 26). *U.S. News & World Report,* pp. 45–53.

Forrest, K. A., Austin, D. M., Valdes, M. I., Fuentes, E. G., & Wilson, S. R. (1993). Exploring norms and beliefs related to AIDS prevention among California Hispanic men. *Family Planning Perspectives, 25,* 111–117.

Fowler, J. D. (1991). Stages in faith consciousness. *New Directions for Child Development, 52,* 27–45.

Fowler, J. W. (1981). *Stages of faith: The psychology of human development and the quest for meaning.* San Francisco: Harper & Row.

Franco, E. L. (1991). The sexually transmitted disease model for cervical cancer: Incoherent epidemiological findings and the role of mis-classification of human papillomavirus infection. *Epidemiology, 2,* 98–106.

Frankel, K. A. (1990). Girls' perceptions of peer relationship support and stress. *Journal of Early Adolescence, 10,* 69–88.

Franklin, A. J. (1985). The social context and socialization variables as factors in thinking and learning. In S. F. Chipman, J. W. Segal, & R. Glaser (Eds.), *Thinking and learning skills* (Vol. 2). Hillsdale, NJ: Erlbaum.

French, S. A., Perry, C. L., Leon, G. R., & Fulkerson, J. A. (1995). Dieting behaviors and weight change history in female adolescents. *Health Psychology, 14,* 548–555.

Freud, A. (1969). Adolescence as a developmental disturbance. In G. Caplan & S. Lebovici (Eds.), *Adolescence.* New York: Basic Books.

Freud, S. (1925a). The dissolution of the Oedipal complex. In J. Strachey (Ed.), *The standard edition of the complete psychological works of Sigmund Freud* (Vol. 19). London: Hogarth Press, 1961.

Freud, S. (1925b). Some psychical consequences of the anatomical distinction between the sexes. In J. Strachey (Ed.), *The standard edition of the complete psychological works of Sigmund Freud* (Vol. 19). London: Hogarth Press, 1961.

Freud, S. (1954). *Collected works, standard edition.* London: Hogarth Press.

Frey, C. U., & Rothlisberger, C. (1996). Social support in healthy adolescents. *Journal of Youth and Adolescence, 25,* 17–31.

Frisch, R. E. (1983). Fatness, puberty, and fertility: The effects of nutrition and physical training on menarche and ovulation. In J. Brooks-Gunn & A. C. Petersen (Eds.), *Girls at puberty.* New York: Plenum Press.

Frisch, R. E. (1991). Puberty and body fat. In R. M. Lerner, A. C. Petersen, & J. Brooks-Gunn (Eds.). *Encyclopedia of adolescence* (Vol. 2, pp. 884–892). New York: Garland.

Fuligni, A. J., & Eccles, J. S. (1993). Perceived parent–child relationships and early adolescents' orientation toward peers. *Developmental Psychology, 29,* 622–632.

Fullerton, H., Jr. (1987). Projections 2000: Labor force projections—1986 to 2000. *Monthly Labor Review.* Washington, DC: U.S. Department of Labor.

Furman, W., & Buhrmester, D. (1992). Age and sex differences in perceptions of networks of personal relationships. *Child Development, 63,* 103–115.

Furstenberg, F. F. (1988). Child care after divorce and remarriage. In E. M. Hetherington & J. D. Arasteh

(Eds.), *Impact of divorce, single-parenting, and stepparenting on children.* Hillsdale, NJ: Erlbaum.

Furstenberg, F. F., Jr., Brooks-Gunn, J., & Morgan, S. P. (1987). *Adolescent mothers in later life.* New York: Cambridge University Press.

Gaddis, A., & Brooks-Gunn, J. (1985). The male experience of pubertal change. *Journal of Youth and Adolescence, 14,* 61–69.

Galambos, N. L., & Maggs, J. L. (1990). Putting mothers' work-related stress in perspective: Mothers and adolescents in dual-earner families. *Journal of Early Adolescence, 10,* 313–328.

Galambos, N. I., Sears, H. A., Almeida, D. M., & Kolaric, G. C. (1995). Parents' work overload and problem behavior in young adolescents. *Journal of Research on Adolescence, 5,* 201–223.

Galotti, K. M., & Kozberg, S. F. (1996). Adolescents' experience of a life-framing decision. *Journal of Youth and Adolescence, 25,* 3–16.

Gamoran, A., & Mare, R. D. (1989). Secondary school tracking and educational inequality: Compensation, reinforcement, or neutrality? *American Journal of Sociology, 94,* 1146–1183.

Garbarino, J. (1980). Some thoughts on school size and its effects on adolescent development. *Journal of Youth and Adolescence, 9,* 19–31.

Garber, J., Robinson, N. S., Valentiner, D. (1997). The relation between parenting and adolescent depression: Self-worth as a mediator. *Journal of Adolescent Research, 12,* 12–33.

Garcia, J. (1993). The changing image of ethnic groups in textbooks. *Phi Delta Kappan, 75,* 29–35.

Gardner, H. (1983). *Frames of mind.* New York: Basic Books.

Gardner, W. M., Roper, J. T., Gonzalez, C. C., & Simpson, R. G. (1988). Analysis of cheating on academic assignments. *Psychological Record, 38,* 543–555.

Garland, A. F., & Zigler, E. (1993). Adolescent suicide prevention: Current research and social policy implications. *American Psychologist, 48,* 169–182.

Gavin, L. A., & Furman, W. (1989). Age differences in adolescents' perceptions of their peer groups. *Developmental Psychology, 25,* 827–834.

Gavin, L. A., & Furman, W. (1996). Adolescent girls' relationships with mothers and best friends. *Child Development, 67,* 375–386.

Ge, X., Conger, R. D., Lorenz, F. O., Elder, G. H., Montague, R. B., & Simons, R. L. (1992). Linking family economic hardship to adolescent distress. *Journal of Research on Adolescence, 2,* 351–378.

Geller, L. G. (1985). *Word play and language learning for children.* Urbana, IL: National Council of Teachers of English.

Gerber, R. W., & Newman, I. M. (1989). Predicting future smoking of adolescent experimental smokers. *Journal of Youth and Adolescence, 18,* 191–201.

Gerstein, M., Lichtman, M., & Barokas, J. U. (1988). Occupational plans of adolescent women compared to men: A cross-sectional examination. *Career Development Quarterly, 36,* 222–230.

Gibbs, J. T. (1989). Black American adolescents. In J. T. Gibbs, L. N. Huang, & Associates (Eds.), *Children of color.* San Francisco: Jossey-Bass.

Gick, M. L., & Holyoak, K. J. (1980). Analogical problem solving. *Cognitive Psychology, 12,* 306–355.

Gilbert, S. F. (1994). *Developmental biology* (4th ed.). Sunderland, MA: Sinaur Associates, Inc.

Giles-Sims, J., & Crosbie-Burnett, M. (1989a). Stepfamily research: Implications for policy, clinical interventions, and further research. *Family Relations, 38,* 19–23.

Giles-Sims, J., & Crosbie-Burnett, M. (1989b). Adolescent power in stepfather families: A test of normative-resource theory. *Journal of Marriage and the Family, 51,* 1065–1078.

Gilligan, C. (1982). *In a different voice: Psychological theory and women's development.* Cambridge, MA: Harvard University Press.

Gilligan, C. (1986). Exit-voice dilemmas in adolescent development. In A. Foxley, M. S. McPherson, & G. O'Donnell (Eds.), *Development, democracy, and the art of trespassing: Essays in honor of Albert O. Hirschman.* Notre Dame, IN: University of Notre Dame Press.

Gilligan, C. (1988a). Adolescent development reconsidered. In C. Gilligan, J. V. Ward, J. M. Taylor, & B. Bardige (Eds.), *Mapping the moral domain.* Cambridge, MA: Harvard University Press.

Gilligan, C. (1988b). Exit-voice dilemmas in adolescent development. In C. Gilligan, J. V. Ward, J. M. Taylor, & B. Bardige (Eds.), *Mapping the moral domain.* Cambridge, MA: Harvard University Press.

Gilligan, C. (1989a). Preface: Teaching Shakespeare's sister. *Making connections: The relational worlds of adolescent girls at Emma Willard School.* Cambridge, MA: Harvard University Press.

Gilligan, C. (1989b). Prologue. In C. Gilligan, N. P. Lyons, & T. J. Hanmer (Eds.), *Making connections: The relational worlds of adolescent girls at Emma Willard School.* Cambridge, MA: Harvard University Press.

Gilligan, C., & Attanucci, J. (1988). Two moral orientations: Gender differences and similarities. *Merrill-Palmer Quarterly, 34,* 223–237.

Gilligan, C., Lyons, N. P., & Hanmer, T. J. (Eds.). (1989). *Making connections*. Troy, NY: Emma Willard School.

Ginsburg, H., & Opper, S. (1988). *Piaget's theory of intellectual development*. (3rd ed.). Englewood Cliffs, NJ: Prentice-Hall.

Ginzburg, E. (1972). Toward a theory of occupational choice: A re-statement. *Vocational Guidance Quarterly, 20,* 169–176.

Ginzburg, E. (1990). Career development. In D. Brown, L. Brooks, & Associates (Eds.), *Career choice and development*. San Francisco: Jossey-Bass.

Glick, P. C. (1989). Remarried families, stepfamilies, and stepchildren: A brief demographic profile. *Family Relations, 38,* 24–27.

Glover, R. W., & Marshall, R. (1993). Improving the school-to-work transition of American adolescents. *Teachers College Record, 94,* 588–609.

Goldstein, A. P., Sprafkin, R. P., Gershaw, N. J., & Klein, P. (1980). *Skill-streaming the adolescent*. Champaign, IL: Research Press.

Goldstein, B. (1976). *Introduction to human sexuality* (p. 80). Belmont, CA: Star.

Golombok, S., & Tasker, F. (1996). Do parents influence the sexual orientation of their children? Findings from a longitudinal study of lesbian families. *Developmental Psychology, 32,* 3–11.

Goode, E. (1984). *Drugs in American society* (2nd ed.). New York: Knopf.

Goossens, L. (1984). Imaginary audience behavior as a function of age, sex, and formal operations. *International Journal of Behavioral Development, 1,* 77–93.

Gordon, M. (1989). The family environment of sexual abuse: A comparison of natal and stepfather abuse. *Child Abuse and Neglect, 13,* 121–130.

Gordon, T. (1972). *Parent effectiveness training*. New York: New American Library.

Grandjean, A. C. (1988). Eating versus inactivity. In K. Clark, R. Parr, & W. Castelli (Eds.), *Evaluation and management of eating disorders*. Champaign, IL: Life Enhancement Publications.

Gray, W., & Hudson, L. (1984). Formal operations and the imaginary audience. *Developmental Psychology, 20,* 619–627.

Greenough, W. T., Black, J. E. & Wallace, C. S. (1987). Experience and brain development. *Child Development, 58,* 539–559.

Greif, G. L., & DeMaris, A. (1990). Single fathers with custody. *Families in Society, 71,* 259–266.

Gross, B. (1990). Here dropouts drop in—and stay! *Phi Delta Kappan, 71,* 625–627.

Grotevant, H. D., & Cooper, C. R. (1986). Individu-

ation in family relationships. *Human Development, 29,* 82–100.

Gwartney-Gibbs, P. A. (1986). The institutionalization of premarital cohabitation: Estimates from marriage license applications, 1970 and 1980. *Journal of Marriage and the Family, 48,* 423–434.

Habenicht, D. J., & Futcher, W. G. (1990). Psychological profile of the female adolescent incest victim. *Child Abuse and Neglect, 14,* 429–438.

Hains, A. A., & Ryan, E. B. (1983). The development of social cognitive processes among juvenile delinquents and nondelinquent peers. *Child Development, 54,* 1536–1544.

Hains, A. A., & Szyjakowski, M. (1990). A cognitive stress-reduction intervention program for adolescents. *Journal of Counseling Psychology, 37,* 79–84.

Hale, J. L. (1987). Plagiarism in classroom settings. *Communication Research Reports, 4,* 66–70.

Hale, S. (1990). A global developmental trend in cognitive processing speed. *Child Development, 61,* 653–663.

Hale, S., Fry, A. F., & Jessie, J. (1993). Effects of practice on speed of information processing in children and adults: Age sensitivity and age invariance. *Developmental Psychology, 29,* 880–892.

Hall, C. S. (1954). *A primer of Freudian psychology*. Cleveland: World Publishing.

Hall, E., & Post-Kammer, P. (1987). Black mathematics and science majors: Why so few? *Career Development Quarterly, 35,* 206–219.

Hall, G. S. (1904). *Adolescence: Its psychology and its relations to physiology, anthropology, sociology, sex, crime, religion, and education* (Vol. 1). New York: Appleton-Century-Crofts.

Hallinan, M. T., & Teixeira, R. A. (1987). Opportunities and constraints: Black-white differences in the formation of interracial friendships. *Child Development, 58,* 1358–1371.

Hamer, D. H., Hu, S., Magnuson, V.-L., Hu, N., & Pattatucci, A. M. L. (1993). A linkage between DNA markers on the X-chromosome and male sexual orientation. *Science, 261,* 321–326.

Hammelman, T. L. (1993). Gay and lesbian youth: Contributing factors to serious attempts or considerations of suicide. *Journal of Gay and Lesbian Psychotherapy, 2,* 77–89.

Hammond, W. R., & Yung, B. (1993). Psychology's role in the public health response to assaultive violence among young African-American men. *American Psychologist, 48,* 142–154.

Hanawalt, B. A. (1986). *The ties that bound: Peasant families in medieval England*. New York: Oxford University Press.

Harris, L. (1988). *Public attitudes toward teenage pregnancy, sex education, and birth control.* New York: Planned Parenthood of America.

Harris, M. G. (1994). Cholas, Mexican-American girls, and gangs. *Sex Roles, 30,* 289–301.

Hart, D., & Fegley, S. (1995). Prosocial behavior and caring in adolescence: Relations to self-understanding and social judgment. *Child Development, 66,* 1346–1359.

Hartup, W. W. (1993). Adolescents and their friends. In B. Laursen (Ed.), *New directions for child development* (pp. 3–22). San Francisco: Jossey-Bass.

Harvey, O. J., & Rutherford, J. (1980). Status in the informal group. *Child Development, 31,* 377–385.

Hass, A. (1979). *Teenage sexuality: A survey of teenage sexual behavior.* New York: Macmillan.

Hatcher, R., Hatcher, S., Berlin, M., Okla, K., & Richards, J. (1990). Psychological mindedness and abstract reasoning in late childhood and adolescence: An exploration using new instruments. *Journal of Youth and Adolescence, 19,* 307–326.

Hatcher, R., Wysocki, S., Kowal, D., Guest, F. J., Trussell, J., Stewart, F., Stewart, G., & Crates, W. (1993). *Contraceptive technology: 1990–1992.* Durant, OK: Essential Medical Information Systems, Inc., and New York: Irvington.

Hauser, S. T., Borman, E. H., Jacobson, A. M., Powers, S. I., & Noam, G. G. (1991). Understanding family contexts of adolescent coping: A study of parental ego development and adolescent coping strategies. *Journal of Early Adolescence, 11,* 96–124.

Havighurst, R. J. (1952). *Developmental tasks and education.* New York: Longman.

Havighurst, R. J. (1972). *Developmental tasks and education.* New York: David McKay.

Hayes, C. D. (Ed.). (1987). *Risking the future: Adolescent sexuality, pregnancy, and childbearing.* (Vol. 1). Washington, DC: National Academy Press.

Hein, K. (1989). Commentary on adolescent acquired immunodeficiency syndrome: The next wave of the immunodeficiency virus epidemic? *Journal of Pediatrics, 114,* 144–149.

Hein, K. (1991). Fighting AIDS in adolescents. *Issues in Science and Technology, 7(3),* 67–72.

Hein, K., & Futterman, D. (1991). Medical management in HIV-infected adolescents. *Journal of Pediatrics, 119,* 518–520.

Held, T. (1986). Institutionalization and deinstitutionalization of the life course. *Human Development, 29,* 157–162.

Helwig, C. C. (1995). Adolescents' and young adults' conceptions of civil liberties: Freedom of speech and religion. *Child Development, 66,* 152–166.

Helwig, C. C., Hildebrandt, C., & Turiel, E. (1995). Children's judgments about psychological harm in social context. *Child Development, 66,* 1680–1693.

Hendrick, C., & Hendrick, S. (1986). A theory and method of love: *Journal of Personality and Social Psychology, 50,* 392–402.

Hendrick, C., & Hendrick, S. (1991). Dimensions of love: A sociobiological interpretation. *Journal of Social Clinical Psychology, 10,* 206–230.

Hendrick, C., Hendrick, S., & Adler, N. L. (1988). Romantic relationships: Love, satisfaction, and staying together. *Journal of Personality and Social Psychology, 54,* 980–988.

Hendry, L. B., Glendinning, A., & Shucksmith, J. (1996). Adolescent focal theories: Age-trends in developmental transitions. *Journal of Adolescence, 19,* 307–320.

Henggeler, S. W. (1989). *Delinquency in adolescence.* Newbury Park, CA: Sage.

Herrera, R. S., & DelCampo, R. L. (1995). Beyond the superwoman syndrome: Work satisfaction and family functioning among working-class, Mexican-American women. *Hispanic Journal of Behavioral Sciences, 17,* 49–60.

Hetherington, E. M. (1989). Coping with family transitions: Winners, losers, and survivors. *Child Development, 60,* 1–14.

Hetherington, E. M., Cox, M., & Cox, R. (1982). Effects of divorce on children and parents. In M. E. Lamb (Ed.), *Nontraditional families.* Hillsdale, NJ: Erlbaum.

Hetherington, E. M., Hagan, M. S., & Anderson, E. R. (1989). Marital transitions: A child's perspective. *American Psychologist, 44,* 303–312.

Higham, E. (1980). Variations in adolescent psychohormonal development. In J. Adelson (Ed.), *Handbook of adolescent development.* New York: Wiley.

Hingson, R. W., Strunin, L., Berlin, B., & Heeren, T. (1990). Beliefs about AIDS, use of alcohol and drugs, and unprotected sex among Massachusetts adolescents. *American Journal of Public Health, 80,* 295–299.

Hirsh, R. H., Paolitto, D. P., & Reimer, J. (1979). *Promoting moral growth: From Piaget to Kohlberg.* New York: Longman.

Hoffman, M. L. (1980). Moral development in adolescence. In J. Adelson (Ed.), *Handbook of adolescent psychology.* New York: Wiley.

Hoffman, M. L. (1988). Moral development. In M. H. Bornstein & M. E. Lamb (Eds.), *Developmental psychology: An advanced textbook.* Hillsdale, NJ: Erlbaum.

Hogan, R. (1980). The gifted adolescent. In J. Adelson (Ed.), *Handbook of adolescence.* New York: Wiley.

Hogan, R., Viernstein, M. C., McGinn, P. V., Daurio, S., & Bohannon, W. (1977). Verbal giftedness and sociopolitical intelligence. *Journal of Educational Psychology, 50,* 135–142.

Hogan, R., & Weiss, D. (1974). Personality correlates of superior academic achievement. *Journal of Counseling Psychology, 21,* 144–149.

Hoge, D. R., Johnson, B., Luidens, D. A. (1995). Types of denominational switching among Protestant young adults. *Journal for the Scientific Study of Religion, 34,* 253–258.

Hogue, A., & Steinberg, L. (1995). Homophily of internalized distress in adolescent peer groups. *Developmental Psychology, 31,* 897–906.

Holland, J. L. (1961). Creative and academic performance among talented adolescents. *Journal of Educational Psychology, 52,* 136–147.

Holland, J. L. (1985a). *Making vocational choices: A theory of vocational personalities and work environments* (2nd ed.). Englewood Cliffs, NJ: Prentice-Hall.

Holland, J. L. (1985b). *Manual for the Vocational Preference Inventory.* Odessa, FL: Psychological Assessment Resources.

Holland, J. L. (1987). Current status of Holland's theory of careers: Another perspective. *Career Development Quarterly, 36,* 24–30.

Hood, K. E. (1991). Menstrual cycle. In R. M. Lerner, A. C. Petersen, & J. Brooks-Gunn (Eds.), *Encyclopedia of adolescence* (Vol. 2, pp. 642–646). New York: Garland.

Horn, J. L., & Cattell, R. B. (1967). Refinement and test of the theory of fluid and crystallized ability intelligences. *Journal of Educational Psychology, 57,* 253–270.

Horner, M. (1968). Toward an understanding of achievement-related conflicts in women. *Journal of Social Issues, 28,* 157–175.

Horney, K. (1937). *The neurotic personality of our time.* New York: Norton.

Horney, K. (1967). *Feminine psychology.* New York: Norton.

Horowitz, F. D., & O'Brien, M. (1986). Gifted and talented children. *American Psychologist, 41,* 1147–1152.

Horowitz, M. (1993, December). In search of Monster. *Atlantic,* pp. 28–37.

Horst, H. J., Bartesh, W., & Derksen-Thedens, I. (1977). Plasma testosterone, sex hormone-binding globulin-binding capacity and percent binding of testosterone and 5a-dihydrosterone in prepubertal, pubertal, and adult males. *Journal of Clinical Endocrinology and Metabolism, 45,* 522–527.

Houston, J. P. (1986). Survey corroboration of experimental findings on classroom cheating behavior. *College Student Journal, 20,* 168–173.

Howard, G. R. (1993). Whites in multicultural education: Rethinking our role. *Phi Delta Kappan, 75,* 36–41.

Howell, F. M., Frese, W., & Sollie, C. R. (1984). The measurement of perceived opportunity for occupational attainment. *Journal of Vocational Behavior, 25,* 325–343.

Hoyt, K. B. (1988). The changing workforce: A review of projections—1986 to 2000. *Career Development Quarterly, 37,* 31–39.

Hoyt, K. B. (1989). The career status of women and minority persons: A 20-year retrospective. *Career Development Quarterly, 37,* 202–212.

Huang, L. N., & Yin, Y. (1989). Chinese American children and adolescents. In J. T. Gibbs, L. N. Huang, & Associates (Eds.), *Children of color.* San Francisco: Jossey-Bass.

Hu-DeHart, E. (1993). The history, development, and future of ethnic studies. *Phi Delta Kappan, 75,* 50–54.

Huelskamp, R. M. (1993). Perspectives on education in America. *Phi Delta Kappan, 74,* 718–721.

Huesmann, L. R., Lefkowitz, M. M., Eron, L. D., & Walder, L. D. (1984). Stability of aggression over time and generations. *Developmental Psychology, 20,* 1120–1134.

Huff, C. R. (1996). The criminal behavior of gang members and non-gang, at-risk youth. In C. R. Huff (Ed.), *Gangs in America* (2nd ed.). Thousand Oaks, CA: Sage.

Huff, C. R., & Trump, K. S. (1996). Youth violence and gangs: School safety initiatives in urban and suburban school districts. *Education and Urban Society, 28,* 492–503.

Huizinga, D., & Elliott, D. S. (1987). Juvenile offenders: Prevalence, offender incidence, and arrest rates by race. *Crime and Delinquency, 33,* 206–223.

Humphrey, L. L. (1989). Observed family interactions among subtypes of eating disorders using structural analysis of social behavior. *Journal of Consulting and Clinical Psychology, 57,* 206–214.

Hunt, J. M. (1961). *Intelligence and experience.* New York: Ronald Press.

Hur, Y., & Bouchard, T. J., Jr. (1995). Genetic influences on perceptions of childhood family environment: A reared apart twin study. *Child Development, 66,* 330–345.

Husbands, C. L. (1970). Some social and psychological consequences of the American dating system. *Adolescence, 5,* 451–462.

Huston, A., McLoyd, V., & Garcia Coll, C. (1994). Children and poverty: Issues in contemporary research. *Child Development, 65,* 275–282.

Huttenlocher, P. R. (1990). Morphometric study of human cerebral cortex development. *Neuropsychologia, 28,* 517–527.

Hyde, J. S. (1981). How large are cognitive gender differences? A meta-analysis using *w*2 and *d*. *American Psychologist, 36,* 892–901.

Hyde, J. S. (1991). *Understanding human sexuality* (4th ed.). New York: McGraw-Hill.

Imbimbo, P. V. (1995). Sex differences in the identity formation of college students from divorced families. *Journal of Youth and Adolescence, 24,* 745–761.

Inderbitzen-Pisaruk, H., Clark, M. L., & Solano, C. H. (1992). Correlates of loneliness in midadolescence. *Journal of Youth and Adolescence, 21,* 151–167.

Inhelder, B., & Piaget, J. (1958). *The growth of logical thinking from childhood to adolescence.* New York: Basic Books.

Insel, P., & Roth, W. T. (1991). *Core concepts in health* (6th ed.). Mountain View, CA: Mayfield.

Insel, P., & Roth, W. T. (1998). *Core concepts in health* (8th ed.). Mountain View, CA: Mayfield.

Irion, J. C., Coon, R. C., & Blanchard-fields, F. (1988). The influence of divorce on coping in adolescence. *Journal of Youth and Adolescence, 17,* 135–145.

Irving, L. M. (1993). The relationship between childhood sexual abuse and subsequent onset of bulimia nervosa. *Child Abuse and Neglect, 17,* 305–314.

Jackson, J. F. (1993). Human behavioral genetics, Scarr's theory, and her views on interventions: A critical review and commentary on their implications for African American children. *Child Development, 64,* 1318–1332.

Jadack, R. A., Hyde, J. S., Moore, C. F., & Keller, M. L. (1995). Moral reasoning about sexually transmitted diseases. *Child Development, 66,* 167–177.

Jahnke, H. C., & Blanchard-Fields, F. (1993). A test of two models of adolescent egocentrism. *Journal of Youth and Adolescence, 22,* 313–326.

Jarrett, R. L. (1995). Growing up poor: The family experiences of socially mobile youth in low-income African American neighborhoods. *Journal of Adolescent Research, 10,* 111–134.

Jensen, A. R. (1969). How much can we boost IQ and scholastic achievement? *Harvard Educational Review, 39,* 1–123.

Jensen, A. R. (1985). The nature of the black-white difference on various psychometric tests: Spearman's hypothesis. *The Behavioral and Brain Sciences, 8,* 193–263.

Jensen, L. C., de Gaston, J. F., & Weed, S. E. (1994). Sexual behavior of nonurban students in grades 7 and 8: Implications for public policy and sex education. *Psychological Reports, 75,* 1504–1506.

Joebgen, A. M., & Richards, M. H. (1990). Maternal education and employment: Mediating maternal and adolescent emotional adjustment. *Journal of Early Adolescence, 10,* 329–343.

Johnson, B. M., Shulman, S., & Collins, W. A. (1991). Systematic patterns of parenting as reported by adolescents: Developmental differences and implications for psychosocial outcomes. *Journal of Adolescent Research, 6,* 235–252.

Johnson, C., Steinberg, S., & Lewis, C. (1988). Bulimia. In K. Clark, R. Parr, & W. Castelli (Eds.), *Evaluation and management of eating disorders.* Champaign, IL: Life Enhancement Publications.

Johnston, D. K. (1988). Adolescents' solutions to dilemmas in fables: Two moral orientations—two problem solving strategies. In C. Gilligan, J. V. Ward, & J. M. Taylor (Eds.), *Mapping the moral domain.* Cambridge, MA: Harvard University Press.

Johnston, L. D., O'Malley, P. M., & Bachman, J. G. (1989). *Drug use, drinking, and smoking: National survey results from high school, college, and young adult populations, 1975–1988* (DHHS Publication No. ADM 89–1638). Washington, DC: U.S. Government Printing Office.

Jones, M. C. (1957). The late careers of boys who were early- or late-maturing. *Child Development, 28,* 113–128.

Jones, M. C. (1958). A study of socialization patterns at the high school level. *Journal of Genetic Psychology, 93,* 87–111.

Jones, M. C. (1965). Psychological correlates of somatic development. *Child Development, 36,* 899–911.

Jones, M. C., & Bayley, N. (1950). Physical maturing among boys as related to behavior. *Journal of Educational Psychology, 41,* 129–148.

Jones, M. C., & Mussen, P. H. (1958). Self-conceptions, motivations and attitudes of early- and late-maturing girls. *Child Development, 29,* 491–501.

Josselson, R. L. (1980). Ego development in adolescence. In J. Adelson (Ed.), *Handbook of adolescent psychology.* New York: Wiley.

Josselson, R. L. (1982). Personality structure and identity status in women as viewed through early memories. *Journal of Youth and Adolescence, 11,* 293–299.

Josselson, R. L. (1987). *Finding herself: Pathways to identity development in women.* San Francisco: Jossey-Bass.

Josselson, R. L. (1988). The embedded self: I and thou revisited. In D. K. Lapsley & F. C. Power (Eds.), *Self, ego, and identity.* New York: Springer-Verlag.

Josselson, R. L. (1992). *The space between us.* San Francisco: Jossey-Bass.

Kagan, J. (1971). A conception of early adolescence. *Daedalus, 100,* 997–1012.

Kahle, J. B. (1982). Can positive minority attitudes lead to achievement gains in science? Analysis of the 1977 National Assessment of Educational Progress, Attitudes Toward Science. *Science Education, 66,* 539–546.

Kail, R. (1991). Developmental change in speed of processing during childhood and adolescence. *Psychological Bulletin, 109,* 490–501.

Kail, R. (1992). Processing speed, speech rate, and memory. *Developmental Psychology, 28,* 899–904.

Kalof, L. (1995). Sex, power, and dependency: The politics of adolescent sexuality. *Journal of Youth and Adolescence, 24,* 229–249.

Kammer, P. P., Fouad, N., & Williams, R. (1988). Follow-up of a pre-college program for minority and disadvantaged students. *Career Development Quarterly, 37,* 40–45.

Kandel, D. B. (1975). Stages in adolescent involvement in drug use. *Science, 190,* 912–914.

Kandel, D. B. (1978). Similarity in real-life adolescent friendship pairs. *Journal of Personality and Social Psychology, 36,* 306–312.

Kandel, D. B., & Yamaguchi, K. (1985). Developmental patterns of the use of legal, illegal, and medically prescribed psychotropic drugs from adolescence to young adulthood. In C. L. Jones & R. J. Battjes (Eds.), *Etiology of drug abuse: Implications for prevention. NIDA Research Monograph 56* (DHHS Publication No. ADM 85–1335). Washington, DC: U.S. Government Printing Office.

Kane, M. J. (1988). The female athletic role as a status determinant within the social system of high school adolescents. *Adolescence, 23,* 253–264.

Kaufman, J. F., Shaffer, H., & Burglass, M. E. (1985). The biological basics: Drugs and their effects. In T. E. Bratter & G. G. Forrest (Eds.), *Alcoholism and substance abuse.* New York: Free Press.

Keating, D. P. (1980). Thinking processes in adolescence. In J. Adelson (Ed.), *Handbook of adolescent psychology.* New York: Wiley.

Kegan, R. (1982). *The evolving self.* Cambridge, MA: Harvard University Press.

Kegan, R. (1994). *In over our heads.* Cambridge, MA: Harvard University Press.

Keith, J. G., Nelson, C. S., Schlabach, J. H., & Thompson, C. J. (1990). The relationship between parental employment and three measures of early adolescent responsibility: Family-related, personal and social. *Journal of Early Adolescence, 10,* 399–415.

Keller, M., & Wood, P. (1989). Development of friendship reasoning: A study of interindividual differences in intraindividual change. *Developmental Psychology, 25,* 820–826.

Kelly, M. L., & Grace, N. (1990). Acceptability of positive and punitive discipline methods: Comparisons among abusive, potentially abusive, and nonabusive parents. *Child Abuse and Neglect, 14,* 219–226.

Keniston, K. (1970). Youth: A "new" stage of life. *American Scholar, 39,* 631–654.

Kennedy, L. W., & Baron, S. W. (1993). Routine activities and a subculture of violence: A study of violence on the street. *Journal of Research in Crime and Delinquency, 30,* 88–112.

Kenny, A. M., Guardado, S., & Brown, L. (1989). Sex education and AIDS education in the schools: What states and large school districts are doing. *Family Planning Perspective, 21,* 56–64.

Kerfoot, M., Harrington, R., & Dyer, E. (1995). Brief home-based intervention with young suicide attempters and their families. *Journal of Adolescence, 18,* 557–568.

Kett, J. F. (1977). *Rites of passage.* New York: Basic Books.

Kingston, M. H. (1977). *The woman warrior.* New York: Vintage Books.

Kinsey, A. C., Pomeroy, W. B., & Martin, C. E. (1948). *Sexual behavior in the human male.* Philadelphia: Saunders.

Kinsey, A. C., Pomeroy, W. B., Martin, C. E., & Gebhard, P. H. (1953). *Sexual behavior in the human female.* Philadelphia: Saunders.

Kirby, D. (1984). *Sexuality education: An evaluation of programs and their effect.* Santa Cruz, CA: Network Publications.

Kitano, H. H. L., & Daniels, R. (1988). *Asian Americans: Emerging minorities.* Englewood Cliffs, NJ: Prentice-Hall.

Klebanov, P. K., & Brooks-Gunn, J. (1992). Impact of maternal attitudes, girls' adjustment, and cognitive skills upon academic performance in middle and high school. *Journal of Research on Adolescence, 2,* 81–102.

Klein, M. W. (1995). *The American street gang.* New York: Oxford University Press.

Klein, S. S. (1985). *Handbook for achieving sex equity through education.* Baltimore, MD: Johns Hopkins University Press.

Klerman, L. V. (1988). The delivery of health services to early adolescents. In M. D. Levine & E. R. McArney (Eds.), *Early adolescent transitions.* Lexington, MA: D. C. Heath.

Knobil, E. (1980). The neuroendocrine control of the menstrual cycle. *Recent Progress in Hormone Research, 36,* 53 88.

Koch, P. B. (1988). The relationship of first intercourse to later sexual functioning concerns of adolescents. *Journal of Adolescent Research, 3,* 345–362.

Kochman, T. (1987). The ethnic component in black language and culture. In M. J. Rotheram & J. S. Phinney (Eds.), *Children's ethnic socialization: Pluralism and development* (pp. 219–238). Beverly Hills: Sage.

Kohlberg, L. (1976). Moral stages and moralization: The cognitive developmental approach. In T. Lickona (Ed.), *Moral development and behavior.* New York: Holt, Rinehart & Winston.

Kohlberg, L. (1984). *The psychology of moral development.* New York: Harper & Row.

Kohlberg, L., & Kramer, R. (1969). Continuities and discontinuities in childhood and adult moral development. *Human Development, 12,* 93–120.

Kohn, P. M., & Milrose, J. A. (1993). The Inventory of High-School Students' Recent Life Experiences: A decontaminated measure of adolescents' hassles. *Journal of Youth and Adolescence, 22,* 43–55.

Kohut, S., Jr. (1988). *The middle school: A bridge between elementary and high schools* (2nd ed.). Washington, DC: National Education Association.

Koss, M. P., Dinero, T. E., Seibel, C. A., & Cox, S. L. (1988). Stranger and acquaintance rape: Are there differences in the victim's experience? *Psychology of Women Quarterly, 12,* 1–24.

Krasnoff, A. G. (1989). Early sex-linked activities and interests related to spatial abilities. *Personal and Individual Differences, 10,* 81–85.

Kratcoski, P. C., & Kratcoski, L. D. (1986). *Juvenile delinquency.* Englewood Cliffs, NJ: Prentice-Hall.

Krisberg, B., Schwartz, I., Fishman, G., Eisiloits, Z., Guttman, E., & Joe, J. (1987). The incarceration of minority youth. *Crime and Delinquency, 29,* 333–364.

Kroger, J. (1986). The relative importance of identity status interview components: A replication and extension. *Journal of Adolescence, 9,* 337–354.

Kroger, J. (1988). A longitudinal study of ego identity status interview domains. *Journal of Adolescence, 11,* 49–64.

Kroger, J. (1992). Intrapsychic dimensions of identity during late adolescence. In G. R. Adams, T. P. Gullotta, and R. Montemayor (Eds.), *Adolescent identity formation.* Newbury Park, CA: Sage.

Kroger, J. (1995). The differentiation of "firm" and "developmental" foreclosure identity statuses: A longitudinal study. *Journal of Adolescent Research, 10,* 317–337.

Kroger, J. (1996). Identity, regression and development. *Journal of Adolescence, 19,* 203–222.

Kroger, J., & Greene, K. E. (1996). Events associated with identity status change. *Journal of Adolescence, 19,* 477–490.

Krohne, H. W., & Rogner, J. (1982). Repression-sensitization as a central construct in coping research. In H. W. Krohne & L. Laux (Eds.), *Achievement, stress, and anxiety.* Washington, DC: Hemisphere.

Krumboltz, J. D. (1991). *Career beliefs inventory.* Palo Alto, CA: Consulting Psychologists Press.

Kuhn, T. S. (1962). *The structure of scientific revolutions.* Chicago: University of Chicago Press.

Kulin, H. E. (1991a). Puberty, hypothalamic-pituitary changes of. In R. M. Lerner, A. C. Petersen, & J. Brooks-Gunn (Eds.), *Encyclopedia of adolescence* (Vol. 2, pp. 900–907). New York: Garland.

Kulin, H. E. (1991b). Puberty, endocrine changes at. In R. M. Lerner, A. C. Petersen, & J. Brooks-Gunn (Eds.), *Encyclopedia of adolescence* (Vol. 2, pp. 897–899). New York: Garland.

Kupersmidt, J. B., & Coie, J. D. (1990). Preadolescent peer status, aggression, and school adjustment as predictors of externalizing problems in adolescence. *Child Development, 61,* 1350–1362.

Kurdek, L. A. (1990). Effects of child age on the marital quality and psychological distress of newly married mothers and stepfathers. *Journal of Marriage and the Family, 52,* 81–85.

Kurdek, L. A., & Fine, M. A. (1994). Family acceptance and family control as predictors of adjustment in young adolescents: Linear, curvilinear, or interactive effects? *Child Development, 65,* 1137–1146.

LaFromboise, T. D., & Low, K. G. (1989). American Indian children and adolescents. In J. T. Gibbs, L. N. Huang, & Associates (Eds.), *Children of color.* San Francisco: Jossey-Bass.

Lamborn, S. D., Dornbusch, S. M., & Steinberg, L. (1996). Ethnicity and community context as moderators of the relations between family decision making and adolescent adjustment. *Child Development, 67,* 283–301.

Lanza-Kaduce, L., & Klug, M. (1986). Learning to cheat: The interaction of moral-development and social learning theories. *Deviant Behavior, 7,* 243–259.

Lapsley, D. K., FitzGerald, D. P., Rice, K. G., & Jackson, S. (1989). Separation-individuation and the "new look" at the imaginary audience and personal fable: A test of an integrative model. *Journal of Adolescent Research, 4,* 483–505.

Lapsley, D. K., Milstead, M., Quintana, S. M., Flannery, D., & Buss, R. R. (1986). Adolescent egocentrism and formal operations: Tests of a theoretical assumption. *Developmental Psychology, 22,* 800–807.

Lapsley, D. K., & Murphy, M. (1985). Another look at the theoretical assumptions of adolescent egocentrism. *Developmental Review, 5,* 201–217.

Larkin, J. H. (1985). Understanding, problem representations, and skill in physics. In S. F. Chipman, J. W. Segal, & R. Glaser (Eds.), *Thinking and learning skills* (Vol. 2). Hillsdale, NJ: Erlbaum.

Larson, R., & Richards, M. H. (1994). *Divergent realities.* New York: Basic Books.

Larson, R. W., Richards, M. H., Moneta, G., Holmbeck, G., & Duckett, E. (1996). Changes in adolescents' daily interactions with their families from ages 10 to 18: Disengagement and transformation. *Developmental Psychology, 32,* 744–754.

Lau, S., & Lau, W. (1996). Outlook on life: How adolescents and children view the life-style of parents, adults and self. *Journal of Adolescence, 19,* 293–296.

LeBlanc, M. (1983). Delinquency as an epiphenomenon of adolescence. In R. R. Corrado, M. LeBlanc, & J. Trepanier (Eds.), *Current issues in juvenile justice.* Toronto: Butterworth.

Ledoux, S., Choquet, M., & Manfredi, R. (1993). Associated factors for self-reported binge eating among male and female adolescents. *Journal of Adolescence, 16,* 75–91.

Lee, J. A. (1973). *The colors of love.* Ontario, Canada: New Press.

Lee, J. A. (1988). Love styles. In R. J. Sternberg & M. L. Barnes (Eds.), *The psychology of love.* New Haven: Yale University Press.

Lee, S. H. (1990). Influence of metacognitive knowledge and aptitude on problem solving. *Journal of Educational Psychology, 82,* 306–314.

Leland, J. (1993, November 29). Criminal records: Gangsta rap and the culture of violence. *Newsweek,* pp. 60–66.

Leland, N. L., & Barth, R. P. (1993). Characteristics of adolescents who have attempted to avoid HIV and who have communicated with parents about sex. *Journal of Adolescent Research, 8,* 58–76.

Lempers, J. D., & Clark-Lempers, D. S. (1992). Young, middle, and late adolescents' comparisons of the functional importance of five significant relationships. *Journal of Youth and Adolescence, 21,* 53–96.

Lempers, J. D., & Clark-Lempers, D. S. (1993). A functional comparison of same-sex and opposite-sex friendships during adolescence. *Journal of Adolescent Research, 8,* 89–108.

Leon, G. R., Perry, C. L., Mangelsdorf, C., & Tell, G. J. (1989). Adolescent nutritional and psychological patterns and risk for the development of an eating disorder. *Journal of Youth and Adolescence, 18,* 273–282.

Lerner, R. M. (1986). *Concepts and theories of human development* (2nd ed.). New York: Random House.

Lerner, R. M. (1996). *America's youth in crisis.* Thousand Oaks, CA: Sage.

Lerner, R. M., Delaney, M., Hess, L. E., Jovanovic, J., & von Eye, A. (1990). Early adolescent physical attractiveness and academic competence. *Journal of Early Adolescence, 10,* 4–20.

LeVay, S. (1991). A difference in hypothalamic structure between heterosexual and homosexual men. *Science, 253,* 1034–1037.

Lever, J. (1976). Sex differences in the games children play. *Social Problems, 23,* 478–487.

Lever, J. (1978). Sex differences in the complexity of children's play and games. *American Sociological Review, 43,* 471–483.

Levesque, R. J. R. (1993). The romantic experience of adolescents in satisfying love relationships. *Journal of Youth and Adolescence, 22,* 219–251.

Levitt, M. J., Guacci-Franco, N., & Levitt, J. L. (1993). Convoys of social support in childhood and early adolescence: Structure and function. *Developmental Psychology, 29,* 811–818.

Levitt, R. A. (1981). *Physiological psychology.* New York: Holt, Rinehart & Winston.

Lewontin, R. (1982). *Human diversity.* New York: Scientific American Books.

Li, X., Sano, H., & Merwin, J. C. (1996). Perception and reasoning abilities among American, Japanese, and Chinese adolescents. *Journal of Adolescent Research, 11,* 173–193.

Licht, B. G., Linden, T. A., Brown, D. A., & Sexton, M. A. (1984, August). *Sex differences in achievement orientation: An "A" student phenomenon?* Paper presented at the meeting of the American Psychological Association, Toronto, Canada.

Lips, H. M. (1993). *Sex and gender: An introduction* (2nd ed.). Mountain View, CA: Mayfield.

Lips, H. M. (1997). *Sex and gender: An introduction* (3rd ed.). Mountain View, CA: Mayfield.

Lo, L. (1994). Exploring teenage shoplifting behavior: A choice and constraint approach. *Environment and Behavior, 26,* 613–639.

Lobel, T., & Levanon, I. (1988). Self-esteem, need for approval, and cheating behavior in children. *Journal of Educational Psychology, 80,* 122–123.

Lonky, E., Roodin, P. A., & Rybasch, J. M. (1988). Moral judgment and sex-role orientation as a function of self and other presentation modes. *Journal of Youth and Adolescence, 17,* 189–195.

LoSciuto, L., Rajala, A. K., Townsend, T. N., & Taylor, A. S. (1996). An outcome evaluation of Across Ages: An intergenerational mentoring approach to drug prevention. *Journal of Adolescent Research, 11,* 116–129.

Lourenco, O., & Machado, A. (1996). In defense of Piaget's theory: A reply to 10 common criticisms. *Psychological Review, 103,* 143–164.

Lovitt, T. C. (1989). *Introduction to learning disabilities.* Boston: Allyn & Bacon.

Lucas, B. (1988). Family patterns and their relationship to obesity. In K. L. Clark, R. B. Parr, & W. P. Castelli (Eds.), *Evaluation and management of eating disorders.* Champaign, IL: Life Enhancement Publications.

Luzzo, D. A., Funk, D., & Strang, J. (1996). Attributional retraining increases career decision-making self-efficacy. *Career Development Quarterly, 44,* 378–386.

Luzzo, D. A., James, T., & Luna, M. (1996). Effects of attributional retraining on the career beliefs and career exploration behavior of college students. *Journal of Counseling Psychology, 43,* 415–422.

Luzzo, D. A., & Ward, B. E. (1995). The relative contributions of self-efficacy and locus of control to the prediction of vocational congruence. *Journal of Career Development, 21,* 307–317.

Lyon, J. M., Henggler, S., & Hall, J. A. (1992). The family relations, peer relations, and criminal activities of Caucasian and Hispanic-American gang members. *Journal of Abnormal Child Psychology, 20,* 439–449.

Maguire, K., Pastore, A. L., & Flanagan, T. J. (1993). *Sourcebook of criminal justice statistics 1992.* U.S. Department of Justice, Bureau of Justice Statistics. Washington, DC: U.S. Government Printing Office.

Major, B., & Forcey, B. (1985). Social comparisons and pay evaluations: Preferences for same-sex and same-job wage comparisons. *Journal of Experimental Social Psychology, 21,* 393–405.

Malina, R. M. (1990). Physical growth and performance during the transitional years (9–16). In R. Montemayor, G. R. Adams, & T. P. Gullotta (Eds.), *From childhood to adolescence.* Newbury Park, CA: Sage.

Malinowski, B. (1925). Magic, science, and religion. In J. Needham (Ed.), *Science, religion and reality* (pp. 18–94). New York: Macmillan.

Mann, L., Harmoni, R., & Power, C. (1989). Adolescent decision-making: The development of competence. *Journal of Adolescence, 12,* 265–278.

Marcia, J. E. (1980). Identity in adolescence. In J. Adelson (Ed.), *Handbook of adolescent psychology.* New York: Wiley.

Marcia, J. E. (1988). Common processes underlying ego identity, cognitive/moral development, and individuation. In D. K. Lapsley & F. C. Power (Eds.), *Self, ego and identity: Integrative approaches.* New York: Springer-Verlag.

Margolin, L., Miller, M., & Moran, P. B. (1989). When a kiss is not just a kiss: Relating violations of consent in kissing to rape myth acceptance. *Sex Roles, 20,* 231–243.

Markstrom-Adams, C., Hofstra, G., & Dougher, K. (1994). The ego-virtue of fidelity: A case for the study of religion and identity formation in adolescence. *Journal of Youth and Adolescence, 23,* 453–469.

Markstrom-Adams, C., & Smith, M. (1996). Identity formation and religious orientation among high school students from the United States and Canada. *Journal of Adolescence, 19,* 247–261.

Markus, H. R., & Kitayama, S. (1991). Culture and the self: Implications for cognition, emotion, and motivation. *Psychological Review, 98,* 224–253.

Martin, B. (1990). The transmission of relationship difficulties from one generation to the next. *Journal of Youth and Adolescence, 19,* 181–199.

Martinez, R., & Dukes, R. L. (1987). Race, gender and self-esteem among youth. *Hispanic Journal of Behavioral Sciences, 9,* 427–443.

Martorano, S. C. (1977). A developmental analysis of performance on Piaget's formal operations tasks. *Developmental Psychology, 13,* 666–672.

Masters, W. H., & Johnson, V. E. (1966). *Human sexual response.* Boston: Little, Brown.

Masters, W. H., Johnson, V. E., & Kolodny, R. C. (1988). *Human sexuality* (3rd ed.). Boston: Little, Brown.

Matuschka, P. R. (1985). The psychopharmacology of addiction. In T. E. Bratter & G. G. Forrest (Eds.), *Alcoholism and substance abuse.* New York: Free Press.

Maynard, R. C. (1990, August 5). An example of how Afro-American parents socialize children. *The Oakland Tribune.*

Mayr, E. (1982). *Growth of biological thought: Diversity, evolution, and inheritance.* Cambridge, MA: Harvard University Press.

Mazor, A., & Enright, R. D. (1988). The development of the individuation process from a social-cognitive perspective. *Journal of Adolescence, 11,* 29–47.

McAdams, D. P. (1990). *The person: An introduction to personality psychology.* San Diego: Harcourt Brace Jovanovich.

McCary, J. L., & McCary, S. P. (1982). *McCary's human sexuality* (4th ed.). Belmont, CA: Wadsworth.

McFarlane, A. H., Bellissimo, A., Norman, G. R., & Lange, P. (1994). Adolescent depression in a school-based community sample: Preliminary findings on contributing social factors. *Journal of Youth and Adolescence, 23,* 601–620

McGue, M., Sharma, A., & Benson, P. (1996). The effect of common rearing on adolescent adjustment: Evidence from a U.S. adoption cohort. *Developmental Psychology, 32,* 604–613.

McLanahan, S. S., Astone, N. M., & Marks, N. (1988, June). *The role of mother-only families in reproducing poverty.* Paper presented at the Conference on Poverty and Children, Lawrence, KS.

McLanahan, S. S., & Booth, K. (1989). Mother-only families: Problems, prospects, and politics. *Journal of Marriage and the Family, 51,* 557–580.

McLaughlin, D., & Whitfield R. (1984). Adolescents and their experience of parental divorce. *Journal of Adolescence, 7,* 155–170.

McLaughlin, R. D., & Ross, S. M. (1989). Student cheating in high school: A case of moral reasoning versus "fuzzy logic." *High School Journal, 72,* 97–104.

Mechanic, D., & Hansell, S. (1989). Divorce, family conflict, and adolescents' well-being. *Journal of Health and Social Behavior, 30,* 105–116.

Meeus, W., & Dekovic, M. (1995). Identity development, parental and peer support in adolescence: Results of a national Dutch survey. *Adolescence, 30,* 931–944.

Meichenbaum, D. H. (1985). *Stress inoculation training.* New York: Pergamon.

Meichenbaum, D., & Deffenbacher, J. L. (1988). Stress inoculation training. *Counseling Psychologist, 16,* 69–90.

Michel, A. (1986). *Down with stereotypes? Eliminating sexism from children's literature and school textbooks.* Washington, DC: UNESCO.

Midgley, C., Arunkumar, R., & Urdan, T. C. (1996). "If I don't do well tomorrow, there's a reason": Predictors of adolescents' use of academic self-handicapping strategies. *Journal of Educational Psychology, 88,* 423–434.

Miller, B. C., Christopherson, C. R., & King, P. K. (1993). Sexual behavior in adolescence. In T. P. Gullotta et al. (Eds.), *Adolescent sexuality.* Newbury Park, CA: Sage.

Miller, B. C., & Fox, G. L. (1987). Theories of adolescent heterosexual behavior. *Adolescent Research, 2,* 269–282.

Miller, G. (1989). Foreword. In J. T. Gibbs, L. N. Huang, & Associates (Eds.), *Children of color.* San Francisco: Jossey-Bass.

Miller, G. A., Galanter, E., & Pribram, K. H. (1960). *Plans and the structure of behavior.* New York: Holt, Rinehart & Winston.

Miller, J. (Ed.). (1973). *Psychoanalysis and women.* New York: Brunner/Mazel.

Miller, J. (1976). *Toward a new psychology of women.* Boston: Beacon Press.

Miller, J. G., & Bersoff, D. M. (1989). When do American children and adults reason in social conventional terms? *Developmental Psychology, 24,* 366–375.

Miller, K. E. (1990). Adolescents' same-sex and opposite-sex peer relations: Sex differences in popularity, perceived social competence, and social cognitive skills. *Journal of Adolescent Research, 5,* 222–241.

Miller, R. L. (1989). Desegregation experiences of minority students: Adolescent coping strategies in five Connecticut high schools. *Journal of Adolescent Research, 4,* 173–189.

Minuchin, S., Rosman, B., & Baker, L. (1978). *Psychosomatic families. Anorexia nervosa in context.* Cambridge, MA: Harvard University Press.

Mischel, W., & Mischel, H. N. (1976). A cognitive social-learning approach to morality and self-regulation. In T. Lickona (Ed.), *Moral development and behavior: Theory, research, and social issues.* New York: Holt, Rinehart & Winston.

Mitchell, L. K., & Krumboltz, J. D. (1987). The effects of cognitive restructuring and decision-making training on career indecision. *Journal of Counseling and Development, 66,* 171–174.

Mitchell, L. K., & Krumboltz, J. D. (1990). Social learning approach to career decision making: Krumboltz's theory. In D. Brown, L. Brooks, & Associates (Eds.), *Career choice and development.* San Francisco: Jossey-Bass.

Moeller, T. P., & Bachmann, G. A. (1993). The combined effects of physical, sexual, and emotional abuse during childhood: Long-term health consequences for women. *Child Abuse and Neglect, 17,* 623–640.

Molina, B. S. G., & Chassin, L. (1996). The parent–adolescent relationship at puberty: Hispanic ethnicity and parent alcoholism as moderators. *Developmental Psychology, 32,* 675–686.

Money, J. (1988). Commentary: Current status of sex research. *Journal of Psychology and Human Sexuality, 1,* 5–16.

Montemayor, R., & Van Komer, R. (1985). The development of sex differences in friendship patterns and peer group structure during adolescence. *Journal of Early Adolescence, 5,* 285–294.

Moore, K. A., & Glei, D. (1995). Taking the plunge: An examination of positive youth development. *Journal of Adolescent Research, 10,* 15–40.

Moran, G. F. (1992). Adolescence in colonial America. In R. M. Lerner, A. C. Petersen, & J. Brooks-Gunn (Eds.), *Encyclopedia of adolescence* (Vol. 1). New York: Garland.

Morrow, K. B., & Sorell, G. T. (1989). Factors affecting self-esteem, depression, and negative behaviors in sexually abused female adolescents. *Journal of Marriage and the Family, 51,* 677–686.

Morrow, L. (1988, August 8). Through the eyes of children. *Time,* pp. 26–45.

Mortimer, J. T., Finch, M. D., Ryu, S., Shanahan, M. J., & Call, K. T. (1996). The effects of work intensity on adolescent mental health, achievement, and behavioral adjustment: New evidence from a prospective study. *Child Development, 67,* 1243–1261.

Mortimer, J. T., Finch, M., Shanahan, M., & Ryu, S. (1992). Work experience, mental health, and behavioral adjustment in adolescence. *Journal of Research on Adolescence, 2,* 25–57.

Mounts, N. S., & Steinberg, L. (1995). An ecological analysis of peer influence on adolescent grade point average and drug use. *Developmental Psychology, 31,* 915–922.

Munroe, R. (1955). *Schools of psychoanalytic thought.* New York: Dryden Press.

Mussen, P. H., & Jones, M. C. (1957). Self-conceptions, motivations and interpersonal attitudes of late- and early-maturing boys. *Child Development, 28,* 243–256.

Muuss, R. E. (1975). Adolescent development and the secular trend. In R. E. Muuss (Ed.), *Adolescent behavior and society: A book of readings.* New York: Random House.

Muuss, R. E. (1990). *Adolescent behavior and society* (4th ed.). New York: Random House.

Nagata, D. K. (1989). Japanese American children and adolescents. In J. T. Gibbs, L. N. Huang, & Associates (Eds.), *Children of color.* San Francisco: Jossey-Bass.

National Assessment of Educational Progress. (1994). http//www.ed.gov/nces/pubs/96814.htm/

National Center for Education Statistics. (1995). *The condition of education, 1995.* Washington, DC: U.S. Department of Education.

National Center for Health Statistics. (1968–1991). *Vital statistics of the United States: Vol. 2. Mortality—Part A* [for 1966–1988]. Washington, DC: U.S. Government Printing Office.

National Institute on Drug Abuse. (1985). National household survey on drug abuse. In the Surgeon General's report, 1988, *The health consequences of smoking: Nicotine addiction.* U.S. Department of Health and Human Services. Washington, DC: U.S. Government Printing Office.

Needle, R. H., Su, S. S., & Doherty, W. J. (1990). Divorce, remarriage, and adolescent substance use: A prospective longitudinal study. *Journal of Marriage and the Family, 52,* 157–169.

Neisser, U. (1967). *Cognitive psychology.* New York: Appleton-Century-Crofts.

Neisser, U. (1976). *Cognition and reality.* San Francisco: Freeman.

Nelson, M. R. (1988). Issues of access to knowledge: Dropping out of school. In L. N. Tanner (Ed.), *Critical issues in curriculum, 87th yearbook of the National Society for the Study of Education.* Chicago: University of Chicago Press.

Newman, J. (1985). Adolescents: Why they can be so obnoxious. *Adolescence, 20,* 635–645.

Ng, S. H. (1990). Androcentric coding of MAN and HIS in memory by language users. *Journal of Experimental Social Psychology, 26,* 455–464.

Nitz, K., Ketterlinus, R. D., & Brandt, L. J. (1995). The role of stress, social support, and family environment in adolescent mothers' parenting. *Journal of Adolescent Research, 10,* 358–382.

Nolin, M. J., & Petersen, K. K. (1992). Gender differences in parent–child communication about sexuality. *Journal of Adolescent Research, 7,* 59–79.

Norton, E. M., Durlak, J. A., & Richards, M. H. (1989). Peer knowledge of and reactions to adolescent suicide. *Journal of Youth and Adolescence, 18,* 427–437.

Nucci, L., Camino, C., & Sapiro, C. M. (1996). Social class effects on northeastern Brazilian children's conceptions of areas of personal choice and social regulation. *Child Development, 67,* 1223–1242.

Nurmi, J.-E., Poole, M. E., & Kalakoski, V. (1996). Age differences in adolescent identity exploration and commitment in urban and rural environments. *Journal of Adolescence, 19,* 443–452.

Oakes, J. (1985). *Keeping track: How schools structure inequality.* New Haven, CT: Yale University Press.

O'Brien, S. F., & Bierman, K. L. (1988). Conceptions and perceived influence of peer groups: Interviews with preadolescents and adolescents. *Child Development, 59,* 1360–1365.

O'Connell, A. N. (1976). The relationship between life-style and identity synthesis and re-synthesis in traditional, neotraditional and nontraditional women. *Journal of Personality, 44,* 675–688.

Offer, D., Ostrov, E., & Howard, K. I. (1981). *The adolescent.* New York: Basic Books.

Ogbu, J. U. (1981). Black education: A cultural-ecological perspective. In H. P. McAdoo (Ed.), *Black families.* Beverly Hills: Sage.

Ogbu, J. U. (1992). Understanding cultural diversity and learning. *Educational Researcher, 21,* 5–14.

Okun, M. A., & Sasfy, J. H. (1977). Adolescence, the self-image and formal operations. *Adolescence, 12,* 373–379.

Orlofsky, J., & Frank, M. (1986). Personality structure as viewed through early memories and identity status in college men and women. *Journal of Personality and Social Psychology, 5,* 580–586.

Orlofsky, J., Marcia, J. E., & Lesser, I. M. (1973). Ego identity status and the intimacy versus isolation crisis of young adulthood. *Journal of Youth and Adolescence, 27,* 211–219.

Ornstein, P. A., Naus, M. J., & Liberty, C. (1975). Rehearsal and organizational processes in children's memory. *Child Development, 26,* 818–830.

Orthner, D. (1990). Parental work and early adolescence: Issues for research and practice. *Journal of Early Adolescence, 10,* 246–259.

Osherson, D. N., & Markman, E. M. (1975). Language and the ability to evaluate contradictions and tautologies. *Cognition, 3,* 213–226.

Osipow, S. H. (1983). *Theories of career development* (3rd ed.). Englewood Cliffs, NJ: Prentice-Hall.

Overton, W. F., Ward, S. L., Noveck, I. A., Black, J., & O'Brien, D. P. (1987). Form and content in the development of deductive reasoning. *Developmental Psychology, 23,* 22–30.

Owings, J., & Stocking, C. (1985). *High school and beyond: Characteristics of high school students who identify themselves as handicapped.* Washington, DC: National Center for Education Statistics, U.S. Department of Education.

Page, R. N. (1990). Games of chance: The lower-track curriculum in a college-preparatory high school. *Curriculum Inquiry, 20,* 249–281.

Palinscar, A. S., & Brown, A. L. (1984). Reciprocal teaching of comprehension-monitoring activities. *Cognition and Instruction, 1,* 117–175.

Panel on High-Risk Youth. Commission on Behavioral and Social Sciences and Education, National Research Council. (1993). *Losing generations: Adolescents in high-risk settings.* Washington, DC: National Academy Press.

Papini, D. R., Farmer, F. L., Clark, S. M., & Snell, W. E., Jr. (1988). An evaluation of adolescent patterns of sexual self-disclosure to parents and friends. *Journal of Adolescent Research, 3,* 387–401.

Papini, D. R., Snell, W. E., Belk, S. S., & Clark, S. (1988, April). *Developmental correlates of women's and men's sexual self-disclosures.* Paper presented at the meeting of the Southwestern Psychological Association, Tulsa, OK.

Pardeck, J. A., & Pardeck, J. L. (1990). Family factors related to adolescent autonomy. *Adolescence, 25,* 311–319.

Parker, J. G., & Gottman, J. M. (1989). Social and emotional development in a relational context. In T. J. Berndt & G. W. Ladd (Eds.), *Peer relationships in child development.* New York: Wiley.

Parker, S., Nichter, M., Nichter, N., Vuckovic, N., Sims, C., & Ritenbaugh, C. (1995). Body image and weight concern among Afro American and White adolescent females: Differences that make a difference. *Human Organization, 54,* 103–115.

Parks, G. (1990). *Voices in the mirror: An autobiography.* New York: Doubleday.

Pasley, B. K., & Ihenger-Tallman, M. (1989). Boundary ambiguity in remarriage: Does ambiguity differentiate degree of marital adjustment and integration? *Family Relations, 38,* 46–52.

Paterson, J. E., Field, J., & Pryor, J. (1994). Adolescents' perceptions of their attachment relationships with their mothers, fathers, and friends. *Journal of Youth and Adolescence, 23,* 579–600.

Patrikakou, E. N. (1996). Investigating the academic achievement of adolescents with learning disabilities: A structural modeling approach. *Journal of Educational Psychology, 88,* 435–450.

Pattatucci, A. M. L., & Hamer, D. H. (1995). Development and familiality of sexual orientation in females. *Behavior Genetics, 25,* 407–420.

Patterson, S. J., Sochting, I., & Marcia, J. E. (1992). The inner space and beyond: Women and identity. In G. R. Adams, T. P. Gullotta, & R. Montemayor (Eds.), *Adolescent identity formation*. Newbury Park, CA: Sage.

Paulson, S. E., Koman, J. J., III, & Hill, J. P., III. (1990). Maternal employment and parent–child relations in families of seventh graders. *Journal of Early Adolescence, 10,* 278–295.

Pearl, R., Bryan, T., & Herzog. (1990). Resisting or acquiescing to peer pressure to engage in misconduct: Adolescents' expectations of probable consequences. *Journal of Youth and Adolescence, 19,* 43–55.

Perkins, D. N. (1987). Knowledge as design: Teaching thinking through content. In J. B. Baron & R. J. Sternberg (Eds.), *Teaching thinking skills: Theory and practice.* New York: Freeman.

Perlmutter, B. F. (1987). Delinquency and learning disabilities: Evidence for compensatory behaviors and adaptation. *Journal of Youth and Adolescence, 16,* 89–95.

Perry, W. G. (1970). *Forms of intellectual and ethical development in the college years.* San Francisco: Holt, Rinehart & Winston.

Peskin, H. (1967). Pubertal onset and ego functioning. *Journal of Abnormal Psychology, 72,* 1–15.

Peskin, H. (1973). Influence of the developmental schedule of puberty on learning and ego development. *Journal of Youth and Adolescence, 2,* 273–290.

Peskin, H., & Livson, M. (1972). Pre- and postpubertal personality and adult psychological functioning. *Seminars in Psychiatry, 4,* 343–353.

Petersen, A. C., Compas, B. E., Brooks-Gunn, J., Stemmler, M., Ey, S., & Grant, K. (1993). Depression in adolescence. *American Psychologist, 48,* 155–168.

Petersen, A. C., & Crockett, L. (1985). Pubertal timing and grade effects on adjustment. *Journal of Youth and Adolescence, 14,* 191–206.

Petersen, A. C., Crockett, L., Richards, M., & Boxer, A. (1988). A self-report measure of pubertal status: Reliability, validity, and initial norms. *Journal of Youth and Adolescence, 17,* 117–134.

Petersen, A. C., & Taylor, B. (1980). The biological approach to adolescence. In J. Adelson (Ed.), *Handbook of adolescent psychology.* New York: Wiley.

Petersen, C. C., & Murphy, L. (1990). Adolescents' thoughts and feelings about AIDS in relation to cognitive maturity. *Journal of Adolescence, 13,* 185–187.

Phelps, L., Johnston, S. S., Jimenez, D. P., Wilczenski, F. L., Andrea, R. K., & Healy, R. W. (1993). Figure preference, body dissatisfaction, and body distortion in adolescence. *Journal of Adolescent Research, 8,* 297–310.

Phelps, S. B., & Jarvis, P. A. (1994). Coping in adolescence: Empirical evidence for a theoretically based approach to assessing coping. *Journal of Youth and Adolescence, 23,* 359–371.

Phinney, J. (1989). Stages of ethnic identity development in minority group adolescents. *Journal of Early Adolescence, 9,* 34–49.

Phinney, J. (1990). Ethnic identity in adolescents and adults: Review of research. *Psychological Bulletin, 108,* 499–514.

Phinney, J. (1993). A three-stage model of ethnic identity development. In M. Bernal & G. Knight (Eds.), *Ethnic identity: Formation and transmission among Hispanics and other minorities* (pp. 61–79). Albany: State University of New York Press.

Phinney, J. (1996). When we talk about American ethnic groups, what do we mean? *American Psychologist, 51,* 918–927.

Phinney, J. S., & Cobb, N. J. (1996). Reasoning about intergroup relations among Hispanic and Euro-American adolescents. *Journal of Adolescent Research, 11,* 306–324.

Phinney, J. S., & Devich-Navarro, M. (1997). Variations in bicultural identification among African American and Mexican American adolescents. *Journal of Research on Adolescence, 7,* 3–32.

Phinney, J., & Kohatsu, E. (in press). Ethnic and racial identity and mental health. In J. Schulenberg, J. Maggs, & K. Hurrelmann (Eds.), *Health risks and developmental transitions during adolescence.* New York: Cambridge University Press.

Phinney, J., & Rosenthal, D. A. (1992). Ethnic identity in adolescence: Process, context, and outcome. In G. Adams, R. Montemayor, & T. Gulotta (Eds.), *Advances in adolescent development* (Vol. 4). Newbury Park, CA: Sage.

Phinney, J. S., & Rotheram, M. J. (1987). Children's ethnic socialization: Themes and implications. In M. J. Rotheram & J. S. Phinney (Eds.), *Children's ethnic socialization: Pluralism and development.* Beverly Hills: Sage.

Phinney, J., & Tarver, S. (1988). Ethnic identity search and commitment in black and white eighth graders. *Journal of Early Adolescence, 8,* 265–277.

Piaget, J. (1952a). *The child's conception of number.* New York: Humanities Press.

Piaget, J. (1952b). *The origins of intelligence in children.* New York: International Universities Press.

Piaget, J. (1954). *The construction of reality in the child.* New York: Basic Books.

Piaget, J. (1965). *The moral judgment of the child,* New York: Free Press.

Piaget, J. (1971). *Biology and knowledge,* Chicago: University of Chicago Press.

Pittman, R. B., & Haughwout, P. (1987). Influence of high school size on dropout rate. *Educational Evaluation and Policy Analysis, 9,* 337–343.

Place, D. M. (1975). The dating experience for adolescent girls. *Adolescence, 10,* 157–174.

Pleck, J. H., Sonenstein, F. L., & Swain, S. O. (1988). Adolescent males' sexual behavior and contraceptive use: Implications for male responsibility. *Journal of Adolescent Research, 3,* 275–284.

Plomin, R., & Daniels, D. (1987). Why are children in the same family so different from one another? *Behavioral and Brain Sciences, 10,* 1–60.

Plomin, R., Reiss, D., Hetherington, E. M., & Howe, G. W. (1994). Nature and nurture: Genetic contributions to measures of the family environment. *Developmental Psychology, 30,* 32–43.

Plummer, D. L. (1995). Patterns of racial identity development of African American adolescent males and females. *Journal of Black Psychology, 21,* 168–180.

Plummer, D. L. (1996). Black racial identity attitudes and stages of the life span: An exploratory investigation. *Journal of Black Psychology, 22,* 169–181.

Pollack, S., & Gilligan, C. (1982). Images of violence in Thematic Apperception Test stories. *Journal of Personality and Social Psychology, 42,* 159–167.

Poole, M. E., & Evans, G. T. (1988). Adolescents' self-perceptions of competence in life skill areas. *Journal of Youth and Adolescence, 18,* 147–173.

Postman, N. (1982). *The disappearance of childhood.* New York: Delacorte.

Powell, G. J. (1985). Self-concepts among Afro-American students in racially isolated minority schools: Some regional differences. *Journal of the American Academy of Child Psychiatry, 24,* 142–149.

Powers, S. I., Hauser, S. T., Schwartz, J. M., Noam, G. G., & Jacobson, A. M. (1983). Adolescent ego development and family interaction: A structural-developmental perspective. In H. D. Grotevant & C. R. Cooper (Eds.), *Adolescent development in the family.* San Francisco: Jossey-Bass.

Price, J., Desmond, S., & Smith, D. (1991). A preliminary investigation of inner city adolescents' perceptions of guns. *Journal of School Health, 61,* 255–259.

Proulx, J., & Koulock, D. (1987). The effect of parental divorce on parent-adolescent separation. *Journal of Youth and Adolescence, 16,* 473–480.

Purcell, P., & Stewart, L. (1990). Dick and Jane in 1989. *Sex Roles, 22,* 177–185.

Putallaz, M. (1983). Predicting children's sociometric status from their behavior. *Child Development, 54,* 1417–1426.

Quay, H. C. (1987). Intelligence. In H. C. Quay (Ed.), *Handbook of juvenile delinquency.* New York: Wiley.

Raja, S. N., McGee, R., & Stanton, W. R. (1992). Perceived attachments to parents and peers and psychological well-being in adolescence. *Journal of Youth and Adolescence, 21,* 471–485.

Ramirez, O. (1989). Mexican American children and adolescents. In J. T. Gibbs, L. N. Huang, & Associates (Eds.), *Children of color.* San Francisco: Jossey-Bass.

Rathunde, K. (1996). Family context and talented adolescents' optimal experience in school-related activities. *Journal of Research on Adolescence, 6,* 605–628.

Raudenbush, S. W., Rowan, B., & Cheong, Y. F. (1993). Higher order instructional goals in secondary schools: Class, teacher, and school influences. *American Educational Research Journal, 30,* 523–553.

Ray, J., & Briar, K. H. (1988). Economic motivators for shoplifting. *Journal of Sociology and Social Welfare, 15,* 177–189.

Reese, H. W., & Overton, W. F. (1970). Models of development and theories of development. In L. R. Goulet & P. B. Baltes (Eds.), *Life-span developmental psychology: Research and theory.* New York: Academic Press.

Regan, P. C., & Berscheid, E. (1995). Gender differences in beliefs about the causes of male and female sexual desire. *Personal Relationships, 2,* 345–357.

Reid, M., Landesman, S., Treder, R., & Jaccard, J. (1989). "My family and friends": Six- to twelve-year-old children's perceptions of social support. *Child Development, 60,* 896–910.

Reinis, S., & Goldman, J. M. (1980). *The development of the brain.* Springfield, IL: Thomas.

Reischl, T. M., & Hirsch, B. J. (1989). Identity commitments and coping with a difficult developmental transition. *Journal of Youth and Adolescence, 18,* 55–69.

Reiss, D., Oliveri, M. E., & Curd, K. (1983). Family paradigm and adolescent social behavior. In H. D. Grotevant & C. R. Cooper (Eds.), *Adolescent development in the family.* San Francisco: Jossey-Bass.

Report of the Secretary's Task Force on Youth Suicide. (1989). *Vol. 1: Overview and recommendations*

(DHHS Publication No. ADM 89–1621). Washington, DC: U.S. Government Printing Office.

Resnick, M., Harris, L., & Blum, R. (1993). The impact of caring and connectedness on adolescent health and well-being. *Journal of Pediatrics and Child Health, 29,* (Suppl. 1), 3–9.

Restak, R. (1984, November). Master clock of the brain and body. *Science Digest,* pp. 54–104.

Reyes, L. H., & Stanic, G. M. (1985, April). *A review of the literature on Blacks and mathematics.* Paper presented at the meeting of the American Educational Research Association, Chicago.

Reyes, O., & Jason, L. A. (1993). Pilot study examining factors associated with academic success for Hispanic high school students. *Journal of Youth and Adolescence, 22,* 57–71.

Rice, K. G., Cole, D. A., & Lapsley, D. K. (1990). Separation-individuation, family cohesion, and adjustment to college: measurement validation and test of a theoretical model. *Journal of Counseling Psychology, 37,* 195–202.

Rice, K. G., & Mulkeen, P. (1995). Relationships with parents and peers: A longitudinal study of adolescent intimacy. *Journal of Adolescent Research, 10,* 338–357.

Riegel, K. F. (1973). *Dialectic operations: The final period of cognitive development.* Princeton, NJ: Educational Testing Service.

Riley, M. W. (1986). The dynamisms of life stages: Roles, people, and age. *Human Development, 29,* 150–156.

Roche, J. P., & Ramsby, T. W. (1993). Premarital sexuality: A five-year follow-up study of attitudes and behavior by dating stage. *Adolescence, 28,* 67–80.

Roeser, R. W., Midgley, C., & Urdan, T. C. (1996). Perceptions of the school psychological environment and early adolescents' psychological and behavioral functioning in school: The mediating role of goals and belonging. *Journal of Educational Psychology, 88,* 408–422.

Rogoff, B. (1990). *Apprenticeship in thinking: Cognitive development in social context.* New York: Oxford University Press.

Rogow, A. M., Marcia, J. E., & Slugowski, B. R. (1983). The relative importance of identity status interview components. *Journal of Youth and Adolescence, 12,* 387–400.

Rollins, J. (Ed.). (1981). *Hidden minorities: The persistence of ethnicity in American life.* Washington, DC: University Press of America, 1981.

Roper, W. L., Peterson, H. B., & Curran, J. W. (1993). Commentary: Condoms and HIV/STD prevention—Clarifying the message. *American Journal of Public Health, 83,* 501–503.

Rosenberg, M., Schooler, C., & Schoenbach, C. (1989). Self-esteem and adolescent problems: Modeling reciprocal effects. *American Sociological Review, 54,* 1004–1018.

Rosenthal, D. A., & Feldman, S. S. (1992). The nature and stability of ethnic identity in Chinese youth: Effects of length of residence in two cultural contexts. *Journal of Cross-Cultural Psychology, 23,* 213–227.

Rosenthal, D. A., & Hrynevich, C. (1985). Ethnicity and ethnic identity: A comparative study of Greek-, Italian-, and Anglo-Australian adolescents. *International Journal of Psychology, 20,* 723–742.

Rosenthal, D., & Peart, R. (1996). The rules of the game: Teenagers communicating about sex. *Journal of Adolescence, 19,* 321–332.

Roth, P. (1969). *Portnoy's complaint.* New York: Random House.

Rotheram, M. J., & Phinney, J. S. (1983). *Intercultural attitudes and behaviors of children.* Paper presented at the meeting of the Society for Intercultural Evaluation, Training and Research, San Germignano, Italy.

Rotheram, M. J., & Phinney, J. S. (1987). Ethnic behavior patterns as an aspect of identity. In J. Phinney & M. Rotheram (Eds.), *Children's ethnic socialization: Pluralism and development.* Beverly Hills: Sage.

Rotheram-Borus, M. J., & Phinney, J. S. (1990). Patterns of social expectations among black and Mexican-American children. *Child Development, 61,* 542–556.

Rowe, D. C., Vazsonyi, A. T., & Flannery, D. J. (1994). No more than skin deep: Ethnic and racial similarity in developmental process. *Psychological Review, 101,* 396–413.

Ruble, D. N., & Brooks-Gunn, J. (1982). The experience of menarche. *Child Development, 53,* 1557–1566.

Rutter, M. (1986). The developmental psychopathology of depression. In M. Rutter, C. E. Isard, & P. B. Read. (Eds.), *Depression in young people.* New York: Guilford Press.

Ryan, J. M., Tracey, T. J. G., & Rounds, J. (1996). Generalizability of Holland's structure of vocational interests across ethnicity, gender, and socioeconomic status. *Journal of Counseling Psychology, 43,* 330–337.

Sanderson, C. A., & Cantor, N. (1995). Social dating goals in late adolescence: Implications for safer sexual activity. *Journal of Personality and Social Psychology, 68,* 1121–1134.

Satter, E. (1988). Should the obese child diet? In K. Clark, R. Parr, & W. Castelli (Eds.), *Evaluation and management of eating disorders.* Champaign, IL: Life Enhancement Publications.

Scarr, S. (1992). Developmental theories for the 1990s: Development and individual differences. *Child Development, 63,* 1–19.

Scarr, S. (1993). Biological and cultural diversity: The legacy of Darwin for development. *Child Development, 64,* 1333–1353.

Scarr, S., & Weinberg, R. A. (1983). The Minnesota adoption studies: Malleability and genetic differences. *Child Development, 34,* 260–267.

Schafer, W. E., Olexa, C., & Polk, K. (1972). Programmed for social class: Tracking in high school. In K. Polk & W. E. Schafer (Eds.), *Schools and delinquency.* Englewood Cliffs, NJ: Prentice-Hall.

Schaie, K. W. (1965). A general model for the study of development problems. *Psychological Bulletin, 64,* 92–107.

Schaie, K. W., & Willis, S. L. (1993). Age difference patterns of psychometric intelligence in adulthood: Generalizability within and across ability domains. *Psychology and Aging, 8,* 44–55.

Schiano, D. J., Cooper, L. A., Glaser, R., & Zhang, H. C. (1989). Highs are to lows as experts are to novices: Individual differences in the representation and solution of standardized figural analogies. *Human Performance, 2,* 225–248.

Schiedel, D. G., & Marcia, J. E. (1985). Ego identity, intimacy, sex role orientation, and gender. *Developmental Psychology, 21,* 149–160.

Schwartzberg, N. S., & Dytell, R. S. (1996). Dual-earner families: The importance of work stress and family stress for psychological well-being. *Journal of Occupational Health Psychology, 1,* 211–223.

Schweder, R. A., Mahapatra, M., & Miller, J. (1987). Culture and development. In J. Kagan (Ed.), *The emergence of moral concepts in young children.* Chicago: University of Chicago Press.

Scott-Jones, D., & Turner, S. L. (1988). Sex education, contraceptive and reproductive knowledge, and contraceptive use among Black adolescent females. *Journal of Adolescent Research, 3,* 171–187.

Sebald, H. (1981). Adolescents' concept of popularity and unpopularity, comparing 1960 and 1976. *Adolescence, 16,* 187–193.

Seiber, J. E. (1980). A social learning approach to morality. In M. Windmiller, N. Lambert, & E. Turiel (Eds.), *Moral development and socialization.* Boston: Allyn & Bacon.

Seixas, P. (1993). Historical understanding among adolescents in a multicultural setting. *Curriculum Inquiry, 23,* 301–327.

Selman, R. L. (1976). Social-cognitive understanding. In T. Lickona (Ed.), *Moral development and behavior.* New York: Holt, Rinehart & Winston.

Selman, R. L. (1980). *The growth of interpersonal understanding.* New York: Academic Press.

Selman, R. L., & Byrne, L. F. (1974). A structural-developmental analysis of levels of role taking in middle childhood. *Child Development, 45,* 803–806.

Selye, H. (1982). Stress: Eustress, distress, and human perspectives. In S. B. Day (Ed.), *Life stress* (Vol. 3). New York: Van Nostrand Reinhold.

Sessa, F. M., & Steinberg, L. (1991). Family structure and the development of autonomy during adolescence. *Journal of Early Adolescence, 11,* 38–55.

Shafii, M., Carrigan, S., Whittinghill, J. R., & Derrick, A. (1985). Psychological autopsy of completed suicide in children and adolescents. *American Journal of Psychiatry, 142,* 1061–1064.

Sheley, J. F., Zhang, J., Brody, C. J., & Wright, J. D. (1995). Gang organization, gang criminal activity, and individual gang members' criminal behavior. *Social Science Quarterly, 76,* 53–69.

Sherman, J. A. (1978). *Sex-related cognitive differences: An essay on theory and evidence.* Springfield, IL: Thomas.

Shifflett-Simpson, K., & Cummings, E. M. (1996). Mixed message resolution and children's responses to interadult conflict. *Child Development, 67,* 437–448.

Shucksmith, J., Hendry, L. B., & Glendinning, A. (1995). Models of parenting: Implications for adolescent well-being within different types of family contexts. *Journal of Adolescence, 18,* 253–270.

Shulman, S., Seiffge-Krenke, I., & Samat, N. (1987). Adolescent coping style as a function of perceived family climate. *Journal of Adolescent Research, 2,* 367–381.

Siegler, R. S. (1991). *Children's thinking.* Englewood Cliffs, NJ: Prentice-Hall.

Silverberg, S. B., & Steinberg, L. (1990). Psychological well-being of parents with early adolescent children. *Developmental Psychology, 26,* 658–666.

Silverstein, B., Perdue, L., Peterson, B., & Kelly, E. (1986). The role of the mass media in promoting a thin standard of bodily attractiveness for women. *Sex Roles, 14,* 519–532.

Simmons, R. G., & Blyth, D. A. (1987). *Moving into adolescence.* New York: Aldine de Gruyter.

Simons, R. L., Robertson, J. F., & Downs, W. R. (1989). The nature of the association between parental rejection and delinquent behavior. *Journal of Youth and Adolescence, 18,* 297–310.

Simpson, G. E., & Yinger, J. M. (1985). *Racial and cultural minorities* (5th ed.). New York: Plenum Press.

Skinner, B. F. (1938). *The behavior of organisms: An experimental analysis.* New York: Appleton-Century-Crofts.

Skinner, B. F. (1953). *Science and human behavior.* New York: Macmillan.

Skinner, B. F. (1961). *Cumulative record* (rev. ed.). New York: Appleton-Century-Crofts.

Slaughter-Defoe, D. T., Nakagawa, K., Takanishi, R., & Johnson, D. J. (1990). Toward cultural/ecological perspectives on schooling and achievement in African- and Asian-American children. *Child Development, 61,* 363–383.

Slavin, R. E. (1985). Cooperative learning: Applying contact theory in desegregated schools. *Journal of Social Issues, 41,* 45–62.

Sloan, J., Kellermann, A., Reay, D., Ferris, J., Koepsell, T., Rivara, F., Rice, C., Gray, L., & LoGerfo, J. (1988). Handgun regulation, crime, assaults, and homicides. *New England Journal of Medicine, 319,* 1256–1262.

Small, M. Y. (1990). *Cognitive development.* San Diego, CA: Harcourt Brace Jovanovich.

Smetana, J. (1988). Concepts of self and social convention: Adolescents' and parents' reasoning about hypothetical and actual family conflicts. In M. R. Gunnar (Ed.), *21st Minnesota Symposium on Child Psychology.* Hillsdale, NJ: Erlbaum.

Smetana, J. G., & Asquith, P. (1994). Adolescents' and parents' conceptions of parental authority and personal autonomy. *Child Development, 65,* 1147–1162.

Smetana, J. G., & Berent, R. (1993). Adolescents' and mothers' evaluations of justifications for disputes. *Journal of Adolescent Research, 8,* 252–273.

Smetana, J. G., Braeges, J. L., & Yau, J. (1991). Doing what you say and saying what you do: Reasoning about adolescent–parent conflict in interviews and interactions. *Journal of Adolescent Research, 6,* 276–295.

Smith, E. A., & Udrey, J. R. (1985). Coital & noncoital sexual behaviors of white and black adolescents. *American Journal of Public Health, 75,* 1200–1203.

Smith, T. E. (1990). Parental separation and the academic self-concepts of adolescents: An effort to solve the puzzle of separation effects. *Journal of Marriage and the Family, 52,* 107–118.

Smolak, L., Levine, M. P., & Gralen, S. (1993). The impact of puberty and dating on eating problems among middle school girls. *Journal of Youth and Adolescence, 22,* 355–368.

Snarey, J. R. (1985). Cross-cultural universality of social-moral development: A critical review of Kohlbergian research. *Psychological Bulletin, 97,* 202–232.

Snow, R. E. (1986). Individual differences and the design of educational programs. *American Psychologist, 41,* 1029–1039.

Sochting, I., Skoe, E. E., & Marcia, J. E. (1994). Career-oriented moral reasoning and prosocial behavior: A question of gender or sex role orientation. *Sex Roles, 31,* 131–147.

Sokolov, E. M. (1963). Higher nervous functions: The orienting reflex. *Annual Review of Physiology, 25,* 545–580.

Solomon, G. (1990). Using technology to reach at-risk students. *Electronic Learning, 9,* 14–15.

Solomon, J., Scott, L., & Duveen, J. (1996). Large-scale exploration of pupils' understanding of the nature of science. *Science Education, 80,* 493–508.

Solso, R. L., & Johnson, H. H. (1994). *Experimental psychology* (5th ed.). New York: HarperCollins.

Sommer, K., Whitman, T. L., Borkowski, J. G., Schellenbach, C., Maxwell, S., & Keogh, D. (1993). Cognitive readiness and adolescent parenting. *Developmental Psychology, 29,* 389–398.

Sonenstein, F. L. (1986). Risking paternity: Sex and contraception among adolescent males. In A. B. Elster & M. E. Lamb (Eds.), *Adolescent fatherhood.* Hillsdale, NJ: Erlbaum.

Sorenson, R. C. (1973). *Adolescent sexuality in contemporary America: Personal values and sexual behavior, ages thirteen to nineteen.* New York: World.

Sowell, T. (1978). Race and IQ reconsidered. In T. Sowell (Ed.), *American ethnic groups.* The Urban Institute.

Speight, S. L., Vera, E. M., & Derrickson, K. B. (1996). Racial self designation, racial identity, and self-esteem revisited. *Journal of Black Psychology, 22,* 37–52.

Spencer, M. B. (1985). Racial variations in achievement prediction: The school as a conduit for macrostructural cultural tension. In H. McAdoo & J. McAdoo (Eds.), *Black children: Social, educational, and parental environments.* Beverly Hills: Sage.

Spires, H. A., Gallini, J., & Riggsbee, J. (1992). Effects of schema-based and text structure-based cues on expository prove comprehension in fourth graders. *Journal of Experimental Education, 60,* 307–320.

Spreen, O. (1988). *Learning disabled children growing up.* New York: Oxford University Press.

Steele, C. M. (1992). Race and the schooling of Black Americans. *The Atlantic Monthly, 269,* pp. 68–78.

Steele, C. M., & Aronson, J. (1995). Stereotype threat and the intellectual test performance of African Americans. *Journal of Personality and Social Psychology, 5,* 797–811.

Stein, J. H., & Reiser, L. W. (1994). A study of white middle-class adolescent boys' responses to "semenarche" (the first ejaculation). *Journal of Youth and Adolescence, 23,* 373–384.

Steinberg, L. (1987). The impact of puberty on family relations: Effects of pubertal status and pubertal timing. *Developmental Psychology, 23,* 451–460.

Steinberg, L. (1989). Reciprocal relation between parent–child distance and pubertal maturation. *Developmental Psychology, 24,* 122–128.

Steinberg, L., with Brown, B. B., & Dornbusch, S. M. (1996). *Beyond the classroom.* New York: Simon & Schuster.

Steinberg, L., Fegley, S., & Dornbusch, S. (1993). Negative impact of part-time work on adolescent adjustment: Evidence from a longitudinal study. *Developmental Psychology, 29,* 171–180.

Steinberg, L., Lamborn, S. D., Darling, N., Mounts, N. S., & Dornbusch, S. M. (1994). Over-time changes in adjustment and competence among adolescents from authoritative, authoritarian, indulgent, and neglectful families. *Child Development, 65,* 754–770.

Sternberg, R. J. (1981). Intelligence and nonentrenchment. *Journal of Educational Psychology, 73,* 1–16.

Sternberg, R. J. (1984). Mechanisms of cognitive development: A componential approach. In R. J. Sternberg (Ed.), *Mechanisms of cognitive development.* New York: Freeman.

Sternberg, R. J. (1985). *Beyond I. Q.: A triarchic theory of human intelligence.* New York: Cambridge University Press.

Sternberg, R. J., & Rifkin, B. (1979). The development of analogical reasoning processes. *Journal of Experimental Child Psychology, 27,* 195–232.

Stevens-Long, J., & Cobb, N. J. (1983). *Adolescence and early adulthood.* Mountain View, CA: Mayfield.

Stevens-Long, J. & Commons, M. L. (1992). *Adult life* (4th ed.). Mountain View, CA: Mayfield.

Stevenson, H. W., Chen, C., & Uttal, D. H. (1990). Beliefs and achievement: A study of black, white, and Hispanic children. *Child Development, 61,* 508–523.

Streitmatter, J. (1993). Identity status and identity style: A replication study. *Journal of Adolescence, 16,* 211–215.

Strong, B., & DeVault, C. (1994). *Human sexuality.* Mountain View, CA: Mayfield.

Strong, B., & DeVault, C. (1997). *Human sexuality: Diversity in contemporary America* (2nd ed.). Mountain View, CA: Mayfield.

Subich, L. M. (1989). A challenge to grow: Reaction to Hoyt's article. *Career Development Quarterly, 37,* 213–217.

Subkoviak, M. J., Enright, R. D., Wu, C., Gassin, E. A., Freedman, S., Olson, L. M., & Sarinopoulos, I. (1995). Measuring interpersonal forgiveness in late adolescence and middle adulthood. *Journal of Adolescence, 18,* 641–655.

Sue, S. (1991). Ethnicity and culture in psychological research and practice. In J. Goodchilds (Ed.), *Psychological perspectives on human diversity in America* (pp. 51–85). Washington, DC: American Psychological Association.

Super, D. E. (1981). A developmental theory: Implementing a self concept. In D. H. Montross & C. J. Shinkman (Eds.), *Career development in the 1980s: Theory and practice.* Springfield, IL: Thomas.

Super, D. E. (1990). A life-span, life-space approach to career development. In D. Brown, L. Brooks, & Associates (Eds.), Career choice and development. (2nd ed., pp. 197–261). San Francisco: Jossey-Bass.

Surgeon General's Report. (1988). *The health consequences of smoking: Nicotine addiction.* U.S. Department of Health and Human Services. Washington, DC: U.S. Government Printing Office.

Swarr, A. E., & Richards, M. H. (1996). Longitudinal effects of adolescent girls' pubertal development, perceptions of pubertal timing, and parental relations on eating problems. *Developmental Psychology, 32,* 636–646.

Switzer, J. Y. (1990). The impact of generic word choices: An empirical investigation of age- and sex-related differences. *Sex Roles, 22,* 69–82.

Szapocznik, J., & Kurtines, W. M. (1993). Family psychology and cultural diversity: Opportunities for theory, research, and application. *American Psychologist, 48,* 400–407.

Tanner, J. M. (1968). Earlier maturation in man. *Scientific American, 218,* 21–27.

Tanner, J. M. (1972). Sequence, tempo and individual variation in growth and development of boys and girls aged twelve to sixteen. In J. Kagan &

R. Coles (Eds.), *Twelve to sixteen: Early adolescence.* New York: Norton.

Tanner, J. M. (1974). Sequence and tempo in the somatic changes in puberty. In M. M. Grumbach, G. D. Grave, & F. E. Mayer (Eds.), *Control of the onset of puberty.* New York: Wiley.

Tanner, J. M. (1991). Menarche, secular trend in age of. In R. M. Lerner, A. C. Petersen, & J. Brooks-Gunn (Eds.), *Encyclopedia of adolescence* (Vol. 2, pp. 637–641). New York: Garland.

Tashakkori, A., & Thompson, V. (1991). Race differences in self-perception and locus of control during adolescence and early adulthood: Methodological implications. *Genetic, Social, and General Psychology Monographs, 117,* 153–174.

Tavris, C., & Wade, C. (1984). *The longest war: Sex differences in perspective* (2nd ed.). San Diego: Harcourt Brace Jovanovich.

Taylor, R. D. (1996). Adolescents' perceptions of kinship support and family management practices: Association with adolescent adjustment in African American families. *Developmental Psychology, 32,* 687–695.

Teddlie, C., Kirby, P. C., & Stringfield, S. (1989). Effective vs. ineffective schools: Observable differences in the classroom. *American Journal of Education, 97,* 221–236.

Terman, L. M. (1925). *Genetic studies of genius. Vol. 1: Mental and physical traits of a thousand gifted children.* Stanford, CA: Stanford University Press.

Thomas, R. M. (1979). *Comparing theories of child development.* Belmont, CA: Wadsworth.

Thornberry, T. P., Krohn, M. D., Lizotte, A. J., & Chard-Wierschem, D. (1993). The role of juvenile gangs in facilitating delinquent behavior. *Journal of Research in Crime and Delinquency, 30,* 55–87.

Thornton, M. C., Chatters, L. M., Taylor, R. J., & Allen, W. R. (1990). Sociodemographic and environmental correlates of racial socialization by black parents. *Child Development, 61,* 401–409.

Tidwell, R. (1988). Dropouts speak out: Qualitative data on early school departures. *Adolescence, 23,* 939–954.

Tillman, R. (1986). *The prevalence and incidence of arrest among adult males in California.* Sacramento, CA: State of California Department of Justice.

Tittle, C. K. (1986). Gender research and education. *American Psychologist, 41,* 1161–1168.

Tobias, A. L. (1988). Bulimia: An overview. In K. Clark, R. Parr, & W. Castelli (Eds.), *Evaluation and management of eating disorders.* Champaign, IL: Life Enhancement Publications.

Tobin-Richards, M. H., Boxer, A. M., & Petersen, A. C. (1983). The psychological significance of pubertal change: Sex differences in perceptions of self during early adolescence. In J. Brooks-Gunn & A. C. Petersen (Eds.), *Girls at puberty.* New York: Plenum Press.

Toch, T. (1993a). Violence in schools. *U.S. News & World Report, 115,* pp. 31–37.

Tolson, J. M., & Urberg, K. A. (1993). Similarity between adolescent best friends. *Journal of Adolescent Research, 8,* 274–288.

Trautman, P. D. (1989). Specific treatment modalities for adolescent suicide attempters. In *Report of the Secretary's Task Force. Vol. 3.* Washington, DC: U.S. Government Printing Office.

Trautman, P. D., & Rotheram, M. J. (1986). Reported in Trautman, P. D. (1989). Specific treatment modalities for adolescent suicide attempters. In *Report of the Secretary's Task Force. Vol. 3.* Washington, DC: U.S. Government Printing Office.

Treboux, D., & Busch-Rossnagel, N. A. (1990). Social network influences on adolescent sexual attitudes and behaviors. *Journal of Adolescent Research, 5,* 175–189.

Trent, W. T. (1983). *Race and sex differences in degree attainment and major field distributions for 1975–76 to 1980–81* (Report No. 339). Baltimore, MD: Johns Hopkins University, Center for Social Organization of Schools.

Tschann, J. M., Adler, N. E., Irwin, C. E., Millstein, S. G., et al. (1994). Initiation of substance use in early adolescence: The roles of pubertal timing and emotional distress. *Health Psychology, 13,* 326–333.

Tschirgi, J. E. (1980). Sensible reasoning: A hypothesis about hypotheses. *Child Development, 51,* 1–10.

Turiel, E. (1983). *The development of social knowledge: Morality and convention.* Cambridge, England: Cambridge University Press.

Turner, C. B., & Cashdan, S. (1988). Perception of college students' motives for shoplifting. *Psychological Reports, 62,* 855–862.

Underwood, B. J. (1957). *Psychological research.* New York: Appleton-Century-Crofts.

Urberg, K. A. (1992). Locus of peer influence: Social crowd and best friend. *Journal of Youth and Adolescence, 21,* 439–450.

Urberg, K. A., Degirmencioglu, S. M., Tolson, J. M., & Halliday-Scher, K. (1995). The structure of adolescent peer networks. *Developmental Psychology, 31,* 540–547.

U.S. Bureau of the Census. (1984). *Current population reports, Series P-25, No. 952, Projections of the population of the United States by age, sex, and race: 1983–2080.* Washington, DC: U.S. Government Printing Office.

U.S. Bureau of the Census. (1986). *Statistical abstract of the United States: 1987* (107th ed.). Washington, DC: U.S. Department of Commerce.

U.S. Bureau of the Census. (1992a). *Current population reports, Series P-20, No. 468, Marital status and living arrangements: March 1992.* Washington, DC: U.S. Government Printing Office.

U.S. Bureau of the Census. (1992b). *Current population reports, Series P-20, No. 467, Household and family characteristics.* Washington, DC: U.S. Government Printing Office.

U.S. Bureau of the Census. (1992c). *Current population reports, Series P-60, No. 185, Poverty in the U.S.: 1990.* Washington, DC: U.S. Government Printing Office.

U.S. Bureau of the Census. (1993). *Statistical abstract of the United States: 1993* (113th ed.). Washington, DC: U.S. Government Printing Office.

U.S. Bureau of the Census. (1994). *Statistical abstract of the United States: 1994* (114th ed.). Washington, DC: U.S. Government Printing Office.

U.S. Bureau of the Census. Baugher, E., & Lamison-White, L. (1996a). *Current population reports, Series P60-194, Poverty in the United States: 1995.* Washington, DC: U.S. Government Printing Office.

U.S. Bureau of the Census. Day, J. C. (1996b). *Current population reports, Series P25-1130, Population projections of the United States by age, sex, race, and Hispanic origin: 1995 to 2050.* Washington, DC: U.S. Government Printing Office.

U.S. Bureau of the Census. (1996c). *Statistical abstract of the United States: 1996* (116th ed.). Washington, DC: U.S. Government Printing Office.

U.S. Department of Education. (1988). *Ninth annual report to Congress on the implementation of the Education of the Handicapped Act.* Washington, DC: OSERS.

U.S. Department of Education. (1996). *Digest of educational statistics 1996, NCES 96-133.* Washington, DC: U.S. Government Printing Office.

U.S. Department of Justice. (1991). *Criminal victimization, 1990* (Special Report No. NCJ-122743). Washington, DC: Bureau of Justice Statistics.

U.S. Department of Labor, Bureau of Labor Statistics. (1994). *The American work force: 1992–2005.* Bulletin 2452, April 1994. Washington, DC: U.S. Government Printing Office.

Vicary, J. R., Klingaman, L. R., & Harkness, W. L. (1995). Risk factors associated with date rape and sexual assault of adolescent girls. *Journal of Adolescence, 18,* 289–306.

Vigil, J. D. (1988). *Barrio gangs.* Austin: The University of Texas Press.

Violato, C., & Kwok, D. (1995). A cross-cultural validation of a four-factor model of adolescent concerns: A confirmatory factor analysis based on a sample of Hong Kong Chinese adolescents. *Journal of Adolescence, 18,* 607–617.

Visher, E. B., & Visher, J. S. (1989). Parenting coalitions after remarriage: Dynamics and therapeutic guidelines. *Family Relations, 38,* 65–70.

Voyer, D. (1996). The relation between mathematical achievement and gender differences in spatial abilities: A suppression effect. *Journal of Educational Psychology, 88,* 563–571.

Vuchinich, S., Angelelli, J., & Gatherum, A. (1996). Context and development in family problem solving with preadolescent children. *Child Development, 67,* 1276–1288.

Vygotsky, L. (1978). *Mind in society.* Cambridge, MA: Harvard University Press.

Wagner, B. M., Cohen, P., & Brook, J. S. (1996). Parent/adolescent relationships: Moderators of the effects of stressful life events. *Journal of Adolescent Research, 11,* 347–374.

Wagner, R. K., & Sternberg, R. J. (1986). Tacit knowledge and intelligence in the everyday world. In R. J. Sternberg & R. K. Wagner (Eds.), *Practical intelligence: Nature and origins of competence in the everyday world.* New York: Cambridge University Press.

Waldman, I. D. (1996). Aggressive boys' hostile perceptual and response biases: The role of attention and impulsivity. *Child Development, 67,* 1015–1033.

Walker, L. J. (1984). Sex differences in the development of moral reasoning: A critical review. *Child Development, 55,* 677–691.

Walker, L. J. (1986). Sex differences in the development of moral reasoning: A rejoinder to Baumrind. *Child Development, 57,* 522–526.

Walker, L. S., & Greene, J. W. (1986). The social context of adolescent self-esteem. *Journal of Youth and Adolescence, 15,* 315–322.

Wallerstein, J. S. (1989). *Second change.* New York: Ticknor & Fields.

Wallerstein, J. S., Corbin, S. B., & Lewis, J. M. (1988). Children of divorce: A ten-year study. In E. M. Hetherington & J. D. Arasteh (Eds.), *Impact of divorce, single-parenting, and stepparenting on children.* Hillsdale, NJ: Erlbaum.

Walters, J. M., & Gardner, H. (1986). The theory of multiple intelligences: Some issues and answers. In R. J. Sternberg & R. K. Wagner (Eds.), *Practical intelligence: Nature and origins of competence in the everyday world.* New York: Cambridge University Press.

Wapner, M. L. (1980). Personal communication.

Wapner, M. L. (1990). Personal communication.

Ward, D. A. (1986). Self-esteem and dishonest behavior revisited. *Journal of Social Psychology, 126,* 709–713.

Ward, S. L., & Overton, W. F. (1990). Semantic familiarity, relevance, and the development of deductive reasoning. *Developmental Psychology, 26,* 488–493.

Wark, G. R., & Krebs, D. L. (1996). Gender and dilemma differences in real-life moral judgment. *Developmental Psychology, 32, 220–230.*

Warren, M. P. (1983). Physical and biological aspects of puberty. In J. Brooks-Gunn & A. C. Petersen (Eds.), *Girls at puberty.* New York: Plenum Press.

Wason, P. C., & Johnson-Laird, P. N. (1972). *Psychology of reasoning: Structure and content.* Cambridge, MA: Harvard University Press.

Waterman, A. S. (1992). Identity as an aspect of optimal psychological functioning. In G. R. Adams, T. T. Gullotta, & R. Montemayor (Eds.), *Adolescent identity formation.* Newbury Park, CA: Sage.

Waterman, A. S. (1993). Two conceptions of happiness: Contrasts of personal expressiveness (Eudaimonia) and hedonic enjoyment. *Journal of Personality and Social Psychology, 64,* 678–691.

Waugh, R. F., Godfrey, J. R., Evans, E. D., & Craig, D. (1995). Measuring students' perceptions about cheating in six countries. *Australian Journal of Psychology, 47,* 73–80.

Wayment, H. A., & Peplau, L. A. (1995). Social support and well-being among lesbian and heterosexual women: A structural modeling approach. *Personality and Social Psychology Bulletin, 21,* 1189–1199.

Weaver, F. M., & Carroll, J. S. (1985). Crime perceptions in a natural setting by expert and novice shoplifters. *Social Psychology Quarterly, 48,* 349–359.

Webster, C. (1994). Effects of Hispanic ethnic identification on marital roles in the purchase decision process. *Journal of Consumer Research, 21,* 319–331.

Wechsler, D. (1981). *WAIS-R Manual: Wechsler Adult Intelligence Scale—Revised.* San Antonio, TX: Psychological Corporation.

Weddle, K. D., McKenry, P. C., & Leigh, G. K. (1988). Adolescent sexual behavior: Trends and issues in research. *Journal of Adolescent Research, 3,* 245–257.

Weiner, I. B. (1980). Psychopathology in adolescence. In J. Adelson (Ed.), *Handbook of adolescent psychology.* New York: Wiley.

Weis, D. (1983). Affective reactions of women to their initial experience of coitus. *Journal of Sex Research, 19,* 209–237.

Wentzel, K. R., & Erdley, C. A. (1993). Strategies for making friends: Relations to social behavior and peer acceptance in early adolescence. *Developmental Psychology, 29,* 819–826.

Werner, E. (1989, April). Children of the garden island. *Scientific American,* pp. 106–111.

Werner, E. (1989). High-risk children in young adulthood: A longitudinal study from birth to 32 years. *American Journal of Orthopsychiatry, 59,* 72–81.

Werner, E., & Smith, R. (1982). *Vulnerable but invincible: A longitudinal study of resilient children and youth.* New York: McGraw-Hill.

Werner, E., & Smith, R. (1992). *Overcoming the odds: High risk children from birth to adulthood.* Ithaca, NY: Cornell University Press.

Westermeyer, J. (1986). *A clinical guide to alcohol and drug problems.* New York: Praeger.

Wetzel, J. (1987). *American youth: A statistical snapshot.* Washington, DC: William T. Grant Foundation.

White, K. L., Speisman, J. C., & Costos, D. (1983). Young adults and their parents: Individuation to mutuality. In H. D. Grotevant & C. R. Cooper (Eds.), *Adolescent development in the family.* San Francisco: Jossey-Bass.

White, L. K., & Booth, A. (1985). The quality and stability of remarriages: The role of stepchildren. *American Sociological Review, 50,* 689–698.

Whitehead, A. N. (1929). *The aims of education.* New York: Macmillan.

Whiteside, M. F. (1989). Family rituals as a key to kinship connections in remarried families. *Family Relations, 38,* 34–39.

Williams, G. H. (1995). *Life on the color line: The true story of a white boy who discovered he was black.* New York: Dutton.

Williams, J. H. (1983). *Psychology of women* (2nd ed.). New York: Norton.

Williams, J. M., & White, K. A. (1983). Adolescent status systems for males and females at three age levels. *Adolescence, 18,* 381–389.

Wilson, S. M., & Medora, N. P. (1990). Gender comparisons of college students' attitudes toward sexual behavior. *Adolescence, 25,* 615–627.

Windle, M., Miller-Tutzauer, C., & Domenico, D. (1992). Alcohol use, suicidal behavior, and risky activities among adolescents. *Journal of Research on Adolescents, 2,* 317–330.

Winer, G. A., Craig, R. K., & Weinbaum, E. (1992). Adults' failure on misleading weight-conservation tests: A developmental analysis. *Developmental Psychology, 28,* 109–120.

Winer, G. A., & McGlone, C. (1993). On the uncertainty of conservation: Responses to misleading conservation questions. *Developmental Psychology, 29,* 760–769.

Wintre, M. G., Hicks, R., McVey, G., & Fox, J. (1988). Age and sex differences in choice of consultant for various types of problems. *Child Development, 59,* 1046–1055.

Wirth, L. (1945). The problem of minority groups. In R. Linton (Ed.), *The science of man in the world crisis.* New York: Columbia University Press.

Witkin, G. (1991, April 8). Kids who kill. *U.S. News & World Report,* pp. 26–32.

Women on Words and Images. (1975). *Dick and Jane as victims: Sex stereotyping in children's readers* (Expanded ed.). Princeton, NJ: Woman on Words and Images.

Wood, K. C., Becker, J. A., & Thompson, J. K. (1996). Body image dissatisfaction in preadolescent children. *Journal of Applied Developmental Psychology, 17,* 85–100.

Wright, L. S., Frost, C. J., & Wisecarver, S. J. (1993). Church attendance, meaningfulness of religion, and depressive symptomatology among adolescents. *Journal of Youth and Adolescence, 22,* 559–568.

Wyche, K., Obolensky, N., & Glood, E. (1990). American Indian, Black American, and Hispanic American youth. In M. J. Rotheram-Borus, J. Bradley, & N. Obolensky (Eds.), *Planning to live: Evaluating and treating suicidal teens in community settings,* 355–389. Tulsa: University of Oklahoma Press.

Wyshak, G., & Frisch, R. E. (1982). Evidence for a secular trend in age of menarche. *New England Journal of Medicine, 306,* 1033–1035.

Yamaguchi, K., & Kandel, D. B. (1984). Patterns of drug use from adolescence to young adulthood: III. Predictors of progression. *American Journal of Public Health, 74,* 673–681.

Yau, J., & Smetana, J. G. (1993). Chinese-American adolescents' reasoning about cultural conflicts. *Journal of Adolescent Research, 8,* 419–438.

Yau, J., & Smetana, J. G. (1996). Adolescent–parent conflict among Chinese adolescents in Hong Kong. *Child Development, 67,* 1262–1275.

Ying, Y. (1994). Chinese American adults' relationship with their parents. *International Journal of Social Psychology, 40,* 35–45.

Yoder, J. D., & Kahn, A. S. (1993). Working toward an inclusive psychology of women. *American Psychologist, 48,* 846–850.

Young, B. J. (1995). Career plans and work perceptions of preservice teachers. *Teaching and Teacher Education, 11,* 281–292.

Youniss, J. (1980). *Parents and peers in social development.* Chicago: University of Chicago Press.

Youniss, J., & Smollar, J. (1989). Adolescents' interpersonal relationships in social context. In T. J. Berndt & G. W. Ladd (Eds.), *Peer relationships in child development.* New York: Wiley.

Youth Indicators: Trends in the Well-Being of American Youth. (1988). Washington, DC: U.S. Government Printing Office.

Youth Indicators: Trends in the Well-Being of American Youth. (1991). Washington, DC: U.S. Government Printing Office.

Youth Indicators: Trends in the Well-Being of American Youth. (1993). Washington, DC: U.S. Government Printing Office.

Youth Indicators: Trends in the Well-Being of American Youth. (1996). Washington, DC: U.S. Government Printing Office.

Zabatany, L., & Hartmann, D. P. (1990). The psychological functions of preadolescent peer activities. *Child Development, 61,* 1067–1080.

Zeldin, S., & Price, L. A. (1995). Creating supportive communities for adolescent development: Challenges to scholars. *Journal of Adolescent Research, 10,* 6–14.

Zeman, J., & Garber, J. (1996). Display rules for anger, sadness, and pain: It depends on who is watching. *Child Development, 67,* 957–973.

Zetlin, A. G. (1993). Everyday stressors in the lives of Anglo and Hispanic learning handicapped adolescents. *Journal of Youth and Adolescence, 22,* 327.

Zimmerman, B. J., Bandura, A., & Martinez-Pons, M. (1992). Self-motivation for academic attainment: The role of self-efficacy beliefs and personal goal-setting. *American Educational Research Journal, 29,* 663–676.

Zimmerman, R. S., Sprecher, S., Langer, L. M., & Holloway, C. D. (1995). Adolescents' perceived ability to say "no" to unwanted sex. *Journal of Adolescent Research, 10,* 383–399.

Zuckerman, M. (1990). Some dubious premises in research and theory on racial differences. *American Psychologist, 45,* 1297–1303.

CREDITS

PHOTO CREDITS

Part One Opener © David Madison 1997; p. 1 (left), © Mary Kate Denny/PhotoEdit; p. 1 (right), © Tony Freeman/PhotoEdit **Chapter 1** p. 2, © Paul Conklin/PhotoEdit; p. 5, © David Toy; p. 9, © Elizabeth Crews; p. 10, © Joel Gordon; p. 16, © Tony Freeman/PhotoEdit; p. 22, © David Madison 1997; p. 25, © Jim West/Impact Visuals; p. 27, © Michelle Bridwell/PhotoEdit; p. 30, © Erich Lessing/Art Resource; p. 35, © Carey/The Image Works **Chapter 2** p. 40, © Mary Kate Denny/PhotoEdit; p. 44, © Mary Kate Denny/PhotoEdit; p. 49, © Joel Gordon; p. 51, © Ken Heyman/Woodfin Camp & Associates; p. 53, © Paul Conklin/PhotoEdit; p. 54, © AP/Wide World Photos; p. 59, © Corbis-Bettmann; p. 62, © UPI/Corbis-Bettmann; p. 63, © UPI/Corbis-Bettmann; p. 67 (top), Courtesy Nancy Chodorow; p. 67 (bottom), © David Young-Wolff/PhotoEdit; p. 68, Photo © Jerry Bauer/Courtesy Carol Gilligan; p. 77, © Sam Forencich **Part Two Opener** p. 82, © Skjold Photographs; p. 83 (left), © Tony Freeman/PhotoEdit; p. 83 (right), © Elizabeth Crews **Chapter 3** p. 84, © David Young-Wolff/PhotoEdit; p. 92, © Michael Newman/PhotoEdit; p. 93, © Phil McCarten/PhotoEdit; p. 95, © David Young-Wolff/PhotoEdit; p. 102, © Dwayne Newton/PhotoEdit; p. 108, © Ulrike Welsch/PhotoEdit; p. 111, © Tony Freeman/PhotoEdit; p. 113, © 1993 B. Bodine/Custom Medical Stock Photo; p. 119, © Tom Prettyman/PhotoEdit; p. 127, © Elizabeth Crews **Chapter 4** p. 130, © David Young-Wolff/PhotoEdit; p. 133, © Nita Winter; p. 136, © Comstock Inc./M. C. Warner; p. 145, © Will & Deni McIntyre/Photo Researchers, Inc.; p. 148, © Suzanne Arms/Jeroboam; p. 151, © Merritt Vincent/PhotoEdit; p. 157, © Elizabeth Crews; p. 161, © Myrleen Cate/Tony Stone Images; p. 163, © Elizabeth Crews; p. 164, © Elizabeth Crews; p. 167 (top left), © Mary Kate Denny/PhotoEdit; p. 167 (right), © David Young-Wolff/PhotoEdit; p. 167 (bottom left), © Roberto Soncin Gerometta/Photo 20-20; p. 172, © Nancy Richmond/The Image Works; p. 174, © Michael Newman/PhotoEdit; p. 181, © Jeff Greenberg/PhotoEdit **Chapter 5** p. 188, © Skjold Photographs; p. 193, © Elizabeth Crews; p. 203, © Skjold Photographs; p. 207, © Myrleen Ferguson/PhotoEdit; p. 210, © David Young-Wolff/PhotoEdit; p. 215, © Elizabeth Crews; p. 220, © Michael Newman/PhotoEdit; p. 224, © Comstock Inc.; p. 231, © Jose Carrillo/PhotoEdit; p. 234, © Jonathan Nourok/PhotoEdit; p. 238, © Roberto Soncin Gerometta/Photo 20-20 **Chapter 6** p. 246, © Michael Newman/PhotoEdit; p. 249, © Skjold Photographs; p. 252, © Michael Newman/PhotoEdit; p. 253, © Elizabeth Crews; p. 257, © David Young-Wolff/PhotoEdit; p. 259, © Skjold Photographs; p. 262, © David Young-Wolff/PhotoEdit; p. 266, © Cleo Photo/The Picture Cube; p. 271, © Cleo Photo/Jeroboam; p. 272, © David Young-Wolff/PhotoEdit; p. 275, © Joel Gordon; p. 277, © Joel Gordon **Chapter 7** p. 282, © Elizabeth Crews; p. 286, © Dennis MacDonald/PhotoEdit; p. 292, © Elizabeth Crews; p. 296, Courtesy of Professor Albert Bandura, Stanford University; p. 298, © Mary Kate Denny/PhotoEdit; p. 302, © Elizabeth Crews; p. 304, © David Young-Wolff/Tony Stone Images; p. 307, © Elizabeth Crews; p. 320, © Michelle Bridwell/PhotoEdit; p. 323, © Jonathan Nourok/PhotoEdit **Part Three Opener** p. 326 (left), © Comstock Inc./Stuart Cohen; p. 326 (right), © Dennis MacDonald/Jeroboam; p. 327, © Michael Newman/PhotoEdit **Chapter 8** p. 328, © Joan Liftin/Actuality, Inc.; p. 331, © Suzanne Arms; p. 334, © Bob Daemmrich/The Image Works; p. 336, © Comstock Inc./T. Dickinson; p. 337, © Robert Eckert/The Picture Cube; p. 339, © Elaine Rebman/Photo Researchers, Inc.; p. 340, © Comstock Inc./Stuart Cohen; p. 345, © Dennis MacDonald/Jeroboam; p. 349, © John Eastcott/Yva Momatiuk/The Image Works; p. 354, © Tony Freeman/PhotoEdit; p. 360, © Jim Corwin/Stock Boston; p. 361, © Joel Gordon; p. 365, © Jeff Greenberg/Photo 20-20; p. 370, © Joel Gordon; p. 371, © Donne Binder/Impact Visuals **Chapter 9** p. 374, © Esbin-Anderson/Photo 20-20; p. 379, © John Boykin/PhotoEdit; p. 389, © 1995 Marilyn Humphries/Impact Visuals; p. 396, © Joan Liftin/Actuality, Inc.; p. 399 (left), © Children's Defense Fund; p. 399 (right), © Drew Crawford/The Image Works; p. 410, © 1996 Roger Mastroianni **Chapter 10** p. 414, © J. Pickerell/The Image Works; p. 421, © David Young-Wolff/PhotoEdit; p. 423, © Joel Gordon; p. 426, © Joel Gordon; p. 431, © Myrleen Ferguson/PhotoEdit; p. 437, © Esbin-Anderson/The Image Works; p. 439, © Warner Brothers, 1988/MP & TV Photo Archive; p. 446, © Mary Kate Denny/PhotoEdit; p. 450, © Michael Newman/PhotoEdit; p. 455, © Jeff Greenberg/PhotoEdit; p. 462, © Jim Prigoff and Henry Chalfant; p. 466, © Michelle Bridwell/PhotoEdit **Chapter 11** p. 470, © David Young-Wolff/PhotoEdit; p. 472, © UPI/Corbis-Bettmann; p. 477, © Skjold Photographs; p. 478, © Jeff Jacobsen/Actuality, Inc.; p. 488, Courtesy Nancy Cobb; p. 491, © Mark Richards/PhotoEdit; p. 496, © David Ryan/Photo 20-20; p. 504, © Bob Daemmrich/Stock Boston **Chapter 12** p. 506, © Catherine Smith/Impact Visuals; p. 509, © Dorothy Littell/Stock Boston; p. 521, © Robert Yager/Tony Stone Images; p. 526, © Ramey/Stock Boston; p. 528, © 1996 New Line Cinema/Photo by Kerry Hates/MP & TV Photo Archive; p. 535, © Christopher Smith/Impact Visuals; p. 537, © Owen Franken/Stock Boston; p. 541, © Michael Newman/PhotoEdit; p. 549, © Frank Siteman/Stock Boston **Chapter 13** p. 554, © Bob Daemmrich/Stock Boston; p. 556, © Robert Brenner/PhotoEdit; p. 561, © Mark Constantini/SF Examiner; p. 565, © Michael Newman/PhotoEdit; p. 570, © Mary Kate Denny/PhotoEdit; p. 572, © Shelley Boyd/PhotoEdit **Chapter 14** p. 574, © Cleo Photography/Jeroboam; p. 577, Courtesy of Richard L. Simmons; p. 581, Courtesy of Robert Cohen; p. 586, © B.D. Lanphere/Stock Boston; p. 587, © B.D. Lanphere/Stock Boston; p. 593, Courtesy of Professor Benjamin Harris

TEXT CREDITS

Chapter 1 **Box 1.1** From R. C. Maynard, The Oakland Tribune, August 5, 1990. Used with permission. **Table 1.1** R. J. Havinghurst, Developmental tasks and education, David McKay,

Author Index

SUBJECT INDEX